Symphony Orchestras of the World

Symphony Orchestras of the World

 SELECTED PROFILES

Edited by
ROBERT R. CRAVEN

Greenwood Press
New York
Westport, Connecticut
London

Library of Congress Cataloging-in-Publication Data
Symphony orchestras of the world.

   Bibliography: p.
   Includes index.
   1. Symphony orchestras.   I. Craven, Robert R.
ML1200.S9   1987   785'.06'61   86-29452
ISBN 0-313-24073-6 (lib. bdg. : alk. paper)

Library of Congress Catalog Card Number: 86-29452
ISBN: 0-313-24073-6

First published in 1987

Greenwood Press, Inc.
88 Post Road West, Westport, Connecticut 06881

Printed in the United States of America

The paper used in this book complies with the
Permanent Paper Standard issued by the National
Information Standards Organization (Z39.48-1984).

10 9 8 7 6 5 4 3 2 1

Copyright Acknowledgments

For permission to use materials, we are indebted to the following:

From the *New Schwann* catalogs for use of discographies, used with permission of *Schwann
Record and Tape Guide*.

From *Gramophone Classical Catalogue*. Used with permission of General Gramophone
Publications, Ltd.

Contents _____

Acknowledgments _____

Several years' worth of correspondence, comprising literally thousands of pieces of mail, has gone into this volume. It would be impossible, therefore, to acknowledge all the help that I received during that time from so many kind correspondents all over the world. With the certain knowledge, then, that a great many more contributed than can be mentioned, I'll try to enumerate some who were of special assistance, giving my thanks to:

First and foremost, Marilyn Brownstein, humanities editor at Greenwood Press, who originated the idea to produce this volume and its companion, *Symphony Orchestras of the United States* (1986). Thanks as well to Greenwood Press editor Cynthia Harris, who offered help and suggestions.

The staffs of the New Hampshire College Shapiro Library and the New Hampshire College Computer Center.

Those who helped make known the search for contributors, especially the editors of *The Horn Call, International Journal of Music Education,* Canadian Association of Music Libraries *Newsletter,* International Society of Bassists *Newsletter,* and the Royal Music Association *Newsletter.*

Those who coordinated the efforts of authors within their respective countries: Dr. Joachim Dorfmüller, Professor of Historical Musicology at the Westfälische Wilhelms-Universität Munster; Dr. Jan Ledeč of the Czech Music Fund Information Center; Prof. Jacek Szerszenowicz, Professor of Aesthetics at the University of Lodz.

Those who commented briefly on the preliminary list of orchestras: David Ewen, author and editor; John Holmes of the Australian Embassy in Vienna; and Robert J. Lurtsema of WGBH-FM Public Radio in Boston.

Those who suggested which orchestras to include from various countries: Mr. Hiram Amarante of the University of Minas Gerais Music School, Brazil; Dr. Stephen Barnes, Dean of the College of Fine Arts of Eastern New Mexico University; Dr. Warren Bebbington, Dean of Music at the University of Queensland, Australia; Prof. Bojan Bujic, Oxford University; Ms. Marjorie Ann Ciarlillo of the China Music Project, Cleveland; Mr. Cesare Corsi of Rome; Dr. Joachim Dorfmüller, Professor of Historical Musicology at the Westfälische Wilhelms-Universität Munster; Dr. Harald Goertz of the Austrian Music Society; Mr. Lev Grigoriev of "Muzykalnaya Zhizh," Moscow; Dr. R. Hausler, General Secretary of the International Musicological Society; Dr. Johannes Heinrich of Siegen, West Germany; Dr. Hempel, Director of the Deutcher Verlag für Musik, Leipzig; J. L. Hyde of the Australian Broadcasting Corporation; Mr. Maurice Leroy of the Belgian Royal Academy; Dr. Jan Ledeč of the Czech Music Fund Information Center; Mr. Per Olof Lundahl of the Swedish Music Information Center; Dr. Siegfried Matthus of the German Democratic Republic Academy of Arts; Mr. Michael Meixner, Head of the International Music Exchange, Budapest; Mrs. Edna Mostarda of Rome; Prof. Yoshihiro Obata of Florida International University; Prof. S. K. Ookerjee of Bombay; Dr. Juan A. Orrego-Salas, Director of the Latin-American Music Institute at Indiana University; Dr. Karel Pech of Prague; Mr. J.-Claude Piguet, Professor of Philosophy, University of Lausanne; Mr. Yakov Platek of "Muzykalnaya Zhizh," Moscow; Dr. Ashok D. Ranade, Bombay University; Mr. Giovanni Ranieri of Tokyo; Mr. Robert Rÿker of the Japan Sinfonia Planning Office; Mr. Karoly Sailer of Interconcert, Budapest; Prof. Guillermo Scarabino of the National University of Cuyo, Argentina; Dr. Shen Sin-Yan, President of the Chinese Music Society; Dr. Jacek Szerszenowicz, Professor of Aesthetics at the University of Lodz; Mr. Jan Taat, Director of the Residentie Orchestra, The Hague; Mr. P. van den Bos, Director, Contactorgaan van Nederlandse Orkesten; Prof. John William Woldt of Texas Christian University; Mr. Roger Wright, Manager, British Music Information Centre.

Those who helped find authors for articles: Mrs. Gerda Alexander of Copenhagen; Prof. Enrique Arias of the American Conservatory, Chicago; Prof. Ian Bartlett of London; Prof. Dorothea Baumann of the University of Zurich; Dr. Robert Begiebing, Professor of English, New Hampshire College; Prof. Bojan Bujic, Oxford University; Ms. Siglind Bruhn of Munich; Mr. Lennart Dehn of the Göteborgs Symfoniker; Dr. Joachim Dorfmüller, Professor of Historical Musicology at the Westfälische Wilhelms-Universität Munster; Dr. Salwa El-Shawan Castelo-Branco of the New University of Lisbon; Prof. James Erb of the University of Richmond, Virginia; Dr. John Fleming, Assistant Professor of English, New Hampshire College; Dr. James Grace, Professor of Law, New Hampshire College; Prof. Ardis O. Higgins of the Santa Barbara Symphony; Mr. Yoshiuki Iida; Prof. Israel Katz of New York City; Mrs. Sibyl Kneihs of Vienna; Mr. Luis Pereira Leal, Director of the Music Department, Gulbenkian Foundation, Lisbon; Ms. Kiri Lee of Harvard University; Prof. David Maves of the College of Charleston, South Carolina; Prof. Denis McCaldin of the University of Lancaster; Mrs. Edna Mostarda of Rome; Rev. Arthur Paré, S. J.; Mr. Helge B. Pedersen of Esbjerg, Denmark; Mr. Lars Pedersen of Esbjerg, Denmark; Mr. Einar Persson of the Association of Swedish Orchestras; Mr. J.-Claude Piguet, Professor of Philosophy, University of Lausanne; J. A. Ritchie,

Secretary General of the International Society for Music Education; Ms. Monica Rivero of New Hampshire College; Prof. Guillermo Scarabino of the National University of Cuyo, Argentina; Mr. Anthony Scelba, bassist, of Bloomfield, New Jersey; Mr. Peter Schindler of The Massachusetts Institute of Technology; Mr. Stephen H. Smith of the Egmont Trio, Manchester, New Hampshire; Mrs. Fumi Tsukahara of Tokyo; Mr. Nils L. Wallin, Executive Secretary of the International Music Council, Paris; Prof. Henri VanHulst, Professor of Musicology at the Free University of Brussels; Prof. John Windhausen, History Department, St. Anselm College, Manchester, New Hampshire.

Those who spoke with me in Europe, providing material for the book's general introduction: Dr. Rolf Dunnwald, Director of the Deutsche Orchestervereinigung e.V. and Mr. David Whelton of the Arts Council, London.

Those who translated correspondence and performed other services: Frank Aguilera, Juan Castillo, George Commenator, Diane Dugan, Julia DiStefano, Robert Fleeson, Jackie Hickox, Carolyn Hollman, Peter Jähne, Richard Pantano, Monica Rivero, Carol West, Walter Zimmermann, all of New Hampshire College; Peter Schindler of The Massachusetts Institute of Technology; Mary Oliveira of Bishop Connolly High School, Fall River, Massachusetts; Camille Ahern, of Digital Equipment Corporation; and Anneliese Yiengst of St. Anselm College.

Those who wrote and/or translated articles. Their names are listed in the Contributors and Translators sections.

Special thanks to my family—Carole, Rob, and Diane—for allowing me the freedom to see this project to its end.

Introduction _____

SCOPE AND PURPOSE

The profiles in this book are intended to provide the general reader with basic information about 122 of the leading or most representative orchestras of the world, exclusive of the United States—whose orchestras are similarly profiled in the companion volume, *Symphony Orchestras of the United States: Selected Profiles* (Westport, Conn.: Greenwood Press, 1986). They are not intended to expose house secrets behind the public facade, nor do they purport to offer definitive critical assessments. They offer historical précis, describe orchestras' seasonal activities, outline their administration, and describe their cultural impact.

The articles' authors are musicologists, conductors, composers, librarians, historians, humanists, music critics, orchestra personnel, and orchestra administrators. Given the diversity of their professional backgrounds, not to mention the cultural diversity of their many national origins or their varied political persuasions, the authors necessarily present their orchestras from a variety of viewpoints. Despite an overriding conformity in scope, coverage, and organization, therefore, some articles will stress certain aspects of orchestral development or activity more than others. Likewise, some authors have adopted a more critical perspective than others, and the reader is advised that opinions and critical judgments are those of the individual authors, not of the editor-in-chief.

The orchestras profiled in this volume were chosen by the editor with the intention of offering a wide geographical diversity while concentrating on ensembles of high quality and historical importance. Each orchestra in the preliminary group considered for inclusion met one of the following criteria: was a full-sized symphony orchestra whose primary role was concertizing (as opposed to opera or ballet work); had been reviewed in the *New York Times* since 1965; was represented in the 1982 *New Schwann Catalog*; was among those orchestra names recognized by a selected panel of American musicians and/or music lovers; or was a leading orchestra of a major city. A bias toward American experience was recognized in these criteria, and care was taken not to exclude orchestras because of it. The resulting long list was then circulated, either in whole or in parts, to numerous correspondents throughout the world. Based largely on their comments and suggestions, a revised list, similar to the grouping in the present volume, was created. A few selected chamber orchestras were added, as were some opera orchestras having long histories of symphonic work.

Unfortunately, several of the orchestras slated for inclusion in the volume did not answer authors' repeated requests for information and so could not be covered. Among them are the Caracas Philharmonic, Estonian State Symphony, Hamburg Philharmonic, Luxembourg Radio Orchestra, Monte Carlo Philharmonic, Oslo Philharmonic, Philharmonic Orchestra of La Scala, Royal Danish Orchestra, Slovak Philharmonic, and the State Orchestra of Athens. The editor sincerely hopes they can all be included in any future editions of this book.

SOURCES

The articles are based on a great many sources, including orchestra-generated materials such as house histories and press materials. However, only the most significant of these are included in the individual bibliographies, which are collectively a very rich compilation, probably the most complete in print. Most authors verified the factual content of their articles with the orchestras themselves. Further secondary sources were considered whenever they were available. In many cases authors conducted interviews and other forms of primary research as well, including work with orchestra archives.

DEFINITIONS AND SYMBOLS

The organization of the volume is alphabetical by country, city, and name of orchestra. The population figures following city names are based on information in the *United Nations Demographic Yearbook* for 1983. An asterisk (*) following the population figure indicates that the figure is for the greater metropolitan area, not just the city proper.

Single asterisks following the names of orchestras are cross references to other orchestras profiled in this volume. Cross references to the companion volume *Symphony Orchestras of the United States* are indicated by two asterisks.

Essentially each profile characterizes its orchestra and offers historical highlights. For the vast majority the entry concludes with data on recording history and/or a selective discography, a chronology of music directors or chief conductors, a bibliography, and an "access" section. Entries in the selective discographies are representative of those recordings by the orchestra that are currently listed in either *The New Schwann* (American) or the *Classical Gramophone* (British) catalogs of December 1985. Other currently available recordings are also included in some cases. The access section ending each profile gives the orchestra's name followed by its address and, whenever available, its telephone number (often with the city code in parentheses) and the name and title of an orchestra administrator. In the profiles and their lists of music directors, the "present" generally reflects the situation as of 1986 (in most cases September 1986), when authors were asked to update their articles for publication.

BRIEF BIBLIOGRAPHIC GUIDE

Orchestras in the United States are profiled in *Symphony Orchestras of the United States,* ed. Robert R. Craven (Westport, Conn.: Greenwood Press, 1986), which also contains a bibliography of other works on American orchestras. Beyond the brief coverage afforded by such standard music encyclopedias as *The New Grove Dictionary of Music and Musicians* (London: Macmillan, 1980) or *Die Musik in Geschichte und Gegenwart* (Kassel: Barenreiter, 1949–1979) and such national references as *The Encyclopedia of Music in Canada* (Toronto: Toronto University Press, 1981), there are few works that provide conveniently centralized information about contemporary orchestras in their cultural settings outside the United States.

Of these the most widely available is probably Michael Hurd's *The Orchestra* (New York: Facts on File, 1980). A highly illustrated work in folio format, *The Orchestra* presents a popularly-accessible treatment of orchestral history, instrumentation, and conductors. It also briefly profiles 25 first-ranked orchestras in Britain, Europe, and the United States. Matsue Nakasone's *Sekai no Okesutora Jiten* [Dictionary of Orchestras of the World] (Tokyo: Geijitsu Gendai Sha, 1984), currently available only in Japanese, offers brief profiles of world-famous orchestras, as well as a number of dictionarylike entries concerning other important ensembles. It also presents material about individual conductors and about orchestral history generally. The most thorough look at the then-current situations of individual orchestras is presented by Howard Taubman in *The Symphony Orchestra Abroad: A Report of a Study* (Vienna, Va.: American Symphony Orchestra League, [1979]), which, though not widely available, provides a penetrating and very candid look at the inner workings of 13 British and European orchestras. Commissioned by the American Symphony Orchestra League, the study takes an analytical point of view rather than a popular or historical one and looks closely at the question of how orchestras outside of the United States deal with common problems of management, finances, personnel, attendance, and other fundamental issues of survival.

The general history of the orchestra is treated in the music encyclopedias, in standard music history texts such as Donald Jay Grout's *A History of Western Music* (New York: Norton, 1975), and in the few volumes devoted entirely to the subject. An examination of the orchestra's history in musicological as well as social and other contexts is provided in *The Orchestra: Origins and Transformations,* edited by Joan Peyser (New York: Scribner's, 1986). The history of the orchestra as a social institution is also addressed in Henry Raynor's *A Social History of Music: From the Middle Ages to Beethoven* (New York: Schocken, 1972) and carried into later years in *Music and Society: Since 1815* (New York: Schocken, 1976). His work *The Orchestra: A History* (New York: Scribner's, 1978) is rather more musicological, treating the complexities of the orchestra as an instrument for musical expression, from the baroque through the twentieth century. An older, though very readable account of the rise and flowering of the symphony orchestra is found in Paul Bekker's *The Story of the Orchestra* (New York: Norton, 1936). More detailed works are Adam von Ahn Carse's, *The Orchestra from Beethoven to Berlioz* (Cambridge: Heffner, 1948) and *The Orchestra in the Eighteenth Century* (Cambridge: Heffner, 1950).

Orchestra histories may be gleaned from other sources as well. Several volumes of national music history, for example, outline the development of orchestral life in their respective countries. Among the better known of these is Reginald Nettel's *The Orchestra in England: A Social History* (1948; rpt. St. Clair Shores, Michigan: Scholarly Press, 1972), first published at the time of major changes in the English orchestral structure. Many of the conductors' biographies and collective biographies also provide insights into the development of the orchestras involved. Examples are *Dictators of the Baton* (Chicago: Alliance, 1943) by David Ewen; Harold C. Schonberg's *The Great Conductors* (New York: Simon & Schuster, 1967); David Wooldridge's *Conductor's World* (New York: Praeger, 1970); and Philip Hart's *Conductors: A New Generation* (New York: Scribner's 1979). Many orchestras have published house versions of their histories, and several others are the subjects of independent historical accounts (see the bibliographies with individual orchestra profiles and the more general Selective Bibliography).

PRIMER OF COMMONALITIES AND DIVERSITIES

Because the orchestra is an instrument of traditional culture and international communication, there are far more basic similarities than differences among the ensembles represented in the following profiles. Yet there is also much diversity in the stories of more than a hundred orchestras from some 40 countries. A brief and very general look at the musical, administrative, social, and political variety among orchestras will help put individual organizations into a larger perspective.

It is generally agreed among Western music critics that the once obvious, often definitive, differences in timbre and other characteristics of sound among orchestras have largely disappeared. Today's conductors typically split their "full time" music directorships among two or more orchestras, and when they are before their "other" orchestra(s) the empty podium is staffed with a cadre of international guest conductors. The result is an increasing uniformity of sound. Yet there remain many subtle exceptions and some that can be noticed by even the nonexpert listener. Such characteristics are most obvious today among the Viennese orchestras, which have long been identified with local schools of instrumental practice, and among chamber orchestras associated for many years with their founding conductors. Some Eastern European orchestras too have kept a recognizable tone quality, particularly in their brass sections, as any professional horn player will attest. Even in tuning protocol, there remain differences. Despite the international agreement setting A at 440 cps., most European orchestras tune higher, in some cases significantly so.

Repertoire is another distinguishing mark of the many orchestras profiled here. One sees varying degrees of nationalism, traditionalism, modernism, diversity, and specialization. Some orchestras concentrate on the large romantic and postromantic works of Central Europe, while others concentrate on the limited repertoire of their own national heritages. Some, such as the radio orchestras of Europe, feature much contemporary music, while others pursue a broad, eclectic repertoire. Of special interest are the orchestras of Asia, where national musical traditions may not be immediately compatible with those of European art music.

The characteristics of repertoire constitute a complex subject, particularly in international terms. In one view, the symphony orchestra is by its nature essentially a keeper of tradition. But in the various countries the tradition has developed in different ways, and regional or national considerations play an important role. For example, the dilemma of what and how much contemporary music to place in the repertoire is clouded on the international scale by the specifics of local values and local perceptions of the role of symphonic music in the larger culture. There is also the Aristotelian question of the role of art in society—should the performance of symphonic music delight or inform? Can (or should) it be wholly aesthetic or need it always be at least partly polemical? The issue of repertoire implies a closely linked issue of audience—for whom does, or should, the symphony orchestra exist? Again we are met by diversity of opinion. The orchestra, like any artistic medium, can be made to serve any number of social, political, or economic functions, which, depending on one's viewpoint, may or may not be considered the proper domain of art.

Repertoire is very much a function of political and economic considerations, particularly since funding for the arts is a government function in many nations. Long recognized as a potent implement of nationalism—and national policy regarding the function of "art"—the dissemination of symphonic music is viewed officially in many nations as an arm of "cultural and educational development." In such cases the repertoire is likely to be not only nationalistic but conservatively so, admitting, alongside the approved works of the past, only that contemporary music best meeting the political goals of the funding entity. On the other hand, some developing and Third World nations—Egypt and Costa Rica, for example—have viewed the symphony orchestra as an implement of westernization or cultural mainstreaming, part of a deliberate policy of cultural expansion. Elsewhere in the developing nations, one finds symphonic music and the orchestras that perform it intimately linked to the many individual histories of European colonization and subsequent independence.

In the more culturally permissive nations one finds the repertoire responsive to the marketplace and/or (here, too) the government. Examples are at one extreme the self-governing, free-enterprise orchestras of London, which, rightly or wrongly, are frequently criticized for attempting to lure audiences through an unadventurous repertoire of romantic favorites played by star soloists; and at the other extreme, the government-funded and administered radio orchestras of some Western European countries. Since the end of the "radio age," the radio orchestra has become—thanks in part to its freedom from market considerations—an instrument for the exposition and encouragement of new music, largely of a national character.

In terms of administration orchestras can be categorized according to at least two major variables: the degree to which the orchestra is autonomous (i.e., free of government control) and the degree to which it is self-funded. In general, the privately managed, not-for-profit, partially self-funded model of most orchestras in the United States is not found outside of North America. In Eastern Europe, to choose an opposite circumstance, orchestral life takes place largely through the auspices of state-administered "philharmonics," institutions that centralize musical performance, often with the inclusion of music education as well. Philharmonics typically include at least one orchestra and/or chorus, concert halls, recording facilities, and sometimes a music library, school, or museum.

In contrast to such state-administered and state-funded organizations are the relatively few self-administered and self-funded private orchestras, such as the Israel Philharmonic, whose prototypes include the four independent major orchestras of London. The London Philharmonic Orchestra, London Symphony, Philharmonia, and Royal Philharmonic are all run by their performing musicians and largely funded through earned income, with between 10% and 20% of the budget deriving from government grants. The economic insecurities of such an arrangement have long been felt in London, but recent events have caused increasing concern: among other things, recent cuts in the London orchestras' Arts Council funding (a total of £280,000 of government money shifted to the development of another regional orchestra in the East of England); the political dissolution as of March 31, 1986, of the Greater London Council (another source of income); and an overall average live attendance rate, according to the Arts Council, of under 70% of capacity. It has been suggested that in such a market-driven environment, only three orchestras will endure.

In West Germany, with its high proportion of fully professional ensembles per capita (95 in a country of 55 million), orchestras are comfortably subsidized by local, state, and federal governments in varying proportions and are administered by Boards of Directors who are usually closely linked to the governmental funding agencies. As with regional orchestras in the United Kingdom, nationally applied contracts for wage minimums and other labor considerations in West Germany are negotiated between an association of orchestras (Deutscher Bühnenverein) and a union of musicians (Deutsche Orchestervereinigung). However, the German schedule of wages also includes classifications for orchestras and authorized allotments of personnel in an elaborate schedule of tariff classes.

Among the different classes of ensembles are radio orchestras, chamber orchestras, state orchestras (mostly concerned with operatic performance and comprising the majority of the ensembles), city orchestras, and orchestras that are privately incorporated (though ultimately government-sponsored and supervised). The exception to the rule—literally in a class by itself—is the Berlin Philharmonic, which, though funded in much the usual manner, is a self-governing, democratic entity. While German orchestras are certainly not immune to organizational and personnel crises—witness the recent turmoil experienced by the Beethovenhalle Orchestra of Bonn—as a group they do seem to enjoy a degree of stability. In Germany, where the orchestra is a central tradition, it is afforded a place of honor and protection in the nation's cultural identity.

A further example of the cultural diversity in administration and funding of orchestras may be found among the nine professional symphonic ensembles of Tokyo. Here symphonic music has, in a relatively few years, become a matter of local and national pride, with each orchestra supported by its corps of loyal subscribers. Most Tokyo orchestras, privately administered by Boards of Directors, are largely self-sustaining, even more so than in London, with less than 5% of the budget derived from government funds. As elsewhere, however, orchestras in Tokyo face problems—for example, the scarcity of concert halls and rehearsal facilities, a unique set of labor tensions, and competition for audience loyalty.

This sketch of commonalities and diversities may serve as a small sampling of the many issues surrounding the orchestra as a musical, social, political, and economic institution. Each facet of orchestral life has a complexity of its own, and each deserves far more discussion than can be given here. It is hoped that the following profiles will—to echo a sentiment expressed in the introduction to *Symphony Orchestras of the United States*—make the many varieties of orchestral experience better known to the institution's global constituencies.

Symphony Orchestras of the World

Argentina ─────────────────────

BUENOS AIRES   (9,927,000*)

Buenos Aires Philharmonic Orchestra

The 117-member Buenos Aires Philharmonic Orchestra (Orquesta Filarmónica de Buenos Aires) is one of the Colón Theatre's (Teatro Colón's) four artistic ensembles, the others being the chorus, the ballet corps, and the Teatro's own orchestra, which plays mainly in the pit for opera and ballet. The Filarmónica is in charge of the Teatro's symphonic season and occasionally provides musical support for ballets and also plays outdoors in the summer in some of Buenos Aires's parks and gardens. The orchestra presents a total of some 130 performances per year. Filarmónica dress rehearsals are usually opened to high school students. Although there are no fixed subgroups within the orchestra, members are actively involved in recital and chamber music playing, especially for the Teatro Colón's educational programs, which reach several thousand students every year.

The Teatro Colón is a source of pride for Buenos Aires due to its architectural, technical, and acoustical characteristics. Opened in 1908, the theatre has a full capacity of about 4,000 and is home to a work force of some 1,300 people, including orchestra, opera, and ballet personnel, and their many-faceted support staff. The hall is horseshoe-shaped after the model of mid-nineteenth-century European halls like the Paris and Vienna opera houses. It has an ample diversity of seating and standing room, allowing a wide range of ticket prices. The orchestra is supported by the Teatro Colón's budget, largely derived from municipal funds and in a much lesser degree by revenues, box-office sales, and private patronage. The musicians are on the city's payroll and hold full-time tenures. They elect delegates to deal with the administration.

The orchestra's repertoire is wide and varied, emphasizing, in addition to the traditional programs, numerous twentieth-century works. It has always been the orchestra's policy to pioneer the work of Argentine composers.

At the end of World War II, Buenos Aires had only one permanent professional orchestra, the Colón's, which had two short symphonic seasons per year (before and after the main opera and ballet subscription series). The rest of Argentina had only three professional orchestras—in La Plata, Córdoba, and Paraná. The war years resulted in an unparalleled bonanza for Argentina because of restricted imports and massive exports of grain and cattle. At the time of the 1946 election, the newly inaugurated authorities of President Perón's regime found vast resources at hand to fund many ambitious cultural projects.

City Hall's new officials had plans for a new orchestra and wanted to engage as its first music director Clemens Krauss, who was available, having had some difficulties in postwar Europe due to his activity during the Nazi years. Negotiations were held, but because of the urgency to start the new orchestra, the post finally went to Lamberto Baldi, an Italian conductor who was active in Montevideo and São Paulo. Jaime Pahissa, a Spanish exile living in Buenos Aires, was appointed as Baldi's codirector.

Auditions began on September 19, 1946, and the orchestra was formally established on November 21, bearing the name "Orquesta Sinfónica de la Ciudad de Buenos Aires." The very first sounds it uttered were those of the Trio of Mozart's Symphony No. 39 (K. 543), conducted by Baldi. The new group boasted some unusual traits. Women occupied prominent seats for the first time in an Argentine orchestra (today's concertmistress is Haydée Francia). There were also many talented teenagers, such as Concertmaster Ernesto Mampaey (18), Assistant Concertmaster Luis Caracciolo (17), and others even younger. Juan Pedro Franze, the orchestra's first manager, recalls one of Baldi's fits of despair, in which he shouted *"Ma che vuoi che faccia io con quest' orchestra che è un Kindergaraten?"* ("What do you want me to do with this kindergarten orchestra?")

The orchestra had its first series of concerts in Argentina's foremost resort, Mar del Plata, during the summer of 1947. Its influence soon led to the building, between 1948 and 1949, of brand new symphony orchestras in Mendoza, Tucumán, Mar del Plata, and the National Symphony in Buenos Aires.* During its first seasons the orchestra's seat was the former Teatro Municipal, headed by Horacio Rabuffetti, one of the driving forces behind the group's birth and organization. The ensemble, honoring J. S. Bach on the bicentennial of his death, set foot on the Colón's stage for the first time during the 1950 season. Its name was changed to "Orquesta Filarmónica de Buenos Aires" in 1958, and three years later it was incorporated as one of the Colón's artistic ensembles.

After Baldi's departure and up to the time of Pedro Ignacio Calderón's appointment as music director in 1966, the orchestra had principal guest conductors who took over sizable portions of its seasons: Manuel Rosenthal, Ferruccio Calusio, Fabien Sevitzky, Jacques Singer, and Mariano Drago. The roster of foreign guest conductors was impressive. Herbert von Karajan, Wilhelm Furtwängler, Otto Klemperer, Clemens Krauss, and Ferdinand Leitner showed a bias toward German traditions, but there were also Sir Thomas Beecham, Pierre Boulez, Lorin Maazel, Sir Malcolm Sargent, and many others. The roll of guest artist has been filled by equally prominent musicians.

The activity of Alberto Ginastera's "Instituto Di Tella" in the 1960s was instrumental in widening the orchestra's repertoire toward music of the twentieth century. Founded by the wealthy Di Tella family and its related industries, the Instituto provided a vehicle within which Ginastera led the Latin American Center for Advanced Musical Studies (Centro Latinoamericano de Altos Estudios Musicales). The Center's students studied with visiting professors such as Aaron Copland, Olivier Messiaen, Riccardo Malipiero, Bruno Maderna, and others. During their stays, the Filarmónica performed many of their works as well as works by other twentieth-century masters. Much of this material found its way into the Filarmónica's regular programs, as did music of Karlheinz Stockhausen, Luigi Nono, Hans Werner Henze, Wolfgang Fortner, Bruno Maderna, and Earle Brown. This trend deepened under the present music director, Pedro Ignacio Calderón, who, in addition to tapping unexplored fringes of traditional repertoire such as Sibelius and Mahler cycles, presented such new works as Krzysztof Penderecki's *St. Luke Passion* and *Te Deum*.

CHRONOLOGY OF MUSIC DIRECTORS: Lamberto Baldi, 1946–1951. Pedro Ignacio Calderón, 1966–1980. Stanislaw Wislocki, 1981. Antonio Russo, 1982. Pedro Ignacio Calderón, 1983-present.

BIBLIOGRAPHY: Interviews with the orchestra's first manager, Juan Pedro Franze, and Music Director Pedro Ignacio Calderón. Roberto Caamaño, *La Historia Del Teatro Colón, 1908–1968,* 3 vols, (Buenos Aires: Cinetea, 1969). Ladislao Kurucz, *Vademecum Musical Argentino* (Buenos Aires: Vamuca, 1983). Teatro Colón archives.

ACCESS: Orquesta Filarmónica de Buenos Aires, Cerrito 618, 1010 Buenos Aires. 35–5414. Pedro Ignacio Calderón, Music Director.

GUILLERMO E. SCARABINO

National Symphony Orchestra of Argentina

Argentina's 101-member National Symphony Orchestra (Orquesta Sinfónica Nacional) is a federally sponsored ensemble normally performing in Buenos Aires. Some of its series concerts are carried live by the national radio network, and all are recorded for the radio's archives. As a national ensemble the orchestra tours the country. In its 35-year existence it has visited most of the state capitals and main cities of inland Argentina. Some tours have reached neighboring countries such as Paraguay and Brazil.

The orchestra's typical 44-week season consists of 20 to 24 repeated programs, a couple of one- to two-week tours, and a number of popular, educational, and promotional concerts, amounting to a total of 60 to 80 performances. The music of Argentine composers has a prominent place in the orchesta's repertoire. From the time of Juan José Castro's leadership on, short autumn series of contemporary music are not infrequent. The 1984 subscription series made a point of drawing its programs from music of this century, with a smaller percentage of unfamiliar works of older masters. The orchestra's short-lived Wind Quintet was established from 1963 to 1967. It was then taken over by the Mozarteum Argentino, under whose sponsorship it pursued a distinguished career in Argentina and abroad.

The National Orchestra was created in 1949 by President Perón's Decree No. 35,879, and it gave its first concert under Roberto Kinsky, its founding music director, at Buenos Aires's Teatro Colón on November 30, 1949. The background and circumstances of the orchestra's birth are very much like those of the Buenos Aires Philharmonic.* The founding players were drawn from the Teatro Colón's Orchestra, from the Orquesta Sinfónica de la Ciudad de Buenos Aires (later known as the Buenos Aires Philharmonic), and from among European émigrés who had settled in Argentina following World War II.

The orchestra's start was impressive, especially the seasons from 1950 through 1953, which were handled by Argentina's oldest management firm, Conciertos Daniel. Guest conductors in those series were Erich Kleiber (8 programs, including a Beethoven cycle), Igor Markevitch (7), Sergiu Celibidache (5), and other first-rate musicians such as Rafael Kubelik, Sir Georg Solti, Paul Paray, Désiré Defauw, Sir Malcolm Sargent, and others. Soloists were of equal prominence: Artur Rubinstein, Ruggiero Ricci, Pierre Fournier, Victoria de los Angeles, and many more.

This powerful drive weakened through the years, as some structural and functional trouble spots began to show. Ever-shrinking funding ran parallel to the country's receding bonanza of the World War II years, and the roster of guest artists grew qualitatively thinner. There were still some luminaries (Jean Martinon, Ernest Ansermet, Isaac Stern, José Iturbi and others), but the dazzling density of the first seasons never returned.

Increasing bureaucracy in the orchestra's management was another inconvenience to be reckoned with. Juan José Castro, the orchestra's music director of more than four years, bitterly exposed it in his resignation letter of October 1960 and sent shock waves through the musical establishment. In mid–1964 *Buenos Aires Musical,* a respected periodical, polled more than 30 prominent members of the musical community—composers, performers, conductors, scholars, critics, and managers. The subject was "basic problems affecting the Orquesta Sinfónica Nacional." The results showed an almost unanimous agreement in four areas: excessively bureaucratized administration, inadequate placement of the orchestra's personnel within the ranks of public employees, budget, and lack of a permanent hall for rehearsals and concerts.

Twenty years later the situation in regard to the inquiry may be summarized as follows: the orchestra's administrative chain of command extends from the President of Argentina through the Minister of Education and Justice, the Secretary of Culture, and the Director of Musical Affairs. Since 1972 orchestra members have had their own proper standing within the Public Administration's personnel. The orchestra's budget is a part of that of the Secretary of Culture's and is split among other departments or activities (museums, choruses, drama, etc.). The orchestra has permanent rehearsal space on the eleventh floor of the Teatro Nacional Cervantes's Annex. Since 1979 the ensemble has performed its subscription concerts at the 1,400-seat Auditorio de Belgrano, thus putting to an end its previous wandering among different halls (the Colón, Gran Rex, Opera, Coliseo, Cervantes, and Presidente Alvear theatres). The relationship with Teatro Colón has been uneven, depending on the Teatro's usually busy schedule and/or the good will of the City toward the federal administration.

RECORDING HISTORY AND SELECTIVE DISCOGRAPHY: Since the leadership of Víctor Tevah the National Orchestra has made commercial recordings, largely comprising Argentine works, for EMI/Angel.

Luis Gianneo, *Variaciones sobre un tema de tango*; Roberto García Morillo, *Variaciones olímpicas*, Op. 24 (Víctor Tevah): Angel SLPA–11201. Alberto Ginastera, *Pampeana No. 3*; Robert Caamaño, *Suite para orquesta de cuerdas*, Op. 9 (Tevah): Angel SPLA–11204. Carlos López Buchardo, *Escenas Argentinas*; Gilardi, *Gaucho con botas nuevas*; Pascual de Rogatis, *Danzas de "Huemac"* (Tevah): Angel SPLA–11203.

CHRONOLOGY OF MUSIC DIRECTORS: Roberto Kinsky, 1949–1953. Carlos Felix Cillario, 1954–1955. Juan José Castro, 1956–1960. Víctor Tevah, 1961–1962. Simón Blech, 1964–1965. Teodoro Fuchs, 1966–1967. Juan Carlos Zorzi, 1968–1969. Jacques Bodmer, 1970–1975. Jorge Fontenla, 1976–1977. Juan Carlos Zorzi, 1978–1984.

BIBLIOGRAPHY: Interview with National Orchestra principal viola and founding member Ernesto Blum. Archives of Conciertos Daniel (Lavalle 1171, Buenos Aires). *Buenos Aires Musical*, especially 2 May 1961 and 16 Sept. 1964. Ladislao Kurucz, *Vademecum Musical Argentino* (Buenos Aires: Vamuca, 1983). *La Nación* newspaper, Buenos Aires, 22 Oct. 1960.

ACCESS: Orquesta Sinfónica Nacional, Córdoba 1155, 1055 Buenos Aires. Iván R. Cosentino, Director Nacional de Música.

GUILLERMO E. SCARABINO

Australia ━━━━━━━━━━━━━━━━━━━━━━━━━

MELBOURNE   (2,803,000)

Melbourne Symphony Orchestra

The oldest and finest of Australia's orchestras, the Melbourne Symphony Orchestra (MSO) plays with a distinctive excitement and unerring clarity. Although it was not established in its present form until 1950, the orchestra is the direct descendant of three ensembles of the early 1900s and heir to a tradition of orchestral concerts that began at Melbourne in the 1860s. Today, after a decade under the vibrant Japanese conductor Hiroyuki Iwaki, the MSO is an orchestra of international rank.

With its full-time strength of 88 players, the MSO gives more than 110 concerts each year. Through four subscription series (April to October), a youth series, 12 free concerts, and 40 school concerts, it reaches an annual live audience of over 250,000; as the permanent Melbourne orchestra of the Australian Broadcasting Corporation (ABC), it also performs regularly on national radio and television and occasionally records film and television soundtracks. The Elizabethan Theatre Trust Orchestra—the only other full-time orchestra in Victoria—is fully occupied with opera and ballet performances. Consequently, as the state's principal provider of orchestral concerts, the MSO performs not only in Melbourne but also in three suburban centers and ten regional cities each year. Additionally, many of its members play in such smaller ensembles as the Philharmonia of Melbourne or the Melbourne String Quartet, while some teach part-time at the Victorian College of the Arts.

Based in Australia's second largest city, the orchestra's home since 1982 has been the Melbourne Concert Hall, set on the banks of the Yarra River in the $200 million Victorian Arts Centre. This auditorium seats 2,600 in a conventional three-tiered structure; its interior is spectacular, but its acoustics are strangely uneven, despite a complex tuning system of moveable perspex discs and woolen banners. The sound is more satisfactory in the Robert Blackwood Hall, Monash University, Clayton, where the orchestra gives one of its suburban series. The orchestra also plays in the open air, giving many of its free concerts at the Sidney Myer Music Bowl, an imposing steel awning with a capacity of 32,000 set near the Arts Centre on the lawns of King's Domain.

The MSO is part of a national network of six ABC orchestras, which together operate on an annual budget of nearly $22 million Australian. Only 30% of its funds come from box-office sales and 10% from subsidies ($175,000 from the Victorian government and $25,000 from the University of Melbourne); 60% comes from the ABC budget. The country's dominant employer of orchestral musicians, the ABC is a federal government enterprise headed by a government-appointed Board of Directors under which there is a general manager. Important contracts may be negotiated by the general manager, but most aspects of orchestral management are delegated to a director of music. Orchestral Advisory Committees and Orchestral Concert Subscribers' Committees are maintained in each state, but these have only limited influence over artistic policy; in practice, programming and the engagement of artists are centrally controlled by the director of music and staff of the Music/Concerts Department.

All ABC orchestras are affected by conditions of service and other factors that tend to inhibit competition among players (see Sydney Symphony Orchestra*); in the MSO, however, recent retirements have dramatically lowered the average age, and outstanding young players have obtained a number of the first desks. A significant part of the present membership is female; indeed, the orchestra was among the world's first to admit women to its ranks. As early as 1940 women occupied nearly half the positions, evidently making such guest conductors as Otto Klemperer rather skeptical of the orchestra's quality.

In their repertoire the ABC orchestras reflect the ABC Music/Concerts policy. Consequently, the MSO plays the standard repertoire, but places a special emphasis on Australian compositions, presenting more than 20 such works each year. Nevertheless, the programs can also be strongly influenced by the director of music. During the period 1963 to 1973, for example, while John Hopkins was director of music, the MSO performed an astonishing number of contemporary European and American works (see Sydney Symphony Orchestra); since then, the programs have become less adventurous.

Orchestral concerts became a feature of Melbourne's life in the 1850s, when the discovery of gold in the state accelerated the city's growth in population and prosperity. Ambitious concerts were presented by such colorful figures as Charles Horsely (1822–1876), an eccentric English composer/conductor, and by the time of the International Exhibition in 1880–1881, an orchestra of 121 players could easily be assembled. For the International Centennial Exhibition of 1888–1889 a first-rate orchestra of 80 players was engaged (with a nucleus of 15 brought from London), and 244 concerts were presented under the distinguished English composer/conductor Sir Frederick Cowen (1852–1935). After this a number of

Cowen's key players stayed on in Melbourne to form a permanent Victorian National Orchestra under the English organist Hamilton Clarke (1840–1912). The Exhibition orchestra, however, had been heavily subsidized by the Victorian government—Cowen had been paid a staggering £5,000 for his services—and without such support a permanent orchestra on the same scale had no chance of survival. Clarke's orchestra soon collapsed.

A more successful scheme was instigated by the young English composer/ conductor G.W.L. Marshall-Hall (1862–1915), who came to Melbourne in 1891 as founding professor of music at the University of Melbourne. With the support of the city's music warehouse Allan & Co., Marshall-Hall conducted an immensely successful orchestral concert in 1892 and then established a series of subscription concerts. Gifted and charismatic, Marshall-Hall for 20 years led performances of startling conviction and remarkable quality. Eventually the orchestra's structure, a part-time amalgam of professional, student, and amateur players, drew opposition from the musicians' union. By 1910 the resulting disputes had almost destroyed the concerts; in 1912 Marshall-Hall returned to England and the orchestra slowly disintegrated.

Two other ensembles, direct forbears of the modern MSO, presented orchestral concerts in Melbourne during this period: the largely-amateur Melbourne Symphony Orchestra, founded in 1906 by local violinist Alberto Zelman, Jr. (1874–1927), and the University of Melbourne Conservatorium Orchestra, founded in 1896 by Marshall-Hall. In 1900 Marshall-Hall's appointment at the university was not renewed, and the Conservatorium, still under his direction, became independent. Subsequently, another University of Melbourne Orchestra was formed, which gave concerts under the Scottish organist Franklin Peterson (1861–1915), who succeeded Marshall-Hall as professor of music, and then under the local violinist William Laver (1866–1940). Widely acclaimed concerts were given by the Australian violinist/conductor Bernard Heinze (1894–1981), who took over the University of Melbourne Orchestra in 1924, and by the English composer/conductor Fritz Hart (1874–1949), who took over the MSO following Zelman's death in 1927. Nevertheless, for 20 years after the demise of the Marshall-Hall Orchestra in 1912, the financing of orchestral concerts remained precarious; little progress was made toward the establishment of a permanent, professional orchestra.

The situation began to improve in 1932, when a prosperous local merchant, Sidney Myer, started to patronize the orchestra. With Myer's help the MSO's mounting debts were paid, the University of Melbourne established an annual series of free concerts, and the two bodies merged their orchestras under the MSO's title. The ABC was formed in the same year, with a set of goals including the cultivation of orchestral music, and a core ensemble of 15 full-time players was established at Melbourne under the local trumpeter Percy Code. The reformed MSO programs were now broadcast regularly on radio, conducted in turn by Heinze and Hart, and in 1934 the orchestra gave four hugely successful concerts under the celebrated Irish conductor Sir Hamilton Harty, brought to Australia by the ABC. After this, guest conductors were regularly featured with the orchestra, including several of front rank (see Sydney Symphony Orchestra). Heinze became musical advisor to the ABC in 1934 (Hart left Australia to become conductor of the Honolulu Symphony Orchestra** in 1935), and the MSO's combination of public subscription concerts, radio broadcasts, and featured celebrities was made the basis of the ABC's orchestral ventures in all other Australian cities.

Heinze urged the ABC to establish full-sized, permanent orchestras in each capital city. To this end the ABC increased its Melbourne core ensemble to 35 in 1936 and took over all aspects of the MSO's management in 1940; but further expansion during World War II was not possible. Finally, in 1950, by securing subsidies from the Victorian government and the Melbourne City Council, the ABC was able to expand its core to 82, and a full-sized orchestra was created, now adopting the title Victorian Symphony Orchestra.

A series of resident conductors was then engaged, beginning with the fiery Italian composer/conductor Alceo Galliera (b. 1910), who led two spirited seasons. He was followed in 1952 by the Argentine composer/conductor Juan José Castro (1895–1968), who introduced many contemporary works to the orchestra, and in 1953 by the Czech-born English conductor Walter Susskind (1918–1980), who brought an engaging warmth to many aspects of Melbourne's musical life. The Austrian conductor Kurt Wöss arrived in 1956; his successor, the eclectic French conductor Georges Tzipine (b. 1907) was popular, not only with the players but also with the audience.

Much of the orchestra's present finesse was developed in the period 1965–1979, while Leonard Dommett (b. 1928) was concertmaster. An Australian with extensive experience in London, Dommett inculcated in his players habits of discipline and unfailing professionalism and laid the technical basis on which outstanding performances could be built. During these years the orchestra made international tours to New Zealand (1965), Canada (1967), and the United States (1970); two of these were led by the Dutch conductor Willem van Otterloo (1907–1978). Holding the chief conductorship of the orchestra jointly with that of the Hague Philharmonic (Residentie-Orkest*) from 1967, van Otterloo gave profoundly penetrating—if rather sober—performances with the orchestra. He was succeeded in 1971 by the revered Bohemian conductor Fritz Rieger (b. 1910), who had to relinquish the post the following year after a series of heart attacks. The orchestra was known by its present title throughout this period, the name Victorian Symphony Orchestra having been abandoned in 1965.

The present chief conductor, Hiroyuki Iwaki (b. 1932), was engaged in 1974, after a stunning guest appearance with the orchestra in 1973. Iwaki brought an impeccable rhythmic sense to the orchestra and continues to produce exciting, often remarkable performances of the most challenging works of such composers as Berlioz, Tchaikovsky, Mahler, Stravinsky, and Olivier Messiaen. One of the few front-rank conductors to accept an extended engagement in Australia in recent years, he commutes between Melbourne and Tokyo, where he conducts Japan's NHK Symphony Orchestra.*

RECORDING HISTORY AND SELECTIVE DISCOGRAPHY: Since 1932 significant performances or studio recordings made by the ABC orchestras, notably more than 100 Australian compositions, have been tranferred to disc or cassette and issued by the ABC to international cultural and educational agencies. Unfortunately, these have seldom been available to the public, and copies preserved in the ABC Music Library and the National Film and Sound Archive are not at present accessible. Few of the recordings of Australian works have been released commercially; the five-disc set *Australian Festival of Music* (Festival SFC 80018–22), for example, is now difficult to obtain.

Britten, *Piano Concerto in D*; Copland, *Piano Concerto* (Gillian Lin/John Hopkins): Chandos ABR 1061. Grainger, *To a Nordic Princess* (Patrick Thomas): EMI OASD 7606. Edmund Rubbra, *Symphony No. 5*; Arthur Bliss, *Checkmate* (Hans-Hubert Schonzeler): Chandos ABR 1018. Walton, *The Bear* (Vanco Cavdarski): Chandos ABR 1052.

CHRONOLOGY OF MUSIC DIRECTORS: Alberto Zelman, Jr., 1906–1927. Fritz Hart, 1927–1932. Bernard Heinze, 1932–1949. Alceo Galliera, 1950–1951. Juan José Castro, 1952–1953. Walter Susskind, 1953–1955. Kurt Wöss, 1956–1959. Georges Tzipine, 1961–1965. Willem van Otterloo, 1967–1970. Fritz Rieger, 1971–1972. Hiroyuki Iwaki, 1974-present.

BIBLIOGRAPHY: Annual Reports of the ABC, 51 vols. (Canberra, 1932–1983). *Australian Encyclopedia*, 10 vols. (Sydney, 1965). James Barrett, *Outline History of Orchestral Music in Melbourne* (Melbourne: Lady Northcote Permanent Orchestra Trust Fund, 1941). Charles Buttrose, *Playing for Australia: A Story about ABC Orchestras and Music in Australia* (Melbourne, 1982). R. J. Cameron, *Year Book Australia*, vol. 67 (Canberra, 1983). Kenneth Hince, "The Melbourne Symphony Orchestra," *ABC Subscription Concert Programme* (Sydney, 1967). Charles Moses, "The Story of the ABC Symphony Orchestras," *ABC Subscription Concert Programme* (Sydney, 1957). Bede Nairn and Geoffrey Serle, *Australian Dictionary of Biography*, 9+ vols. (Melbourne, 1966 –). M. Thérèse Radic, *G. W. L. Marshall-Hall: Portrait of a Lost Crusader*, vol. 5 of *Music Monographs* (Perth, W.A.: University of Western Australia, 1982). Concert programs in Grainger Museum, University of Melbourne; Melba Memorial Conservatorium, Melbourne; Latrobe Library, Melbourne; National Library of Australia, Canberra.

ACCESS: Melbourne Symphony Orchestra, ABC Studios, 92 Waverly Road, East Malvern, Vic., 3145. (61–3) 528-4444.

WARREN A. BEBBINGTON

SYDNEY   (3,280,000)

Sydney Symphony Orchestra

The largest and busiest of Australia's orchestras, the Sydney Symphony Orchestra (SSO) has 97 full-time players and gives more than 150 concerts each year. It reaches a live audience of over 310,000 a year through five subscription series (April to October), ten free concerts, a youth series, and 36 school concerts. As the permanent Sydney orchestra of the Australian Broadcasting Corporation (ABC), the SSO also reaches a much wider audience through national radio and television broadcasts.

Based in Australia's oldest and largest city, the SSO is at the hub of Australian cultural life. Since 1973 its home has been the $100 million Sydney Opera House, a complex of billowing canopies, dramatically sculptured in white against the waters of Sydney Harbor. The concert hall in the Opera House complex has 2,700 seats arrayed in boxed tiers on all sides of the platform and a wooden ceiling of sweeping curves that contributes to the clear (if unremarkable) acoustics.

Of the three orchestras in New South Wales, the Elizabethan Theatre Trust Orchestra devotes itself to opera and ballet, and the ABC Sinfonia is a training orchestra; the SSO thus provides most of the state's orchestral concerts and travels to ten regional centers each year. Some of its members teach part-time at the N.S.W. State Conservatorium, and many participate in chamber ensembles such as the Sydney Wind Quintet or the Sydney String Quartet.

Although orchestral concerts began in Sydney in the 1880s, the SSO was not securely established until 1936, and its present title was not definitively adopted until 1946. Today it is part of a national network of six ABC orchestras centrally managed as a federal government enterprise (see Melbourne Symphony Orchestra*). Thirty percent of the SSO's funding comes from box-office sales and 10% from subsidies ($270,000 Australian from the N.S.W. government and $30,000 from the Sydney City Council); 60% is from the ABC budget. ABC Music/Concerts Department policy informs SSO programming, as with all ABC orchestras. Its repertoire may be described as standard, but with the addition of more than 20 works by Australian composers each year, usually including some written for ABC commissions.

A full, well-balanced, and homogeneous sonority, reliable horns, and a tradition of impressive woodwind soloists are the SSO's most enduring characteristics. Admittedly, the difficulty of obtaining resident visas for Australia means that competition for places in ABC orchestras is less international than in comparable ensembles; and once engaged, players enjoy tenure and conditions similar to those of the Australian Public Service. Older players are therefore not easily displaced, and an element of stagnation, particularly among ABC string players, is a recurring problem. Furthermore, while in the 1930s and 1940s many legendary conductors were attracted to Australia, today's towering conductors do not appear with the ABC orchestras. Australia's great distance from Europe and the United States seems to discourage such outstanding conductors as Herbert von Karajan or Karl Böhm; and Sir Charles Mackerras has refused to continue as the SSO's chief conductor beyond 1985, rather than "virtually give up a career in Europe or America, as commuting is costly and exhausting" (Melbourne

Age, 7 July 1984). These factors profoundly affect the quality not only of the
SSO but of all the ABC orchestras. Nevertheless, the SSO undoubtedly ranks
among the world's better ensembles.

The various forerunners of the SSO were all occasional ensembles of bandsmen, students, and amateurs. An orchestra of 57 players was assembled in 1889
for a pair of concerts under one Roberto Hazon; and probably some of its members
subsequently appeared in Hazon's Amateur Orchestral Society, which gave concerts intermittently from 1891 for some years. The title Sydney Symphony
Orchestra was adopted in 1908 by an ensemble of 65 players that presented
seasons of five or six concerts under the leadership of the English musician W.
Arundel Orchard (1867–1960), who had conducted a group of similarly provincial quality in London.

Unquestionably, the most important precedent for a permanent Sydney orchestra was that created by the Belgian violinist and former conductor of the
Glasgow Choral Union Henri Verbrugghen (1873–1934), who came to Sydney
in 1916 as founding director of the Conservatorium. By 1917 Verbrugghen had
assembled a largely professional orchestra of 70; in 1918 he obtained a N.S.W.
government subsidy and adopted the title N.S.W. State Orchestra. He found an
audience in Sydney for more than 25 orchestral concerts a year and took the
orchestra on tours interstate and to New Zealand. However, in 1922, a newly
elected N.S.W. government withdrew the subsidy and the orchestra was disbanded. Verbrugghen resigned his position in disgust and spent the remainder
of his career in the United States, where he was conductor of the Minneapolis
Symphony [now Minnesota] Orchestra.** Orchard became director of the Conservatorium, and for a decade Sydney's orchestral life consisted of the eight
concerts given each year by the Conservatorium's predominantly student
orchestra.

The present orchestra's development began with the creation of the ABC in
1932. From the first, the ABC made orchestral music one of its major features;
its opening broadcast included items by a National Broadcasting Symphony
Orchestra (under Orchard). In 1934 the mercurial Irish conductor Sir Hamilton
Harty was brought to Sydney for five concerts with the ABC Symphony Orchestra, which now included a core of 25 full-time players. Harty had made the
Hallé Orchestra* perhaps the finest in England, and he soon showed what could
be done in Australia when a major talent was employed. After this the ABC
adopted a plan of featuring celebrity conductors in its broadcasts. While subsequent directors of the Conservatorium, such as Edgar Bainton and Joseph Post,
continued to appear with the orchestra, the major conducting for the next ten
years was done by a series of outstanding guest artists, including Sir Malcolm
Sargent, George Szell, Sir Thomas Beecham, Antál Doráti, Otto Klemperer,
Georg Schnéevoigt, Eugene Ormandy, and Walter Susskind.

In 1934 the talented Australian violinist/conductor Bernard Heinze (1894–
1981) became musical adviser to the ABC. Following the pattern of Heinze's
successful orchestral ventures in Melbourne, regular subscription concerts were

established in Sydney and the core ensemble was increased to 45 in 1936. Heinze himself appeared regularly with the orchestra, serving as ABC conductor-in-chief during World War II, and remaining an important influence on the ABC's development for more than three decades. His plans for a full-sized, fully-professional orchestra were shelved during the war, but in 1946, by obtaining subsidies from the N.S.W. government and Sydney City Council, the core ensemble was augmented to 72 players. At that time the present title was purchased from George Plummer (who had founded the 1908 group of that name), and all managerial functions remaining with the Conservatorium were absorbed by the ABC.

Now the ABC sought to establish a salary large enough to attract a resident conductor of international stature to the orchestra. By combining the stipend of the directorship of the Conservatorium with that allocated for the SSO conductor, a salary of £8,000 was created—at a time when the Australian prime minister was earning £5,000—and this was sufficient to obtain the services of the distinguished English composer/conductor Sir Eugene Goossens (1893–1962), then conductor of the Cincinnati Symphony Orchestra.** Magnetic and exceptionally gifted, Goossens gave the orchestra the prospect of attaining international rank and astonished the public with performances of unprecedented accomplishment. Under his direction the SSO made its first commercial recording (for EMI, 1953) and the N.S.W. government laid its plans for the future Sydney Opera House. Important guest conductors continued to appear. The number of subscription series was increased from three to five, yet concerts remained completely sold out. Goossens gave the SSO the most brilliant decade in its history; his abrupt and widely publicized departure from Australia in 1956, absurdly precipitated by his being charged, at Sydney Airport, with importing pornographic literature, was a tragedy.

A series of less flamboyant conductors followed. Nikolai Malko, the first of the SSO's conductors not shared with the Conservatorium, was, despite his thoughtful interpretations and amiable personality, past his best when he arrived at Sydney in 1957. He was in poor health and died in Sydney in 1961. The American conductor Dean Dixon (1915–1976) gave a dazzling and urbane tour in 1962, but once appointed chief conductor in 1964 failed to maintain his earlier sparkle and was not reengaged after 1967. The youthful Israeli conductor Moshe Atzmon (b. 1931) arrived in 1969 and restored some measure of life to the orchestra.

That concert attendance continued to rise under these conductors was largely due to the work of the English cellist/conductor John Hopkins (b. 1927), the ABC director of music from 1963. Hopkins promoted imaginative programs, multiplying the number of Australian compositions being performed by the ABC orchestras, and introducing many new works by such composers as Michael Tippett, Gian-Carlo Menotti, Iannis Xenakis, Peter Maxwell-Davies, Mario Davidovsky, and Milton Babbitt. He extended Heinze's policy of concerts for young people through a series based on the London Proms and initiated many commercial recordings of Australian works, including revivals of earlier scores by such Australians as Percy Grainger. He made numerous appearances himself, but also engaged first-class guest conductors.

Consistently sensitive, reliable, and polished performances, however, did not reappear in the SSO until the Dutch conductor Willem van Otterloo (1907–1978) was appointed chief conductor in 1973. Occupying the post jointly with that of the Hague Philharmonic (Residentie-Orkest*), Otterloo had a keen sense for the SSO's capacity and steadily improved its level of accomplishment. He was killed in a car accident in Melbourne in 1978. Under his successor, the French conductor Louis Frémaux (b. 1921), the orchestra gave stylish—if not quite exuberant—performances. Sir Charles Mackerras (b. 1925), appointed chief conductor in 1982, was the first Australian to hold the post; he had once been principal oboist in the SSO under Goossens. As well as a vital sense for rhythms and color, Mackerras brought a scholarly interest in authentic texts and styles to the orchestra and a convincing sense of dramatic pace and shape.

Nevertheless, attendances at SSO concerts have been static since Hopkins's departure from the ABC in 1973, and the engagement of such frankly popular guest conductors as Willy Boskovsky (1974) and Arthur Fiedler (1975) has failed to arrest a general decline in public patronage. The SSO has made three international tours: in 1965 to Asia and Britain; in 1968 to New Zealand; and in 1974 to Asia, Britain, and Europe.

RECORDING HISTORY AND SELECTIVE DISCOGRAPHY: As with all ABC orchestras, few of the SSO's many recordings are available to the public (see Melbourne Symphony Orchestra).

Bach/Stokowski, *Orchestral Transcriptions* (John Lanchberry): RCA RL 10168. Coates, *Three Men, London Calling,* and other works (Otterloo): EMI/HMV ESD 7062. Debussy, *Danses sacrae et profane*; Ravel, *Introduction and Allegro* and other works (Robert Pickler): Chandos ABR 1060. Dvořák, *Symphony No. 8* (José Serebrier): RCA ARL 1-3550; Grainger, *Tribute to Foster* and other works (John Hopkins): EMI OASD 7608.

CHRONOLOGY OF MUSIC DIRECTORS: Bernard Heinze (Adviser, 1934–1943), 1943–1946. Eugene Goossens, 1947–1956. Nikolai Malko, 1957–1961. Dean Dixon, 1964–1967. Moshe Atzmon, 1969–1971. Willem van Otterloo, 1973–1978. Louis Frémaux, 1979–1981. Sir Charles Mackerras, 1982–1985.

BIBLIOGRAPHY: Annual Reports of the ABC, 51 vols. (Canberra, 1932–1983). *Australian Encyclopedia,* 10 vols. (Sydney, 1965). Charles Buttrose, *Playing for Australia: A Story about ABC Orchestras and Music in Australia* (Melbourne, 1982). R. J. Cameron, *Year Book Australia,* vol. 67 (Canberra, 1983). Concert programs in National Library of Australia, Canberra; Mitchell Library, Sydney. Glen Hamilton, "The Sydney Symphony Orchestra," *ABC Subscription Concert Programme* (Sydney, 1966). Charles Moses, "The Story of the ABC Symphony Orchestras," *ABC Subscription Concert Programme* (Sydney, 1957). Bede Nairn and Geoffrey Serle, *Australian Dictionary of Biography,* 9+ vols. (Melbourne, 1966-). W. Arundel Orchard, *Music in Australia* (Melbourne, 1952). Joseph E. Potts, "The Sydney Symphony Orchestra, *Strad* 79 (1969), 457–461.

ACCESS: Sydney Symphony Orchestra, Arcadia Theatre, Victoria Avenue, Chatswood, N.S.W., 2760. (61–2) 31–0211.

WARREN A. BEBBINGTON

Austria ⸺

LINZ (197,000)

Linz Bruckner Orchestra

The performances of the Linz Bruckner Orchestra are limited principally to
its home town and the state of Upper Austria, of which Linz is the capital.
Consisting of just under 100 musicians, the Linz Bruckner Orchestra plays all
the opera and operetta productions of the Upper Austrian Theatre (Oberöster-
reichischer Landestheater) in Linz. It also gives some 40 symphonic concerts
each year in town and throughout the province.

On the banks of the Danube in Linz stands the Brucknerhaus, a successful
combination of modern glass-and-steel architecture and traditional, good concert-
hall acoustics. The Brucknerhaus, along with LIVA, Linz's main concert booking
agency, employs the Bruckner Orchestra for three or four concerts each season
in its Gesellschaftskonzert and Sunday afternoon concert series. The International
Bruckner Festival engages the orchestra for two concerts every year, for aria
concerts, concert performances of stage works, and special events (like a Hoff-
nung Festival concert). Four further concerts are given for the national Workers'
Organization (an important institution in socialist Austria), as well as four young
people's concerts, and two choral accompaniments. All in all, the ratio of theatre
works to concerts stands at 55 to 45.

All concert planning is done by the principal conductor, who sets the dates
for concerts together with the general manager and a representative of the theatre.
The Bruckner Orchestra's yearly budget is 46 million schillings and is derived
almost entirely from the government of the Province of Upper Austria.

Although founded in 1803, the orchestra really began to emerge as an autonomous ensemble only as late as 1961 under the direction of Kurt Wöss. In 1803
the orchestra existed mainly for theatre productions, and only rarely did it perform

in concert in Linz. Nevertheless, the orchestra had close contact with both Beethoven and Bruckner. Beethoven was often in Linz visiting his brother; he finished his Eighth Symphony there. Much more important for the orchestra, however, was its relationship with Bruckner, who spent a large part of his life in Linz—composing, teaching, and working as Regens Chori for the Linz choral group Frohsinn. Bruckner conducted the Linz orchestra in his own Mass in D Minor and Mass in E Minor, as well as the final chorus from Richard Wagner's *Die Meistersinger*.

The name Bruckner Orchestra was applied to the group some 50 years after the composer's death. During the German domination of Austria in the 1940s, the Reichs Radio in Linz put together a first-class orchestra of musicians from throughout the region. Their conductor was Georg Ludwig Jochum. After the war only 39 out of the orchestra's 104 musicians were left, but they were able to resuscitate the theatre. The orchestra slowly grew, and in 1968, after many fruitful years under Kurt Wöss, it was finally given the name Bruckner Orchestra.

One cannot underestimate the importance of Kurt Wöss to the Bruckner Orchestra. He built it into one of the leading ensembles in a country already rich in fine groups. Wöss led the orchestra in the world premieres of Bruckner's *Studiensymphonie* in F Minor and the 1887 version of his Eighth Symphony. Heavy emphasis was also placed on works of Mahler and Richard Strauss. In Brucknerhaus Wöss was responsible for concert performances of Debussy's *Pelléas et Mélisande* and Wagner's *Tristan und Isolde* and *Die Walküre*.

The orchestra toured for the first time outside Austria under Wöss's baton, to Italy, Poland, and Germany. In later years the Bruckner Orchestra added tours to Czechoslovakia, Hungary, and Yugoslavia, as well as return visits to Italy. Theodor Guschlbauer was principal conductor from 1976 to 1983. From 1983 to 1985 Dr. Roman Zeilinger was principal conductor, and the Bruckner Orchestra is now in the hands of Manfred Mayrhofer.

The Bruckner Orchestra has spawned some excellent chamber music groups: the Linz Wind Quintet, the Linz Woodwinds (an octet), a string quartet carrying Bruckner's name, and the Linz Chamber Ensemble, an amorphous group capable of performing everything from duets to works for chamber orchestra.

RECORDING HISTORY AND DISCOGRAPHY: The Bruckner Orchestra began recording under Theodor Guschlbauer and has produced two commercial recordings to date:
Bruckner, "Nullte" Symphony (Guschlbauer): Amadeo AVRS 501. Fridolin Dallinger, First Symphony (*Bauernkriegssymphonie*) (Guschlbauer): Preiser Records SPR 142 ("Zeitgenössische Musik 25").

CHRONOLOGY OF PRINCIPAL CONDUCTORS: (Guest conductors to 1940.) Georg Ludwig Jochum, 1940–1945. (Guest conductors, 1945–1961.) Kurt Wöss, 1961–1976. Theodor Guschlbauer, 1976–1983. Roman Zeilinger, 1983–1985. Manfred Mayrhofer, 1985-present.

BIBLIOGRAPHY: Correspondence with Bruckner Orchestra administration. Bruckner Orchestra Linz, miscellaneous documents.

ACCESS: Bruckner Orchestra Linz, Promenade 39, Linz 4020. 77651.

                                                              JANET TURKOVIĆ

SALZBURG   (138,000)

Mozarteum Orchestra

The Mozarteum Orchestra consists of 90 musicians and performs not only at the Salzburg Festival in the summer but all through the regular season as well. It has two major subscription series, one in the Festival Hall and one in the large concert hall of the Mozarteum. It also has two smaller series, one centering on youth concerts and the other comprising concerts in factories and industrial concerns.

During the summer festival the Mozarteum Orchestra plays the Mozart Matinees, two "Serenade" concerts, and three church operas. Opera is not only a summer pastime, however, as the orchestra plays for six music productions during the year, whether opera, operetta, or musical comedy. The year 1985, for instance, saw a first-rate production of *Wozzeck* in Salzburg. This function consumes nearly half of all the orchestra's services. Altogether, the orchestra plays 66 concerts and 123 opera, operetta, or musical theatre performances each year.

The Mozarteum Orchestra's relationship with the Hochschule Mozarteum is purely historical. Although their names are the same, the only thing bringing them together is the one public subscription series the orchestra gives in the Hochschule Mozarteum's concert hall. The Mozarteum Orchestra's administration consists of a Board of 11 members, representing the city and province of Salzburg. Responsible to this Board are the general manager and the general music director. The general music director (principal conductor) is responsible for program selection, in coordination with the concert hall's needs and wishes. The orchestra tours regularly. In 1985 the ensemble toured the United States, and recent years had taken them to South America and throughout Europe (the latter an annual event).

As its name suggests, the Mozarteum Orchestra is known for its interpretation of Mozart. It plays more Mozart than of any other composer, and it now uses exclusively in its performances the new editions of Mozart's works (based on autographs where available) being published by Barenreiter Verlag, Kassel. In addition to its Mozart tradition, the orchestra relies heavily on the classical, romantic, and contemporary repertoire to fill out its performances. A recent example of programming is a 1985 concert with Hans Graf conducting: Mozart's Symphony No. 38 ("Prague"), the four last songs of Richard Strauss, and Béla Bartók's Concerto for Orchestra. Groups within the Mozarteum Orchestra are three string quartets, two larger chamber groups, and a wind octet.

The annual budget of the Mozarteum Orchestra is 55 million Austrian schillings, of which 36 million schillings is subsidized from municipal and province sources.

Musical life in Salzburg had been practically nonexistent since the death of Michael Haydn in 1806. Interest was reawakened only in 1841, the 50th anniversary of Mozart's death. Mozart's widow, Constanze von Nissen, used that occasion to urge Salzburg to erect a conservatory in his memory, with her son, Franz Xaver Wolfgang Mozart, as director. Her ideas were to be realized, although the first director of the Mozarteum conservatory was Aloys Taux, not Mozart's son.

The year 1841 saw the official imperial approval for the predecessor of today's Mozarteum Orchestra. The name was the "Salzburg Dommusikverein und Mozarteum Orchester" (Salzburg Cathedral Music Association and Mozarteum Orchestra), its music director was Aloys Taux, and the guiding light behind it was Franz Edler von Hilleprandt. Financial backing for the project came from all over Europe. Especially noteworthy was the interest of many prominent music publishers in the orchestra's development. One of the first works the new orchestra performed was Mozart's *Requiem*, at the funeral of Mozart's widow.

Many of the first orchestra members came from Bohemia, the contact between Salzburg and Prague having been stronger than that with Vienna. Not the least impressive of the Prague imports was to be violinist and concertmaster Otokar Sevčik. As late as 1917 the Mozarteum Orchestra was recognizable for its Bohemian flair. In 1846 the organization of a pension fund gave the orchestra members some sense of financial security, although their services at that time were certainly not those of a full-time orchestra. Performances were largely limited to the cathedral and the theatre, with only minimal concert activity outside of these.

The work of conducting the orchestra and directing the conservatory proved too much for Taux, and he died at an early age. The next music director, Hans Schläger, choral director by profession, was able to procure Joseph Joachim and Clara Schumann for concerts, but his enthusiasm for his assignment soon faded under insufficient funds and a dearth of talent in the orchestra itself. When Schläger moved over to the more administrative side of Salzburg's musical life in 1868, the Mozarteum passed over Anton Bruckner's application to promote Otto Bach as its new music director. Although Bach was the first to bring Beethoven's Ninth Symphony and Verdi's *Requiem* to Salzburg, he eventually felt it necessary to leave, under public and internal pressures.

In 1880 Josef Friedrich Hummel became music director, and a new era began for the Mozarteum Orchestra and its organization. Hummel conducted all the orchestra's concerts; its theatre (opera and operetta) performances were conducted by Karl Muck or his assistant, Hugo Wolf. Every summer 106 promenade concerts were given in the Mirabell Gardens and nine concerts in Klessheim Castle. During his 28 years at the head of the orchestra, Hummel concentrated above all else on raising the quality and standards of playing.

In 1908 the orchestra underwent a revision. The contractual connection with the cathedral was ended and the orchestra's offical new name was Mozarteum Orchestra. The new music director, also in that year, was Joseph Reiter. His term was limited to three years; his extravagance proving too much for Salzburg's financial resources. A succession of four additional short-term music directors followed until the Vienna-born Bernhard Paumgartner came to the orchestra and moved to Salzburg in 1917. Musical life there was never to be the same again. Singlehandedly he shaped and led the Salzburg Festival, directed the Conservatory, conducted orchestra concerts, and took the Mozarteum Orchestra for the first time on tour outside Austria. The Mozarteum Orchestra had always considered Mozart's music its own, and now under Paumgartner, even more Mozart was to be heard.

Although the stature of the orchestra was raised by Paumgartner's ensuring its inclusion in Salzburg Festival programs, the actual working conditions of individual musicians were far from satisfactory. They had no security, financial or otherwise, and intrigue reigned. Only after World War I were musicians from Salzburg given the recognition they deserved.

The period between the two world wars was a good one for the orchestra, which gave some excellent concerts during this time, including one with Siegfried Wagner in honor of his 60th birthday. In that same year, 1929, Herbert von Karajan began his conducting career in Salzburg, performing *Salome, Tosca, Josephslegende* and *Cavalleria Rusticana* all with the Mozarteum Orchestra. There were tours abroad, guest appearances in Czechoslovakia (1931), and a tour in 1937 in Europe. The orchestra enjoyed great success, especially with its Mozart interpretations.

At the time of Austria's joining the German Reich in 1938, Paumgartner was relieved of his post. In 1944 all cultural institutions were banned. At about the same time Paumgartner left, the orchestra had become incorporated as such, with a full season, social security, and full legal status. The new director in 1939 was Willem van Hoogstraten. At the time there were 47 orchestra members, and van Hoogstraten limited activities just to concerts so as not to conflict with the theatre musicians in town.

Immediately after the war Salzburg fell into the hands of the Americans, who were responsible for the occupation of that section of Austria. They were concerned that the Salzburg Festival be reinstated as quickly as possible. Since the Vienna Philharmonic,* the former backbone of the Festival, was not allowed to leave Vienna under the terms of the occupation, the Mozarteum Orchestra was reactivated to fill the need.

Postwar conditions were difficult for the musicians. It took all of the orchestra manager's business acumen to bring the orchestra's services (rehearsals and performances) up to 42 a month. The musicians banded together to found their own corporation. Conductors there were aplenty, due to the reigning travel restrictions. The orchestra enjoyed working under Clemens Krauss, Karl Böhm, Hans Knappertsbusch, and Josef Krips, to name only a few.

By 1950, however, the orchestra was in grave financial straits. Public appeal was made, and Salzburg responded generously. Municipal and provincial funds were forthcoming. By 1951 the musicians were again under contract, and again travelling—this time to Moscow, Kiev, Prague, and Greece under Bernhard Paumgartner's direction. In 1952 Hermann von Schmeidel took the orchestra on a tour of Germany. Then, in 1953, Ernst Märzendorfer, known as a perfectionist, took over the post of music director. The orchestra went on tour to the United States in 1966. Märzendorfer left the orchestra after five years and in 1959 Mladen Basic took his place. A particularly selfless conductor, known and loved for putting the orchestra's interests before all else, Basic concentrated on conducting opera. He brought, among others, *Salome, Die Walküre, Ariadne auf Naxos,* and *Fidelio* (absent many years) to Salzburg. His eight-year tenure was terminated with the arrival of a new opera director in Salzburg (at the theatre). Basic, not wanting to limit himself only to concertizing, moved on.

The year 1969 brought Leopold Hager to the orchestra as principal conductor for 12 years—years devoted to raising the artistic level of the ensemble. During his regime the orchestra toured Europe, the United States, Japan, and South America. It also made a great many recordings. Emphasis was on Mozart, both in concert and opera productions. Hager's successor, Ralf Weikert, continued the tradition and went so far as to perform the rarely heard Mozart operas during his three-year tenure with the orchestra. The present music director, Hans Graf, arrived in 1984.

RECORDING HISTORY AND SELECTIVE DISCOGRAPHY: Most of the Mozarteum Orchestra's recordings were done with its former music director Leopold Hager. These include all the Mozart piano concertos (Karl Engel), the youth operas of Mozart, and his concert arias, all for Deutsche Grammophon. On the Teldec label the orchestra appears with Gustav Kuhn doing the Salzburg Symphonies of Mozart and, again with Hager, Mozart's horn, oboe, and bassoon concertos.

Mozart, Bassoon Concerto and Oboe Concerto (Milan Turković and Jurg Schaeftlein/ Hager): Teldec 642361. Mozart, Symphonies No. 40 and 41 (Hager): Euphoria 2009. Mozart, Violin Concerto No. 1 (Thomas Zehetmair/Hager: Teldec 642537.

CHRONOLOGY OF MUSIC DIRECTORS: Aloys Taux, 1841–1861. Hans Schläger, 1861–1868. Otto Bach, 1868–1880. Josef Friedrich Hummel, 1880–1908. Joseph Reiter, 1908–1911. Paul Graener, 1911–1913. Robert Hirschfeld, 1913–1914. Eugen Schmitz, 1914–1915. Franz Ledwinka, 1915–1917. Bernhard Paumgartner, 1917–1938. Willem van Hoogstraten, 1939–1945. Robert Wagner, 1945–1947. Paul Walter, 1947–1953. Ernst Märzendorfer, 1953–1958. Meinhard von Zallinger, 1958–1959. Mladen Basic, 1959–1967. Leopold Hager, 1969–1981. Ralf Weikert, 1981–1984. Hans Graf, 1984-present.

BIBLIOGRAPHY: Joseph Schröcksnadel, *Salzburgs Musikalische Botschafter: Das Mozarteum Orchester* (Salzburg: Verlag Alfred Winter, 1984).

ACCESS: Mozarteum Orchestra, Schwarzstrasse 4, Salzburg 5020. (0622)72–3–30. Dr. Sigune Neureiter, Manager.

JANET TURKOVIĆ

VIENNA (1,515,000)

Austrian Radio Symphony Orchestra

A major broadcasting ensemble, the Austrian Radio Symphony Orchestra (ORF: Österreichisches Rundfunk Symphonie Orchester), has had an important role in cultural life in Austria and beyond its borders as well.

Although the orchestra's main mission is broadcasting, it also presents two subscription concert cycles of about six programs each in both the Musikverein and Konzerthaus in Vienna. The orchestra's own six-concert annual series in the Radio Concert Hall is free or costs a minimal admission, and all programs are taped for broadcast. Annually about 60 live concerts are on the ORF Symphony's performance schedule. It presents about ten hours of music per week on Austrian Radio.

The ensemble's home auditorium in Vienna's Radio Center was conceived, acoustically speaking, for live broadcasting and tapings. Clemens Holzmeister, Austria's most important prewar architect, designed the hall, considered one of Europe's most beautiful for this purpose. Completed in 1936, it comfortably seats 300 people in wide, thickly padded leather chairs. In January of 1983 a new, four-manual, 60-stop mechanical organ by the West German builder Karl Schuke was dedicated in the hall to replace an earlier instrument dating from 1938. The instrument is expected to broaden the orchestra's repertoire possibilities; dedicatory ceremonies included, for example, the world premiere of Peter Eben's Organ Concerto. The auditorium also serves as rehearsal room, although the schedule varies according to the preparation necessary for particular works. Rehearsals, except the final dress, are strictly closed to the public.

From its inception in 1969 the orchestra has by policy devoted one-third of its repertoire to twentieth-century composers. Premieres in Austria of contemporary composers are the rule at the ORF Symphony, and these have included works of Luciano Berio, Ernst Křenek, Roman Haubenstock-Rumati, Witold Lutosławski, and Krzysztof Penderecki, in addition to Radio-commissioned works.

It would seem that the orchestra's style is distinguished by a sound necessary for interpreting the modern classics—Bartók, Stravinsky, Kodály, the Second Viennese School—but as in all of the Viennese ensembles, one cannot overlook the so-called Viennese warmth, particularly evident in the orchestra's strings. This tradition of tone culture, passed on by orchestra members and teachers to their substitutes and students, is a hallmark of the ORF Symphony Orchestra. The orchestra does not use period instruments or the D trumpet (although the Viennese School expects facility on this instrument), but it does require the Viennese technical approach to reeds and horns. For some years the ORF horn section has used an innovative "double" version of the traditional Vienna horn.

The orchestra's annual budget is drawn directly from that of the Austrian Radio. Today it amounts to 85 million Austrian shillings. The orchestra employs its 100 members, four administrators in the orchestra bureau, a general manager, and a principal conductor from this budget. Guest conductors and soloists are selected for specific performances and not on a regular basis by the general manager, although the orchestra, through its spokesman, can make suggestions. It is not, however, an independent ensemble. Its members are employed to serve the Austrian Radio, and as a result the determination of artistic questions is left in the hands of the administration and, to an extent, the principal conductor.

The same policy applies regarding tours, recording contracts, and innovative projects beyond the orchestra's broadcasting demands. Since Austria has a socialistic political and economic system, all salaries as well as working conditions are regulated. Employees are entitled to four weeks' paid vacation; health care and a retirement fund are an automatic result of consistent employment.

Additional operating monies are gleaned from regular local and international tours, set up at the discretion of the manager, as well as yearly participation in Austria's music festivals: the Vienna Festival, the Styrian Autumn in Graz, the International Bruckner Festival in Linz, and the Carinthian Summer. A major aspect of the ORF Symphony's work has been the creation of special programs for the Salzburg Festival. Here the orchestra has gained a permanent place in the Festival planning with performance of major twentieth-century works such as Franz Schmidt's *Book of the Seven Seals,* Ernst Křenek's *Charles the Fifth,* and Othmar Schoeck's *Penthesilea.*

The ORF Sinfonietta is a flexible chamber music group of 23, whose unusual programs and instrument groups allow performances of works outside the fixed boundaries of the larger orchestra. The ensemble has made significant musical contributions in its broadcast work and also has its own performance series of some six concerts per season in the Radio Music Hall.

The present ORF Symphony Orchestra was founded in 1969 to replace the Vienna Radio Orchestra, which had existed since 1945. The ORF Symphony thus grew out of an established orchestra whose members were not only well seasoned musicians but also excellent sight readers, practitioners who learned quickly and who had played under some of Europe's greatest postwar conductors. Half of the Vienna Radio Orchestra's repertoire consisted of Austrian entertainment or light music of a higher standard, such as that of Johann Strauss, and half was of symphonic literature, baroque to modern.

With the reorganization of the Austrian Radio in 1969, Director General Gerd Becher, orienting himself on British and German principles of broadcasting, recognized the need for the Radio's own permanent orchestra—one that would perform additionally outside the radio studios. New orchestra members recruited from the opera, from other symphony orchestras, and from the finer Viennese groups were added to players remaining from the older orchestra. With musical competition high among the already existing excellent Viennese ensembles, the newly formed ORF Symphony Orchestra was to devote only one-third of its repertoire to lesser-known classic and romantic works, one-third to twentieth-century music (emphasizing contemporary Austrian), and the remaining third to the daily requirements of specific broadcast purposes.

Three permanent and many guest conductors have shaped and influenced the ORF Symphony in its short existence. The first principal conductor, Milan Horvat, was Yugoslavian. Actualizing the mandate of the orchestra's charter, he built up an enormous repertoire. Horvat was replaced in 1975 by the Finnish conductor Leif Segerstam. Through the years many of the world's most illustrious conductors have appeared with the orchestra, and all introduced works from

their respective national backgrounds. A younger generation of Austrian conductors has also appeared in recent years, as have other important musicians,
such as composer/conductors Rudolf Barshai, Gunther Schuller, and Cristóbal
Halffter, to name but a few.

In 1982 Lothar Zagrosek became the orchestra's third principal conductor and
immediately aroused interest by placing emphasis on specific works, including
performances of Alexander von Zemlinsky's *Lyric* Symphony (with ongoing
work on his operas) in Salzburg, Frank Martin's *Golgotha,* and the first performance of Josef Matthias Hauer's opera *Salambo.* Zagrosek continues his
special interest in twentieth-century music in addition to maintaining the orchestra's normal activity with the classical-romantic repertoire.

RECORDING HISTORY AND SELECTIVE DISCOGRAPHY: In addition to an enor-
mous number of radio and festival tapes available in the listeners' archives, the ORF
Orchestra has produced to date 15 commercial recordings on Orfeo, Philips, Polydor,
Amadeo, Atlantis, and Teldec labels. Its most outstanding release was for Philips in 1974
(6700–084), the first year the orchestra recorded, with Michael Gielen conducting Arnold
Schoenberg's *Moses and Aaron.*

Gottfried Von Einem, *Danton's Death* (Zagrosek): Orfeo S102–842 H. Ernst Křenek,
Charles the Fifth (Albrecht): Amadeo AVRS 305. Handel, *Messiah* (Charles Mackerras):
DG ARC–2710016 (3 records).

CHRONOLOGY OF PRINCIPAL CONDUCTORS: Milan Horvat, 1969–1975. Leif
Segerstam, 1975–1982. Lothar Zagrosek, 1982-present.

BIBLIOGRAPHY: ORF Symphony Orchestra, miscellaneous fact sheets and taped interviews in archives of the Austrian Radio, Vienna. Erhard Seyfried, "Concerning the
. . . Vienna Horn," *The Horn Call,* Oct. 1985.

ACCESS: ORF Symphonie Orchester, Argentinierstrasse 30a, 1040 Vienna. (0222) 65–
95/420. Gottfried Kraus, General Manager.

                                                                    CAROL KOCH

Vienna Philharmonic

The Vienna Philharmonic (Wiener Philharmoniker) is not only one of the main
pillars of musical life in Vienna but is also among the most revered orchestras
in the world. Soon to celebrate the 150th anniversary of its foundation, the
orchestra has from the very beginning been built on the performance of music
of the masters of the Viennese Classical School.

The Vienna Philharmonic still maintains many of its original traditions, notably
that of being an exclusively male orchestra. Many of the orchestra's approximately 140 musicians teach privately and in various music schools in Vienna
(Hochschule für Musik und darstellende Kunst, Konservatorium der Stadt Wien)
and participate in various constellations of independent chamber music groups.
The orchestra's most important regularly scheduled activities outside of Vienna
take place in Salzburg, where the Mozart Week (in January) and the famous
Summer Festival (July/August) would not be the same without the Philharmonic.

The small number of concerts per season (approximately 70 in 1985–1986) is deceptive. About half of these take place in Vienna, mostly in the Golden Hall of the Society of Friends of Music (Gesellschaft der Musikfreunde), where the eight annual subscription concerts (plus eight dress rehearsal performances) are traditionally held. The most important concerts outside the subscription concerts are the Nicolai Memorial Concert, which emphasizes the works of Beethoven, as was Otto Nicolai's original intention, and the immensely popular New Year's Concert, devoted to works of the Strauss dynasty. Other performances in Vienna usually take the form of concerts during the annual Festival of Vienna (May/June). The orchestra also makes several concert tours each season, but these are often defined by the orchestra's duties at the Vienna Opera, where it is the pit orchestra during the Opera's ten-month season. In addition, numerous recordings both as an opera and concert orchestra keep the Philharmonic very busy—and solvent. The Vienna Philharmonic receives only insignificant state subventions and is supported by its concerts and other activities.

The organization of the Vienna Philharmonic dates back to Nicolai's original idea of representing each group of instruments—11 in all—with an elected delegate. By 1862 these representatives assumed certain organizational functions, and the conductor of the subscription concerts, who was also general director of the orchestra, was chosen by vote too. This system of democratic choice still lives on today although the orchestra is formally and legally a society and not a mere concert organization.

The Vienna Philharmonic stands apart from other orchestras not because of the instruments its members play, but rather by virtue of its special homogeneity and fluid sound. Almost all of the musicians are Austrian born and trained, and many are born Viennese. Some peculiarities, perhaps also explained by tradition, are the use of special Viennese varieties of the oboe and horn, the latter often the scapegoat for bad mistakes although there is no talk of parting with it (see also Austrian Radio Symphony Orchestra* and Vienna Symphony Orchestra*). An interesting outgrowth of this preoccupation with a special sound is the existence of an Institute for Viennese Musical Style (Wiener Klangstil) at the Music Academy.

The Vienna Philharmonic was founded in 1842 by the German composer Otto Nicolai (1810–1849) as an answer to the dilletantism that seemed rampant on the Viennese concert scene. Nicolai's solution was to raise the quality of concert life by hiring professional musicians for orchestral performances. As the music director of the Imperial Opera House (Kärntnertortheater), his logical choice was the opera orchestra, thus creating a duality of functions that still exists today. Nicolai's original handwritten announcement of the first concert of March 28, 1842, is still preserved in the Philharmonic archive (a collection distinct from the archive of the Society of the Friends of Music). Indeed, the Philharmonic has always insisted on being an independent organization, even though it has rented its rooms in the Society Building and performed there since the building was opened in 1870.

Nicolai conducted 12 concerts between 1842 and 1847, at which time he left his position at the Imperial Opera House. The organization of the Philharmonic dates back to his ideas, although these were modified in 1860 when a directorate with a general director, archivist, business manager, treasurer, and other members was specified. Such precepts as the democratic choice of the directorate and the resident conductor (a position coincident with that of general director until after Mahler), and the commitment to the classical repertoire have made the orchestra what it is today. Although Nicolai planned only two concerts per season, the reorganization of 1860 set the number of subscription concerts at four, which soon became the present norm of eight. The reorganization of the Philharmonic came after a period of six years under the direction of Karl Eckert (1820–1879), who kept the Philharmonic concerts going and was the conductor of the first subscription concert (January 15, 1860). Otto Dessoff (1835–1892) was the first elected resident conductor.

It was during Dessoff's era that the orchestra enjoyed direct contact with two great composers who lived in Vienna at the time: Johannes Brahms (who had moved to the city in 1862) and Anton Bruckner. The first work by Brahms to be played by the Philharmonic was his Serenade No. 2 in D Major (Dec. 12, 1869). On January 22, 1871, Brahms played the solo part in his D Minor Piano Concerto, and on November 2, 1873, he conducted the first performance of his Variations on the "Chorale of St. Anthony," better known as the *Haydn Variations*. Anton Bruckner conducted the Philharmonic for the first time on October 26, 1873. This was the first performance of his Symphony No. 2 in C Minor; a special concert outside the subscription series was necessitated by the length of the work.

Brahms and Bruckner lived and died in Vienna; the Philharmonic's contact with two other famous composers of the period was shorter. Richard Wagner conducted the orchestra in 1862–1863 in three concerts, which he had organized in the "Theater an der Wien" and later, on May 12, 1872, he conducted Beethoven's Third Symphony together with his own works in a benefit concert for needy musicians. Giuseppe Verdi, who had already appeared in Vienna in April 1843 for two performances of his opera *Nabucco,* returned to the city for the last time in 1875 to conduct his *Requiem* four times and *Aïda* twice in the new Imperial Opera House. Under Dessoff the orchestra made its first concert trip, albeit not far from home, to Salzburg, where the Philharmonic first performed on July 17, 1877.

With Hans Richter (1843–1916), who conducted the first performances of Wagner's *Ring* in Bayreuth, a former member of the Philharmonic took over the orchestra's direction. His era lasted from the season of 1875–1876 until 1897–1898. At the beginning of that period the Society of the Friends of Music organized its own concerts of musical novelties under the direction of Johann Herbeck, thus presenting the Philharmonic concerts with a certain rivalry. Richter interrupted his activities with the orchestra for the 1882–1883 season, but as a whole his era has been called the "Golden Age" of the Philharmonic. Works of Bach, Handel, Gluck, Mozart, Beethoven, Schumann, and Louis Spohr formed the basis of Richter's concert programming, but those of Bruckner, Brahms, and Dvořák appeared regularly. The highpoint of the Bruckner concerts was clearly the world premiere of the Eighth Symphony on December 18, 1892. That same year saw the first inclusion of explanatory notes in the programs; they have become a little-known medium for original musicological research. A memorial concert on November 8, 1896, featuring Bruckner's Seventh Symphony emphasized the special relationship the Philharmonic has maintained with the works of this Austrian composer right up to the present day. Brahms too remained close to the Philharmonic; among the more important products of the relationship was the first performance of Brahms's Third Symphony on December 2, 1883. This Golden Age was also marked by a new appreciation of the managerial aspects of a musical organization, the establishment of a pension fund for retired orchestra members (1886–1887), and the institution of the Nicolai Memorial Concerts.

When Gustav Mahler (1860–1911) took over his first concert of the Vienna Philharmonic (November 6, 1898), it was obvious that a new era had begun. He soon took the orchestra on its first foreign tour, to Paris, where the Philharmonic gave five concerts during the World's Fair. On this occasion Camille Saint-Saëns, as president of the Commission for Musical Performance, presented the orchestra with a crown of golden oak leaves as a symbol of the Commission's appreciation. Unfortunately, the material prospects of this trip were not bright, since it was possible to finance the trip back only with the aid of a donation by Albert Rothschild. Mahler's short era—he resigned in 1901—was notable not so much for a change in programming as for its abrupt change in interpretation. Mahler emphasized this fact by putting the very work in his first concert that Richter had conducted in his last one: Beethoven's *Eroica* Symphony.

Mahler never developed a warm relationship with the Philharmonic, which he conducted in the Opera until 1907. His doctor's advice to restrict his activities is generally viewed as a convenient excuse for terminating the orchestral association. The Viennese violinist and operetta composer Josef Hellmesberger (1855–1907) was the next conductor-in-residence, but after his first season he shared his duties with Ernst von Schuch, Vassily Safonoff, Richard Strauss, Karl Muck, and Felix Mottl. In this period Arthur Nikisch and Bruno Walter also conducted occasionally.

Felix Weingartner (1863–1942) was named director of the Imperial Opera in 1907 and was soon chosen by the Philharmonic as its next director. He stayed in this position for 19 years, long after he had ceased to direct the opera. Weingartner emphasized French music and travelled widely with the orchestra (Switzerland, 1917; Berlin, 1918; South America, 1922). Richard Strauss, who shared the directorship of the Vienna State Opera with Franz Schalk from 1919 to 1924, took the Philharmonic on a second South American tour in 1924. Strauss had conducted the orchestra for the first time on December 16, 1906, in Salzburg. This was to be the first of 85 concerts in all, and his close ties to the orchestra are evidenced by the fact that he celebrated both his 75th and 80th birthdays with the Philharmonic. Other important developments in the Weingartner era were the opening of the Salzburg Festival in 1925 and the performance of the dress rehearsals of the subscription concerts as second subscription concerts. (The Philharmonic concerts are normally Sunday morning matinees preceded by a Saturday afternoon "Dress Rehearsal," as it is still called.)

In 1922 Wilhelm Furtwängler (1886–1954) joined the Philharmonic in a Brahms Memorial Celebration. Five years later he accepted the direction of the subscription concerts, initially with Schalk (1927–1928) and then alone until 1930. Furtwängler expressed great satisfaction in performing with the orchestra. The last resident conductor of the Philharmonic was Clemens Krauss (1893–1954), who served in the position from 1930 to 1932. He introduced the New Year's Concerts as part of the standard concert activities and was the conductor of the first Philharmonic concert after the Second World War.

Since 1932 the Vienna Philharmonic has relied on guest conductors, many of whom have been affiliated with the orchestra for 20, 30, or more years. While maintaining a basically classical repertoire, the orchestra has included works of contemporary composers—for example, Schoenberg's *Gurrelieder* with the composer conducting (June 12 and 13, 1920) and Ravel's Piano Concerto under the composer's direction on February 2, 1932. The Austrian composers Joseph Marx and Franz Schmidt remained in close contact with the Philharmonic, and the orchestra even actively helped provide for the financial security of the German composer Hans Pfitzner's last days. Pfitzner (1869–1949) was made an honorary member of the Vienna Philharmonic, and as a token of his appreciation he dedicated the original score of his masterpiece, the opera *Palestrina*, to the orchestra.

In spite of the Austrian Civil War (1934) and continuous political strife, the 1930s were a period of intense musical activity during which the circle of guest conductors was enriched by Arturo Toscanini, Bruno Walter, and Hans Knappertsbusch. Toscanini first conducted the Philharmonic in Budapest in October 1933 and then went on to lead another 46 concerts from 1934 to 1937, although he refused to include in his programs the works of two great Austrian masters, Bruckner and Mahler. Bruno Walter (1876–1962), who conducted his first subscription concert on March 4, 1934, had his own ideas about the special quality of the orchestra's sound: "The sound of 1897 is the same today although not one musician from those days is still active in the present orchestra. . . . This is how Vienna sounds!" The third of the new guest conductors, Hans Knappertsbusch (1888–1965), dubbed the orchestra "The Incomparable" ("*Die Unvergleichlichen*"). He conducted a subscription concert on November 18, 1934, and was soon as famous for his short rehearsals and his rough language as for the superb quality of his concerts.

The Philharmonic managed to stay together in Vienna during the war years mostly due to Furtwängler's intervention, and it gave concerts as late as April 1945. Despite seemingly insuperable difficulties, the subscription concerts were already resumed in the 1945–1946 season with Josef Krips, Rudolf Moralt, Felix Prohaska, Karl Krueger, and Herbert von Karajan. Of course the orchestra could not participate in the 1945 Salzburg Festival, but that has remained the only exception to the Philharmonic's presence there since the festival was founded in 1925. Soon many of the already mentioned conductors were reunited with the orchestra. Furtwängler played an important role again and took the Philharmonic to England on its first postwar tour, in 1948. This marked a new beginning in the orchestra's travels, and it has since toured widely, including visits to Africa in 1950 under Clemens Krauss; Japan in 1956 with Paul Hindemith; the United States in 1956 with Carl Schuricht and André Cluytens; a world trip in 1959 with Karajan; Moscow in 1962 with Karajan and Willy Boskovsky; Japan, China, and Korea in 1973 with Claudio Abbado; and Mexico in 1981 with Carlos Kleiber.

Although virtually every world-renowned conductor has conducted the Vienna Philharmonic, the decades since World War II have seen special relationships develop between the orchestra and several conductors in particular: Herbert von Karajan, Sir Georg Solti, Karl Böhm, and Leonard Bernstein. They have all received the orchestra's highest award, the Ring of Honor of the Vienna Philharmonic.

RECORDING HISTORY AND SELECTIVE DISCOGRAPHY: The VPO's recording activities date back to the 1920s when Schalk and Weingartner used the new possibilities offered by the founding of the Austrian Broadcasting System (RAWAG) to document the orchestra's sound. These and most other recordings before the end of World War II were either studio recordings or live concert performances without much editing. A thorough study of the VPO's recording history is being prepared for its 150th anniversary in 1992.

The most recent (1986) catalog of presently available recordings of the Philharmonic, produced by a private Austrian firm (Neustidler Paper Mills), lists approximately 350 titles, many in re-release, with the orchestra conducted by some 40 conductors. Although many of these are opera recordings, the conductors include many who have also headed Vienna Philharmonic subscription concerts. The orchestra has recorded regularly for Deutsche Grammophon and EMI; its works appear also on the CBS, Orf, Philips, and RCA labels. Some of its Decca recordings are available in Japan on King records.

Beethoven, Complete Symphonies (Bernstein): DG 2740216; also issued separately. Beethoven, Complete Symphonies (Böhm): DG; also issued separately. Beethoven, Complete Piano Concertos (Backhaus/Schmidt-Isserstedt): Decca SPA403; also issued separately. Brahms, Complete Symphonies (Bernstein): DG 2741023; also issued separately. Brahms, Symphony No. 4 (Carlos Kleiber): DG 2532003. Bruckner, Complete Symphonies (Karajan): DG, issued separately. Bruckner, Symphonies Nos. 4, 7, 8, and 9 (Furtwängler): DG 2740201 (5 records). Haydn, *The Creation* (Karajan): DG 2741017 (2 records). Mahler, *Das Lied von der Erde* (Walter): Decca ACL 305. Mozart, Symphonies Nos. 29, 35, 38–41 and *Maurerische Trauermusik* (Böhm): DG 2740268 (3 records); also issued separately. Mozart, Piano Concertos Nos. 20 and 21 (Gulda/Abbado): DG 2530548. Schubert, Symphony No. 9 (Solti): Decca SXDL 7557; London LDR–71057. [Johann Sr., Johann Jr., and Joseph Strauss], *Neujahrskonzerte der Wiener Philarmoniker* (Boskovsky): Decca D147D4 (3 records). Strauss, *Also Sprach Zarathustra*,

Don Juan, and *Till Eulenspiegel* (Karajan): Decca JB27; London 41017 (3 records). Verdi, *Requiem* (Reiner): Decca DJB 2003 (2 records).

CHRONOLOGY OF MUSIC DIRECTORS: Otto Nicolai, 1842–1848. Georg Hellmesberger, 1848–1850. Karl Eckert, 1854–1860. Otto Dessoff, 1860–1875. Hans Richter, 1875–1898. Gustav Mahler, 1898–1901. Josef Hellmesberger, 1901–1903. Ernst von Schuch, Felix Mottl, Franz Schalk, Richard Strauss, Arthur Nikisch, and Bruno Walter, 1903–1908. Felix Weingartner, 1908–1927. Wilhelm Furtwängler, 1928–1930. Clemens Krauss, 1930–1932. (Guest conductors after 1932.)

BIBLIOGRAPHY: Interview with Vienna Philharmonic Archivist Dr. Clemens Hellsberg, 1986. Otto Biba, *Die Wiener Philharmoniker Botschafter der Musik* Exhibition Catalog (Linz, 1976). Otto Biba, *Die Unvergleichlichen: Die Wiener Philharmoniker und Salzburg* (Vienna: Herder, 1977). Herta and Kurt Blaukopf, *Die Wiener Philharmoniker: Wesen, Werden, Wirken eines grossen Orchesters* (Vienna and Hamburg: Paul Zsolnay, 1986). Kurt Dieman, *O Ye Millions, I Embrace Ye* (Vienna: Österreichischer Bundesverlag, 1983). *Briefe an di Wiener Philharmoniker,* ed. Franz Endler, Harry Weber, and Margit Munster, *Die Wiener Philharmoniker* (Vienna: Edition Wien, 1986; also in English: *The Vienna Philharmonic,* trans. Charles Kessler. Wilhelm Jerger (Vienna, 1942). H. Fitzpatrick, ''Notes on the Vienna Horn,'' *Journal of the Galpin Society* 14: 1961. Wilhelm Furtwängler, *Ton und Wort: Aufsatze und Vorträge 1918 bis 1954,* 10th ed. (Wiesbaden: Backhaus, 1982). Franz Grasberger, *Die Wiener Philharmoniker bei Johann Strauss* (Vienna: Rosenbaum, 1963). Eduard Hanslick, *Geschichte des Concertwesens in Wien* (Vienna, 1869–1870). Rudolf Hanzl and Alfred Boskovsky, *Die Wiener Philharmoniker: ein Stück Welgeschichte* (Vienna, 1947). Wilhelm Jerger, *Die Wiener Philharmoniker: Erbe und Sendung* (Vienna, 1942). Josef Kaut, *Festspiele in Salzburg* (Salzburg, 1965). Heinrich Kralik, *Die Wiener Philharmoniker und ihre Dirigenten* (Vienna, 1960). Erwin Mittag, *Aus der Geschichte der Wiener Philharmoniker* (Vienna: Gerlach & Weidling, 1950). Richard von Perger, *Denkschrift zur Feier des fünfzigjährigen ununterbrochenen Bestandes der philharmonischen Konzerte in Wien 1860–1910* (Vienna, 1910). Alfred Planayavsky et al., ''125 Jahre Wiener Philharmoniker,'' *Österreichische Musikzeitschrift,* 22: Feb./Mar., 1967. Carl Ferdinand Pohl, *Festschrift aus Anlass der Feier des 25jährighen ununterbrochenen Bestandes der im Jahre 1842 gegründeten philharmonischen Concerte in Wien* (Vienna, 1885). Richard Rickett, *Music and Musicians in Vienna* (Vienna: Prachner, 1973). Christl Schönfeldt, *Die Wiener Philharmoniker* (Vienna, 1956); in English: *The Vienna Philharmonic Orchestra* (1957). Otto Strasser, *Und dafür wird man noch bezahlt: Mein Leben mit den Wiener Philharmonikern* (Vienna & Berlin: Neff, 1974). Otto Strasser, *Sechse is': Wie ein Orchester musiziert und funktioniert* (Vienna: Neff, 1981). Joseph Sulzer, *Ernstes und Heiteres aus dem Leben eines Wiener Philharmonikers* (Vienna, 1910). Hans Weigel, *Das Buch der Wiener Philharmoniker* (Vienna, 1967). *Wiener Philharmoniker 1842–1942. Ein Festschrift,* 2 vols. (Vienna, 1942). Alexander Witeschnik, *Seid umschlungen, Millionen: Mit den Wiener Philharmonikern unter Herbert von Karajan auf Weltreise* (Vienna, 1960). Alexander Witeschnik, *. . . diesen Kuss der ganzen Welt. Mit den Wiener Philharmonikern unter Herbert von Karajan von Moskau bis Paris* (Vienna, 1962). Alexander Witeschnik, *Musizieren geht ubers Probieren oder Viel Harmonie mit kleinen Dissonanzen: Die Geschichte der Wiener Philharmoniker in Anekdoten und Geschichten* (Vienna and Berlin: Neff, 1967).

ACCESS: Wiener Philharmoniker, Bosendorferstrasse 12, A–1010 Vienna. (0222) 65–65–25. Professor Alfred Altenburger, Vorstand.

ROBERT M. LINDELL

Vienna Symphony Orchestra

In a city abounding with concerts, the Vienna Symphony Orchestra (Wiener Symphoniker) is the most active concert orchestra. It was founded for this purpose, and in a city as tradition-minded as Vienna, circumstances have not changed since the turn of the century. Whereas the Vienna Philharmonic's* primary function is that of an opera orchestra (giving just under 25 concert hall performances in a season), the 127-member Vienna Symphony averages 120 evening performances. It has three concert subscription series in the Musikverein, the oldest and most historic of Vienna's concert halls; one subscription series in the Konzerthaus; and numerous other concerts outside of these series.

The orchestra records copiously and tours frequently. Its tours in recent years have included a 1980 anniversary tour to all four compass points of Europe, separate tours to Japan and the United States in 1982, to South America in 1983, and a tour of England in 1984–1985.

Since 1946 the Vienna Symphony has been affiliated with the Bregenz Festival during the summer months. In 1980 a new Festival Hall was dedicated, where the Symphony traditionally plays three concerts. Here also one of the major operas of the standard repertoire is annually performed. The Symphony also provides music for an operetta or musical show produced on the lake stage.

One tradition the Vienna Symphony is careful to nurture is its distinctive sound. It tunes to an A of 445 cps, and its string sound is distinctively sweet. Like other Viennese ensembles, the orchestra employs the Viennese horn, a single-F instrument (unlike the "double" F/B-flat horns commonly in use elsewhere) that affords the player fewer technical ways to correct intonation. The increased importance of the embouchure contributes to cultivating a characteristic style of slurring often described as gracefully "liquid." The Symphony also employs the Viennese oboe, which is of unique construction, with distinctive keying, bore, and reed. Its upper register is difficult to articulate, but the lower register is known for its deep, rich sound.

The Vienna Symphony has a prolific array of smaller ensembles, including the Prisma Brass Ensemble and the Bella Musica group, the latter devoted to the Viennese light classical repertoire. Many of the members of Nikolaus Harnoncourt's Concentus Musicus Wien come from the Symphony. The well-known Johann Strauss Ensemble is a Symphony group, as are the chamber music ensembles Musica Instrumentalis, Eight Cellists of the Vienna Symphony, the Vienna String Trio, Chamber Orchestra of the Vienna Symphony, and the Vienna Instrumental Soloists.

In 1976 the Symphony's governing Board initiated a thorough reorganization by including on its Board for the first time representatives of the two major concert halls, the Austrian Radio, City Hall, the Vienna Festival, the Bregenz Festival, and selected representatives from the orchestra itself. It was an unusual arrangement, but one dictated by the unusual role the Vienna Symphony plays within the city. The desired result would be direct cooperation between the

Symphony, its financial backers (principally the city), and local concert promoters. The one person responsible for coordination of all these varied elements is the general secretary, an appointee responsible to the Board. Programming decisions for the subscription series are made by the concert halls that hire the Symphony—but the Board, the conductor in question, and the music director (or principal guest conductor) play a role in these decisions.

The Vienna Symphony is proud of its numerous premiere performances of new orchestral works, many of them composed expressly for the orchestra. One typical example of the orchestra's programming might be the 1980 Wolfgang Sawallisch concert with Mozart's Symphony No. 36 (*Linz*), Gottfried von Einem's *Ludi Leopoldini,* and the Brahms Violin Concerto (with Christian Altenburger).

The total budget of the Vienna Symphony comes to approximately 100 million Austrian schillings, a figure not untypical for major European orchestras. Seventy-five percent of the budget is provided by a municipal subsidy and 10% from the federal government.

The orchestra dates back to 1900, when Vienna was bursting with new artistic activity. The Jugendstill (art nouveau) movement was in full swing, with artists like Gustav Klimt, Josef Hoffmann, and Otto Wagner making their mark on the city and a whole new generation of younger artists as well. Gustav Mahler was the famed director of the State Opera. The new music of Brahms, Bruckner, Wagner, Richard Strauss, and Mahler was making audiences sit up and take notice. It was a time of great growth and an almost insatiable musical hunger among the Viennese. Curiously enough, out of all levels of the citizenry, and not just the elite, came a cry for orchestral music and orchestra concerts. Out of this need grew the Wiener Konzertverein and its orchestra.

The financial backing for the venture came from prominent Viennese families, and the Musikverein (Gesellschaft der Musikfreunde) contributed vital organizational help. The list of supporters from 1900 includes names like Auersperg, Liechtenstein, Thun-Hohenstein, Rothschild, and Ludwig Wittgenstein.

The first season of this Konzertverein orchestra (later to become the Vienna Symphony) consisted of two subscription series of six programs each. One series was devoted to the complete orchestral works of Beethoven. The orchestra met with an enthusiastic response from public and critics alike. And from its earliest beginnings it was to become (as it remains today) associated with the music of Anton Bruckner. The first music director of the orchestra was Ferdinand Löwe. A student of Bruckner's, he was devoted to bringing his teacher's orchestral works before a public still torn in fierce and demonstrative loyalty between Bruckner and Brahms. Without interruption (as was the case with performance of Mahler's music, which in consequence of wartime anti-Semitism was neglected), the traditional way the Symphony performs Bruckner has been handed down intact from one musical generation to the next. Löwe performed Beethoven and Brahms as well as his beloved Bruckner.

He also held concerts outside in the Volksgarten and made available low ticket prices for the regular Sunday pops concerts. The orchestra's musicians in 1900 had guaranteed posts, with summer spa concerts (alone averaging 320 performances) to pad their pockets. The winter performances ranged between 300 and 350.

In those early years the new music of Franz Schmidt, Paul Dukas, Hugo Wolf, Tchaikovsky, Richard Strauss, and Mahler were brought before a thankful public. Guest conductors of those years were Bruno Walter, Felix Weingartner, Claude Debussy, and Pietro Mascagni; among other soloists were heard Wilhelm Backhaus, Béla Bartók, Pablo de Sarasate, Bronislaw Huberman, and Fritz Kreisler.

The year 1907 saw a new orchestra on the Viennese scene, the Wiener Tonkünstlerorchester. Later, in 1914–1915, due to the economic exigencies of World War I, it would merge with the Wiener Konzertverein Orchestra to become the Vienna Symphony Orchestra. Before that, in 1913, Wilhelm Furtwängler was to make his Viennese debut with this new orchestra. The piano soloist was 16-year-old George Szell.

Vienna's burgeoning concert life demanded a second concert hall, and in 1910 the Wiener Konzerthausgesellschaft filled the bill with an enormous new hall in a building that housed Vienna's conservatory as well. For the formal opening in 1913 Richard Strauss composed a *Festliches Präludium*. Aldolf Busch was the concertmaster on that occasion.

After the war Furtwängler became the Vienna Symphony's first permanent conductor. The formal incorporation of the Vienna Symphony was to follow in the 1921–1922 season, the same season that saw Hans Knappertsbusch make his Viennese debut. The early 1930s were a time of reorganization for the orchestra. A spin-off orchestra under the aegis of the Austrian Radio was responsible for the more popular, light classical repertoire. The Symphony itself made its first foreign tour, travelling to Italy under its new music director, Oswald Kabasta. In 1936 Eugene Ormandy returned from America for a guest appearance in which he conducted Arnold Schoenberg's *Verklärte Nacht*. The Vienna Symphony also made its first tour to England, once again bringing "their" Bruckner to a wider public.

At the time Austria joined the German Reich in 1938, the Vienna Symphony was declared to be the official city orchestra. As such, it was to provide background music for many ordinary and uninteresting functions like openings of trade fairs. The concert promoters in Vienna saw to it, however, that a balance was reached by engaging a roster of illustrious conductors and soloists, and the Vienna Symphony remained active until 1944, when the war made it impossible to perform.

After World War II permanent conductor Hans Swarowsky was responsible for great artistic strides made by the orchestra. Names standing out from the list of conductors in the late 1940s include Josef Krips, Rafael Kubelik, Paul Hindemith, Clemens Krauss, Erich Leinsdorf, Otto Klemperer, Karl Böhm, and Malcolm Sargent. Herbert von Karajan's long association with the orchestra began in 1948.

The Symphony was not without its difficulties, however. The orchestra functioned by being rented out by its Board to the various concert halls. Its musicians were mere employees of the Symphony's governing organization and were in no way its members. Financial straits in 1949 threatened the orchestra's existence. Eventually, the city of Vienna, under great public pressure, redirected other funds to the orchestra in the form of an annual subsidy. There was also an agreement whereby the federal government would underwrite one-third (today it is 10%) of the orchestra's total budget.

The 1950s brought the Viennese debuts of Lorin Maazel, Carlo Maria Giulini, and Wolfgang Sawallisch, all with the Vienna Symphony. Although the orchestra profited by work with these conductors (and Karajan and Klemperer), it was again searching for a permanent music director, and in 1959 Sawallisch took that post, to usher in a new era for the Symphony. The next 11 Sawallisch years took the orchestra around the world, including an appearance at the General Assembly of the United Nations. After Sawallisch's departure the Symphony worked often with Josef Krips until, in 1973, Carlo Maria Giulini agreed to become the new music director. His association with the Symphony in that capacity lasted until 1976, and it was not until 1982 that the orchestra again had a music director. Gennady Rozhdestvensky assumed that post for one year, the high point of which was a South American tour under his baton. In 1985 Georges Prêtre was appointed as principal guest conductor.

RECORDING HISTORY AND SELECTIVE DISCOGRAPHY: The Vienna Symphony has more than 400 recordings to its credit. In 1948 orchestra members built their own recording studio in Vienna's Konzerthaus. Funds for the project came from the members themselves. The orchestra also recorded the film music for numerous movies being made after the war. VSO recordings appear on all major European labels. The conductors appearing most often with the orchestra are Rudolf Moralt, Bernhard Paumgartner, and more recently, Wolfgang Sawallisch.

Beethoven, Piano Concerto No. 5 (Arturo Benedetti-Michelangeli): DG 2531 385. Brahms, Symphony No. 3 and *Tragic Overture* (Sawallisch): Philips 412290–4. Bruckner, Symphony No. 9 (Matačić): Amadeo 410 963–1. Copland, *Appalachian Spring Suite*; Ives, *Three Places in New England* (Walter Hendl): Desto 6403E. Mozart, Piano Concertos Nos. 22 and 19, K. 482 and K. 459 (Alicia de Larrocha/Uri Segal): Decca SXDL 7566, London LDR–71066 (CD). Ravel, *Shéhérezade*; Berlioz, *Nuits d'été* (Francis Travis/Hildegard Behrens): Decca 411 895–1. Smetana, *Die Moldau* (Gerd Albrecht): Atlantis 95 005. Stravinsky, *The Firebird* (Sawallisch): Orfeo S–044831-A. Tchaikovsky, Piano Concertos Nos. 1 and 3 (Rozhdestvensky/Viktoria Postnikova): Decca DH410 112–1.

CHRONOLOGY OF MUSIC DIRECTORS: Ferdinand Löwe, 1900- (date uncertain). Wilhelm Furtwängler, 1914- (date uncertain). Oswald Kabasta, 1933–1944. Hans Swarowsky, 1946–1948. Herbert von Karajan, 1948–1958. Wolfgang Sawallisch, 1958–1969. (Guest conductors, 1969–1973.) Carlo Maria Giulini, 1973–1976. (Guest conductors, 1976–1983.) Gennady Rozhdestvensky, 1982–1983. Georges Prêtre (Principal Guest Conductor), 1985- present.

BIBLIOGRAPHY: *80 Jahre Wiener Symphoniker* (Vienna: Doblinger, 1980.) Franz Endler, *Musik auf Reisen* (Vienna: Österreichischer Bundesverlag, 1982) (description of a tour with the Vienna Symphony). *Hundert Jahre Goldener Saal: Das Haus der Gesellschaft der Musikfreunde am Karlsplatz* (Vienna: Gesellschaft der Musikfreunde, 1970). Maximilian Piperek, Scientific Coordinator, *Stress and Music* (Vienna: Wilhelm Braumüller, 1981) (analysis of stress factors among professional symphonic musicians, commissioned by Vienna Symphony).

ACCESS: Vienna Symphony, Lehargasse 11, A–1060 Vienna. (0222) 56–35–50. Dr. Lutz Lüdemann, General Secretary.

JANET TURKOVIĆ

Belgium ────────────────

BRUSSELS (997,000*)

Belgian National Orchestra

Although the Belgian National Orchestra occupies an important position in the Belgian musical world, it can no longer claim the monopoly it had when it was created. Now five other orchestras also play concerts of symphonic music. The political evolution of Belgium toward a federation of two language communities has led to the creation of a Walloon and a Flemish Symphonic Orchestra, which work, respectively, in Liège and Antwerp. It has also caused the split of the Radio Orchestra into two new ensembles, each converted into a full-size orchestra. What's more, since the 1981–1982 season, the National Opera has organized a series of symphonic concerts with its own orchestra in Brussels.

In the nineteenth century concert life was flourishing in Belgium, but it was rather a long time before a permanent orchestra with professional musicians was established. The initiative was taken by Désiré Defauw, who had occupied, since 1925, a prominent position in the musical world of Brussels. He created his own concert society, conducted the concerts of the Royal Music Conservatory, and was the musical director of the Belgian Radio. In 1931 he reached an agreement with the concert societies of Brussels: the Philharmonic Society, the Ysaÿe Concerts, and the Spiritual Concerts. For all the performances of orchestral music, they agreed to engage the ensemble founded by Defauw, the Symphonic Orchestra of Brussels.

In May of 1936 the Belgian Government decided to grant Defauw's orchestra an annual subsidy and to transform it into the Belgian National Orchestra (BNO), under the protection of Queen Elisabeth. Under its new name the orchestra played its first concert in September 1936; Defauw conducted the orchestra in the Brussels Palace of Fine Arts. It consisted of 62 musicians, who had each passed a competitive examination. Orchestra members were no longer paid according to the number of performances they played, but received fixed salaries. As the BNO was not allowed to organize concerts itself, it was hired by those societies that could offer enough artistic and financial guarantees. The orchestra was in fact still managed by the concert societies of Brussels under the supervision of a government commissioner who had veto power. Since it was the concert organizer who engaged the conductor, Defauw lost the privileged position he had occupied at the head of the Symphonic Orchestra of Brussels.

During the first season (1936–1937) the BNO gave 81 performances, of which only three were outside Brussels. Even during later years the orchestra worked chiefly in the capital. It played mainly the concerts of the Philharmonic Society established in 1927 on the occasion of the construction of the Palace of Fine Arts. This building, designed by Victor Horta, was intended to become the center of cultural life in Brussels—a task it still fulfills. A society was created for each artistic field, and the Philharmonic Society has been responsible for classical music for more than 50 years. Symphonic concerts are given in the large hall, today called Henry Le Boeuf Hall. It was inaugurated in 1929 and contains more than 2,000 seats. Now the BNO also rehearses there.

From 1932 on, the Philharmonic Society frequently invited the Austrian conductor Erich Kleiber to lead its concerts. Before 1940 he conducted the BNO several times, raising it to a very high level. With its Beethoven concerts the BNO reached the first peak in its history. After World War II it lacked the stimulating influence of a long cooperation with a famous conductor; for 15 years guest conductors succeeded each other, and this lack of continuity resulted in a difficult period for the orchestra.

In 1958 the situation was drastically changed. The BNO ceased to be a private institution and was recognized by the Belgian Government as "an organization of general benefit." From then on it has been supervised by the minister of education and run by a Board of Directors, of which the first members were the musicology professors of the four Belgian universities. From 1960 to 1973 the Board was assisted by a musical adviser, the eminent musicologist Paul Collaer. Today the Board consists of eight members appointed by the government for a period of three years. Two secretaries and a small administrative team are permanently at their assistance. The 1958 statute, adapted in 1966, turned the musicians into public servants. They are still recruited in the same way as previously stated and are subsequently appointed by the minister. They are paid according to a legal scale and are entitled to a pension at the age of 65.

On May 23, 1960, a law was passed requiring the appointment of a conductor/ music director who by virtue of his permanence was expected to inspire the BNO with new enthusiasm and cohesion. The music director had to conduct a certain number of performances, but the opportunity to invite guest conductors still existed. Although the BNO was still not allowed to organize its own concerts, the organizing societies usually consulted with the music director about programs, and this usage has been maintained until now.

It was a wise idea to appoint the French conductor of Belgian descent, André Cluytens, as conductor/music director in 1960. He succeeded both in giving new élan to the BNO and in attracting large audiences with his colorful and sensitive interpretations. He devoted his attention mainly to the music of Claude Debussy, Maurice Ravel, Richard Strauss and the romantic composers, but the orchestra also performed works by composers from J. S. Bach to our contemporaries. Under the direction of Cluytens the BNO toured Western Europe for the first time. In 1963 it performed in West Germany, Austria, and Switzerland; in 1965 in Spain and Portugal; and two years later again in West Germany and Austria.

The excellent cooperation with Cluytens ended with his sudden death in 1967. The Austrian Michael Gielen was appointed as his successor for the period 1969 to 1973. Very soon it became apparent that the audiences were less attracted by the taste and interpretation of the new conductor/music director. He showed preference for music of the twentieth century, but the average concertgoer was still little acquainted with the works of Webern, Schoenberg and others of their bent. The performances of the traditional repertoire, moreover, appeared too cool and intellectual to the Belgian public. However, these performances were of an outstanding quality, proven by the BNO's 1972 tour of the United States. Gielen endeavored to render truthfully every detail in the score and to make the audience feel the musical form as clearly as possible.

Gielen was succeeded by the Belgian conductor André Vandernoot, who had often worked with the BNO. When he resigned at the end of the 1974–1975 season, the Board decided to appoint Georges Octors, BNO concertmaster, as provisional conductor/musical director. The interim of Octors, who had already conducted quite a number of BNO concerts, lasted until the end of the 1982–1983 season, longer than expected. It cannot be denied that this long interregnum created a feeling of despondency among the musicians, chiefly because at the same time the government was making all kinds of plans that might have meant the end of the BNO. An amalgamation with the orchestra of the National Opera was considered, but eventually no decision was taken. In those difficult circumstances Octors tried to keep the musicians motivated; nevertheless, some of the BNO's concerts were badly reviewed in the press.

Since September 1, 1983, the Israeli of Romanian origin, Mendi Rodan, has been the new conductor/music director of the BNO, whereas Georges Octors was appointed conductor. The first results are hopeful, and it may be assumed that the quality of the performances will improve in the near future. Moreover, the BNO has been offered new opportunities: the national lottery increases by 10% the orchestra's government subsidy, which amounted to $2,200,000 for 1984. Another Maecenas is the organization "The Friends of the BNO," founded in 1960. It buys valuable string instruments and places them at the disposal of orchestra members, who in principle play their own instruments. The value of these acquisitions, among which is a violin by Stradivari, is estimated at about $6 million.

The most recent change in the status of the BNO came into effect on January

1, 1984. Since then the 90-piece orchestra is not only rented out at a sum fixed by the government, but is allowed to organize concerts itself. For the 1984–1985 season the BNO planned a cycle of ten concerts for which it tries to attract large audiences mainly by the international reputation of the participating soloists. With the addition as well of concerts of the Royal Music Conservatory of Brussels (French Section) and concerts outside the capital, the playing season has increased. Of an average of 80 performances a year (of which a minimum of 24 are directed by Rodan), about half are played in the provinces. Such concerts may be organized by the Festival of Flanders or the Festival of Wallonia, but also on the initiative of Youth and Music, or a concert society in Antwerp, Liège, or elsewhere—even by an organization aiming to improve the local cultural life by a BNO performance, which is always considered to be an event.

In alternation with the Orchestra of the Belgian Radio (French Section), the BNO accompanies soloists in the finals of the Queen Elisabeth Contest at the Palace of Fine Arts. The BNO also cooperates with the first winners in concerts given on the occasion of the contest. Finally, the BNO plays an important part in the distribution of the music of Belgian composers. It regularly performs Belgian compositions during its concerts and has been active in recording Belgian soloists and works.

RECORDING HISTORY AND SELECTIVE DISCOGRAPHY: Performances of the finals in the Queen Elisabeth Contest are recorded, and the best are released through Deutsche Grammophon. These are the BNO's only commercially available recordings. The BNO has also made more than 100 records dedicated to Belgian composers of the late-nineteenth and twentieth centuries, played only by Belgian soloists and conductors. Not for commercial release, these records are financed by the Belgian Government and distributed abroad via diplomatic channels.

Bartók, Violin Concerto No. 2 (Zazofsky/Octors): DG 2535012. Chopin, Piano Concerto No. 1 (J. Swann/Defossez): DG 2530287.

CHRONOLOGY OF MUSIC DIRECTORS: (Guest conductors, 1936–1960.) André Cluytens, 1960–1967. Michael Gielen, 1969–1973. Andre Vandernoot, 1974–1975. Georges Octors (Interim Conductor), 1976–1983. Mendi Rodan, 1983-present.

BIBLIOGRAPHY: Henri Vanhulst, ''Orchestres et concerts,'' in Robert Wangermee and Philippe Mercier, eds., *La musique en Wallonie et à Bruxelles*, vol. 2 (Brussels, 1982), pp. 43–91.

ACCESS: Belgian National Orchestra, Place E. Flagey 18, 1050 Brussels. (32–2) 640–0288. Paul Evrard and Jan Symoens, Managers.

                                                                        HENRI VANHULST

LIÈGE   (214,000)

The Philharmonic Orchestra of Liège and of the French-Speaking Community of Belgium

The Philharmonic Orchestra of Liège and of the French-Speaking Community of Belgium (Orchestre philharmonique de Liège et de la Communauté française de Belgique) plays an average of 75 performances a year in a season lasting from September to June. About half of these performances are given in the large hall of the Conservatory of Liège, which has 1,900 seats. The orchestra also rehearses there. Furthermore, the orchestra regularly plays in other Walloon towns, and in the 1985–1986 season it played for the first time a complete concert series in Charleroi and Verviers. The orchestra is occasionally asked to play in Brussels and important Flemish towns, as well as in France and the Netherlands. It has toured Europe several times, in 1984 travelling to West Germany, Austria, and Spain.

In 1980, on the occasion of its 20th anniversary, the word "Philharmonic" was added to the orchestra's name. In 1983 the name was finally changed to "The Philharmonic Orchestra of Liège and of the French-Speaking Community of Belgium," since from then on the Ministry of the French-Speaking Community contributed more than half of the orchestra's budget, which in 1985 amounted to 130,000,000 Belgian francs. A quarter of this sum is paid by the City Council of Liège, and the national lottery increases the orchestra's annual subsidy by 10%. The Friends of the Orchestra association also contributes; in 1983 they financed the release of a recording.

The Board of the orchestra consists of nine representatives from the Ministry of the French-Speaking Community and seven from the city of Liège. The Executive Committee consists of five members who are assisted by an administrative team. Prior to January 1, 1984, the law did not allow Belgian orchestras to organize their own concerts, and so the city of Liège created a special committee at the foundation of the orchestra. Beginning with the 1985–1986 season the orchestra began organizing concerts on its own, including chamber music performances for which it divides itself into small ensembles (String Quartet, Philharmonietta Nova, etc.).

Fernand Quinet, the then director of the Royal Music Conservatory of Liège, played an important part in the foundation of the orchestra. In 1947 he was able to convince the local authorities to found a 24-member chamber orchestra that would not only perform independently, but could also occasionally join forces with the 54 musicians of the local opera to play symphonic concerts. In those circumstances it was impossible to give the ensemble the necessary cohesion, and Quinet was well aware that the performances he conducted had not been prepared satisfactorily. In March 1960 Liège decided to found a full-size orchestra with permanent activities. Quinet was put in charge and commissioned to engage 71 musicians. The new ensemble played its first concert on October 16, 1960.

Since 1960 the orchestra has been led consecutively by four permanent conductors, and as a result the quality of performances has improved greatly. Fernand Quinet's health was not very strong, and he had to be replaced on several occasions by other Belgian conductors. His programs showed a preference for Brahms and the French composers of the late nineteenth and early twentieth centuries. In 1965 Quinet was succeeded by a Frenchman, Manuel Rosenthal, who was able to enlarge the orchestra. He programmed composers of the nineteenth and twentieth centuries, among whom Maurice Ravel and Igor Stravinsky proved his favorites. Under his direction quite a number of pieces were performed for the first time in Liège, but the result was not always satisfactory. The orchestra had difficulties coping with the high demands of an unfamiliar repertoire, and audiences grew smaller each year.

Between 1967 and 1977 the American conductor Paul Strauss succeeded in reversing the situation by imposing strict discipline upon the orchestra, resulting in considerable improvement in its performances. The orchestra then consisted of 89 musicians, on the demand of Strauss. In those years the first commercially available recordings were made, although the orchestra has also made recordings for the Ministry of the French-Speaking Community. Strauss's programs, which were expected to include performances of Mahler and the Russian composers, were less radical than Rosenthal's and consequently his concerts had a growing success. Although he took into account the musical taste of the average concertgoer, he nevertheless performed the most important works of quite a number of twentieth-century composers.

In 1977 Pierre Bartholomée was appointed conductor. In Belgium and its neighboring countries he had a considerable reputation as a composer of avantgarde music and as leader of the Musique Nouvelle Ensemble. It is not surprising, then, that he has been able to turn the orchestra into a first-class performer of the most modern compositions. It is now invited to play at specialized festivals at Angers, Metz, and Strasbourg. Simultaneously, Henri Pousseur, director of the Liège Conservatory, has made his institution an important center of contemporary music, a perfect cooperator for the orchestra. Bartholomée's contemporary programming includes works of both Belgian and foreign composers, among whom may be mentioned Philippe Boesmans and Luis de Pablo. He also dedicates much of his attention to less-performed pieces, mainly from the nineteenth century. The traditional repertoire, from Bach to Debussy, however, is never omitted from the programs.

RECORDING HISTORY AND SELECTIVE DISCOGRAPHY: The first commercially available recordings were made under Strauss for HMV. Under Bartholomée the Liège orchestra records mostly for Ricercar, a local company. The following selections are both first recordings.

Philippe Boesmans, Violin Concerto (R. Piéta/Bartholomée): RIC 014. Villa-Lobos, *Chôros XII* (Bartholomée): RIC 007.

CHRONOLOGY OF MUSIC DIRECTORS: Fernand Quinet, 1960–1965. Manuel Rosenthal, 1965–1967. Paul Strauss, 1967–1977. Pierre Bartholomée, 1977-present.

BIBLIOGRAPHY: Jacques Mairel, *Quatre organimes culturels wallons* (Brussels: Ministère de la Communauté française, 1979), coll. ''Documents et Enquêtes,'' 17.

ACCESS: The Philharmonic Orchestra of Liège and of the French-Speaking Community of Belgium, 11 rue Forgeur, 4000 Liège. (41) 23 63 60. Roger Pernay, General Manager. Paul-Emile Mottard, Director of Public Relations.

HENRI VANHULST

Brazil

RIO DE JANEIRO (5,093,000)

Symphony Orchestra of Brazil

The 102-member Brazilian Symphony Orchestra (OSB: Orquestra Sinfônica Brasiliera) is among the most important orchestras in South America. Other important Brazilian orchestras are the Orquestra Sinfônica Nacional (an entity of the Brazilian Ministry of Education and Culture) in Rio de Janeiro, the São Paulo State Symphony Orchestra, and the São Paulo City Orchestra, the latter two residing in the city of São Paulo.

The orchestra's home season lasts from April 15 to the end of December. Its performance series in Rio de Janeiro's Theatro Municipal includes some 30 concerts featuring standard works from the Romantic and later periods. It also undertakes a series of about ten concerts of a lighter nature in outlying districts. A pops series is now in the planning stages. In addition to its home and tour concerts, the orchestra presents a long-standing series of youth concerts. It also records for television rebroadcast, bringing its concerts to remote parts of the vast Brazilian hinterlands. It supports the Colégio Preparatório de Instrumentalistas, where several of its members teach, thereby adding to the growth of orchestras elsewhere in the country. Members of the OSB hail from Brazil and other countries, including the United States.

Since 1965 the OSB's subsidies from the federal and state governments of Brazil have declined, and in recent years the OSB has widened its base of support by extending its services to the private sector, particularly in alliance with such large businesses as Mercedes Benz, Grupo Yerdan, and Souza Cruz. Today it claims distinction as the only Brazilian orchestra of its size receiving only 10% of its support from federal funding.

The orchestra's artistic standards are among the highest on the continent, and it has been received favorably on its tours, which have included, in addition to South American countries, visits to Europe and North America. The OSB is the only major South American orchestra to have visited the principal music capital of the United States, New York City.

Dating back to the eighteenth century, opera has been a staple of Brazilian-European cultural life, and not only in the largest cities. (Brazil's most famous opera house is probably the extravagant hall in Manaus, 1,000 miles up the Amazon; the fruit of a booming economy based on rubber plantations, it was completed just as the local economy began to wane, and consequently its days of glory were few.) Symphonic music was much slower in establishing a foothold in Brazil. Although sources differ as to their exact dates, earlier ensembles included a Sociedade de Concertos Populares under Carlos de Mesquita (1880s), an Associação de Concertos Populares (1896), the Sociedade de Concertos Sinfônicas (early 1900s), the Filarmônica do Rio de Janeiro founded by Walter Burle Max (1931), and the Orquestra Villa Lobos (1931–1935).

Without a permanent and public orchestra of its own, the city of Rio de Janeiro played host in 1940 to the NBC Symphony under Arturo Toscanini and to the All-American Youth Symphony under Leopold Stokowski. According to the brief history of the OSB published on the occasion of the orchestra's 40th anniversary, these two events combined to further the momentum felt as the city moved toward the establishment of its own major ensemble. The present Orquestra Sinfônica Brasiliera was founded on July 11, 1940, at the instigation of city musicians (among them its founding conductor, José Siqueira), and with the cooperation of the musicians' union (Ordem dos Músicos) and the support of a wide range of civic and cultural leaders. Among these were the writer Guilherme Figueiredo and the impresario Arnaldo Guinle, both of whom sought and received the support of Brazilian President Vargas and the federal government. The orchestra's first concert was held at Rio's Municipal Theater on August 17, 1940.

In 1944 the Hungarian conductor Eugen Szenkar was appointed *regente titular* (titled [music] director). Szenkar presided over symphonic concerts at home as well as on tour in Argentina and also led a series of concerts as part of the Rio de Janeiro opera season. The late 1940s were a high point in the orchestra's history. With its audiences swelling to unprecedented sizes, the OSB presented over 100 concerts in 1949 under Szenkar and guest conductors such as Serge Koussevitzky, Charles Munch, Eugene Ormandy, William Steinberg, and others. The orchestra initiated a series of youth concerts, given at the Cine Rex, with the idea of extending an interest in symphonic music to future audiences. Its national role was also fulfilled during this period by its frequent visits to neighboring and far-flung Brazilian states.

According to the OSB's anniversary history, however, the early 1950s saw a period of decline for the orchestra as it passed through a series of guest conductors and suffered both financially and artistically. The musicians kept the organization afloat by volunteering their services and maintaining the organization's structure through lean times. The orchestra emerged from this difficult time, however, following the advent of Music Director Eleazar de Carvalho in the mid–1960s. Carvalho's disciplined approach and reinstatement of artistic standards raised once again the ensemble's national status. Youth concerts were reinstated.

In 1965 the OSB, formerly a privately constituted society, was declared a nationally subsidized foundation, and its precarious existence was thus greatly stabilized. Three years later the present music director, Isaac Karabtchevsky, was appointed *regente titular*, a position he still holds. Karabtchevsky, a São Paulo native of Russian extraction, sought to widen the orchestra's scope, which he did both musically and geographically. He diversified the repertoire, including standard Germanic and Russian romantic works as well as works from the modern Brazilian mainstream. He also took the OSB to Europe in 1974 and to the United States and Canada in 1977. Youth concerts continued, as they still do, and Karabtchevsky took the orchestra to another wide audience as well. Under the auspices of Roberto Marinho's "Project Aquarius," the orchestra was able to reach a great many people, as in the memorable Quinta da Boa Vista Concert of 1972. According to orchestra sources, since Karabtchevsky's ascendance the OSB has led a stable existence and has maintained a high level of musical quality in the context of its geographical and cultural situation.

RECORDING HISTORY AND SELECTIVE DISCOGRAPHY: The OSB has released some 30 records, including an historic recording, *Barroco Miniera* (1957). Its recordings have provoked critical praises; however, the OSB is hampered from embarking on commercial recording activities by the lack of suitable recording facilities. An OSB recording has been distributed by the Organization of American States in its "Music of the Americas" series of Inter-American Musical Editions.

Villa-Lobos, *Bachianas Brasileiras* No. 4; Marlos Nobre, *In Memoriam*; Claudio dio Santoro, *Asymtolic Interactions* (Karabtchevsky): OAS 002.

CHRONOLOGY OF MUSIC DIRECTORS (Regentes titulares; data incomplete): José Siqueira, 1940–1944. Eugen Szenkar, 1944–1950. Eleazar de Carvalho, 1964(?)–1968. Isaac Karabtchevsky, 1969–present.

BIBLIOGRAPHY: Peter G. Davies, "Recordings: Latin American Music—An Overview on Disks," *New York Times*, 20 July 1980. Donal Henahan, "Brazil Symphony In New York Debut," *New York Times*, 7 December 1977. *New Grove Dictionary of Music and Musicians* (New York: Macmillan, 1980). "OSB 40 Anos," in OSB pamphlet, n. d. [ca.1980]. Thanks to Dr. Lawrence Kinsman and Mary Oliveira for helping to secure information.

ACCESS: Orquestra Sinfônica Brasiliera, Avenido Rio Branco 135, Room 918–920, Rio de Janeiro. (021) 222–4592, 222–5842. João Carlos Alvim Correia, Executive Director.

ROBERT R. CRAVEN

Canada _____

HAMILTON   (542,000*)

Hamilton Philharmonic Orchestra

The Hamilton Philharmonic (HPO), with 30 permanent resident musicians and 30 to 40 contracted players, presents an average of 60 annual concerts to over 10,000 regular subscribers. An additional 150 school performances are presented annually by the full orchestra and smaller ensembles.

The orchestra's organizational structure consists of a president, a Board of Directors, and a Board of Governors, with operations directed by a general manager and staff of ten. Its 1986 budget was approximately $2.3 million, of which 40% derived from ticket sales; 43% from federal, provincial, and municipal grants; and 17% from corporate and private support.

In 1973, after presenting concerts in several temporary locations, the HPO finally moved to Hamilton Place, a multi-purpose concert facility with a seating capacity of 2,183. The orchestra's regular concert series include: Celebrity Series, pops concerts, Candlelight Concerts, Saturday children's concerts, and Music Alive (a contemporary music series). Its core of permanent musicians form smaller chamber groups to give in-school performances and clinics. This group also presents concerts and workshops throughout the Hamilton-Wentworth region.

The HPO's founding in 1949 was the culmination of many years of orchestral activity in the city. The year 1884 marked the beginning of regular orchestral performances in Hamilton. Among the organizations involved were the Hamilton Philharmonic Society and its successor, the Hamilton Orchestral Club, under the conductors Frederick Torrington (1837–1917), John Aldous (1853–1934), and finally Charles Harris (1863–1925), who renamed it the Harris Orchestral Club. A typical concert from this period was one given at the Grand Opera

House, which featured two movements from Haydn's "Surprise" Symphony, selections from Donizetti's *Lucia di Lammermoor*, and a Strauss waltz.

In the twentieth century the organization was named successively the Hamilton Symphony Orchestra, Hamilton Orchestral Club, and Hamilton Symphony Orchestra. Graham Godfrey (1890–1955), who had been assistant to Adrian Boult in the direction of the Birmingham Festival Choral Society before coming to Canada, became conductor and directed the first concert of the HSO in 1931. His programming of complete Mendelssohn, Beethoven, and Dvořák symphonies indicated that the ensemble was finally ready to perform the major orchestral repertoire.

World War II caused the temporary disbandment of the orchestra, but with the appointment of Jan Wolanek (b. 1895) in 1949 the orchestra once again continued to develop. At the outset the orchestra featured only Canadian soloists and by its 1952–1953 season offered three subscription concerts. Wolanek's successor, after a season of temporary conductors, was Victor di Bello (b. 1933), who had founded the Toronto Pro Arte Orchestra. He raised the standards of the orchestra, reduced its size, and continued to expand its repertoire.

With the appointment of Lee Hepner (b. 1920) in 1962, the orchestra entered an important new stage in its development. Hepner, who had founded the Edmonton Symphony Orchestra in 1952, gave the ensemble the strong leadership it needed. Under his directorship the number of concerts increased and the annual budget grew from $20,000 in his first year to $100,000 in the 1968–1969 season. Hepner programmed many standard orchestral works and introduced audiences to contemporary compositions, including major Canadian works. A youth orchestra and in-school concerts were initiated by him.

Boris Brott (b. 1944) took over in 1969 as artistic director and conductor. With experience as conductor of the Northern Sinfonia (Newcastle-on-Tyne), Lakehead Symphony Orchestra, and Regina Symphony Orchestra, he was prepared to expand the Hamilton orchestra's activities. He began by building the orchestra around a nucleus of resident professional musicians who formed the basic ensemble of 30 players and core chamber groups. The Czech String Quartet and Sentiri Wind Quintet are examples of these chamber ensembles, as is Canadian Brass, which became independent of the orchestra in 1977. Brott actively promoted the orchestra in the community, often utilizing novel methods to introduce classical music to new audiences. His concerts inside the Dofasco steel mill and his use of narrators, cartoonists, dancers, actors, mime, and film demonstrate his innovative approach to the programming and promotion of classical music.

The increase in the number of concerts and the growth of audiences coincided with the orchestra becoming a fully-professional group. During Brott's tenure the orchestra has continued to perform the standard repertoire, including cycles of Mahler and Bruckner symphonies. Brott has commissioned new Canadian works, produced programs of contemporary compositions, and featured numerous international soloists. BMI awards have recognized these contributions to contemporary programming. In addition, the orchestra has joined forces with popular musicians such as Tranquility Base and trumpeter Chuck Mangione for recordings and performances. The HPO has also become a leader among Canadian orchestras in its commitment to educating young audiences.

RECORDING HISTORY AND SELECTIVE DISCOGRAPHY: Among the orchestra's earlier recordings are *Land of Make Believe* (Chuck Mangione/Brott) and two recordings by the Hamilton Phiharmonic Virtuosi, featuring works of Sibelius, Ravel, and Stravinsky.

A Fifth of Broadway (Brott): CBC SM–5022. Works of Bizet, Gellman, Fauré, Delius (Brott): CBC SM–195.

CHRONOLOGY OF MUSIC DIRECTORS: Jan Wolanek, 1949–1957. Leonard Pearlman and Bryden Thomson, 1957–1958. Victor di Bello, 1958–1962. Lee Hepner, 1962–1969. Boris Brott, 1969-present.

BIBLIOGRAPHY: Interviews with HPO administration and conductors. *Encyclopedia of Music in Canada* (Toronto: University of Toronto Press, 1981). *Hamilton Philharmonic Orchestra: 100 Years of Music* (Hamilton: Wentworth Publishing, 1984).

ACCESS: Hamilton Philharmonic Orchestra, Box 2080, Station A, Hamilton, L8N 3Y7. (416) 526–8800. Paul Eck, General Manager.

FREDERICK A. HALL

MONTREAL   (2,828,000)

Montreal Symphony Orchestra

The Montreal Symphony Orchestra (MSO) is comparable in national significance to the symphony of the other metropolis in Canada, Toronto (see Toronto Symphony Orchestra*). The MSO has a regular season of about 70 concerts, including four subscription series and a summer festival, with a total annual live audience of about 500,000. Each year it also goes on several international tours, makes at least half a dozen recordings, records for broadcast via the Canadian Broadcasting Corporation, is hired for the production of a dozen operas, and cooperates with the municipal adiminstration for the production of several free concerts in parks and other public places. The MSO's home is the 3,000-seat Place des Arts, completed in 1963. Its adequate acoustics were welcome to the orchestra, which had hitherto performed in various halls and arenas.

The MSO is headed by a Board of Overseers including the general manager and the music director as well as a special counselor to the music director. There is also a Women's Committee that is particularly active in the organization of symphonic matinees and in the MSO Competition, which gives young soloists the opportunity to be heard with the orchestra. The orchestra runs on a budget of approximately $9.6 million Canadian per year. Of that, about 20% comes from government grants (municipal, federal, provincial), about 45% from operating revenues (ticket sales, radio, television), and the rest is from individual and corporate donations.

Under Music Director Charles Dutoit the MSO has shown a marked preference for French music, including that of Camille Saint-Saëns, Maurice Ravel, Édouard Lalo, Charles Gounod, and Hector Berlioz. The orchestra's growing prestige is owed in some measure to its success with such repertoire, and the ensemble has become known as one of the world's foremost French orchestras. Although the Austro-German classical and romantic repertoire is still present, Dutoit is sincerely engaged in the promotion of Canadian music, as can be seen by the frequent programming of composers such as Roger Matton, Clermont Pepin, George Crumb, and R. Murray Schafer. He also does not hesitate to include other modern works such as Oliver Messiaen's *Turangalila* Symphony or Edgar Varèse's *Ameriques*.

The call for a symphonic society in Montreal, heard as early as 1845, went unheeded until 1863, when a 30-member orchestra performed works by Daniel Auber and Gioacchino Rossini. Sporadic performances followed, but a professional orchestra was not gathered until the 1894–1895 season, when one of the first French-Canadian composers, G. Couture, led a series of ten concerts played by a group that included a core of 20 European musicians imported for the occasion. Again in 1898, under J. J. Goulet, an orchestra performed in a series of 12 concerts. Through the years of World War I and shortly thereafter, the formation of a permanent orchestra continued to be stymied, and it would be until the years of the Great Depression.

Canada's artistic life had always been characterized by a latent conflict between the two founding cultures of the country, the French and the English. Montreal, at the heart of the French province of Quebec, has always felt this tension most acutely, the main part of its population being French speaking, with key economic positions being held at the time by an English-speaking elite. In the early 1930s there was a small orchestra whose members were mostly, if not exclusively, English speaking. In reaction and reflecting public opinion, local French newspapers launched a press campaign leading to a government grant of $3,000 toward an orchestra representative of the French majority. The Montreal Symphony Orchestra's first concert took place on January 14, 1935.

The choice of an artistic director was obvious: Wilfrid Pelletier, assistant director at the Metropolitan Opera in New York, who had the necessary experience and knowledge combined with an energetic personality. He initiated a number of programs that he hoped would bring classical music closer to the general public. These included the Children's Symphonic Matinee series, an Annual Award of Composition, an Annual Festival in the suburbs, and finally a series of summer concerts. The orchestra's soloists were largely from Quebec, and a work by a French-Canadian composer was performed at each concert. Although German music had a good part of the programming, French music also had a considerable share of the repertoire. The sixth concert of the first season, for example, was devoted exclusively to French composers.

When Pelletier's position at the Metropolitan Opera necessitated a new MSO director, the position was taken by Désiré Defauw, who had been a guest conductor in the 1940–1941 season. His considerable experience in Belgium and other European countries made him the man the ensemble needed to ameliorate its technical difficulties; it soon reached a technical standard comparable to that of other North American orchestras. It was during this period that the MSO began inviting top conductors—Sir Thomas Beecham, Charles Munch, Sir Georg Solti, and others—as well as soloists of a similar calibre, to perform in Montreal. Their appearance with a still relatively modest ensemble can be accounted for by the political tensions in Europe and by the more-than-dynamic public relations practices of a man who literally gave his life to the orchestra—one of the prime movers in its history—Pierre Béique, who has held several key positions in the organization from 1936 to the present.

Defauw organized special events such as a complete cycle of Beethoven symphonies and the presentation of a Spring Festival with works like *Boris Godounov* and *La damnation de Faust*. He was also particularly interested in new music, as can be seen in the programming of Richard Strauss's *Metamorphosen* and Dmitri Shostakovich's Symphony No. 9 less than three years after their world premieres. The years following Defauw's departure in 1953 saw a period of guest conductors, opted for by Béique in view of financial constraints and a still-limited concert season. During 1951–1952 and the following season Otto Klemperer, immobilized in Montreal by an accident that prevented his departure, often led the orchestra, although he had no official title.

The appointment of Igor Markevitch in 1957 was a new departure for the ensemble, for in his brief years with the MSO he helped instigate contracts for its members and brought new challenges in repertoire. Markevitch led the orchestra in its first performance of Stravinsky's *Sacre du Printemps* and commissioned a work by a Canadian composer (Harry Somer's *Fantasia*), thus beginning a tradition of annual commissions.

Markevitch's failing health a few weeks before the beginning of a new season made a replacement most unlikely, but Béique succeeded in securing the services of Zubin Mehta, who was to conduct the orchestra at the inauguration of the Place des Arts. Mehta also led the orchestra during its first two international tours, which were to include Moscow, Leningrad, Paris, and Vienna (1962) and France, Belgium, and Switzerland (1966). It was also under Mehta that the orchestra began participating in the production of major operas.

The galvanizing personality of Zubin Mehta was difficult to match, and Franz-Paul Decker had a considerable task before him when he succeeded Mehta in 1967. Under him the orchestra learned to pay attention to every detail of a work, and each nuance was carefully rehearsed. Coming from the German tradition, Decker was fond of programming the gigantic works of late romanticism, so that works of composers such as Richard Strauss, Anton Bruckner, and Gustav Mahler were often performed.

His successor in 1975, Rafael Frühbeck de Burgos, was to stay only 18 months with the orchestra; several misunderstandings between him and members of the MSO making his departure inevitable. He was nevertheless to conduct the orchestra in its first appearance at Carnegie Hall and on its third European tour, which brought the ensemble to France, Switzerland, Great Britain, and Czechoslovakia.

In 1978 came Charles Dutoit, with a totally new approach to the role of the orchestra in the cultural community. With first-rate public relations, Dutoit undertook to popularize the MSO. He achieved this by very intense rehearsals for the musicians, appearances with the orchestra at free concerts in parks and sports arenas, participation on popular television talk shows, and numerous appearances with his ensemble in the company of popular commercial artists. He was also to return the orchestra to Carnegie Hall and to conduct it during further successful tours. His most notable initiative, though, probably consisted in signing an exclusive recording contract with Decca/London. The recordings and their awards have contributed greatly to the orchestra's reknown both internationally and at home, particularly in respect to its French repertoire.

RECORDING HISTORY AND SELECTIVE DISCOGRAPHY: Since 1982 the MSO has issued 15 highly acclaimed records, many of which have won international prizes. Its recording of Ravel's ballet *Daphnis et Chloé*, for example, has won the Grand Prix du Disque de l'Académie Charles Cros, the Prix mondial du disque de Montreux, and the Japan Record Academy Award; the record of Manuel de Falla's ballet *El sombrero de tres picos (Three-cornered Hat)* has won the Prix Georges-Auric de l'Académie du disque français and the High Fidelity International Record Critics Award.

Falla, *El sombrero de tres picos* and *El amor brujo* (Colette Boky, Huguette Tourangeau/Dutoit): London LDR 71060. Lalo, *Symphonie espagnole*; Saint-Saëns, Violin Concerto No. 1 (Kyung-Wha Chung/Dutoit): London LDR 71029. Ravel, *Daphnis et Chloé* (Dutoit): London 400055 (2 CDs). Joaquin Rodrigo, *Concierto de Aranjuez* and *Fantasia para un gentilhombre* (Carlos Bonell/Dutoit): London LDR 71027. Saint-Saëns, Symphony No. 3 (Hurford/Dutoit): London LDR 71090.

CHRONOLOGY OF MUSIC DIRECTORS: Wilfrid Pelletier, 1936–1941. Désiré Defauw, 1941–1953. (Guest conductors, 1953–1957.) Igor Markevitch, 1957–1961. Zubin Mehta, 1961–1967. Franz-Paul Decker, 1967–1975. Rafael Frühbeck de Burgos, 1975–1976. (Guest conductors, 1976–1978.) Charles Dutoit, 1978-present.

BIBLIOGRAPHY: Interviews with MSO Director of Public Relations Claudette Dionne, 1984. Cecile Huot and Gilles Potvin, "Montreal Symphony Orchestra," *Encyclopedia of Music in Canada* (Toronto: University of Toronto Press, 1981). Eric McLean, "Montreal Symphony, No More Hussars," *Musical America*, Sept. 1963. Montreal Symphony Orchestra, miscellaneous documents, 1984. Gilles Potvin, *Les 50 premières années* (Montreal: Editions A. Stanke, 1984).

ACCESS: Montreal Symphony Orchestra, 200 de Maisonneuve Boulevarde West, Montreal, Que. H2X 1Y9. (514) 842–3402. Zarin Mehta, General Manager. Claudette Dionne, Director of Public Relations.

FRANÇOIS VANASSE

OTTAWA

National Arts Centre Orchestra

Canada's National Arts Centre Orchestra (NACO), a 46-member, classical-size ensemble, has been ranked with the best in the world and consistently praised for performing with refinement and precision. The orchestra is part of the National Arts Centre (NAC) organization, a project first conceived by the federal government in celebration of Canada's centenary in 1967. The NAC was designed to encourage excellence in the performing arts and to foster the country's bilingual (French and English) heritage.

The Centre complex, located alongside Confederation Square in downtown Ottawa, consists of a series of hexagonal structures thrusting up through terraces at different levels. The main foyer of the building serves as a *hall d'entrée* from which radiate foyers servicing three performing halls: the 2,326-seat Opera/ Concert Hall, the 969-seat Theatre, and the 350-seat Studio.

The orchestra runs on a 46-week contract, including the summer season, and performs as the instrumental accompanist for visiting presentations; the year comprises 36 main series performances, 12 pops and four children's concerts, five or six specials, normally 10 broadcasts, and one major recording. In addition, the musicians are active providing concerts in the National Capital Region and chamber music at the Centre in a series entitled "Music for a Sunday Afternoon." National tours are an important function of the orchestra. Generally the touring pattern comprises one to the east, one west, and one abroad; thus the NACO spends more time on the road than any other Canadian orchestra.

The legal entity of the National Arts Centre is that of a crown corporation directly accountable to Parliament through the minister of communications (NAC Act of July 15, 1966). A 16-member Board of Trustees is responsible for the administration of the Centre "at arm's length" from Parliament and consists of a chairman, vice-chairman, the mayors of Ottawa and Hull, the director of the Canada Council, the president of the Canadian Broadcasting Corporation, the government film commissioner, and nine other members. With the exception of those who hold their appointment by virtue of position or elected office, Board members are appointed to a renewable three-year term through an order-in-council issued by the Cabinet. The Board of Trustees exercised the full powers of the NAC Act and took the unprecedented step of creating resident companies in music and theatre at the Centre. Consequently, unlike most other North American arts organizations, these companies require very little public solicitation of funds.

The music policy of the National Arts Centre was established prior to the passage of the NAC Act. Under the chairmanship of Louis Applebaum, a well-known composer and music administrator, a music committee was organized in 1964 to formulate plans for opera, music, and ballet. Applebaum and Ezra Schabas of the University of Toronto proposed the formation of a classical-sized ensemble that would provide a variety of musical services, including public and children's concerts, broadcasting, touring, chamber music, teaching, and opera and ballet accompaniment. Acting on these suggestions, the committee formulated plans for a 45-member orchestra, a size determined by a number of factors: financially, the Centre could only afford a first-rate small ensemble; touring would be more feasible with a smaller group; the virtuoso nature of the baroque, classical, and contemporary repertoire would attract high-calibre players; and the chamber concept would provide alternative programming to that provided by the larger symphony orchestras. Despite the objections of the Montreal Symphony Orchestra* and the Toronto Symphony Orchestra,* who were concerned about the formation of another orchestra in the nearby area, Louis Applebaum successfully convinced the Board of the advantages of such a project for all of Canada. On October 2, 1976, Jean-Marie Beaudet completed a feasibility study that supported Applebaum, and on October 10, 1967, Judy LaMarsh, the secretary of state, approved the formation of the National Arts Centre Orchestra.

Beaudet, the first director of music at the Centre, was responsible for the choice of Mario Bernardi, an outstanding Canadian conductor (formerly with the Sadler's Wells—now English National—Opera), as the first and founding conductor of the NACO. On October 7, 1969, Bernardi and the new orchestra (46 members, average age 27) made their debut performance to rave reviews. In that opening season the orchestra presented 18 concerts and experienced difficulty finding full-time employment for its members, who ten years later presented 54 subscription concerts, six nonsubscription concerts, and 13 more on tour.

Tours had become an important part of the season, and in its first ten years of operation the orchestra performed concerts in a total of 210 communities. A very successful 1972 debut at New York's Carnegie Hall led to tours of England, the U.S.S.R., and Italy (1973); Mexico and the United States (1975); France, Germany, and Italy (1978); and Scotland (1980). Rave reviews followed wherever the NACO performed.

During his 13-year tenure, Bernardi created a fastidious classical orchestra with a refined, transparent sound. Morale among the players remained strong, and many became soloists and chamber artists who made a substantial contribution to the country's cultural life. Economic stability, extra rehearsal time, generous working conditions, and high-calibre talent provided Bernardi the opportunity to create a connoisseur's orchestra. However, there were inherent limitations. Romantic and post-romantic works for large orchestra were virtually unplayable. Bernardi left the orchestra in 1982 to accept the musical directorship of the Calgary Philharmonic and the CBC Vancouver Orchestra. Of the 450 works performed in 500 concerts under Bernardi, 74 had been by Canadian composers and 20 were new commissions.

After a careful search the administration chose the Italian composer/pianist/conductor Franco Mannino as the NACO's new music director. His 1982 debut provoked a standing ovation, and he has since continued to win the admiration of audiences and critics.

RECORDING HISTORY AND SELECTIVE DISCOGRAPHY: The first recording contract for the NACO was signed with RCA (Canada) Ltd. in February of 1970. From 1973 to 1977 the CBC recorded six discs including a number of new Canadian works. During the 1977–1978 season Bernardi recorded an album of Italian opera arias for Columbia records. During the early 1980s the orchestra recorded lighter works of Haydn and Beethoven and various opera overtures for the CBC.

Beethoven, Symphony No. 1; Forsyth *Sagittarius* (Canadian Brass/Bernardi): CBC SM328. Mozart, *Eine Kleine Nachtmusik*, K. 525; Symphony No. 40, K. 550 (Bernardi): CMC SM5018. Mozart, Symphony No. 39, K. 453; Tchaikovsky, *Variations on a Rococo Theme for Cello* (Dennis Brott/Bernardi): CBC SM306.

CHRONOLOGY OF MUSIC DIRECTORS: Mario Bernardi, 1968–1982. Franco Mannino, 1982–1985.

BIBLIOGRAPHY: Ulla Colgrass, "Mario Bernardi Moves On," *Music Magazine*, Toronto, Aug. 1981. Federal Review Committee, *Report to the Minister of Communications from National Arts Centre* (Ottawa, 9 Jan. 1981). Hilary McLaughlin, "Mario's Last Bow," *Ottawa Magazine*, July 1982. National Arts Centre Orchestra, miscellaneous press releases and press clippings, 1982–1984.

ACCESS: National Arts Centre, Music Office, Ottawa, Ont. K1P 5W1. (613) 996–5051. Harold Clarkson, Orchestra Manager.

BERNARD W. ANDREWS

TORONTO   (3,067,000*)

Toronto Symphony

The Toronto Symphony (TS) is based in the capital city of the province of Ontario. It was named successively the Toronto Conservatory Symphony Orchestra (1906–1908), Toronto Symphony Orchestra (1908–1918), New Symphony Orchestra (1922–1927), Toronto Symphony Orchestra (1927–1967), and Toronto Symphony (1967-present). A Board of Directors, representative of community interests and headed by a president, is responsible for the TS organization, which consists of the music director and principal conductor, managing director, and support staff of 39. Since its formation in 1906 the orchestra has been at the center of Toronto's musical activities and has been the leading musical organization in English-speaking Canada.

The 101-member ensemble now presents approximately 150 concerts each season to audiences numbering 600,000. A concert season comprises ten different series, including evening subscription concerts, matinee performances, young people's concerts, promenades, and pops concerts. In addition, there are summer series at Roy Thomson Hall and at Ontario Place. The TS performed in Massey Hall from 1966 to 1982. For its 1982 season the TS moved to the newly built Roy Thomson Hall with a seating capacity of 2,812. Its 1985 budget of $10 million Canadian derived from ticket sales, government grants (municipal, provincial, federal), and donations both corporate and private. Based on a recent American Symphony Orchestra League report, it claims more subscribers (41,000 for 1985–1986) than any other orchestra on the continent.

Members of the Toronto Symphony contribute in various ways to the musical life of the Toronto region and of Canada. Some perform in chamber groups, tour as soloists, and teach at the University of Toronto, Royal Conservatory of Music, and other educational institutions, including many summer camps. The TS presents 20 school concerts annually at Roy Thomson Hall, and performers tour schools and libraries with educational programs that reach more than 100,000 children.

For 30 years prior to the founding of the Symphony, attempts were made to establish a permanent orchestra in Toronto. However, these organizations generally lasted for a few concerts or, at best, one concert season. Finally, Frank Welsman (1873–1952) formed the Toronto Conservatory Symphony Orchestra in 1906. Renamed the Toronto Symphony Orchestra in 1908, it presented annual concert series in Massey Music Hall (called Massey Hall after 1933), which for many years was the only Canadian concert hall specifically designed for musical performances.

Symphonies by Mendelssohn, Tchaikovsky, and Beethoven, plus the obligatory overtures and incidental orchestral music, entertained audiences of this period. Some of the world's leading soloists—Fritz Kreisler, Wilhelm Backhaus, Sergei Rachmaninoff—appeared with the TSO as part of their North American tours. Even Edward Elgar conducted his own oratorio *The Dream of Gerontius* (1911) in Toronto. Popular concerts were introduced in 1909, and the orchestra toured to nearby Ontario towns and cities. The TSO's ranks were depleted during World War I, and finally the organization was discontinued in 1918.

In 1912 Luigi von Kunits (1870–1931) turned down the conductorship of the Philadelphia Orchestra** to take up a teaching position in Toronto. He had studied in Vienna with Otokar Sevčik and Anton Bruckner before teaching in Chicago and Pittsburgh and becoming concertmaster and assistant conductor of the Pittsburgh Symphony Orchestra.** In 1922 von Kunits organized an orchestra and conducted the inaugural concert of the New Symphony Orchestra in April, 1923. In 1927 the name was changed to "Toronto Symphony Orchestra." Von Kunits and the TSO were the Canadian pioneers in broadcasting live weekly radio concerts in 1929–1930. The orchestra's repertoire was conservative, featuring well-known nineteenth-century European compositions.

Sir Ernest MacMillan (1893–1973) became the first Canadian-born conductor of the TSO in 1931. He systematically expanded the orchestra's repertoire to include more English composers, Béla Bartók, Carl Nielsen, and many others. During his tenure the orchestra matured musically, attained economic stability, increased its season to 26 weeks, and performed in regular national radio broadcasts, which were important unifying events in such a large country. Under MacMillan's direction the first recordings were made and children's concerts instituted. By the 1940s Canadian compositions were programmed regularly and Canadian performers were featured. In 1951 the TSO gave its first U.S. concerts in Detroit. In addition to its own concert season, the TSO performed regularly with the Toronto Mendelssohn Choir. MacMillan retired at the end of the 1955–1956 season after 25 years as conductor.

Walter Susskind (1913–1980), who had held conducting posts with the Carl

Rosa Opera, Scottish Orchestra (now the Scottish National Orchestra),* Melbourne Symphony Orchestra,* and Philharmonia Orchestra of London,* succeeded MacMillan. He programmed many British compositions and introduced Luciano Berio, Arnold Schoenberg, and Anton Webern to Toronto audiences. Under Susskind's direction the TSO appeared in Carnegie Hall in 1963 with Canadian Lois Marshall as soloist. After ten seasons Susskind resigned in 1965, leaving behind a versatile ensemble that presented 30 weeks of concerts.

The mercurial conductor Seiji Ozawa (b. 1931), who had captivated Toronto audiences with earlier guest appearances, became the new conductor. Ozawa's adventurous programming included composers such as Toru Takemitsu, Charles Ives, and Olivier Messiaen. He took the orchestra on tour, in 1966 to Great Britain and France and in 1969 to Japan, and gave the TS a new international prominence. After only four seasons Ozawa resigned. He was replaced by Karel Ančerl (1908–1973).

Ančerl's disciplined approach and exacting standards underlined the differences between the TS's new conductor and Ozawa. The less-dynamic Ančerl set about the task of instilling his concept of disciplined ensemble playing. He introduced Czech composers such as Leoš Janáček and Bohuslav Martinů to Toronto and returned to a more conservative repertoire. A Beethoven-centenary festival in 1970 and a Brahms festival one year later were outstanding successes. In 1971, under Ančerl, the TS began to present outdoor concerts at the Ontario Place Forum that introduced the orchestra and classical music to thousands. Despite Ančerl's sudden death in 1973, the TS went ahead with its planned tour of England, Austria, West Germany, and Belgium.

In 1975, after a number of guest conductors and during the tenure of Victor Feldbrill (b. 1924) as resident conductor (1973–1977), the TS appointed Britishborn Andrew Davis (b. 1944). Davis returned to the practice of more varied programming. He included many British composers such as Edward Elgar and Michael Tippett, and explored systematically the works of Alexander Borodin and Gustav Mahler. The TS returned to touring and visited New York, Washington, California, and various parts of Canada. The tour in 1978 to China and Japan with Canadians Maureen Forrester (contralto) and Louis Lortie (piano) was received with critical acclaim. The TS was only the fourth orchestra in the world to tour China. Under Davis the Toronto Symphony has continued to develop its true potential, and he has expanded the group's recording activities with several major companies. Davis has recently announced that he will not renew his contract, resigning as of June 1988.

RECORDING HISTORY AND SELECTIVE DISCOGRAPHY: Under Sir Ernest MacMillan's direction the TSO made more than ten recordings, including Gustav Holst's *The Planets* and Elgar's *Pomp and Circumstance Marches* on 78 rpm records for RCA Victor. Susskind, Ozawa, and Ančerl made recordings during their conductorships, and Davis has been very active in recording orchestral works since becoming music director and conductor. More than 30 records have been produced in recent years by RCA, Radio Canada International, Columbia, CBC, and CRI.

Berlioz, *Symphonie fantastique* (Ozawa): Odyssey Y31923. Janáček, Suite from *The Cunning Little Vixen, Taras Bulba* (Davis): Columbia M35117. Martinů, Symphony No. 5 (Ančerl): CBC SM-218. Roger Matton, Concerto pour deux pianos (Susskind): CRI SD317.

CHRONOLOGY OF MUSIC DIRECTORS: Frank Welsman, 1906-1918. (Operations suspended, 1918-1922.) Luigi von Kunits, 1922-1931. Sir Ernest MacMillan (1931-1956). Walter Susskind, 1956-1965. Seiji Ozawa, 1965-1969. Karel Ančerl, 1969-1973. Victor Feldbrill (Resident Director), 1973-1977. Andrew Davis, 1975-1988.

BIBLIOGRAPHY: Phone interviews with TS administration, 1985. Arnold Edinborough, *A Personal History of the Toronto Symphony* (Toronto, 1972). *Encyclopedia of Music in Canada* (Toronto: University of Toronto Press, 1981).

ACCESS: Toronto Symphony, 60 Simcoe Street, Suite C116, Toronto M5J 2H5.

FREDERICK A. HALL

VANCOUVER (1,310,000*)

Vancouver Symphony Orchestra

The Vancouver Symphony Orchestra (VSO), designated a Major Orchestra by the American Symphony Orchestra League, performs in Vancouver's Orpheum Theatre, a refurbished vaudeville and movie theatre built in 1927 in the conservative Spanish Renaissance style of its contemporaries around North America. The VSO was a part-time tenant until 1959, when it moved to the new Queen Elizabeth Theatre, a multi-purpose hall still used by the VSO for its ballet series, but which proved to be acoustically inadequate for symphony concerts. It was not until 1977, however, that the Orpheum had been purchased by the city, renovated, refurbished, and made available, primarily for orchestral concerts by the VSO. The excellent acoustics and visual grandeur of the nearly 3,000-seat facility add greatly to concerts.

The performance season of the VSO runs from early September to mid-June, providing 43 weeks of employment for 80 contracted musicians. Six different series of performances are available to the public: the main or Jubilee series of standard orchestral repertoire, the Musically Speaking series featuring a guest lecturer, a Great Composers series dealing with one composer per program, a family Pops series aimed at young people and families, and a later series á la Boston Pops for adults. In addition, the Vancouver Symphony Society acts as an impresario, bringing in five ballet companies for runs in the city, with the VSO in the pit of the Queen Elizabeth Theatre, as well as a recital series featuring international artists in solo recital at the Orpheum.

The orchestra and its concerts are managed by an administrative staff of 25, with an annual budget of $6.5 million Canadian. The Vancouver Symphony Society, through its official Board and Executive Committee, governs the entire operation as a nonprofit organization allowed certain tax advantages under Canadian law. While the VSO plays for more than 300,000 people annually and has 40,000 ticket subscribers, only 50% of funds come from ticket sales. The rest derives from various levels of government (30%) and from the private sector (20%) through corporate sponsorship programs, foundations, endowments, fundraising projects such as radiothons ($140,000 in 1984), and individual donations.

The impact of the VSO and its musicians radiates throughout the Vancouver area. Many orchestra members teach privately or through the universities and colleges in the community, and many lead or coach ensembles. Several ensembles from within the orchestra perform during the year, and many of its players take part in separate recital series. Some VSO musicians pursue further freelance playing in the Canadian Broadcasting Corporation (Radio) Chamber Orchestra and for the several commercial recording studios located in Vancouver.

The Vancouver Symphony Orchestra has been the "cultural flagship" on the west coast of Canada since its inception in 1931. Previous attempts at forming an orchestra had foundered due to the character of the young city whose economy was based on resource exploitation and shipping. With the growth and maturation of Vancouver after World War I, however, the needs of the community for the arts prompted the founding of the Vancouver Symphony Society and the beginning of regular concerts. Although Vancouver is not the capital city of the province of British Columbia, it is the largest center and economic hub for a vast hinterland and Oriental trade.

The growth of Vancouver in recent decades is reflected in the expansion of its arts community, which now includes a major public gallery and many private ones, several dance companies, the Vancouver Opera, numerous theatre companies and choral societies, a professional chamber choir, a radio orchestra of the CBC, an opera/freelance orchestra, and numerous chamber music and recital groups, all in addition to the VSO. Vancouver in the 1980s is now an office/technical economic center whose people demand a high cultural component in their leisure-time activities.

Over the years the VSO's conductors have each contributed to the orchestra's growth, starting in 1931 at its inception with Allard de Ridder, who came to Vancouver from Los Angeles and stayed until 1940. During World War II and until 1946 the orchestra was without a permanent conductor but had guests of the highest order—Sir John Barbirolli, Leonard Bernstein, Otto Klemperer, and others. From 1946 to 1950 Jacques Singer led the VSO and initiated regular Pops concerts in Vancouver. Irwin Hoffman led the orchestra from 1952 to 1964 and began touring throughout British Columbia, making it a resource for the whole province.

In 1964 the appointment of Meredith Davies as conductor and music director began a considerable growth in the VSO, which molded it into a tight, cohesive ensemble. This was achieved in part by attracting many top-level players, one of whom was Simon Streatfield as principal violist. Upon Davies's departure in 1971 Streatfield became the interim conductor and then associate conductor with the arrival of Kazuyoshi Akiyama in 1972.

It is Akiyama who has brought the VSO to the forefront of Canadian musical life, molding it into one of the top orchestras in the country. Its profile has been raised greatly due to several factors, the first being regular broadcasting of its concerts over CBC Radio. In addition, the orchestra has toured more frequently under Akiyama: to various parts of British Columbia (1979, 1980, 1981), across Canada (1976), through the western United States (1978), and to Japan (1974 and 1985). Further exposure has been made through recordings on the CBC's SM5000 series.

Rudolf Barshai succeeded Akiyama as music director and conductor in the 1985–1986 season, although Akiyama will return regularly as Conductor Laureate. Barshai, the founder and conductor of the Moscow Chamber Orchestra* for 20 years, emigrated from the U.S.S.R. in 1977 and is now conductor of the Bournemouth Orchestra* in Britain, a post he will retain along with the VSO. A greater emphasis on the classics and less familiar Russian works may be the future direction of the VSO, as well as increased emphasis on the string sound of the orchestra, due to Barshai's background as a fine violist.

SELECTIVE DISCOGRAPHY: Berlioz, *King Lear*; Franck, Symphony in D Minor (Akiyama): CBC SM5033. Strauss, *Death and Transfiguration* and *Salome's Dance* (Akiyama): CBC SM5015. Tchaikovsky, *Romeo and Juliette* and *Francesca da Rimini* (Barshai): CBC SM5038. Tchaikovsky, Symphony No. 4 (Akiyama): CBC SM5006.

CHRONOLOGY OF MUSIC DIRECTORS: Allard de Ridder, 1931–1940. Jacques Singer, 1946–1950. Irwin Hoffman, 1952–1964. Meredith Davies, 1964–1971. Simon Streatfield, 1971–1972. Kazuyoshi Akiyama, 1972–1985. Rudolf Barshai, 1985–present.

BIBLIOGRAPHY: Chuck Davis, *The Vancouver Book* (Vancouver: Evergreen, 1976). Vancouver Symphony Orchestra, miscellaneous fact sheets, 1984.

ACCESS: Vancouver Symphony Society, 400 E. Broadway, Vancouver, B.C. V5T 1X2. (604) 875–1661. Edward P. Oscapella, Executive Director.

BRIAN G'FROERER

WINNIPEG   (584,000*)

Winnipeg Symphony Orchestra

The Winnipeg Symphony Orchestra (WSO) presents a musically varied, 34-week season (September to May) comprising over 60 concerts. It performs in the 2,263-seat Manitoba Centennial Hall (1968). Built for the orchestra's use and designed for acoustical quality, the hall is owned by the province and rented to the orchestra. The 12-program Masterworks series of 24 performances is supplemented with the Musically Speaking series of six concerts (sponsored by the du Maurier Council for the Arts), a seven-program, 14-performance Pops series (sponsored in part by Seagram Distillers Ltd.), and five concerts specifically for children. An additional series brings the orchestra to Brandon, Manitoba.

The Masterworks series, led by WSO Music Director Kazuhiro Koizumi and guest conductors, features well-known soloists in programs that strike a balance among the periods, occasionally presenting unusual works side by side with standard favorites. A 1985–1986 program, for example, presented works of Alan Ridout, Beethoven, Dvořák, and Stravinsky. Mahler's Symphony No. 2 ("Resurrection") was the sole offering in the season's final Masterworks concert. The Musically Speaking series, under Koizumi and guest conductors (including in recent years, Erich Kunzel) adds verbal commentary to programs centering on familiar symphonies and concertos. In these and its other series the orchestra almost never performs without a soloist. Pops programming mixes works such as overtures, concertos, or suites of standard symphonic composers with those of theatre or popular composers for programs such as "Springtime in Vienna," "Kunzel on Broadway," or "Fiedler's Favourites."

With a nucleus of 67 musicians, the WSO can expand to over 80 as the music requires. WSO musicians comprise the core of the Manitoba Chamber and Rainbow Stage Orchestras, and the WSO acts as pit orchestra for the Royal Winnipeg Ballet and the Manitoba Opera Association. Its budget of just under $3 million Canadian is funded by ticket sales, the Canada Council, province of Manitoba, Manitoba Arts Council, city of Winnipeg, Winnipeg Foundation, and both private and corporate donations.

According to the orchestra's typescript history, the WSO was founded in 1947, though it was not the first orchestra to bear that title. Winnipeg symphony orchestras—formed in 1923, 1930, 1932, and other years—had all failed for various reasons, and it was not until after World War II that a concerted attempt was made to found a lasting, professional symphonic ensemble in Winnipeg. Under auspices of the Winnipeg Civic Music League (1946), the Winnipeg Symphony Orchestra was organized in 1947 as a joint stock company, an appeal for support was made to the citizens, and a conductor, Dr. Walter Kaufmann, was engaged. The first performance was held in December of 1948 at the Winnipeg Civic Auditorium.

Kaufmann stayed for ten years, to be followed in 1958 by the 34-year-old Canadian conductor Victor Feldbrill, formerly assistant conductor of the Toronto Symphony Orchestra* and a possessor of considerable guest conducting experience. By this time the orchestra was capable of a season of 36 performances as well as 17 school appearances. The orchestra also became more closely affiliated with the CBC. For the first time musicians were contracted on an extended (24-week) basis, with weekly salaries and union status.

Simultaneous with the WSO's move in 1968 to the Centennial Concert Hall was the accession of a new music director, George Cleve. When Cleve resigned at the end of 1969/1970, a season of guest conductors produced the appointment of the Italian conductor Piero Gamba. Under Gamba the orchestra began to tour more extensively, visiting small communities in Manitoba, several Canadian cities, and, in 1980, New York.

The overall picture, however, was far from bright. Indeed, by 1980 declining ticket sales and community support had brought the orchestra to the edge of bankruptcy. A reported deficit of $1.2 million in 1980–1981, programming that has been described as "repetitive and unimaginative," and a resultant lack of enthusiasm both within and surrounding the ensemble seemed like a death sentence. In an emergency meeting the Board of Trustees decided to take measures: change the artistic and operational management, follow a path of fiscal restraint, program for audience appeal, and look to the future.

The plan was a success. Under Executive Director Jack Mills and with the help of grants from municipal, provincial, and federal governments, corporate sponsors, and individuals, the orchestra in 1984 was for the first time able to show an accumulated surplus. An 18-month search for a new music director yielded the experienced Japanese conductor Kazuhiro Koizumi, who was appointed in 1982 and to whom the orchestra attributes its musical renaissance (an opinion corroborated by recent, positive critical notices). The orchestra has publicized its current crest of achievement, as in its 1983–1984 program booklet, which invites subscribers to "Discover the New Winnipeg Symphony Orchestra."

RECORDING HISTORY AND SELECTIVE DISCOGRAPHY: Although the WSO became associated with the CBC in 1958, most of its available recordings are of recent vintage.

Kunzel on Broadway (Kunzel): Fanfare Records. Morawetz, *Carnival* Overture; Tchaikovsky, *Mozartiana*; Kodály, *Dances of Galanta*; Dvořák, *Legend* (Koizumi): CBC SM5039. *An Evening With Rodgers and Hammerstein* (Kunzel): Moss Music/CBC DMMG 114.

CHRONOLOGY OF MUSIC DIRECTORS: Walter Kaufmann, 1948–1958. Victor Feldbrill, 1958–1968. George Cleve, 1968–1970. (Guest conductors, 1970–1971.) Piero Gamba, 1971–1980. (Guest conductors, 1980–1982.) Kazuhiro Koizumi, 1982-present.

BIBLIOGRAPHY: Correspondence with WSO Director of Public Relations Darlene Ronald, 1986. Peter Carlyle-Gordge, "Variations on a Theme of Discord," *Macleans*, 22 Sept. 1980. Peter Carlyle-Gordge and Jane Mingay, "Winnipeg's Upbeat Note," *Macleans*, 24 Jan. 1983. *Encyclopedia of Music in Canada* (Toronto: University of Toronto Press, 1981). "A History of the Winnipeg Symphony Orchestra" (Winnipeg: WPO typescript, 1985). Roger Newman, "Symphony Sounds Sweet Notes after Reversing Financial Crisis," *Manitoba Business*, June 1985. Darlene Ronald, "Facing the Music: The Winnipeg Symphony Orchestra Turnaround," *Mid-Canada Commerce*, April 1985. WSO fact sheets and program booklets.

ACCESS: Winnipeg Symphony Orchestra, Room 101, 555 Main Street, Winnipeg, Manitoba R3B 1C3. (204) 942–4576. Max Tapper, Executive Director.

ROBERT R. CRAVEN

Chile ───────────────────────────

Symphony Orchestra of Chile

The present Symphony Orchestra of Chile (OSC: Orquesta sinfónica de Chile) was formed as such in 1940 when, by Law of the Republic No. 6696, one of the most original and effective cultural institutions in South America was created: the Musical Extension Institute (IEM: Instituto de Extensión Musical) of the University of Chile.

In addition to its season of regular symphonic concerts, the OSC and its chamber ensembles participate in festivals of Chilean music, one of the IEM's activities most profoundly influencing national culture. In general, the regular season concerts are each repeated once, and there are approximately six to ten separate programs presented.

Under Music Director Victor Tevah the orchestra continues its historical commitment to a repertoire emphasizing new works of Chilean composers along with the customary classical and romantic repertoire. It also participates in festivals held every two years, in which a public jury judges the quality and importance of works presented after a technical preselection by specialists (composers, musicologists, performers, etc.) assembled as a special committee. Foreign conductors and soloists frequently perform with the orchestra.

One problem faced by the OSC and other university groups such as ballet and theatre ensembles is the lack of a suitable venue of their own. The orchestra has performed in the Municipal, Central, Gran Palace, and Victoria Theatres, which, with the exception of the Municipal, must be rented. From 1940, by agreement between the Musical Extension Institute and the Municipal Theatre, the orchestra has performed its concerts there and also accompanied the opera seasons of the university's Faculty of Arts.

The OSC is under separate administrative and artistic management. A standing committee composed of musicians, concertmaster, and regular conductor sees to decisions of programming and of engaging guest conductors. Administrative matters are handled by a staff of approximately seven. The OSC budget is administered by the Faculty of Arts, who in turn receive funding from the university. To this is added the revenue resulting from ticket sales.

Between 1930 and 1940 there existed in Santiago the Orchestra of the Symphonic Concerts Association and ensembles supported both by official organizations (such as the Faculty of Fine Arts of the University of Chile) and by private initiative. Because of the ability, technical musical training, and dedication of its conductor, Professor Armando Carvajal, there was now a focal point where the Chilean people could become acquainted with symphonic music, although many of them had been previously exposed to opera.

Despite economic conditions not always sufficiently favorable, the spirit of this organization and its outward expression, demonstrated by regularly performed concerts, show its intention of educating the public with many outstanding symphonic works from the baroque to the modern age, including, of course, the most important Chilean works.

This activity, maintained with regularity and with appropriate publicity and programming, was educating a public of diverse social character to contemporary and modern composers outside the operatic tradition to which it was accustomed. The performance in those concerts of the most qualified Chilean soloists (42 in all) provided powerful encouragement for musical performance, a circumstance that was reinforced by the incorporation of superior musical teaching within and outside of the university.

All this led to the inspired creation of the Musical Extension Institute (IEM), an accomplishment that has been attributed in its totality to the composer and formidable backer of music in Chile, Domingo Santa Cruz Wilson. The purpose of the Institute was to foster and spread musical activity in every way. The formation and maintenance of a symphony orchestra (and other suitable organizations) was fundamental to its aim of bringing about various high-quality musical activities. The first step that the IEM (as it would later be known) took was to form the Symphony Orchestra of Chile. Thus, without interruption of concert activities, the OSC was born on January 7, 1941, out of the Symphonic Concerts Association Orchestra, with a concert in the Municipal Theatre of Santiago under the direction of its regular conductor, Armando Carvajal.

Soon chamber ensembles comprising musicians chosen from the OSC grew in the shadow of the parent ensemble, allowing the inclusion of chamber concerts of the most diverse sorts within the orchestra's seasons. The success of the orchestra and its allied activities may be attributed in part to its administrative and financial soundness, enacted by law and ensured with a 2½% tax on all film admissions. That stability, combined with Carvajal's tireless work, the careful maintenance of musical quality and orchestral efficiency through annual auditions, and, finally, the prestige brought to the OSC by the university, all combined to create circumstances that attracted the attention and interest of two important conductors of the age, Erich Kleiber and Fritz Busch. Both performed many memorable seasons, trained and encouraged musicians, and, in short, left as their legacy to the orchestra a demand for discipline and a dynamism that has carried the group to a permanently high artistic level.

Between 1941 and 1952 the OSC performed, without interruption, 241 concerts in its respective annual seasons, 162 free or reduced-price popular concerts, 144 educational concerts with programs appropriate for various school levels, outdoor summer concerts, 24 tours of the country, and winter seasons in Viña del Mar and Valparaiso. Not included in this list are the performances of the OSC in the opera season of the Municipal Theatre.

In addition to Kleiber and Busch, who must be considered developers of the orchestra, many first-ranked foreign conductors have visited the OSC. From 1941 to the present the OSC has sustained its performances and especially its spirit. It has had a profound influence on the cultural life of the country. Between 1943 and 1984, for example, 309 foreign and 198 Chilean works have been premiered.

Victor Tevah, formerly a violinist in the OSC, succeeded Armando Carvajal in 1947 as the OSC's regular conductor. His work has been tireless, of a high level, and he has shown a special dedication to Chilean music. He has premiered practically every work of quality for orchestra or chamber ensemble that has been written in the country.

Recent conductors have included the young Francisco Rettig, who studied in Germany under Volker Wangenheim. Premieres under Rettig include the Concerto for Guitar and Orchestra (1985) and the Symphony "El Hombre ante la Ciencia" (1986) by Alfonso Letelier.

RECORDING HISTORY AND SELECTIVE DISCOGRAPHY: The OSC has made numerous recordings of Chilean music, encompassing works of Pedro Humberto Allende, Gustave Becerra, Próspero Bisquert, Acario Cotapos, Alfonso Leng, Alfonso Letelier, Juan Orrego Salas, Domingo Santa-Cruz, Enrique Soro, Darwin Vargas, and Jorge Urrutia.

Three Chilean Composers: Santa-Cruz, Letelier, Soro (Tevah): Inter-American Musical Editions AS–011 (Organization of American States).

CHRONOLOGY OF MUSIC DIRECTORS: Armando Carvajal, 1940–1947. Victor Tevah, 1947-present.

BIBLIOGRAPHY: Domingo Santa-Cruz, "Principales estrenos de la orquesta sinfónica de Chile," typescript, University of Chile, 1984.

ACCESS: Orquesta Sinfónica de la Universidad de Chile, Casilla 2100, Compañia 1264, Santiago.

ALFONSO LETELIER
TRANS. DAVID BRADT

China (People's Republic) ___

Central Philharmonic Orchestra

The Central Philharmonic Society, established in 1956, is one of China's largest musical organizations. Within the umbrella organization of the Society fall the Central Philharmonic Orchestra, a chorus, two small groups of solo and duet performers, a chamber music ensemble, and several composers.

Since its beginning the Central Philharmonic Orchestra of Beijing has presented both Western and Chinese music. Western selections range from the classical period through the contemporary. The Chinese repertoire consists of music by Chinese composers who utilize strictly Western forms, instruments, and techniques, but incorporate some Chinese elements. In addition to public concerts, the orchestra performs music for films and television programs, makes recordings, broadcasts concerts over radio and television, and carries on musical exchanges with international cultural organizations. The objective of the orchestra is to satisfy the demands of the cultural life of the people through carrying out the Chinese Communist Party's goal of the prosperity of socialist art.

The concert season differs from year to year, with regular concerts being reestablished in 1982. While the majority of concerts are given in Beijing, the orchestra periodically travels around the country giving performances in the major cities of most provinces and stopping at factories, mines, villages, and outlying territories. In recent years it has performed in North Korea, Japan, Southeast Asia, Romania, Yugoslavia, Latin America, and Africa. In 1978 some of its members toured the United States as part of the China Performing Arts Troupe, and several—Liu Shikun (piano), Liu Dahai (pipa/pear-shaped lute), Han Zhongjie (conductor)—have appeared and/or recorded with the Boston Symphony

Orchestra.** Some Western musicians have conducted and/or performed with the Central Philharmonic Orchestra.

All members of the Central Philharmonic Orchestra have been trained in conservatories and university music departments. Some have studied abroad, and some have received prizes in international competitions for composing, conducting, or performing. There is a balance of experienced older musicians and promising young talents.

From 1951 to 1956 the Central Philharmonic Orchestra was part of a musical troup that included Chinese traditional singing, dancing, and instruments. When the Central Philharmonic Society was established, the traditional music performers formed a separate organization. The orchestra was inactive during the Cultural Revolution (1966–1976). Its first public performance of Western music thereafter was a presentation in Beijing on March 26, 1977, of the Beethoven Fifth Symphony, Premier Zhou Enlai's favorite piece. Since then the orchestra has consistently expanded its repertoire of Western music—the Chinese premiere of the Verdi *Requiem* took place in the spring of 1986. The orchestra continues to promote new works by Chinese composers.

SELECTIVE DISCOGRAPHY: *Boston Symphony, Sergi [sic] Ozawa, People's Republic of China*, Philips 9500–692.

CHRONOLOGY OF CHIEF CONDUCTORS: Li Delun, 1957-present. Han Zhongjie, 1961-present. Chen Xieyang, 1982-present (part-time basis, on loan from Shanghai Ballet).

ACCESS: Central Philharmonic Orchestra, Central Philharmonic Society, Heping Li, Beijing.

MARJORIE ANN CIARLILLO

Costa Rica ─────────────────

SAN JOSÉ (395,000*)

National Symphony Orchestra of Costa Rica

Founded in 1926, the Costa Rican National Symphony Orchestra (OSN: Orquesta Sinfónica Nacional de Costa Rica) is at the forefront of Costa Rica's national policy of cultural and economic growth. This unusual emphasis upon culture, especially music, is advocated by the Ministry of Culture, Youth, and Sports, whose goal it is to spread quality music throughout the country, to encourage the support of national composers, and to establish an educational infrastructure that will provide the necessary musicians to maintain a continuing national musical organization. The OSN is designed to be the principal group carrying out this policy through its function as a national symphony orchestra of professional standards and through subsidiary and allied groups such as the National Youth Symphony and various smaller chamber groups like the Orquesta da Camera de Heredia.

The regular concert season of the OSN consists of eight concerts each month from April to November. All of these subscription concerts are performed in the Teatro Nacional, an elegant theatre constructed in 1897 as a copy of the Opéra Comique in Paris and having a capacity of 1,000 people. The OSN performs principally in San José, the capital, but also tours each of Costa Rica's seven provinces annually. In addition, it has made a tour to Colombia. The OSN has 72 permanent professional musicians, including a number of foreigners, mostly Americans. Membership is also drawn from the National School of Music, which is under the auspices of the National University Faculty of Fine Arts and whose teachers are drawn from the OSN. The orchestra is entirely state supported, with an annual budget of ¢21,588,000. The administration is carried out through the

Ministry of Culture, Youth, and Sports, though internal matters such as repertoire are the responsibility of the music director.

Following the construction of the Teatro Nacional at the end of the last century, various opera troupes performed in Costa Rica, the orchestra being supplied upon demand from among local musicians. It was not, however, until 1926 that an attempt to form a permanent symphonic orchestra was made. This group, also called the OSN, lasted but a single season and was disbanded until 1941, when an Argentinian, Hugo Mariani, reconstructed the orchestra. This organization, composed mainly of amateurs, was more successful and performed sporadically until 1961, when a firm administrative and economic foundation was laid. Between 1966 and 1971 the OSN lacked any clear direction as a succession of permanent "guest conductors" attempted to keep the orchestra functioning. Finally, in 1972, the government stepped in and ordered a complete reorganization of the OSN. It was put on a permanent professional basis through the hiring of an American conductor, Gerald Brown, the recruiting of foreign musicians, and the reshuffling of Costa Rican personnel (which resulted in the establishment of minimum performance standards). Since 1982 the OSN has been under the leadership of a Costa Rican conductor, Agustin Cullell.

The OSN performs a repertoire similar to other major symphony orchestras throughout the world. Guest conductors and first-rank soloists appear on the program each season. A recording featuring the OSN and violinist Dylana Jehson was made in 1973.

CHRONOLOGY OF MUSIC DIRECTORS: Juan Loots, 1926–1927. Hugo Mariani, 1941–1964. Ricardo del Carmen, 1964–1966. Carlos E. Vargas, Benjamin Guiterrez, and others, 1966–1971. Gerald Brown, 1972–1982. Agustin Cullell, 1982-present.

BIBLIOGRAPHY: Interview with Agustin Cullell, 1985. Richard Biesanz, *The Costa Ricans* (Englewood Cliffs: Prentice Hall, 1982). Samuel Rovinski, *Cultural Policy in Costa Rica* (Paris: UNESCO, 1977). Frank Stalzer, "Orchestras of Guatemala and Costa Rica," *Woodwind World*, June 1976. Kerman Turner, "Why Tractors Without Violins? Costa Rica's Music Revolution," *Americas*, Feb. 1973.

ACCESS: Orquesta Sinfónica Nacional, Aportado 1035, San José, Costa Rica. 22–26–82. Agustin Cullell, Music Director.

BERTIL H. VAN BOER, JR.
MARGARET L. FAST

Czechoslovakia _____

PRAGUE   (1,183,000)

Czech Philharmonic Orchestra

The Czech Philharmonic Orchestra is generally recognized today as the leading concert orchestra in Czechoslovakia. Besides its concert activity in Prague it fulfills the role of a representative orchestra at most significant cultural events of state-wide importance as well as in numerous tours abroad.

The Czech Philharmonic considers its concert activity in Prague as its main mission. Each season it organizes six series of subscription concerts, each with usually eight concerts. Some seasons feature composers' cycles (Mozart, Dvořák, Mahler) or cycles for gala occasions (Czech Philharmonic Jubilee, Czech Music Year, etc.). Each season the orchestra performs in other Czechoslovak towns and goes on several foreign tours organized in cooperation with the Pragokoncert agency. About 50 of its 95 to 110 annual concerts are held in Prague.

In Prague the Czech Philharmonic plays mostly in the Dvořák Hall of the House of Artists. Originally called the Rudolfinum, it was built in 1876–1884 as a counterpart to the National Theatre designed by the same architects, Josef Zítek and Josef Schulz. Originally it was intended as a picture gallery of the Society of Patriotic Friends of Art and for the Music Conservatory. In 1918 it housed the Parliament. In 1946 it became the headquarters of the Czech Philharmonic, with its large hall renamed Dvořák Hall. With 1,050 seats and a platform for 120 musicians, it has excellent acoustics (additionally perfected by Antonín Engel) and is often used for recording purposes. Its present organ, built by Rieger & Kloss of Krnov in 1975, has a mechanical system, four manuals, 63 key-stops, and 5,050 pipes.

High standards for newly accepted Philharmonic musicians are assured by exacting competition in admission. All first players are virtuosic on their instruments, and all are active as soloists. The instruments used by Philharmonic musicians are of the finest makers and are owned by the orchestra. The normal distribution of strings is 14, 12, 10, 10, 8; in recordings and on foreign tours two players are added to each group. The orchestra tunes to an A of 443 cps.

Composer and musicologist Ctirad Kohoutek has been artistic director of the Czech Philharmonic since 1980. The director, who has a deputy for economic affairs, is in charge of the secretariat and the repertory adviser, who is in turn responsible for the preparation and realization of concerts. Four officials of the artistic operation section assure concert realization. The Czech Philharmonic Orchestra and Prague Philharmonic Choir have their respective secretaries, assuring operation in the course of the season. A third secretary handles the affairs of chamber ensembles. The Czech Philharmonic has an archive of sheet music consisting of almost 6,000 items, mostly orchestral materials, and a collection of recordings—mostly its own—as well as extensive documentation of its activities.

The core repertoire of the Czech Philharmonic includes the cycle of symphonic poems by Bedřich Smetana (*My Country*), symphonies by Antonín Dvořák and Bohuslav Martinů, compositions by Leoš Janáček, the best works of other twentieth-century Czech composers, and the finest works of foreign composers from the baroque to the present.

The movement for the regeneration and independence of the Czech nation, which lived for almost three centuries under the yoke of the Austro-Hungarian monarchy, developed broadly in all spheres of life at the end of the nineteenth century. The need for an independent Czech symphony orchestra was very topical then, and the constitution in 1894 of a society of members of the National Theatre orchestra under the name of the Czech Philharmonic was a logical step in the process of achieving cultural independence. The society's mission was to hold Czech Philharmonic concerts as a counterweight to German ones. The income produced would go to its treasury. The first concert organized by the society, on January 4, 1896, is considered the founding act of the Czech Philharmonic Orchestra: the National Theatre orchestra under Dvořák played a program of his compositions in the present-day Dvořák Hall. Twenty-three concerts were held under various conductors between 1896 and 1901.

The Czech Philharmonic Orchestra was independently reconstituted in 1901 from among National Theatre orchestra members dismissed after an abortive strike against Karel Kovařovic, the new opera chief, who had been introducing an unusually rigorous and exacting regime. The orchestra's first representative concert was conducted on October 15, 1901, by Ludvík Vítězslav Čelanský, who was succeeded for a short time by Oskar Nedbal. At Čelanský's recommendation Dr. Vilém Zemánek was put at the head of the orchestra; he maintained that position until 1918.

The Czech Philharmonic owed its financial underpinnings largely to Zemánek's organizational skills. Nevertheless, a succession of popular concerts, even in restaurants, to assure a more regular income; the departures of personnel to better-off orchestras; a disunity in leadership, especially during the war years; and Zemánek's insufficient artistic capabilities all led to a wavering artistic level followed by more serious (mostly financial) troubles. The immediate threat of extinction, however, was always warded off by gifts from affluent supporters. They included two prominent artists: Oskar Nedbal, who led the first successful tour to Vienna in 1901 and conducted concerts at the 1902 coronation celebrations in London; and Jan Kubelik, who negotiated those concerts. Such tours did not bring the expected financial rewards but did gain a good name for the orchestra, which (despite its remarkable level under Nedbal's conducting and with Kubelik's violin playing) was yet quite unknown abroad.

At the Philharmonic concerts, conducted in Prague by Nedbal and later by Karel Kovařovic, the Czech public was acquainting itself more intimately with works by Smetana, Dvořák, and Zdeněk Fibich. It was also hearing premieres of key works by Vítězslav Novák, Josef Suk, and Josef B. Foerster, works that otherwise would have had little chance of performance and perhaps would not have been composed at all, without the prospect of performance by the Czech Philharmonic.

After the foundation of the independent Czechoslovak Republic, the Czechoslovak Philharmonic Society was established (1919) and Václav Talich (1883–1961) became the chief of the Czech Philharmonic Orchestra. He had conducted it for the first time in 1917, and on October 30, 1918, he won general acclaim for his brilliant first presentation of Josef Suk's symphonic poem *The Ripening*. In spite of constant economic difficulties (reduced by Talich through assured state subsidies), and in the face of many organizational changes, the orchestra was growing under Talich's artistic leadership and acquiring the reputation of the first musical ensemble of its kind in the awareness of the Czechoslovak cultural public. Tours of Slovakia, especially in Smetana's jubilee year of 1924, contributed to that growth.

Participation in the festivals organized by the International Society for Contemporary Music in Prague in 1924 and 1925 brought the orchestra to the attention of a number of prominent musical personalities; its international renown was growing. Prominent composers, conductors, and soloists came to Prague to meet the orchestra. Thanks to Talich, the ensemble achieved an unusually impressive string sound, supple and lilting, which since then has become a characteristic feature of the Czech Philharmonic Orchestra. In Talich's time the orchestra was acquainting listeners with key works of world music, but domestic repertoire was its basis. His productions of compositions by Smetana, Dvořák, and Suk are still benchmarks of Czech performing art. On May 12, 1925, the Philharmonic began appearing on Czechoslovak Radio, and the revenues generated by live relays of its performances furnished an important source of income.

In the prewar period the most important conductors of the Czech Philharmonic were František Stupka (1879–1965). Karel Šejna (1896–1982), Jaroslav Řídký (1897–1956), and Rafael Kubelik, who led large tours of Great Britain and Belgium in 1937 and 1938. The Philharmonic succeeded in maintaining the continuity of concert life throughout the German occupation of Czechoslovakia, and some 70% of the compositions played were Czech.

The decree of the president of the Republic on October 22, 1945, was an important milestone in the history of the Czech Philharmonic Orchestra: it was declared a state orchestra. By organizing the first Prague Spring International Music Festival in 1946, the year of its 50th Jubilee, the Czech Philharmonic founded the tradition of the country's most important annual musical event. Starting in 1948 the Czech Philharmonic began turning into an artistic institution, with the founding of the Czech Philharmonic Soloists (today comprising piano, violin, and cello). In 1951 the Smetana Quartet, the Czech Nonet, and the Czech Choir (now the Prague Philharmonic Choir, chief choirmaster, Lubohír Mátl) became institutional parts of the Philharmonic. The Kühn Children's Choir was added in 1952 (chief choirmaster, Jírí Chvála).

On October 20, 1950, the orchestra again secured a prominent artist to be its head for many years: Karel Ančerl (1908–1973). Under his guidance the Czech Philharmonic reached a world level of performance and scored great successes in many tours abroad, including its first overseas tour of Australia, New Zealand, Japan, China, and India in 1959. The number of concerts was also increasing. Between 1945 and 1970 the orchestra appeared in 2,169 concerts, of which 563 occured in 30 countries on four continents. In 1954 and again in 1985 the Philharmonic was awarded the State Prize, first class, for outstanding performances and propagation of Czech music, and in 1956 it received the Order of the Republic, a high state distinction.

Since December 1, 1955, the Czech Philharmonic has been headed by a director. Until 1958 it was cellist Karel Pravoslav Sádlo, then until 1980 composer Jiří Pauer. After Karel Ančerl's departure in 1968 Václav Neumann took over as chief conductor. Significant contributions have been made as well by Zdeněk Košler (second conductor), František Vajnar (guest conductor; also conductor on a tour of Japan), and at present Libor Pešek and Jiří Bělohlávek (conductors).

The Philharmonic keeps expanding. Since 1975 it has included the Talich Quartet, since 1977, the vocal-instrumental ensemble of Prague Madrigalists, and since 1979, the Due Boemi di Praga ensemble (bass clarinet and piano). The Czech Philharmonic also incorporates two smaller ensembles comprising members of the orchestra: the Czech Philharmonic Consort wind ensemble, winner of the Wiener Flötenuhr prize for its recording of Mozart divertimentos and serenades, and the Philharmonic Chamber Orchestra, a string ensemble devoted mainly to baroque music.

RECORDING HISTORY AND SELECTIVE DISCOGRAPHY: The Czech Philharmonic Orchestra made its first records under Václav Talich for His Master's Voice, namely Smetana's *My Country* (1929) and Dvořák symphonies (1935–1937). At present the orchestra produces records for the two Czech recording companies, Supraphon and Panton, often in cooperation with foreign companies (Decca, Teldec, Nippon Columbia, and others). Since 1960 its records have won 40 prizes internationally. For instance, its recording of Arthur Honegger's oratorio *Jeanne d'Arc au bûcher* under Serge Baudo won four important prizes, and its recording of Smetana's *Bartered Bride*, conducted by Zdeněk Košler, won the prize of German critics in 1983. Its recording of Dvořák's Symphony No. 9 under Neumann on a compact disc won the first Nippon Columbia gold record awarded to a record of this kind.

Dvořák, *Stabat Mater* (Wolfgang Sawallisch): Supraphon 1112 3561–62. Dvořák, Symphony No. 9 (Neumann): Supraphon CDS 7002 (CD). Honegger, *Jeanne d'Arc au bûcher* (J. Veselka/Baudo) Supraphon 1–12–1651/52. Mahler, Symphonies Nos. 1–9 (Neumann): Supraphon 1110 4001–15 released individually by Pro Arte. Martinů, Symphonies Nos. 1–6 (Neumann): Supraphon 1410 3071–74. Prokofiev, Symphonies Nos. 2 and 4 (Košler): Supraphon 1110 3731/32 (2 records). Smetana, *My Country* (Smetáček): Pro Arte 201, Supraphon 1110 3431–32 (2 records).

CHRONOLOGY OF CHIEF CONDUCTORS: Ludvík Vítězslav Čelanský, 1901–1902. Oskar Nedbal, 1902. Vilém Zemánek, 1902–1918. Ludvík Vítězslav Čelanský, 1918–1919. Václav Talich, 1919–1941. Karel Šejna, 1941–1942. Rafael Kubelík, 1942–1948. Václav Neumann, 1948–1949. Karel Šejna, 1949–1950. Karel Ančerl, 1950–1968. Václav Neumann, 1968-present.

BIBLIOGRAPHY: V. Holzknecht, *Česká filharmonie, příběh orchestru* (The Czech Philharmonic: The Story of an Orchestra) (Prague, 1963). V. Pospíšil, *S Ceskou filharmonií třemi světadíly* (With the Czech Philharmonic Orchestra through Three Continents) (Prague, 1961). R. Veselý, *Dějiny České filharmonie v letech 1901–1924 (History of the Czech Philharmonic, 1901–1924)* (Prague, 1935).

ACCESS: Česká filharmonie, Alšovo nábřeží 12, 110 01 Praha 1. 231–68–12. PhDr. Ctirad Kohoutek, CSc., Artistic Director. Jaroslav Tvrzský, Head of Artistic Operations.

JAROSLAV HOLEČEK

Prague Chamber Orchestra

This first-ranked ensemble is one of the oldest Czechoslovak chamber orchestras, and therefore its representation abroad is considered an important feature of its activity. Based in Prague, the orchestra presents a series of six subscription concerts in Dvořák Hall of the House of Artists, the headquarters of the Czech Philharmonic Orchestra.* The orchestra participates regularly in domestic festivals of international character—the Prague Spring Festival, the Brno Festival, and the Bratislava Music Festival. It also makes extended (usually two-month) tours abroad. It has visited the United States nine times, Canada three times, Japan twice, and South America twice. It also undertakes shorter visits to many European countries, especially traditional festival centers such as Salzburg, Würzburg, Montreux, Dubrovnik, San Sebastian, and Santander. In all, it averages 90 concerts per year. It regularly features the most prominent Czech and foreign soloists.

Playing without a conductor has become the basic specific feature of the ensemble, an exacting task due to the group's relatively large size. Its 36 players are apportioned as follows: six first violins, six seconds, four violas, four cellos, and two double basses; flutes, oboes, clarinets, bassoons, horns, and trumpets in pairs; percussion; and harpsichord. The ensemble uses stringed instruments by the best domestic makers; its brasses are of American and West German origin. It currently tunes to an A of 440 cps. Its reviewers unanimously emphasize the ensemble's sweetness of sound.

The group's composition reflects its focus on classical works, primarily those of Haydn, Mozart, and early Beethoven. However, music of neoclassicism and early romanticism is performed regularly. A model program includes a classical symphony, a concerto, and a twentieth-century composition. Every concert usually includes at least one work by a Czech composer—from old masters through Antonín Dvořák, Leoš Janáček, and Bohuslav Martinů, to contemporaries. The ensemble's outstanding qualities have given rise to many new works dedicated to it.

The Prague Chamber Orchestra's beginnings are connected with the Czechoslovak Radio Symphony Orchestra. A chamber ensemble was formed from among its members for recordings that did not require large symphony apparatus—above all scores by baroque, early classical, and old Czech masters (Franz and George Benda, Jan Dušek, Johann Stamitz, Anton Reicha, Johann Worzischek, Josef Mysliveček, Leopold Koželuh, the masters of Citoliby). Because the members considered it necessary to study these works from the chamber-music point of view, with each member being aware of mutual musical connections, they decided to play without a conductor. The orchestra made its first recording in 1951 and considers that year as the date of its foundation.

The orchestra's history has been characterized by gradual emancipation from the Radio Orchestra, as public concerts started to prevail over studio recordings and tours became more numerous. In 1955 the Prague Chamber Orchestra started to operate under the sponsorship of the National Museum, and it has enlarged its repertoire from the Museum's archives of scores. However, this linkage was not very satisfactory, and in 1964 the orchestra came under the Administration of Cultural Establishments of the Ministry of Culture and in 1967 under the Music Studio of the Czech Music Fund, whose mission is to give practical support to the development of artistic talents. The Prague Chamber Orchestra helps to introduce young soloists and performs the best works of young composers. It influences cultural development also by the organization of instructive concerts. It also offers special programs for people with impaired vision.

Organizationally, the Prague Chamber Orchestra has no director but rather an administrative manager. Artistically, the orchestra is guided by the concertmaster (at present Oldřich Vlček), who personally supervises the study of all compositions. The ensemble is financed from state subsidies through the Ministry of Culture of the Czech Socialist Republic. It is represented through the Pragokoncert Czechoslovak artistic agency. An 11-member group of string players was established within the ensemble in 1976, led by Oldřich Vlček. Under the name of Virtuosi di Praga, it has a repertoire representative of the orientation of the Prague Chamber Orchestra as a whole.

RECORDING HISTORY AND SELECTIVE DISCOGRAPHY: The orchestra cooperates regularly with Supraphon, averaging six records per year. The orchestra also makes both live and special recordings for radio broadcast, mostly of contemporary music. Cooperation with Czechoslovak television is also important. In all, the orchestra has made some 150 records for Supraphon, Panton, Slovak Opus, Deutsche Grammophon, Nippon Columbia, Telarc, IMA, and others. Some records have won distinctions, such as the Wiener Flötenuhr and the Grand Prix du Disque de l'Académie Charles Cros.

Bach, Concertos for Harpsichord and Strings, BWV 1052–1058 (Růžičková): Supraphon 1110 3421–23 (3 records). Dvořák, *Czech Suite* and Serenade for Strings: Pro Arte 1033. Jan Hanuš, *Little Suite for Nine Instruments*: Seraphim 10283. Haydn, Symphonies No. 95 and 102: Supraphon 1110 3186. Haydn, Symphonies No. 99 and 103: Supraphon 1110 2969. Mozart, Violin Concertos (Suk): Supraphon 1110 1521–25 (5 records).

BIBLIOGRAPHY: *20 Let Prazškého Kohorního Orchestru (1951–1971)* (Prague: PCO, 1971).

ACCESS: Prague Chamber Orchestra, Valdštejnské nám. 1, 118–00 Prague 1. (422) 513.

MILENA DOSOUDILOVÁ

Prague Symphony Orchestra

Besides the Czech Philharmonic Orchestra,* the Prague Symphony is the most important representative of symphonic culture in the contemporary musical life of Bohemia. The orchestra holds three annual subscription cycles and a series of special concerts for a total of some 100 performances per year. Since 1947 it has appeared annually in the Prague Spring International Music Festival, it has toured abroad regularly since 1957, and it frequently makes commercial and rebroadcast recordings.

The orchestra has its headquarters in Prague's Municipal House, a large, representative art nouveau building of 1911. Rehearsals and concerts are held in the 1,400-seat Smetana Hall, which has good acoustics, a large platform, an organ, and a balcony that can serve a large choir. The Prague Symphony has its subscription concerts on Tuesdays and Wednesdays, while Thursdays and Fridays are reserved for the Czech Philharmonic (in its own hall). The Prague Symphony organizes morning concerts at Smetana Hall for the city's students, and the hall also serves as the scene for most of the Prague Spring Festival's concerts, hosting the most prominent world orchestras.

At present the Prague Symphony comprises 118 players, with a complement of five players for each woodwind instrument and double rosters of brasses. The orchestra has some genuine virtuosos among its ranks; some appear as prominent soloists, and many others are professors at the Prague Conservatory. Wind instruments in the orchestra are altogether of foreign manufacture (largely American and French), the strings are of Czech, German, and Austrian makers. The orchestra tunes to an A of 443 cps.

The Prague Symphony's repertoire, both at home and on tour, is founded on Czech national music (Bedřich Smetana, Antonín Dvořák, Leoš Janáček, Zdeněk Fibich, Josef Suk, Vitězslav Novák, Otakar Ostrčil, Josef B. Foerster). In recent years it has dedicated itself intensively to new creations (Bohuslav Martinů, Jiří

Pauer, Oldřich Flosman, Josef Matěj, Otmer Mácha, Jindřich Feld). The orchestra is especially disposed to perform works by Mahler, Prokofiev, Bartók, and Shostakovich (Bartók's Concerto for Orchestra, for example, or Shostakovich's last three symphonies).

Since 1971 the orchestra has been gradually turning into a large musical institution, including the Suk Chamber Orchestra (13 strings), the Prague Quartet, the Foerster Trio, the Prague Male Choir (60 members), the Musica Bohemica vocal-instrumental ensemble (12 members), the Linha Singers vocal-instrumental ensemble (18 members), and the Bambini di Praga children's choir (various groupings by age). A variety of groups are freely attached to the orchestra on a contractual basis: the Collegium Musicum Pragense (8 winds), the Prague Chamber Soloists (14 strings), the Corni di Praga horn quartet, and the Kuhn Mixed Choir. Five soloists (violinist, violist, cellist, two pianists) have permanent contracts with the orchestra.

The orchestra also includes a concert agency (Koncertní jednatelství FOK), which organizes 12 to 15 cycles of concerts in Prague each season, dedicated mostly to chamber, school, and summer performances. In 1984 these totaled 500 concerts, including those of the Prague Symphony and visiting orchestras. Institutionally, the Prague Symphony thus accounts for 25% of professional musical activity in the Czech Socialist Republic. The institution is headed by a director who has undivided artistic and administrative responsibility. The chief repertory adviser is his deputy.

The institution's activity also cooperates with concert organizers outside Prague. It offers repertory advice and appearances of its own ensembles to festival-like events in the towns of Trutnov, Kladruby u Stříbra, Beroun, Sedlčany, and others. Of great importance for the musical life of Prague is the contract of cooperation between the Prague Symphony Orchestra and the Dresden Philharmonic Orchestra,* which allows for mutual exchanges of ensembles and individual members. The orchestra also cooperates on a long-term basis with the Faculty of Music of the Prague Academy of Arts and Music; at the end of each academic year the orchestra performs works and is conducted by Academy graduates.

The orchestra was founded in the autumn of 1934 as a voluntary cooperative of qualified musicians without permanent jobs. Under its organizer, Rudolf Pekárek (1900–1974), the orchestra, then consisting of 25 members, sought performance opportunities in films, operas, and concert halls: thus its name, F-O-K (film/opera/koncert). Until 1942 the FOK orchestra recorded music to almost all of the nearly 200 films produced in Czechoslovakia. As it participated only rarely in opera performances and appeared in concerts only until 1936, radio broadcasting was its main source of income. In its radio work (several hours of live performances weekly from 1934 to the beginning of World War II), the orchestra developed its musical characteristics of flexibility, technical virtuosity, and vivid expression.

During the Nazi occupation, Rudolf Pekárek was deported to a concentration camp, and in the same year (1942) the FOK orchestra became, by official decree, the Prague German Operetta Orchestra. With the halt of operetta activity in 1944, FOK members were sent as laborers to the Ostmark Werke factory.

After the War the FOK—still a cooperative minimally subsidized by the state—joined Prague's musical life, guided and conducted by Dr. Václav Smetáček, who already in 1936 premiered with the FOK works by the then-young Czech composers František Bartoš, Pavel Bořkovec, Jaroslav Ježek, Hans Krása, Isa Krejčí, and Bohuslav Martinů. Smetáček headed the orchestra from May 1942 through 1972. On January 1, 1952, the FOK orchestra was nationalized and attached to the Prague National Committee, which has guided and financed it since then. Its name was accordingly changed to the Prague Symphony Orchestra.

Various outstanding Czech conductors have cooperated with the orchestra, but the profile and style of the ensemble were established by Václav Smetáček, one of the greatest personalities of Czech postwar music. Smetáček ideally combined intellect and education with natural musicality and temperament. An outstanding oboe virtuoso and chamber player himself, he led the orchestra to a high technical level of rendition and, as an experienced teacher, he led all its groups to a cultured, modern mode of expression. After his retirement from his permanent engagement he appeared as guest conductor with the orchestra almost until his death in 1986.

Among its achievements the orchestra counts national awards such as the Order of Labor (1962) for its service in educating the younger generation, and the Victorious February Order (1984), a high state distinction awarded on the occasion of its 50th anniversary, in recognition of its service to the development of musical culture. In its foreign tours the orchestra has made many visits in Eastern and Western Europe, the U.S.S.R., the Mediterranean region, and the United States (four times). It has appeared with conductors and soloists of the very highest order.

RECORDING HISTORY AND SELECTIVE DISCOGRAPHY: The orchestra's systematic cooperation with record producers started after 1947. The first recordings (of small entertaining orchestral compositions) were gradually taken over by ever more important tasks, and the orchestra eventually accompanied outstanding domestic and foreign instrumentalists and began recording the great symphonic repertoire. An example of such an early symphonic recording is the Supraphon record of symphonies by Johannes Brahms and Robert Schumann conducted by Dean Dixon. Today the orchestra has a contract for regular cooperation with Supraphon but also makes records for the more recently established Panton of the Czech Music Fund.

Bartók, Concerto for Orchestra (Jiří Bělohlávek): Supraphon 1111 03189. Martinů, *The Miracle of Our Lady (Hry o Marii)*, complete opera (soloists of the Prague National Theatre/Bělohlávek): Supraphon 1116 3401. Suk, *Praga* and *Fantasie for Violin and Orchestra in G Minor* (Čeněk Pavlík/Vladimír Valék): Panton 81100149. Tchaikovsky, *Capriccio Italien*; Rimsky-Korsakov, *Capriccio Español* (Bělohlávek): Supraphon 1110 2817.

CHRONOLOGY OF CHIEF CONDUCTORS: Rudolf Pekárek, 1934–1942. Václav Smetáček, 1942–1972. Ladislav Slovák, 1972–1976. Jiří Bělohlávek, 1977-present.

BIBLIOGRAPHY: O. Novotná and Petar Zapletal, comps., *The Prague Symphony Orchestra* (Prague: Prague Symphony, 1984). Petar Zapletal, *FOK: Fifty Years of the Prague Symphony Orchestra* (Prague: Editio Supraphon, 1984).

ACCESS: Prague Symphony Orchestra, Náměstí republiky 5, 110 00 Prague 1. 23–15–981 and 23–16–662. Dr. Ladislav Šíp, Director.

LADISLAV ŠÍP

Denmark _____

COPENHAGEN   (1,374,000*)

Danish Radio Symphony Orchestra

The Danish Radio Symphony Orchestra (DRSO; also known abroad as the Danish National Orchestra), is one of the world's oldest broadcasting ensembles. Other permanent, professional orchestras in Denmark are the venerable Royal Danish Orchestra (Det Kongelige Kapel, belonging to the Royal Opera and Ballet in Copenhagen), and five regional orchestras, including the Sjaellands Symphony Orchestra, which has a renowned summer season at Copenhagen's Tivoli Gardens.

With 92 players, the DRSO is funded and administered by the Danish Government through the state-run radio authority. Its repertoire has historically been rich in contemporary works of both Danish and foreign composers, a tradition it has recently revitalized.

On its tours the orchestra features Danish music, frequently including one or more pieces by Carl Nielsen, a composer with whom the orchestra has long been associated. Frequently visiting the neighboring Scandinavian countries, the orchestra also makes occasional longer tours, the most notable in recent years being its visit to the United States, where it played 23 concerts under the direction of Sixten Ehrling. In 1986 it visited Great Britain, playing eight concerts under the direction of its new chief conductor, Lamberto Gardelli.

The DRSO's season of approximately 35 regular home concerts takes place at Copenhagen's 1,074-seat Radio House Concert Hall. In addition to approximately 20 productions per year for the State Radio and an average of five annual commercial recordings, the orchestra also performs occasional opera productions and maintains a summer season at Tivoli Gardens.

The DRSO began in 1925 as an 11-piece ensemble auditioned and hired on behalf of the Danish State Radio by the station's founder, Emil Holm. The orchestra had grown to comprise 60 players by 1931, when it came under the leadership of its first chief conductor, Launy Grøndahl. A permanent choir was added in 1932, and in 1933 the orchestra began to offer public concert performances in addition to its broadcasting work. Two important periods in the orchestra's early history were its associations with conductors Nikolai Malko and Fritz Busch, both of whom were instrumental in building the ensemble's repertoire and musicianship.

The postwar years saw the inauguration of the Radio House Concert Hall and the establishment of the orchestra's commercial recording activities. Without a regular chief conductor, the orchestra was led until 1967 by a succession of guests, among them many of the period's most highly regarded conductors and, in the case of contemporary works, composer/conductors such as Pierre Boulez, Witold Lutosławski, Krzysztof Penderecki, and others. The year 1965 saw the installment of the triennial International Nikolai Malko Competition for Young Conductors, which continues today.

In 1967 the orchestra came under the leadership of its first permanent music director in many years, Herbert Blomstedt, who remained in that capacity until 1977, and whose most tangible legacy with the group is his recording of the complete orchestral works of Carl Nielsen. The following years again saw guest conductors, particularly ''permanent guest conductor'' Yuri Ahronovitch.

Recent developments have included a recommitment to the twentieth-century repertoire, including contemporary works both Danish and foreign. At the same time, the orchestra has reduced its number of studio productions in favor of live concerts. A partial list of recent guest conductors gives the flavor of the orchestra's approach: Peter Eötvös, Karlheinz Stockhausen, Oliver Knussen, Michael Tabechnik, and Jan Latham-Koenig. The period of guest conducting since the departure of Herbert Blomstedt in 1977 came to an end with the appointment of Lamberto Gardelli as chief conductor in a three-year contract effective August 1986.

RECORDING HISTORY AND SELECTIVE DISCOGRAPHY: The DRSO has a long history of recordings, at first by virtue of its broadcast activities, and later for commercial labels. Collections of historic recordings have been released in LP format, among them ''Great Singers in Copenhagen: Live-optagelser 1931–39'' in a three-record set by Danacord and ''Great Soloists in Copenhagen: Live-optagelser 1931–35'' in a five-record set, also by Danacord. The orchestra's recorded repertoire is rich in works of twentieth-century Danish composers, particularly Nielsen, whose works the orchestra began recording commercially in the 1950s under Erik Tuxen and Thomas Jensen. Some of these performances are available on rereleases from EMI. The orchestra has recorded for Bis, Danacord, DMA, EMI (with releases on Seraphim and Turnabout), Erato, Poco, and Unicorn.

Nielsen, Symphony No. 2 (Jensen): EMI EM290443–3 (2 records). Nielsen, Symphony No. 4 (Grøndahl): EMI EM290443–3 (2 records). Nielsen, Symphony No. 5 (Tuxen): EM290443–3 (2 records). Nielsen, Symphonies No. 1, No. 2, No. 3, and other works (Blomstedt): Seraphim S–6097 (3 records). Nielsen, Symphonies No. 4, No. 5, No. 6, and other works (Blomstedt): Seraphim S–6098 (3 records): also released with previous selection as *Carl Nielsen: Komplette orkestervaerker*: EMI. Per Nørgaard, *Iris; Voyage into the Golden Screen* (Tamas Veto): Caprice 1054.

CHRONOLOGY OF PERMANENT CONDUCTORS: Launy Grøndahl, 1925–1956. Erik Tuxen, 1936–1957. Mogens Woldike, 1950–1967. Thomas Jensen, 1957–1963. Herbert Blomstedt, 1967–1977. Lomberto Gardelli, 1986-present.

Frequent Guest Conductors: Nikolai Malko, 1929–1961. Fritz Busch, 1933–1951. Yuri Ahronovitch (Permanent Guest Conductor).

BIBLIOGRAPHY: Correspondence with DRSO administrators Hans Henrik Holm and Kjeld Neiiendam, 1986. DRSO miscellaneous documents. Christopher Follett, "Almost 60 Years on the Air," *Scanorama*, June 1982.

ACCESS: Danish Radio Symphony Orchestra, Radiohuset, 1999 Copenhagen V. (01) 36–06–47. Kjeld Neiiendam, manager.

ROBERT R. CRAVEN

Dominican Republic _____

National Symphony Orchestra of the Dominican Republic

Generally regarded as being of the highest musical quality in the country, the National Symphony Orchestra (OSN) approaches a half century of existence having achieved goals toward which it had set out: professionalism; enhancement of national music through performance of Dominican composers and by Dominican soloists; annual concert seasons; and the raising of popular cultural tastes. A recent innovation is the creation of the OSN Foundation, dedicated to channeling private funding to the orchestra for the purpose of bettering its facilities, salaries, and seasonal activities.

Presenting some 100 symphonic concerts per year, the OSN is under the jurisdiction of the General Office of Fine Arts, an institution responsible to the Secretary of State for Education, Fine Arts, and Culture. Its personnel includes an artistic director, three associate directors, a manager, 78 musicians, and personnel responsible for public relations, archives, staging, and other technical/ administrative functions. As government employees, the members of the OSN are entitled to receive life insurance, disability leave, pension, and various social programs implemented by the government.

In recent years a system of competition has been established for hiring new members, including a regular procedure for internal promotion. The greatest organizational concern of the present management is bettering working conditions and balancing out the musicians' salaries in accordance with their responsibilities and their professional competence. Since 1983, 17 foreign musicians have joined the OSN; they are fulfilling two-year contracts that include teaching at the National Conservatory of Music. OSN members teach at the Conservatory as well as at other institutions, both public and private. They frequently perform in the country's major concert halls as soloists, chamber players, and conductors.

Beginning at the turn of the present century, in Santo Domingo and other important cities, various groups were being formed by musicians to popularize symphonic and chamber music. In 1932 the Symphonic Orchestra of Santo Domingo was formed. It performed benefit concerts and commemoratives, but at the end of eight years of constant work, economic and artistic difficulties compelled a pause in their labors. Then, thanks to the efforts of the Secretary of Education and the Director of Fine Arts, it was possible to create a more stable institution, one with official status. Thus the OSN was born on August 5, 1941.

The group's first conductor was the Spanish composer Enrique Casal Chapí. Under his baton the OSN began regular programming, performing several series of concerts with works of Beethoven and baroque composers; it also premiered contemporary works. Casal Chapí arranged for the works of Dominican composers to be performed in inaugural concerts; during the years he remained in the country, he achieved remarkable educational success and always offered encouragement to composers, in particular his assistant conductor, Enrique Mejía Arredondo.

The Mexican maestro Abel Eisenberg conducted the Symphony in 41 concerts between 1946 and 1951, sharing conducting in seven of them with Arredondo. During this time the orchestra continued to show preference for the Viennese classics, the romantics, and the nationalistic music of Russia and Spain.

An Italian, Maestro Roberto Caggiano, occupied the post of conductor from 1951 to 1959, conducting 106 concerts, in the programs of which he left room for numerous works authored by Dominicans. Dominican soloists, including singers, participated in a major way. In the mid–1950s the ensemble was joined by several prestigious European instrumentalists who helped raise the level of the orchestra's programs.

At the beginning of 1959 Manuel Simó, a composer, was named conductor. He was a disciple and understudy of Casal Chapí and heir to his aesthetic restlessness. Under Simó's guidance the number of annual concerts was increased considerably, as well as the number of appearances of the OSN in various cities around the country. Furthermore, annual seasons were established and a contemporary and avant-garde repertoire was successfully introduced. Approached at first with some distrust, as years passed Simó educated both musicians and public, producing progress in musical perceptions.

Both foreign and Dominican conductors invited to perform with the orchestra between 1959 and 1978 contributed to its development and to its maturity. The founding of the 1,600-seat National Theatre in 1973 demanded of the OSN great dedication and more varied performances. The OSN now had to alternate its symphonic programming with performances of opera, ballet, and theatrical events. In the mid–1970s the OSN began to present educational concerts and succeeded in gaining a new public and the participation of popular groups. This has been the OSN's most important recent cultural contribution.

In 1980 the Dominican violinist Jacinto Gimbernard became conductor. He succeeded in hiring some 17 foreign musicians to strengthen the orchestra. Since March of 1984 Carlos Piantini, a Dominican conductor with international experience and exposure, has directed the OSN. A student in Vienna of Hans Swarowsky and a violinist with the New York Philharmonic for 15 years, Piantini is at present initiating a process of reorganization and renovation of the image of the nation's foremost orchestra. Starting in 1985 he has offered, from January through April, a grand season with invited soloists and conductors, both national and international. In the summer a series of pops concerts will be presented, and the orchestra will tour nationally. He proposes to hold concerts from October through December at places of historical or cultural interest in the capital, in hospitals and parks, and in the provinces. He also foresees educational concerts directed by students.

RECORDING HISTORY: Under sponsorship of The Reserve Bank and the Central Bank of the Dominican Republic, the OSN has made two recordings of works by Dominican composers, both under Simó, and both produced by Industria de Discos Salón Mozart with technical assistance from Licinio Mancebo, director of the National Music Archives.

CHRONOLOGY OF MUSIC DIRECTORS: Enrique Casal Chapí, 1941–1945. Abel Eisenberg, 1946–1951. Roberto Caggiano, 1951–1959. Manuel Simó, 1959–1980. Jacinto Gimbernard, 1980–1984. Carlos Piantini, 1984-present.

BIBLIOGRAPHY: *Isla Abierta*, Suplemento Periódico Hoy, Ano III, 14, 21, and 28 April 1984 (Santo Domingo). Bernarda Jorge, *La Música Dominicana, Siglos XIX-XX* (Santo Domingo: Editora UASD, 1982). Bernard Jorge, "Bases ideológicas de la Práctica Musical durante la Era de Trujillo," *Revista Eme-Eme Estudios Dominicanos*, March/April 1982. *Memoria 25 años Orquesta Sinfónica Nacional, 1941–1966* (Santo Domingo: Editorial Arte y Cine, 1966). *Memoria 10 años Orquesta Sinfónica Nacional, 1966–1976* (Santo Domingo, 1976).

ACCESS: National Symphony Orchestra of the Dominican Republic, Palacio de Bellas Artes, Partado Postal No. 2692, Oficina Correo Principal, Zona Colonial, Santo Domingo. (819) 682–8542. Marino S. Mieses, Manager.

BERNARDA JORGE
TRANS. DAVID BRADT

Egypt _____

CAIRO (5,074,000)

Cairo Symphony Orchestra

The Cairo Symphony Orchestra (CSO) is the only ensemble of its kind in the Arab region. First established by the Egyptian Radio in 1956 and named the Radio Orchestra, it was transferred in 1959 to the administrative domain of the Egyptian Ministry of Culture and renamed the Cairo Symphony Orchestra. The CSO's goals have always been to disseminate Western "art music" to Egyptian audiences, to encourage Egyptian composers of symphonic music, and to provide training for young Egyptian instrumentalists, soloists, and conductors.

The 50-member CSO performs weekly to Cairene audiences during a yearly concert season of approximately nine months. Due to its lack of a permanent concert hall, the ensemble has alternated between several performance locations, including the Cairo Opera House, the Sayid Darwish Concert Hall, and the Jumhuriyyah Theatre. A segment of the CSO also accompanies Egyptian and/ or foreign ballet and opera companies during their yearly two- to three-month seasons. In addition, the entire ensemble presents occasional performances in other Egyptian cities and has performed in Beirut and Damascus. Thus far, the CSO's recording activites have been limited to a few long-playing records produced by the government-owned record company Sono Cairo.

The CSO's repertoire includes works from the baroque era to the twentieth century, excluding dodecaphonic and post-World War II compositions. Classical and romantic compositions predominate. The orchestra also frequently performs works by Egyptian composers, most notably Yusif Greis, Abu Bakr Khairat, Aziz El-Shawan, Gamal Abd El-Rahim, and Rif'at Garranah.

The CSO is administered by a director. Artistic matters and programming are in the hands of a permanent or semipermanent conductor who collaborates with a small committee of specialists. All CSO activities are sponsored by the Egyptian Government.

The nucleus of the CSO was first formed under auspices of the Egyptian Radio shortly after it first began broadcasting in 1934. Members of this initial ensemble were mostly European musicians residing in Egypt. It was conducted by Joseph Hüttel. In 1956 the Egyptian Radio decided to expand and improve upon available elements by contracting additional musicians and a new conductor (the Austrian, Franz Litschauer). During the same year it officially established this improved ensemble as the Radio Orchestra. In January of 1959 the Radio Orchestra was transferred to the administrative and financial domain of the Ministry of Culture and given its present name.

The Egyptian Government's early guarantees of the CSO's continuity, expansion, and improvement reflect the cultural policy designed and implemented by the leaders of the 1952 revolution. This policy stressed the revival and preservation of Egypt's national heritage but also encouraged receptivity to influences from foreign cultures, and when it was enacted, Western cultural products received priority. Government patronage of the arts was also ensured. Several new institutions were thus dedicated to the dissemination of Western Music, among them the Cairo National Conservatory and the Cairo Symphony Orchestra.

During its first decade the CSO relied heavily on foreign musicians and conductors. Seventy percent of its members were Europeans contracted temporarily. A good number of the remaining 30% were Egyptian wind players who had previously performed in military bands. During this period several European conductors led the orchestra for extended periods of time ranging from one to several years. They include Franz Litschauer, Gika Zdravkovitch, José Feriz, and Tibor Frešo. The only Egyptian who (occasionally) conducted the orchestra was Ahmad Ebeid. Several renowned conductors and soloists were invited, among them Yuri Bukov, Aram Khachaturian, and Charles Munch. With the permanent conductors' efforts and the Ministry's continued support, the ensemble's artistic level improved, and today many Egyptian musicians and music critics regard the 1960s as the Golden Era of the CSO and of Western art music in Egypt. During this time the orchestra's most notable chamber music activities also occurred, including those of the Cairo Quartet (1964–1966) and the Cairo Chamber Orchestra (ca. 1966–ca.1969).

During the 1970s inflation and the Ministry's ensuing budgetary restrictions forced many foreign musicians to leave Egypt before there were enough Egyptians to replace them. The CSO's artistic level and schedule of activities both suffered. At the same time, however, many Egyptian musicians and several conductors were being trained both in Egypt and abroad. By the 1980s they constituted 70% of the orchestra. In addition, a handful of Egyptian conductors were able to carry on the orchestra's activities, and several Egyptian soloists enriched its concert season.

The orchestra's cultural impact has been considerable, considering its difficult mission. Although it has had a relatively small following, the CSO has succeeded in establishing Western art music as a permanent part of Cairene life. Many of its members have contributed their expertise through teaching both at the Cairo National Conservatory and privately. The CSO has also been a catalyst in the development of an Egyptian school of symphonic composers.

CHRONOLOGY OF MUSIC DIRECTORS (Permanent Conductors): Complete information is unavailable, due in part to the destruction of the orchestra's archives in the burning of the Cairo Opera House in the early 1970s. Some years saw guest conductors and no permanent directors. The following was supplied by orchestra administrators. Franz Litschauer, 1959–1960. Sacha Popov, 1963–1964. Gika Zdravkovitch, 1964–1971. Yusif El-Sisi, 1976–1978 and 1982-present.

BIBLIOGRAPHY: Interviews CSO Chief Conductor/Director Yusif El-Sisi and former CSO Artistic Committee Member and former Director, Ahmad Al-Masri, 1984. Wizārat Al-Thaqāfah wa Al-Irshād Al-Qawmī [Ministry of Culture and National Guidance], Ur-qistra Al-Qāhirah Al-Simfūni [The Cairo Symphony Orchestra] (Cairo: Ministry of Culture, 1960).

ACCESS: Cairo Symphony Orchestra, 27 Shari' Abd El-Khaliq Tharwat, Cairo. (20–2) 752409. Mo Yusif El-Sisi, Chief Conductor and Artistic Director.

SALWA EL-SHAWAN CASTELO-BRANCO

El Salvador _____

El Salvador Symphony Orchestra

Established in 1922, the El Salvador Symphony Orchestra (OSES: Orquesta Sinfónica de El Salvador) is the oldest symphony orchestra in Central America. It is the parent group for two professional orchestras in this small but densely populated country, the National Symphony Orchestra (Orquesta Sinfónica Nacional) and the El Salvador Chamber Orchestra (Orquesta da Camera de El Salvador). As such it is a major force in El Salvador's cultural life.

The OSES performs ten months per year, divided into four seasons: from February to April it fulfills an educational function in a School Season sponsored by the Ministry of Education; from April to June, the so-called Popular Season, it tours the country and also presents open-air concerts in the capital city of San Salvador; from July to October it performs biweekly in the regular subscription series season; and in December it presents a short Christmas season. Although one of the duties of the OSES is to present concerts in outlying provinces and cities, the recent civil unrest has made such tours infrequent. Virtually all concerts are held in the Teatro Nacional in San Salvador. The OSES has toured Honduras and Costa Rica.

Many of the musicians comprising the OSES are native-born Salvadorians, though some foreigners (mostly Americans) fill in on various instruments. The musicians perform both in the regular orchestra and the chamber orchestra according to need. There is also a popular orchestra, the Barrientos Orchestra, which has achieved some fame for its performance of popular and ethnic arrangements of Salvadorian music, though its membership differs from that of the OSES. The OSES has been funded at various times by both the government and private sectors. Most recently, its administration and funding have been supplied by the Ministry of Education. The musical director is in charge of the daily administration of the orchestra. The budget is currently 974,811 colones per year.

The repertoire of the OSES is largely similar to that of major orchestras elsewhere in the hemisphere. Guest conductors and soloists are brought in both locally and from other countries. Each year a concert is dedicated solely to the performance of Salvadorian works; in addition, native composers are presented throughout the rest of the year. The OSES does not record.

The present organization was established in 1922 by a German immigrant, Paul Müller, with the goal of offering quality music throughout the country on a permanent basis. The OSES, however, had a number of predecessors in the post-colonial period of the nineteenth century. In 1859 Rafael Orozco founded the first orchestra, which continued until about 1880 under his successors Alfredo Lowenthal, Alejandro Coussin, Emilio Dresner, and Enrique Drews. In 1906 Juan Aberle and Antonio Gianoli created the Sociedad Orchestral Salvadoreño, which was superseded shortly thereafter by the Orquesta Sinfónica de los Supremos Poderes. The OSES's primary turning point from a regional orchestra into a national symphony came in 1940 with the appointment of Mexican violinist and composer Humberto Pacas as conductor. Since then all of the musical directors have been native Salvadorians.

CHRONOLOGY OF MUSIC DIRECTORS: Paul Müller and Richard Hünterranch, 1922–1939. Humberto Pacas, 1940–1950. Alejandro Muñoz Ciudad Real, 1950–1961. Esteban Servellon, 1962–1973. Gilberto Orellana H., 1974-present.

BIBLIOGRAPHY: Interview with Gilberto Orellana H., 1985. Howard Bentstein et al., *Area Handbook for El Salvador* (Washington, D.C.: GPO, 1971). Luis Ramon y Rivera and Helen Hyers, "El Salvador," *New Grove Dictionary of Music and Musicians*. Nicholas Slonimsky, *Music of Latin America* (New York: Da Capo, 1972).

ACCESS: Orquesta Sinfónica de El Salvador, 8a Avenida Norte No. 228, San Salvador. (503) 22–8690. Gilberto Orellana H., Music Director.

BERTIL H. VAN BOER, JR.
MARGARET L. FAST

Finland ⸻⸻⸻⸻⸻⸻

HELSINKI (905,000*)

Helsinki Philharmonic Orchestra

In a regular concert season extending from September through early June, the Helsinki Philharmonic performs about 50 concerts in three separate series: Favorites Series I and II (also known as "Popular," with repeated programs) and a Symphony Series. Despite their titles, the two series are not widely divergent in repertoire: a 1985 Symphony Series program presented works of Beethoven, Shostakovich, and Sibelius, while the following week's Favorites Series program offered works of Prokofiev, Britten, and Sibelius. Special concerts round out the season, and further performances are offered under the title of "Helsinki Summer Concerts" and under the auspices of the Helsinki Festival. Touring is an increasingly important function of the ensemble, and about one-third of its performances are broadcast. The Philharmonic sponsors numerous chamber music activities from within its ranks, including the Philharmonic Brass Quintet, the Finlandia Sinfonietta (comprising 20 to 25 members), the Finnish String Quartet, and a variety of occasional groupings.

At the Philharmonic's 1,718-seat Finlandia Hall (1971), an imposing, modernistic structure by Alvar Aalto, audiences hear a wide-ranging repertoire, with no lack of Finnish music. Contemporary and modern composers (particularly those of Finland) are represented in full-orchestra concerts. Nevertheless, the most frequently played composer in the 1984–1985 season was Mozart.

As of 1985 the orchestra comprises 97 players. A support staff of two stage managers and five office personnel, all officials of the city of Helsinki, administer day-to-day operations. An institution of the city, the orchestra has as its leadership a Board of Trustees of nine members elected to four-year terms. This body is roughly equivalent in political status to the Helsinki City Council, which is also elected to four-year terms. The orchestra and its Board fall under the control of the deputy mayor of culture and education and are not formally tied to the national government of Finland. Annual budgeting is funded largely through the city, with ticket sales accounting for only 14% to 15% of the total; other government contributions are about 2%, and there are no private contributions.

Finland was a part of the Russian Empire when Robert Kajanus founded the Helsinki Orchestral Society in 1882. According to the orchestra's self-published materials, Kajanus conducted the Society's orchestra of some 36 players and from the first held both symphony concerts (at Helsinki University) and popular concerts (at the Seurahuone Hotel). In these early years Kajanus was the orchestra's principal financial supporter. State functions and theatre performances were also part of the season, the orchestra being Helsinki's only regular symphonic ensemble.

Following the organization's change of name in 1895 to the Helsinki Philharmonic Society, its growth enabled the orchestra to tour abroad in 1900, visiting Scandinavia, Germany, Holland, Belgium, and France—with a notable success at the Paris World's Fair.

Beginning in 1899, however, Czar Nicholas II set about an increasingly stringent policy of "Russifying" the heretofore semi-independent Finnish state as well as Finnish culture. Embroiled in the politics of Russification and nationalism, the orchestra fell into a difficult time in the early twentieth century. A visit by Kajanus to St. Petersburg to lobby for renewed funding was perceived in political terms, and despite help from the Helsinki city government, there arose a rival orchestra, the Helsinki Symphony under Georg Schnéevoigt. Finland achieved independence in 1918, and with the new political climate, the city consolidated the ensembles in 1919 under auspices of the Helsinki Philharmonic Orchestra, with Schnéevoigt and Kajanus equally sharing the podium.

By the time Kajanus retired in 1932, after 50 years as conductor, the orchestra had established an impressive history as an instrument of Finnish national pride. Works of Finnish composers were regularly featured (as they are today), and their chief craftsman, Jean Sibelius, had premiered many of his compositions with the Helsinki Philharmonic. Schnéevoigt, now principal conductor, took the orchestra to England (1934) and Sweden (1936) and increased the organization's activities in new music, education, and opera.

On the eve of World War II, the Soviet Union, having made demands for certain Finnish lands, invaded the country; the following years saw Finland fighting on the German side in an effort to expel the Soviets. Schnéevoigt departed, and despite the destruction of its university concert hall by air raids, the depleted orchestra continued under Armas Järnefelt. Following four years under Martti Similä (1946–1950), the organization sought the services of Tauno Hannikainen, who had left Finland at the onset of the war and become a naturalized American citizen. Hannikainen energized the organization, with new school concerts and request concerts being inaugurated. The orchestra toured Switzerland and the German Federal Republic in 1960.

In 1965, Sibelius's anniversary year, the orchestra again toured Europe, visiting many countries under the direction of its new principal conductor, Jorma Panula, and with the assistance of Sir John Barbirolli. A two-month tour of 49 American cities followed in 1968. Ensconced in the new Finlandia Hall in 1971, the orchestra has since, under conductors Paavo Berglund and Okko Kamu, expanded its tours, making them nearly annual events. These include visits to Japan in 1982, the United States in 1983, and the British Isles in 1984.

In its recent programming the orchestra has responded to the many anniversary years of major composers and has also continued its policy of featuring Finnish composers. It hosted the European Music Year (EMY 1985) and has emphasized commissioned pieces as well as works by women. The 1984–1985 season saw an emphasis on music by Russian and Soviet composers as well as visits to Sibelius Hall by Soviet ensembles as part of the Helsinki Festival's "Soviet Music Days." The Helsinki Philharmonic made a week's tour of the Soviet Union in March of 1985, with visits to Tallinn, Leningrad, and Moscow. For 1985–1986 the orchestra held a musical celebration of the 150th anniversary of the *Kalevala*, Finland's national epic.

RECORDING HISTORY AND SELECTIVE DISCOGRAPHY: The Philharmonic has made numerous recordings of Finnish music and has in recent years entered the commercial recording field, with plans afoot for a broadening, under direction of Okko Kamu, of its recorded repertoire. In 1984, under Paavo Berglund, the orchestra began a series of Sibelius recordings for EMI, expected to continue for five years for a total of nine recordings.

Uuno Klami, *Fantasie Tscheremisse* and *Kalevala Suite* (Panula): Finlandia 302 PSI. Sibelius, Symphony No. 4 and Symphony No. 7 (Berglund): EMI EL 27–0099–1.

CHRONOLOGY OF PRINCIPAL CONDUCTORS: Robert Kajanus, 1881–1932. Robert Kajanus and Georg Schnéevoigt, 1914–1916, 1919–1932. Georg Schnéevoigt, 1932–1941. Armas Järnefelt, 1941–1945. Martti Similä, 1946–1950. Tauno Hannikainen, 1951–1965. Jorma Panula, 1965–1972. Paavo Berglund, 1975–1978. Paavo Berglund and Ulf Söderblom, 1978–1979. Okko Kamu, 1981–   .

BIBLIOGRAPHY: *Concerto* (Helsinki Philharmonic General Program, 1984). Benjamin Epstein, "Helsinki Philharmonic," *Los Angeles Times*, 7 Mar. 1983. *Helsinki Philharmonic Orchestra 1882–1982* (Helsinki Philharmonic, 1982). *Helsinki Philharmonic Orchestra* (Helsinki Philharmonic, n.d.). Reijo Jyrkiainen, HPO Manager, correspondence with author, 1985. Harold C. Schonberg, "Music: An Orchestra of Finland," *New York Times*, 17 Feb. 1968. Thanks to Pirkko Moisala of the Sibelius Academy in Helsinki for helping to secure information.

ACCESS: Helsinki Philharmonic Orchestra, Finlandia Hall, Karamzininkatu 4, SF–00100 Helsinki. (358–0) 40 241. Reijo Jyrkiainen, Manager.

ROBERT R. CRAVEN

France ────────────────────────

(1,170,000*)

Lyon Symphony Orchestra

The Lyon Symphony Orchestra (OSL: Orchestre Symphonique de Lyon) was founded in 1969 for the sole purpose of promoting symphonic music in Lyon (the second largest city in France) and the surrounding region of the Rhône-Alpes in eastern France. The OSL is a relative newcomer to the French orchestral scene, though Lyon itself has had a long tradition of symphonic music dating back to the seventeenth century.

The OSL is a permanent professional orchestra with a 52-week season and regular subscription concerts performed in the modern Maurice Ravel Auditorium in Lyon. Each summer it also provides the major portion of the annual Festival Berlioz, founded in 1976, and in addition tours the surrounding region extensively. Members of the orchestra also perform with the Lyon Opera. The administration of this 94-member orchestra is overseen by a professional board of directors. Musical administration is in the hands of the music director, who decides matters of repertory policy. The OSL is state-supported, with half its budget coming from the French Ministry of Culture and the other half from the City and Province of Lyon as well as box office receipts.

The musical tradition of Lyon dates back to the Academy Royale de Lyon, a group of 20 violins and bass, which was gathered under royal privilege in the middle of the seventeenth century. In 1714, an academy for vocal and instrumental music was founded, as was a concert society; this group performed irregularly until 1736, when Étienne Mangean organized a series of subscription concerts. Beginning in 1756, music publishers such as A. le Goux moved to Lyon, and the town achieved a substantial reputation as a musical center until the time of the French Revolution. It was not until 1835 that the musical life in this city was reestablished through regular concerts inaugurated by Joseph Hainl. Until the 1960s the orchestra remained a local municipal group with no steady support. In 1967 André Malraux proposed a complete restructuring of musical life in France, and Lyon responded through the mayor, Louis Pradel, and parliamentary representative Proton de la Chapelle. These men announced the formation of a regional orchestra under the direction of the well-known conductor Louis Frémaux.

The OSL has since achieved an international reputation for its dynamism, spontaneity, and sensitivity. In 1982 the orchestra made a successful tour of central Europe. It regularly appears in other French cities. The OSL's repertoire is largely traditional, though efforts are being made to promote contemporary music.

CHRONOLOGY OF MUSIC DIRECTORS: Louis Frémaux, 1969–1971. Serge Baudo, 1971-present.

BIBLIOGRAPHY: Frank Dobbins, "Lyons," *New Grove Dictionary of Music and Musicians* (New York: Macmillan, 1981). John Holmes, *Conductors on Record* (Westport, Conn.: Greenwood, 1982). Stefan Jaeger, *Das Atlantisbuch der Dirigenten* (Zurich: Atlantis, 1985).

ACCESS: Orchestre Symphonique de Lyon, Auditorium M. Ravel, 149 rue Garibaldi, F–69 003 Lyon. Claude Jacquemin, Manager.

BERTIL H. VAN BOER, JR.

PARIS (8,510,000*)

Lamoureux Orchestra

The Lamoureux Orchestra, formerly known as the Society of New Concerts (Société des Nouveaux Concerts), was established in 1881. Presently the orchestra comprises 95 professional musicians (many under 30 years of age) and talented soloists who also perform in various Lamoureux chamber ensembles (wind quintet, octet, etc.) and/or other Paris orchestras.

The Lamoureux subscription season includes 14 to 18 orchestral concerts and separate chamber music subscription series, in a season from October to March, under guest conductors, there being no permanent conductor since 1969. Concerts are held in Pleyel Hall, which has 2,300 seats and excellent acoustics. Choral/orchestral performances take place in two Paris churches, Église de la Madelaine and Église de la Trinité. The orchestra's performance characteristics include a high quality of execution, precision, and expressiveness.

The orchestra is administered by a nine-member Artistic Council, elected every three years, and now led by Lamoureux Association President Jean-Claude Bernède and an administrator. The council is responsible for selection of guest conductors, for concert programs, and for orchestral auditions. The Lamoureux Orchestra's budget of upward of 3 million francs derives mostly from ticket sales, with a 25% subsidy from the city of Paris. Orchestral musicians are paid per concert. To supplement the budget additional performances are scheduled in the Parisian suburbs, especially with the Paris Ballet Company. The orchestra also participates in various other musical events, such as the Soviet Music Week, the Musical Spring (Printemps Musical) programs, and diverse competitions. It has a long and illustrious list of recordings.

Lamoureux concert programming continues to follow the direction of the founder's philosophy, namely the promotion of French composers' works of the early twentieth century (excepting the contemporary avant-garde) in addition to standard repertoire of the eighteenth to twentieth centuries. In the past, Lamoureux concerts were distinguished by numerous premieres of works of Claude Debussy, Paul Dukas, Édouard Lalo, Maurice Ravel, Albert Roussel, and others. For the last ten years, however, it has performed no premieres. Lamoureux programming is diverse and geared to audience appeal: all-French programs (with special emphasis on Berlioz); single-composer programs devoted to works of Beethoven, Mozart, Wagner, or Gershwin; choral programs of favorite composers from Handel to Verdi; or a series of "French Classics of the Twentieth Century."

In late-nineteenth-century Paris the motto "Gallic Art" (Ars Gallic) bore fruit in an active musical life including numerous chamber and symphonic concerts regularly performed by Paris's three symphony orchestras, the Society of Conservatory Concerts (Société des Concerts du Conservatoire) established in 1828 by François Habeneck, the Popular Concerts of Classical Music (Concerts Populaires de Musique Classique) founded in 1861 by Jules Pasdeloup, and the Artistic Association of Édouard Colonne (l'Association Artistique d'Edouard Colonne) created in 1874. All three prompted a strong national awareness and enthusiasm for French music.

The demand was strong enough to justify the formation of a new orchestra in 1881 by Charles Lamoureux, award-winning violinist, past member of the Pasdeloup Orchestra, and experienced conductor of the Paris Opéra House. Under the name "Society of New Concerts" the orchestra presented on October 23 at the Théâtre du Château-d'Eau, Place de la République, a program of Beethoven, Antonio Sacchini, Berlioz, Handel, Gluck, and Domenico Cimarosa.

For 16 years, until 1897, Lamoureux nurtured the orchestra with works of Wagner, whom he ardently admired, Berlioz, and other romantics. Contemporary French composers' new works were also well represented on Lamoureux's concert programs: César Franck's *Les Eolides* (1882), Vincent d'Indy's *Symphonie sur un chant montagnard français* (1887), Emmanuel Chabrier's *España* (premiere, 1883), Ernest Chausson's *Viviane* (1888), and Gabriel Fauré's *Pavane* (1888). Lamoureux also led early performances of Richard Strauss, Johannes Brahms, and Alexander Borodin. Although Lamoureux never shared the podium with other conductors, famous contemporary soloists frequently appeared with the orchestra. The orchestra began to tour, visiting Russia in 1893. In 1896 yearly London visits were established.

Upon his illness and consequent retirement in 1897, Lamoureux chose as his successor Camille Chevillard. Reorganized as an association, the orchestra took the name of its founder, who continued to conduct on occasion and to greatly influence the preparation of concert programs until his death in 1899. Under Chevillard the Lamoureux Orchestra began to invite guest conductors and also to include works of the new generation of French composers. Among the premieres Chevillard conducted were Debussy's *Nocturnes* (Nos. 1 and 2: *Nuages* and *Fêtes*; 1901) and the solo orchestral version of Fauré's *Pélleas et Mélisande* (1901). In 1913 the orchestra presented the first concert versions of three grand French ballets, Ravel's *Daphnis et Chloé*, Dukas's *Le Péri*, and Roussel's *Le Festin de L'araignée*. The orchestra's repertoire was diversified with symphonic cycles of the masters as well as works by non-French contemporaries such as Gustav Mahler, Edward Elgar, and Richard Strauss.

By 1907, after several years of changing venues (the Eden Théâtre, Cirque d'Été, Théâtre de la République, Nouveau-Théâtre, Théâtre Sara-Bernhardt, and Salle Gaveau), the orchestra settled into its present home, the Salle Pleyel. Now enjoying an international reputation, the Lamoureux's overseas tours multiplied. With the coming of World War I, however, the orchestra's ranks were decimated, and from 1914 to 1919 the Lamoureux merged with the Orchestra of the Concerts Colonne, with Chevillard and the Colonne's Gabriel Pierné alternating at the podium. Following the war Chevillard, who was also music director of the Opéra and a Conservatory professor, proposed the Lamoureux conductorship to the young Paul Paray, who assumed the post in 1920. Chevillard remained active with the orchestra, however, and led the group in its first recordings shortly thereafter.

In 1923 the 37-year-old Paray was elected president-conductor after Chevillard's death. Paray had a brilliant career with the Lamoureux Orchestra. Performances were increased to include matinees on Saturdays and Sundays, and programs placed even greater emphasis on contemporary French composers such as Georges Migot, Louis-François-Marie Aubert, Jean Rivier, and Jacques Ibert. From this period on, however, the orchestra no longer made an effort to plan programs of avant-garde composers such as *Les Six*, Stravinsky, or the Second Viennese School, but rather performed those "new" works that had already been accepted by the concert-going public.

In 1928 Albert Wolff succeeded Paray at Lamoureux. Because the performance of avant-garde French music had now shifted to other Parisian orchestras (such as the National Orchestra of France*), Wolff concentrated on large-scale symphonic works of the earlier generation. Mahler's Fourth Symphony was performed in 1931 to a disconcerted public. At the insistence of Lamoureux musicians, d'Indy, Georges Georgescu, Ottorino Respighi, Ravel, and Prokofiev conducted concerts of their own works. Premieres during this period included Ravel's *Bolero* (1932) and Concerto in G for Piano and Orchestra (1932), the latter performed by Marguerite Long with Ravel conducting. When Wolff left the orchestra in 1934 to conduct Concerts Pasdeloup, a year's interim was followed by the election of Eugène Bigot, who once again featured recent composers, albeit those more appealing to the public: Florent Schmitt, Jean Rivier, Francis Poulenc, and others.

Following the Second World War, during which Lamoureux activities ceased, a new public had to be courted, and for several years the programs consisted largely of Beethoven, Wagner, other romantics, and some already approved twentieth-century composers. When Jean Martinon replaced Bigot in 1951 he reinstated a somewhat more adventurous programming policy, admitting works of Bartók and Prokofiev. Martinon developed a transparent orchestral texture and virtuosic technique. Celebrated guest conductors led the orchestra during these years: Sir Georg Solti, Josef Krips, Pierre Monteux, and many others. Nevertheless, financial pressures compelled Lamoureux musicians to secure jobs with other performance groups. Musicians now elected representatives to a committee that gave them representation in the association.

Martinon departed in 1957, after which the president-conductor's dual position was split between two individuals. Composer Georges Auric was elected Lamoureux president and Russian-born conductor/composer Igor Markevitch became the permanent conductor. Now reestablished with the Parisian public, the orchestra under Markevitch expanded the concert programming, adding Russian works, choral works of Mozart and Berlioz, and works of contemporary French composers, among them Darius Milhaud and Pierre Boulez. Guest conductors continued to appear, among them Leonard Bernstein, Lorin Maazel, and Bernard Haitink. A successful concert tour to the United States in 1960 was followed by others throughout Europe, including England and Greece. In recognition of its accomplishments the French Government in 1961 awarded the orchestra the title "Utilité Publique."

Following the 1962 election of Jean-Baptiste Mari as Lamoureux conductor (and composer André Jolivet as president), orchestral programs remained primarily traditional. Paul Paray frequently conducted in the 1960s, and he added some works from the early twentieth century. To encourage attendance, questionnaires were distributed to the audiences at concerts with a view to programming according to their wishes. Some changes occurred in the orchestra's personnel, and it became increasingly difficult to make replacements within the ranks of the orchestra. Lamoureux musicians' principal employment remained outside of the orchestra. In 1969 the decision was made to no longer appoint a permanent orchestral conductor, but to rely on guests, among whom have been established conductors such as Jean-Pierre Jacquillat (who appeared frequently from 1975 to 1977) as well as talented young conductors such as (in the early years of the policy) Seiji Ozawa. In 1979 the artistic council (Conseiller artistique) was created. Two years later the orchestra celebrated its 100th anniversary, having performed almost 5,000 concerts.

RECORDING HISTORY AND SELECTIVE DISCOGRAPHY: The Lamoureux Orchestra's first recordings were made in the early 1920s by Chevillard (of Debussy, Borodin, and Wagner). Wolff recorded exclusively on the Polydor label. Many Lamoureux recordings of the early years were made "without labels" and have been permanently lost. In the 1930s Ravel and the orchestra made recordings, among which was a 1932 live performance of his *Bolero*. Martinon made numerous recordings in the 1950s, and Markevitch made over 40 recordings on the Philips label. Guest conductors who have recorded with the orchestra include Antál Doráti, Charles Munch, and Roberto Benzi. The orchestra has recorded for Erato, Deutsche Grammophon, Everest, and Pathé-Marconi, among others. No recordings have been made in the last six years.

Bizet, *L'Arlésienne* Suites No. 1 and No. 2; Carmen Suites No. 1 and No. 2 (Doráti): Philips, 41175–4 (4 records) or (Markevitch): Phi. Fest. 6570107. Joseph Canteloube, *Songs of the Auvergne*; Chausson, *Poeme de l'amour et de la mer* (De los Angeles/ Jacquillat): Angel S–36898. Ibert, Concerto for Flute (Rampal/Fromert): RCA AGL–1– 3658. Roussel, *Bacchus et Ariadne* (Ballet) Suite No. 2 (Markevitch): DG 2543807.

CHRONOLOGY OF MUSIC DIRECTORS: Charles Lamoureux, 1881–1897. Camille Chevillard, 1897–1923. Paul Paray, 1923–1928. Albert Wolff, 1928–1934. (Transitional season, 1934–1935). Eugène Bigot, 1935–1951. Jean Martinon, 1951–1957. Igor Markevitch, 1957–1962. Jean-Baptiste Mari, 1962–1969. No permanent conductors after 1969.

BIBLIOGRAPHY: Interview with Lamoureux Administrator Annie Foultier, Paris, 1985. Alain Pâris, *Concerts Lamoureux* (Paris: Guerin, 1981). "Lamoureux, Charles," *The New Grove Dictionary of Music and Musicians*, 6th ed. (London: Macmillan, 1980). Lamoureux Orchestra, miscellaneous programs.

ACCESS: Association des Concerts Lamoureux, 252, rue du Faubourg Saint-Honoré, Paris 75008. (011–331) 562–59–93 or 563–44–34. Marcel Naulais, Lamoureux General Secretary. Annie Foultier, Lamoureux Administrator.

                                                       VIOLET VAGRAMIAN-NISHANIAN

National Orchestra of France

Founded in 1934, the National Orchestra of France (ONF: Orchestre National de France), is one of the formations of the Office de Radio-diffusion Télévision Française (ORTF). The ONF consists of 117 musicians, some of whom also perform in chamber ensembles such as the double bass quartet, the woodwind quintet, or the brass quintet.

The ONF annually performs between 50 and 55 concerts during the September to June concert season, which includes four subscription series and two series coproduced with the Théâtre des Champs Elysées and Ademma. Additionally, the orchestra plays free concerts in the Maison de Radio France (built in 1963). The ONF's widely diverse concerts are often held in the Théâtre des Champs Elysées, the Salle Pleyel, and other concert halls. All ONF programs are broadcast live or prerecorded on the France-Musique channel, reaching an audience estimated at several million.

The orchestra's budget is derived from the Ministry of Culture's Bureau of Music subvention (85%), ticket sales (10%), and patron donations (5%). The ONF has both administrative and artistic representation elected from within its own ranks. Concert programming for the season is the responsibility of the orchestra's music director (a position distinct from that of principal conductor, though sometimes manned by the same individual).

The ONF performs various kinds of concert programs encompassing all the musical periods; however, it especially favors contemporary works and the works of French composers, past and present. A representative all-French program played in January 1986 presented Gabriel Fauré's *Masques et Bergamasques*, Op. 112; Maurice Ravel's Concerto No. 1 in D for Piano and Orchestra; and Henri Dutilleux's Symphony No. 2 (*"Le Double"*). Additionally, Radio France and the Ministry of Culture regularly commission new works. For example, during the 1985–1986 season, 60 works by 55 European and French composers were premiered, many by the ONF, throughout Parisian concert halls.

The orchestra regularly makes worldwide tours and has travelled throughout Europe, to the U.S.S.R., the United States (with a return engagement planned for March 1987), South America, and Japan. It frequently plays at major music festivals. The ONF is renowned for high performance standards, as a broadcast and concert orchestra, and as one of the powerful and active forces in Parisian and international concert life.

The emergence and historical development of the National Orchestra of France, which would become a champion of avant-garde works, is directly related to the growing list of achievements that occurred in radio broadcasting during the 1920s. By 1923 regular broadcasts linked France and America from the top of the Eiffel Tower. In 1926 all existing French stations combined into a network of the national government. The formation of an orchestra for the State Radio was the idea of Jean Mistler, the French Minister of Posts from 1933–1934. An avid music lover, Mistler envisioned a high-quality ensemble that would be financially secure as a result of license fees paid by radio listeners. The Orchestre du Fédération Nationale de Radio-diffusion was thus established with 80 young, talented musicians, competitively chosen and placed under the noted conductor Désiré Émile Inghelbrecht.

On March 13, 1934, the orchestra's first concert was broadcast from the Salle du Conservatoire; it consisted of works by Beethoven, Mendelssohn, Debussy, César Franck, and others. Inghelbrecht nurtured the orchestra until 1944, exposing the public to the classics, romantics, and especially the works of Debussy, Ravel, and Albert Roussel. One of the first broadcasts of the original setting of Modest Mussorgsky's *Boris Godunov* was on French radio in 1935. Initially a select studio audience was invited to the ONF's performances, which grew considerably, eventually constituting a loyal following. Without the constraints of a box office, the orchestra expanded its repertoire to include numerous avant-garde works. By 1938 the orchestra had completed its 500th radio broadcast.

Orchestral activities were suspended during World War II; many musicians were evacuated to Rennes and later Marseilles. Remobilization took place with resumption of orchestral activities, from 1944 to 1947, with conductor Manuel Rosenthal. Since 1945 the orchestra, under control of the Radio-diffusion Télévision Française, has established a role of leadership in its new educational programs as an active patron of new music. This means increased performances of the works of established twentieth-century masters—such as Arthur Honegger, Darius Milhaud, Bartók and Stravinsky—and especially premieres of newly written French and non-French composers' works. The ONF's first tours began in 1946, and two years later it visited the United States under Charles Munch, establishing its reputation as a fine orchestra with special performance skills, especially in the French repertoire.

The ONF played numerous premieres under the direction of its capable conductor Roger Désormière from 1947 to 1951, including Milhaud's Second and Third Symphonies (1947, 1948), André Jolivet's Concerto pour ondes Martenot (1949), Francis Poulenc's Concerto for Piano (1949), and Pierre Boulez's Le Soleil des eaux (1949). Désormière was especially known for performances of both contemporary and preclassical music.

From 1951 to 1958 D. E. Inghelbrecht reassumed directorship of the ONF. During these and the following years numerous international artists and conductors made guest appearances with the orchestra—Ernest Ansermet, Serge Koussevitzky, David Oistrakh, and many others. Inghelbrecht was followed in 1959 by Maurice Le Roux. In his time premieres included Jean Rivier's Sixth and Seventh Symphonies (1958, 1962), Charles Koechlin's La Cité nouvelle (1962), Gustave Charpentier's Concerto pour ondes Martenot (1964), and Gilbert Amy's Antiphonies (1965).

In 1968 Jean Martinon (a composer in his own right) became the ONF's conductor, remaining until 1973. His repertoire included the classics, contemporary compositions, and a special concern for works of Bartók, Prokofiev, and French composers. His performances emphasized the translucency of orchestral texture.

Since Martinon the post of ONF chief conductor has not necessarily been filled by the same person who has acted as its music director. Martinon was followed in 1973 by the gifted Romanian, Sergiu Celibidache, as chief conductor. Celibidache's two years with the ensemble saw artistic strides. The music director during Celibidache's years was Serge Blanc. Alain Bancquart served both roles from 1975 to 1976. Alain Moène (music director, 1977–1983) was succeeded by the present music director, Marc Thomson.

Also from 1977 to the present, the orchestra came under the baton of Chief Conductor Lorin Maazel, who has led it since 1977. Under Maazel the ONF has maintained its stature with innovative programming and regular recordings for radio and major record companies. A series of 17 unusual concerts occurred from May through June of 1980, with Isaac Stern as performer/teacher/adviser. Each season the ONF participates in diverse programs sponsored by the ORTF under the title "Perspectives of the Twentieth Century." Performances in 1985 of newly commissioned works included Luciano Berio's Homage à Scarlatti, Carlos Roque-Alsina's Concerto for Piano and Orchestra, Cristóbal Halffter's Parafrasis, and Dutilleux's Concerto for Violin and Orchestra.

RECORDING HISTORY AND SELECTIVE DISCOGRAPHY: The ONF made its first recording in 1936—Milhaud's Suite française conducted by Inghelbrecht. Since then it has recorded regularly on many major labels, recently for Erato, EMI, CBS, Deutsche Grammophon, Angel, RCA, and others. Works of the standard repertoire and twentieth-century French composers are well represented, under guest conductors such as Charles Munch, Leonard Bernstein, Seiji Ozawa, and Mstislav Rostropovich; regular conductors Le Roux, Martinon, Maazel and others may also be heard on ONF recordings. The ONF makes 52 radio performance recordings for Radio France as well as five to ten commercial disc recordings. Among its historical recordings are the *Cinquantenaire de L'Orchestre National de France* (works of Beethoven, Brahms, Debussy, Haydn, and others) released by Erato, and a six-volume edition (on 24 LPs) comprising the orchestral works of Debussy conducted by Martinon (Angel S–37064–68, 37124).

Berlioz, *Symphonie Fantastique* (Conlon): Erato NUM–75106. Bizet, *Carmen* (Mignenes-Johnson, Domingo/Maazel): Erato ECD–88037 (3 records). Milhaud, *Création du monde*, *Le Boeuf sur le toit*, and *Saudades* (Bernstein): Angel S–37442. *Musique Fran-çaise* "La Callas a Paris," Angel S–3950 (2 records). Milhaud, *Les Maries de la Tour Eiffel* and other works (Milhaud): Adès 14007. Ravel, *Alborado del gracioso, Bolero, Rapsodie*, and *La Valse* (Maazel): CBS 37289. Stravinsky, *Le Sacre du printemps* and *Etudes* (Boulez): Nonesuch 71093. Iannis Xenakis, *Metastasis* and *Pithoprakta* (Le Roux): Vanguard C–10030.

CHRONOLOGY OF CHIEF CONDUCTORS: Désiré Émile Inghelbrecht, 1934–1944. Manuel Rosenthal, 1944–1947. Roger Désormière, 1947–1951. D. E. Inghelbrecht, 1951–1958. Maurice Le Roux, 1959–1967. Jean Martinon, 1958–1973. Sergiu Celibidache, 1973–1975. Alain Bancquart, 1975–1976. Lorin Maazel, 1977-present.

BIBLIOGRAPHY: Correspondence with ONF Program Adviser Christophe Mandot, 1985–1986. "Behind the Scenes," *High Fidelity and Musical America*, Jan. 1976. Jean Yves Bras's article reduction from "Orchestre National de France," by Alain Pâris, *Dictionnaire des Interpretis* (Paris: n.d., n.p.). Pierre Fauchaux, *Orchestre National de France* (Paris, 1981)—brochure. Orchestre National de France, miscellaneous documents.

ACCESS: Orchestre National de France, Radio France, Société Nationale de Radiodiffusion, Pièce 63–14, Maison de Radio France, 116 Avenue du President Kennedy, Paris 75016. (011–331) 230–30–28. Dany Marguin, Administrator.

VIOLET VAGRAMIAN-NISHANIAN

Orchestre de Paris

The Orchestre de Paris is the leading orchestra of France, serving the large and culturally sophisticated French capital and its environs. The annual budget is 70 million French francs. The season consists of about two dozen doubles on Wednesdays, Thursdays, and some Fridays at 8:30 P.M., a total of about 50 concerts annually. The orchestra presently consists of 115 players.

Since 1981 the home of the Orchestre de Paris has been the Salle Pleyel, successor to the recital hall of the noted piano manufacturers and publishers Pleyel. Chopin made his Paris debut in the old Salle Pleyel; the new hall was inaugurated in October 1927 by a concert of the Société des Concerts du Conservatoire, predecessor of the Orchestre de Paris, during which Stravinsky conducted his *Firebird* Suite and Ravel led *La Valse*. Now owned by the Crédit Lyonnais (a French bank), the Salle Pleyel was refurbished in the last decade according to the specific needs of tenancy by a major symphony orchestra. The Salle Pleyel has thus been the first hall to afford the Orchestre de Paris rehearsals and performances in the same room. It seats 2,300.

Also located in Paris are the National Orchestra of France* and the Nouvel Orchestre Philharmonique (the two radio/television orchestras); the Orchestre de l'Île de France; the Lamoureux Orchestra*; and the Ensemble Orchestral de Paris, a chamber orchestra sponsored by the city of Paris. Other French orchestras include the Orchestre du Capitole de Toulouse, Strasbourg Philharmonic Orchestra,* Lyon Symphony Orchestra,* Orchestre de Bordeaux, Orchestre des Pays de la Loire, and the Orchestre Philharmonique de Lille. But just as no other French city approaches Paris in cultural importance, so no other orchestra in the nation quite enjoys the illustrious history of the Orchestre de Paris and its predecessor.

The Orchestre de Paris assumed its name in 1967 during a full-scale restructuring of the national commitment to arts and letters following the political upheavals during the late 1960s. One of the critical issues in French music was the demand for a much larger and presumably better orchestra than the historic Société des Concerts du Conservatoire, which it replaced. Due in large measure to its antiquated constitution of 1828, the Société had grown stagnant from nearly every point of view. The call of the politicians was for a new society "of national stature . . . to create and administer a great orchestra, which, by its exceptional quality, [would] convey the musical prestige of Paris and the nation to all countries." The most significant provisions of the new constitution were three: the post of permanent musical director, with sole authority for the artistic affairs of the orchestra; quadrennial auditions of each player; and an exclusivity clause that requires each musician to devote virtually full time to the Orchestre de Paris.

The formal dissolution of the Société des Concerts on June 21, 1967, and the immediate creation of the Orchestre de Paris was a diplomatic triumph of the Directeur-Général de la Musique, Marcel Landowski (b. 1915; also known for his work as a composer), and of the celebrated writer André Malraux (1901–1976), Minister of Culture at the time. Despite the fact that some tenured members of the Society were to lose their jobs, the vote for dissolution carried, 51 for, 13 opposed, 1 abstention. The first concert of the new Orchestre de Paris was on November 14, 1967, with Charles Munch conducting.

In September 1975 Daniel Barenboim (b. 1942; he was 33 at the time) was officially named principal conductor, and the long and successful reign of a musical talent that was prodigious from the outset has been marked by consistent growth in his own musical understanding and in the sonority and technique of his orchestra.

The orchestra enjoys a substantial subsidy from the nation and from the city of Paris. It is a nonprofit society formed under French law of 1901.

The Orchestre de Paris has since its inception been active in a broad spectrum of activities beyond its main subscription series. The 150th anniversary in 1978 of the founding of the Société des Concerts was the occasion for a national commemoration in which it joined the Conservatoire, Bibliothèque Nationale, and a specially constituted committee in offering a gala commemorative concert, chamber concerts, exhibitions, and a variety of luxurious publications. In May 1979 the Orchestre de Paris and its chorus travelled to the Kennedy Center, Washington, D.C., to present a substantial part of the Berlioz repertoire in the course of a festival called "Paris: The Romantic Epoch"; there were also concerts in Carnegie Hall, New York. The group has travelled widely in Western Europe and Japan. Mozart festivals given in the three seasons 1982–1984 (and the highly successful 1979 appearances in Washington, D.C.) led in due course to a co-production by the Washington Opera and the Orchestre de Paris of the Mozart/ Da Ponte operas, staged by Jean-Pierre Ponnelle.

During the 1985–1986 season the tenth anniversary year of Barenboim's leadership coincided with the European Musical Year. A gala season included appearances by many individual artists, as well as the National Symphony Orchestra** with Mstislav Rostropovich and the Munich Philharmonic Orchestra* with Sergiu Celibidache, the latter as part of an exchange whereby the Orchestre de Paris appeared in Munich as well. There were also pre- and mid-season appearances in Scotland, Sweden, Finland, Spain, Russia, and Czechoslovakia.

Related musical concerns sponsored by the Orchestre de Paris include an annual cycle of a half dozen or more concerts of chamber music, many of them with Barenboim at the piano. Young people's concerts are produced in conjunction with the Jeunesses-Musicales de France (roughly, "French Youth-in-Music Federation"); the orchestra is also a major sponsor of the Orchestre Français des Jeunes (French Youth Orchestra). One of Barenboim's boldest strokes was his early call for a 250-voice amateur chorus to be affiliated with his orchestra; this was founded and is led by Arthur Oldham.

Each season the orchestra travels for a week to one of the large cities in France for a series of traditional concerts, public workshops, chamber music, and concerts devoted to new music. It also hosts appearances in Paris of major visiting ensembles. Since 1986 the orchestra has engaged in co-productions of new music with the Ensemble InterContemporain, the celebrated contemporary music group led by Pierre Boulez.

The Orchestre de Paris plays with the assurance characteristic of a well-conceived modern institution with roots extending well into the past. Much of the best teaching of instrumental technique and craft, after all, has long been associated with the Paris Conservatoire; the resulting quality of the orchestral sound might best be characterized as suave and technically superb, with the most fetching textures coming from the violins and upper woodwinds. Of particular interest is the confluence in one orchestra of French-built woodwinds, for Paris is the most important European locus of woodwind manufacture. In former decades, the most unusual tone quality was doubtless that of the French bassoon, uncommonly played outside France—an instrument of lighter, hollower tone-quality than the German Heckel instrument, and favored by those who play it as being considerably more agile. Now the Heckel bassoons are used exclusively. French violins reached their zenith in the nineteenth century with the work of Jean-Baptiste Vuillaume, five of whose instruments are in use by the Orchestre de Paris. The traditional double-bass bow (the ''French'' bow or ''Bottesini'' bow) is similar to the violin (or cello) bow and is held overhand, palm downward, as opposed to the underhand-bow technique used by most orchestras in German- and English-speaking countries. The orchestra's pitch standard is A at 442 cps.

The orchestra has been scrupulous in its attention, both in live performances and recordings, to the French masters: above all Berlioz (at last recognized as a national treasure, and at least partly through the efforts of Barenboim and his orchestra), Gounod, Saint-Saëns, Bizet, Lalo, Franck, Fauré, Debussy, Ravel, Roussel, and Milhaud. The Orchestre de Paris is on the whole less recognizably French than its predecessor (to judge, at least, from recordings of the Société des Concerts); the great guest conductors expect in Paris (as in Berlin, Vienna, and Amsterdam) a uniformity of style and accomplishment that mutes the old distinctions. But there remain unquestionably French predilections, as manifest, for example, in the regular programming of modern composers of the ilk of Witold Lutosławski, Luciano Berio, Pierre Boulez, Hans Werner Henze, and Henri Dutilleux.

The Société des Concerts du Conservatoire was founded in March 1828 by François-Antoine Habeneck, Luigi Cherubini (the composer and, at the time, director of the Conservatoire), and their followers, with the principal intent of offering Beethoven's symphonies to the French public. The connection with the Paris Conservatoire was relatively informal; the by-laws specified that the director of the Conservatoire would chair the governing committee of the Society and that all members of the Society should be former students or present staff members of the Conservatoire. Originally there were some 59 strings and 31 wind players, a full chorus of about 70, and guest soloists, a structure that changed infrequently until 1967. The Société was one of the first European orchestras to be governed by its members.

Conductors were elected by a vote of the members (sociétaires); this process tended to assure elevation of the assistant conductor to the full podium—at times the outgoing chef simply named his successor—and thus the continuation of established practices, both good and bad, of the past. Nearly all the early conductors served simultaneously as chief conductor at the Opéra, where most were already employed.

Habeneck conducted with his bow, from a cued violin part; despite this seemingly primitive custom, his accomplishments, particularly in introducing French audiences to Beethoven, were legion. Several decades later E.-M.-E. Deldevez, a staunch proponent of conducting with the bow, led the orchestra from his seat at the head of the violin section.

The early repertoire relied heavily on Beethoven symphonies, but always there was emphasis on indigenous compositions, including those of Gluck, Luigi Cherubini, Rossini, and Meyerbeer. The works of Haydn and Mozart had a decent place in the concerts of the first decades. "At nearly every concert," wrote violinist Eugene de Sauzay, "we were able to offer an unfamiliar work, exciting the curiosity and the enthusiasm of a public who would always ask to hear it again."

Because it was formed anew, the Society had little by way of ancestry, little connection to continuo practice, and a concomitant receptivity to new ways of doing things. The Society became much admired and imitated as a setter of precedents. It is said, for example, that the Paris Orchestra was the first to adopt uniform bowing as a practice. Although Berlioz was not otherwise much involved in the group, two developments that he pioneered—carefully marked orchestral parts with rehearsal letters and the practice of rehearsing by sections—appear to have been adopted by the orchestra in due course.

The provision for a chorus in the structure of the Society made possible the inclusion in the repertoire of important French church music as well as scenes from works in vogue at the Opéra, Opéra-Comique, and Théâtre-Italien (Italian Opera). Programming with chorus included many excerpts from the operas of Weber, a good deal of Rossini (especially the *Stabat Mater* and some wildly popular scenes from *Moïse*), Haydn's *Creation*, Mendelssohn's *St. Paul*, and some epochal performances of Beethoven's Ninth. The chorus was abandoned for reasons of economic stricture after World War I.

The many distinguished instrumentalists affiliated with the orchestra as regular members or by virtue of frequent solo appearances included, especially among the wind players, some of the most influential innovators and teachers of the day, many of whom were on the Conservatory faculty—the oboist Henri Brod, for example, who developed and manufactured oboes with the modern Boehm-like key system; the clarinettist Hyacinthe Klosé, author of a celebrated treatise; the hornist Pierre-Joseph Meifred, an avid proponent of the valved horn; or the trumpeter/cornettist J. B. Arban ("Arban's Famous Trumpet Method"). For all the virtuoso wind playing, however, it was the string sonority and technique that most pleased the Society's attentive listeners.

Leading soloists, of course, frequently appeared with the orchestra, among them Chopin, Mendelssohn, Clara Schumann, Saint-Saëns (frequently), Joseph Joachim, Pablo de Sarasate, and Marguerite Long. All the great French singers appeared as well, including the tenors Adolphe Nourrit and Gustave Roger, the noted mezzo Pauline Viardot, and, later, the soprano Claire Croiza. Many of the visiting artists commented on the orchestra's precision—Mendelssohn, for example, and Wagner (who years later still remembered the Society's performance of the Ninth Symphony as indescribably beautiful), and Beethoven's associate Anton Felix Schindler, who affirmed that nowhere else in the world could one hear a better Pastoral Symphony.

Concerts were offered on Sundays at 2:00 P.M.; this was because the members were also employed at theatres with evening performances. The site of the performances was the old Salle des Concerts of the Conservatoire (capacity 1,084) in the rue Bergère, a hall of unparalleled acoustic character. Tickets for the small room were so scarce and highly valued that for a century they were passed on from generation to generation of family subscribers. In a season lasting from mid-January until just after Easter, the Society offered at first six or seven subscription concerts plus extraordinary concerts, command performances, and benefits (for members, the pension fund, and occasionally, the conductor). By the turn of the century the season had extended to ten concert pairs.

By the 1860s the Society had more than its share of significant rivals. A series of Concerts Populaires in the Cirque d'Hiver (known popularly as the Concerts Pasdeloup after Jules Pasdeloup [1819–1887]) were similar to the London Prom concerts. Concert series by Édouard Colonne (1838–1910; concerts from 1878) and Charles Lamoureux (1838–1910; concerts from 1881) dominated the late nineteenth century, and such organizations as the Société Nationale, in promoting new music, gave many more important first performances than did the Société des Concerts. Nevertheless, under Jules Garcin the Society gave the first performance of César Franck's D-Minor Symphony in 1889, and he introduced the Paris public to Beethoven's *Missa Solemnis* (1888), Brahms's Fourth Symphony (1890), and Bach's B-Minor Mass (1891). Indeed, the (usually) friendly rivalry of the several orchestras and the crossover of musicians from group to group guaranteed a wholesome musical climate and a healthy atmosphere for new music.

After a disastrous fire in a public building in May 1897, the Salle des Concerts (and a number of other public places) was closed to assure the public safety, and the orchestra's home for the season 1897–1898 was the Palais Garnier, the present opera house at the head of the Avenue de l'Opéra. With the removal of the Conservatoire to the rue de Madrid, completed in 1911, it became clear that the days of the Salle des Concerts were numbered, though public outcries to preserve it were ultimately successful. (The hall still exists, though it is little used.) Meanwhile, the orchestra began increasingly to search out more spacious venues for performance.

In the early twentieth century André Messager emerged as an especially influential conductor; among his great triumphs was the first performance of Debussy's *Pélleas et Mélisande* (1902). He led the Society in first performances of works by Paul Dukas, Ernest Chausson, Florent Schmitt, and Richard Strauss (*Taillefer*, 1912). In October 1918 Messager took the orchestra on a tour of the United States, during the course of which 50 American cities, from New York to Texas, hosted concerts. Columbia Records issued recordings of some of these performances.

From there the history of the Société des Concerts is tied up with the unhappy course of events in twentieth-century Europe. The economic and cultural desolation between the wars, followed by the Nazi occupation, had profound adverse effects on the orchestra, though Munch managed to keep things alive from 1938 to 1946 with diligent attention to its style of playing and with first performances of works by Roussel, Schmitt, Arthur Honegger, Stravinsky, and even Olivier Messiaen.

By the 1950s and 1960s, however, there were growingly heeded urges in French culture to be done with relics of the past and to promote instead avatars of contemporary civilization. It was in this climate that the Société des Concerts at length declined and fell.

The library of the Orchestre de Paris/Society des Concerts is one of the glories of French patrimony. It includes the great French editions of Beethoven, Haydn, and Mozart, used and carefully marked by Habeneck and his successors. Among its many treasures is the complete set of manuscript performance material given by Berlioz to the Société in 1863. During the 1970s the archives and most of the old performing materials were transferred to the Bibliothèque Nationale.

RECORDING HISTORY AND SELECTIVE DISCOGRAPHY: Barenboim and the Orchestre de Paris record primarily for the Deutsche Grammophon Gesellschaft and, since 1986, Erato, with earlier records by Columbia (CBS) and Angel. Approximately 100 discs are in print. Records of the Société des Concerts du Conservatoire (usually identified in English as the Paris Conservatory Orchestra) were issued by Pathé-Marconi, Angel/ EMI, and London; some historic recordings are to be found on the Turnabout label. Recent recordings of the Orchestre de Paris have garnered the Grand Prix du Disque and a number of prizes of the French Académie Charles Cros.

Historic recordings of the Société des Concerts deserving special notice are the Bloch Violin Concerto (Szigeti/Munch), Turnabout THS–65007; Ravel's Concerto for the Left Hand and Saint-Saëns's Piano Concerto No. 4 (Cortot), Pathé 2C051–43370; and Berlioz's *L'Enfance du Christ* (Cluytens et al.), Seraphim 6125. Readers may wish to compare Orchestre de Paris recordings of the Berlioz *Symphonie fantastique* under Munch (Angel RL–32061) and Barenboim (DG 2531–092).

Berlioz, *Te Deum* (Dupouy), CBS M–34526. Berlioz, *Les Nuits d'Été* (Te Kanawa/ Barenboim) and *Cléopâtre* (Jessye Norman/Barenboim)(DG 253204). Debussy, *Images* and *Prélude à L'Après-midi d'un faune*, DG 2532058. Fauré, *Requiem* and *Pavane* (Fischer-Dieskau), Angel S–37077. Lalo, *Symphonie espagnole*; Berlioz, *Rêverie et Caprice* (Perlman), DG 2532–011. Ravel, *Bolero, La Valse, Pavane pour une infante défunte*, Suite No. 2 from *Daphnis et Chloé* (Barenboim) DG 2532041; DG 400061–2 GH (CD).

CHRONOLOGY OF MUSIC DIRECTORS: Société des Concerts: François-Antoine Habeneck, 1828–1849. Narcisse Girard, 1849–1860. Théophile Tilmant, 1860–1864. François George-Hainl, 1864–1873. E. -M. -E. Deldevez, 1873–1885. Jules Garcin, 1885– 1892. Paul Taffanel, 1892–1901. Georges-Eugène Marty, 1901–1908. André Messager, 1908–1918. Philippe Gaubert, 1918–1938. Charles Munch, 1938–1946. André Cluytens, 1946–1967.

Orchestre de Paris: Charles Munch, 1967–1968. Herbert von Karajan ("Conseiller musical"), 1969–1972. Serge Baudo, 1969–1971. Georg Solti, 1972–1975. Daniel Barenboim, 1975-present.

BIBLIOGRAPHY: Berlioz, *Mémoires* (Paris, 1870). Élisabeth Bernard, "A Glance at the Archives of Some Parisian Orchestral Societies," *19th-Century Music* 7 (1983), 104– 6 (trans. D. Kern Holoman). Henri de Curzon, "History and Glory of the Concert-Hall of the Paris Conservatory," *Musical Quarterly* 3 (1917), 304–318. Arthur Dandelot, *La Société des Concerts du Conservatoire de 1828 à 1897* (Paris, 1898); 2d ed. titled . . . *(1828–1923)* (Paris, 1923). E. -M. -E. Deldevez, *La Société des Concerts, 1860–1885*

(Paris, 1887). Antoine Elwart, *Histoire de la Société des Concerts du Conservatoire Imperial de Musique* (Paris, 1860; 2d ed., 1864)—includes by-laws and programs through 1863. D. Kern Holoman, "Orchestral Material from the Library of the Societe des Concerts," *19th-Century Music* 7 (1983), 106–118. D. Kern Holoman, "The Emergence of the Orchestral Conductor in Paris in the 1830s," in *Paris in the 1830s: Proceedings of the Smith College Colloquium* (New York: Pendragon Press, 1986). Jean-Michel Nectoux, *Association pour le 150ᵉ anniversaire de la Société des Concerts du Conservatoire* (Paris, 1978). Jean-Michel Nectoux, "Deux Orchestres Parisiens en 1830: L'Opéra et la Société des Concerts du Conservatoire," in *Paris in the 1830s: Proceedings of the Smith College Colloquium* (New York: Pendragon Press, 1986). Orchestre de Paris, press materials, 1982–1986. "La Vie musicale à Paris à travers les *Mémoires* d'Eugène Sauzay (1809–1901)," ed. Brigitte François-Sappey, *Revue de musicologie* 60 (1974), 159–210.

Concert programs, handbills, minutes, and other primary materials regarding the Société are held at the Bibliothèque Nationale.

ACCESS: Orchestre de Paris, Salle Pleyel, 252 rue de Faubourg St. Honoré, 75008 Paris. 563–07–40 (box office), 561–96–07 (public information). Bruno Brochier, General Manager.

D. KERN HOLOMAN

STRASBOURG   (373,000*)

Strasbourg Philharmonic Orchestra

Established in 1855, shortly after the founding of the Strasbourg Conservatory of Music (1848), and founded by that institution's teachers, the Strasbourg Philharmonic Orchestra (OPS: Orchestra Philharmonique de Strasbourg) is today an important regional orchestra, ranked by critics as France's premier ensemble outside of Paris. The OPS serves a large region comprising the northeastern area of France (Alsace) as well as portions of Germany and Switzerland.

The OPS presently consists of 109 musicians, and its overall structure follows the traditional Germanic *grosses Orchester* pattern. It is a permanent professional group that is active throughout the entire year. Due to the popularity of its concerts, the OPS divides its season into three series, Cycles A and B consisting of 12 concerts apiece, and a shorter series, Cycle C, which offers five concerts between May and October. In addition, the regional duties of the OPS include about six concerts per season in neighboring cities such as Colmar, as well as three school concerts. The OPS also provides musicians for the Opera du Rhin, and, more recently, it has given rise to smaller groups such as the famous Percussions de Strasbourg and a chamber ensemble dedicated to contemporary music, Studio III. In June the OPS is one of the principal participants in the annual Festival International de Musique de Strasbourg. The orchestra has toured widely during recent years, performing in the Soviet Union (1972), Japan (1979), the United States (1975, 1980), and throughout Europe. It makes regular appearances on radio and television.

The OPS previously performed in the Palais des Fêtes, a multi-purpose hall seating 1,100. Since 1975 its home has been the modern Palais de la Musique et des Congres, a concert and conference hall seating 1,908 people. This hall, based upon an expanded, fan-shaped audience chamber, has both excellent acoustics and visual perspectives of the orchestra.

The OPS is administered by both an artistic and an administrative division, working in close cooperation with each other. Administrative employees work for the city of Strasbourg. The artistic division is responsible for program selection and the determination of repertoire and guest artists, while the administrative division manages a budget of 30 million French francs. This budget is divided as follows: 33% from the French government as part of a government-sponsored grant to all French orchestras, 20% from receipts, and the remaining 47% from the city of Strasbourg. Private donations are solicited for gifts of permanent value to the orchestra, such as concert pianos. Strasbourg Philharmonic musicians are hired on a tenured basis.

Strasbourg has had a long and illustrious history of music. The first public concerts were inaugurated in 1730 as the Académie de Musique. The city itself boasted important musical figures such as Franz Xaver Richter and Ignaz Pleyel. The latter in 1781 participated in a series of public performances with Johann P. Schönfeld before the French Revolution called a halt to musical activity. The first Alsatian music festival sponsored by the Union Alsacienne de Musique commenced in 1830 and shortly thereafter, with the founding of the Conservatory of Music in 1848, the need for a permanent professional orchestra was recognized.

The present orchestra was formed in 1855 with the teachers of the conservatory and has since maintained continuous operation even during the two world wars and despite the changes in territorial boundaries between Germany and France. In 1972 the French government issued a cultural directive reorganizing and reestablishing numerous orchestras, among them the OPS, on a firm, government-supported foundation. Under this directive the OPS became a regional orchestra, expanding its audience support beyond the city of Strasbourg.

The repertoire of the OPS is largely traditional, in both the German and French mainstreams, in the context of its regular concerts. The music director decides upon the programs to be given, based upon feedback from both the musicians and public response. Its repertoire is supplemented, particularly during the Festival Musica each September, by new works and music composed by young composers of the region.

The OPS has gained a reputation based upon a happy blend of both French and Germanic orchestral sonority, due primarily to Strasbourg's location in the Alsace, within the sphere of influence of both nationalities. The city belonged to France until 1872, to France from 1918 to 1940, and from 1945 to the present; in the intervening years it was on German soil. Due to the influence exercised by leading German conductors such as Franz Stockhausen, Otto Klemperer, and Hans Rosbaud, as well as an increase in size in 1940 from 50 members to over

80, the OPS has taken on the proportions of the traditional large Germanic orchestra; yet the French influence is found in the lightness of response and the choice of repertoire. The two traditions are so evident that when the OPS performs in Germany it is praised for its "French" sound, while in Paris it is said to have a "German" sound, thus making it virtually unique in this respect. The standard tuning of the orchestra is A at 443 cps.

RECORDING HISTORY AND SELECTIVE DISCOGRAPHY: The OPS has recorded exclusively with Erato since its first recording, Hector Berlioz's *Symphonie Fantastique*, in 1972. Alain Lombard, conductor for a period of a decade during the 1970s and 1980s, vigorously promoted the OPS as a recording orchestra and set the tone for an almost continuous series of releases, mostly of traditional repertoire. This tradition continues today under Lombard's successor, Theodor Guschlbauer.

   Frank, Symphony in D Minor (Lombard): Erato STU 71019. Mendelssohn, Violin Concerto (Guschlbauer): Erato ST U 70803. Prokofiev, Violin Concertos Nos. 1 and 2 (Amoyal/Lombard): Erato STU 70866. Stravinsky, *Le Sacre de Printemps* (Lombard): Erato STU 71019.

CHRONOLOGY OF MUSIC DIRECTORS: Josef Hasselmans, 1855–1871. Franz Stockhausen, 1871–1907. Hans Pfitzner, 1907–1915. Otto Klemperer, 1915–1918. Hans Pfitzner, 1918–1919. Guy Ropartz, 1919–1929. Paul Paray, 1929–1940. Hans Rosbaud, 1940–1945. Paul Bastide, 1946–1950. Ernest Bour, 1950–1964. Alceo Galliera, 1964–1971. Alain Lombard, 1971–1983. Theodor Guschlbauer, 1983-present.

BIBLIOGRAPHY: Interviews with OPS Administrative Director Albert Moritz and Director of Public Relations Sylvain Frémaux, 1986. John Holmes, *Conductors on Record* (Westport, Conn.: Greenwood, 1982). Stefan Jaeger, ed., *Das Atlantisbuch der Dirigenten* (Zurich: Atlantis, 1985). Albert Moritz, *Orchestre Philharmonique de Strasbourg* (Strasbourg: n.d.), pamphlet. "Strasbourg," *New Grove Dictionary of Music and Musicians* (New York: Macmillan, 1980).

ACCESS: Orchestre Philharmonique de Strasbourg, Hôtel de Ville, 9 rue Brulée, F–67000 Strasbourg. 88–22–15–60. Albert Moritz, Administrative Director. Sylvain Frémaux, Public Relations Director.

BERTIL H. VAN BOER, JR.
MARGARET L. FAST

German Democratic Republic ——————————————

Berlin State Orchestra

Known until 1918 as the Royal Prussian Court Orchestra (Königlich Preussische Hofkapelle) and then until 1945 as the Prussian State Orchestra (Preussische Staatskapelle), the Berlin State Orchestra (Berliner Staatskapelle) is, next to the Berlin Philharmonic Orchestra,* the most important ensemble of the divided city of Berlin.

Although today the 149-member State Orchestra is largely an opera orchestra performing with the Berliner Staatsoper to which it is attached, it has a long history of symphonic playing as well. In addition to its nearly-nightly engagements with the opera, the Berlin State Orchestra presents each season a series of eight to ten symphonic concerts, each of which is repeated. Programs are frequently dedicated to the music of the present day as well as to single composers. Some eight additional concerts are also held with the venerable Berliner Singakademie. Additionally, a chamber ensemble of the State Orchestra (Kammerorchester "Carl Philipp Emanuel Bach") plays five to eight programs per year. Other chamber music ensembles formed under State Orchestra auspices include seven string quartets (Streichquartett der Deutschen Staatsoper, Berliner Streichquartett, etc.) and several brass ensembles.

Until 1984 Berlin State Orchestra symphonic concerts took place at the 1,352-seat Deutsche Staatsoper/Lindenoper and its smaller Apollo-Saal with 270 seats; since October of that year they have been given in the reconstructed Schauspielhaus at the Platz der Akademie (in earlier times the "Gendarmenmarket"). The Schauspielhaus has two rooms, a large concert hall with approximately 1,700 seats and a chamber music hall (the Apollo-Saal) with 450 seats.

The antecedents of the Berlin Staatskapelle date from 1572, 30 years after the

Elector of Brandenburg, Joachim II, ordered a *Kunstpfeifferei* (12 trumpeters, 1 zinkenist, one tympanist). Aside from this group, music in the Cathedral and the castle was taken care of by a *Hofkapelle* consisting of a choir and organist. In 1572 Johannes Wesalius, the first Kapellmeister documented by name, was asked to expand the instrumental group. Strings were added, and Hans Schreider, the inventor of the contra-bassoon, was called to be the instrument builder. In the separate fields of church and chamber music, the repertoire predominantly embraced music of German, French, and Dutch origin. The orchestra's importance grew under the leadership of Wesalius's successors, Johannes Eccard and Nicolaus Zangius, and especially under the English composer William Brade. Brade took over the conductorship in 1619 but was not able to stop the decline that came as a result of the Thirty Years' War; in 1640 there were only seven members left.

It was not until the beginning of the eighteenth century, after the Electoral Residence was transformed into the Royal Residence, that the orchestra's stature began to rise—the first of numerous ups and downs in response to the whims of an everchanging political environment. By 1712 the ensemble was equipped with over 27 musicians, to which brass players of the hunting and court trumpet corps were added, ad libitum. This brief bloom under Queen Sophie Charlotte was followed by a new decline under Friedrich Wilhelm II, who in 1713 dismissed all court musicians with the exception of the trumpeters.

It was his son Friedrich the Great who stopped the stagnation by calling a new Hofkapelle with famous instrumentalists like the violinists Johann Gottlieb Graun or Franz and Georg Benda; Bach's son Carl Philipp Emanuel as cembalist; and the flute virtuoso Johann Joachim Quantz, who instructed Friedrich the Great in both flute and composition. Friedrich saw to the construction of a new opera house, opening ceremonies for which took place in 1742 under the artistic direction of Karl Heinrich Graun. Graun remained Kapellmeister until his death in 1759. The repertoire under Graun and Johann Adolf Hasse was dominated by Italian opera.

War—the Seven Years War with Austria—again ended the flourishing orchestra. Only in 1775, when Johann Friedrich Reichardt became Hofkapellmeister was the court orchestra again revived. Its new ascension was much helped by a Concert Spirituel series (1783) based on the Parisian prototype, which admitted symphonic music on days when the opera was closed. Thus a certain broad attraction was garnered within middle-class circles, as had already been aimed at in 1749 with the constitution of a Society for the Practice of Music (Musikubenden Gesellschaft). Its members, with the help of Hofkapelle musicians, played the latest symphonies and overtures—at first in private homes and later in hotel halls, such as the "Stadt Paris." Reichardt's sympathy for the French Revolution led to his suspension in 1794, after he spoke out against Italian opera in 1789 by presenting Berlin's first exposure to a Mozart opera in German.

Reichardt's successor with the Hofkapelle, Bernhard Anselm Weber, favored the German repertoire for his entire life (he died in 1821)—as the premiere performance of Beethoven's *Fidelio* testified. His successor was Gasparo Spontini, the first Music Director General (Generalmusikdirektor), who got the king's sympathy by offering French and Italian operas and emphasizing the spectacular. A proclivity for the baroque was introduced into Berlin's sense of musicality at this time as well. It was brought by Zelter's Singing Academy (Singakademie) and their interest in Bach, documented by Felix Mendelssohn's conducting the 1829 reintroduction of the *St. Matthew Passion*.

By 1801 the ensemble had begun a tradition of playing two or three orchestral concerts each year to benefit widows and orphans, and foreign orchestral pieces appeared occasionally as opera entr'acts, but real interest in symphonic music did not come until 1824, when the Hofkapelle gave Berlin premieres of Beethoven's Third and Fifth Symphonies under Carl Moeser. Subscription concerts of the Opernkapelle were offered for the first time in 1842. Motivated by the opera conductor Wilhelm Taubert and titled "Sinfonie-Soiréen," this series was occasionally conducted by Felix Mendelssohn, who was also conductor at the Leipzig Gewandhaus Orchestra.* Taubert stayed with the Hofkapelle until 1833. In 1871 he invited Richard Wagner as guest conductor, thus adopting a futuristic stance. Also joining the conducting staff were Robert Radecke and Ludwig Deppe, followed by Josef Sucher, who did not provoke the resonance of his predecessors among an audience that demanded a classical and early romantic repertoire.

With the advent of Felix Weingartner from Mannheim as Hofkapellmeister in 1891, the Hofkapelle was to reach a peak. Weingartner was aided by Karl Muck (from 1892). Considered a sovereign of the baton, Weingartner was associated with the Kaim Concerts in Munich (1891–1903); he assured the Berlin ensemble of a high standard of interpretation. The lofty performance standards of the Berlin Staatskapelle, as it was now called, was assured by conductors such as Richard Strauss (Weingartner's immediate successor in 1908) and Wilhelm Furtwängler (who simultaneously led the city opera and Museum Orchestra of Frankfurt am Main*). Hermann Abendroth and Erich Kleiber followed, the latter especially reasserting the classical tradition and works of Richard Strauss in the repertoire. Staatskapellmeister from 1923, Kleiber quit in 1934 and emigrated in protest against the cultural politics of the National Socialists.

Otto Klemperer worked with Kleiber from 1927 to 1931, bringing a radical change in policies. He arranged Staatskapelle symphonic concerts in the Kroll Opera House that allowed contemporary music to be heard, including that of Arnold Schoenberg, Igor Stravinsky, and Paul Hindemith. The policy extended to the opera as well. Kleiber had already made a sensation with the performance of Alban Berg's *Wozzeck* (1925), a decisive step in the history of the Staatskapelle. In 1936 Herbert von Karajan had come to Berlin, where he became closely associated with the Philharmonic. From 1941 until the closing of the Staatsoper in 1944, he led the symphonic concerts of the Staatskapelle, while at the same time holding the office of Staatsopernkapellmeister. The home of the Staatskapelle, the Staatsoper (State Opera House), was bombed in 1941 but quickly rebuilt; however, shortly before the capitulation in 1945 it was devastated.

Nevertheless, the Staatskapelle reactivated itself with impressive speed, offering a large opera concert on June 26, 1945 (seven weeks after the capitulation) at the Radio Hall in West Berlin's Masurenallee under Karl Schmitz. Karajan's successor as the "General" of the Deutschen Staatsoper Berlin until 1948–1949 was Johannes Schüler. He was followed until 1955 by a long line of guest conductors, including Hermann Abendroth, Wilhelm Furtwängler, Joseph Keilberth, Fritz Lehmann, and Sir Georg Solti. When the reconstructed opera building (Unter den Linden) was opened on September 4, 1955, as home of the Deutsche Staatsoper Berlin, the artistic responsibility of the Staatskapelle was given over to Franz Konwitschny, who had by then six years' experience as music director of the Leipzig Gewandhaus Orchestra. He remained with the State Orchestra (and the Gewandhaus) until his death in 1962. Konwitschny's credits include his cultivation of both Mozart and Richard Strauss in the repertoire. In the opera he oversaw the production in Berlin of an entire *Ring* cycle. He also publicized the orchestra by greatly increasing its production of symphonic records for distribution both within and outside the D.D.R. Konwitschny and the orchestra also began touring, most notably to the Soviet Union.

A brief interregnum under conductors Helmut Seydelmann, Heinz Fricke, and Heinz Rögner ended in 1964 with the appointment of Otmar Suitner, who has, with the exception of 1971–1974, presided ever since. His goals were to tighten up playing standards and expand the orchestra's international renown. The Staatskapelle engaged itself more and more with contemporary music of the D.D.R., presenting works by Paul Dessau, Jean Kurt Forest, Günter Kochan, Rudolf Wagner-Régeny, and Ruth Zechlin, among others. A favored soloist with the State Orchestra since the days of Konwitschny has been David Oistrakh. At present Suitner holds the position of Geschäftsführender Generalmusikdirektor and is assisted by two Generalmusikdirektoren, Heinz Fricke and Siegfried Kurz. The orchestra has toured with increasing frequency under Suitner, with visits in the last five years to the Soviet Union, Japan, France, Italy, Australia, New Zealand, and Switzerland.

SELECTIVE DISCOGRAPHY: Beethoven, Complete Symphonies (Suitner): Denon (also issued separately). Beethoven, Symphony No. 5 (Strauss, 1928): InSynch 4128. Brahms, Violin Concerto (Kreisler/Blech): Pearl 250/1. Paul Dessau, *Einstein* (Suitner): NOVA 885103/104 (2 records). Dessau, *Puntila* (Dessau): NOVA 885127/128 (2 records). Dvořák, Symphony No. 7 (Suitner) Spectrum 181.

CHRONOLOGY OF MUSIC DIRECTORS: (Various titles): Johannes Wesalius, 1572–1607. William Brade, 1618–1619. Karl Heinrich Graun, 1735–1759. Johann Friedrich Reichardt, 1775–1794. Bernhard Anselm Weber, 1792–1821. Gasparo Spontini, 1820–1842. Felix Mendelssohn Bartholdy, 1841–1845. Gottfried Wilhelm Taubert, 1845–1883. Robert Radecke, 1883–1887. Ludwig Deppe, 1887–1888. Josef Sucher, 1888–1899. Felix von Weingartner, 1891–1908. Richard Strauss, 1908–1920. Wilhelm Furtwängler, 1920–1922. Hermann Abendroth, 1922–1923. Erich Kleiber, 1923–1935. Otto Klemperer,

1927–1931. Herbert von Karajan, 1941–1944. Johannes Schüler, 1945–1949. Franz Konwitschny, 1955–1962. Otmar Suitner, 1964–1971 and 1974-present.

BIBLIOGRAPHY: Correspondence with Berlin Staatskapelle *Konzertdramaturg* Horst Richter. Berlin Staatskapelle, miscellaneous documents. Horst Seeger and Ulrich Bokel, *Musikstadt Berlin* (Leipzig: VEB Deutscher Verlag für Musik, 1974).

ACCESS: Deutsche Staatsoper Berlin, Unter den Linden 5–7, DDR–1068 Berlin. 00372–20540. Gunter Rimkus, Intendant.

JOACHIM DORFMÜLLER
TRANS. PETER JÄHNE AND ANNELIESE YIENGST

DRESDEN   (515,000)

Dresden Philharmonic

The city of Dresden, situated near the borders of Poland and Czechoslovakia, has long been a center for the arts. The Dresden Philharmonic (die Dresdner Philharmonie) is one of East Germany's major orchestras, well into its second century.

The 102-piece ensemble performs about 100 concerts annually in the Dresden area as well as 20 to 30 concerts on foreign tours. It participates in many international music events, particularly with the international Dresden Music Festival. Its Dresden season includes three different subscription series (one of which concentrates on a particular composer), a series of chamber concerts, several youth concerts, and a summer season in the Schlosspark. The Dresden Philharmonic also has an expanded audience via radio and television broadcasts and numerous recordings. An affiliation with the Dresden Kreuzchor in addition to work with its own Philharmonic Chorus has resulted in many fine performances of major choral/symphonic literature. The Philharmonic Chorus performs not only with the orchestra, but in special ensemble performances as well.

At its inception the orchestra was closely identified with its first (and most longstanding) place of performance, Dresden's Commerce Hall. Hence it was known at first as the "Commerce Hall Orchestra" (das Gewerbehausorchester). Not until 1885, when the noted concert agent Hermann Wolff aided the group, modelling its organization and focus after that of the Berlin Philharmonic Orchestra,* did it become known as the Dresden Philharmonic. Further refinements in its governance in 1924 set it up as a cooperative entity until the inception of the German Democratic Republic, when it came under the authority of the national government.

Since its earliest days in the Commerce Hall, the Dresden Philharmonic has traditionally been a more affordable alternative to the long-established Dresden Opera House and the Court Orchestra (Hofkapelle), both of which presided over the musical scene before the First World War. It developed and continues an educational mission with a history of youth, popular, and historic concerts spanning over a century. Orchestra members are active in leading various musical

groups of the city, including those for schools, trade groups, and other organizations. Introductory educational discourses for each concert series foster musical understanding among Dresden concertgoers, furthering the longstanding
effort toward audience education. It is in this light that the present orchestra
leadership views government control as most beneficial; within the doctrine of
"socialist realism" the Dresden Philharmonic perceives itself as an enlightener
and educator for the masses.

The orchestra's development is the subject of a number of works from the
pen of its chief historian, Artistic Manager Dr. Dieter Härtwig. According to
Dr. Härtwig, the Dresden Philharmonic was founded on November 29, 1870.
The first artistic director was Moritz Erdmann Puffholdt, who after a year was
followed by Hermann Gustav Mannsfeldt. Mannsfeldt remained as director from
1871 until 1885, during which time the "Commerce Hall Orchestra" made its
first foreign tours to Petersburg, Warsaw, and Amsterdam. The first inroads
toward audience education were made in 1883, when Mannsfeldt instituted "historical concerts," which traced musical development via chronological programming (encompassing, for instance, the musical styles from Bach to Wagner).

The year 1885 was a major turning point for the orchestra. Hermann Wolff
helped the group to reorganize and define its artistic direction. It is at this juncture
that it took on its present title, the Dresden Philharmonic. Appropriate to this
transformation from the more parochial Commerce Hall days, a number of guest
artists were invited to conduct the orchestra, including Jean-Louis Nicodé, Tchaikovsky, Dvořák, Brahms, Hans von Bülow, Strauss, Rubinstein, and
Rachmaninoff.

The position of artistic director during these years passed among four capable,
but somewhat undistinguished musicians: M. Zimmermann (1885–1886); Ernst
Stahl (1886–1890); August Trenkler (1890–1903); and Willy Olsen (1903–1915).
During Olsen's tenure local programming was developed, especially for young
people and for workers and tradespeople, beginning in 1912. Paul and Eva
Büttner were instrumental in the success of these programs. Olsen's successor,
the Austrian-born Edwin Lindner, brought considerable vision and enthusiasm
to the ensemble. He was instrumental in engaging guest artists of the highest
caliber.

The year 1923 witnessed considerable upheaval. Leadership shifted briefly to
Dresden's composer/conductor Joseph Gustav Mraczek. The orchestra, no
stranger to economic hardship, fell victim to the staggering inflation plaguing
Germany, and although it still enjoyed considerable international acclaim, the
Philharmonic suffered its worst season in 1923–1924.

Eduard Mörike took over as resident conductor in 1924. Known internationally
as a Beethoven and Wagner specialist, he also had a missionary zeal for educating
his audiences. Thus were added additional performances at the Dresden People's
Theater (Dresdner Volksbühnenkonzerten) and numerous school concerts, with
programming reminiscent of Mannsfeldt's "historical concerts" of nearly 40
years earlier.

Paul Scheinpflug (1929–1932) and Werner Ladwig (1932–1934) led the orchestra after Mörike left, and Dutch-born Paul van Kempen took over as artistic director in 1934. Under his leadership, the Dresden Philharmonic attained world-class stature among musicians and also began its long recording career. However, van Kempen left in 1942 because of difficulties with the Nazis. From then until the end of the war, several people conducted, most notably Otto Matzerath, Bernardino Molinari, Kurt Eichhorn, and Carl Schuricht. The latter was finally appointed artistic director, remaining in the post until September 1944, when war conditions dictated an end to the orchestra's work.

On February 13, 1945, Dresden was heavily bombed. Among the areas destroyed was the Dresden Philharmonic's home and one-time namesake, the Commerce Hall, complete with the orchestra's archives and library. Yet the postwar Dresden Philharmonic was performing again within four months—on June 8, 1945, under the direction of Gerhart Wiesenhütter, who remained artistic director until early 1946. The orchestra's new home was Dresden's "Steinsaal," where it would remain until 1957, when it moved again to the Congress Hall of the Dresden Health Museum. Here it remained until 1970.

A new era began on July 1, 1947, with the appointment of Professor Heinz Bongartz as artistic director. His energetic, consistent, purposeful direction contributed tremendously to the orchestra's quality, bringing it new international recognition. Under Bongartz the Philharmonic toured 14 countries, including Egypt and China. Bongartz remained an active force with the orchestra even after stepping down in 1964. He continued as guest conductor until late 1977, not long before his death, and he was influential as a mentor for other orchestra leadership. His contributions to the orchestra spanned 30 years.

As of January 1, 1950, control of the Dresden Philharmonic was assumed by the East German government. This new state of affairs naturally had ramifications for the orchestra, but the new regime was quick to affirm its support, elevating the orchestra to the rank of "special class" (Sonderklasse) in 1951. Since 1954 it has been a member of the "top class" (Spitzenklasse) of East German orchestras, a distinction it shares with the national ensembles (Staatskapellen) of Dresden and East Berlin and with the Leipzig Gewandhaus Orchestra.* Other honors awarded during the 1950s and 1960s include the "Fatherland's Silver Order of Merit" (Vaterländische Verdienstordens in Silber), its appointment by Prague's Dvořák Society as the primary orchestra for a competitive Dvořák Series, and the gold Mahler Medal awarded by the International Gustav Mahler Society of Vienna.

Prof. Horst Förster took over from Bongartz in 1964, remaining as director until 1967, when a student of Bongartz, Kurt Masur, took the podium. Previously the associate director of the Dresden Philharmonic (1955–1958), Masur's musicianship with the ensemble was characterized as dramatic, expressive, bold, and passionate.

A noteworthy event of this era was the fruition of a plan that had been espoused by both former directors Bongartz and Förster—the formation of a Philharmonic

Chorus, an amateur group with both adult and children's choruses. Directors of this chorus have included Wolfgang Berger, Hartmut Haenchen, and Matthias Geissler. The chorus first sang with the orchestra in the October 7, 1970, performance of Beethoven's Ninth Symphony conducted by Masur in celebration of the opening of the orchestra's new home, the 2,400-seat concert hall of the Dresden Palace of Culture (Dresdner Kulturpalast).

The orchestra's Centennial Concerts took place November 22–29, 1970. Widely broadcast on radio and television, the celebration included a return performance of Bongartz on the podium as well as other guest performances and several premieres. The festival week was closed with Masur conducting Beethoven's Ninth Symphony.

Masur left the Dresden Philharmonic in 1972. His successor, Günther Herbig, was as analytical and meticulous as Masur had been expressive and bold. Herbig's style was reminiscent of Bongartz's, and among his memorable symphonic performances with the orchestra were works of Mahler, Anton Bruckner, and Carl Nielsen. Extensive touring in 13 countries characterized this era.

The 1977–1978 season marked the beginning of the most recent chapter in the Dresden Philharmonic's history with the appointment of Prof. Herbert Kegel as artistic director. Kegel has an extensive background in choral literature, opera, and contemporary works. Hence the orchestra's repertoire in major choral literature has expanded under Kegel. It has recently included Mahler's Eighth Symphony; Beethoven's Ninth; Mozart's *Requiem*; Schubert's Mass in A-flat Major; a premiere of Rainer Kunad's cantata, *Metai*; concert performances of Ravel's opera *L'Enfant et les Sortilèges* and Wagner's *Parsifal*; and a joint production in the Dresden Cathedral of Benjamin Britten's *War Requiem* by the BBC and East German Television (DDR-Fernsehen). Understandably, the Philharmonic Chorus increased in stature and ability by working with such professional groups as the Leipzig Radio Chorus and the Dresden State Opera Chorus.

Hindemith and Mozart cycles and a two-year series of Beethoven symphonies and overtures have been features of the Kegel era. The repertoire of the orchestra has expanded considerably, especially in twentieth-century music. This has not been at the expense of earlier masters, and Kegel's affinity for Mahler is well documented; however, his work with modern music has been said to influence his approach toward earlier classics, fine tuning, attention to rhythms, and technical detail.

RECORDING HISTORY AND SELECTIVE DISCOGRAPHY: The Dresden Philharmonic first recorded in 1937 as the "Dresdner Philharmoniker," under Paul van Kempen. Among its notable recordings are the centennial recordings of Prokofiev's *Classical* Symphony and Tchaikovsky's Second Symphony, both under Masur; the series of Haydn's "London" Symphonies under Herbig; a complete cycle of Mozart Piano Concertos under Masur (Annerose Schmidt, soloist); and a cycle of Beethoven symphonies under Kegel. These, however, are just a few of the titles, and the orchestra's recorded repertoire on Eterna (1970–1984) includes at least three dozen classical, romantic, and twentieth-century composers. More particularly, recordings have been many under Kegel, with

works by Brahms, Mahler, Berg, Stravinsky, Hindemith, Boris Blacher, Krzysztof Pen-
derecki, and Manfred Weiss, to name a few. Of all these recordings, only a few of the
Beethoven symphonies are currently in print and available in Western countries.
Beethoven, Symphonies Nos. 1 and 8 (Kegel): Pro Arte S 614. Beethoven, Symphony
No. 5 (Kegel): Pro Arte S 601. Beethoven, Symphony No. 7 (Kegel): Pro Arte S 600.

CHRONOLOGY OF MUSIC DIRECTORS: Moritz Erdmann Puffholdt, 1870–1871.
Hermann Gustav Mannsfeldt, 1871–1885. M. Zimmermann, 1885–1886. Ernst Stahl,
1886–1890. August Trenkler, 1890–1903. Willy Olsen, 1903–1915. Edwin Lindner,
1915–1923. Joseph Gustav Mraczek, 1923–1924. Eduard Mörike, 1924–1929. Paul
Scheinpflug, 1929–1932. Werner Ladwig, 1932–1934. Paul van Kempen, 1934–1942.
Carl Schuricht (with Otto Matzerath, Bernardino Molinari, Kurt Eichhorn), 1942–1944.
Gerhart Wiesenhütter, 1945–1946. Heinz Bongartz, 1947–1964. Horst Förster, 1964–
1967. Kurt Masur, 1967–1972. Günther Herbig, 1972–1976. Herbert Kegel, 1977–
present.

BIBLIOGRAPHY: Correspondence between Dresden Philharmonic Artistic Manager
Dieter Härtwig and Robert R. Craven, 1983–1984. Dresden Philharmonic Program Notes
and Prospectus, 1983–1984. Dieter Härtwig, *Die Dresdner Philharmonie: Eine Chronik
des Orchesters 1870–1970* (Leipzig: Deutscher Verlag für Musik, 1970). Dieter Härtwig,
Die Dresdner Philharmonie—Einst und Heute (N.p., 1983), pamphlet. Dieter Härtwig,
Die Dresdner Philharmonie (Leipzig: Bibliographischer Institute, 1985).

ACCESS: Dresden Philharmonic, Kulturplast am Altmarkt, PSF 368, 8012 Dresden.
4866–285. Dieter Härtwig, Artistic Manager.

KRISTIN E. CARMICHAEL

Dresden Staatskapelle

One of the oldest orchestras in Europe, the Dresden Staatskapelle can claim
a continuous history of more than four centuries. It preserves in its name the
term *Kapelle* (chapel), denoting that originally its duty was providing choral
music for the religious observances of its ducal patron; since the seventeenth
century, however, it has been occupied principally with opera and concert music.
Today the ensemble is famous for the distinctive tone color it brings to the
dramatic works of Carl Maria von Weber and Richard Wagner (which it learned
directly from the composers) and the operas of Richard Strauss (most of which
it gave as premieres).

The Kapelle's home has traditionally been the Semper Opera House, an opulent
neo-Renaissance structure with a circular auditorium whose level floor and four
galleries hold 1,326 seats. The building was bombed in the last days of World
War II but reopened in 1985 completely restored. Save for a larger fly tower
and more modern stage mechanics, the building today appears exactly as it did
in the nineteenth century, with even its wall and ceiling paintings and allegorical
stage curtain undisturbed. Subtle adjustments to the audience space have improved sight lines and enhanced the already notable acoustics, while a modern
annex has been added, housing a box office, cloakroom, and administrative
offices, connected to the original auditorium by a bridge. As well as its schedule

with the Kapelle, the Opera House accommodates regular performances by visiting opera and ballet companies and by concert artists from all over the world.

Since the seventeenth century the Kapelle has had a complex administrative structure, involving not one music director but a hierarchy of officials with various titles and functions. Generally, a Hofkapellmeister or general music director has been in overall control of musical matters and director of the major operatic performances, while up to two Kapellmeisters have conducted opera and concerts, and Vice Kapellmeister or music directors have had charge of music for the principal church services and lesser entertainments. Consequently, several figures in the chronology at the end of this entry have overlapping terms; moreover, substantial work was done by conductors who never obtained official rank. The Czech composer Jan Dismas Zelenka (1679–1745), for example, though untitled, undertook many directorial duties while the ailing Johann David Heinichen (1683–1729) was Kapellmeister.

Overall artistic policy was traditionally in the hands of an Intendant, a Saxon nobleman appointed by the court, and the Kapelle was prey not just to the whims of royal taste but also to the wiles of courtly intrigue. Today the Kapelle is part of a network of 88 state-run ensembles in the German Democratic Republic (East Germany); under its present conductor, Herbert Blomstedt, it maintains a comprehensive repertoire, with emphasis on composers whose works it once pioneered, such as Hans Pfitzner, Mahler, Weber, Wagner, and Richard Strauss.

Situated on the banks of the Elbe, Dresden was once a picturesque city of historic churches, palaces, and academies. When the Kapelle was established in 1548 by the Elector of Saxony, its 19 members were at first chiefly choristers whose duty was to provide music for the Lutheran services; they performed choral works by their early Kapellmeister, Johann Walter (1496–1570) and Matthaeus Le Maistre (d. 1557). During more than 20 years under the singer-composer Rogier Michael (1552–1611), the ensemble grew to 40 singers and instrumentalists and the duties began to include music for court ceremonies, banquets, comedies, and festivals. Michael's assistants included such influential younger composers as Michael Praetorius, Johann Schein, and Heinrich Schütz, and when Schütz succeeded him in 1617 the Kapelle was the largest and most important musical body in Protestant Germany.

Throughout its subsequent history, however, the Kapelle's development was periodically disturbed by the conflicts in which Dresden became enmeshed, several of which destroyed historic auditoriums within the city and dispersed the ensemble's members. Schütz was at first able to develop large-scale performances for the court ceremonies, involving multiple choirs of voices, wind, and stringed instruments; but the Thirty Years' War took a devastating toll, and by 1639 only ten musicians remained at the Kapelle. In the aftermath of the war, Schütz worked tirelessly at reorganizing musical life, not just in Dresden, but throughout Germany. Sadly, by the 1660s, when a revival of the Kapelle gathered momentum, he was already an old man, relieved of active duties and living on a reduced stipend.

Schütz, the greatest German composer of his day, had spent two periods studying at Venice, and he was responsible for appointing a number of Italian musicians to the Kapelle and introducing various Italian idioms and techniques to its work. Italian influences at Dresden intensified with the accession of Elector Johann Georg II in 1665; an opera enthusiast, the new Elector built an opera house on the Taschenberg, combined his own musicians with those of his predecessor to bring the Kapelle to a strength of 35, and engaged the Italian castrato-composer Angelini Bontempi (1674–1701) to open the opera house in 1667 with a performance of his *Tesea*. Italian opera was secured as the Kapelle's central activity after the accession of Friedrich August I (the Strong) in 1694, who converted to Catholicism. More Italians achieved the rank of Kapellmeister, including Vincenzo Albrici (1631–1696) and Giovanni Alberto Ristori (1692–1753). A more elaborate, 814-seat opera house was built in the Zwinger and opened in 1719 with a performance of *Giove in Argo*, under its composer Antonio Lotti (1667–1740). By this time Dresden had become the major conduit through which Italian styles and genres spread northward in Germany; both Handel and Telemann held its performances in high regard.

With the appointment of Johann Adolf Hasse as Hofkapellmeister in 1734, the orchestra entered the most dazzling phase of its history. Hasse (1699–1783) was already internationally acclaimed as the leading composer of *opera seria* of the age, and he continued to make numerous tours abroad to supervise performances of his works throughout the two decades of his activity at Dresden. In his direction of the Kapelle he insisted on placing artistic excellence before all else. Ignoring pressures for German membership in the orchestra, he recruited internationally famous players, including the flutists Pierre Buffardin and Johann Joachim Quantz. The violinist Johann Georg Pisendel (1687–1755), who Hasse made concertmaster, was the greatest violinist of the day, a pupil of Torelli and Vivaldi for whom Bach, Vivaldi, and Albioni had written works. Pisendel introduced the concertos and chamber works of Albioni, Vivaldi, and Tartini, as well as works by such German composers as Telemann; Johann Fasch; Christoph Graupner; Gottfried Stölzel; Johann Joachim Quantz; Franz and Georg Benda; and August, Carl, and Johann Graun. Hasse's organization of the orchestra, his standards, and his method of seating became models for other orchestras established in these years at Berlin, Mannheim, Prague, and Leipzig. The Kapelle in his time was described by Quantz as the best in Germany and by Jean-Jacques Rousseau as one of the two best in Europe.

Hasse's achievements, however, were rapidly undone by the Seven Years War, during which, in 1756, Saxony was defeated. The Zwinger Opera House was used by the military during the fighting, and the salaries to the Kapelle members were suspended. Pisendel died in 1755, and after the war even the salary offering for the Kapellmeister was too low to attract a musician of distinction. The obscure composer Domenico Fischietti (1725–1810) was engaged as music director, and when Charles Burney visited Dresden in 1772 he found few of the distinguished figures of Hasse's time remaining in the Kapelle.

Matters improved with the appointment of the Dresden-trained composer Johann Gottlieb Naumann (1741–1811) as Kapellmeister in 1786. Naumann began to rebuild the membership of the Kapelle, and he established a series of subscription concerts, at which the new concert works of Haydn and Mozart were introduced. In the theatre, however, the repertoire rarely ventured beyond Italian *opera buffa*, the highly esteemed works of Hasse, and inconsequential imitations of Hasse by Naumann and his colleagues. The Dresden-born Joseph Schuster (1748–1812) gained a following with *Singspiel*; Ferdinando Paër (1771–1839) was less successful in the theatre than in the church; the singer-composer Vincenzo Rastrelli (1760–1839) largely worked at directing music for the liturgy; and Naumann's pupil Franz Seydelmann (1748–1806), once he obtained official rank in the Kapelle, was usually too drunk to be productive. None of the reform operas of Gluck or Luigi Cherubini was attempted, and by the first years of the nineteenth century both the orchestra's playing and its repertoire were indifferent.

Naumann died, absurdly, of drowning after falling in a ditch while out walking. In 1813 the Napoleonic campaigns brought another war to Dresden, and a terrible battle was fought under the city walls; nevertheless, the Kapelle's fortunes were now improving under the direction of Francesco Morlacchi (1784–1841), appointed Kapellmeister in 1811. Arriving at Dresden after a distinguished career in Italy, Morlacchi was a dynamic director and a brilliant musician who played most orchestral instruments himself. When he arrived the concertmaster was Cristofero Babbi (1745–1814), a player of taste and feeling but hardly of the front rank; Morlacchi saw to it that he was succeeded by an internationally known figure, Giovanni Polledro (1781–1853), the finest violinist since Giovanni Battista Viotti. Morlacchi made many outstanding appointments to the orchestra; on Polledro's departure in 1824 he secured a no less distinguished figure in Giuseppe Antonio Rolla (1798–1837), and then in 1839 Karol Lipinski (1790–1861), a virtuoso for a time thought to rival Paganini, and whose pupils included Joseph Joachim and Henryk Wieniawski. Morlacchi established a tradition of annual pension fund concerts in 1829 in which he led such rare performances as Bach's *St. Matthew Passion*, and he expanded the orchestra to nearly 50. At his death in 1841 the Kapelle's reputation from the days of Hasse had largely been restored.

Significantly, Morlacchi's term coincided with the rise of an indigenous reaction against the Italian dominance of Dresden's musical affairs. Carl Maria von Weber was appointed to direct the "German Opera," and despite numerous intrigues by Morlacchi and his supporters at court, Weber's *Der Freischütz* achieved a success that could not be contained. Karl Reissiger (1798–1859), appointed music director after Weber's untimely death in 1826, eventually outpaced Morlacchi with excellent performances of Weber's *Oberon* and *Euryanthe* and the hugely successful premiere of Wagner's *Rienzi*; and when Wagner joined Reissiger as Kapellmeister in 1843, the repertoire included the newest German and French works as well as the Italian favorites.

Adherence in the Kapelle to practices established by Hasse was now a vice rather than a virtue. Many of the scores of the early nineteenth century demanded a method of orchestral directions and seating different from those of the eighteenth century. Both Weber and Wagner had petitioned the Dresden court for changes, and Wagner succeeded in instituting a more modern method of seating for opera, as well as in abolishing the Kapelle's old habit of playing concert music with the instruments arranged in semicircular rows. Wagner also obtained an increase in the orchestra's size to 60 and for his legendary Beethoven concerts directed the orchestra from the front in the modern manner. Still, he was obliged to continue directing opera from the footlights, with the orchestra behind him; it was not until the days of Ernest von Schuch that this practice was abandoned at Dresden. Guest conductors in these years included Berlioz, Louis Spohr, Johann Nepomuk Hummel, Mendelssohn, Schumann, Liszt, and Hans von Bülow.

The 1849 Dresden Revolution saw the Zwinger Opera House burned down, but it had only been used for concerts and lesser entertainments since the 1841 opening of the predecessor to the present building, designed by Gottfried Semper. Wagner had been implicated in the Revolution, and after he fled Dresden Karl Krebs (1804–1880) was appointed. Krebs gave excellent performances of the grand operas of Giacomo Meyerbeer and Gaspare Spontini, but in general the next three decades were not an outstanding period for the orchestra.

The cellist-conductor Julius Rietz (1812–1877), who succeeded Reissiger in 1860, proved a fine administrator but a lackluster conductor, and his reputation declined during his Dresden years; Franz Wüllner (1832–1902), who had been an important figure at the Munich Opera, became enmeshed in endless difficulties with the court at Dresden, and eventually was forced to relinquish his position.

The most brilliant period for the Kapelle after the time of Hasse was its 40 years under Ernst von Schuch (1846–1914). After his debut with the orchestra in 1872, Schuch was appointed Kapellmeister with Rietz and Wüllner in 1873, achieved sole charge of the establishment in 1882, and became General Music Director in 1889. The Semper Opera House had burned down in 1869 but was rebuilt in 1878, and Schuch greatly expanded the repertoire of works presented there: he conducted 51 world premieres, including Strauss's *Salome*, *Electra*, and *Rosenkavalier*. He also added 117 works to the Dresden repertoire, including many by Wagner, Puccini, Ernö von Dohnányi, Ignacy Padereweski, and Ermanno Wolf-Ferrari. He gave regular subscription concerts in the opera house, introducing new scores by Elgar, Debussy, Hans Pfitzner, Max Reger, Mahler, and Sir Charles Villiers Stanford, as well as by younger German composers. Schuch was a conductor of unusual intelligence and refinement; when he left, the orchestra had a worldwide reputation.

Schuch's tradition of operatic premieres continued for some years after his death. Fritz Reiner introduced Strauss's *Die Frau ohne Schatten*, and Fritz Busch conducted the premieres of Strauss's *Intermezzo* and *Die Aegyptische Helena*, Busoni's *Doktor Faust*, Weill's *Der Protagonist*, and Hindemith's *Cardillac*. Busch was at first coolly received a Dresden, but his revivals of Verdi and his championship of such younger composers as Pfitzner eventually won him great esteem; inevitably, his vocal opposition to the Nazis drove him from his position in 1933. Karl Böhm, appointed to succeed Busch after a brilliant debut, conducted the premieres of Strauss's *Daphne* and *Die schweigsame Frau*, as well as new works of Rudolf Wagner-Régeny and Heinrich Sutermeister; Karl Elmendorff (1891–1962) introduced Joseph Hasse's *Die Hochzeit des Jobs* and Hermann Goetz's *Der Wilderspeistiger.*

The devastating bombing of Dresden in 1945 largely destroyed the Semper Opera House, and after the war the Kapelle performed in temporary halls or, from 1948, in the reopened Schauspielhaus. A series of conductors now held three- or four-year terms with the orchestra, including Franz Konwitschny, who was also engaged at the Leipzig Gewandhaus Orchestra*; Rudolf Neuhaus (b. 1914), who conducted the premieres of Fidelio Finke's *Der Zauberfisch* and Rainer Kunad's *Maître Pathelin*, and Kurt Sanderling, who also led the Berlin Symphony Orchestra. The present conductor, Herbert Blomstedt, has occupied the position for 11 years; on February 13, 1985, he opened the restored Semper Opera House with a performance of Weber's *Der Freischütz.*

RECORDING HISTORY AND SELECTIVE DISCOGRAPHY: The orchestra has made numerous recordings since 1950 including many on labels with international distribution, such as Deutsche Grammophon, Angel/HMV/Seraphim, Philips, and RCA. Although the currently-available recordings of the Dresden Staatskapelle include opera performances, symphonic music is more widely represented than opera.

Beethoven, Overtures (Karl Böhm): DGG Priviledge 253513. Borodin, *In the Steppes of Central Asia* (Sanderling): DGG 2535664. Mahler, Symphony No. 1 (Suitner): DGG Heliodor 2548; DG/Japan MGW–5108 PSI. Mozart, Symphonies Nos. 39 and 41 (Colin Davis): Philips 410046–2 PH (CD). Schubert, Complete Symphonies (Sawallisch): Philips Fest. 6770015 (5 records). Strauss, *Alpine* Symphony (Kempe): HMV SLS 861. Strauss, *Also Sprach Zarathustra* (Kempe): HMV Greensleeve ESD 7026; Seraphim S–60283. Strauss, *Aus Italian* (Kempe): HMV ASD 3319; Seraphim S–60301. Strauss, Horn Concertos Nos. 1 and 2 (Damm/Kempe): Angel S–37004. Wagner, *Die Meistersinger* (Karajan): HMV SLS 957. Wagner, *Rienzi* (Hollreiser): HMV SLS990.

CHRONOLOGY OF MUSIC DIRECTORS: (Various titles, some overlapping): Johann Walter, 1548–1554. Matthaeus Le Maistre, 1554–1557. Antonio Scandello, 1568–1580. Pinello di Ghirardi, 1580–1584. Rogier Michael, 1587–1613. Heinrich Schütz, 1617–1672. M. G. Peranda, 1672–1675. Sebastiano Cherici, 1675. Vincenzo Albrici, 1675–1680. Christoph Bernhard, 1681–1692. Nicolaus Adam Strungk, 1692–1697. Johann David Heinichen, 1717–1729. Giovanni Alberto Ristori, 1718–1733. Johann Adolf Hasse, 1734–1756. Domenico Fischietti, 1765–1772. Johann Gottlieb Naumann, 1776–1801. Joseph Schuster, 1787–1812. Franz Sydelmann, 1787–1806. Ferdinando Paër, 1804–1806. Francesco Morlacchi, 1811–1832. Carl Maria von Weber, 1817–1826. Karl Reissiger, 1826–1859. Richard Wagner, 1842–1849. Karl Krebs, 1850–1872. Julius Rietz, 1860–1877. Franz Wüllner, 1878–1882. Ernst von Schuch, 1873–1914. Hermann Kutzschbach, 1898–1906, 1909–1936. Kurt Striegler, 1909–1945, 1952–1953. Fritz Reiner, 1914–1921. Fritz Busch, 1922–1933. Karl Böhm, 1934–1942. Karl Elmendorff, 1943–1944. Joseph Keilberth, 1945–1949. Rudolf Kempe, 1949–1952. Franz Konwitschny, 1953–1955. Rudolf Neuhaus, 1955–1956. Lovro von Matačić, 1956–1958. Otmar

Suitner, 1960–1964. Kurt Sanderling, 1964–1967. Martin Turnovsky, 1967–1968. Siegfried Kurz, 1971–1974. Herbert Blomstedt, 1975-present.

BIBLIOGRAPHY: Warren A. Bebbington, "The Orchestral Conducting Practice of
Richard Wagner," Ph.D. Diss., City University of New York, 1983. Hans von Brescius,
*Die Königliche musikalische Kapelle von Reissiger bis Schuch (1826–1898): Festschrift
zur Feier des 350-jährigen Kapelljubiläums* (Dresden: C. C. Meinhold & Söhne, 1898).
Adam Carse, *The Orchestra in the Eighteenth Century* (1940; rpt., New York: Broude,
1969). Adam Carse, *The Orchestra from Beethoven to Berlioz* (New York: Broude, 1948).
F. W. Marpurg, *Historisch-Kritische Beyträge zur Aufnahme der Musik* (Berlin, 1754–
57), vol. I, p. 206ff. Robert Prölss, *Geschichte des Hoftheaters zu Dresden* (Dresden:
W. Boensch, 1878). Articles in *Panoram DDR*.

ACCESS: Staatskapelle Dresden, Semperoper, 8010 Dresden.

WARREN A. BEBBINGTON

LEIPZIG   (557,000)

Leipzig Gewandhaus Orchestra

Among the oldest of all full-time symphony orchestras, the Leipzig Gewandhaus Orchestra (LGO) is the direct descendant of a concert ensemble formed
in 1743 and heir to a performing tradition at Leipzig dating back to the 1680s.
The orchestra's title comes from its original auditorium, the Gewandhaus, completed in 1781, the first purpose-built concert hall in Europe. This building was
outgrown long ago, but its name, redolent with two centuries of distinctive music
making, has been proudly preserved.

Although seldom numbering more than 90 on stage, the LGO employs 191
players, for its members also form the orchestra of the Leipzig Opera, the Leipzig
Bach Orchestra, the Neues Bachisches Collegium, and such chamber groups as
the Gewandhaus Quartet and the Gewandhaus Brass Quintet. Each of these
ensembles has an intensive schedule of its own. The Bach Orchestra, for example,
formed in 1962 by Gewandhaus Chief Concertmaster Gerhard Bosse, gives
concerts of Mozart and Bach in period style and frequently tours in its own right.
Additionally, members of the orchestra have teaching responsibilities at the
Leipzig Hochschule für Musik, as they have done since the founding of that
institution in 1843.

The LGO's home since 1981 has been the Neues Gewandhaus, a modern glass
and sandstone structure facing Karl Marx Platz. Here the main auditorium has
1,905 seats whose raked wedges completely encircle the platform. Maroon up-
holstery and dark green, oak-panelled walls contribute to highly satisfying visual
ambience and acoustics. A four-manual, 89-rank Schuke organ holds the listener's eye, its 6,638 pipes arrayed above the platform in glistening silver ensembles,
with horizontal trumpets displayed in striking clusters. A second auditorium
holds 493 moveable seats on a level, wooden floor for the 32 chamber music
concerts given each year. The main foyer, beneath steep balcony walls with

frescoes by Sighard Gille, provides space for informal concerts held on Mondays at 6:00 P.M. The orchestra's choral concerts, particularly those featuring the choir of the Thomasschule and conducted by its cantor, Hans-Joachim Rotzch, are occasionally held in the historic Thomaskirche, once presided over by the city's most revered musical forefather, Johann Sebastian Bach.

Once managed for the citizens of Leipzig by a committee of lawyers and shopkeepers, the LGO is today one of 88 orchestras fully funded and administered by the government of the German Democratic Republic. The orchestra gives 100 concerts each year, arranged in three subscription series (Thursdays and Fridays), a Tuesday series, a new works series, a special series, an autumn festival, school concerts, and workers' concerts. Through these appearances it reaches a live audience of over 100,000 each year; through its other ensembles and radio or television broadcasts it reaches an audience many times larger still.

During more than 16 years under its present conductor, Kurt Masur, the orchestra has relied on thematic programming, such as cycles of works by Beethoven, Mendelssohn, Bruckner, Max Reger, or Mahler; nevertheless, a place has always been found for new music, and Masur has propagated scores by such contemporary German composers as Fritz Geissler, Siegfried Matthus, Wilhelm Weissmann, Thomas Heyhn, and Reinhardt Pfundt. Masur has also increased the orchestra's touring activities, and the LGO has now appeared in almost every European capital from Moscow to London, as well as extensively in North and South America, Canada, and Japan.

Seventeenth-century Leipzig was a particularly likely city for the early establishment of a symphony orchestra. In most German towns the oversight of a court meant that symphony concerts were given in the shadow of opera and depended on the availability of theatre musicians. Unless they were given on Fridays or during Lent, when the theatres were closed, orchestral concerts had to be largely amateur affairs. Leipzig, however, was free of the influence of a court. A thriving commercial center and university town with a civic government, it was fertile soil for the seeding and growth of public concerts. From 1688 regular concerts were given in a coffeehouse by Kuhnau's Collegium Musicum, formed from university students and city bandsmen; Georg Philipp Telemann's Collegium Musicum, formed in 1704 with some of the same players, is remembered for the many performances it gave of new works, particularly after Bach assumed its directorship in 1729.

The beginning of the LGO can be traced to March 11, 1743, when 16 of the best Collegium Musica musicians were combined to form the Grosses Concert; aside from an interruption during the Seven Years War, this ensemble gave concerts at the Drei Schwänen tavern each Thursday for the next 30 years. At first directed by a certain Zehmisch, in 1763 the Grosses Concert was taken over by the indefatigable Johann Adam Hiller (1728–1804). A prolific composer who virtually founded *Singspiel*, Hiller immensely increased the popularity of the concerts by introducing vocal items performed by well-known singers of the day. Leaving the orchestral numbers to his concertmaster, Georg Häser, who rehearsed and led them from the first desk of the violins, Hiller concentrated on preparing the vocal numbers, which included both popular songs and favorites from the operas of Johann Adolf Hasse, Karl Heinrich Graun, Christoph Willibald Gluck, and many Italian composers of the time. Hiller introduced a subscription scheme and expanded the season to include concerts of sacred works in Lent; within three years he was the most prominent musician in the city, and his concerts were an unassailable feature of Leipzig's musical life.

The Grosses Concert was taken over in 1771 by its clavier player, Georg Simon Löhlein (1725–1781), and attention soon shifted to the Musikübende Gesellschaft, which Hiller founded in 1775 from his students and followers. A permanent home for Hiller's concerts soon became desirable, and as a new *Gewandhaus* (Cloth Hall) was to be built by the clothmakers and wool merchants for their trade fairs, the designer Carl Friedrich Dauth developed an upper floor especially for concerts. This flat-floored, oblong room, later decorated with murals by Johann Ludwig Giesel and ceiling frescoes by Adam Friedrich Oeser, had a low, railed-off platform for the orchestra at one end and 700 seats arranged in lengthways rows to face a central aisle. When Hiller and the orchestra, now numbering 25, presented the first concert there on November 25, 1781, the flat, wooden walls proved to supply fine acoustics for orchestral music.

Hiller's players were neither first-rate musicians nor even specialists on single instruments. His own skills included basic proficiency on every instrument from the flute to the string bass, and his players were often equally dilettante; obviously, the standard of his ensemble did not compare with the major opera orchestras of his time. Still, regular concentration on orchestral works brought a unity of ensemble and precision of execution that became the hallmark of the LGO. A visit to Mitau secured for Hiller the position of Kapellmeister to the Duke of Courland, and in 1785 he was succeeded at Leipzig by Johann Gottfried Schicht (1753–1823), who had played violin in Hiller's ensembles for many years. By the time of Hiller's departure, the orchestra's basic traditions and loyalties had been securely established.

The difficult new symphonies of Beethoven made an early appearance at Leipzig during Schicht's tenure. Led by Bartolomeo Campagnoli, Schicht's concertmaster from 1797, Beethoven's First Symphony was performed at Leipzig in 1801—only a year after its Vienna premiere; his Second in 1804, his Third in 1807, and his Fifth and Sixth in 1809. Campagnoli introduced the Seventh Symphony in 1816, by which time Schicht had been appointed cantor of the Thomasschule and had passed the directorship of the orchestra to his pupil, the song composer Johann Philipp Christian Schulz (1773–1827).

During Schulz's term Beethoven's Eighth Symphony was introduced in 1818 and his Ninth in 1826, both led by Karl Matthäi (1781–1826), who became concertmaster when Campagnoli outstayed a period of leave in 1817. All these performances were unconducted, and obviously, little more than steady pace and smooth tone were achieved. Nevertheless, such visitors to Leipzig as Louis Spohr and Ignaz Moscheles were impressed by what they heard, accustomed as they were to the slipshod arrangements still customary for symphonic music elsewhere. In these years the LGO undoubtedly helped lay the foundation of the Beethoven performance practice and helped make Beethoven's music the staple of orchestral concert programs.

When Schulz died in 1827, the orchestra numbered 38 and was fully professional, its players' duties embracing concerts, operas, and various church and civic ceremonies. During the directorship of the jovial Christian August Pohlenz (1790–1843), the players also formed the Euterpe, at whose meetings they read through the earliest works of such novices as the young Felix Mendelssohn and the completely unknown Richard Wagner. The orchestra's routines rapidly changed, however, once Mendelssohn became director in 1835.

Although remembered chiefly as a composer, Mendelssohn was an outstanding conductor who had developed his accomplishment through directing weekly concerts at his parents' home. The death of Matthäi in the year of Mendelssohn's appointment allowed him to assume control of the rehearsals for the orchestral works—a task that, as a fine violinist, he was able to carry out with undisputed authority. Unprecedented though it was, he conducted all works himself, being one of the first conductors to use a baton. His concertmaster, Ferdinand David, filled a role more akin to his modern equivalent than to his Leipzig predecessors.

Mendelssohn introduced many new works to the repertoire, including Schumann's First, Second, and Fourth Symphonies and Schubert's Ninth, and he restored to the programs many long-neglected works of Bach. He increased the orchestra's size to nearly 50, and partly in an effort to raise its standards, he established the Leipzig Hochschule für Musik, drawing on the orchestra members for teaching staff. Although summoned to a court position at Berlin in 1841, he continued as conductor at Leipzig and in 1842 saw another story added to the Gewandhaus auditorium, providing galleries for the expanding audience. Mendelssohn's rapid-paced, sparkling performances, if not so technically flawless as those achieved by the Paris or London orchestras, were unsurpassed in warmth of spirit and suppleness of execution; his premature death in 1847 was a loss from which the orchestra did not fully recover for 50 years.

Although he had raised salaries in the orchestra, Mendelssohn had been unable to attract players of front rank; particularly in its wind sections the orchestra remained imperfect. Nevertheless, certain habits of rehearsal routine and ensemble had become unshakeable. Tradition by this time was so important in the LGO that even long-standing idiosyncrasies were conservatively retained: the practice, for example, of having the violins and violas play standing remained unchanged until 1905. In the hands of Mendelssohn's successor, conservatism also began to affect the repertoire: the cellist-composer Julius Rietz (1812–1877) revered the scores of Handel and Bach and avoided newer composers such as Liszt. Rietz's attention was never far from popular Italian and French opera; he held the conductorship of the Leipzig Opera for most of his time with the LGO, and in 1860 he left to become conductor of the Dresden Opera.

Even more conservative was the Leipzig-born composer Carl Reinecke (1824–

1910), who for 30 years circumscribed the orchestra's repertoire to Bach, Schumann, Spohr, and others of similar age. Admittedly, Reinecke was a champion of Brahms—he frequently included all four Brahms symphonies in the season, sternly instilling clarity and disciplined ensemble in his performances—but the most adventurous programs during his tenure were those of guest conductors, who included Berlioz, Wagner, Grieg, Richard Strauss, and Tchaikovsky.

That a larger building became necessary during these years owed less to Reinecke than it did to external factors—the population of Leipzig quadrupled between 1850 and 1890. A Neues Gewandhaus, comprising a 1,700-seat concert hall and a 640-seat chamber music hall, was constructed at Königsplatz in the southwestern Music Quarter and opened on December 11, 1884; its opulent decorations and neoclassic lines, designed by Martin Gropius and Heinrich Schmieder, became a model for Symphony Hall, Boston.

Possibly the most dazzling period for the LGO began when the conductor of the Leipzig Opera, Arthur Nikisch (1855–1922), took control of the orchestra in 1895. One of the greatest figures in the history of conducting, Nikisch exacted from the orchestra great beauty of string tone and, through extraordinary control, an uncanny rhythmic freedom, which together generated overwhelmingly passionate readings. He excelled at romantic works and brought forward scores by Berlioz, Liszt, and Wagner long disdained by his predecessors. His interpretive flights on the podium were matched by imaginative programming: he pioneered works by Strauss, Max Reger, Frederick Delius, and Arnold Schoenberg; his premiere of Bruckner's Seventh Symphony brought its composer wide attention; his legendary reading of Tchaikovsky's Fifth Symphony rescued the work from the disastrous impression it had created under its composer's direction. Nikisch developed a thematic style of programming, giving cycles of Brahms, Beethoven, and Bruckner; he inaugurated workers' concerts; and he gave public rehearsals for students. He took the orchestra on its first tour, while during his own absences conducting abroad his guests at Leipzig included Fritz Steinbach, Willem Mengelberg, Ernst von Schuch, Karl Muck, Max Reger, Richard Strauss, and Max von Schillings.

Nikisch had successfully directed the LGO and the Berlin Philharmonic Orchestra* simultaneously for many years, and after his death the fiery young Wilhelm Furtwängler, already in demand in New York, Berlin, and Vienna, was appointed. Furtwängler's absences, however, proved disruptive for the orchestra, and in 1928 he was succeeded by Bruno Walter. Walter's unalloyed, fresh readings of standard repertoire were immediately welcomed at Leipzig, but in 1933 he was forced by the Nazis to resign, and a colorless decade began under Hermann Abendroth (1883–1955), his repertoire constrained by Nazi cultural policy. On February 20, 1944, the Neues Gewandhaus was struck in a bombing raid and completely destroyed.

After the war the austere Kongress-Halle at the Leipzig Zoo, damaged but not destroyed in the bombing raids, was fitted with 1,800 seats. It served as home to the LGO for the next 30 years. The work of restoring the orchestra's reputation was begun by Herbert Albert (b. 1903), and after his appointment to the Graz Opera in 1948 it was continued by the Moravian-born conductor Franz Konwitschny (1901–1962). An expansive conductor who strove to escape from the mundanities of rhythmic beating, Konwitschny gave notable performances of Mahler, Bruckner, and Reger, introduced new scores by such contemporary German composers as Hanns Eisler, Paul Dessau, and Robert Gerster, and made many recordings with the orchestra. After Konwitschny died on tour in Yugoslavia in 1962, the versatile Czech conductor Václav Neumann (b. 1920) provided both satisfying performances of the orchestra's existing repertoire and notable additions of major modern works.

The orchestra's present conductor, Kurt Masur (b. 1927), was appointed when Neumann left to take over the Stuttgart Opera in 1970. Trained at the Leipzig Hochschule für Musik, Masur has a comprehensive repertoire and gives equally dynamic and emotional performances of Bach and Beethoven as he does of Serge Prokofiev and Aram Khachaturian. Conducting a performance of Siegfried Thiele's *Hymn to the Sun* and Beethoven's Ninth Symphony, he proudly presided over the opening of the present Neues Gewandhaus on October 8, 1981.

SELECTIVE DISCOGRAPHY: Beethoven, Complete Symphonies (Konwitschny): Fontana K71BA6DO. Beethoven, *Fidelio* Overtures (Masur): Philips 4162740–4PH6. Brahms, Complete Symphonies, etc. (Masur): Philips 7699109 (4 records). Brahms, *Hungarian Dances* (Masur): Philips 6514305. Mahler, Symphony No. 5 (Neumann): Vanguard C–10011/2. Mendelssohn, Complete Symphonies (Masur): Vanguard 10133/6 (4 records). Prokofiev, Piano Concertos (M. Beroff/Masur): EMI EG290261.

CHRONOLOGY OF MUSIC DIRECTORS: Johann Adam Hiller, 1775–1785. Johann Gottfried Schicht, 1785–1810. Johann Philipp Christian Schulz, 1810–1827. Christian August Pohlenz, 1827–1835. Felix Mendelssohn-Bartholdy, 1835–1847. Julius Rietz, 1848–1860. Carl Reinecke, 1860–1895. Arthur Nikisch, 1895–1922. Wilhelm Furtwängler, 1922–1928. Bruno Walter, 1928–1933. Hermann Abendroth, 1934–1945. Herbert Albert, 1946–1949. Franz Konwitschny, 1949–1962. Václav Neumann, 1964–1968. Heinz Bongartz, 1969. Kurt Masur, 1970-present.

BIBLIOGRAPHY: Warren A. Bebbington, "The Orchestral Conducting Practice of Richard Wagner," Ph.D. Diss., City University of New York, 1983. Adam Carse, *The Orchestra from Beethoven to Berlioz: A History of the Orchestra* (New York: Broude, 1948). Alfred Dörffel, *Geschichte der Gewandhausconcerte zu Leipzig vom 25. November 1781 bis 25 November 1881* (Leipzig: Breitkopf und Härtel, 1884). *Gewandhaus zu Leipzig: Konzertjahr 1985–1986* (Leipzig: Gewandhaus, 1986). Steffen Lieberwirth, *Dokumente zur Gewandhausegeschichte* (Leipzig: Gewandhaus, 1986), 3 vols. Elise Polko, *Reminiscences of Felix Mendelssohn-Bartholdy: A Social and Artistic Biography*, trans. Lady Wallace (New York: Leypoldt & Holt, 1869). August Schmidt, *Musikalische Reise-Momente auf einer Wanderung durch Norddeutschland* (Hamburg: Schuberth, 1846). Louis Spohr, *Louis Spohr's Autobiography* (1865; rpt., New York: Da Capo, 1969).

ACCESS: Leipziger Gewandhaus, Karl-Marx-Platz, 7020 Leipzig. 7796.

WARREN A. BEBBINGTON

WEIMAR   (70,000)

Weimar State Orchestra

In Weimar, a Thuringian town with many cultural connections including links to Goethe, Schiller, and Liszt, concert life is dominated by the State Orchestra. Well known for its operatic achievements, the orchestra has been associated with historic movements in symphonic literature as well. It currently maintains an 11-month season that includes ten symphonic concerts on Thursdays, with repeat performances on Fridays. The State Orchestra maintains several ancillary groups, including the Chamber Orchestra of the Weimarischen Staatskapelle, the Bätzel-Quartett, and the Weimar State Orchestra Wind Quintet.

The beginnings of court music in Weimar date to the year 1482, when a court band of trumpets and tympani is documented. Political events prevented the appearance of a well-established corps of vocal and instrumental musicians until 1650, but the court band nevertheless progressed by fits and starts during the sixteenth century, as seen in the ensemble of 11 trumpeters and four violinists, plus lutenist and tympanist. After the capitulation of Mühlberg in 1573, however, court music was interrupted. The presence of Johann Hermann Schein as Ka-pellmeister in 1616 seemed to offer hope in a time of crisis, but the Thirty Years' War intervened, bringing the music once again to a halt. Within four years of the war's close, however, the court orchestra had been reestablished under Adam Drese, a follower of composers Heinrich Schütz and Johann Rosenmüller. He conducted for only a decade, until 1662, when the court orchestra was once again dissolved, this time upon the death of Duke Wilhelm IV. A new, more permanent ensemble was formed in 1683 under Johann Samuel Drese, Adam's cousin. His 20 musicians were soon faced with the new task of performing as a theatre orchestra in the Weimar Opera founded in 1684. The enterprise was unpropitious, however, for church music would gain ascendency over the theatre in the Court of Weimar.

In 1703 Johann Sebastian Bach joined the court orchestra as a violinist; by 1708 he had become a chamber musician, and by 1714 he was Konzertmeister. His hope to succeed Johann S. Drese (d. 1716), however, did not come true, for Johann Wilhelm Drese, the untalented son of the deceased, was called, and Bach left to become Kapellmeister at the nearby court of Köthenh.

The following years were not happy ones for the court orchestra, as nearly all its musicians were dismissed on political grounds. Two decades passed before new life was seen, little by little—first from 1756 to 1758 under Johann Ernst Bach (distantly related to Johann Sebastian) and then under Ernst Wilhelm Wolf, Kapellmeister from 1768 to 1792. The latter, an opera composer himself, fought on behalf of Mozart, whose operas with the exception of *Idomeneo* were all replayed in Weimar. A sympathy for Mozart was also felt by Johann Wolfgang von Goethe, court theater director from 1791 to 1817; he nevertheless could not work with Wolf, who was followed in the Kapellmeister position by two of

Haydn's pupils, Johann Friedrich Kranz and Franz Seraph von Destouches. Wolf's enthusiasm for Mozart was taken up by a later Kapellmeister, August Bernhard Müller (1810–1817), who was also a champion of Beethoven. *Fidelio* was presented in Weimar in 1816.

Nearly two decades under the next Kapellmeister, the composer Johann Nepomuk Hummel, saw a rise in performance standards and the solidification of a steady repertoire. Operatic offerings expanded to include, in addition to Mozart and Beethoven, Gluck, Weber, and even Rossini. In 1828 a new court theatre was inaugurated, replacing the hall that had burned three years previously, and the program included Beethoven's Ninth Symphony. Although this was the most fertile period of Hummel's career, none of his orchestral compositions seem to have had premiere performances at Weimar; rather they were first presented in Vienna.

Hummel's tenure ended in 1837, and five years later, first on an occasional basis and then full-time from 1848, the position was filled by Franz Liszt, who was just ending an itinerant career as virtuoso soloist. His Konzertmeister from 1849 was the celebrated Joseph Joachim, and other of his friends, notably Hans von Bülow, Ferdinand Hiller, and Joachim Raff, joined him in Weimar as well. With the presence of Liszt, Weimar became a center of European musical culture. A succession of new works were heard there, including in 1850 the premiere performance of Wagner's *Lohengrin*, early performances of *Tannhäuser* and *Fliegende Holländer* in 1852 and 1855, and a Wagner festival in 1853. Considerable reinforcements were certainly needed, because the orchestra was allocated only 38 playing posts as of 1851 (21 strings, 16 winds, one percussion). Liszt's years in Weimar were among his most productive. In addition to major piano works such as most of the *Hungarian Rhapsodies*, the Weimar era saw the production—and premiere performances in the town—of his most memorable orchestral works as well. These included *Les Préludes* (performed under Liszt in 1854), the *Faust-Symphony* (under Liszt in 1857), and two piano concertos— in E-flat Major (under Berlioz, with Liszt as soloist in 1855), and in A Major (under Liszt, with Bronsart playing).

Politics, fashion, and personalities eventually conspired against Liszt. His championship of the avant-garde (and the politically suspect Richard Wagner in particular), antagonism against his relationship with Princess Carolyne von Sayn-Wittgenstein, the death of Grand Duke Charles Frederick and Duchess Marie Pavlovna (both of whom were Liszt supporters), a cadre of musical opponents (including former friends Hiller and Joachim as well as the opera *intendant* Dingelstedt), failure to secure funds for his long-hoped-for production of the *Ring*, and a general shift in taste away from musical expression to the theatre— all made Weimar an increasingly inhospitable environment for Liszt. When in 1858 Liszt's premiere performance of Peter Cornelius's opera *The Barber of Baghdad* was hissed, it was clear that his days in Weimar would soon come to an end.

Following Liszt, the artistic temperature in Weimar was considerably reduced under a triumvirate of directors, Eduard Lassen, Carl Stöhr, and Karl Müller-hartung. Subscription concerts were begun, however, and Müllerhartung, director from 1869, founded in 1872 the Ducal Orchestral School, which later grew into the Hochschule für Musik, whose tradition of orchestral training is carried on today in the State Music School of Weimar under auspices of the Thuringian Ministry of Education. Opera premieres in this period include Camille Saint-Saëns's *Samson and Delilah* (1877), a performance arranged in absentia by Liszt.

The latter years of the court orchestra were distinguished by seasons under Richard Strauss (1889–1894), who was responsible for the introduction in Weimar of Engelbert Humperdinck's *Hänsel und Gretel* in 1893. Strauss's first-composed tone poem, *Macbeth* (performed 1890), and one of his most enduring, *Don Juan* (1889), both received their premiere performances in Weimar. Strauss was followed by Bernhard Stavenhagen (1896–1902) and Peter Raabe (1907–1919), the musicologist who dedicated himself to a chronicle of Liszt's life and works. In addition to producing a two volume biography (1931) containing an extensive catalog, Raabe edited Liszt's works and became the curator of Weimar's Liszt Museum, which remains one of the city's cultural resources.

After World War I the orchestra was renamed the State Orchestra of Weimar, and in the years between the wars the orchestra maintained a roster of some 60 musicians. Under Ernst Praetorius the orchestra's classical heritage was reinforced, in addition to its long association with romantic music. Anton Bruckner's symphonies were played in the orchestral programs. Praetorius stayed until 1933 and was followed by Paul Sixt, who was at the same time directing the Musikhochschule in Weimar. Sixt's efforts were destroyed, however, along with much of Weimar, in the air raids of March 1945.

The orchestra's renaissance was entrusted to Hermann Abendroth, who was previously associated with the Berlin State Orchestra* and the Leipzig Gewandhaus Orchestra.* He cared for the standard repertoire but also saw to the backlog of worthy music that had been unplayed in the years since 1933 and filled his seasons with first performances.

When Abendroth died in 1956 the post of conductor went to Gerhard Pflüger, whose repertoire included contemporary composers such as Dessau and a much-noted Dimitri Shostakovich cycle. The orchestra also took up touring, with trips to various countries of Eastern Europe. Other innovations under Pflüger were school and youth concerts, often preceded by introductory lectures. Pflüger's successor, Lothar Seyfarth, was director at the time of a complete refurbishing of the National Theatre. Two years under Rolf Reuter (1978–1980) were followed by another two under the Weimar native Peter Gülke. In 1983 Rudolf Bräuer, who had been conducting symphonic concerts and a good portion of the operatic programs as well, was called to take Gülke's position when Gülke left for the German Federal Republic. Gülke became the director of the Wuppertal Symphony Orchestra* in 1986.

CHRONOLOGY OF MUSIC DIRECTORS: Johann Hermann Schein, 1615–1616. Johann Samuel Drese, 1683–1716. Georg Christoph Strattner, 1695–1704. Johann Ernst

Bach, 1756–1758. Ernst Wilhelm Wolf, 1768–1792. Johann Friedrich Kranz, 1799–1803. Franz Seraph von Destouches, 1803–1810. August Bernhard Müller, 1810–1817. Johann Nepomuk Hummel, 1819–1837. Hippolyte André Chelard, 1840–1847. Franz Liszt, 1848–1858. Eduard Lassen, 1858–1895. Carl Stöhr, 1868–1889. Karl Müllerhartung, 1869–1889. Richard Strauss, 1889–1894. Bernhard Stavenhagen, 1895–1898. Emil Nikolaus von Rezniczek, 1896–1902. Peter Raabe, 1907–1919. Carl Leonhardt, 1920–1922. Julius Prüwer, 1922–1924. Ernst Praetorius, 1924–1933. Paul Sixt, 1933–1945. Hermann Abendroth, 1945–1956. Gerhard Pflüger, 1957–1973. Lothar Seyfarth, 1973–1978. Rolf Reuter, 1978–1980. Peter Gülke, 1981–1983. Rudolf Bräuer, 1983-present.

BIBLIOGRAPHY: *Festschrift 100 Jahre Abonnementskonzerte der Weimarer Staatsorchester* (Weimar, 1963). *Grove Dictionary of Music and Musicians*, 5th ed. (New York: St. Martins, 1954). Hans John, *Musikstadt Weimar* (Leipzig: VEB Deutscher Verlag für Musik, 1984). *New Grove Dictionary of Music and Musicians* (New York: Macmillan, 1980). Victor Seroff, *Franz Liszt* (New York: Macmillan, 1966).

ACCESS: Weimarische Staatskapelle, Postschliessfach, 5300 Weimar.

JOACHIM DORFMÜLLER
TRANS. PETER JÄHNE

German Federal Republic ——

BADEN-BADEN (40,000)

Southwest Radio Symphony Orchestra

Since 1946 Baden-Baden, a thermal spa at the northern edge of the Black Forest area, has been the seat of the Südwestfunk (Southwest Radio). The Southwest Radio Symphony Orchestra (Sinfonieorchester des Südwestfunks Baden-Baden), with 97 members, is an important seat of the musical avant-garde, a function the orchestra has maintained since its earliest days. It had achieved as of 1984 a list of more than 250 premiere performances, comprising works by a most impressive catalog of contemporary composers.

In addition to its many broadcasting commitments, the orchestra presents about 30 live-audience concerts each season. It also records frequently and tours widely. Recent tours have brought it through France, Austria, the Netherlands, Switzerland, Hungary, Portugal, and Italy. Its primary concert venue at home is Hans-Rosbaud Hall, named after the orchestra's former music director. The orchestra is administered and funded through the Southwest Radio of Baden-Baden.

Ensembles formed from within the orchestra include a brass quintet, the Südwest-Deutsche Bläservereinigung (Southwest German Wind Ensemble), Riedel String Quartet, Aurelia String Quartet, and the Glinka Trio.

In 1946 the Southwest Radio was an institution started by the French occupation forces, and since 1952 it has been a radio station of the government of the State of Baden-Württemberg. The head of the main music department of the station was from the beginning the musical author and publisher of *Melos*, Heinrich Strobel. The newly created Radio Orchestra consisted mainly of members of the Symphony and Resort Orchestra of Baden-Baden (Symphonie- und Kurorchester Baden-Baden), which had dissolved toward the end of World War II.

Decisively taking part in planning for an indigenous symphony orchestra, in 1948 Strobel appointed as its leader Hans Rosbaud (b. Graz, 1895), who was until then chief conductor of the Munich Philharmonic Orchestra.* His engagement signalled an interest in contemporary music in addition to the classical and romantic symphonic literature. Rosbaud and Strobel conceived of programs that since 1950 have brought the orchestra the highest praises in its participation at the annual Donaueschingen Music-Days, especially for its rendering of the most difficult, avant-garde scores. Rosbaud was chief conductor of the orchestra for more than 14 years, after 1957 simultaneously with his residence at the Zurich Tonhalle Orchestra,* until his death on December 29, 1962.

On January 1, 1964, Ernest Bour (b. Thionville, France, 1913) became Rosbaud's successor. Bour had been working at the Strasbourg opera as well as with the French National Orchestra* and had also been guest conductor at the Southwest Radio Station. He had long been involved with modern and experimental music, but he was also especially well versed in the works of Haydn, Mozart, Schubert, and Ravel. Bour believed that musicians, indebted to the progress of music, must devote part of their time to the latest works. Together with Strobel, and since 1965 with Gerth-Wolfgang Baruch, Bour designed a program that continued Rosbaud's concept and even went a step further.

The third chief conductor in the history of the Orchestra, Kazimierz Kord (b. Silesia, Poland, 1930) was formerly the head of the National Philharmonic Orchestra in Warsaw.* He assumed the podium as of January 1, 1980. Baruch's successors, Otto Tomek (1976), Friedrich Hommel (1977), and Christoph Bitter (since 1981), have kept the orchestra guided on the course set by Strobel and Rosbaud. Kord stayed in office until June 30, 1986, when he was succeeded by the chief conductor of the City Opera and Museum Orchestra of Frankfurt am Main,* Michael Gielen (b. Dresden, 1927). An expert in constructing programs combining the classical and contemporary, Gielen was perceived as an optimal candidate for the chief conductorship at Baden-Baden.

RECORDING HISTORY AND SELECTIVE DISCOGRAPHY: The Southwest Radio Orchestra office does not have an official discography. The orchestra has recorded for MGM, Deutsche Grammophon, Orion, Turnabout, and other labels, and is well known around the world for its recordings.

Beethoven, Sextets (Southwest Radio Wind Ensemble): Vox SVBX–579 (3 records). Bruckner, Symphony No. 7 (Rosbaud): Turnabout 34083. Ernst Křenek, *Horizon Circled* (Křenek): Orion 78290. Gyorgy Ligeti, *Atmosphères* (Bour): MGM S-1E13. Karlheinz Stockhausen, *Trans* (Bour): DG 2530726 PSI.

CHRONOLOGY OF MUSIC DIRECTORS: Hans Rosbaud, 1948–1962. Ernest Bour, 1964–1979. Kazimierz Kord, 1980–1986. Michael Gielen, 1986-present.

BIBLIOGRAPHY: Christoph Bitter, *Sinfonieorchester des Sudwestfunks Baden-Baden* (Baden-Baden, 1980).

ACCESS: Sinfonieorchester des Südwestfunks, Orchesterburo, Postfach 820, D–7570 Baden-Baden 1. 07221.2761. Olaf Seesemann, Manager.

JOACHIM DORFMÜLLER
TRANS. ANNELIESE YIENGST

BAMBERG   (70,000)

Bamberg Symphony

A 102-piece orchestra since May 20, 1974, the Bamberg Symphony has parity with the Munich State Opera Orchestra. Well-known conductors such as Werner Egk, Robert Heger, Eugen Jochum, Clemens Krauss, Hans Rosbaud, Hermann Scherchen, and Sir Georg Solti have served as guest conductors, engaged either in Bamberg or on tour. The Bamberg Symphony was the first German orchestra to tour internationally after the Second World War, giving concerts in France (1949), Spain, Portugal, Switzerland, and the Netherlands (1950). It has worked under a recording agreement with Bavarian Broadcasting since 1950, when it began regular radio broadcast programming. In 1963 the orchestra began television broadcasting as well. The orchestra supports a string quintet (formed in 1974), a wind ensemble (oboes, clarinets, horns and bassoons in pairs; formed in 1965), and a percussion quartet (formed in 1984).

The orchestra's repertoire has included standard works from the baroque to the present. While classical and romantic works dominate the repertoire, more than half of all the composers whose works have been rehearsed and performed belonged to the twentieth century. Upon taking into account broadcast productions, it is clear that there has been considerable emphasis upon modern works.

Today, as in the past, the orchestra faces a problem in finding a suitable concert hall. This world renowned and highly respected orchestra has used Bamberg's 1,065-seat Dominican Church as a "temporary" home since 1951. Its concerts in Bamberg are thus limited to about 10 per year. However, the Symphony has acquired a building site (called "An der Weide"), and architectural bids have been pursued. Lack of funds comprises the only remaining obstacle between the orchestra and a badly needed, formal, 1,500-seat concert hall.

The city of Bamberg is situated in northern Bavaria. Despite an intellectual and political history dating to the eleventh century, it is only in the immediate past that Bamberg has possessed an orchestra of any more than regional significance—to say nothing of international renown. Because of political reasons, such an orchestra was not established until immediately after World War II.

On May 5, 1945, just three days before the German surrender, a final rehearsal conducted by Joseph Keilberth in Prague's Rudolphinum was abruptly cut short. The musicians fled—many to the French Zone (which lay near the American Zone, just east of the French border). Keilberth went to Dresden, where he became general music director and chief of the opera. The musicians found a new conductor, Herbert Albert from Leipzig, and began to concertize in the area around Bamberg, constantly expanding their radius of performance.

Hans Knappertsbusch, general music director in Munich, agreed to work with this orchestra as guest conductor, and he was a source of considerable artistic stimulus. It was under his direction that the first major concert tour was undertaken, September 14–27, 1948; the orchestra performed in cities throughout southern Germany as well as in Feldkirch, Austria.

The Bamberg Symphony's association with Joseph Keilberth resumed in 1949, when he agreed to conduct for them as well as for Dresden. On September 7, 1949, the group established itself legally as an association; this action, and the formation ten years later of a Board of Trustees, gave the Bamberg Symphony some certainty of regular support; for it was then possible to exert some influence over the existing subsidy sources—the city of Bamberg and the Bavarian Ministry of Education and Culture.

During the Keilberth era the Bamberg Symphony performed some 70 to 80 concerts each year, with regular foreign tours that included the Benelux countries and the four Scandinavian countries as well as France, Great Britain, Ireland, Yugoslavia, Austria, Spain, and the United States. Under Keilberth's direction the orchestra performed in 150 cities—this along with performances conducted by many of the world's most renowned artists, among them Sergiu Celibidache, André Cluytens, Antál Doráti, Paul Hindemith, Rudolf Kempe, Václav Neumann, Fritz Rieger, Horst Stein, and Lovro von Matačić. Keilberth died in Munich at the age of 60, on July 20, 1968. Thereafter, until 1973, Eugen Jochum took over as chief conductor. The orchestra toured in the Mediterranean region and Hungary as well as North and South America.

When Jochum resigned at the age of 71, Istvan Kertész assumed the post; unfortunately, Kertész himself died shortly afterward (April 16, 1973), and the directorship was again open. For six years the orchestra was again in the hands of leading guest conductors, the post being filled in 1979 by James Loughran (b. Glasgow, 1931), resident conductor of the Hallé Orchestra* in Manchester, England. Loughran remained with the Bamberg Symphony until 1983; he contributed much from his main area of expertise, English music, to the group's considerable classical and romantic repertoire.

The 1983 to 1985 seasons have featured Witold Rowicki (b. Tagenrog, U.S.S.R, 1914), former director of the National Philharmonic in Warsaw.* The 1985–1986 season commenced under the direction of Horst Stein, who was born in Wuppertal-Elberfeld in 1928 and has been associated with the Orchestra de la Suisse Romande.* The orchestra continues to perform with leading soloists and guest conductors of international fame.

RECORDING HISTORY AND SELECTIVE DISCOGRAPHY: The Bamberg Symphony began recording in 1950 under a contract with Bavarian Broadcasting. In 1951 it won the "Grand Prix du Disque" for its recording of Mozart symphonies. Since then it has recorded over 250 performances, largely of music by classical and romantic composers. The orchestra has recorded for Ariola, CRI, Deutsche Grammophon, EMI, Entr'-acte, Erato, Orfeo, Philips, Phonoklub, RCA, Teldec, Turnabout, Vox, and other labels.

Bruckner, Symphony No. 4 (Heinrich Hollreiser): Turnabout 34107. Glazunov, *The Kremlin* and other works (Aldo Ceccato): Arabesque 8091. Mozart, Symphonies Nos. 39, K. 543 and 41, K. 551; *Masonic Funeral Music* (Eugen Jochum): Orfeo S–045832 H (2 records). Tchaikovsky, Symphony No. 5 (Stein): Entr'acte 6511. Wagner, Symphony in C (Otto Gerdes): DG 2543817.

CHRONOLOGY OF MUSIC DIRECTORS: Herbert Albert, 1946–1948. Georg Ludwig Jochum, 1948–1949. Joseph Keilberth, 1949–1968. (Guest conductors, 1968–1971.) Eugen Jochum (Artistic Director), 1971–1973. Istvan Kertész, 1973. (Guest conductors, 1973–1983.) James Loughran (Chief Conductor), 1979–1983. Witold Rowicki, 1983–1985. Horst Stein, 1985-present.

BIBLIOGRAPHY: Lutz Besch, *Bamberger Symphoniker, 1946–1976* (Bamberg, 1973).

ACCESS: Bamberger Symphoniker, Altes Rathaus, D–8600 Bamberg. 0951/57950. Rolf Beck, Intendant.

JOACHIM DORFMÜLLER
TRANS. KRISTIN E. CHARMICHAEL

BERLIN   (WEST: 1,869,000)

Berlin Philharmonic Orchestra

Berlin, onetime capital of the German Empire, today is a divided metropolis in the heart of both the German-speaking world and Europe. With a combined (East-West) population of 3.4 million, Berlin is still one of the world's major cities, with a dynamic economy offering a rich academic and cultural environment. West Berlin has three orchestras of high calibre: the Berlin Philharmonic Orchestra (Berliner Philharmonisches Orchester), the German Opera Orchestra (Orchester der Deutschen Oper), and the Radio Symphony Orchestra (Radio-Sinfonieorchester). Of these, the Philharmonic has the richest history and— because of its high quality—it carries the greatest international significance. Having been led by such conductors as Hans van Bülow, Arthur Nikisch, Wilhelm Furtwängler, and Herbert von Karajan, the Berlin Philharmonic Orchestra is generally acknowledged as one of the world's most polished and influential ensembles.

The organization of the orchestra is unique. It is a democratic entity with all of the attendant rights and responsibilities, or, as Furtwängler described it, "a republic in miniature." The orchestra's most visible self-governing practice is seen in the choice of the resident conductor and the orchestra manager. New members are admitted by vote of the membership after a one-year probationary period, although the resident conductor maintains veto rights. Orchestra members are represented by a two-member executive committee, which is aided by a five-member liaison board that keeps contact with the members at large. Berlin Philharmonic musicians are highly esteemed by their colleagues throughout West Germany and indeed all of Europe.

The orchestra gives approximately 100 concerts in Berlin each year, plus opera performances; it also offers special series with its music director, Herbert von Karajan. Much of the orchestra's funding is self-generated from ticket sales, television productions, broadcasting revenues, and recording royalties.

The Berlin Philharmonic Orchestra travels widely, having by 1984 logged, among others, six United States tours, four to Japan, and virtually annual tours among the metropolitan centers of Europe. It has also taken part in festivals in Athens, Edinburgh, Leningrad, Lucerne, Moscow, Prague, Salzburg, and Vienna.

Since the advent of Herbert von Karajan in 1955, the orchestra has recorded extensively (under the title "Berliner Philharmoniker"), making it one of the world's most prolific recording ensembles. Its historic recordings now available in re-release comprise a major historical document in the practice of orchestral performance.

Currently there are several ensembles formed from within the 114-member Philharmonic. They include three string quartets (Bottger, Brandis, and West-phalian), the Philharmonic Soloists (a quintet), the Philharmonic Octet, and the Twelve Philharmonic Cellists.

The Berlin Philharmonic Orchestra has its origins in a group known as "Bilse's Band" (die "Bilsesche Kapelle"), which was founded in 1862 and directed by Benjamin Bilse, music director for the royal court. Over the next 20 years this group gave some 3,000 concerts, earning it considerable popularity. From these 60 or so musicians and from a comparable number of other musicians, another group emerged under the leadership of hornist Otto Schneider and violinist Richard Jäger. However, after a guest performance of the Court Orchestra of Meiningen (Meininger Hofkapelle) under the direction of Hans von Bülow, this newly formed group decided that their artistic standards should be higher and that their financial situation should be improved. This was something of which Bilse was incapable, and on March 16, 1882, the group chose Ludwig von Brenner as their principal conductor. They retained the services of Hermann Wolff (founder of a concert agency in Berlin in 1880); he would be an important adviser in their financial and organizational considerations. Wolff had the highest artistic standards, and he managed to engage such conductors as Franz Wüllner, Karl Klindworth, and Joseph Joachim, as well as guest conductors Johannes Brahms and Hans von Bülow.

With the latter, whom Wolff managed to engage as principal conductor in 1887 (with the first subscription concert on October 21), begins the actual history of the orchestra that had already been in existence for five years. Von Bülow, born in Dresden in 1830, had long been a pianist and conductor of renown; he is today seen as a pivotal force in the history of the art of conducting. From the beginning of his tenure, he concentrated on a classical and romantic symphonic repertoire. His high standards laid the foundation for the orchestra's later world fame. His guest conductors also added to the orchestra's growth—among them were Tchaikovsky (1888), Brahms and Grieg (1889), and Strauss (1891). Finances improved considerably and a pension fund was begun; those members of the Philharmonic with ten years' service were eligible to receive benefits. The orchestra's inadequate home in the Bernburger Street roller skating rink (secured under Wolff) was totally renovated under von Bülow. It reopened on October 5, 1888.

Citing personal reasons, von Bülow terminated his contract at the end of the

1891–1892 season, but he returned the following season along with guest conductor Richard Strauss and others. On February 12, 1894, von Bülow died in Cairo, where he had gone because of ill health. Two days later, Franz Mannstaedt, the resident conductor of the Berlin popular concerts, led the Philharmonic at the funeral ceremony. On February 19 Ernst von Schuch conducted the memorial concert. For the next few years Wolff engaged Hans Richter and Felix von Weingartner, among others; Richard Strauss was also contracted to conduct ten Philharmonic concerts.

On October 14, 1895, the Hungarian-born Arthur Nikisch (b. 1855) made his debut as resident conductor. His repertoire was founded in Beethoven and Brahms, but he also devoted energy to works by Tchaikovsky, Bruckner, Liszt, Schumann, Mahler, and Strauss. Composers of the Haydn-Mozart era were seldom heard; nor were those of the current avant-garde. Guest conductors were Brahms, Karl Muck, Wilhelm Furtwängler, Mahler, Bruno Walter, Strauss, and especially for contemporary music, Hermann Scherchen, Otto Klemperer, and Oskar Fried. During the Nikisch era the instrumentalists who came to Bernburger Street to perform with the orchestra numbered among the absolute elite.

International acclaim followed tours to France and Belgium (1897), Russia and Poland (1899), and Austria and southern and western Europe (1900–1901). The "Berliner" soon became the most widely known and respected touring orchestra of the Continent. During the summer months they made regular guest appearances (until 1911) in the Casino (Kursaal) of the Dutch city of Scheveningen; during the regular concert season there were regular Sunday and Tuesday pops concerts (Populäre Konzerte). These latter were led by Josef Rebiček from 1897 to 1903; then by Ernst Kunwald until 1912; until 1919 by Camillo Hildebrand; and until 1925 by Richard Hagel. When Hermann Wolff died in 1902, management of the now-incorporated orchestra passed into the hands of his widow, Louise Wolff.

Nikisch last conducted the Philharmonic on January 9, 1922, just 14 days before he died. Fundamentally different in personality and directing technique from his predecessor, Nikisch was the prototype of the romantic-sentimental, genuinely expressive conductor. If von Bülow could be credited with imparting a distinct sense of the logic of musical structures, Nikisch was the one who brought out the poetry, the color, the mystery. This was to be his most lasting contribution.

Nikisch's death came during difficult times, for there were the German defeat of World War I, the Weimar Republic, and an advancing artistic avant-garde that caused a rift between the romantic and the radical. Every Nikisch follower no doubt had strong opinions regarding the new music. It was in the midst of these conditions that Wilhelm Furtwängler, a native Berliner born in 1886, came to conduct the Nikisch memorial concert on February 6, 1922. Known to the Philharmonic by virtue of his 1918–1919 music cycle with them, he became Nikisch's successor on October 9, 1922. His programs concentrated heavily on Beethoven, Brahms, and Bruckner. He dedicated with his unique artistry ten

Philharmonic concerts every year to these composers and set standards of international scope. He was acclaimed as an interpreter of Beethoven's *Eroica* and other odd-numbered (*ungerade*) symphonies. His devotion extended to Schubert, Schumann, Richard Strauss, and Hans Pfitzner, but not Mahler.

Nevertheless, many world and orchestra premieres were part of Furtwängler's era: Debussy, Honegger, Stravinsky, Hindemith, Bartók, Kurt Weill, Prokofiev, and Arnold Schoenberg—the heretofore suppressed demand was considerable. Furtwängler conducted 432 concerts during the two decades until 1942. This was along with 54 tours in 24 countries, visiting 145 cities to perform 653 concerts (34 in Paris alone, 26 in London). Of these, 229 were directed by guest conductors, chief among whom were Knappertsbusch, Eugen Jochum, Clemens Krauss, and Hermann Abendroth. The Berlin concerts were regularly repeated in Hamburg.

Klemperer and Kleiber appeared in Berlin as guest conductors with their own series of concerts, as did Bruno Walter, who conducted Mozart, Beethoven, Schumann, and Mahler and also gave exemplary performances of Shostakovich, Stravinsky, Prokofiev, and Janáček. Also, Oskar Fried had a special engagement for the modern music, as did Felix von Weingartner, Hermann Scherchen, Fritz Busch, and Klaus Pringsheim, who conducted the first Mahler cycle. Conducting their own works were Alexander Glazunov, Ferruccio Busoni, Carl Nielsen, Erich Korngold, Ottorino Respighi, Igor Stravinsky, Hans Pfitzner, Hermann Zilcher, Fritz Büchtiger, and Paul Höffer. In 1922 the first concert of the International Society for New Music (die Internationale Gesellschaft für Neue Musik) took place under the direction of Ernest Ansermet. No less illustrious are the names of the guest soloists during the Furtwängler era, among them Bartók, Rachmaninoff, Karol Szymanowski, Yehudi Menuhin (with a debut at age 12), Hindemith, Pierre Fournier—and more of similar rank.

The worldwide economic crisis of 1929 brought the orchestra to difficult times; only with the help of subsidies from the city of Berlin, the national regime, and the Berlin Radio Network was it able to survive. Hitler's seizure of power in 1933 brought new problems to the orchestra: Walter was no longer allowed to conduct; Klemperer and Kleiber emigrated. In an article entitled "Hindemith's Downfall" ("Der Fall Hindemith") written for the newspaper *Deutsche Allgemeine Zeitung*, Furtwängler supported the man whom he felt was the most significant German composer of the time. In any case, he included therein a strong personal reprimand to Propaganda Minister Goebbels; and he saw no other recourse than to resign all of his posts: leadership of the Philharmonic and of the Prussian State Opera (der Preussische Staatsoper), as well as the vice presidency of the German National Department of Music (Reichsmusikkammer).

Furtwängler returned to the podium after four months' absence (in March 1935) to great public acclaim. Enticing invitations came his way, such as Toscanini's recommendation to the New York Philharmonic,** but Furtwängler was to stay in Berlin. He continued to strengthen the already proverbial standards of the orchestra, which became an oasis of pure art of the highest order, standing above political power struggles. Most helpful to the orchestra was the restructuring of the position of artistic leader and later that of manager. After the death of Louise Wolff, this latter position went to Hans von Benda (1935–1939) who was followed by Gerhart von Westerman—first until 1945 and then after 1952. In 1933 the position of pops concert conductor (filled after Karl Nagel by Julius Prüwer) was abolished. It was felt that the orchestra should no longer be responsible for two such different endeavors (striving for perfection with the resident or guest conductors on the one hand and the routine performance of simple material on the other). It seemed that the important task of exposing wide segments of the population to good music was being taken over by radio broadcasting.

On January 30, 1944, the Philharmonic building was totally destroyed by a bombing raid. The orchestra had to seek out other performance spaces at the State Opera; the Cathedral; at the Admiral's Palace, where Furtwängler's last concert before the surrender took place on January 22, 1945; and at the Beethoven Concert Hall, where, under Heger's direction, the last Philharmonic concert before the surrender took place on April 6, 1945.

Just six weeks later, May 26, 1945, the Philharmonic resumed its work in the postwar environment under the direction of Leo Borchard, who had been named as the new resident conductor. The orchestra began in the Titania-Palast, a movie theatre, and for nearly a decade this edifice would be the center for West Berlin's musical life. The conditions under which the orchestra had to work were the most primitive in its history. But regained freedom and the hopes for a better future inspired the musicians, and with them, the Berliners who came in droves to those first concerts.

But Borchard was shot and killed by an Occupation soldier on August 23, 1945 (as was Anton Webern one month later in Mittersill, Austria). Furtwängler was still unavailable because of continuing political vindication proceedings. Hence, Sergiu Celibidache took over leadership beginning with the concert scheduled by Borchard for August 29, 1945. The 33-year-old conductor was received with tumultuous praise and was seen as the one most worthy to carry on after Furtwängler. This succession was legitimized by prolific work in Berlin as well as by numerous German tours. These programs concentrated much on Beethoven and primarily on the music of Eastern Europe; but there was also an increasing preoccupation with the music that had been banned between 1933 and 1945—contemporary work of the 1920s through 1940s.

On May 25, 1947, Furtwängler, released at last, conducted once again in Berlin. He remained and led the orchestra along with Celibidache both at home as well as on tours that included more and more foreign ventures. Not until February 1952, however, did Furtwängler make a firm commitment to the Berlin Philharmonic. At about this time also, the orchestra came under the jurisdiction of the government of Berlin. While fully acknowledging the merits of Celibidache, the Berliners honored "their" Furtwängler as the authority on Beethoven, Bruckner, and Brahms. This long-honored conductor, renowned not only in

Europe but throughout the world, took the podium for the last time on September 24, 1954, in Berlin.

The upcoming October tour to Hamburg, the Netherlands, and Belgium was taken over by Karl Böhm. Furtwängler was then sick with a lung inflammation from which he was never to recover; he died November 30, 1954, in Baden-Baden. Memorial concerts took place on December 9, 1954 (Keilberth conducting), and January 23, 1955 (Sawallisch conducting). It was also Keilberth who, on the anniversary of Furtwängler's 70th birthday on January 26, 1956, conducted a posthumous world premiere of his Third Symphony.

Herbert von Karajan (b. Salzburg, 1908) was appointed Furtwängler's successor, effective April 5, 1955. Despite Celibidache's merits at the podium, the members of the orchestra decided in the spirit of "independent artistic consensus" in favor of Karajan—a decision inspired by his absolute precision, sense of style, temperament, and directional abilities, as well as by his openness to the media (Celibidache had refused all LP production offers). Having made a bravura debut with the Philharmonic on April 8, 1938, Karajan had shortly before his appointment also completed a very successful first tour of the United States and Canada with the orchestra, in which he conducted 26 concerts. Karajan's reputation had been well established in his work with the Vienna Symphony Orchestra,* the London Philharmonic Orchestra,* and Milan's La Scala.

The foundation of Karajan's repertoire remained with the major classical and romantic symphonies; however, these were augmented by every significant representative of twentieth-century music up to Krzysztof Penderecki, Luigi Nono, and Hans Werner Henze. The orchestra gave about 100 concerts annually in Berlin, along with another 30 on tour; of these, Karajan directed about 20 per year in Berlin as well as all of the touring concerts. He also conducted every recording session. Touring increased under Karajan as well.

Karajan had to make do with the concert hall at the Berliner Musikhochschule for eight years. On October 15, 1963, the construction of the new Philharmonic Hall (Philharmonie) was officially begun. Designed by architect Hans Scharoun to accommodate 2,000 listeners at a maximum 30 meters distance from the stage, it is located in the center of the entire city of Berlin, in the vicinity of the Brandenburg Gate. Among the innumerable, stellar guest artists to perform with the orchestra here was Anton Heiller, the first to play its new Schuke organ.

An ongoing tradition (since 1963) has committed five evenings per season to music of the twentieth century. Conductors for these have included Boris Blacher, Pierre Boulez, Luigi Dallapiccola, Werner Egk, Hans Werner Henze, Paul Hindemith, Witold Lutosławski, Frank Martin, Krzysztof Penderecki, Goffredo Petrassi, Karlheinz Stockhausen, and Igor Stravinsky, all of whom have brought their own works to the Berlin public. From 1981 to 1984 there were 42 world premieres and 24 other premiere performances under Philharmonic auspices.

Management duties grew constantly under Karajan, as the orchestra evolved into its present size and functional configuration. Until 1963 management was in the hands of Dr. Gerhart von Westerman, when Dr. Wolfgang Stresemann took over. His successor in 1978 was Dr. Peter Girth. Stresemann returned to the management in 1984, to be followed in 1986 by Hans Georg Schäfer.

RECORDING HISTORY AND SELECTIVE DISCOGRAPHY: The Berlin Philharmonic has one of the longest and most illustrious recording histories of all the world's orchestras. Among its achievements is the first recording of a full symphony, Nikisch's rendering of Beethoven's Fifth (1913) on eight record sides. Other early recordings by Karl Böhm, Erich Kleiber, Hans Knappertsbusch, Richard Strauss, Bruno Walter, and others make the Philharmonic legacy central to the history of recorded music. The Fuirtwängler era was well documented, including some landmark performances (of Schumann's Fourth, Beethoven's Fifth, and Tchaikovsky's Sixth, for example). Some of Karajan's finest older performances (from the 1950s and 1960s) are available in standard re-releases, and the orchestra continues an enormous output of recordings. The 1985 *New Schwann Artists Catalog* lists approximately 300 currently available entries—mostly under Karajan—with performances of a vast portion of the standard repertoire.

The orchestra's 100th anniversary in 1982 was celebrated with an outpouring of historic re-releases, most notably by EMI and Deutsche Grammophon. EMI's set of five records, *Berlin Philharmonic: 100 Years* (IC 137–54095/9) includes works of Beethoven, Bruckner, Liszt, Mozart, Nicolai, Prokofiev, Schubert, Schumann, Strauss, Tchaikovsky, and Wagner. Among these are Nikisch's 1913 recording of Beethoven's Fifth as well as performances by Walter, Böhm, Furtwängler, Lehmann, Celibidache, Karajan, and others. The DG set *Berlin Philharmonic: 100 Years* is much more extensive, comprising 33 discs in six albums arranged chronologically and by genre: Volume 1, *Early Recordings*, DG 2740–259; Volume 2, *Furtwängler*, DG 2740–260; Volume 3, *Karajan*, DG 2740–261; Volume 4, *Celebrated Soloists*, DG 2740–262; Volume 5, *Eminent Guest Conductors*, DG 2740–263; Volume 6, *Digital Recordings* DG 2741–008. A similar collection of works by the Chamber Music Alliance of the Philharmonic is also available (DG 2741011) in a set of five records.

CHRONOLOGY OF MUSIC DIRECTORS: Ludwig von Brenner, 1882–1887. Hans von Bülow, 1887–1892. Arthur Nikisch, 1895–1922. Wilhelm Furtwängler, 1922–1945. Leo Borchard, 1945. Sergiu Celibidache, 1945–1952. Wilhelm Furtwängler, 1952–1954. Herbert von Karajan, 1955-present.

BIBLIOGRAPHY: Joseph Horowitz, "Sixty-Eight Years of the Berlin Philharmonic," *Musical America*, Dec. 1982. Peter Muck, *100 Jahre Berliner Philharmonisches Orchester I-III* (Berlin and Tutzing, 1982). Werner Oehlmann, *Das Berliner Philharmonisch Orchester* (Berlin and Kassel, 1974). Klaus Schultz and Peter Girth, *Philharmonischer Almanach I/II* (Berlin, 1982–1983). Howard Taubman, *The Symphony Orchestra Abroad: A Report of a Study* (Vienna, Va.: American Symphony Orchestra League, [1971]).

ACCESS: Berliner Philharmonisches Orchester, Matthäikirchstrasse 1, D–1000 Berlin 30. 030–254880. Hans Georg Schäfer, Manager.

JOACHIM DORFMÜLLER
TRANS. KRISTIN E. CARMICHAEL

BONN   (293,000)

Beethovenhalle Orchestra

Bonn's symphony orchestra, whose namesake, Beethoven, was a native of the city, was a long time in establishing its own identity separate from that of the orchestra of the neighboring cultural center in Cologne, the town that for many years dominated the cultural growth of its smaller neighbor. Today the capital of the German Federal Republic, Bonn is still a relatively small city, but with an allocation for 130 musicians, its orchestra has risen to the top ranks of the West German system of orchestral pay scale and size classifications.

The orchestra is administered and funded by the city of Bonn. It is currently undergoing changes in artistic direction that have weakened its yearly activities, with the Cultural Department of the city of Bonn redistributing its configuration of concert series and subscription system. A consolidation of direction in repertory management is expected after 1988.

Symphonic activity in Bonn began in earnest in the mid-nineteenth century, though its roots go somewhat further back. Military conflicts in 1794, following just after the French Revolution, put a sudden end to Bonn's musical life, which had been centered at the court of the electorate of Cologne (Kurkölnische Kurfürsten). The last elector, Max Franz, had to abdicate. The group of court musicians, which had already performed the operas of Mozart in Bonn and comprised more than 30 players, was disbanded. Ludwig van Beethoven, the most renowned of Bonn's court musicians, had left two years earlier to study with Joseph Haydn.

The loss of the electoral seat at the Court thus affected the continuance of the cultivation of music in Bonn during the entire nineteenth century. Church music and music history were adopted as curricula by the university (founded in 1818), but the development of an orchestra progressed slowly, beginning with the founding of the Bonner Bürger-Singerverein (People's Choral Society, 1840) and an amateur orchestral society (1843). This association, built up with outside musicians (primarily from Cologne), numbered 162 players as it took part, two years after its inception, in Bonn's first music festival. Louis Spohr and Franz Liszt conducted at this festival, which was attended by the English Queen Victoria and the Prussian King Friedrich Wilhelm IV. The concerts were centered around the dedication of the Beethoven memorial on the Münsterplatz, and the master's works were their focus.

During the following period the Städtische Gesangverein (City Choral Society), which had evolved from the Bürger-Singerverein, and its administrator/music director were chief influences on musical life in Bonn. Attempts to develop a long-range commitment to an orchestra out of the Beethoven Society (founded 1850) at first ran aground. One reason was the engagement of an orchestra comprised of top-notch outside musicians under the direction of Cologne's music director, Ferdinand Hiller, to appear at the Beethoven Festival in 1871 (because of the Franco-Prussian War, the Centenary Jubilee was postponed a year). The first "Beethovenhalle" was constructed for this festival, which gave Bonn's present orchestra its name. There were repeated appeals in contemporary Bonn newspapers supporting the idea of a city orchestra. However, not the further music festivals in 1883 and 1885, the setting up of the Beethoven house in 1889, nor even the establishment of a Bonn concert society in 1899 were to result in the hoped-for orchestra. Bonn's chamber music evenings and church concerts had made the city famous in the musical world, but symphonic concerts were still supplied by guests—for example, regular concerts by Cologne's Gürzenich Orchestra,* as documented by the presentation of all nine Beethoven symphonies under the direction of Franz Wüllner in May of 1894.

The necessary impetus came first in 1903 with a guest appearance by the Philharmonic Orchestra of Coblenz, under its director, Heinrich Sauer. The then 37-year-old Sauer was contracted in 1907 with his 38-member ensemble to spend the winter months in Bonn. However, responsibilities for the Bonn city orchestra, including philharmonic concerts (in the Beethovenhalle and in the Town Hall), opera productions in the City Theatre (with guest direction and productions from Cologne and Düsseldorf), and choral society concerts, were time-consuming enough to require a full year's commitment.

Considerably better conditions, relating to the programming of orchestral works, were achieved for the production of music festivals in 1910 (Schumann/ Brahms), 1912 (Mahler), and 1913 (Mid-Rhineland Festival). Following 1907 the two individuals who shared responsibility for laying the groundwork for the future of musical culture in Bonn were Music Director Hugo Grüters and Conductor Heinrich Sauer, who presented all of the Bruckner Symphonies. Grüters gave a conservative impression; however, his direction of the Mahler festival and the fact that Max Reger dedicated to him his *Romantic Suite*, op. 115, proved that he was in close contact with contemporary composers. Immediately following the orchestra's first regular symphony concert in 1907, the first important guest conductor took the podium: Richard Strauss, directing a performance of his *Sinfonia Domestica* on November 2, 1907. Many well-known guests conducted in Bonn prior to the First World War.

Shortly after the war began the Beethovenhalle began to serve as a military hospital. Because of the draft, the orchestra was heavily reduced, and finally, in 1916, it was disbanded. After difficult negotiations and only with the financial support of Bonn's Friends of Music, was the city orchestra reestablished in its old form in 1920. The orchestra had its first major task to fulfill as early as December of 1920: a music festival commemorating Beethoven's 150th birthday.

Grüters left in 1922 and was replaced by Max Anton, who had previously worked in Osnabrück. By taking over the symphony concerts and the city choral society, the new director had a broader jurisdiction than Sauer, who concentrated on opera productions (still imported from Cologne) and popular concerts. Anton introduced then-contemporary composers (Hindemith and Schoenberg, among others) in exemplary concerts and led the orchestra for Bonn's 1,000th anniversary celebration in 1925. The orchestra then expanded to 46 members. After 1927 the Beethoven Festival was held every two years (every three after 1967). Anton began the engagement of renowned guest conductors with Hindemith, Erich Kleiber, and Max von Schillings. Following Anton's retirement in 1931 due to ill health, and in the midst of an economic depression, the Bonn orchestra was led provisionally by Hermann Abendroth (director at Cologne) for the 1931–

1932 season. It was kept going by contributions, especially the profits from the "Volkstumlichen Beethovenfeste" begun by Elly Ney.

For the 1932 celebration of the orchestra's 25th anniversary, a noticeable consolidation began with the hiring of the new music director, Gustav Classens, a student of Abendroth. At the same time, an independent musical theatre was built in Bonn. Classens promoted a mainly classical and romantic repertoire, with a few moderate modern compositions mixed in. He was replaced during the war years by then over–70-year-old Heinrich Sauer and by Eugen Papst (orchestra director in Cologne). After the Beethovenhalle became the victim of bombings in 1943, symphony and choral concerts were carried on in the Metropol Theatre and in churches. The first postwar season was organized in similar makeshift concert halls—the auditorium of Bonn University or the Salon at the Museum König. Despite the obvious difficulties, a Beethoven festival was organized in 1946.

After Classens, Otto Volkmann led as general music director of the Bonn Orchestra for 14 years, until 1963. For the 50th anniversary of the ensemble in 1957, a promising young city music director was chosen: Volker Wangenheim, who then took over as general music director of the now officially named "Orchestra of the Beethovenhalle, Bonn" in 1963. Wangenheim's engagement coincided with the dedication of the rebuilt Beethovenhalle in 1958–1959, with which Bonn assumed her new cultural role. The grand opening to contemporary music (works of Tadeusz Baird, Hans Werner Henze, Rudolf Kelterborn, György Ligeti, Isang Yun, and Bernd Alois Zimmermann, among others) was matter-of-fact under Wangenheim's masterful leadership. So too was a turn toward the late-romantic, which culminated in a complete Gustav Mahler cycle. Krzysztof Penderecki's *St. Luke Passion* was included on the program of the 1974 Beethoven Festival. During Wangenheim's years the orchestra appeared with increasing frequency at important music festivals in Salzburg, Vienna, Budapest, and elsewhere.

Wangenheim took a professorship at the Cologne Conservatory in 1979 and was replaced for three years by Jan Krenz, the longtime director of the Warsaw Opera. During that short period the number of places authorized in the budget for orchestra members was raised from 99 to 130 and the pay-scale classification of the orchestra placed it among the top orchestras in West Germany. The 75th Jubilee was celebrated without a chief music director after Krenz did not renew his contract for 1982–1983.

Gustav Kuhn, a student of Herbert von Karajan and Bruno Maderna, was appointed for the 1983–1984 season, and he took the elevated musical expectations of metropolitan Bonn into account. After two years the orchestra had adopted a new and apparently successful configuration of seasonal activities, combining a variety of concert series, special classical programs, workshops, and studio concerts. The focal point of the workshops in 1983–1984 was works of composers Bruno Maderna and Erik Satie. The cultural life of Bonn could carry out such ambitious projects up until the end of Gustav Kuhn's last contracted season. The orchestra began the 1985–1986 season, however, without a principal conductor.

It has been announced that in the autumn of 1987 Dennis Russell Davies will become the new music director of the Beethovenhalle Orchestra, marking a new impulse in the city's musical life.

CHRONOLOGY OF MUSIC DIRECTORS: Heinrich Sauer (Principal Conductor) and Hugo Grüters (Music Director), 1907–1916 and 1920–1922. Max Anton, 1922–1931. Gustav Classens, 1932–1949. Otto Volkmann, 1949–1963. Volker Wangenheim, 1957–1979. Jan Krenz, 1979–1982. Gustav Kuhn, 1983–1985. (Guest conductors, 1985–1987.) Dennis Russell Davies (to begin duties in 1987).

BIBLIOGRAPHY: E. Bücheler, "Zur Musikgeschichte der Stadt Bonn," in *Jahrtausendfeier der Stadt Bonn, Musikfest am 19–20 und 21 Mai 1925* (Bonn, 1925)—program book. Joseph Schmidt-Görg, "Bonn," in *Die Musik in Geschichte und Gegenwart*, vol. 2 (Kassel, 1963). Heinz-Dieter Terschüren, *75 Jahre Orchester der Beethovenhalle, vormals Stadtisches Orchester Bonn (1907–1982)* (Bonn, 1982).

ACCESS: Die Beethovenhalle Orchester Bonn, Wachsbleiche 17, Beethovenhalle, D–5300 Bonn 1. 0228–773685. Luis Wüst, Business Manager.

FRANK REINISCH
TRANS. SUSAN ELIZABETH HOAGLUND

COLOGNE   (977,000)

Gürzenich Orchestra of the City of Cologne

Not far from Cologne lies the village of Gürzenich, which entered the history of music in a very curious way. In the fifteenth century the council of the city of Cologne built a large ballroom and dancehall on a piece of land that had, at one time, belonged to the lords of Gürzenich. As with the famous cathedral of Cologne, this building fell into oblivion over the centuries. It was first used again in 1800, at first in its original function as a ballroom, then for art exhibitions, and finally also as a concert hall. The hall figures importantly in the history of the Cologne orchestra that bears its name.

A scientific and cultural center between the significantly smaller federal capital of Bonn and the state capital of Düsseldorf, Cologne has a rich musical heritage complemented by the highly rated Cologne Opera, the Musikhochschule Rheinland (College of Music of the Rhineland), and two radio stations (West German Radio and Radio Germany). The 123-member Gürzenich Orchestra (also known as the Cologne Orchestra) enjoys a preeminent role with its commitment to the Opera, a season of 30 symphonic concerts, and extensive travel for guest performances. The orchestra is administered and funded by the city of Cologne. Programming decisions are made in cooperation with the office of the city's cultural director.

As early as the beginning of the eighteenth century, the Kölner Ratsmusik (Council Band of Cologne) had made a name for itself as a prominent ensemble.

As Cologne came under Prussian administration after the 1814 withdrawal of Napoleon's armies, an active musical life developed in many half-private, half-public amateur circles. Around 1820 theatre, cathedral, and military musicians, as well as a few amateurs, formed a 40-person orchestra, which led to the founding of a concert society in 1827. The orchestra was considerably expanded for the large oratorio performances of the Niederrheinischen Musikfeste (Lower Rhine Music Festival), which at regular intervals was also held in Cologne. This music festival now found the Gürzenich to be an appropriate venue. The public orchestra concerts, the "society concerts," took place at first in its casino hall.

In 1840 the well-known opera composer, Konradin Kreutzer (who wrote *Das Nachtlager von Granada*) was named as the first city conductor—probably also with a view to placing his directive personality at the head of the multifarious cultural life of Cologne. Within a year Kreutzer, with 182 musicians and 500 choir members, presented Beethoven's Ninth Symphony to the Cologne public for the first time.

Although by the middle of the nineteenth century the Cologne city conductor would simultaneously claim the title of "Gürzenich Conductor," the assumption of the orchestra into city service was still by no means a closed matter. Indeed such negotiations were carried out by each Cologne conductor for many years. Kreutzer's successor, Heinrich Dorn, founded a concert union, which should have given financial security to musicians who were not permanently employed. (Later, when the Cologne cathedral no longer used orchestra musicians, this function was taken over by a "pension institute.") An important event of this period was the founding of the Rheinischen Musikschule, which until the Second World War was closely connected with the leader of the Cologne orchestra. Out of this school, which was soon designated a "conservatory," emerged today's internationally important Musikhochschule Rheinland (College of Music of the Rhineland).

The composer/conductor Ferdinand Hiller relieved Dorn after a few years and set about the lengthy work of laying the ground for a stabilized repertoire. Next to the major works of the Viennese classics, Hiller preferred to follow the school of Brahms. Characteristically, Hiller's recommendation would be to make Brahms his successor in Cologne.

The desire to maintain the Gürzenich as a representative concert hall for all large musical presentations had become so strong in Cologne by the mid-nineteenth century that in 1857 an architectural modification was attempted, but it was neither acoustically nor stylistically satisfying. Nevertheless, the Gürzenich became an enduring shelter for the orchestra and a point of recognition for Cologne, in the manner of the Gewandhaus for Leipzig, the Salle Pleyel for Paris, or the Philharmonie for Berlin. Ferruccio Busoni even wrote once of the "Gürzenich style" that distinguished the Cologne orchestra. In Hiller's years, Cologne became an attractive podium to the most influential and finest of Europe's musicians. At mid-century one could see and hear at the Gürzenich the likes of Berlioz, Brahms, von Bülow, Gounod, Liszt, Mendelssohn, Ignaz Moscheles, Paganini, Clara Schumann, Bedřich Smetana, Louis Spohr, Sigismond Thalberg, Verdi, and Wagner. To Hiller may also be attributed the institution of public chamber concerts.

Under Franz Wüllner, who succeeded the 73-year-old Hiller in 1884, a city orchestra at the Gürzenich was finally realized. It was made up of 43 professional musicians and held the title still in effect today, "Gürzenich Orchestra of the City of Cologne." Wüllner now offered works of the "composers of the future" whom Hiller had largely neglected—namely Wagner and Strauss, who witnessed the original performances of *Till Eulenspiegels lustige Streiche* and *Don Quixote* in Cologne's Gürzenich under Wüllner's direction. Wüllner also initiated the orchestra's first tours and first pops concerts (which took place during theatre recesses).

Another of Wüllner's innovations was the Cologne Summer Opera Festival, which was one of the major musical events of its time and drew the early twentieth century's most gifted conductors to Cologne. The Cologne opera was later to be led in a more permanent fashion by Otto Klemperer and Wolfgang Sawallisch. The Gürzenich concerts at the century's start were led by Fritz Steinbach, the Meiningen-schooled conductor who brought the orchestral works of Brahms and of Max Reger more to the fore. (Reger's *Hiller Variations*, op. 100, was dedicated to Steinbach.) The first performance of Gustav Mahler's Fifth Symphony, under the direction of the composer, occurred at the Gürzenich in 1904.

Certainly the preference of Steinbach's successor Hermann Abendroth lay with the symphonic creations of Anton Bruckner, for whom Abendroth worked with great intensity in Cologne. Nevertheless, Abendroth supported a wide, representative repertoire of contemporary orchestral compositions—among them works of Walter Braunfels, Ferruccio Busoni, Alfredo Casella, Erich Wolfgang Korngold, Max von Schillings, and Ernst Toch. The performance of Arnold Schoenberg's *Five Pieces for Orchestra*, op. 16, created much controversy. In 1933 Schoenberg held his last performance in Germany in Cologne, "Style and Idea, New and Antiquated Music"; thereafter events of that sort, or even performances of the avant-garde, were hardly possible in Cologne, as the exhibition "Decadent Art" ("Entartete Kunst") showed in 1938.

Eugen Papst, the next Cologne orchestra director and a friend of Richard Strauss, made a name for himself with monumental oratorio performances during the war years. In 1943 the Gürzenich was completely destroyed during an air raid and was erected again in 1955 in modern style.

The first three postwar decades were determined by the personality of Günter Wand, whose exemplary recording practice and resolute dedication to contemporary music provided the Gürzenich Orchestra once again with an international standing. It was also Wand who resumed the title of "Gürzenich Conductor" which Wüllner laid aside in 1888. Istvan Kertész, Cologne's opera director at the time, was foreseen as Wand's successor. His death in 1973 prevented the appointment. Under Yuri Ahronovitch's decade of leadership, the orchestral culture of Cologne was stamped with the conductor's special commitment to late romantic symphonic works. In this period the orchestra's international travels widened considerably.

In 1986, with the opening of a new 2,000-seat comprehensive concert hall, the Gürzenich Orchestra obtained the wherewithal for a program of expansion that it envisions for the future. Its new director, Marek Janowski, began his work in Cologne in the 1985–1986 season.

RECORDING HISTORY AND SELECTIVE DISCOGRAPHY: Although the orchestra recorded with much success under Günter Wand, it has in recent years stood in the shadow of the Cologne Radio Symphony Orchestra (Kölner Rundfunk Sinfonie Orchester) in this regard and has released no important records.

Beethoven, *Missa Solemnis* (Wand): Nonesuch 73002 (2 records). Webern, Cantata No. 1; Schoenberg, *Five Pieces for Orchestra* (Wand): Nonesuch 71192.

CHRONOLOGY OF MUSIC DIRECTORS: Konradin Kreutzer, 1840–1842. Heinrich Dorn, 1843–1849. Ferdinand Hiller, 1850–1884. Franz Wüllner, 1885–1902. Fritz Steinbach, 1902–1914. Hermann Abendroth, 1915–1934. Eugen Papst, 1936–1944. Günter Wand, 1946–1975. Yuri Ahronovitch, 1975–1985. Marek Janowski, 1985-present.

BIBLIOGRAPHY: W. Kahl, "Köln," *Musik in Geschichte und Gegenwart (MGG)*, Vol. 7. H. Kipper, "Das Kölner Gürzenich-Orchester," *Die Musik*, 1, 1901, pp. 187–197. H. Kipper, *Zur Geschichte der Gürzenich-Konzerte* (Cologne, 1907). H. Unger, *Festbuch zur Hundertjahrfeier der Concert-Gesellschaft in Köln 1827–1927* (Cologne, 1927). H. J. Zingel, *Das Kölner Gürzenich-Orchester* (Cologne, 1963). H. J. Zingel, *Das Gürzenich-Orchester: 75 Jahre Stadtkölnisches Orchester* (Cologne, 1963).

ACCESS: Gürzenich-Orchester der Stadt Köln, Offenbachplatz, Postfach 180241, D–5000 Köln 1. (0221) 2076–236. Friedrich Wilhelm Jung, Director.

FRANK REINISCH
TRANS. GEORGE COMMENATOR

FRANKFURT AM MAIN   (620,000)

City Opera and Museum Orchestra of Frankfurt am Main

The cultivation of music in this important commercial center is traced back into the twelfth century. It first noted a splendid highpoint, however, with Georg Philipp Telemann's "Collegium Musicum," from 1712 to 1721.

Today, with an authorized size of 116 musicians, Frankfurt's City Opera and Museum Orchestra (Städtisches Opernhaus- und Museumsorchester Frankfurt am Main) offers some 250 performances per year (30 stage productions and ten ballets), plus ten pairs of symphonic concerts. Its music-theatre performances take place in the city Opernhaus, but symphonic programs are presented in the Konzertsaal, known also as the Old Opera House (Alte Opernhaus), completely reconstructed out of the rubble of World War II, and inaugurated on August 28, 1981, with a performance of Mahler's Eighth Symphony.

Under its principal conductor, Michael Gielen, the Frankfurt orchestra's symphonic programming has been characterized by a contrast of the traditional with the avant-garde. An example is the juxtaposition of Arnold Schoenberg's *Survivors from Warsaw* and Beethoven's Ninth. Recent programs have featured the works of Tadeusz Baird, Luciano Berio, Pierre Boulez, Paul-Heinz Dittrich, Hans Werner Henze, Mauricio Kagel, Luigi Nono, and Bernd Alois Zimmermann. Gielen's contract runs until 1987, when the conductorship will pass to Gary Bertini, presently chief director of the West German Radio (Westdeutsche Rundfunk) Symphony Orchestra, Cologne.

The orchestra is funded and governed by the city of Frankfurt, and although its historic links to the old "museum" from which it takes its name long ago disappeared, there remains a town Museumgesellschaft, which arranges about 20 symphonic concerts per season.

The Frankfurt National Theatre was founded in 1792. To it was attached a 28-member orchestra led by Carl August Cannabich, the son of Mattias Cannabich of Mannheim. In 1799 it was strengthened by ten members from the dissolved private orchestra of Peter Bernard, the snuff manufacturer who resided in neighboring Offenbach. Its development into the modern city orchestra was closely bound to the development of the "Museum," an academy of four sections: Literature, Visual Arts, Musical Arts, and Friends of Art. Lectures, discussions, presentations, concerts with improvised programs—at first amateur and then increasingly professional—were at the disposal of the institution's registered members. The director of the Musical Arts section was Carl Josef Schmitt, a follower of Cannabich, who appeared occasionally with his theatre orchestra and who could, according to the status of the box office, engage artists who were passing through town. Concerts of the orchestra, which included at most 40 musicians, took place in the English Square (Englischer Hof).

In 1818 Schmitt was replaced by Louis Spohr, who became director of the opera of the Frankfurt Theatre. Spohr, one of the age's most celebrated musicians, established a tradition of relatively high performance standards in a repertoire based on the Beethoven symphonies. After Spohr departed the Theatre (and so the Musical Arts section as well), an interim period was concluded with the 1821 appointment of Karl Wilhelm Ferdinand Guhr, who continued Spohr's Beethoven tradition and strengthened it with presentations of symphonic works of Haydn and Mozart. Contemporary music was virtually never heard under Guhr. After 1829 concerts took place at the Red House on the Zeil (Rothes Haus auf der Zeil), and after 1832 at the hotel "Zum Weidenbusch."

Over the years the Museum's visual arts and literature functions succumbed, and by 1861 only its Musical Arts section remained viable. It had succeeded to the extent of establishing a fund for musicians' widows and orphans; a pension fund was established later. After Guhr's death in 1848 the orchestra's direction was taken over by Franz Messer (b. Hofheim, 1811), the director of the Frankfurt Cecilia Society (Frankfurter Caecelienverein). He produced up to six works of Beethoven per season, and though he devoted himself to Mozart and Cherubini, he left space as well for Mendelssohn, Schubert, and Schumann. In his era the first noteworthy guest soloists of the orchestra appeared, among them Clara Schumann, Joseph Joachim, and Julius Stockhausen.

The decision to erect a new building dedicated solely to concert presentations was made during Messer's directorship. He died, however, in 1860, a year before the dedication of the building, the "Saalbau" on Junghofstrasse. His successor, Karl Müller, was simultaneously the director of the Cecilia Society, and under him the orchestra presented purely concert performances in the 2,200-seat Saalbau. Müller concentrated on the classics, with a special preference for Beethoven. He intensively cultivated the works of Schumann, especially after Clara Schumann had accepted an appointment in 1873 to the Conservatory (Hochsches Konservatorium) of Frankfurt; during this period Brahms too was in Frankfurt as conductor and soloist at the Saalbau.

Müller was responsible for many innovations in the orchestra. The Frankfurt public was afforded more and more access to newer music under Müller, who conducted Liszt and Wagner and also invited Eugene d'Albert, Antonín Dvořák, Edvard Grieg, Joachim Raff, Anton Rubinstein, Richard Strauss, and Tchaikovsky as interpreters of their own works. The orchestra also participated in the revitalization of chamber music toward the end of the century, with performances in the 1870s and 1880s by its own Heermann Quartet. Following its association with the Opera in 1880, the orchestra grew to 70 members and its work load increased significantly.

The following years saw many guest conductors of the highest order—among them Felix Mottl, Gustav Mahler, Arthur Nikisch, and Richard Strauss. A period of artistic growth came with the appointment in 1906 of Willem Mengelberg, who was simultaneously the principal conductor of the Concertgebouw Orchestra* in Amsterdam, whose reputation he did much to raise. Mengelberg remained in Frankfurt until 1920, during which time he played much Mahler, whose music he held in high esteem. In addition to the standard repertoire, Mengelberg also presented contemporaries such as Claude Debussy, Max Reger, and especially Richard Strauss, for whom he also had a special affinity. The 20-year-old Paul Hindemith was concertmaster during the Mengelberg era.

When, in 1921, Mengelberg went to New York (where he would become associated with the New York Philharmonic**), he left behind a gap filled for two seasons by Wilhelm Furtwängler. Guest conducting appearances by Fritz Busch, Bruno Walter, and Hans Knappertsbusch were followed by the appointment of Hermann Scherchen. A disciple of Schoenberg, Scherchen brought to Frankfurt authentic interpretations of the Second Viennese School. Frankfurt in those years heard much new music, for Scherchen also favored Busoni, Honegger, Pfitzner, and Stravinsky.

When Scherchen left in 1924, Clemens Krauss (b. 1893) was hired from the State Opera (Staatsoper) of Vienna, his home city, as director of the Frankfurt Opera. As his predecessors Spohr and Guhr had done, Krauss applied himself to the theatre and concert podiums simultaneously. Krauss took up Scherchen's commitment to contemporary composers and in particular paid attention to the increasingly prominent former colleague of the orchestra, Paul Hindemith.

When Krauss returned to the Vienna State Opera in 1929, the Frankfurt position was vacant for five years. Following three seasons under Georg Ludwig Jochum, the orchestra came under the direction in 1937 of Franz Konwitschny (b. Nordmahren 1901), who sought to maintain the musical life of Frankfurt until such hopes were ruined in the destruction of the opera and the old Saalbau on January 29, 1944.

The postwar season of 1945–1946 brought the orchestra into the Börsensaal with a total of ten concerts under Bruno Vondenhoff of Cologne (b. 1902). His successor, Georg Solti, changed the concert venue to the large hall on Theaterplatz. With his international reputation, Solti would move on in several years (he would later conduct the Covent Garden Opera and the Chicago Symphony**), and his farewell concert at Frankfurt in 1961 was a performance of the Mahler Sixth Symphony. Following interim periods under Lovro von Matačić (until 1966) and the American Theodore Bloomfield (until 1968), the opera/concert position was taken over by Christoph von Dohnányi. Dohnányi's classical/romantic repertoire was enhanced with much contemporary music as well as his commitment to the music of Mendelssohn. He was followed by Michael Gielen, and, according to plans, Gary Bertini in 1987. Under Bertini the orchestra will rise to the highest scale classification of German orchestras and increase step by step to 130 members.

SELECTIVE DISCOGRAPHY: Mahler, Symphony No. 8 (Gielen): CBS Masterworks 79238. Mendelssohn, Symphony No. 1 and *Die Erste Walpurgisnacht* (Dohnányi): Turnabout 34651. Schoenberg, *Pelleas und Melisande* (Gielen): Mediaphon 59011.

CHRONOLOGY OF MUSIC DIRECTORS: Carl Josef Schmitt, 1808–1817. Louis Spohr, 1818–1819. Karl W. F. Guhr, 1821–1848. Franz Messer, 1848–1860. Karl Müller, 1860–1891. Gustav F. Kogel, 1891–1903. Siegmund von Hausegger, 1903–1906. Willem Mengelberg, 1907–1920. Wilhelm Furtwängler, 1920–1922. Hermann Scherchen, 1922–1924. Clemens Krauss, 1924–1929. (Guest conductors, 1929–1934). Georg Ludwig Jochum, 1934–1937. Franz Konwitschny, 1937–1945. Bruno Vondenhoff, 1945–1952. Georg Solti, 1952–1961. Lovro von Matačić, 1961–1966. Theodore Bloomfield, 1966–1967. Christoph von Dohnányi, 1968–1977. Michael Gielen, 1977–1987. Gary Bertini, to begin in 1987.

BIBLIOGRAPHY: Dieter Rexroth, "Zur Geschichte des 'Museums' und der 'Frankfurter Museums-Gesellschaft," in *Museum: 175 Jahre Frankfurter Museums-Gesellschaft* (Frankfurt: Lembeck, 1984).

ACCESS: Frankfurter Opernhaus- und Museumorchester, Untermainanlage 11, D–6000 Frankfurt/Main 1. 0611–25621. Günter Hempel, Managing Director.

JOACHIM DORFMÜLLER
TRANS. GEORGE COMMENATOR

HAMBURG   (1,623,000)

North German Radio Symphony Orchestra

With an authorized allotment of 115 playing members, the North German Radio Symphony Orchestra (NDRSO: Norddeutsche Rundfunks Sinfonie-Orchester) is among West Germany's most illustrious radio and concert ensembles. Its activities include radio productions, commercial recordings, numerous tours, and a subscription series that is an important part of Hamburg's musical season. Its concerts in the 1,700-seat Grosser Saal of Hamburg's Musikhalle comprise a series of 12 performances, each given at 11:00 A.M. on Sunday and repeated on Monday at 8:00 P.M.. Eight to ten additional concerts are also presented in Hamburg, including performances in conjunction with the NDR Chorus, concerts at Hamburg's Stadthalle, and studio concerts at the Hamburg Hochschule für Musik, featuring new works. Additional performances are held at Kieler Castle and at towns in northern Germany.

The NDR Symphony Orchestra has long made its reputation on its performances on tour. In the 1986–1987 season it was scheduled to visit Florence and Sofia, in addition to longer tours of Spain (in August), Italy/France/etc. (in November and December), Japan (in April), Austria (in May), and East Germany (in June).

In addition to its symphonic performances, the NDRSO maintains a schedule of chamber concerts, featuring the "Soloists of the North German Radio Symphony Orchestra," at the Rudolf-Steiner-Schule, Farmsen.

Although the orchestra prides itself on widely praised performances of Brahms, Beethoven, and the other German masters, it also frequently presents works of modern and contemporary composers. The orchestra also points with pride to its record of having presented over 80 world premiere performances, of which more than 40 were commissioned by the NDR. Its 1986–1987 subscription concert season, however, was dominated by romantic and early twentieth-century composers, although it did also feature works of more recent years. Opening with a performance of Bruckner's Fifth Symphony and closing with his Eighth, the season presented Brahms and Beethoven as the most-performed composers, and the series included works of Barber, Bartók, Arthur Benjamin, Debussy, Henri Dutilleux, Dvořák, Haydn, Janáček, György Ligeti, Gustav Mahler, Bohuslav Martinů, Mendelssohn, Oliver Messiaen, Carl Nielsen, Prokofiev, Ravel, Saint-Saëns, Schumann, Strauss, Stravinsky, and Karol Szymanowski. Chief conductor Günter Wand was scheduled to lead the orchestra in four of the twelve concerts, with the remainder to be led by Jiří Bělohlávek, Rafael Frühbeck de Burgos, Charles Dutoit, Jan Krenz, Lorin Maazel, Esa-Pekka Salonen, David Shallon, and Horst Stein as guest conductors.

The NDR Symphony Orchestra was founded under auspices of the newly created North German Radio in 1945 by conductor Hans Schmidt-Isserstedt.

Schmidt-Isserstedt's plan was to create a major broadcasting ensemble, and his high criteria in a search for personnel took him beyond the borders of Germany. Immediately setting off on a performance policy that included touring, Schmidt-Isserstedt soon brought the orchestra to nearby sites and then, in the early 1950s, the group travelled more widely in Europe, to the USSR, and the United States. Also under Schmidt-Isserstedt the orchestra established a policy of attention to recent music, within the context of a wide-ranging overall repertoire. The year 1954 saw two important performances: Schoenberg's *Moses and Aaron* and Mahler's Eighth Symphony. Under successive chief conductors the orchestra continued to tour widely. The orchestra has appeared with a very long list of renowned guest conductors. In 1983 the NDR broadcast a long series of historic recordings documenting Schmidt-Isserstedt's 26 years with the orchestra.

RECORDING HISTORY AND SELECTIVE DISCOGRAPHY: The NDRSO records both in the Musikhalle in Hamburg and in NDR Broadcasting studios. Since its recording of the Berlioz *Symphonie Fantastique* in 1964 under Pierre Monteux won the Grand Prix du Disque Académie Charles Gros, the orchestra has consistently won recognition for its commercial recordings, of which it has made more than 80. Significant recent rereleases include a 1948 recording of the Brahms Violin Concerto with Ginette Neveu. Among its most recent important recording projects under Wand are a just-completed Brahms cycle (Schmidt-Isserstedt also made one) and a projected Beethoven cycle.

Berlioz, *Symphonie fantastique* (Monteux): Turnabout 34616. Brahms, Symphony No. 1 (Wand): Pro Arte 626; EMI/Deutsche Harmonia Mundi 1C 067 199774–1. Brahms, Symphony No. 2 (Wand): EMI/Deutsche Harmonia Mundi 1C 067 169519–1. Brahms, Symphony No. 3 (Wand): EMI/Deutsche Harmonia Mundi 1C 067 169506–1. Brahms, Symphony No. 4 (Wand): EMI/Deutsche Harmonia Mundi 1C 067 169530–1. Brahms, Symphony No. 4 (Schmidt-Isserstedt): Vox 512270. Stockhausen, *Carré* (Stockhausen, et al.): DG 137002 PSI.

CHRONOLOGY OF MUSIC DIRECTORS: Schmidt-Isserstedt, 1945–1971. Moshe Atzmon, 1972–1976. Klaus Tennstedt, 1979–1981. Günter Wand, 1982.

BIBLIOGRAPHY: Correspondence with NDR Publications Editor Dr. Ulf Thomson. *Hans Schmidt-Isserstedt* (Hamburg: NDR, 1983), pamphlet. NDR Sinfonieorchester, Miscellaneous documents, 1986. *Das Sinfonie-Orchester des Norddeutschen Rundfunks 1945–1985*, ed. Dr. Ulf Thomson (Hamburg: NDR, 1985), pamphlet.

ACCESS: Das Sinfonie-Orchester des Norddeutschen Rundfunks, Rothenbaumchaussee 132–134, 2000 Hamburg 13. (040) 413–2401 and 413–2708. Friedrich Wilhelm Rauker, Intendant.

ROBERT R. CRAVEN

HEILBRONN   (111,000)

Württemberg Chamber Orchestra

The Württemberg Chamber Orchestra of Heilbronn (also known as the Heilbronn Chamber Orchestra) gives annual subscription concerts in Heilbronn's

"Harmonie" hall, an 1,800-seat building constructed in 1958. The orchestra's other main activities consist of large concert tours throughout West Germany and the rest of Europe. The group also travels overseas with well-known soloists. Of the 80 concerts performed outside Heilbronn, some 30 are in foreign countries. The orchestra participates regularly in European festivals. In addition to its many recordings, the group is heard on some 30 radio stations. It has frequently worked with the world's most renowned instrumental and vocal soloists.

The repertoire naturally focuses on the baroque, but Haydn, Mozart, and their contemporaries are also frequently performed. Other works are also presented, including contemporary works, all with a view to authentic interpretation, not so much in terms of playing on period instruments, but in terms of articulation and ensemble practice. Numerous premieres and first performances have also been presented.

Heilbronn is located approximately 60 kilometers southeast of Heidelberg and is the seat of the state of Württemberg. Here a man named Jörg Faerber established, in December 1960, a chamber orchestra that first performed under him in Stuttgart on January 13, 1961. Faerber (b. Stuttgart, 1929), who was educated in the State Music School, had been musical director at the theater in Heilbronn. Taking some members from the earlier state orchestra of Heilbronn and adding some music students, he put together the chamber orchestra, which today comprises a core of 15 string players. Württemberg Chamber Orchestra musicians come from several different countries (both European and non-European) and are engaged for annual contracts under the wage parity agreement Tarifklasse A. As required, some musicians may be engaged from foreign countries. It is administered under the Heilbronn Orchestra Society e.V.

Within a few years of its founding, the Württemberg Chamber Orchestra had begun travelling, and its trips soon brought it to a great many countries on several continents. It visited the U.S.S.R. in 1979; North America in 1974 and 1981; the Far East in 1979, 1983, and 1986; and South Africa in 1971 and 1973. The orchestra still works only with its founder and mentor, Jörg Faerber.

RECORDING HISTORY AND SELECTIVE DISCOGRAPHY: The orchestra began recording upon its first tour to Great Britain in 1963–1964, under auspices of the BBC. Since then it has recorded more than 350 works, with emphasis on the baroque and classical repertoires. Helmuth Rilling engaged the orchestra for the closing record of his series recording the complete Bach Cantatas. The Heilbronn Chamber Orchestra has recorded for EMI Electrola, Erato/RCA, FSM, Intercord, Tudor, Turnabout, Vox, and other labels. Its current list of records in print contains in excess of 50 titles.

Mendelssohn, Complete Symphonies (Faerber): Vox QSVBX 5147. Mozart, Symphonies Nos. 14, K. 114; 23, K. 181, and 33, K. 319 (Faerber): Schwann LC 1038. Mozart, Violin Concertos Nos. 3, K. 216, and 5, K. 219. (Fr.-P.Zimmermann/Faerber): EMI-Electrola 067 270075–1.

CHRONOLOGY OF MUSIC DIRECTORS: Jörg Faerber, 1961-present.

BIBLIOGRAPHY: Württemberg Chamber Orchestra, Miscellaneous documents.

ACCESS: Württembergisches Kammerorchester Heilbronn, Orchesterverein Heilbronn e.V. Postfach 3730, D–7100 Heilbronn. 07131/87272. Karl Nagel, Manager.

JOACHIM DORFMÜLLER
TRANS. PETER JÄHNE

MARL   (90,000)

Philharmonia Hungarica

The Philharmonia Hungarica was formed in 1959 by a group of Hungarian émigrés in an effort to establish a first-rate orchestra, an objective that would be fulfilled in a very few years.

The Philharmonia Hungarica has travelled widely and is well known for its recordings. By the end of 1984 the orchestra had travelled a total of some 800,000 kilometers, completed 120 tours outside of Germany, and made 12 television appearances and 80 radio broadcasts. In addition to its busy schedule of tours and recordings, the Philharmonia Hungarica serves as the city orchestra of Marl. From its founding to the 1984–1985 concert season the Philharmonia Hungarica had performed 250 concerts in Marl alone, testifying to an active schedule. The orchestra is supported by the city and is governed by a general manager who is responsible to the town administration.

As of 1984 the orchestra's complement of musicians was 87, with 50 of these from Hungary. However, a variety of nationalities is represented within the group, including members from Germany, Japan, Israel, Austria, Poland, Canada, and Scotland. In 1965 the Hungarian Soloists, a chamber ensemble, was formed from among regular members of the Philharmonia Hungarica. This group, no longer active today, was under the leadership of solo violist Andreas Sandor, and it concertized frequently throughout much of Europe.

The orchestra's beginnings may be traced to the 1956 Budapest uprising and an ensuing two-year odyssey for many musicians who fled Hungary. Their idea, shared by the group's first music director, Zoltán Rozsnyai, was to find a new musical home and build an orchestra of the highest standards. But there were obstacles to overcome: the most difficult was to prove to the world that this ensemble was in a position to produce music of superior quality. In addition, the orchestra had to gain audience acceptance. Numerous international organizations provided generous influential support: the Ford and Rockefeller Foundations, the International Rescue Committee, the United Nations High Commission on Refugees, and the Swiss Committee for Aid to the Freedom Fighters of Hungary. The orchestra was also aided by a number of illustrious persons, among them the Viennese conductor Karl Böhm; Secretary to the Viennese Concerthouse Dr. Egon Seefehlner; and the composer Gottfried von Einem. Antál Doráti served as mentor for the emerging orchestra.

The orchestra first rehearsed in Vienna in February 1958 and gave performances in May of that year with cellist Janos Starker in the Viennese Concerthouse and in June with violinist Yehudi Menuhin in the Great Music Society Hall, also in Vienna. The response to these performances was very enthusiastic.

A step toward full musical status was taken when the ensemble appointed Dr. Georg Fürstenberg and Yehudi Menuhin president and honorary president, respectively. But it was still felt necessary to further prove the group's abilities before the world, so a series of guest appearances was planned. There were several concerts in Munich (1957); a tour of France, Belgium, and the Netherlands (1958); and a visit to Canada and the United States (1960).

In 1959 the city of Marl, known chiefly for its large chemical industries, possessed a modest amateur orchestra called the Music Society of Marl, which performed in an 818-seat theatre. The city had at this time no full-scale symphony orchestra. In July 1958 Dr. Heinrich Kraus served as host and director for Hungarian refugees entering Germany; he was, along with Peter Csobadi, instrumental in helping musicians of the Philharmonia Hungarica settle in Marl.

Once it was certain that the city was to become the orchestra's permanent second home, the group realized the need for additional financial support from prominent, politically influential leaders. Carlo Schmid, vice president of the German Federal Diet; Felix von Eckardt, state secretary to the federal chancellor; and Rudolf Heiland, mayor of Marl; took an interest and provided essential support. So too did Konrad Adenauer, who was at the time chancellor of the German Federal Republic. With this kind of recognition and commitment, the Philharmonica Hungarica was now in a position to look to the future and make plans to develop fully its musical potential.

On March 4, 1959, the Philharmonia Hungarica performed its first concert in Marl. Shortly afterwards (March 23), the orchestra was officially registered—with Felix von Eckardt listed as president, Antál Doráti as honorary president, and Zoltán Rozsnyai as music director.

The year of the International Refugee, 1960, was of special importance to the orchestra. Its members first received the loan of temporary housing in Marl. By the mid-1960s they were able to move into permanent quarters specifically constructed for orchestra members and families. Arrangements for this musical settlement were facilitated in part by special emissary Yul Brynner.

During the 1960s the number of performers in the orchestra grew to 86; most of them were Hungarians. It was also during this period that the members joined a musical union that officially gave the orchestra a "Class B" designation. In 1960 Miltiades Caridis succeeded Zoltán Rozsnyai as music director. Under his leadership the orchestra became very active, participating in various musical festivals throughout the world, including performances in Athens and at London's Royal Festival Hall, tours through Spain and Portugal, and a 16-day special series of concerts for UNESCO (14 performances in ten European cities). In addition, the cities of Cologne and Düsseldorf in the German Federal Republic made the Philharmonia Hungarica their permanent guest orchestra. And for five working weeks out of every year, the group was to be at the disposal of the Cologne West German Radio Broadcasting network.

Caridis was succeeded by Alois Springer, who served as music director from 1968 to 1971. After Springer's departure in 1971, the position of music director remained vacant for three years. Orchestra members created a search committee, and with the help of the orchestra's manager, Gerhard Hellwig, the search ended in 1974 with the appointment of Reinhard Peters. It was during the interim period that the orchestra's reputation reached its highest point, particularly in its recording activities.

Under Peters's five-year artistic management (1974–1979), the orchestra travelled widely, with 33 tours to other countries and four separate visits to America. In view of the group's increasing renown, its status was upgraded to "A." In 1979 the orchestra came under the direction of Uri Segal, with Dr. Herbert Tobischek as its chief administrator. Segal left the orchestra in 1984, and Gilbert Varga was named his successor. Dr. Tobischek was succeeded by Gerhard Fabian.

RECORDING HISTORY AND SELECTIVE DISCOGRAPHY: Beginning in 1960, during its visit to the United States, the Philharmonia Hungarica undertook, with Antál Doráti, the enormous task of recording all of Haydn's symphonies. Efforts toward this project were intensified in the 1970s, still with Doráti's leadership, and the resulting recordings, which won numerous awards (including the Grand Prix du Disque and the German Recording Prize), did much to further the orchestra's reputation. The Haydn symphonies comprise 48 LP discs, produced by Decca-Teldec and conducted by Doráti; they are available in the United States on the London label in single albums and in sets of from four to six discs. Another recording project, also under Doráti and for Decca-Teldec, documents the orchestral works of Kodály. Other recordings of the Philharmonia Hungarica on Vox, Turnabout, Candide, DBX, Euphoria, Mercury and other labels cover a wide repertoire.

Glazounov, Violin Concerto (Ricci/Peters): Mercury 344621. Haydn, Symphonies Nos. 93–104 (Doráti): London STS 15319–24 (6 records). Rossini, Overtures; Berlioz, *Rakoczi March* (Rozsnyai): RealTime 204.

CHRONOLOGY OF MUSIC DIRECTORS: Zoltán Rozsnyai, 1957–1960. Miltiades Caridis, 1960–1968. Alois Springer, 1968–1971. (Guest conductors, 1971–1974.) Reinhard Peters, 1974–1979. Uri Segal, 1979–1984. Gilbert Varga, 1985-present.

BIBLIOGRAPHY: Herbert Tobischek, *25 Jahre Philharmonia Hungarica* (Marl: Breitfeld & Biermann, 1982).

ACCESS: Philharmonia Hungarica, Theater der Stadt Marl, Postfach 1920, D-4370 Marl. 02365/13031 and 14007. Gerhard Fabian, General Manager.

JOACHIM DORFMÜLLER
TRANS. DON W. SIEKER

MUNICH   (1,287,000)

Bavarian Radio Symphony Orchestra

The Bavarian Radio Symphony Orchestra, also known abroad as the Munich Symphony (Symphonieorchester des Bayerischen Rundfunks), with 115 playing members, is one of the principal broadcasting ensembles in West Germany.

In addition to its other broadcasting duties, its season includes 12 public programs, each presented twice on a subscription basis; two special concerts with world-famous soloists; and four "Musica Viva" concerts of contemporary music. Since the 1984–1985 season an additional four concerts have brought the ensemble to various towns of West Germany under direction of its chief conductor, Sir Colin Davis. Its home halls are the 1,200-seat Herkules-Saal of the Munich Residenz and, since 1986, the 2,400-seat Philharmonie Munich am Gasteig. The orchestra is funded and administered by the Bavarian Radio of Munich. Tours and recordings are important functions of the orchestra.

Several ensembles have been created from within the ranks of the orchestra, including the Koeckert-Quartet, the Röhn-Trio, the Werner-Egk-Quartet, the Bach Collegium Munich, and the Munich Brass Ensemble.

The Bavarian Radio Station was established by law on August 10, 1948, in Munich, the successor to the "Deutsche Stunde in Bayern G.m.b.H." (German Hour in Bavaria Association, founded 1922). The Bavarian Radio Station has had its own symphony orchestra since 1949. Negotiations that had been in progress concerning taking over the Munich Philharmonic Orchestra,* which was left in the lurch after Hans Rosbaud's departure, were broken off in 1950. On July 13, 1949, the newly created Radio Symphony Orchestra was conducted by Richard Strauss in a radio production of the Intermezzo of his opera *Capriccio*. In September of that year Eugen Jochum (b. 1902) was appointed chief conductor. Bavarian Radio Symphony Orchestra concerts took place at first in the auditorium of the Munich University until the Hercules Hall in the Munich Residence (which was helped financially by the radio station during reconstruction after the Second World War) could be used again by March of 1953.

During the Jochum decade the orchestra took several foreign tours—to Austria, Italy, Switzerland, Belgium, Great Britain, and the Netherlands, among others. Since 1952 the orchestra has also participated in the "International Competition of the Association of the Radio Broadcasting Stations in the Federal Republic of Germany." In the Musica Viva series founded by Amadeus Hartmann, the orchestra devoted time during the early years to contemporary music. Among others, Stravinsky and Hindemith both conducted, in 1951 and 1955, respectively. Guest conductors included Clemens Krauss, Dimitri Mitropoulos and Rafael Kubelik.

Jochum left the orchestra in 1960, turning his attention to the Concertgebouw Orchestra* in Amsterdam. One outstanding event during the ensuing vacancy was a concert-version performance of Alban Berg's *Lulu* conducted by Georg Solti on May 5, 1961. Jochum's successor, Rafael Kubelik (b. 1914), continued the tradition of a repertoire based on the classical and romantic periods.

Under Kubelik the orchestra travelled repeatedly through western and northern European countries and also three times to the United States and Canada (1968, 1975, 1978). It participated in the Osaka Festival (1965) as well as festivals in Vienna and Lucerne. The orchestra participated in many high quality productions for radio, television, and the recording industry, and its work spanned a wide range of forms and styles. Its guest conductors were among the world's finest, and several worked closely with the orchestra. One, Kiril Kondrashin, was designated as successor to Kubelik in 1979 but his reign lasted only until 1981, when he died. Leonard Bernstein has appeared repeatedly with the orchestra since 1976 (for instance, in a television coproduction of Wagner's *Tristan und Isolde* in 1981). Kubelik resigned from his office on September 30, 1979, but he conducted the orchestra several times in the following years.

In this period the orchestra was quite active for the Bavarian Radio Station, with numerous concerts and recordings (for example symphonies by Bruckner, Mozart, and Schumann as well as the operas *Freischütz* and *Parsifal*). Other productions (i.e. broadcasts and/or recordings) were Wagner's *Feen* with Sawallisch, Strauss's *Intermezzo*, the complete secular and sacred vocal works of Schubert, Mozart's *Magic Flute*, Strauss's *Daphne*, and Wagner's *Tannhäuser* under Haitink.

On the first day of September 1983, Sir Colin Davis became chief conductor. Under Davis the orchestra participated in the Berlin Festival weeks, and plans for recordings of Gounod's *Margarethe* and a complete cycle of the Mendelssohn symphonies were undertaken. In addition to its European tours, the orchestra visited Japan in 1984 and the United States in April 1986.

RECORDING HISTORY AND SELECTIVE DISCOGRAPHY: The Bavarian Radio Orchestra has recorded since 1950. Under Kubelik the orchestra twice received the highest German decorations, in 1966 for Schoenberg's *Gurrelieder* and in 1973 for Pfitzner's *Palestrina*. The orchestra devotes 20 weeks a year to LP productions (mostly coproductions) and live productions. Its repertoire covers all periods of music, from baroque through contemporary.

Pfitzner, *Palestrina* (Kubelik): DG 2711013. Schubert, *Vocal Works* (Sawallisch): EMI 157–43300/05 and 157–143607 (six records). Schoenberg, *Gurrelieder* (Kubelik): DG 2726046. Strauss, *Daphne* (Haitink): EMI 165–143582/83 (2 records). Strauss, *Intermezzo* (Sawallisch): EMI 165–30983/85 (3 records).

CHRONOLOGY OF MUSIC DIRECTORS: Eugen Jochum, 1949–1960. Rafael Kubelik, 1961–1979. Kiril Kondrashin (Designated successor), 1979–1981. Sir Colin Davis, 1983-present.

BIBLIOGRAPHY: Correspondence with Bavarian Radio Symphony Orchestra manager Friedrich Welz. Miscellaneous documents.

ACCESS: Symphonieorchester des Bayerischen Rundfunks, Abteilung Klangkörper, Rundfunkplatz 1, 8000 München 2. 089–59002736. Friedrich Welz, Manager.

JOACHIM DORFMÜLLER
TRANS. ANNELIESE YIENGST

Bavarian State Orchestra

Munich, the capital of Bavaria, one of West Germany's states (Bundesländer) situated in the southwestern part of the country, is the third largest city of the Federal Republic. An important economic center, it is also the seat of a university and numerous academies. In addition to the Bavarian State Orchestra (Bayerische

Staatsorchester), other Munich-based orchestras of professional stature include the Munich Philharmonic Orchestra,* the Bavarian Radio Symphony Orchestra,* and the Kurt Graunke Symphony Orchestra. In past years Munich acquired an association in musical history especially as a "Wagner and Richard Strauss City," a fact it owes exclusively to the Bavarian Court and State Orchestra (Das Bayerische Hof- und Staatsorchester München), whose tradition goes back to the year 1530.

Today, under the name Bayerische Staatsorchester, the ensemble plays in four places: the National Theatre, with 2,100 seats; the "Old Residence" or "Cuvilliés Theatre" (reopened after reconstruction in 1958), with 500 seats; the "Prinzregententheater," with 1,122 seats; and an experimental stage known as the "Theater im Marstall" (Theatre in the Former Royal Stable), with 200 seats.

The orchestra is run and funded by the Free State of Bavaria, which absorbs its deficits. The city of Munich also gives subsidies. Further support is given by user organizations, including the Theatergemeinde (Theatre Community), Volksbühne (People's Stage), and Freie Volksbühne (Free People's Stage) with some 60,000 members. Occasionally the orchestra performs in double performances and therefore double services.

Although it is currently identified primarily with the Bavarian State Opera, for which it serves as the accompanying ensemble, the Bavarian State Orchestra has a long and distinguished history as a concert ensemble. Today the orchestra also plays for ballet performances and presents an orchestral season of some 12 concerts between September 15 and July 31.

In 1523 Duke Wilhelm IV of Bavaria had called to Munich as court composer and "Musicus intonator" Ludwig Senfl (1490–1549), born in Zurich and trained by Heinrich Isaac in Vienna. As such, Senfl was to institutionalize court music, a task that he essentially completed in seven years. The Bavarian State Orchestra thus considers 1530 as the year of its founding. The beginning was rather modest: Senfl had at his disposal no more than seven instrumentalists, later joined by about 20 choristers. But on this basis the French-Flemish musician Orlando di Lasso, who carried the artistic responsibility from 1563 to his death, could gradually shape Munich into a center of sacred and secular music. The instrumental body gradually increased to 21 members who indulged predominantly in the music of the Netherlands and Belgium, the home region of their leader, di Lasso.

Based on this tradition, the first opera performance took place in 1653, in the Hercules Hall (Herkulessaal) of the Munich Residence complex. A year later there was another performance for the consecration of the first free-standing opera house on German soil. Leading in the cultivation of the Italian repertoire was especially Johann Kaspar Kerll, head of the court orchestra from 1656 to 1677 and (after a stint at St. Stephen's Cathedral in Vienna) again from 1684 until his death in 1694.

In 1692, however, the orchestra faced a crisis of continuity: Elector Maximilian Emanuel II became governor general of the Netherlands and so drew the majority of the then 34 musicians to Brussels. He tried, however, to make up for the damage by generous financial contributions after his return to Munich in 1705. His conductor by then was Giuseppe Antonio Bernabei (in office from 1688 to 1732), followed by Pietro Torri (to 1737) and Giovanni Parta (to 1755), all outstanding Italians who systematically raised the level of the orchestra. They also succeeded in enlarging the orchestra to 54 members and, in 1753, they were able to move into the Residence Theatre (part of the court proper) built by François de Cuvilliés. Since that time the orchestra has regularly participated in opera productions.

Among the applicants for the position of conductor was W. A. Mozart, though in vain—even though his opera *Idomeneo* had its world premiere (under his baton) in Munich in 1781 and was a splendid success. This was under the reign of Elector Karl Theodor, who had come to Munich in 1777 from Mannheim and who was instrumental in combining the Mannheim and Munich orchestras both stylistically and in shared personnel.

With the coronation of Elector Maximilian IV Joseph as king of Bavaria in 1806, the orchestra officially became the Royal Court Orchestra. Ten years later it moved into the 2,600-seat Royal Court and National Theatre under the leadership of Court Conductor Peter von Winter, who was installed in 1801. Unfortunately this theatre was destroyed only five years later by flames, but, in 1825, the year of von Winter's death, it was renovated and again put to full use. The repertoire of this quarter century under von Winter was oriented predominantly toward the symphonies of Haydn and Beethoven, and less toward those of Mozart, with whom von Winter's relationship is said to have been less than congenial. Concert subscriptions were offered again, but this time more successfully than in 1714, when the same idea miscarried. Famous virtuosos performed with the orchestra—among them the violinists Jacques-Féréol Mazas, Pierre Rode and Louis Spohr, as well as the pianist Johann Nepomuk Hummel. The orchestra now grew to 110 members, among them 22 contracted soloists (one of them was the famous flutist Theobald Böhm). During these years—1825 to 1837—Joseph Hartmann Stuntz was conductor.

The orchestra received increasing international recognition after Franz Lachner was established as its leader in 1836. During 31 years under his artistic leadership, he widened the repertoire of both classical and romantic symphonic literature while also performing vocal/orchestral compositions from Bach to Haydn and much opera, especially Verdi and Wagner. Lachner created the basis in Munich for Wagner world premieres after he conducted the very first performance of *Lohengrin*. So it was possible, under Hans von Bülow, to experience in Munich brilliant premieres of *Tristan and Isolde* in 1865, *Die Meistersinger* in 1868, and—with an enlarged orchestra pit—*Das Rheingold* in 1869. Moreover, the social position of the musicians improved. In 1867 the functional income was changed into a regular salary, and in 1873 the court musicians were put on an equal footing with the esteemed court servants. Consequently, the security of the orchestra members, who now bore the title "Royal Chamber Musicians," was guaranteed for life.

After Lachner, in 1870, it was Franz Wüllner who was commissioned by Wagner personally to conduct his *Ring des Nibelungen*. Two years later Wüllner was assisted by Hermann Levi, who became an actively engaged advocate of Wagner's "Bayreuth idea" and who made the Munich orchestra, as the "Bayreuth Festival Orchestra," into the Wagner Orchestra par excellence. In the city of Munich itself there were, under Levi, between 1867 and 1892, no less than 731 Wagner performances; and the German romantic opera, as a matter of principle, rose to a zenith at the Isar River. Many interesting events happened during Levi's era: Brahms performed his own compositions, the orchestra engaged itself with Bruckner's works, as well as with an important Mozart renaissance. Before leaving in 1896, Richard Strauss was court conductor for two years; his symphonic poem *Aus Italien* had already been presented for the first time in 1887 by the orchestra. It was practically a matter of course that soon all essential stage and concert pieces from Strauss's pen were part of the regular orchestra repertoire.

Among Levi's successors several stood out: Herman Zumpe after 1901, Felix Mottl after 1904, and Bruno Walter from 1913 to 1922. Mottl became the first nominated opera director in 1906 and as such, head of an orchestra with 115 members. He initiated a raise in salaries, realized in 1909, making orchestras positions more attractive but at the same time more competitive and strenuous.

With the political changes after the end of the First World War, the orchestra changed from a "Court" to a "State" service. The position of the Munich Court Conductor (Hofkapellmeister) was, after 399 years, replaced by the Bavarian Music Director General in the person of Hans Knappertsbusch, who held it until he was banned from conducting in 1935 by the National Socialists. Knappertsbusch brought the orchestra immense world recognition and was considered one of the truly great conductor personalities of his century, especially in the cultivation of the great classical and romantic inheritances.

In 1937 Clemens Krauss became his successor, continuing the tradition and finally leading more than 138 musicians. He suffered tremendous mental anguish at the destruction of the National Theatre (Opera House) during a night bombing raid in 1943, and, one year later, the demolition of the Cuvilliés-Residence Theatre. After the occupation of Germany in 1945, opera performances were held in the temporarily refurbished Deutsches Museum (German Technical Museum), which included a large rectangular hall and, after 1947, in the also temporarily fixed up Prinzregententheater. Krauss was by then forbidden to conduct in Germany and Knappertsbusch had regained his post as opera director. But the occupation forces removed him also, and he later came back to Munich only as a guest conductor.

With Georg Solti a new era began on September 1, 1946. Solti functioned as music director until 1952, at first together with Ferdinand Leitner. Solti was followed by Rudolf Kempe for two seasons, and after a two-year interim Ferenc Fricsay conducted a pair of seasons. Under Kempe the orchestra resumed touring, with a London visit in 1953 with the Strauss operas *Arabella, Die Liebe der Danaë,* and *Capriccio.*

Fricsay's successor, Joseph Keilberth, previously head of the Bamberg Symphony,* stood at the podium in Munich from 1959 until 1968; he collapsed during the "Love Duet" in the second act of a *Tristan* performance and died shortly afterward. His forte in Munich was the romantic period, especially the works of Hans Pfitzner, with which he identified completely. During Keilberth's time there were more tours, the world premiere of Henze's *Elegy,* the first appointment of a woman as orchestra member, and the longed-for opening of the rebuilt National Theatre in Munich in the 1963–1964 season.

The orchestra then consisted of 140 members, two more than under Clemens Krauss. Since 1971 Wolfgang Sawallisch has had the directorship. With wide experience with such organizations as the Vienna Philharmonic,* Hamburg Philharmonic, and Salzburg and Bayreuth Festivals, Sawallisch has done much to increase the orchestra's international reputation. In 1974 Sawallisch and Leitner brought the orchestra to Japan in productions of operas and symphonic works by Mozart, Wagner, and Strauss.

SELECTIVE DISCOGRAPHY: Strauss, *Die Frau ohne Schatten Meistersinger* (Keilberth): Deutsche Grammophon 2721161. Wagner, *Meistersinger* (Keilberth): AR XI 70851-R.

CHRONOLOGY OF MUSIC DIRECTORS (Selective): Ludwig Senfl, 1523–1540. Orlando di Lasso, 1563–1594. Johann Kaspar Kerll, 1656–1673. Giuseppe Antonio Bernabei, 1686–1732. Giovanni Porta, 1738–1755. Andrea Bernasconi, 1755–1784. Peter von Winter, 1801–1825. Franz Lachner, 1836–1867. Hans von Bülow, 1866–1869. Friedrich Wilhelm Meyer, 1869–1882. Franz Wüllner, 1870–1877. Hermann Levi, 1872–1896. Joseph von Rheinberger, 1877–1894. Franz Fischer, 1880–1913. Richard Strauss, 1894–1896. Joseph Becht, 1894–1918. Max Erdmannsdörfer, 1896–1889. Hugo Röhr, 1896–1918 and 1934. Bernhard Stavenhagen, 1889–1902. Herman Zumpe, 1901–1903. Felix Mottl, 1904–1911. Bruno Walter, 1913–1918 and 1922. Otto Hess, 1913–1918 and 1920. Hans Knappertsbusch, 1922–1933 and 1945. Clemens Krauss, 1937–1944. Bertil Wetzelberger, 1945–1946. Ferdinand Leitner, 1946–1947. Sir Georg Solti, 1946–1952. Rudolf Kempe, 1952–1954. Ferenc Fricsay, 1956–1958. Joseph Keilberth, 1959–1968. Wolfgang Sawallisch, 1971-present.

BIBLIOGRAPHY: Hans-Joachim Nösselt, *Ein Ältest Orchester: 450 Jahre Bayerisches Hof- und Staatsorchester* (Munich: Bruckmann, 1980).

ACCESS: Bayerisches Staatsorchester, Max Joseph-Platz 2, D–8000 München 22. (089) 2185354. Klaus Einfeld, Orchestra Office Director.

JOACHIM DORFMÜLLER
TRANS. ANNELIESE YIENGST

Munich Philharmonic Orchestra

The Munich Philharmonic Orchestra is one of the city's leading ensembles dedicated primarily to symphonic concerts. In addition to the brief symphonic season of the Bavarian State Orchestra,* concert life in Munich is enriched as well by productions of the Bavarian Radio Symphony Orchestra,* the Kurt Graunke Symphony, and the activities of many smaller ensembles.

In a season running from September to July, the Munich Philharmonic offers approximately 110 concerts, until 1985 presented largely at Munich's National Theater, which since its opening in 1963 has been a great source of pride to the city. Since November 1985 the orchestra has had at its disposal a new concert hall, the 2,400-seat Philharmonie in the Cultural Center at the Gasteig. In the same building is the Orff-Saal, a 600-seat hall suitable for chamber music performances, in which Philharmonic musicians frequently perform.

At the present time the following chamber music ensembles are formed from among the Munich Philharmonic's 129 members: the Munich Baryton-Trio, the Nymphenburg and the Gasteig String Quartets, the Philharmonic Woodwind Quintet, the Philharmonic Octet, the Munich Philharmonic Soloists, the Baroque Ensemble, and the Chamber Ensemble of the Munich Philharmonic Orchestra.

The orchestra is funded through its subscriptions as well as subventions from the municipal government of Munich. It is administered by the city, through the municipal Department of Culture.

In 1891, Franz Kaim (1856–1935), representative of the well-known Augsburg piano factory in Munich, had begun so-called Kaim Concerts in the Bavarian capital. From these soloistic presentations developed the Philharmonic Concerts, with 60 fully engaged musicians. Begun on October 13, 1893, these were the origin of the Munich Philharmonic Orchestra, called at first "Kaim's Philharmonic Orchestra" and after 1895 simply the "Kaim Orchestra."

Hans Winderstein (1856–1925) was hired to direct the Philharmonic's concerts in the Royal Odeon Theatre. His successor in 1895, Herman Zumpe (1850–1903), was able to consecrate the new Kaim Concert Hall on Türkenstrasse. At the same time he founded the Kaim Choir, nowadays the Philharmonic Chorus of Munich. A former assistant to Wagner in Bayreuth, Zumpe laid the foundation to an increasingly important Mahler tradition. But the orchestra soon received the honorary name "Bruckner Orchestra," a distinction it owed to the student of Bruckner and successor to Zumpe, Ferdinand Löwe (1865–1925). Löwe stayed in Munich only one season, leaving to conduct three concerts as a guest in Vienna and unaware that he would return to Munich ten years later. In the meantime, Felix von Weingartner (1863–1942) took over until 1905 and under him the Kaim Orchestra flourished. Constantly sold out performances and subscription concerts in Augsburg, Frankfurt am Main, Mannheim, and Nuremburg, as well as several guest tours to neighboring countries, strengthened its reputation under the prominent conductor who would eventually succeed Mahler at the podium of the Vienna Philharmonic.*

In 1898 Kaim introduced so-called People's Symphony Concerts (Volkssymphonie-Konzerte) with extremely low prices. One can see here the beginning of an engagement of public support for the orchestra as well as in a series of concerts conducted by Siegmund von Hausegger and dedicated to the promotion of a municipally subsidized organization. The Munich Mahler tradition had its first high points during this period: the Second Symphony had its very first performance in 1900, the Fourth was heard under Mahler's direction in 1901. Von Weingartner institutionalized a series of Modern Evenings and travelled with the orchestra through Germany, Italy, and Switzerland. Hans Pfitzner, Max Reger, and Richard Strauss acted as conductors, leading, for the most part, their own works.

The early years of the twentieth century were to be traumatic for the orchestra, which was undergoing a change of leadership and function while at the same time experiencing some musical firsts. In spite of Kaim's resistance, the concert hall (named after him) was renamed "Tonhalle." In 1905 the German-Finnish conductor Georg (Lennart) Schnéevoigt (1872–1947) came to Munich from Riga, Latvia, as a successor to Weingartner. Schnéevoigt brought, aside from the typical classical and romantic programs, a series of Retrospective Concerts dedicated to interpretation in original orchestration. In 1906 the 20-year-old Wilhelm Furtwängler made his debut in Munich.

Orchestral administration was nevertheless precarious, and a year later the Tonhalle was threatened by the necessity for a liquidation auction. In the wake of such dramatic incidents, Kaim resigned but remained an honorary member of the Munich Concert Association (Konzertverein Munich) founded in 1908. Acting as the orchestra's governing body, the Association renamed the ensemble the Konzertverein Orchestra and recalled Ferdinand Löwe from Vienna to Munich. Under Löwe's leadership the Porges Choir Association and the Orchestervereins-Chor (built from the Kaim Chorus) were combined to form the Konzertgesellschaft für Chorgesang (Concert Association for Choral Singing), concentrating their efforts especially on works of Bach.

The orchestra was lauded nevertheless for its performances of Bruckner and Mahler. Löwe led the Munich premiere of the Mahler Fifth Symphony (1910), and the composer himself conducted in the same year the first performance of his Eighth Symphony ("Symphony of a Thousand"). In memoriam of Mahler's death, Bruno Walter conducted in 1911 the world premiere of *Das Lied von der Erde*. Also heard in the 1911 season was the first performance of a complete cycle of Bruckner's symphonies—an impressive accomplishment for both orchestra and conductor.

Occasionally the orchestra ventured to other countries, for example to music festivals in Salzburg and Vevey, where it played under Camille Saint-Saëns and Gustave Doret in 1913. After the First World War broke out, Löwe's contract could not be renewed. He conducted only as a guest, as did Hermann Abendroth, Siegmund von Hausegger, Max Reger, Fritz Steinbach, and Felix von Weingartner. Conscription finally paralyzed the orchestra from 1915 on. Only in the season of 1919–1920, under Hans Pfitzner, did any serious consideration of reconstruction become possible.

Building on its successes, the orchestra, under Siegmund von Hausegger

(1872–1948), began to pick up where it had left off before the war. With more than 20 years' experience with the People's Concerts, von Hausegger felt drawn toward Beethoven, Liszt, and especially Bruckner, whose symphonies he introduced after 1932 in their original versions. Guest conductors of the era included, among others, Fritz Busch, Leopoldo Casella, Eugen Jochum, Hans Knappertsbusch, Hans Pfitzner, Richard Strauss, and Hans Weisbach. Many contemporary works were heard, including music by Walter Braunfels, Paul Hindemith, Anthony Honegger, Hans Pfitzner, Igor Stravinsky, and others. The venerable, 66-year-old conductor said goodbye to Munich on April 4, 1938, with a performance of Beethoven's Ninth, passing the leadership on to Oswald Kabasta (1896–1946).

In spite of the beginning of the war in 1939, the new music director was able to retain the ensemble's high level, at first even adding a few new positions and guest tours (including visits to the German occupied regions). Kabasta's great Munich era ended suddenly when, on April 25, 1944, the Tonhalle became a heap of rubble. The orchestra was soon disbanded and its members made to play concerts in civilian and military hospitals.

The first postwar concert took place on July 8, 1945, under Eugen Jochum in the Prinzregenten-Theatre. Here too, on September 21, 1945, the first German opera production after the unconditional surrender took place—Engelbert Humperdinck's *Hänsel und Gretel*, with the Philharmonic Orchestra and the Regensburger Domspatzen (a renowned boys choir) and Theobold Schrems conducting.

From autumn 1945 to the end of the 1947–1948 season, Hans Rosbaud (1895–1962) led the Philharmonic Orchestra. In 1946 he offered the complete Beethoven symphonies three times and began with a Bruckner cycle. Interested predominantly in the music of the twentieth century, the position offered him by the Southwest Radio Symphony Orchestra (Baden-Baden)* was too attractive for him to pass up, and so he left after three years of extremely fruitful musicianship. The Philharmonic Orchestra, meanwhile, could assert itself very successfully with the city of Munich as sponsor and in view of its regained high artistic level—not only locally but also on various tours, to the 1947 Schwetzingen Festival, for example.

The artistic palette became international under Rosbaud's successor, Fritz Rieger (1910–1978). Munich stayed the center of all work, but after Rieger assumed the podium in 1949, there was a steady stream of tours to all important cultural centers of Europe. The most important of the era's conductors appeared as guests, particularly Knappertsbusch, who was at that time conducting the Bavarian State Opera; occasionally Rudolf Kempe, from the same house, also conducted. Kempe was later to lead the Philharmonic regularly, following very admirably a tradition from Rieger's years that manifested itself in a classical/romantic repertoire punctuated with numerous premieres of modern music. Among these were works of Günther Bialas, Werner Egk, Karl Amadeus Hartmann, Bernard Herrmann, Karl Höller, Karl Michael Komma, and Mark Lothar.

The opening of the reconstructed National Theatre in 1963 marked a period of intensive and highly productive cooperation with the Opera, especially during the Summer Festivals.

The next music director, Rudolf Kempe (1910–1976), led the orchestra in a wide repertoire ranging from baroque to contemporary music. He also greatly expanded the ensemble's recording activities and led it on its tour of the Soviet Union. Following Kempe's sudden death the orchestra was in the hands of a succession of guest conductors, most importantly Karl Böhm, William Steinberg, Wolfgang Sawallisch, Günter Wand, Gennady Rozhdestvensky, Eric Leinsdorf, Sir Georg Solti, Václav Neumann, and Witold Rowicki.

The period of guest conductors came to an end in February 1979, when Sergiu Celibidache (b. 1912) became music director and took under his control the orchestra's artistic development. Celibidache has had many successes, among others, the orchestra's annual appearances since 1983 at Munich's "Festive Summer," and in 1981, 1983, and 1986 during the "Berlin Festive Weeks." Under Celibidache the orchestra has toured widely in Western and Eastern Europe, becoming the first West German Orchestra to perform in East Germany. The orchestra visited North America under Maazel in 1985 and Japan in October 1986 under Celibidache.

RECORDING HISTORY AND SELECTIVE DISCOGRAPHY: Although not primarily known as a recording orchestra, the Munich Philharmonic began making recordings under Rieger. Kempe recorded complete cycles of Beethoven and Brahms symphonies. His death, however, prevented the planned completion of a Bruckner cycle. The orchestra has recorded little under Celibidache, who on principle does not care for recording.

Beethoven, Symphonies Nos. 1–9 and other works (Kempe): Classics for Pleasure [EMI] 4406 (8 records). Miklos Rozsa, Concerto for Cello (Starker/Atzmon): Pantheon FSM 53901.

CHRONOLOGY OF MUSIC DIRECTORS: Hans Winderstein, 1893–1895. Herman Zumpe, 1895–1897. Ferdinand Löwe, 1897–1898. Felix von Weingartner, 1898–1905. Georg Schnéevoigt, 1905–1908. Ferdinand Löwe, 1908–1914. Hans Pfitzner, 1919–1920. Siegmund von Hausegger, 1920–1938. Oswald Kabasta, 1938–1945. Hans Rosbaud, 1945–1948. Fritz Rieger, 1949–1966. Rudolf Kempe, 1967–1976. Sergiu Celibidache, 1979–present.

BIBLIOGRAPHY: Alfons Ott, "Chronik eines Orchesters. Die Geschichte der Münchner Philharmoniker," in Ernst W. Faehndrich, *Die Münchner Philharmoniker 1893–1968*, ed. Alfons Ott (Munich: Winkler, 1968). Regina Schmidt, ed., *Die Münchner Philharmoniker von der Gründung bis heute* (Munich: Wolf, 1985).

ACCESS: Münchner Philharmoniker, Rindermarkt 3–4, 8000 Munich 2. Artistic Management: Anneliese Riedl, Kellerstrasse 4, 8000 München 80. (089) 41810.

JOACHIM DORFMÜLLER
TRANS. ANNELIESE YIENGST

STUTTGART (573,000)

State Orchestra of Stuttgart

The State Orchestra of Stuttgart (Württembergisches Staatsorchester Stuttgart; since 1985 Staatsorchester Stuttgart) with 109 members, is a leading orchestra of the German Federal Republic (GFR) and also among the oldest musical entities in the world.

The orchestra appears primarily in opera and ballet performances, giving some 30 different operas with the Staatsoper Stuttgart and 30 different ballets each year, for a total of about 215 performances. Its season runs virtually year-round, from August through July. It also appears in eight symphonic concerts on a subscription basis. The orchestra is funded largely by the state of Baden-Württemberg and is administered by the state as well, through the office of the orchestra's general manager. Its main performance site is the Liederhalle, which has two concert rooms, the 1,984-seat Beethoven-Saal and the 752-seat Mozart-Saal.

In recent years several ensembles were formed from within the orchestra, among them the Süddeutschen Kammersolisten (South German Chamber Soloists), the Camerata Stuttgart, the Trio Parnassus, and the Alt-Wiener-Strauss-Ensemble (Old Vienna Strauss Ensemble).

Stuttgart, the capital of the southwestern state of Baden-Württemberg, is one of the most industrialized cities in the GFR. It is also the seat of many national and international institutions, among them the headquarters of the American troops in Europe.

The first climax in the musical history of this city, whose founding dates to 1170, came under Duke Ulrich, who engaged singers and instrumentalists in his court at the beginning of the sixteenth century. Leonhard Lechner worked there from 1595 to 1606 as a court conductor. Creator of the actual Stuttgart orchestra, however, was Tobias Solomon, who was engaged in 1606 as conductor to the court. In 1617, under Duke Johann Friedrich, he completed the transformation of a group of instrumentalists organized primarily for musical performance into a tightly organized *opus musicum*. The orchestra therefore considers this year—1617—to be its founding date.

The era of the Thirty Years' War brought enormous problems for the orchestra's existence, but thanks to the Basilius Froberger "conductor dynasty," they were overcome again and again. The first opera performance occurred under conductor Samuel Capricornus in approximately 1660. A consistent opera tradition did not form, however, until the time of Johann Sigismund Cousser, who arrived in Stuttgart from the Hamburg stage. His successors, Nicolo Jommelli (1753–1769) and Agostino Poli (1782–1792), cultivated especially the Italian operas, while Johann Rudolf Zumsteeg committed himself from 1793 to his death in 1802 to German-language musical drama.

With the political changes in 1806 the orchestra was no longer responsible to the duke but to the king of Württemberg. Fortunately, it was possible to engage famous artists and composers for the office of conductor. At first Konradin Kreutzer (1812–1816) brought brilliance to the post, to be followed by Johann Nepomuk Hummel (to 1818). However, the Stuttgart orchestra rose to new heights under Peter Joseph von Lindpaintner (b. Koblenz, 1791), a student of Michael Haydn. After his appointment in 1820 he soon made a wide reputation for himself and the orchestra, which outperformed other court ensembles. Lindpaintner instituted subscription concerts. He was raised to the peerage in 1844, but resigned in 1856 following a dispute concerning the employment of a second conductor in Stuttgart, a Friedrich Wilhelm Kücken, who was dismissed in 1861 because of inability.

The former court opera director from Vienna, Karl Eckert, reorganized the orchestra between 1860 and 1867; the consecration of the Stuttgart Liederhalle (Song Hall, 1864) took place in Eckert's time; the largest German concert hall, the 4,000-seat Liederhalle was destined to become the absolute center of musical life in the Württemberg metropolis.

After Eckert the position of court conductor was divided: Johann Joseph Abert worked until 1887; he was followed by Paul Klengel until 1891, by Wagner's assistant, Herman Zumpe (to 1895), Aloys Obrist (to 1900), and Karl Pohlig (to 1907); the second line of succession in the divided leadership began with Karl Doppler (to 1898), followed by Hans Reichenberger (to 1902). As long as King Karl reigned, the musical scene was conservative. After Wilhelm II came to power in 1891, the situation changed to a more progressive outlook, as the new ruler was a friend and benefactor of music. When the court theater burned on July 1, 1902, after a performance of *Die Meistersinger*, the king asked Theodor Littmann to build the much admired double building of "large" and "small" halls with room for 106 and 46 musicians, respectively. The opening— with a "Festival Week of Richard Wagner," October 25 to November 3, 1912— was put into the very capable hands of the opera composer Max von Schillings (b. Düren, 1868), who had been called to Stuttgart in 1908. In Stuttgart this former Bayreuth assistant reorganized the repertoire, preferring more modern music (including his own operas), with a total of 45 premiere performances. Of 100 Liederhall Concerts, he conducted 84 himself during his stay in Stuttgart, which lasted until 1918. In these concerts he preferred Beethoven and Mozart, but also turned to Brahms, Richard Strauss, Hans Pfitzner, and Max Reger, and even Mahler and Debussy. Von Schillings became director at the Berlin State Opera in 1919.

After World War I the court orchestra became the Staatssorchester (State Orchestra) and the conductor, Fritz Busch (from Siegen), was made State Music Director at the age of 28. He was very interested in Pfitzner and Reger, and under him the orchestra played the classical composers as well as Wagner (with three complete "Ring" cycle performances), brief compositions by Paul Hindemith, and spectacular premieres.

Busch's successor, Carl Leonhardt (b. Coburg, 1886) came from Bayreuth, where he had been assistant. Leonhardt tried to bring about a Handel renaissance and cycles of both Weber and Wagner. He played a large amount of new music with the orchestra, including works of Ferruccio Busoni, Paul Hindemith, Leoš Janáček, Ernst Křenek, Arnold Schoenberg, Franz Schreker, and Kurt Weill. He also travelled with the orchestra throughout the State of Württemberg. In spite of the Great Depression and the reduction of the orchestra to 74 members, Leonhardt kept the orchestra at a high level, as attested by the 130 subscription concerts in Stuttgart. He did not and could not follow the politics of the Hitler regime and asked to resign in 1937. Under his successor, Herbert Albert, the orchestra shrank during the war to 60 musicians. After the widespread destruction of Stuttgart by fire bombs in 1943, the orchestra toured as best it could.

In 1946 the Munich State Kapellmeister Bertil Wetzelsberger was asked to rebuild the Stuttgart Orchestra. He immediately started a Bruckner festival, and in 1947 (in addition to the premiere of Carl Orff's *Bernauerin*) a ten-day festival of contemporary music. In 1949 Wetzelsberger handed the offices of orchestra and opera direction over to Ferdinand Leitner (b. Berlin, 1912). Leitner brought the Stuttgart Orchestra honors not only at home but in foreign countries as well— the orchestra visited festivals in many European countries and was given honorable titles as ''Orff-Bühne'' (''Orff-Stage,'' having given four Orff premieres) and ''Winter-Bayreuth.''

There followed as music director in 1970 Václav Neumann, chief conductor of the Czech Philharmonic Orchestra,* in 1973 Silvio Varviso, and in 1980 Dennis Russell Davies, formerly conductor of the St. Paul Chamber Orchestra** in the United States. Davies, who also conducts the American Composer's Orchestra** in New York City, is deeply committed to new music. In recent years Cristóbal Halffter, Hans Werner Henze, and Krzysztof Penderecki have interpreted their own works with the Stuttgart orchestra. When Davies leaves the orchestra in 1987, Garcia Navarro is expected to be his successor.

RECORDING HISTORY: The orchestra does not record as prolifically as some German orchestras. Although its recording history dates to 1950, its current list of in-print records is short and is limited largely to vocal accompaniment.

CHRONOLOGY OF MUSIC DIRECTORS (selective): Tobias Salomon, 1611–1621. Basilius Froberger, 1621–1631, 1633–1634. Samuel Capricornus (Bockshorn), 1657–1665. Johann Sigismund Cousser, 1700–1704. Nicolo Jommelli, 1753–1769. Agostino Poli, 1782–1792. Johann Rudolf Zumsteeg, 1793–1802. Konradin Kreutzer, 1812–1816. Johann Nepomuk Hummel, 1816–1818. Peter Joseph von Lindpaintner, 1819–1856. Karl Eckert, 1860–1867. Johann Joseph Abert, 1867–1887. Karl Doppler, 1867–1898. Paul Klengel, 1887–1891. Herman Zumpe, 1890–1895. Aloys Obrist, 1895–1900. Hans Reichenberger, 1891–1902. Karl Pohlig, 1901–1907. Max von Schillings, 1908–1918. Fritz Busch, 1919–1922. Carl Leonhardt, 1922–1937. Herbert Albert, 1937–1943. Bertil Wetzelsberger, 1946–1949. Ferdinand Leitner, 1947–1969, Václav Neumann, 1970–1972. Silvio Varviso, 1973–1979. Dennis Russell Davies, 1979-present. Garcia Navarro, to begin in 1987.

BIBLIOGRAPHY: Hansmartin Decker-Hauff, "300 Jahre Instrumentalmusik am Stuttgarter Hof," in *350 Jahre Württembergisches Staatsorchester* (Stuttgart, 1967). Jürgen-Dieter Waidelich, "Die Entwicklung des Württembergischen Staatsorchesters von 1908 bis 1966," in *350 Jahre Württembergisches Staatsorchester* (Stuttgart, 1967).

ACCESS: Staatsorchester Stuttgart, Oberer Schlossgarten 6, D-7000 Stuttgart 1. 0711–20320. Wolfgang Gronnenwein, General Manager.

JOACHIM DORFMÜLLER
TRANS. ANNELIESE YIENGST

Stuttgart Chamber Orchestra

The Stuttgart Chamber Orchestra (Stuttgarter Kammerorchester) is closely linked in its history and character to its founding director, Karl Münchinger (b. 1915).

The orchestra is widely known through its many tours, which it has undertaken annually since its founding in 1945. Indeed, of its 70 to 90 concerts per season, the great majority are held outside of Stuttgart. Although the orchestra did not go much beyond West Germany in the 1985–1986 season, recent tours have brought it to Mainland China (1977); Japan, Hong Kong, and Taiwan (1982); and North America (1981, 1984, 1987). The orchestra's four to eight annual Stuttgart concerts are held in one of the rooms of the city's main concert hall, the Liederhalle.

The ensemble's administrative seat is situated in the building of the International Bach Academy in Stuttgart. The orchestra rehearses in the Academy's hall, and the Academy's director, the renowned Bach authority Helmuth Rilling, has appeared occasionally as guest conductor; however, there are no formal links between the two organizations. An 11-member Board of Directors oversees the orchestra's budget of DM 1.7 million, which is largely subsidized, half by the city of Stuttgart and half by the state of Baden-Württemberg. Additional funds are realized through ticket sales, recording fees, and other earned income. Bookings and programming are undertaken by Münchinger in association with the orchestra's agent in Stuttgart, Michael Russ of Sudwestdeutsche Konzertdirektion. Administrative matters are seen to by a general manager and office staff.

A core ensemble of 17 strings (5,4,4,3,1) is supplemented on an as-needed basis from among West Germany's many orchestras. This arrangement well suits the orchestra's tradition of a repertoire limited largely to well-known works written by Bach, Mozart, and their contemporaries. A typical program might include the Pachelbel *Kanon*, a Bach Brandenburg Concerto, or a Mozart Divertimento. Modern works appear only occasionally, and, especially in recent years, cannot be considered a significant part of the group's repertoire. A staple of its home season is the orchestra's long-standing tradition of an annual Christmastime "Dreikönigskonzert" ("Three Kings Concert"), which in 1986 comprised two symphonies by Haydn (No. 88 and No. 92) plus the Haydn C Major Oboe Concerto, with Lajos Lencsés as soloist. For larger-scale works (such as later Mozart symphonies), the core orchestra is significantly enlarged, performing (and recording) as the "Stuttgart Klassische Philharmonie."

Karl Münchinger, a native of Stuttgart, returned to his hometown after World War II to put into practice his ideal of a chamber orchestra dedicated to the works of J. S. Bach and freed from the romantic heaviness that often attended orchestral renderings of his works. In effect, Münchinger sought and attained what has been called a "golden mean" between emotion and intellect in the interpretation of Bach, with a purity and clarity that illuminated Bach's polyphony, but at the same time with a modicum of "spirit." Münchinger relied on modern instruments and tempered his understanding of baroque performance practice with an equal consideration for the cultural moment in which the music must be realized.

Gathering together 15 musicians and finding a small practice room in the devastated city, Münchinger was able to present a first Stuttgart Chamber Orchestra concert on September 18, 1945, at the Furtbachhaus. An immediate success, the orchestra soon found support in both the city of Stuttgart and the state of Baden-Württemberg. The resulting "Münchinger style" has been said to have retrained the ears of its hearers; in any event, the ensemble was soon playing to enthusiastic audiences in France and elsewhere in Europe, where its success was no doubt enhanced by the emotional atmosphere of the times. Erwin Schwarz quotes one French critic's comment in 1949 to the effect that the ensemble allowed one to see the "forgotten but true face of Germany rise from the ruins and rubble." The orchestra was soon acting the role of cultural ambassador, with annual tours that eventually took it to nearly every region of the world.

After several seasons with a repertoire limited to the few orchestral compositions of J. S. Bach, Münchinger began to experiment with other works, passing by the Italian baroque composers in favor of Haydn and Mozart. A few contemporary works, particularly by Benjamin Britten and Paul Hindemith, were heard from time to time as well. Fiscally unable to expand the ensemble in a permanent fashion for such programs, Münchinger created a separate entity in 1966, the Klassische Philharmonie, comprising the Stuttgart Chamber Orchestra plus additional strings and paired winds.

Despite the Stuttgart Chamber Orchestra's rise to the top rank of pay and size classification among similar German ensembles, Münchinger has had to learn to deal with a relatively rapid turnover in personnel, as the ensemble's restricted repertoire and busy touring schedule have taken their toll. Although some members remain for quite a long time, it is estimated, according to Schwarz, that in its 40 years of existence the orchestra has seen its personnel replaced ten times. Münchinger nevertheless maintains the Stuttgart sound, insisting on adherence to the principles upon which the orchestra was founded some 40 years (and 4,000 concerts) ago.

Now entering his seventies, Münchinger has voiced his opinions about retirement. He is in "no hurry," but neither does he fear it. Whatever decisions are made in that regard, both Münchinger and "his" orchestra are committed to the ensemble's future.

RECORDING HISTORY AND SELECTIVE DISCOGRAPHY: The Stuttgart Chamber Orchestra has recorded since the early 1950s, when it was among the first ensembles to record for the then-new Decca label. Its first recording (for Decca) was a complete and award-winning Brandenburg Concerto cycle (1950), an undertaking it has twice repeated. It has made, in all, some 30 discs, including a recent series of compact discs for the Stuttgart-based firm of Intercord. Its recorded repertoire closely parallels that of its concert presentations. Many of its Decca (London) productions are still in print as re-releases.

Bach, Six Brandenburg Concertos (Münchinger): London STS 15366/7 (2 records). Bach, B Minor Mass (Münchinger): London 1287 (2 records); Decca 414 251–1D2J. Handel, *Water Music* (Münchinger): London LDR 71050; Decca 411 973–1DH2. Mozart, "Nachtmusiken"—serenades and divertimenti (Münchinger): Intercord 180.856 (2 records); 860.953 (CD). Vivaldi, *Four Seasons* (Münchinger): London STS 15403.

CHRONOLOGY OF MUSIC DIRECTORS: Karl Münchinger, 1945-present.

BIBLIOGRAPHY: Interviews with SCO Secretary Mrs. Häfner and Violinist Manfred Wetzler, 1986. Erwin Schwarz, *Humanität durch Musik: Vierzig jahre Karl Münchinger* (Stuttgart: Stuttgart Chamber Orchestra, 1985). Wolfram Schwinger, "Karl Münchinger," *The New Grove Dictionary of Music and Musicians* (New York: Macmillan, 1981).

ACCESS: Stuttgart Kammerorchester, 1 Hasenbergsteige, Stuttgart. 61–06–27. Andreas Keller, Manager.

ROBERT R. CRAVEN

WUPPERTAL   (387,000)

Wuppertal Symphony Orchestra

Wuppertal, the cultured, major city of Nordrhein-Westfalen, is heir to a disjointed history in which its professional orchestra partook for many years.

With 89 budgeted chairs the orchestra has in the past decade been increasingly able to perform large symphonic scores. The former general music director, Hanns-Martin Schneidt, committed himself to bring to his audiences works from the entire breadth of musical history. He especially highlighted Bach, Mozart, and Schubert, but also Anton Bruckner and Gustav Mahler, who have emerged in complete cycles. The orchestra performs about 50 symphony and choir concerts, 180 opera evenings, and 20 trips annually. Schneidt was, as of the 1985–1986 season, supported by conductors Peter Gülke, David Shallon, Jean-François Monnard, and Lothar Knepper.

Orchestra members are employees and officeholders of the city (Städtische Angestellte und Beamte) and are overseen by a management team comprising a Geschaftsführer (since 1960 Heinz Lürhmann, principal oboist) assisted by three or four orchestra members. The orchestra is funded by general ticket receipts and by organizations (Konzertgesellschaft Wuppertal, Kulturgemeinde Volksbühne, and Theatergemeinde) representing in various configurations audiences of the Opera House, Town Hall, and Wuppertal's churches. The cultural life of the town of Wuppertal is administered by its Kulturdezernent, a political officeholder.

Ensembles formed from within the Wuppertal Symphony Orchestra are the Brand Quartet (1950–1970), the live/electronic Mega-Hertz-Group (1969–1975), the Martfeld Quartet (since 1979), and the salon orchestra "Nostalgie" (since 1981).

Elberfeld and Barmen, cities noted for the textile and machine industries, were merged in 1929 with their smaller neighbors, Cronenberg, Ronsdorf, and Vohwinkel, into a "Metropolis of the Mountain Region," known thereafter as Wuppertal. The cities had neither a common orchestra nor common choral and concert societies. In Elberfeld laymen founded an instrumental society in 1830, which still exists today as the "Wuppertaler Instrumentalverein." In 1849 the Langenbach Orchestra, named for Julius Langenbach, a disciple of Louis Spohr, took its place on a professional basis. This orchestra developed through the cooperation of singing societies, the Elberfeld Gesangverein, founded in 1811, and the Barmen Gesangverein, founded in 1816. It was organized under the management of impresario Abraham Küpper.

With the end of the 1861–1862 season, financial dissatisfaction among the Elberfeld orchestra's musicians had spread so far that a total of 18 separated from the artistically incompetent Küpper and, under the leadership of R. Schultz, established their own orchestra, which as the "Elberfelder Orchestra" comprised the germ of today's Wuppertal Symphony. In 1865 Willy Gutkind became the conductor; he was in office until 1883 and worked closely with Hermann Schornstein and (after 1879) with both Julius Buths of the Elberfeld Gesangverein and Anton Kraus of the Barmen Gesangverein. Organizationally, Gutkind was supported by the concert societies of both cities. Cooperation with the Instrumental Society continued. The Heckmann Quartet of Cologne was engaged for principal chairs, and famous artists such as Johannes Brahms, Max Bruch, Joseph Joachim, and Clara Schumann were contracted as guest performers.

Elberfeld's new municipal hall was truly done in major city dimensions; built in the style of the Italian Renaissance, the building (today nearly unchanged) holds nearly 1,800 people in its great hall alone. Buths's successor, Hans Haym, and guest director Richard Strauss presented the formal opening in the framework of the first "Bergischen Musikfestival" in June of 1900. Barmen made do thereafter, as before, with the approximately 600 seats of the "Concordia" hall, which had been outfitted in 1861 with the first European concert-hall organ, an instrument from the local firm of Ibach.

In the meantime, the cities had undertaken efforts to take both orchestras into their own hands; this occurred for the Elberfeld Orchestra in 1886; for the Barmen Orchestra Society (founded 1874) it occurred piecemeal in 1889, with both orchestras now referred to as "city" orchestras. By 1919 a "Barmen-Elberfeld United City Orchestra" was a reality. They had, after all, played the theatres of both cities for a long time. In the following five years the conductors were still separately appointed. For Barmen they were Erich Kleiber, Otto Klemperer, and Hans Weisbach; for Elberfeld, Hermann von Schmeidel. Franz von Hoesslin, the disciple of Max Reger, became the first general music director in 1926; he was avant-garde in repertoire with his commitment to the baroque (a first performance of *Art of the Fugue* among others) and to the modern (Paul Hindemith, Arthur Honegger, Arnold Schoenberg, and Igor Stravinsky, among others).

The Great Depression brought the orchestra many problems, but thanks to private initiative, catastrophe was avoided; benefit concerts were held, led by (among others) Hans Knappertsbusch, himself an Elberfelder. After a combined concert society was formed in 1932, Helmut Schnakenburg became Hoesslin's successor as music director. Fritz Lehmann followed in 1938. In 1944 he was drafted to serve at the Cologne radio station, and he returned to the post of general music director in Wuppertal in November of 1945. In the meantime, Helmut Schaefer, the choir director of the stage, and Hermann Inderau of the Instrumentverein sustained the life of the orchestra in the mostly destroyed city.

Hans Weisbach, whom Wuppertalers knew already from 1924–1926, continued the orchestra's reconstruction. He dedicated himself especially to the symphonies of the nineteenth century (in the "Bruckner Days" of 1948, for example). He also, however, committed himself to contemporary music with the support of the concert society and of the cultural organization known as the People's Stage. Under Weisbach Wuppertal committed itself in 1950 and 1955 to the Nordrhein Music Festival, which had first been organized in Elberfeld in 1817 by Hermann Schornstein. Weisbach also consolidated cooperation with the West German Radio Network in Cologne. A merger with the theatre house of the neighboring city of Solingen went into effect in 1950. Since then the Wuppertal Orchestra and Stage Ensemble have travelled there regularly.

Hans Georg Ratjen became general music director in 1955. With the formal opening of the new opera house in Spinnerstrasse, the orchestra began to highlight the works of Claudio Monteverdi and Mozart and their contemporaries. Ratjen collaborated successfully with Martin Stephani, the leader of the concert society's choir, who was appointed to that office in 1951 and who took over as his successor for four years in 1959. In the fall of 1963 Hanns-Martin Schneidt took over the orchestra (then known as the Wuppertal City Orchestra; since June 1976 it has called itself the Wuppertal Symphony Orchestra). In 1985 the town cultural committee announced that Dr. Peter Gülke (b. Weimar, 1934) would succeed Schneidt as general music director.

SELECTIVE DISCOGRAPHY: Mahler, Symphony No. 3 (Schneidt): MD & G, Detmold/Wuppertal MDG 1032. Mozart, Symphony No. 40 (K. 550); Becker, *Transformationen* (Schneidt): Mediafon Solingen/Wuppertal F 60590-B.

CHRONOLOGY OF MUSIC DIRECTORS: Franz von Hoesslin, 1926–1932. Helmut Schnakenburg, 1932–1938. Fritz Lehmann, 1938–1944, 1945. Hans Weisbach, 1946–1955. Hans Georg Ratjen, 1955–1959. Martin Stephani, 1959–1963. Hanns-Martin Schneidt, 1963–1985. (Guest conductors, 1985–1986.) Peter Gülke, 1986–present.

BIBLIOGRAPHY: Alfred Mayerhofer, *Städtisches Orchester Wuppertal, 1862–1962* (Wuppertal: Girardet, 1962).

ACCESS: Sinfonieorchester Wuppertal, c/o Kulturamt der Stadt Wuppertal, Friedrich-Engels-Allee 83, 5600 Wuppertal 2. 0202–5631. Heinz Lührmann, General Manager.

JOACHIM DORFMÜLLER

TRANS. GEORGE COMMENATOR

Guatemala —————————————

GUATEMALA CITY (800,000)

Philharmonic Orchestra of Guatemala

The Philharmonic Orchestra of Guatemala (OFG: Orquesta Filarmónica de Guatemala) is one of the best established and most active professional orchestras in Central America. This group, founded in 1944, is a continuation of several predecessor ensembles and part of a rich musical heritage that dates back several centuries.

The OFG, like all the other orchestras in the region, is a state-sponsored institution whose principal task is to provide culture not only in the capital, Guatemala City, but in outlying rural areas as well. The regular season of the OFG, performed in the new Mayanesque Teatro Nacional, involves about 20 concerts spread out over an eight-month period from April to December. In addition, the orchestra performs on tour throughout the country and for students in secondary schools. It has one of the oldest Latin American broadcast traditions, with concert programs heard on the Voz de Guatemala radio since 1945.

General administration of the group is the responsibility of the Directorate General of Fine Arts of the Ministry of Culture, whose music department also coordinates the activities of the national chorus. While matters of repertoire are usually left up to the music director, the Directorate is responsible for the promotion of the season and the engagement of various guest artists. The budget for the entire year is approximately 300,000 Quetzals.

European music in Guatemala has a long history. As capital of the entire Spanish province of Central America, Guatemala City hosted an active musical establishment as early as 1500, particularly at the cathedral. Composers like Miguel Pontaza and Vincente Saez wrote and performed there, and during the eighteenth century, Italian operas were a popular form of entertainment. The

National Conservatory, founded in 1880, is the oldest in Central America. But it was not until 1934 that a permanent concert orchestra existed. That year a group known as Ars Nova was formed primarily to perform contemporary nationalistic compositions. Two years later the ensemble was superseded by the Orquesta Progresista, which performed regularly for almost ten years. This group formed the core of the OFG, which presented its first performance on September 8, 1944.

The OFG comprises a smaller group of 45–50 musicians, to which additional players from the National Conservatory may be added upon demand. The orchestra is unique in Central America in that all of its members are Guatemalan. Furthermore, virtually all have been trained at the National Conservatory. The conductors are also native-born, but for the most part trained in the United States. Each season includes both foreign soloists and guest conductors. The main repertoire emphasizes standard works, though Guatemalan works such as Ricardo Castillo's *Xibalba*, based upon Mayan themes, appear regularly on concert programs.

CHRONOLOGY OF MUSIC DIRECTORS: Ricardo del Carmen, 1964–1983. Jorge Sarmiento, 1984-present.

BIBLIOGRAPHY: Edna Nuñez de Rodas, *Cultural Policy in Guatemala* (Paris: UNESCO, 1981). Jorge Sarmiento, "Raices y futuro de la música en Guatemala y latino américa," *Revista Musical Chileña* 33 (1979): 58–65. Nicolas Slonimsky, *Music of Latin America* (New York: Da Capo, 1972). Frank Stalzer, "Orchestras of Guatemala and Costa Rica," *Woodwind World* 15/6 (1976): 12, 34. Rafael Vásquez, *Historia de la música en Guatemala* (Guatemala: Tipografia Nacionale, 1950).

ACCESS: Jorge Sarmiento, Orquesta Filarmónica de Guatemala, 3a, Ave 4–61, Zona 1, Guatamala City, Guatemala. (502–2) 20176.

BERTIL H. VAN BOER, JR.
MARGARET L. FAST

Hong Kong —————————————

HONG KONG (3,674,000*)

Hong Kong Philharmonic Orchestra

Each year the Hong Kong Philharmonic gives 24 pairs of symphonic concerts offering the same program on two consecutive evenings to audiences averaging 1,300 per performance. In addition, pops concerts attract a substantial following—more than 150,000 attendees in 1983–1984.

The orchestra receives support from the Hong Kong government and the Urban Council, which together provide 70% of the Philharmonic's income. Only 10% comes from ticket sales because ticket prices are kept low so most people can afford them. Further support comes from the Royal Hong Kong Jockey Club, patrons, and sponsors. Chair and other endowments have been made by clubs, business firms, and philanthropic individuals. In 1984 a new policy to place endowments under one funding was launched with a capital fund target of HK$50,000,000. A Ladies Committee was established in 1978 to raise HK$500,000 annually, and a Friends of the Philharmonic group was formed in late 1984 to support the orchestra in a number of ways. Expenditures in 1984 were HK$18,000,000, and in 1984 there were 83 players and a support staff of 50. Two subgroups of Philharmonic players, the Tononi String Quartet and the Allegro Woodwind Quintet, performed in chamber music concerts in 1984.

The Hong Kong Coliseum, which seats nearly 12,000, was opened in 1983 and is now used by the orchestra for playing popular music (both Chinese and European), television and film music, and ballet music. Programs of ballet music, with the conductor introducing the works, have drawn audiences to symphonic concerts. Hong Kong is musically bilingual, and a cross-cultural appreciation of Chinese and European music is reflected in the works of Hong Kong composers. New compositions by local composers have been commissioned by sponsors and performed by the orchestra at recent concerts.

The Tsim Sha Tsui Cultural Centre being built on a prominent waterfront site is scheduled for completion in 1987 and will be the administrative and professional home of the orchestra. Its 2,300-seat concert hall (with pipe organ), 1,860-seat multi-purpose theatre, repertory theatre, and comprehensive support facilities have been designed to meet the highest international standards. These auditoriums provide venues for major works to be performed with the full scale of resources envisioned by the composers.

Although the Hong Kong Philharmonic Orchestra completed its first decade as a professional orchestra in 1984, its roots are found in the Hong Kong Philharmonic Society, which gave its first orchestral concert in 1895 under the baton of George Lammert. Concerts were held in 1903 and again in 1907, with Denman Fuller as conductor, and for many years the orchestra continued as a rather casual band of music-making amateurs.

Solomon Bard, who came to Hong Kong in 1934 to study medicine, was a violinist and a dynamic figure in the orchestra's history. His musical ingenuity was heightened during the war years, which he spent in Shamshuipo Prison Camp. Here Bard's "camp music" was arranged for a motley selection of instruments brought into the camp by the Japanese, according to Harry Rolnick in *Celebration*, for "the most harmless of hobbies."

The orchestra was re-formed after the war as the Sino-British Orchestra with Bard as conductor, but in 1953 he handed the baton to Arrigo Foa, an Italian-trained conductor from Shanghai. It was while Foa was conductor that Louis Kentner, the first international artist to perform with the orchestra, came to play Beethoven's Piano Concerto No. 3. Early in 1957 the Hong Kong Philharmonic Society and Orchestra was reborn, and at the end of the year the orchestra broke away, becoming the Hong Kong Philharmonic Orchestra. The new city hall was opened in March 1962, and in April the orchestra gave its first performance in the new venue. By 1964 it was receiving widespread support, local artists were making their concert debuts, and works by Hong Kong composers were being performed.

Lim Kek-tjiang, who was appointed conductor in 1969, achieved the development needed to take the orchestra from amateur to professional status, and plans to turn professional were laid in early 1973. He began auditioning, and by the end of that year seven Hong Kong and 20 overseas musicians were engaged, 15 of whom were still playing with the Philharmonic in 1984.

Following Lim Kek-tjiang's resignation in 1975 and the appointment of Hans Gunter Mommer as conductor, a more refined style of playing was encouraged. The number of full-time musicians increased, and to provide the professional musicians needed to play most of the symphonic repertoire—and the stability required to reach international standards—an orchestral development plan was prepared. By 1978 the number of players on contract had reached 67.

The year 1978 was one of crisis. Adverse press reports brought problems of morale, discipline, and funding and resulted in Mommer's resignation. Ling Tung was appointed conductor and, being Chinese, he seemed an ideal choice. Unfortunately, relationships between players and conductor became strained: Ling Tung dismissed many, and others resigned; however, some fine musicians joined as replacements. In 1981 Ling Tung left, and the orchestra relied on guest conductors until 1984. Fortunately, Carl Pini of the Philharmonia Orchestra* of London had become concertmaster by 1980 and in two years made an enormous contribution by regaining stability within the ensemble.

In 1980 the city hall venue (with its 1,450-seat auditorium) was supplemented by a new town hall in Tsuen Wan, and the 3,300-seat Queen Elizabeth Stadium (its acoustics and atmosphere unsuited to classical programs) was an ideal location to start a series of Philharmonic pops concerts.

Only months after they had both defected from Russia, Maxim Shostakovich and his son Dmitri performed with the orchestra at the 1982 Hong Kong Arts Festival. Later in 1982 Maxim accepted the post of principal guest conductor of the Hong Kong Philharmonic.

Prior to the opening of the 1980–1981 season, 50 players flew to Malaysia to accompany the Sadlers Wells Royal Ballet. This was the orchestra's first overseas tour. In April 1983 the full orchestra toured to Singapore, Bangkok, and Osaka, where it was invited to perform at the 25th Osaka Festival. Its performances on this tour firmly established it as one of the finest orchestras in Asia. In 1986 the orchestra toured the People's Republic of China. Kenneth Schermerhorn was appointed music director in 1984. A regular guest conductor in Hong Kong since 1980 and the orchestra's conductor at the Osaka Festival, Schermerhorn is concurrently the music director of the Nashville (Tennessee) Symphony Orchestra** in the United States. This post of principal guest conductor is shared by Kenneth Jean and Jorge Mester.

RECORDING HISTORY AND SELECTIVE DISCOGRAPHY: The orchestra made its first digital recording in 1982, when it recorded 12 Chinese folk-melodies. The recording was entitled "Colorful Clouds Chasing the Moon" and earned for the Philharmonic its first gold and platinum discs. The orchestra had made seven further digital recordings by the end of 1984. All were made in the Tsuen Wan Town Hall and bear the Hong Kong Records Company Limited label.

Brahms, Hungarian Dances Nos. 1 and 2 (Kenneth Jean): Hong Kong Records/BOSE 4–220118. *Under the Silver Moon* (Chinese folksongs) (Jean): Hong Kong Records 4–240279.

CHRONOLOGY OF MUSIC DIRECTORS: Solomon Bard, 1947–1953. Arrigo Foa, 1953–1969. Lim Kek-tjiang, 1969–1975. Hans Gunter Mommer, 1975–1978. Ling Tung, 1978–1981. (Guest conductors, 1981–1984.) Kenneth Schermerhorn, 1984-present.

BIBLIOGRAPHY: Cynthia Hydes, Amy Chu, John Duffus, and Sun-man Tseung, *Celebration* (Hong Kong Philharmonic Society, 1984).

ACCESS: Hong Kong Philharmonic Orchestra, GPO Box 3858, Hong Kong. 5–7907521. John Duffus, General Manager. Cynthia Hydes, Public Relations Manager.

DALE P. DICKIE

Hungary _____

BUDAPEST (2,064,000)

Budapest Philharmonic Orchestra

The Budapest Philharmonic Orchestra (BPO: Budapesti Filharmóniai Társaság Zenekara) was founded in 1853. It presently consists of 154 professional musicians (115 men, 39 women), many of whom also teach in various music schools or the Liszt Academy of Music. Several also perform in chamber music groups independently of the orchestra.

The orchestra's concert season is from September through June and includes 20 to 30 concerts, with a great many performances each year as the orchestra of the Hungarian State Opera House. The BPO, like the other symphony orchestras of Budapest, has no permanent concert hall. It holds its concerts either in the Erkel Theatre of the Hungarian State Opera House (which seats 2,500 people and is acoustically uneven); the Academy of Music (which seats 1,000 and is acoustically very good); the 680-seat Redoute/Pesti Vigado (with uneven acoustics); or the Patria Hall of the Budapest Congress Center, which opened in 1985 and seats 1,800 persons.

The BPO is an association with a president/conductor, a post filled since 1976 by András Kóródi. It is administered by an executive director and a Board of eleven members elected by ballot every three years at a general assembly of the orchestra. BPO concert programs are jointly arranged by the orchestra itself in collaboration with the Hungarian State Concert Management and guest conductors both Hungarian and foreign. The orchestra's budget is funded in part by ticket sales and is subsidized by the Hungarian State Concert Management, which is subsidized by the state.

BPO concert programming strives to maintain its musical traditions, to render the highest standards of interpretation, and to expose the masses to masterworks of all musical periods. The BPO has the distinction of having premiered many works of eminent Hungarian composers, among them Béla Bartók and Zoltán Kodály.

Budapest, the capital of Hungary, is an important cultural center with 20 theatres, numerous music schools, universities, and colleges. As a republic in its own right, it was created in 1873 with the unification of three towns: Buda and Obuda on the right bank of the Danube, and Pest, on the left bank. Cultural life in Budapest flourished under the rule of the Habsburgs, and by the nineteenth century music societies and instrumental groups were formed alongside diverse theatre and opera companies. A German population had settled in Buda and would influence artistic life there. In 1867 a dual monarchy, Austro-Hungarian, was established, which lasted until the end of World War I, when the city was once again returned to Hungary. In 1948 Hungary became a socialist state.

During the second half of the nineteenth century, famous Hungarian musicians contributed to a new blossoming of culture. One of these was the acclaimed composer, conductor, and concert pianist Ferenc Erkel. Gathering together 46 musicians from the Budapest National Theatre (which he founded in 1838), Erkel organized an orchestra, which he conducted at its inaugural concert on November 20, 1853. They performed works of Beethoven, Mozart, Mendelssohn, and Meyerbeer in the Hungarian National Museum's Hall of Celebration, where they would perform until 1865. The importance of this newly formed organization was immense, as it would be the sole interpreter of Budapest's orchestral achievements for a very long time.

Eventually Erkel established the Philharmonic Society (Filharmóniai Társaság), whose purpose it was to nurture symphonic music in Hungary. As president of the Society and as principal conductor of the Opera House (1831–1874), Erkel effectively influenced the cultural development of Hungary for the next 40 years.

A concert season with celebrated guest artists was begun with performances of compositions by classical and romantic composers, as well as by Hungarians. The orchestra was also responsive to the Wagnerians, who had developed something of a cult in Hungary. In the early years audiences demonstrated great enthusiasm, but as time passed audience interest declined, especially between 1861 and 1864, resulting in a financial crisis. A small group of music lovers sustained the orchestra with donations and by administering its affairs. In 1865 a new concert hall, Redoute, was inaugurated by the orchestra with a performance of Beethoven's Ninth Symphony. Two years later the Society became known as the Hungarian Philharmonic Association (Magyar Filharmóniai Társulat). In 1870 the orchestra celebrated Beethoven's centenary with Franz Liszt at the podium conducting his Beethoven-Cantate, newly written for the occasion. Liszt's musical activities contributed significantly to the cultural growth of Budapest during the second half of the nineteenth century, and the city grew to be an important European music center.

From 1871 to 1875 Hans Richter conducted the Philharmonic and frequently returned thereafter to lead the Philharmonic. He was followed in 1875 by Sándor Erkel, the son of Ferenc Erkel. During his tenure the repertoire was expanded, with first performances in Budapest of works of Bach, Dvořák, Brahms, Tchaikovsky, Saint-Saëns, and others. The Association was reorganized to further expose the public to symphonic music. Stellar guest artists began appearing with the group, among them Fritz Kreisler, Joseph Joachim, Brahms, and others. In 1879 two Liszt programs were performed in collaboration with the composer. The first Budapest performance of Berlioz's *Requiem* took place in 1888, at which time the orchestra adopted the title "Philharmonic Society of Members of the [Budapest] Opera" (A Magyar Királyi Operaház Zenekarából Alakult Filharmóniai Társaság). Erkel's extended illness necessitated the frequent appearance of guest conductors, among them Arthur Nikisch (who gave nine notable concerts with the orchestra from 1893 to 1895), Hans Richter, Felix Mottl, Gustav Mahler, and others.

In 1900 István Kerner, a highly capable conductor, became the orchestra's director. He was especially noted for his Mozart interpretations and became known for performances of new Hungarian works by the young Kodály and Bartók, for all-Hungarian programs, and for music festivals. In 1904 Sunday matinee performances were begun especially for students. Kerner's Hungarian tours with the orchestra began in 1908, and foreign tours began in 1915 with a trip to Vienna.

The orchestra gained further stature with the appointment in 1919 of Ernö Dohnányi as president/conductor. Throughout his 24-year leadership Dohnányi further emphasized the new Hungarian works, such as Bartók's *Miraculous Mandarin Suite*, *Cantata Profana*, and *Music for Strings, Percussion and Celesta*; Kodály's *Háry János Suite*, *Marosszék Dances*, *Galánta Dances*, and *Budavár Te Deum*; and other works. The list of guest artists during this period includes such names as Igor Stravinsky, Maurice Ravel, Ottorino Respighi, Serge Prokofiev, Wilhelm Furtwängler, and Herbert von Karajan. The orchestra frequently toured Europe and England and participated in many music festivals. The 50th anniversary of the unification of Buda and Pest was commemorated in 1923 with a concert gala on November 19, at which Dohnányi's *Festival Overture*, Bartók's *Dance Suite*, and Kodály's *Psalmus Hungaricus* received their first performances. All had been written for the occasion.

From 1943 to 1953 the orchestra was without a chief conductor, and the financial difficulties in the aftermath of World War II forced the cancellation of concerts. A concert took place in 1945 with the surviving members of the orchestra. After the group's reorganization, orchestra concerts, including Hungarian premieres, were led by Hungarian conductors János Ferencsik, Ferenc Fricsay, László Somogyi, and an Italian, Sergio Failoni, who had settled in Hungary. Despite the difficulties of the postwar period, the 1947–1948 concert season encompassed seven concerts plus a visit to Vienna with János Ferencsik. From 1947 to 1950 Otto Klemperer gave numerous successful performances with the orchestra. In 1950 the organization was renamed the Budapest Philharmonic

Society (Budapesti Filharmóniai Társaság). Orchestral programs were then designed to reach a wider public, as for example in 1951's First Hungarian Music Festival.

In 1956 János Ferencsik began a 23-year association with the organization. Ferencsik (who concurrently led the Hungarian State Symphony Orchestra) widened BPO activities, bringing it to international festivals, making recordings, and expanding its programming. In 1953 the BPO's one hundredth anniversary was celebrated with a gala concert at which time Zóltan Kodály was made its honorary president. A festive cycle of programs was performed by the BPO in 1962 to mark Kodály's eightieth birthday, and the composer's *Psalmus Hungaricus* was performed with a chorus of several thousand.

In 1967 András Kóródi assumed the post of conductor, and in 1976 the orchestra elected him conductor/president. He was also principal conductor of the Hungarian State Opera at the time, where he led numerous premieres of newly written Hungarian operas and ballets as well as a full opera repertoire. His programs are widely varied. Under his baton the BPO has performed in Mexico, Japan, and throughout Europe. Its tours have done much to enhance the BPO's international reputation, and its critical reception has been very enthusiastic, with especially kind commentary about the rich timbre of its strings, its flexibility, and the virtuosity of its winds.

RECORDING HISTORY AND SELECTIVE DISCOGRAPHY: The BPO has made numerous recordings. Conductors Ferencsik, Kodály, Kóródi, and others have recorded under a variety of labels including Hungaroton, Deutsche Grammophon, London, Philips, and Angel. Its recordings include several award winners. From 1969 to 1981 the orchestra made 30 recordings of Hungarian works, among them noteworthy performances of music by Erkel, Kodály, and Bartók.

Bartók, *Four Pieces for Orchestra*, Op. 12; *Images*; and *Two Portraits* (Erdélyi): Hung, 1302. Bartók, *Miraculous Mandarin* Suite, Op. 19; *Dance Suite*; and *Hungarian Peasant Songs* (Sándor): Hung. 11319. Bartók, *Romanian Dances*; Violin Concerto, Op. Post.; and *Wooden Prince Suite* (Kóródi): Hung. 11314. Kodály, Concerto for Orchestra and *Summer Night* (Kodály): DG 2543809. Kodály, Concerto for Orchestra and *Háry János* Suite (Ferencsik): Hung. 12190, Qualiton 1194.

CHRONOLOGY OF MUSIC DIRECTORS: Ferenc Erkel, 1853–1871. Hans Richter, 1871–1875. Sándor Erkel, 1875–1900. István Kerner, 1900–1919. Ernö Dohnányi, 1919–1943. (Guest conductors, 1943–1953.) János Ferencsik, 1953–1976. András Kóródi, 1976-present.

BIBLIOGRAPHY: Correspondence with Association of Hungarian Musicians Executive Secretary Eva Csebfalvi, 1985. János Breuer, *The Budapest Philharmonic Orchestra* pamphlet (Budapest, 1981). "Budapest," *Grove Dictionary of Music and Musicians*, 5th ed. (New York: St. Martin's Press, 1954). Budapest Philharmonic Orchestra, miscellaneous programs.

ACCESS: Budapest Philharmonic Orchestra, c/o Hungarian State Opera, Népköztársaság utja 22, 1061 Budapest. (011–361) 312–550. Arpád Wittmann, Philharmonic Executive Director.

VIOLET VAGRAMIAN-NISHANIAN

Hungarian State Symphony Orchestra

The Hungarian State Symphony Orchestra (HSSO; Magyar Allami Hangver-
senyzenekar) was founded in 1923. It includes 117 musicians (87 men, 30
women), most of whom are teachers in music schools or the Academy of Music
and/or members of various Budapest chamber orchestras, among them the Hungarian Chamber Orchestra.

The HSSO's concert season begins at the end of September and lasts until the
beginning of June. Additionally, open-air concerts take place from June to mid-
August. In all, 85 to 100 concerts are performed per year, including tours. HSSO
concerts are held in various concert halls in Budapest, such as the 1,800-seat
Patria Hall of the Budapest Congress Center. The orchestra regularly plays to
audiences of 95% to 100% of house capacity. The HSSO has appeared at many
major European music festivals, and every other year it takes an extensive tour
of West Germany. It also tours with regularity throughout Europe and the world.
The HSSO has a most impressive recording history

The orchestra's budget is provided by the Hungarian State Concert Management, which organizes its concerts, from state subvention. The HSSO has an
Orchestral Committee of seven members who act as an advisory board on matters
of orchestral activities. Five of its members are elected by the orchestra and two
are nominated. The organization's managing director is from the ranks of the
orchestra. Since 1984 the HSSO has not had a permanent music director. Guest
conductors from Hungary and abroad have appeared regularly with the orchestra.

The orchestra's purpose from its inception has been to foster symphonic music
in Hungary. HSSO orchestral concerts offer a balance of the classical and romantic masterworks, twentieth-century works, and works of Hungarian composers, which are sometimes presented in all-Bartók, all-Dohnányi, or similar
programs. Premieres of contemporary Hungarian composers' orchestral works
are frequent. The following program performed by the HSSO in April of 1985
is representative: Dohnányi, Suite in F-sharp Minor, Op. 19; Manuel de Falla,
Noches en los jardines España; and Maurice Ravel, Piano Concerto in G Major
and *Bolero*.

The Hungarian State Symphony Orchestra, originally the Budapest Municipal
Orchestra (Fovárosi Zenekar), a semi-amateur group, was first led by Dezsö
Bor, its conductor for 16 years, from 1923 to 1939. The orchestra became
professional in 1939, at which time its conductor was Béla Csilléry, who remained until 1944, when he left Hungary.

Following World War II the orchestra was reconstituted due to severe losses
sustained among its members. Conductors Ferenc Fricsay and László Somogyi
were significant contributors to the reorganization, and Fricsay remained with
the orchestra until 1948. A student of Bartók and Zoltán Kodály, he was regarded
as an outstanding interpreter of their music. He expanded the ensemble's repertoire considerably, and his performances were noted for their clarity and precision. A dynamic performer, he conducted the familiar classics with great

vividness, and he was admired as well as an exponent of contemporary music. Fricsay also frequently conducted the Budapest Philharmonic Orchestra.* László Somogyi remained with the HSSO until 1952 and continued to develop the orchestra's programming. A municipal organization, the ensemble had been receiving its support from the city of Budapest, but in 1952 this changed, along with the name of the orchestra, which would henceforth be known as the Hungarian State Symphony Orchestra.

The HSSO's new conductor, János Ferencsik, had an international reputation and was to guide the group for the next 32 years, during some of which he was concurrently the music director of the Hungarian State Opera. He preferred the classics: Haydn, Mozart, and Beethoven, and the venerable Hungarians Liszt, Bartók, and Kodály. He also introduced numerous contemporary Hungarian composers' works. His performances with the HSSO were praised for a subtlety of nuance that allowed the ensemble and conductor to become one entity.

Extensive tours brought the group to the United States, Australia, Japan, and many European countries. These tours provoked high acclaim and established the group's worldwide reputation. Ferencsik also made frequent guest appearances at the Bayreuth, Edinburgh, and Salzburg Festivals, as well as at the Vienna Opera House. The HSSO's repertoire continued to expand, but under Ferencsik the orchestra was especially known for vibrant performances of Hungarian music, which Ferencsik frequently premiered and recorded. Since Ferencsik's death in 1984, the HSSO has been without a music director, and has been led by guest conductors both Hungarian and foreign. The orchestra has long been associated with a panoply of guest conductors, however, including Leonard Bernstein, Antál Doráti, Zubin Mehta, and especially Otto Klemperer, who gave 41 concerts with the orchestra.

RECORDING HISTORY AND SELECTIVE DISCOGRAPHY: The Hungarian State Symphony Orchestra has made well over 100 recordings, mainly on the Hungarian label, Hungaroton, with some released on the Fidelio label as well. Numerous recordings were made under Ferencsik, and although his recorded repertoire is wide-ranging, his outstanding discs feature works of the Hungarian composers Erkel, Liszt, Bartók, and Kodály. Among guest conductors who have recorded with the HSSO are András Kóródi, who recorded works of Gounod, Verdi, Bartók, and Prokofiev; Iván Fischer, who recorded Karl Goldmark, Mendelssohn, Mahler, and Donizetti; Giuseppe Patané, whose recordings include works of Puccini, Dvořák and Verdi; and Ferenc Szekeres, who recorded Haydn, Vivaldi, and Antonio Soler. Reviewers have commented on the superior engineering of HSSO recordings.

Bartók, Concerto for Orchestra, *Dance Suite* (Ferencsik): Hung. 12346. Bartók, Suite No. 1, Op. 3 (Ferencsik): Hung. 11480. Erkel, *Festival Overture* (Ferencsik): Hung. 12041. Kodály, *Psalmus Hungaricus*, Op. 13, and other works (Kodály): Hung. 12410/ 12 E (3 discs). Liszt, *Rákóczi March* and other works (Németh): Hung. 12249. Liszt, *Les Préludes, Tasso, Orpheus* (Ferencsik): Hung. 12446 (also in CD, 12446).

CHRONOLOGY OF MUSIC DIRECTORS: Dezsö Bor, 1923–1939. Béla Csilléry, 1939–1944. Ferenc Fricsay, 1945–1948. László Somogyi, 1945–1952. János Ferencsik, 1952–1984.

BIBLIOGRAPHY: Correspondence with Association of Hungarian Musicicans Executive Secretary Eva Csebfalvi, 1985. "Ferencsik, János," *The New Grove Dictionary of Music and Musicians*, 6th ed. (London: Macmillan, 1980). Hungarian State Symphony Orchestra, miscellaneous programs and catalogs. *The Hungarian State Symphony Orchestra* pamphlets (Budapest: HSSO).

ACCESS: Hungarian State Symphony Orchestra, c/o Orzágos Filharmónia, 1051 Budapest, Vörösmarty tér 1, Hungary. (011–361) 180–104. Zsolt Bartha, Managing Director.

VIOLET VAGRAMIAN-NISHANIAN

Orchestra of the Hungarian Radio and Television

The Orchestra of the Hungarian Radio and Television (A Magyar Rádió és Televízió Szimfónikus Zenekara), known abroad as the Budapest Symphony Orchestra, consists of 106 musicians, 82 men and 24 women, many of whom perform in other chamber formations and/or teach in music schools or the Academy of Music. The orchestra was founded in 1945 when the Hungarian Radio was reorganized after World War II.

The concert season of the Budapest Symphony Orchestra is from the end of September to the beginning of July and includes 60 concerts held at various concert halls of Budapest. The orchestra regularly plays to full or nearly full houses.

The Budapest Symphony Orchestra is under the direction of the Music Department of the Hungarian Radio, subsidized by the state. Concert programming is organized by the Hungarian Radio's Music Department in collaboration with its orchestral conductors and the Hungarian State Concert Management. Programs include the Viennese classics and earlier masterworks, works of the romantics and of twentieth-century composers, and especially the works of distinguished contemporary Hungarian composers, whose works the orchestra regularly premieres.

The orchestra's budget derives from that of the Hungarian Radio. More than 60% of the Hungarian Radio broadcast time is devoted to music. Of special importance is educational programming for youth, stressing musical culture.

The Budapest Symphony Orchestra reaches a vast audience through its live broadcasts made either from the studio or the concert hall, and it is credited with having a significant cultural impact within Hungary. Additionally, 50 foreign countries hear taped rebroadcasts of its concerts. Since 1962 the orchestra's music director has been internationally renowned conductor György Lehel, one of Hungary's foremost musicians. Lehel has toured extensively with the orchestra, which is regarded as one of Europe's leading ensembles. Its guest conductors and soloists have consistently been among the very finest.

State broadcasting was already established in Hungary by the mid–1920s under post office control. Commercial broadcasting, developed during the early 1930s, was abandoned after World War II, to be replaced by a nationwide service set up in Budapest under government control. The Budapest Symphony Orchestra was begun in 1945 as an arm of this service. Its first conductor was János Ferencsik. Known for his interest in the classics and Hungarian composers, particularly Liszt, Kodály, and Bartók, Ferencsik nevertheless provided programs that demonstrated a balance between musical periods. Ferencsik made many recordings with the orchestra and established its high standing worldwide. In 1952 László Somogyi followed Ferencsik as the Budapest Symphony Orchestra's music director, remaining with the orchestra until 1956. From 1957 until 1961 the orchestra was led by Tamás Bródy.

György Lehel joined the Budapest Symphony Orchestra as a conductor in 1958 and became its music director and chief conductor in 1962. His role in Hungary's musical life has been decisive. Under Lehel the orchestra advanced further artistically, and its repertoire expanded to give particular emphasis to the performance of new works by present-day Hungarian composers. Lehel's strengths lie also in his interpretations of the late romantic and modern composers. A number of Hungarian composers have dedicated their works to him.

Under Lehel the Budapest Symphony Orchestra makes several major tours annually, in addition to regular appearances at European music festivals. The orchestra made its British debut in 1968 at the Cheltenham Festival, at which it premiered Gordon Crosse's Chamber Concerto, op. 8, and Elizabeth Maconchy's *Three Cloudscapes*. Numerous successful tours have brought the orchestra to the United States, Canada, all of Europe, and Japan. It has won high critical praises in its travels, with special notice of its homogeneity, nuance of shading, and rich sound. A representative program in one of the Budapest Symphony Orchestra's overseas visits included Haydn's Symphony No. 95, Bartók's Concerto No. 3 for Piano and Orchestra. András Szöllösy's *Transfigurazioni*, and Stravinsky's *Firebird* Suite.

RECORDING HISTORY AND SELECTIVE DISCOGRAPHY: The Budapest Symphony Orchestra records regularly. As a radio ensemble it makes all the recordings of contemporary Hungarian composers' works for the Hungarian Radio. The orchestra has made over 100 recordings under the Hungaroton label as well as numerous releases on Deutsche Grammophon, Pathé-Marconi, Westminster, Sefel, Seraphim, and other labels. Recorded works include classical, romantic, twentieth-century, and contemporary works, with emphasis on Hungarian composers. Under Ferencsik's direction many recordings were made of composers such as Liszt, Kodály, and Bartók. Lehel's recordings include complete Bartók and Kodály collections, and he has received critical acclaim for his authoritative interpretations. He has also recorded Brahms's symphonies and overtures and an extensive number of new Hungarian works. Many guest conductors have also recorded with the orchestra.

Bartók, Music for Strings, Percussion and Celesta, *Miraculous Mandarin Suite* (Lehel): Hung. 1301, Dohnányi, *Ruralia Hungarica*, op. 32b; *Variations on a Nursery Song*, op. 25 (Lehel): Hung. 12149. Kodály, *Budavári Te Deum, Missa Brevis* (Ferencsik): Hung. 11397. Kodály, *The Peacock, Galánta Dances, Marosszék Dances* (Lehel): Hung. 12252. Rezso Sugár, *Savonarola, Metamorfosi* (Lehel): Hung. 12518–19. Endre Szekely, *Sounds Arising and Disappearing*, Horn Concerto (Tarjani/Lehel): Hung. 12129. András Szöllösy, *Transfigurazione* (Lehel): Hung. 11733.

CHRONOLOGY OF MUSIC DIRECTORS: János Ferencsik, 1945–1952. László Somogyi, 1952–1956. Tamás Bródy, 1957–1961. György Lehel, 1962-present.

BIBLIOGRAPHY: Correspondence with Association of Hungarian Musicians' Executive Secretary Eva Csebfalvi, 1985. "Lehel, György," *New Grove Dictionary of Music
and Musicians* (London: Macmillan, 1980).

ACCESS: Budapest Symphony Orchestra, c/o Hungarian Radio Music Department,
Bródy S. u. 5–7, H–1800 Budapest. (361) 338–330. István Bogár, Manager.

VIOLET VAGRAMIAN-NISHANIAN

Iceland _____

Iceland Symphony Orchestra

The Iceland Symphony Orchestra, founded in 1950, is among the youngest national orchestras in Europe. Iceland's unique cultural heritage is founded in the literature of the medieval Sagas, while the history of its performing arts is short. Geographically isolated, the island historically had sustained only a small, widely scattered rural population of farmers and fisherman. It was not until the middle of the nineteenth century, when urban development increased prosperity, and improved international communications paved the way for greater cultural exchange, that the centuries-old isolation was broken. Iceland had been unaffected by the baroque and classical eras of music, and it was not until very late in the romantic period that conditions had allowed the establishment of an active musical life.

First attempts to form an orchestra started around 1920. Some Icelanders acquired orchestral instruments and either studied abroad for short periods or were taught by visiting musicians. The main influence was from Germany, by way of Denmark, and in 1926 an orchestra from Hamburg was the first to be heard in Iceland. The years 1930–1932 were crucial. In 1930 Iceland celebrated the 1,000th anniversay of its Parliament (Althing) and the celebrations included the performance of an Icelandic cantata using an orchestra of 50 musicians. Also in 1930 the State Radio and the first music school were established, followed in 1932 by the Philharmonic Society and the Musicians Union. Finally, in 1950, after several abortive attempts, the Symphony Orchestra was established with 40 musicians, funded primarily by the State Radio. The orchestra grew slowly but surely over the years, though its future was often uncertain. It was not until 1982 that parliamentary legislation finally gave it security. Since 1983 the orchestra has been financed by the State (56%), the State Radio (25%), the city of Reykjavik (18%), and Seltjarnarnes, a suburb of the city (1%). The budget for 1986 is $1.1 million.

As of 1986 there are 70 permanent players, mostly Icelandic, and the orchestra can be augmented to about 100 when necessary. The working week is 27.5 hours and orchestra members have two months summer holiday on full pay.

No music director has ever been appointed, but the post of chief conductor has been filled by several musicians who have greatly influenced the orchestra's development. Among them are Olav Kielland (Norwegian; 1956–1960), Bohdan Wodiczko (Polish; 1960–1970), Karsten Andersen (Norwegian; 1970–1980) and Jean-Pierre Jacquillat (French; 1980–1986). Three conductors resident in Iceland, Dr. Victor Urbancic (d. 1958), Dr. Robert A. Ottosson (d. 1974), and Páll P. Pálsson, have also been influential.

The orchestra holds 16 fortnightly subscription concerts in a season from September to June, and about 650 subscribers buy season tickets. Subscription concerts offer a mostly traditional repertoire drawn from all periods. Concert performances of operas and choral works, as well as many symphonic works requiring a large orchestra, have been possible only during the last 20 years. Soloists and conductors are both Icelandic and foreign. The great majority of rehearsals, concerts, and recordings are held in Haskolabio, a cinema seating almost 1,000 and owned by the University of Iceland. A concert house, which will be the future home of the orchestra, is planned.

The orchestra also holds hospital concerts, light music and family concerts, and special events. Audiences are drawn from all age groups and all walks of life, and special student rates are available. Almost all concerts are recorded by the radio; the orchestra also records selected works for both radio and television. In addition to making semiannual (spring and autumn) tours to different parts of Iceland, the orchestra has three times toured abroad—to the Faroes, Germany/ Austria, and France.

The orchestra has a great impact on the musical life of Iceland. Apart from their work as members of the orchestra, the musicians also play for performances of operas and musicals both with the Icelandic Opera Company and in the National Theatre. Much of the teaching in the 12 local music schools is done by orchestra members. As of 1986 two string quartets, a chamber orchestra, two woodwind quintets, and two brass quintets rely mainly on orchestra members for their personnel. The orchestra's domestic tour concerts are a great incentive to musical life outside the capital, particularly to the 8,000 students of the country's 60 music schools. Several times during the season the orchestra visits the schools of Reykjavik and surrounding towns, and these concerts have become increasingly popular. An active group of composers writes for the orchestra, producing both orchestral works and concertos for individual members. It is the orchestra's policy to perform Icelandic works regularly.

In addition to a manager and office staff, the Iceland Symphony's administrative structure includes an Orchestra Committee of five members appointed as follows: the chairman by the Ministry of Education and Culture; one member by the city of Reykjavik; one member by the Ministry of Finance; one member by the radio; and one member by the members of the orchestra. This Committee is responsible for all finances. An Advisory Program Committee of seven members includes one appointed by the Ministry of Education and Culture, one appointed by the city of Reykjavik, and one appointed by the radio, in addition to a composer, an orchestra member, the chief conductor, and the concertmaster.

Over the last 20 years the standards of music education in Iceland have greatly improved, and many students have studied abroad, both in Europe and the United States, for longer periods than were previously possible. On their return they have brought new influences and a wide range of experience to the great benefit of the orchestra. Plans for the immediate future include enlarging the orchestra, especially the string section, and continuing the progress and development already underway.

RECORDING HISTORY AND SELECTIVE DISCOGRAPHY: Disc recordings to date are mostly of Icelandic works made in collaboration with the Iceland Music Information Centre and the radio. A series of recordings of American and Icelandic works was made for CRI.

Cowell, Symphony No. 16; works of Páll Isolfsson and Jon Leifs (Strickland): CRI 179, Ives, "Thanksgiving" from *Symphony: Holidays* (Strickland): CRI S–190 and CRI 177. Jon Leifs, "Saga" Symphony (Jalas): ITM2. Askell Masson, Clarinet Concerto (Pallson): ITM5–01. Atli Heimir Sveinsson, Concerto for Flute and Orchestra (Pálsson); Leifur Thorarinsson, Concerto for Violin and Orchestra (Andersen): ITM3.

CHRONOLOGY OF CHIEF CONDUCTORS: Olav Kielland (1952–1960). Bohdan Wodiczko (960–1970). Karsten Andersen (1970–1980). Jean-Peirre Jacquillat (1980–1986).

BIBLIOGRAPHY: Iceland Symphony Orchestra, miscellaneous documents.

ACCESS: Iceland Symphony Orchestra, Gimli, Laekjargata 3, 101 Reykjavik; PO Box 707, 121 Reykjavik. 622255. Sigurður Björnsson, Manager. Gunnar Egilson, Office Manager.

RUT MAGNÚSSON

Irish Republic _____

DUBLIN

Radio Telefís Éireann Symphony Orchestra

Since 1981, when the Radio Telefís Éireann Symphony Orchestra (RTÉSO) moved to its new home, the National Concert Hall (NCH), it has had a major impact on the social and cultural life of Ireland. Because of the location of the hall in the heart of Dublin, a new audience has been exposed to serious music.

The main hall of the NCH, formerly the University College Dublin Hall, which opened in 1865, has no center aisle and can accommodate 1,260 people. In the recent renovation a balcony with no supporting piers was added, as were special speakers and amplifiers on the side walls to accommodate the hard of hearing. Frequent recitals are held in an adjoining smaller, foyerlike concert hall, the John Field Room, which houses John McCormick's piano and the largest crystal chandelier ever made by Waterford—their £30,000 gift to the newly renovated hall.

Yearly activities of the RTÉSO include two concerts a week from May through September (excluding August)—a Tuesday luncheon program and Friday evening concert. During the remainder of the year, recording sessions are held for radio and television programs, and the orchestra accompanies local choral societies (including the RTÉ Philharmonic Choir) and performs special programs. Children's concerts are given in Galway (one per year) and Cork on Thursdays (four per year). From September to May six recording sessions of children's music with children in the audience are made. A Society of Music for the Young (Ceol Chumann na nÓg), consisting of a committee of volunteers, presents music with explanations to children in the schools of Ireland.

In late October the RTÉSO plays for the Wexford Festival opera season, and in Dublin, during the grand opera season, it accompanies the opera in the Gaiety

Theatre. In December it returns to the NCH for several Christmastime performances of *Messiah*, after which there is a leave; scheduling resumes in January, with a New Year's Eve concert. In late April it performs at the spring opera season at the Gaiety Theatre. All rehearsals and concerts are taped for radio performance.

The RTÉSO includes 71 professional players and is augmented frequently as required. The orchestra's expenses are included in the RTÉ Music Department budget. Salaries are over a million pounds per year. Players are paid about £12,000—a total of some £900,000 yearly. Annual rental of the hall comes to £120,000. Salaries and fees of guest conductors and soloists are funded by RTÉ and paid through television and radio revenues. Players are appointed to full-time positions, and at age 65 receive a pension upon retirement.

The conductor, whose position is distinct from that of the RTÉ music director, has an input as to the choice of works to be performed. Audience consideration is given to most programming. The specific programs often depend upon the expertise of the guest soloists, who are chosen by the RTÉ Music Department and are booked two or three years in advance. There is also a biannual twentieth-century music festival. The orchestra performs a large repertoire from classical works to very recent music, including contemporary Irish music.

There are several subgroups within the RTÉSO. The Irish Brass Ensemble, RTÉ Horn Ensemble, and a wind group known as the Ulysses Wind Ensemble all perform outside of the regular orchestra's schedule. The orchestra performs as closely as possible to the intentions of the composer. For example, natural horns are used for baroque music, a chamber group for *Messiah*, and a reduced orchestra for Mozart.

The RTÉSO grew out of the RÉ Orchestral Players of the 1920s. When Radio Telefís Éireann was formed in 1960, it took over Radio Éireann and was run by the ministers of Post and Telegraph. The original Music Department of Radio Éireann was formed in 1925 with Vincent O'Brien as a part-time first music director, who held auditions for a Station Orchestra of four players, which began performing the following year. In November of 1927 Vincent O'Brien conducted an augmented orchestra especially recruited for the occasion to perform a Beethoven Symphony and some lighter works. The orchestra grew steadily, reaching 24 players by 1936. In 1941, when O'Brien resigned, a complimentary concert was presented at the Gaiety by an augmented Station Orchestra led by Terry O'Connor and conducted by John F. Larchet, Captain J. M. Doyle, and Vincent O'Brien, whose work *Miniature Overture* was performed.

Michael Bowles succeeded O'Brien as music director, and he became the first full-time conductor of the RÉ Orchestra, then numbering 29 players. "Mansion House" Symphony concerts were offered fortnightly with added players who continued to perform each spring and autumn until 1945, when they moved to the 1,800-seat Capitol Theatre on Sunday afternoons. In 1942 the orchestra numbered 40. Bowles was given a two-year leave of absence in 1947 and was replaced by Fachtna Ó Hannracháin, acting music director. In 1949 Phoenix

Hall became the home of the Symphony Orchestra, then numbering 62 players. The Dublin Grand Opera season engaged orchestra members to play for the spring and winter seasons. In 1950 the first provincial concerts were given in Cork, Galway, Limerick, and Waterford. By 1958 the RÉ Orchestra numbered 71 players.

Bowles remained as music director until 1961. He was replaced in 1962 by Tibor Paul, who held the position until Dr. Gerard Victory was appointed in 1967. When Victory retired in 1982, John Kinsella was appointed music director. In recent years the main conductors of the RTÉSO were Albert Rosen, Colman Pearce, Bryden Thomson, and starting in 1987, Janos Furst.

RECORDING HISTORY AND SELECTIVE DISCOGRAPHY: As the Radio Éireann Orchestra, the ensemble recorded in 1956 a two-volume collection of *Music from Old Erin* under the direction of Milan Horvat for Decca Gold Seal. Under direction of the composer the RTÉSO recorded Seán Ó Riada's incidental film music *Mise Éire* for Gaellinn in 1979.

Brian Boydell, *Symphonic Inscapes*, Op. 64 (1968); Gerard Victory, *Jonathan Swift: A Symphonic Portrait* (1970) (Albert Rosen): New Irish Recording Co. NIR 011 (1973). Seóirse Bodley, *Ceol* (Symphony No. 3); Archie J. Potter, *Sinfonia de Profundis* (Colman Pearse): Pickwick Records, Ltd., 70 Dublin Industrial Estate, Finglas, Dublin 11, Ireland (1981).

CHRONOLOGY OF PRINCIPAL CONDUCTORS: Vincent O'Brien, 1925–1941 (RÉ Music Director). Captain Michael Bowles, 1941–1948. Milan Horvat, 1953–1962. Tibor Paul, 1962–1968. Albert Rosen, 1968–1981. Colman Pearse, 1981–1983. Bryden Thomson, 1984–1986. Janos Furst, to assume duties in 1987.

BIBLIOGRAPHY: Interviews with NCH Manager Frank Murphy, RTÉ Head of Music John Kinsella, and RTÉSO Manager Frank Young, 1985. Brian Boydell, "Dublin," *The New Grove Dictionary of Music and Musicians* (London: MacMillan, 1981). Louis McRedmond, ed., *Written on the Wind: Personal Memories of Irish Radio, 1926–1976* (Dublin: Gill and MacMillan, 1976). Frederick May, "Radio Eireann Symphony Concerts," in Aloys Fleischmann, *Music in Ireland: A Symposium* (Cork: Cork University Press, 1952). Séumas Ó Braonáin, "Music in the Broadcasting Service," in Aloys Fleischmann, *Music in Ireland: A Symposium* (Cork: Cork University Press, 1952). Gerard Victory, "What Broadcasting Contributes to Music in Ireland," and "RTÉSO Impresses Foreign Audiences," *Irish Broadcasting Review* (Summer 1979).

ACCESS: Radio Telefís Éireann Symphony Orchestra, National Concert Hall, Earlsfort Terrace, Dublin 2, Ireland. 718402. Frank J. Young, Manager. Radio Telefís Éireann, Donnybrook, Dublin 4, Ireland. 693111. John Kinsella, Head of Music, RTÉ.

CATHERINE DOWER

Israel _____

Jerusalem Symphony Orchestra

The Jerusalem Symphony Orchestra (JSO) is the official orchestra of the Israel Broadcasting Authority (IBA). It is part of the IBA's Classical Music Division, which comprises both the orchestral administration and the radio's music programming function. Being an official ensemble sponsored by the government and situated in the country's capital city, the orchestra is expected to fulfill national and educational duties. It therefore supports Israeli composers and performers through performances and concert engagements, enhancing interest in and understanding for contemporary music. It also initiates special productions of large-scale symphonic and choral works of special historical or national interest, such as Biblical oratorios.

The orchestra runs several series of subscription concerts in Jerusalem, with a regular audience of about 6,000 subscribers. The 1984–1985 season consisted of 32 subscription concerts as well as a series of guided youth concerts, a series of popular classics, and a special series called "Liturgica Week," consisting of performances of large choral works. The orchestra also participates in special events such as the "Testimonium" project of premieres of commissioned works related to Jewish history. Each program is heard all over the country through a live, stereophonic FM broadcast on the classical music channel and is also recorded for taped rebroadcasts. The orchestra is also active in recording new and rare music for the Israeli radio, enriching the broadcast programs and making the recording library of the Israeli radio a valuable sound archive of Israeli works and rare performances.

JSO musicians are civil servants receiving regular salaries from the Broadcast Authority. They are represented by an elected committee, which officially negotiates labor and personnel matters with the orchestra director. In addition to the salary budget, which is determined by national policy, the orchestra receives an operating budget of about $200,000 (1984–1985). Income derives from ticket sales and a proportionate amount derived from the broadcast tax paid by all television-set owners in the country, as well as from special projects commissioned by outside organizations. Visiting soloists and conductors contribute their fees to the Musicians' Trust on certain occasions.

Until 1971 the orchestra suffered from the lack of any adequate concert auditorium in Jerusalem, having had to perform initially at the Addison Movie Theatre and later at the small YMCA auditorium. With the completion of the beautiful, 900-seat Jerusalem Theatre, the orchestra made it its home, albeit shared with theatre groups. Some of the orchestra's larger productions, such as the Berlioz *Requiem*, are held at the spacious Binianei Ha'uma (National Hall), which holds nearly 3,000 listeners. The orchestra will move during its 1987–1988 season into its regular symphonic hall, being built adjacent to the Jerusalem Theatre. This structure holds a 750-seat concert hall and a smaller auditorium for chamber music. It is hoped that it will prove acoustically superior to the somewhat dry Jerusalem Theatre.

Historically, the JSO has closely reflected the social, political, and economic environment in which it has grown. The orchestra originated as a small ensemble in 1936, when the Palestine radio, then under the British mandate, initiated broadcasts in the Hebrew language alongside programs in Arabic and in English, all on a single channel. The beginnings of Hebrew broadcast were hailed all over the country as an important step toward the formation of new national Jewish culture in the ancient homeland. Hebrew broadcasts, followed by the establishment of the Israel Philharmonic Orchestra* a few months later, soon became a symbol of national pride in view of the deteriorating situation in Europe.

Since broadcasting in those days meant live concerts, a small instrumental ensemble was formed, directed, and organized by energetic musicians such as the singer and composer Carl Salomon (later named Shalmon) and the pianist and harpsichordist Arie Sachs. This was the core of the small Radio Orchestra that would be conducted mainly by Salomon; such local figures as composer Hanan (Hans) Schlesinger conducted as well. Shimon Mishori has been the orchestra's concertmaster for most years since its founding. Its members were active in the musical life of Jerusalem, which, during World War II and the 1948 war, was frequently cut off from the remainder of the country.

Following the foundation of the State of Israel, the orchestra regularly broadcast only one weekly concert live. The orchestra's small budget and size hampered its competition in the standard repertoire with the prestigious Palestine (now Israel) Philharmonic in Tel-Aviv, and it took the path of specialization in rare and Israeli compositions. The radical social and economic changes that affected the city of Jerusalem after the 1967 war would profoundly change the orchestra, as would the large wave of immigration of fine professional musicians in the 1960s, mostly from the Soviet Union and the United States. With new resources the orchestra was totally reorganized, expanding into a full-scale symphonic ensemble with an increased schedule of concerts and amibitious programs, though without abandoning its traditional obligation to Israeli and contemporary works.

Following Carl Salomon, who directed the orchestra during its first years, there arose the need for an internationally renowned music director. From 1954 to 1959 the Swedish conductor Heinz Freudental and the Israeli conductor George Singer collaborated as permanent conductors. During the period 1962–1971 the young emigré conductor from Romania, Mendi Rodan, directed the orchestra and strongly affected its method of work and playing style with his meticulous and demanding approach. The American conductor Lucas Foss served as director for two seasons (1971–1974), during which he embarked (as he had done widely in the United States) on innovative ideas such as marathon concerts dedicated to particular stylistic periods. Foss was followed in 1977 by the Israeli conductor Gary Bertini, although his extensive guest conducting duties elsewhere allowed him to conduct only a few concerts each season; prominent guest conductors led the orchestra in his absence. Bertini's contract expired in 1986.

While the orchestra regularly invites soloists from abroad, Israeli musicians still enjoy priority. The orchestra sponsors a yearly performance competition for young musicians, the winners performing as soloists with the orchestra. Some JSO members are active in chamber music ensembles such as the Jerusalem String Trio, the Jerusalem String Quartet, and the Jerusalem Baroque Orchestra. Many of the orchestra's musicians teach at the Jerusalem Academy and Conservatory. In the 1980s the orchestra embarked upon a series of nearly annual international tours.

RECORDING HISTORY AND SELECTIVE DISCOGRAPHY: While the orchestra is very active in radio recordings, no regular production of commercial records has been started yet. Two of the records mentioned here are of special interest due to the inclusion of outstanding Israeli compositions.

Kopytman, *Memory* and *Rotations* (Bertini): Jerusalem Records ATD 8506. *Music from Jerusalem*: works of P. Ben Haim, Y. Gilboa, and M. Castelnuovo Tedesco (Foss, Singer, Ostrovsky): IMP LP 30–81/01/OM. Weill, *Mahagonny* (Foss): Turnabout 34675.

CHRONOLOGY OF MUSIC DIRECTORS: Carl Salomon, 1936–1954 (?). Heinz Freudental and George Singer, 1954–1959. (Guest conductors, 1959–1962.) Mendi Rodan, 1962–1971. Lucas Foss, 1972–1974. (Guest conductors, 1974–1977.) Gary Bertini, 1977–1986.

BIBLIOGRAPHY: Jerusalem Symphony Orchestra, miscellaneous documents.

ACCESS: Jerusalem Symphony Orchestra. The Jerusalem Theatre, 20 Marcus Street, Jerusalem 91010. (02) 215425.

JEHOASH HIRSHBERG

TEL-AVIV   (1,305,000*)

Israel Philharmonic Orchestra

The Israel Philharmonic Orchestra (IPO) maintains a highly prestigious position in Israel. The core of IPO activity is its season of 11 series of subscription concerts. Each series consists of eight concerts in Tel-Aviv, three in Haifa, and one in Jerusalem. In order to avoid repetitiveness a series is often divided into two separate programs. A sample analysis of the 1983–1984 season shows that the orchestra performed 128 subscription concerts, to which were added six concerts of a light classics series and six of a rare music series. The season also contained five fully staged opera performances, one concert for the armed forces, three special events, and 19 international tour concerts. Including its season of five subscription youth concerts (which it has maintained since its beginning), the orchestra thus presented a total of 179 performances.

The IPO enjoys sold-out houses, thanks to a loyal subscription audience of 36,000 members. Subscribers have the special privilege of maintaining their same seats as long as they renew their membership. They also have the right of first choice of tickets for special events. In addition, they participate in yearly meetings in which they are encouraged to express their wishes and opinions with regard to the programs. Many of the subscribers keep their seats for life and even pass on subscription rights as wedding gifts, inheritances, and the like.

The IPO is a self-governing institution owned and ruled as a cooperative of the permanent members, all of whom are full-time players in the orchestra. They elect their executive committees in a general meeting. An elected management of three musicians who serve for a two-year term is responsible for all aspects of policy, programs, contracting conductors and soloists, tours, and public relations. A six-member Musicians' Council deals with personal problems and complaints of the members. Admission procedure to the orchestra is long and demanding. The candidate who passes a solo audition is invited to take part in a rehearsal or a concert during which he is seated in a front chair of his section and followed closely by the conductor. The musician may then be admitted to a probation period of up to three years. If the player passes the trial period his candidacy is put before the general meeting of the IPO permanent members, who consider not only competence but also his or her personality and social integration in the musicians' community. Only then can the candidate become a full member, in which case the position is assured for life, with all retirement benefits included. Some 80 of the 106 IPO players are currently full members. The self-governing system has generally proven itself with regard to self-discipline and the sense of collective responsibility that characterizes the work of the ensemble. The orchestra has recently begun a policy of encouraging the best players to organize regular chamber ensembles, who are allowed to take leaves of absence of up to two months if invited for concert tours abroad.

The overall economic situation in Israel has made it very difficult for the IPO to offer internationally renowned conductors and soloists the fees they usually receive in Europe and in the United States. It has been a reflection of their special attitude toward the IPO, toward its audience, and toward Israel in general that many of them have agreed to perform for much-reduced fees or even for no fee at all. The budget for the 1980–1981 season, as an example, was $4,142,000, of which 55% was allocated to salaries; 11% to fees of conductors, soloists, and choruses; and the rest to maintenance of the Tel-Aviv auditorium and to other expenses. The orchestra's heavy reliance on its audience was reflected by the overwhelming share of (mostly subscription) ticket sales, amounting to 56% of the budget, with 26% covered by the Israeli government, 3% by a donation of the America-Israel Foundation, and a 12% deficit passed on to the next season.

The orchestra performs at an A pitch of 442 cps. In addition to its single-F horns, Wagner Tuben, and rotary-valve trumpets, the orchestra's instrument collection includes oboe d'amore, basset horns, and mandolins.

It was during the first stages of Nazi rule and the spread of anti-Semitism in Europe that many professional Jewish musicians were dismissed from their regular positions in leading orchestras in Central Europe. The eminent Jewish violinist Bronislaw Huberman, whose recitals in Palestine in 1929 and 1931 had met with an unprecedented success, conceived of a new symphony orchestra situated in Palestine and providing haven for the best Jewish musicians. The large wave of immigration into Palestine in the 1930s increased the Jewish population from 175,000 in 1931 to 389,000 in 1936 and provided a highly educated musical audience capable of supporting a fully professional symphony orchestra.

The first stages of the organization of the new ensemble were a one-man venture, with Huberman raising funds mostly through benefit concerts, auditioning musicians, and encouraging them to immigrate to Palestine. Huberman insisted on the highest professional standards, admitting only the finest musicians. He considered the orchestra not only as a tool to help Jewish musicians but mostly as a major step in the fulfillment of the Zionist dream of a new, humanistic society in Palestine. As he wrote in one of his letters: "To beat the world campaign of anti-Semitism it is not enough to create material and idealistic prosperity in Palestine, we must create there new gospels and carry them throughout the world. And the Symphony Orchestra, as I visualize it, would be perhaps the first and easiest step toward that highest aim of Jewish humanity."

The first performance of the Palestine Orchestra took place in a vast exhibition hall at the Levant Fair in Tel-Aviv in December 25, 1936, and was applauded all over the country as a major historical event. The conductor was Arturo Toscanini, who had dramatically cancelled his contract with the Bayreuth Festival, then used as a tool for Nazi propaganda, in order to inaugurate the new orchestra. The orchestra then began a series of subscription concerts, featuring the most famous conductors and Huberman himself, thus forming high standards as well as a lasting pattern of preference for internationally renowned guests.

During the years of World War II, the orchestra persisted in its regular activities despite all difficulties, performing with local conductors and even conducting itself on several occasions. It was but two weeks after its first concert that the orchestra had its first international tour, performing in Egypt under Toscanini. Yearly tours in Egypt and Lebanon continued until 1945, when the political situation in the Middle East rendered such trips unfeasible.

Though virtually cut off from the musical centers in Europe during the years of World War II, the new orchestra enjoyed the advice and expertise of the distinguished educator and pianist, Professor Leo Kestenberg (1882–1962), who immigrated to Israel in 1938, having been removed from his high position in the Prussian Ministry of Education. Kestenberg was the artistic director of the IPO during the years 1938–1945.

Following the foundation of the State of Israel in May of 1948, the Palestine Orchestra renamed itself "The Israel Philharmonic Orchestra." During the first turbulent period of the State, the orchestra took part in many historical events, such as playing the national anthem at the memorable ceremony of the declaration of independence. During a brief cease-fire in the 1948 war, the conductor Leonard Bernstein travelled with the players for eight hours on a dangerous dirt road 45 miles from Tel-Aviv to the besieged city of Jerusalem to play a concert there. The orchestra was described as an "ambassador of good will" when it made its first ambitious tour in the United States and Canada in 1951 under Serge Koussevitzky and Leonard Bernstein. A tour in Europe in 1955 was followed by a world tour in 1960, and nearly-annual tours since have brought the IPO to all regions of the world.

The emergence of the orchestra effected a major change in musical life and musical education in the country. The immigration of nearly 100 highly experienced performers within the short period of three years led to the formation of new chamber groups and encouraged instrumental instruction on a professional level, providing fine teachers for existing and new conservatories.

For its first 20 years, suffering a lack of adequate concert halls, the orchestra played in small theatres and movie houses (with their poor acoustics and inferior facilities) all over the country. The situation changed with the inauguration in 1957 of the Fredric Mann Auditorium in Tel-Aviv (now the orchestra's permanent home), and the completion of the spacious "Binianei-Ha'uma" hall (National Hall) in Jerusalem, both seating some 3,000 listeners. New halls have also been completed in Haifa and other locations in the country.

For more than ten years the IPO performed under guest conductors and with no music director. William Steinberg acted as home conductor during the first season, coaching the new ensemble prior to the arrival of the uncompromising Toscanini and conducting four of the ten subscription concerts. Afterward the orchestra preferred great guest conductors to a regular music director. The ill effects of the discontinuity among conductors led to constant attempts to appoint a music director despite the difficulties in convincing a truly great conductor to make a protracted stay, far away from the great music centers of Europe and the United States. Paul Paray stayed as music director for one season only (1949–1950). Jean Martinon for two (1958–1960).

In 1961 Zubin Mehta made his first, enormously successful performance with the IPO, establishing a deep friendship with the orchestra as well as with Israel and Israeli society generally. In 1969 he received the position of music adviser, and in 1977 he accepted the post of music director, which he has held since then. Still, Mehta continued to direct the Los Angeles Philharmonic** and later the New York Philharmonic** as well, so that the number of his performances in Israel has been limited and the orchestra has continued to perform widely under guest conductors. Still, Mehta's role in reshaping the orchestra, hiring new musicians, and effecting its policy has been considerable.

From its inception the orchestra followed the Central European model of programming, with the classic and romantic German/Austrian repertoire prevailing in concerts. The nature of the audience and the reliance on ticket sales has forced the IPO to limit performances of twentieth-century works in general and of local, Israeli compositions, in particular. This has invited angry criticism from the circles of music teachers, composers' unions, and music critics.

Still, an objective inspection of the repertoire indicates that despite its prevailing conservatism the orchestra has performed many new and rare compositions. An analysis of the repertoire performed from 1936 to 1948 shows that while the so-called standard symphonic repertoire predominated, there was nevertheless much variety. Works of the classic and romantic German/Austrian composers comprised 49% of the programming; modern and contemporary (Arnold Schoenberg, Ernst Toch, etc.) 16%, romantic Italian/French/English 13%, romantic Russian 9%, baroque 8%, Israeli (Paul Ben-Haim, Alexander Boscovitch, etc.) 4%, and Jewish (Ernest Bloch, Alexander Weprick) 1%. Moreover, Israeli symphonic music only started to be composed around 1940, and the representation of local composers was quite satisfactory.

Since 1943 the orchestra has performed often with the Tel-Aviv Chorus, later named the Philharmonic Chorus, a large community group founded and coached by E. Lustig, with which numerous oratorios and masses have been performed. In view of the difficulties of maintaining an opera company of the highest quality in Israel, the IPO has produced several important operas with prominent international casts.

A special aspect of IPO repertoire has been the spontaneous boycott of the music of Wagner (because of his anti-Semitism and in response to the persecutions of Jews in Germany in 1938) and of the music of Richard Strauss due to his collaboration with the Nazi regime. The orchestra itself has tried on several occasions to terminate the boycott following the establishment of diplomatic relations between Israel and the Federal Republic of Germany, but by then the boycott had become so entrenched in public opinion that all attempts met with emotional reactions. Although Wagner and Strauss are freely distributed on records and studied in music history classes, they still cannot be performed by the IPO in regular concert programs. Controversial as such a situation may be, the magnitude of the problem indirectly reflects the salient position of the IPO as a national institution.

RECORDING HISTORY AND SELECTIVE DISCOGRAPHY: The IPO has made numerous recordings, mostly for Decca and Polydor. Among the rare titles one should mention the *Israel Music Anthology*, Vol. 4, with works of J. Tal, A. Majani, T. Avni, J. Kaminsky (Mehta): Jerusalem Records, ATD 8402.

Bernstein, *Serenade* (Bernstein): DG 7802070. Bloch, *Schelomo, Voice in the Wilderness* (Janos Starker/Mehta): London 6661. J. Tal, Symphony No. 2; A. Majani,

Overture Solenelle; T. Avni, *Program Music* 1980; J. Kaminsky, Symphonic Overture (Mehta): Jerusalem Records, ATD 8402 (*Israel Music Anthology*, vol. 4). Mahler, Symphony No. 4 (Barbara Hendricks/Mehta): London LDR–10004.

CHRONOLOGY OF MUSIC DIRECTORS: (Guest conductors, 1936–1949.) Paul Paray, 1949–1950. (Guest conductors, 1950–1958.) Jean Martinon, 1958–1969. Zubin Mehta (Music Adviser), 1969–1977. Zubin Mehta, 1977-present.

BIBLIOGRAPHY: I. Ibbeken and Tzvi Avni, *An Orchestra Is Born*, compiled from the Huberman Archives (Tel-Aviv, 1969). The IPO Archives.

ACCESS: The Tel-Aviv Philharmonic Orchestra, Huberman Street, P.O. Box 11292, Tel-Aviv. 295092.

JEHOASH HIRSHBERG

Italy _____

ROME   (2,830,000)

I Musici

I Musici (I Musici di Roma) is a conductorless chamber orchestra of twelve players organized in a partnership association whose aim is to perform and propagate music for chamber orchestra.

The ensemble's yearly activities include three major overseas tours, five or six European tours, and three or four recordings. The group is based in Rome, but it currently performs abroad more than at home. In 1985, for example, I Musici's 93 concerts included 15 in the United States and Canada, 24 in Japan, 12 in Australia, 41 in foreign European countries, and ten in Italy. Consequently, the ensemble claims no one home hall and has no set subscription series.

Although the group's repertoire ranges from the late seventeenth through twentieth centuries, the emphasis is on works of the eighteenth-century Italian masters, and I Musici has earned a reputation as a pioneer in the renaissance of such music. Predominant in its repertoire is the work of Antonio Vivaldi, whose imaginative genius with groupings of voices and tonal colors has found the ideal medium in such a group as I Musici, where each member can undertake a solo role, allowing a pleasant flexibility and variety in programming. The group's poetic and yet authoritative rendering of the celebrated *Four Seasons*, which they have played many times all over the world, has gained them praise and numerous awards. The many other composers frequently played by the group cover a wide span of styles and periods, from Corelli/Bach/Albinoni to Haydn/ Mozart and Schubert/Mendelssohn through Albert Roussel, Ottorino Respighi, Béla Bartók, Paul Hindemith, Frank Martin, and such Italian contemporaries as Valentino Bucchi, Guido Turchi, and Nino Rota.

The core of I Musici comprises six violins (three firsts, three seconds), two violas, two cellos, a double bass, and keyboard. I Musici members are blessed to be playing an astonishing array of rare eighteenth-century instruments by Stradivari, Gagliano, Goffriller, Guarnieri, Guadagnini, and others. Nevertheless, I Musici has resisted an indiscriminant rush to "authenticity," avoiding what it considers a fetishistic reconstruction of the hypothetical conditions in which music was played two centuries ago. They believe that true philology consists in realizing the inner essence of the work, and they eschew concepts such as "originalinstrumente" as inventions of the cultural industry that excite our need of the antique without guaranteeing any authenticity. No good performer, nor any cultured listener, they argue, can eliminate the significance that two centuries of history and human thought have added to music's wealth.

The idea to form a small and agile orchestra without a conductor, specialized but not limited in repertoire, came about at the end of 1951 to a group of talented instrumentalists who were also social companions, mostly former students of the "Santa Cecilia" Music Conservatory in Rome (an organization not to be confused with the Orchestra of the National Academy of St. Cecilia*). They saw the opportunity to return orchestral chamber music (i.e., Corelli, Bach, Vivaldi, Albinoni, etc.) to its correct dimensions; at the time when it generally was incorrectly played by big symphony orchestras or, much worse, not played at all.

Such an initiative required courage and imagination. In this they were helped by the violinist Remy Principe and composer Barbara Giuranna, both teachers in Rome's Conservatory. Principe was the teacher of most of the group's violinists, and Barbara Giuranna is the mother of Bruno Giuranna, one of the group's founders, an excellent viola/viola d'amore player. Encouraging the open discourse on technical and aesthetic issues that is customary among smaller chamber groups, the members felt a freedom of individual participation in a collective effort that is rare in larger ensembles.

The Roman musical circle, stimulated by such an original enterprise, was already moving in their favor; the National Academy of St. Cecilia invited them for the official presentation concert which took place, with great success, on March 30, 1952, with a program of Leonardo Vinci, Antonio Vivaldi, Giuseppe Tartini, Giovanni Paisello, and Benedetto Marcello. The debut was made under the prolix name of "Gruppo Strumentale Giovani Concertisti di Roma." Luckily, the composer Giorgio Federico Ghedini heard the debut in Rome and suggested they adopt the title, "I Musici," a poetic and obsolete word meaning "the musicians." Upon hearing the rehearsal for I Musici's second performance (with the Italian Radio, RAI), Toscanini is said to have exclaimed, "A perfect chamber ensemble which plays without a conductor! I applauded them, I thanked them. . . . No, Music shall not die!" (Raffaele Calzini, *Corriere della Sera*, June 17, 1952).

I Musici's travels soon brought it farther and farther from home, a circumstance of joy to some members but of concern to others, for whom such a life style was incommodious. Accordingly, it took some time before the ensemble could count on a firm membership capable of guaranteeing long-term planning of important engagements, such as the group's three-month tour of the United States under the auspices of impresario Sol Hurok. By 1953–1954, however, the membership had stabilized. It was in 1954 that the complement "di Roma" was added to the name "I Musici" for the debut tour in Germany, at the insistence of impresario C. W. Winderstein, to attract the attention of German-speaking audiences. The change, in effect only in certain European countries, has since provoked some confusion as to the congruity of "I Musici" and "I Musici di Roma."

The ensemble was shaped over the years by its several concertmasters. The first was Franco Tamponi, whose meticulous approach to ensemble playing in the group's early years, expressed in a large number of long tutti and sectional rehearsals, laid the foundations of the ensemble's rigorous precision. He was succeeded by Felix Ayo, whose 16 years with the group saw many successes, among them a prize-winning recording of Vivaldi's *Four Seasons*.

The lyrical and sensitive violin playing of the next concertmaster, Robert Michelucci, changed somewhat I Musici's approach to musical and performance problems. Michelucci was keen to chisel, while Ayo liked to sculpt. With Michelucci the ensemble's impact on big audiences was perhaps less spectacular, but the more sophisticated listeners declared that I Musici now displayed a more mature sensibility. When Michelucci left in 1972 to carry on a solo career, the post was assumed by the young and enthusiastic Salvatore Accardo, who, playing a Stradivarius, integrated into the ensemble with authority and simplicity. He was equally at home playing a solo concerto, a tutti passage, or simply the accompaniment to another soloist. This kind of adaptability has become a general hallmark of I Musici.

By 1975 it had become difficult for Accardo to juggle his outside solo engagements with the heavy schedule of I Musici, and another marvelous violinist, Pina Carmirelli, (also with a Strad) joined the group in alternation with Accardo. In 1976, however, Accardo's solo career led him to finally leave I Musici, and Carmirelli remained as concertmaster. Twenty-seven-year-old Frederico Agnostini was appointed concertmaster in 1986. The ensemble sees a bright future and is looking forward to its 35th anniversary season in 1987.

RECORDING HISTORY AND SELECTIVE BIBLIOGRAPHY: By 1954 the ensemble had contracted six LP's for "His Master's Voice," and an exclusive contract with Philips was effected in 1955. One of the group's first records of importance for Philips was Vivaldi's *Four Seasons*, featuring Felix Ayo (Grand Prix du Disque and other awards). In all, more than 100 discs have been released, collectively an important force in the rebirth of interest in chamber music, particularly that of the eighteenth century.

Bach, *Brandenburg Concertos*: Philips 412–790–1; Philips 412–790–2 (CD). Vivaldi, *L'Estro armonico*, op. 3: Philips 412–128–1; Philips 6768–8307 (2 records); Philips 412–128–2 (CD). Vivaldi, *Four Seasons* (Carmirelli): Philips 6514–275; Philips 6514–372; Philips 410–0012 (CD).

ACCESS: I Musici, Via Valle Viola, 6, 00141 Rome. (06) 896506. Lucio Buccarella, President.

LUCIO BUCCARELLA

Orchestra of the National Academy of St. Cecilia

Responsible for the artistic expressions of one of the world's most venerable musical organizations, 'the Orchestra of the National Academy of St. Cecilia (OANSC), is among Italy's most important symphonic organizations.

Likewise, the annual symphonic seasons organized by the Institute for the Concerts of ANSC (which the orchestra has served since its founding) are among Italy's most prestigious. The orchestra's regular season is based on a wide repertoire encompassing a spectrum of periods and genres, including difficult and infrequently heard scores, often in collaboration with the Chorus of the ANSC. Contemporary music, however, has in recent years been less frequently heard than in the past. The concerts, about 50 in number, are held annually in two principal seasons: a spring subscription season at the Auditorium di Via della Conciliazione and an outdoor summer season in the Piazza del Campidoglio. In both series the orchestra has a firm tradition of hosting important soloists and is led in two-thirds of its concerts by Italian and foreign guest conductors of the first rank. The Academy also presents an important season of chamber concerts.

Founded in 1907, the orchestra has been guided by an administrative council that supervises planning and programming for the ANSC's musical groups (orchestra, chorus, and chamber ensembles). The council includes representatives from the Academy and unions, as well as public financing agencies that participate with only advisory powers. A separate association of auditors, made up of representatives from the municipal ministry and the prefecture of Rome, controls the financial accounts. The ANSC institution comprises 260 employees of the Institution of Concerts of the ANSC, of whom 200 make up the permanent musical body (including 113 orchestral musicians, 84 chorus members, and a conducting staff of four). Funding has been guaranteed since the ANSC's founding, first by the municipality of Rome and then directly by the state. Such support, channeled through the Ministry of Tourism and Entertainment, provides a generous annual contribution, up to 10 billion lire. In 1946 parliamentary law designated the Institute of the Concerts of the ANSC as the principal symphonic institution of Italy, putting it on a funding par with the major operatic institutions. Minor support comes from local (municipal, provincial, and regional) agencies and a fee paid by Italian Radio and Television (RAI). About 70% of the ANSC's budget is devoted to maintaining the orchestra.

The ANSC Orchestra is an important cultural influence. Its symphonic seasons play to a large live audience, greatly increased by its television broadcasts on the "Third Network" of the RAI. Students of the Conservatory have liberal access to general rehearsals, and the orchestra participates in concerts for children in the schools of Rome. The orchestra's influence extends beyond Rome as well, to the cultural centers of Lazio, where its visits are the high points of the local cultural seasons. The orchestra's activities also include foreign concert tours, recordings (once again taken up after a long interruption), and participation in festivals and other cultural events. Orchestra members frequently teach at the conservatories and are employed in further concert activities in the two chamber concert groups composed of orchestra personnel—a woodwind ensemble and the Chamber Orchestra of the ANSC.

The immediate basis and principal motivation for founding the orchestra and the symphonic seasons was the institutional renewal initiated by the National Academy of St. Cecilia in the last decades of the nineteenth century. Political events and the general decline of sacred music, starting in the first decades of the nineteenth century, had caused a decline of the institutional functions that it exercised since its founding (traditionally fixed in the year 1566). Gradually, the institution evolved from its ancient form as a mutual benefit society with charitable aims and corporate functions to its modern form as a musical institution with national and international contacts and educational and scientific objectives. The visible results of this process were started in 1872 with the founding of a school (*liceo*) for music (a state institution since 1918) and the beginnings of the Library of St. Cecilia, today one of the most important music collections in Italy.

The concert activity inaugurated by the Academy in 1895 had no precedents in the musical life of Rome, for the concerts were public, regularly scheduled, and of high quality. The concerts, held in a large hall built within the Convento delle Orsoline between Via Vittoria and Via dei Greci, now the site of the Academy, quickly became among the most important musical events of the time. Previous concert activity in Rome was provided by a series of musical groups and institutions that grew haphazardly in the 1870s. Among these was the Roman Orchestral Society of 1874 with the personnel of the orchestra of the Apollo Theatre. Governed according to the corporate models of the great German symphonic complexes, it guaranteed, in the climate of the renewal of the musical tastes of those years, annual series of symphonic concerts. When it declined in 1898, its personnel were then primarily employed in the concert activities of the Academy in occasional symphonic-choral performances; they were reconvened in 1905 by the municipality of Rome as the Permanent Municipal Orchestra (Orchestra Stabile Municipale).

This group, the first Italian example of a symphonic entity financed entirely by public subvention, represented the immediate basis for the constitution of the ANSC Orchestra and its symphonic seasons, for when in 1907 the Municipal Orchestra ceased to function as such, it was immediately reconstituted under the aegis of the ANSC. However, the municipality guaranteed the survival of the symphonic season by providing the ANSC an ample endowment for the establishment of a season of at least 25 concerts. For such activity the municipality also endowed the Academy with the Corea Theatre, an ample hall immediately renamed the Augusteo. The new ANSC Orchestra thus began life known as the Augustan Symphonic Orchestra and was blessed with a membership already experienced in symphonic literature.

To the main body of experienced personnel were added young instrumentalists provided directly by the state music school. The orchestra's strength and versatility were proven even in its first season of 25 concerts, however, for the guest conductors of that year included Richard Strauss, Gustav Mahler, Vincent d'Indy, Bruno Walter, Arthur Nikisch, Arturo Toscanini, and Luigi Mancinelli. While the criterion of variety was vigorously maintained, there emerged a tendency to plan cycles of monographic concerts under the direction of single conductors or in groups designated according to nationality. Examples are the 1909 Beethoven festival of six concerts directed by Michael Balling and the Hungarian and Russian festivals of contemporary music (1911–1912) under the direction of Jenö Hubay and Vassily Safonoff, respectively.

The need for consistency in performance standards and programming was addressed in 1912 with the establishment of the post of permanent conductor, which was entrusted to Bernardino Molinari, who continued as permanent director until 1946. In addition to preparing and rehearsing the orchestra, he acted as consulting artist for the programming of the concert seasons and frequently conducted the orchestra as well. Under Molinari the orchestra gave more attention to contemporary music than it has since.

The 1920s particularly saw the orchestra turn toward a modern symphonic repertoire. The more than 50 first performances directed by Molinari in these years included the most important musical scores of modern symphonic music. Among the most shocking must have been the February 1923 first performance in Italy of *The Rite of Spring*. After the music of Stravinsky and Debussy, which Molinari had already begun to introduce in 1914, followed scores by Arthur Honegger, Paul Hindemith, and Arnold Schoenberg. The practice of inviting composers to the Augusteo concerts increased, and between 1914 and 1933 the orchestra invited as soloists or conductors Debussy, Camille Saint-Saëns, Darius Milhaud, Jean Sibelius, Stravinsky, Hindemith, Ernest Bloch, and Sergei Rachmaninoff.

Molinari also gave major attention to the new school of Italian symphonic music, including in his programs the most important works of the so-called generation of the '80s: Gian-Francesco Malipiero, Alfredo Casella, and especially Ottorino Respighi, whose work has remained in the orchestra's permanent repertoire. *The Pines of Rome*, for example, directed by Molinari in its first Italian performance (1924), became a mainstay of the orchestra's repertoire and a virtual theme song for its foreign tours, which had begun in 1918 and climaxed in a 16-concert tour of Germany in 1937. Another element in the orchestra's attention to newer Italian music was its collaboration with the National Union of Musicians and the National Society of Modern Music founded by Casella. An effort of direct promotion was the orchestra's annual presentation to the Augusteo public of unedited works of young composers selected by the "Commissione Permanente di Lettura" instituted by the ANSC in 1914.

Thus in the years of Molinari's direction the orchestra had acquired a clear artistic identity and a sense of purpose. The 25-concert limit was raised to an annual average of 35, and the addition of a community endowment in 1927 provided the basis for such further increases in activity as a series of concerts at popular prices and an educational series for students. Summer concerts were added in 1936 under guarantee of the state at the Basilica di Massenzio.

With the demolition of the Corea Theatre, decreed by the Municipality of Rome in 1936 in order to isolate the original seat of Augustus's tomb, the orchestra was deprived of its home and forced to move periodically, as it still does—first to the Teatro Adriano, then in 1946 to the Teatro Argentina, and in 1958 to the Auditorium di Via della Conciliazione, where it now resides. A return to the Teatro Argentina is foreseen as part of a larger plan (in abeyance since the 1950s) to construct a community theatre on the Via Flaminia—finally a permanent home for the orchestra.

Following Molinari and after a six-year vacancy, the direction of the orchestra was entrusted in 1952 to Ferdinando Previtali. In the interim, however, the orchestra did not cease its touring and participation in festivals, having appeared in Edinburgh under Wilhelm Furtwängler (1948) and at the International Exposition of the Arts in Paris (1952) under Igor Markevitch. Under Previtali the orchestra solidified its already high performance standards and extended its international prestige through two of the most important orchestral tours in its history: to the U.S.S.R. (1967) and the United States (1971). In the regular seasons Previtali dedicated one-composer concerts to Stravinsky, Respighi, Hindemith, and Berg. He also introduced both the orchestra and its audience to Aaron Copland, Benjamin Britten, Dimitri Shostakovich, and, among Italian composers, Goffredo Petrassi, Luigi Dallapiccola, Mario Zafred, Gian-Carlo Menotti, and Ennio Porrino. Luigi Nono and Karlheinz Stockhausen conducted their own compositions in 1967 and 1971, respectively. To satisfy a desire for diversity, the orchestra's programming was pushed in the Previtali era toward the most disparate directions. Relief came with the performance of symphonic-choral works that included oratorios and unstaged operas. Guest conductors of this era once again included the greatest of the age.

The trend toward variety in repertoire increased in succeeding years, in particular during the period under Markevitch (1973–1975). Markevitch showed a great respect for the taste of his predecessors and exhibited a particular preference, with regard to modern repertoire, for the music of Malipiero and Dallapiccola. His successor, Thomas Schippers, a frequent guest conductor in preceding years, was never able to exercise the role of permanent director, and at his death in 1977 there followed a long vacancy ending finally with the appointment of Giuseppe Sinopoli, the orchestra's present permanent director.

In the years prior to Sinopoli the orchestra had noticeably modified its activities, following a tendency already manifested in the Markevitch period, curtailing its recording activities and its traveling concert tours abroad. Nonetheless, the vitality of its members was shown in the formation of the two ANSC Orchestra chamber groups, which have developed an appreciable following and international recognition. Sinopoli became music director in 1983 (the same year in which Leonard Bernstein was named honorary president of the orchestra), and as its conductor he has dedicated concerts to works of Petrassi and Berg and directed the orchestra for the first time in Schoenberg's Chamber Symphony. However, Sinopoli, who is simultaneously principal conductor of the Philharmonia Orchestra (London),* has generally worked within a context of the romantic and late-romantic German repertoire. Under Sinopoli the orchestra is rapidly returning to the levels of its past standards and obligations. After resuming its recording activities in 1984, the orchestra has also begun touring abroad once more.

RECORDING HISTORY AND SELECTIVE DISCOGRAPHY: A first important series of recordings was realized by the ANSC Orchestra between 1948 and 1950 for His Masters Voice. It comprised, in addition to numerous overtures and theatre preludes, the Sixth Symphony of Beethoven, Debussy's *Nuages*, Respighi's *Fountains of Rome*, and *Paganiniana* by Casella. After a second cycle of recordings made under Previtali for Decca from 1952 to 1954 and some recordings for CRI under Antonini, the recording activities of the orchestra underwent a long interruption, only recently ended. Since 1984 the orchestra has recorded for Deutsche Grammophon and Philips (*Il Trovatore* and *Rigoletto*).
    Casella, *La Giara*; Respighi, *Pines of Rome* (Previtali): London STS–1515024. Riegger, *Dance Rhythms* and other works (Antonini): CRI 117. Verdi, *Rigoletto* (Sinopoli): Philips, 412 592. Verdi, *Il Trovatore* (Domingo, etc./Giulini): DG 413–355.

CHRONOLOGY OF MUSIC DIRECTORS: Bernardino Molinari, 1912–1946. (Guest conductors, 1946–1952.) Ferdinando Previtali, 1952–1971. (Guest conductors, 1971–1973.) Igor Markevitch, 1973–1975. (Guest conductors, 1975–1977.) Thomas Schippers, 1977. (Guest conductors, 1977–1983.) Giuseppe Sinopoli, 1983-present.

BIBLIOGRAPHY: E. Calvi, "L'Augusteo (il teatro Corea)," *Nuova Antologia*: 218 (1908): 103–109. *I concerti dal 1895 al 1933*, 2 vols., pubblicazione in occasione del XXV anno dell-Augusteo (16 Feb. 1933) (Rome: Regia Accademia di Santa Cecilia, 1938). A. De Angelis, *La Musica a Roma nel secolo XIX* (Rome, 1934; 1944). A. De Angelis, "Roma attende il suo Auditorio," *Capitolium* 28 (1953): 49–53. A. De Angelis, "Rom: von der Klassik bis zur Gegenwart," in *Die Musik in Geschichte und Gegenwart* (Kassel, 1963), XI: 739–750. E. Di San Martino Valperga, "Le grandi istituzioni musicali: l'Augusteo," *Nuova Antologia* 254 (1931): 217–223. R. Giazotto, *Quattro secoli di storia dell-Accademia Nazionale di Santa Cecilia*, 2 vols. (Milan: ANSC, 1970). R. Meloncelli and N. Pirrotta, "Rome II: the Christian Era," in *The New Grove Dictionary of Music and Musicians* (London, 1980), XVI:153–162. G. Monaldi, "Orchestre e direttori del secolo XIX," *Rivista Musicale Italiana* 16 (1909). National Academy of St. Cecilia, miscellaneous documents, annual reports, and programs. G. Parisotti, *I 25 anni della Societa orchestrale romana* (Rome, 1899). *Santa Cecilia: Rivista bimestrale dell'Accademia Nazionale di Santa Cecilia*, I-VII (1952–1958). I. Valletta, "I concerti orchestrali a Roma," *Rivista Musicale Italiana* 17 (1910): 665–670.

ACCESS: Orchestra dell'Accademia Nazionale di Santa Cecilia, Auditorium Pio, Via della Conciliazione 4, 00193 Roma. (06) 6541044. Accademia Nazionale di Santa Cecilia, Gestione autonoma dei concerti, Via Vittoria 6, 00187 Rome. (06) 6790389 and 6783996. Paola Fontecedro, Official-in-Charge.

CESARE CORSI
TRANS. JULIA DISTEFANO

Symphony Orchestra of the RAI of Rome

The RAI Rome Symphony Orchestra (also known abroad as the "Rome Symphony") plays a wide repertoire encompassing many genres, styles, and periods. Continually changing, the orchestra's programming is determined by requests from Radiodue (the radio network affiliated with the orchestra), orchestra musicians, the chorus, and the public. With the other three RAI orchestras (in Turin, Naples, and Milan), the RAI Rome Symphony Orchestra is a most qualified instrument for the broadcasting of symphonic music.

More than half the direct transmissions planned for radio broadcasting, some 50 each year, are made before live audiences; the majority of these concerts are performed within the context of the symphonic season called "The Concerts of Rome." This November-to-June concert season comprises one RAI concert per week at its mid-season height. The orchestra supplements these performances with many others produced in collaboration with important agencies and institutions, including annual symphonic concerts for His Holiness the Pope (reinstituted in 1955); concerts at the Duomo di Orvieto, broadcast on Eurovision on Easter Sunday (since 1977); and lyric opera productions. Other activities include collaboration with the cultural commissions of Rome and the region of Lazio and with the Bureau of Tourism of Viterbo and of Orvieto. The RAI Rome Symphony is present at important international festivals and occasionally tours abroad.

The orchestra was firmly established in 1950 in its present home, the Auditorium of the Foro Italico, which was furnished by the RAI and modified to make it suitable for the recording of symphonic music. Owned by the state, it is at present the best room of this type in Rome. Public seating is limited to 750 places, but until 1978 admission to the studio had been restricted to a few invited guests. Before then the paying public was not admitted for fear of drawing patrons from the activities of the other musical institutions of Rome.

Since the institution of the reform of the RAI (in the law of April 14, 1975, no. 103), the personnel of the orchestra have become partly integrated into the structure of the Regional Seat of the RAI of Rome, under the direct supervision of its administrator, along with the Lyric Chorus and the Polyphonic Chorus of the RAI of Rome. The artistic direction of the orchestra and the choruses was entrusted to an outside expert contracted every other year, with the advice of the administrator of the Seat. The programming of the entire season of concerts is up to the artistic director. The structure of the orchestra includes also a director of production, one responsible for operations, an internal musical consultant, and other regular and auxiliary personnel. The orchestra members and other employees of the organization are under contract with the RAI. Funding for the orchestra's radio activities is furnished by the RAI and its Regional Seat, while collateral activities are financed by the sponsors initiating them.

The orchestra officially subscribes to the international standard ("recommended laws" of Brussels) of A at 440 cps, although in practice the pitch is often raised slightly. Some of the 98-member orchestra's most noted instrumentalists are its principal wind players, considered the best in Italy. Chamber groups are formed from within the orchestra's ranks, but strictly on an occasional, unofficial basis. Since 1973 the orchestra has been without a permanent chief conductor, and it is limited to rehearsing its weekly concert program in the few days preceding the performance, with the performance conductor present only part of the time. The dress rehearsal is usually open to public-school audiences under the auspices of the AGIMUS organization.

The nucleus of the orchestra was formed following the institution of the EIAR (Office of Italian Broadcasting) on October 2, 1924. An ensemble of 20 musicians was called together under the direction of Riccardo Santarelli to perform music as requested by the administration—classical music, light music, and selections from operettas. The group grew from year to year until 1934, when it reached a full complement of 90 musicians and was charged with the performance of symphonic music.

In 1936, with the official establishment of the orchestra, the RAI named Fernando Previtali permanent conductor, and to him fell the final responsibility of selecting the orchestra's membership. Undoubtedly Previtali did more than anyone else for the orchestra's development. At the beginning there were very few live performances due to inadequate space, but in the autumn of 1944, shortly after the fall of Fascism, its first public symphonic season took place in the Teatro Argentina. Those eight concerts were dedicated to performances of musical compositions that, because of political or ethnic discrimination, had theretofore been prohibited in Italy: music of Mendelssohn, Mahler, Milhaud, Elgar, Barber, Shostakovich, and Gershwin. The public's indifferent attitude toward the orchestra—the product of their having heard only a poor electronic representation of its actual sound—began to improve, and the concerts soon enjoyed a great public and critical acclaim.

A distinct preference for the performance of contemporary music was evident under Previtali, and, while not ignoring standard works, the repertoire featured music by more than a hundred twentieth-century composers. A short, summer lyric season was begun, and the musicians also formed themselves into chamber groups, including a complete chamber orchestra and several smaller ensembles. In order to encourage such ventures, Previtali originated the system (no longer in use) of doubling all the principal string parts, thus allowing alternation of personnel. The practice was later extended to a system of rotation within the string sections at large.

After his first decade with the orchestra, Previtali was helped and later replaced by Carlo Maria Giulini, under whom the orchestra expanded its programming of the standard repertoire. It still, however, maintained its own identity, not wanting to conform to the newly formulated plan of the government (1947), under which the Rome RAI Orchestra would perform traditional music while the Turin RAI Orchestra would concentrate on lesser-known and newly created works. In 1948, for example, the chamber orchestra performed compositions by Gian-Francesco Malipiero, Darius Milhaud, Goffredo Petrassi, and Roman Vlad, all commissioned by Radio Italia. Following Giulini, Ferruccio Scaglia (substitute director under Previtali) took over, and he maintained the direction laid down by his mentor. In 1953 the orchestra performed the entire Wagner *Ring* cycle under Wilhelm Furtwängler, and with a prestigious German cast. This was Furtwängler's last great recording of his interpretation, and it is preserved in the RAI-Rome archives. The following year Igor Stravinsky conducted the orchestra in his own works during an international convention of contemporary music.

After four years under direction of Massimo Freccia and during a long period under Francesco La Rosa Parodi, the role of permanent conductor began to diminish in the orchestra, which was frequently visited by many of the world's great conductors, among them Herbert von Karajan, Leonard Bernstein, and Wolfgang Sawallisch, who in 1970 conducted a performance of Beethoven's *Missa Solemnis* in St. Peter's Basilica, filmed for television by Antonio Zeffirelli.

Parodi was the last permanent conductor, and six years after his departure in 1973 the position was changed to principal conductor, with similar responsibilities. Jerzy Semkow, the first to assume this position (in 1979), was especially noted for his interpretation of late romantic music. Gianluigi Gelmetti held the position in 1981, along with the title of "artistic director."

Today the orchestra is going through a difficult period characterized by some indifference among its public, an attitude interpreted by the current artistic director as a request to follow the current taste of the majority. While satisfying its constituencies that the orchestra is "sustaining the legitimacy of the musical revolution developed after World War II," attention is given to the "historical continuity in the musical events of the last two centuries."

RECORDING HISTORY AND SELECTIVE DISCOGRAPHY: In addition to the recordings preserved in the archives of the RAI of Rome, the orchestra has produced many records, mostly with Fonit-Cetra, but also with such recording companies as Melodram, Atlantis, and others. The first cuts were 78 rpm discs produced by the State Record Library, such as Puccini's *Hymn to Rome*, or by Cetra, as was Anatoli Liadov's *Eight Popular Russian Songs*, op. 58 directed by Vittorio Gui (Cetra BB 25074–5). Subsequently the orchestra recorded numerous lyrical and symphonic works with Cetra, many of which have been preserved in the series "From the Archives of RAI" by Fonit-Cetra, documenting the orchestra's characteristics in its best years. Included in this series are Mozart Piano Concertos K. 415, K. 466, and K. 488 (Benedetti Michelangeli/Vittorio Gui, 1951) LAR 26; Brahms's *Requiem* Op. 45 and *Song of Destiny* (Bruno Walter, 1952) LAR 7: and orchestral works of Stravinsky (Stravinsky, 1957) LAR 25. The Furtwängler *Ring* cycle (1953), the first complete, uncut recording of the entire work, was issued on EMI Seraphim (IS–6100), comprising *Rheingold*, (IC–6076, 3 records), *Walküre*, (IE–6077, 5 records), *Siegfried* (IE–6078, 5 records), and *Gotterdämmerung* (IE–6079, 5 records).

Copland, Piano Concerto (Smith/Copland): Varèse/Sarabande 81098. Sciarrino, *Un'immagine di Arpocrate*, for piano and orchestra with chorus (M. Damerin/G. Gelmetti): Fonit-Cetra, "Italia," ITL 70088.

CHRONOLOGY OF MUSIC DIRECTORS: Permanent Conductors: Fernando Previtali, 1936–1946. Carlo Maria Giulini, 1946–1950. Ferruccio Scaglia, 1953–1959. Massimo Freccia, 1959–1963. Francesco La Rosa Parodi, 1964–1973.

Principal Conductors: Jerzy Semkow, 1979–1982. Gianluigi Gelmetti, 1982–1984.

BIBLIOGRAPHY: *Annuario RAI 1951–1975* (Torino: RAI, 1952–1977). *L'Orchestra Sinfonica di Roma della Radio Italiana* (Rome: RAI-Radio Italiana, ca. 1949). Mario Rinaldi, *Due secoli di musica al Teatro Argentina* (Florence, 1978). Giuseppe Spataro, *La Radio Italiana dalla Liberazione ad oggi* (Dalla relazione al comitato consultivo per le direttive di massima culturali, educative ed artistiche) (Torino, 1947).

ACCESS: Orchestra sinfonica e Coro di Roma alla RAI, Auditorium del Foro Italico, Piazza Lauro de Bosis, 00194 Roma. (06) 3686–6416. Vittorio Bonolis, Operations Manager; Piergiovanni Antonelli, Production Manager.

LUCA TUTINO
TRANS. JULIA DISTEFANO

Japan ─────────────────────────────────

OSAKA (2,623,000)

Osaka Philharmonic Symphony Orchestra

The Osaka Philharmonic Symphony Orchestra (OPSO: Osaka Philharmonic Kokyo Gakudan) has roots going back to 1947, making it the fourth oldest orchestra in Japan. Situated in the second largest city in the nation, it provides some 150 live concerts per year for an estimated audience of over 200,000 people.

Only a few of the concerts are produced directly by the Osaka Philharmonic. More than 25 percent of them are contracted by musical appreciation societies in the Osaka region, and a slightly lesser percentage are sponsored by the government of Osaka Prefecture for its citizenry. School concerts account for more than 10 percent, and there are equal numbers of tour concerts in the western area of Japan and seasonal performances of the Beethoven Ninth, so popular in Japan at year's end. A smaller percentage are sponsored by the Japanese Cultural Affairs Agency. The smallest proportion, eight concerts, constitute the subscription concerts offered by the Osaka Philharmonic.

The orchestra performs two or three times a month in the 2,800-seat Osaka Festival Hall. The largest facility of its kind in Osaka, it is heavily booked and rehearsal time there is limited. More frequently performances are held in the new and attractive, 1,700-seat Symphony Hall, constructed and maintained by the Asahi Broadcasting Corporation.

For its rehearsals, storage, and library facilities, the orchestra rents inexpensive space below the stands of the Osaka city swimming pool. Since rehearsals are always held there until immediately prior to the performances, soloists and musicians are forced to change nuances at the last moment, a problem besetting all the orchestras of Japan.

The OPSO is conceived to be regional in scope and operations. Its offices serve also as the administrative focus of the Regional Symphony Orchestra Association (Chiho Kokyo Gakudan Remmei), representing the symphony orchestras of Gumma (founded in 1945), Hiroshima (1972), Kanagawa (1978), Kyushu (1973), Kyoto (1956), Miyagi (1978), Nagoya (1966), Sapporo (1961), and Yamagata (1972). On the average each of these orchestras performed approximately 135 times during 1984 on a budget in excess of ¥300 million paying an average of 56 players a salary of about ¥3 million.

The Osaka Philharmonic, by contrast, employs a total of 109 people: 97 musicians and a staff of 12. Total expenses for the 1985 season were nearly ¥500 million. Income earned through ticket sales, recording fees, and fees from private concerts accounted for about ¥300 million, fully 60 percent of the budget. Corporate donations from the 120 member companies of the Osaka Philharmonic Society accounted for ¥55 million, and similar amounts were received in operating subsidies from the governments of Osaka City and of Osaka Prefecture. An operating subsidy of ¥35 million was received from the Japanese Cultural Affairs Agency.

The OPSO is the highest paid of the regional orchestras in Japan. In 1984 players earned an average of about ¥4 million. Many musicians also teach privately and in institutions such as the Osaka College of Music and the Osaka University of the Arts. Roughly one-third of the players are graduates of the Osaka College of Music.

The Osaka Philharmonic, as well as its predecessor, the Kansai Symphony Orchestra, has had only one general music director, Takashi Asahina. He was supported by a trio of principal guest conductors in 1985—Kazuyoshi Akiyama, Hiroyuki Iwaki, and Yuzo Toyama—and an assistant conductor, Chitaru Asahina, his son.

The Osaka Philharmonic Symphony Orchestra is headed by a Board of Directors. Its administration is in the hands of a general manager (Kosuke Noguchi) who oversees policy, a Steering Committee chairman (Takashi Hashimoto) who supervises operations, and a staff of 11. Former Sumitomo Bank President Kyonosuke Ibe serves as chairman of the Board. The major goal of the administration is to increase the level of support from the business community to equal the level of earned revenue.

The birth of Japan's foremost regional orchestra was due to the efforts of Takashi Asahini, who had first studied philosophy and law at Kyoto Imperial University. A violinist, he also took up conducting while at the university. In 1934, at age 26, he was invited to make his debut as a conductor with the New Symphony Orchestra, predecessor to the NHK Symphony Orchestra.* He later went to China to conduct and returned to Osaka after the war.

In 1947 Asahina succeeded in founding as a collective an orchestra of some 70 musicians, half of whom came from the NHK Osaka broadcasting orchestra, the Kansai Symphony Orchestra (Kansai Kokyo Gakudan). Asahina made himself conductor and shortly thereafter brought in as manager one of his students who had gone on to form his own music office, Kosuke Noguchi. Under the sponsorship of NHK Osaka, the orchestra performed broadcasts, concerts, and accompaniments for opera and ballet.

Three years later the NHK withdrew sponsorship and this orchestra was broken up. At Asahina's urging, the Kansai Symphony then came under the support of a symphony society formed under the leadership of Sumitomo Bank Chairman Ko Suzuki, president of the Osaka Business Circle. A handful of musicians carried over into the new 70-member orchestra, which rehearsed in the Merchandise and Industrial Committee Room and performed background music for historical Japanese movies.

Under Asahina's leadership the orchestra disbanded once again in 1960 to reform with 60 younger musicians of the Osaka region as the Osaka Philharmonic Symphony Orchestra. The Society and management remained intact, and support was further extended to encompass the municipal and prefectural governments of Osaka as well as the business community. From this time, after 13 years, Asahina's musical aspirations were realized with the performance of the first subscription concerts in Osaka.

Since then the orchestra has considerably matured. Its repertoire has broadened, it has been heard in broadcasts, and it has become an important recording ensemble. In 1975 the OPSO made the first of its international tours and performed 20 concerts during a month in five countries of Europe under Asahina. In 1980 the orchestra toured North America and performed 17 concerts in 14 cities during three weeks under Asahina and Kazuyoshi Akiyama. In 1985 a one-week tour of five concerts was made in China under Takashi Asahina and Chitaru Asahina.

In 1985, his 37th year with the orchestra, despite a heavy schedule of guest-conducting appearances (with more than 50 orchestras to date), Asahina still conducted the majority of the OPSO's subscription concerts. His repertoire concentrates on the Austro/German romantics; he is a champion of the works of Anton Bruckner, and his lengthy list of directorships, presidencies, and honors includes the office of president of the Japan Bruckner Society. For his services to music the president of the Federal Republic of Germany presented Asahina with the Commander's Cross of the Order of Merit.

RECORDING HISTORY AND SELECTIVE DISCOGRAPHY: In 1973 and again in 1985 the Osaka Philharmonic recorded the nine symphonies of Beethoven, and in 1977 under the Victor label it recorded a Beethoven album of the nine symphonies and two masses, which became one of the best sellers of the year. The OPSO also released the same year a series of live recordings of the ten symphonies of Bruckner, which sold out. The four symphonies of Brahms were recorded, as well as works of Tchaikovsky, Dvořák, Shostakovich, Richard Strauss, and Wagner, all under the baton of Takashi Asahina.

Beethoven, Nine Symphonies (Asahina): Victor VIC 4170/8. Bruckner, Symphony No. 7 (Asahina): Victor VDC511. Furtwängler, Symphony No. 2 (Asahina): Victor VIC 2397/8. Mahler, Symphony No. 9 (Asahina): King K25C361/2.

CHRONOLOGY OF MUSIC DIRECTORS: Takashi Asahina, 1947–present.

BIBLIOGRAPHY: Jun Asaka, ed., *Ongaku Nenkan* (Music Yearbook) (Tokyo: Ongaku-no-Tomo Sha, 1984). Keiji Masui, ed., *Data Ongaku Nippon* (Music Data Japan) (Tokyo: Minon Music Library, Minshu Ongaku Kyokai, 1980). Matsue Nakasone, ed., *Sekai no Okesutora Jiten* (Dictionary of Orchestras of the World) (Tokyo: Geijitsu Gendai Sha, 1984). Arihiko Nakata, "Osaka Philharmonic Orchestra: From its Foundation to the Present," in *Expo '70 Classics* (Osaka: Japan Association for the World Exposition, 1970). Takashi Ogawa, ed., *Nippon no Kokyo Gakudan* (Symphony Orchestras of Japan) (Tokyo: Minon Music Library, Minshu Ongaku Kyokai, 1983). *Osaka Philharmonic Orchestra* (Osaka: OPSO, 1983). Masahisa Sakisaka, "Orchestras in Japan," in *New Japan* (Tokyo: Mainichi Shimbun Sha, 1968). Kazuko Yasukawa, gen. ed., *Ensokai Nenkan 1984* (Concert Yearbook) (Tokyo: Shadanhojin Nippon Enso Remmei, 1985).

ACCESS: Osaka Philharmonic Symphony Orchestra, Kitahara 4–55, Higashi-ku, Osaka-fu 541. (81) 06–231–7459. Kosuke Noguchi, Managing Director.

ROBERT RŸKER

TOKYO   (11,676,000*)

New Japan Philharmonic Symphony Orchestra

The New Japan Philharmonic Symphony Orchestra (NJPSO: Shin Nihon Philharmonic Kokyo Gakudan) was founded in 1972. It provides some 160 live concerts per year for an estimated audience of over 200,000 people.

Only a proportion of the concerts are produced directly by the New Japan Philharmonic. More than half are contracted by managements of concert halls wishing to service their local publics and by concert managements who wish to produce performances for their solo artists. School concerts account for more than 10 percent and there are an equal number of concerts performed on tours throughout Japan. Seiji Ozawa conducts a special series of about five concerts scheduled according to his availability, and there are equal numbers of recording sessions and year-end performances of the Beethoven Ninth. Ten concerts constitute the subscription series offered by the NJPSO.

As there is a very great premium on concert halls in the metropolitan area, the orchestra has no real home. The NJPSO performs its subscription concerts at Tokyo Festival Hall, a good hall seating 2,300. Much more frequently, however, performances are held in such concert halls as the 1,300-seat Green Hall in the Chofu district of Tokyo and in the ward halls of Shibuya, Setagaya, Edogawa, and other districts of metropolitan Tokyo.

For its rehearsals, storage, and library facilities, the orchestra is able to rent inexpensive facilities in the Josenji Buddhist Temple in the Shibuya district of Tokyo. For rehearsals occasional use is made also of the Hitomi Memorial Hall at the National Women's University. Inevitably, soloists and musicians are forced to change nuances at the last moment, since only final rehearsals are held in Tokyo concert halls prior to performances.

Such problems indeed beset all the orchestras of Tokyo. The total of 120 existing concert halls, if filled simultaneously would accommodate less than 1/2 of 1 percent of the people who live in the greater Tokyo area (some 22 million people, one-fifth of the entire population of Japan). Even the NHK Symphony Orchestra* is only resident in NHK Hall, and the Tokyo Metropolitan Symphony Orchestra* is able to perform in Tokyo Festival Hall no more frequently than any other orchestra.

The NJPSO competes for space and for its audiences with the eight other professional orchestras resident in Tokyo and with scores of orchestras and other ensembles visiting from abroad, as well as with approximately 50 university and amateur orchestras, 100 bands, and 5,000 choruses.

The New Japan Philharmonic may be thought to be representative of the private orchestras of Tokyo, which receive virtually no enabling subsidies and thus must sustain their activities almost exclusively through earned concert income. These include the Japan Philharmonic Symphony Orchestra (founded in 1956), the New Star Japan (Shinsei Nihon) Symphony Orchestra (1969), the Tokyo City Philharmonic Symphony Orchestra (1975), the Tokyo Philharmonic Symphony Orchestra (1952), and the Tokyo Symphony Orchestra (1946). On the average these orchestras each gave approximately 180 performances during 1984 on a budget of nearly ¥500 million, paying an average of 78 players a salary of about ¥2.2 million.

The New Japan Philharmonic, not included in the figures above, employs a total of 93 people, including 81 musicians and a staff of 12. Total expenses for the 1985 season were over ¥400 million. Income earned through subscription ticket sales accounted for about ¥60 million, and fees from contracted engagements for about ¥350 million, totaling virtually the entire budget. Sustaining donations from NJPSO subscribers accounted for another ¥8 million, and ¥10 million was received as an operating subsidy from the Japanese Cultural Affairs Agency.

The NJPSO pays its musicians on an aggressive level for the private orchestras of Tokyo: during 1984, players earned an average of nearly ¥3 million. Most of the musicians teach privately, and some also teach in institutions such as the Tokyo College of Music. A number of chamber ensembles exist, including a chamber orchestra normally conducted by Michiyoshi Inoue. Almost two-thirds of the players are graduates of the Toho School of Music, and most of the remainder come from the Tokyo National University of Fine Arts; thus, as in other Japanese orchestras, there are strongly stabilizing common denominators among the orchestra members, a pervasive feature of Japanese culture.

The orchestra's music director since 1983 is Michiyoshi Inoue, a prize-winner of the Guido Cantelli Conductor's Competition in Milan. Much of the ascendency of the New Japan Philharmonic, however, must be attributed to the orchestra's first music director, Seiji Ozawa, who continues his abiding support by conducting a number of "Seiji Ozawa Special Concerts" with the NJPSO each year.

The repertoire of the NJPSO is perhaps the most progressive of all the Tokyo orchestras, embracing a high proportion of contemporary music amid the conservative mix of concerto repertoire and standard pieces that characterize its many contracted engagements. The adventurous bent is shown in its performances of opera in concert style, which have included *Bluebeard's Castle*, *Salome*, and *Wozzeck*, conducted by Ozawa, and the entire *Ring*, conducted over four years by Takashi Asahina.

The NJPSO is headed by a Board of Directors, under whom serve its conductors and management. Administration is in the hands of a general manager and a staff of 11. The orchestra's spirited philosophy is concisely stated by General Manager Chiyoshige Matsubara, a former NJPSO horn player: "the orchestra must care first for its standard of performance. The management feels its responsibility to help the orchestra strive for the highest artistic level possible."

The New Japan Philharmonic Symphony Orchestra was formed from the then 15-year-old Japan Philharmonic Symphony Orchestra, which still exists, in a rancorous dispute between the players. Union and nonunion members had worked side by side in the orchestra until two significant events forced their differences to divide them fatefully.

In December 1971 union members of the Japan Philharmonic walked out on strike against the Festival Broadcasting Corporation (Bunka Hoso Kaikan) and Fuji Television, choosing as their vehicle for protest a performance of the popular Beethoven Ninth. They were upset that the orchestra's sponsors had voiced concern about the musicians' performance standard and declining audience ratings and had threatened to withdraw financial support. Union members were agitated also with the orchestra's music director, Seiji Ozawa, who they felt was authoritative in rehearsal to members of the orchestra more senior (older) than himself. The interpersonal relationships fundamental to Japanese society are rigidly vertical, based on seniority. An art form that thrives on individual excellence therefore runs counter to the traditional Oriental respect for authority deriving from age.

For their part, nonunion members of the orchestra tended to comprise the wind players, with a handful of strings and staff. They were impatient with players who placed protection and security before artistic excellence. Then, in March 1972, the financial subsidy withdrawn from the Japan Philharmonic by Bunka Hoso and Fuji Television indicated the orchestra's complete demise. The nonunion musicians separated from their colleagues formally in an attempt to build a new orchestra infused with their own ideals.

The musicians took on the management responsibilities, paid themselves equally a flat salary of ¥50,000 monthly, and asked Ozawa to continue as their music director during the first year, while they sought concert opportunities to put the orchestra together. They welcomed young players into the orchestra, including women—who comprise more than one-third of the musicians—and created an ensemble in a self-consciously American style. The first performance of the new orchestra took place on September 15, 1972, under Ozawa, with an all-Haydn program. Subsequently the management has scrupulously monitored the musicians' performance and instituted an on-going process of reseating individuals.

The NJPSO now claims a high reputation for a sound which is clear, transparent, and bright. In 1973, less than a year after its formation, the orchestra took part in the Hong Kong Arts Festival. The following year it made its first international tour, performing under Ozawa and Kazuyoshi Akiyama in the United States at Carnegie Hall, the Kennedy Center, and the United Nations, and then in London, Paris, Cologne, and Munich.

RECORDING HISTORY AND SELECTIVE DISCOGRAPHY: The New Japan Philharmonic has plans to record all of the concert performances of the Wagner *Ring* tetralogy under Takashi Asahina. A private recording was made under Seiji Ozawa of the Mahler Second Symphony during the orchestra's 100th subscription concert

Violin Pieces: Works of Beethoven, Chausson, Ravel, Saint-Saëns, Sarasate (Jean-Jacques Kantorow/Inoue): Denon CD7005 (CD).

CHRONOLOGY OF MUSIC DIRECTORS: Seiji Ozawa, 1972–1973. Kazuhiro Koizumi, 1975–1979. Conductors committee (Takashi Asahina, Seiji Ozawa, Yukinori Tezuka, and Yaozumi Yamamoto), 1979–1983. Michiyoshi Inoue, 1983–present.

BIBLIOGRAPHY: Jun Asaka, ed., *Ongaku Nenkan* (Music Yearbook) (Tokyo: Ongaku-no-Tomo Sha, 1984). Marcel Grilli, "The New Japan Philharmonic" in *The Japan Times* (Tokyo, 1983). Keiji Masui, ed., *Data Ongaku Nippon* (Music Data Japan) (Tokyo: Minon Music Library, Minshu Ongaku Kyokai, 1980). Matsue Nakasone, ed., *Sekai no Okesutora Jiten* (Dictionary of Orchestras of the World) (Tokyo: Geijitsu Gendai Sha, 1984). Takashi Ogawa, ed., *Nippon no Kokyo Gakudan* (Symphony Orchestras of Japan) (Tokyo: Minon Music Library, Minshu Ongaku Kyokai, 1983). Masahisa Sakisaka, "Orchestras in Japan," in *New Japan* (Tokyo: Mainichi Shimbu Sha, 1968). Kazuko Yasukawa, gen. ed., *Ensokai Nenkan 1984* (Concert Yearbook) (Tokyo: Shadanhojin Nippon Enso Remmei, 1985).

ACCESS: New Japan Philharmonic Symphony Orchestra, Toya Building 5F1, Shibuya 3–16–3, Shibuya-ku, Tokyo 150. (81) 03–499–1631. Chiyoshige Matsubara, General Manager.

ROBERT RŸKER

NHK Symphony Orchestra

The Nippon Hoso Kyokai Kokyo Gakudan (NHK: Japan Broadcasting Corporation Symphony Orchestra), founded in 1926, is the largest, oldest, and best established of Tokyo's nine professional orchestras. It provides over 150 live concerts per year for an estimated audience of 350,000. It offers 30 yearly subscription series during the fall and winter season, as well as special concerts and major tours.

The orchestra gives subscription concerts at the 3,700-seat NHK Hall in Shibuya, Tokyo, a hall with some acoustical problems. The largest facility of its kind in Tokyo, it is very heavily booked, and so the orchestra's rehearsal time there is limited. The orchestra is fortunate to have its own rehearsal hall in

Takanawa, Tokyo, but nevertheless, soloists and musicians are forced to change ensemble balance and nuances at the last moment, since rehearsals are held there until immediately prior to performances. Such problems, however, beset all of Tokyo's orchestras.

Ticket sales are indeed very competitive in Tokyo because of the competition among eight other resident professional ensembles and the many groups that visit from abroad. Some observers point out that a diversity of audience taste has been developing over recent years and that there has been a decline in the number of symphony orchestra concertgoers.

The NHK is headed by a Board of Directors, under whom serve its conductors and a general manager. Management staff hire and negotiate with musicians and soloists. The orchestra employs some 130 people (108 musicians and a staff of 22) on an annual budget in excess of ¥1.6 billion. The orchestra is funded through ticket sales, recordings, private and corporate donations, and a subsidy of about ¥600 million from the Japan Broadcasting System (NHK). In return the orchestra grants the NHK exclusive broadcasting rights. This unique subsidy and the exclusive broadcasting arrangements have had an enormous cultural impact on Japan because the orchestra broadcasts nationwide over the NHK television and radio network. These programs are thus accessible and free to nearly 120 million Japanese people. Over the years (since 1951) the subsidy has also nurtured the orchestra's artistic and financial growth.

The NHK Symphony Orchestra's musicians teach privately and in neighboring schools, such as Tokyo University of the Arts, the Toho School of Music, Musashino College of Music, and the Kunitachi College of Music. They also appear as conductors, concertmasters, or soloists in other orchestras, not only in Tokyo but throughout the country. Even though the NHK Symphony Orchestra's musicians are the best paid in Japan, low salaries still persist—or at any rate, salaries are considerably lower than those of other professions. Although NHK players earned an average of about ¥5.5 million in 1984, many players are compelled to take part-time jobs, and the resulting overwork and fatigue may threaten to jeopardize artistic standards. For a number of years, however, the NHK Symphony Orchestra has been the national model in terms of repertoire selection, artistic quality, and working conditions; it has drawn superior musicians from throughout the country.

One of the orchestra's most significant cultural contributions is the annual Odaka Prize for composition. The winning composition is premiered by the orchestra, a tradition since the competition's inception in 1953. The prize is recognized as one of the most prestigious cultural achievements in Japan, and its recipients have become trendsetters for other Japanese composers. Among them are Akira Mayoshi (four times), Toshiro Mayuzumi and Toru Takemitsu (each twice), and Yuzo Toyama.

Another important contribution is an internship program for young conductors, which enables them to sit in on rehearsals and concerts to study the repertoire— with major conductors, if the intern wishes—and to use the orchestra library.

Interns also receive a monthly stipend for a period of two years. Some graduates from this program now hold major positions with orchestras in Japan and abroad. They include Hiroyuki Iwaki, Tadaaki Otaka, Yuzo Toyama, and Hiroshi Wakasugi.

The NHK Symphony Orchestra has not had a music director as such since the departure of Joseph Rosenstock in 1946. It relies rather on a trio of conductors to fulfill the main conducting duties, as do both other orchestras among the "big three" (the Yomiuri Nippon Symphony Orchestra* and Tokyo Metropolitan Symphony Orchestra*). Principal guest conductors for the 1985–1986 season were Zdenek Kosler, Horst Stein, and Otmar Suitner. The principal resident conductor is Hiroyuki Iwaki.

Details about the first symphony orchestra in Japan are sketchy. According to an article in the Tokyo *Nichinichi* newspaper, the first symphony orchestra made a public appearance on February 19, 1887, at the School of Music at Ueno Park in Tokyo. The orchestra performed, as part of the school's second commencement exercises, the second and third movements of Beethoven's First Symphony. This marked the first formal presentation of a symphony by a Japanese symphony orchestra. Reportedly, the orchestra was a chamber ensemble consisting of strings and woodwinds instead of a full-scale symphony orchestra.

The birth of Japan's first professional orchestra was due to the efforts of Kosaku Yamada, a Japanese composer, and Hidemaro Konoe, a conductor who studied music in Germany. Together, they were the driving force behind a "Japanese-Russian Goodwill Symphony Concert" in April 1924 at the Kabuki Theatre in Tokyo. The success of the concert further enhanced their desire for a new orchestra. Konoe talked to some 40 fellow musicians and succeeded in founding on October 5, 1926, a new ensemble called the Shin Kokyo Gakudan (New Symphony Orchestra).

Konoe was made its first conductor and subsequently led the orchestra until 1935. His repertoire included a wide range of works in the Viennese classical and romantic, French impressionist, and post-romantic styles, as well as works by Igor Stravinsky. Under Konoe's leadership the orchestra firmly established a high standard of performance. It also provided Japanese audiences with the opportunity to hear some of the world's most celebrated soloists, including Jospeh Szigeti, Artur Rubinstein, Efrem Zimbalist, and Emanuel Feuermann. A good many guest conductors, both Japanese and foreign, appeared with the orchestra.

Konoe's successor, Jospeh Rosenstock, occupied the podium from 1936 to 1946 and expanded the repertoire. The orchestra was incorporated in 1942 and renamed the Nippon Kokyo Gakudan (Japan Symphony Orchestra). During the peak of the Second World War the Interior Ministry and the War Ministry coined the term *Tekisei Ongaku*, which means "enemy music," and banned the performance of music of the West other than that of Germany and Italy, with whom the Japanese were allied.

Immediately after the war life was very harsh for the Japanese people, owing to a shortage of food, to unemployment, and to rampant inflation. The orchestra and its musicians underwent some very trying years. Rosenstock left the orchestra in 1947 and it subsequently operated under a number of guests; it has been without a permanent music director since then. Mr. Daigoro Arima, the orchestra's general manager, was instrumental in keeping the orchestra afloat, both during and after the war. Financial stability was at last attained in 1951 when the NHK became a sponsor and the orchestra's name was changed accordingly.

Since then the orchestra has considerably matured. It is recognized internationally as a fine ensemble; it has toured extensively throughout Japan, Europe, North America, the USSR, and Africa. Its repertoire has broadened, it has become an important recording ensemble, its management has stabilized, and it has been heard regularly in broadcasts. Its long list of guest conductors includes some of the world's finest, among them Ernest Ansermet, Daniel Barenboim, Herbert von Karajan, Neville Mariner, Seiji Ozawa, Wolfgang Sawallisch, and many more of equal renown.

In spite of the NHK's success story, there still exist a number of problems: the lack of a suitable concert hall for rehearsals and concerts, modest salaries for musicians, poor attendance at some concerts, and labor disputes. Nevertheless, supporters of the orchestra predict a bright future and expect these problems will ultimately be solved.

RECORDING HISTORY AND SELECTIVE DISCOGRAPHY: The NHK Symphony Orchestra's first recording (1961), under Hiroyuki Iwaki was recorded at Bunkyo Kokaido (Bunkyo Public Hall), Tokyo. Produced and distributed by King Records, Tokyo, it includes *Rhapsody* by Yuzo Toyama, *Kobikiuta* by Shigeki Toyama, and the Concerto for Flute and Orchestra by Naotaki Otaka. Since then a number of recordings have been released on Japanese Columbia, Philips, CBS Sony, EMI, and King labels. The orchestra also recorded an album of 23 records of various Italian operas, which were recorded from live performances in 1963. In 1982 it released a series of recordings featuring works of Japanese composers. Many NHK Symphony Orchestra members record individually as soloists or as chamber music performers.

Beethoven, Symphonies Nos. 5 and 8 (Sawallisch): RCA RCL–8341. Beethoven, Symphony No. 9 (Iwaki): Vox CT2123. Toshiro Mayuzumi, *Nehan* (Toyama): Philips PH–8536. Mozart, Symphonies Nos. 38 (K. 504) and 39(K. 543) (Suitner): Denon CD–7051 (CD). Yuzo Toyama, *Rhapsody* (Iwaki): King SKR–1012.

CHRONOLOGY OF MUSIC DIRECTORS: Hidemaro Konoe, 1926–1935. Joseph Rosenstock, 1936–1946. (Guest conductors, 1946-present.)

BIBLIOGRAPHY: Jun Asaka, ed., *Ongaku Nenkan* (Who's Who in Music) (Tokyo: Ongaku-no Tomo Sha, 1984). Keiji Masui, ed. *Data Ongaku Nippon* (Music Data Japan) (Tokyo: Minon Music Library, Minshu Ongaku Kyokai, 1980). Matsue Nakasone, ed. *Sekai-no Orchestra Jiten* (Dictionary of Orchestras of the World) (Tokyo: Geijyutsu Gendai Sha, 1984). NHK Symphony Orchestra, *Subscription Guide on NHK Symphony Orchestra for Foreign Residents in Japan* (Tokyo, 1980). ''NHK Symphony Orchestra,'' *Tokyo Ongaku Daigaku News* 22 (1984), 24–28. Takashi Ogawa, ed., *Nippon-no Kokyo Gakudan* (Symphony Orchestras of Japan) (Tokyo: Minon Music Library, Minshu Ongaku Kyokai, 1983).

ACCESS: NHK Symphony Orchestra, 2–16–49, Takanawa, Minato-ku, Tokyo 108. (81) 03–443–0271. Takao Hase, General Manager.

YOSHIHIRO OBATA

Tokyo Metropolitan Symphony Orchestra

The Tokyo Metropolitan Symphony Orchestra (TMSO: Tokyo-to Kokyo Gak-udan) is maintained by the Metropolitan Government of Tokyo as a nonprofit foundation under the Department of Education, as is Tokyo Festival Hall, where it resides. The orchestra performs about 140 concerts per year. Fully half of these are educational concerts for junior high school students of the Tokyo Metropolitan Board of Education, which oversees the compulsory education of approximately 5 million students.

Some 70 educational concerts are complemented by a series of 20 subscription concerts, all performed in the 2,300-seat Tokyo Festival Hall. A second series of 12 family concerts is offered in various halls throughout the city. A small series of three concerts is performed in a hall in the Shinjuku district of Tokyo, and the orchestra is also called to perform similar numbers of opera performances, private concerts, and other special concerts, as well as at least half a dozen year-end performances of Beethoven's Ninth Symphony, which is heard widely in Japan at that season.

With the slogan "It's your orchestra," the TMSO has a formal policy to be of service to the Tokyo community; hence its trips to perform in other parts of Japan account for but a few concerts. Two additional unspoken policies are seen to guide the orchestra. Its members are almost entirely Japanese, and its principal conductors are foreigners.

A number of chamber ensembles, including a chamber orchestra, exist within the orchestra and are organized by the members themselves. Roughly two-thirds of the 105 players are graduates of the Tokyo National University of Fine Arts, and most of the remainder come from the Musashino Music Academy.

Three conductors fulfill the main conducting duties, as is also the case in both of the other orchestras among Tokyo's "big three" (the NHK Symphony Orchestra* and the Yomiuri Nippon Symphony Orchestra*). Principal guest conductors for the 1985 season were Jean Fournet, Zdenek Kosler, and Peter Maag. For the large number of educational concerts, orchestra members rotate, with about 70 players performing at a time. Conducting duties too are divided among many young Japanese conductors.

For the backbone of its repertoire, the TMSO leans heavily on the German romantics, who account for about two-thirds of its programming. Programming for the educational concerts is developed by the artistic administrator in consultation with educational committees from the 23 districts of Tokyo. Their decisions, however, are strongly influenced by the guidelines for repertoire laid down by the Japanese Ministry of Education.

This conservative approach highlights also the administration's no-deficit operation of TMSO finances, which involves no individual or business contributions. Total expenses for the 1985 season amounted to ¥1.16 billion. Approximately ¥220 million was realized in subscription ticket sales and ¥40 million from the schools. The operating subsidy from the Metropolitan Government of Tokyo, ¥900 million, nearly 80% of the orchestra's budget, was the largest such subsidy in Japan.

Tokyo Festival Hall rents to the orchestra its administrative offices as well as the orchestra's large and comfortable rehearsal facilities. All rehearsals are held in this rehearsal hall, making the TMSO perhaps the most favorably housed orchestra in Japan. The orchestra has access two or three times per month to the building's main hall (of two), which is otherwise engaged by numerous Japanese and foreign orchestras (see New Japan Philharmonic Symphony Orchestra*).

The TMSO is headed by a Board of Directors, under whom are a managing director (Kiyoshi Kosugiyama) who oversees policy, an artistic administrator (Akira Imamura) who supervises operations, and 15 staff members. The governor of Tokyo appoints a vice-president (Teruo Takano), who maintains liaison with the Metropolitan Government, and Governor Shunichi Suzuki himself serves as honorary president.

In observation of the 500th anniversary of the founding of Tokyo, Tokyo Festival Hall (Tokyo Bunka Kaikan) was built in 1961 to serve the cultural needs of the people. Three years later the city played host to the 1964 Olympics. Tokyo Governor Ryotaro Azuma, then serving as a member of the International Organizing Committee, proclaimed his government's wish to establish a metropolitan symphony orchestra in Tokyo Festival Hall as a memorial to perpetuate the spirit of those celebrations.

Tokyo Department of Education head Torao Obi stated, "The need for the Metropolitan Government to have its own orchestra is due to its obligation to foster the spiritual education of the young, making use of Tokyo Bunka Kaikan, which is a concert hall of world standards. It should meet also the demands of Tokyo's ever-growing musical population."

Only two years prior to that, however, the Yomiuri Group had established the Yomiuri Nippon Symphony Orchestra, increasing the number of professional orchestras in the city at that time to five. There was heated debate about a city project that would result in further exacerbating the competition for survival of the private orchestras in Tokyo. The financial situation of the Metropolitan Government was also called into question. In the end the establishment of the orchestra was conceived as an instrument of the cultural policy of the nation's capital city, raising the spiritual education of the citizenry.

The new orchestra was required to take a neutral position, not to damage any of the private orchestras, in view of its official status in the city. Its members were to be recruited from Japanese musical society without enticing away members from other orchestras. In fact, this made it a difficult birth. The TMSO was founded in February 1965 and began rehearsals in April. Within six months, on October 1, Tokyo Citizens Day, the first concert, a program of Mozart and

Hindemith, was heard under Yoichiro Ohmachi and German conductor Heinz Hoffmann, who served as music director during the first season.

The early years of the orchestra were beset with difficulties. Its basic organization was criticized and its future outlook questioned. A special committee was set up to investigate the various organizations attached to the Metropolitan Government, and a shift in political power in the Metropolitan Assembly created a situation in which the very existence of the orchestra was in doubt. Four years after its founding an appeal was made to the people of Tokyo under a slogan proclaiming, "The Metropolitan Symphony Orchestra is your orchestra." Finally, in 1967, when its popular concerts had already reached their fifth season, the orchestra was able to inaugurate its series of subscription concerts.

The TMSO made its only international tour during its twelfth season, 1977. Twenty-five concerts were performed under Akeo Watanabe and Kenichiro Kobayashi during a month-and-a-half tour of eight countries in Eastern Europe. The orchestra realized its ¥90 million tour budget through earned concert income, supplemented by ¥20 million from the Japan Foundation for International Relations and ¥40 million from the Metropolitan Government of Tokyo.

In order to carry out Governor Azuma's wish to create a fine orchestra for the people of Tokyo, the TMSO offers one of the three highest salaries in the country (with NHK and Yomiuri). During 1984 players earned an average of about ¥4.8 million. Over the years the early problems caused by youth and lack of experience among the newly recruited musicians have been overcome, and the TMSO now claims a high reputation for its flexibility. Its slogan embodies the concept that the TMSO is the property of the people of Tokyo, and it is always aware of its artistic responsibility to them.

RECORDING HISTORY AND SELECTIVE DISCOGRAPHY: The TMSO has made several dozen discs under the Columbia, Victor, CBS Sony, and other labels in Japan. Works by Japanese composers and standard works featuring Japanese soloists make up the bulk of the programming.

Berlioz, *Symphonie Fantastique* (Fournet): Columbia OF7089ND. *Music of Russia* (*Capriccio Italien, Capriccio Espagnol, Steppes of Central Asia*) (Atzmon): Columbia OF7088ND, Denon 7068. Saint-Saëns, *Introduction and Rondo Capriccioso*; Beethoven, *Romance* (Teiko Maehashi/Kazuhiro Koizumi): CBS Sony 28AC1637.

CHRONOLOGY OF MUSIC DIRECTORS: Heinz Hoffmann, 1965–1966. Tadashi Mori, 1967–1972. Akeo Watanabe, 1972–1978. Moshe Atzmon, 1978–1982. Jean Fournet, Zdenek Kosler, Peter Maag (Principal guest conductors), 1982–1986. Hiroshi Wakusugi, 1986–present.

BIBLIOGRAPHY: Jun Asaka, ed., *Ongaku Nenkan* (Music Yearbook) (Tokyo: Ongaku-no-Tomo Sha, 1984). Yoshiyuki Fujita, "Your Orchestra," in *Ongaku-no-Tomo* (Tokyo: Ongaku-no-Tomo Sha, 1981). Keiji Masui, ed., *Data Ongaku Nippon* (Music Data Japan) (Tokyo: Minon Music Library, Minsu Ongaku Kyokai, 1980). Matsue Nakasone, ed., *Sekai no Okesutora Jiten* (Dictionary of Orchestras of the World) (Tokyo: Geijitsu Gendai Sha, 1984). Takashi Ogawa, ed., *Nippon no Kokyo Gakudan* (Symphony Orchestras of Japan) (Tokyo: Minon Music Library, Minshu Ongaku Kyokai, 1983). Masahisa Sakisaka, "Orchestras in Japan," in *New Japan* (Tokyo: Mainichi Shimbun Sha, 1968).

Tokyo: Ensokai Kiroku 1965–1984 (Metro Sounds: Concert Record) (Tokyo: TMSO, 1984). Kazuko Yasukawa, gen. ed., *Ensokai Nenkan 1984* (Concert Yearbook) (Tokyo: Shadanhojin Nippon Enso Remmei, 1985).

ACCESS: Tokyo Metropolitan Symphony Orchestra, Tokyo Festival Hall, Ueno Park 5–45, Taito-ku, Tokyo 110. (81) 03–822–0726. Kiyoshi Kosugiyama, General Manager.

ROBERT RŸKER

Yomiuri Nippon Symphony Orchestra

The Yomiuri Nippon Symphony Orchestra (YNSO: Yomiuri Nippon Kokyo Gakudan) owes its status to its creation and maintenance by the Yomiuri News (Yomiuri Shimbun) Group. The orchestra performs about 120 concerts per year, approximately half of these outside of Tokyo.

As there is a very great premium on concert halls in the metropolitan area (see New Japan Philharmonic Symphony Orchestra*), the orchestra has no home except for its own rehearsal facilities located at Yomiuriland in adjacent Kawasaki. Its main series of 11 concerts is offered monthly at Tokyo Festival Hall (2,300 seats). A second series of 12 concerts is performed at the 2,400-seat Kosei Nenkin Hall in the Shinjuku district of Tokyo, and a third series of six concerts is played at the 2,500-seat Kanagawa Kemmin Hall in Yokohama, a part of the contiguous metropolitan area. The orchestra also performs about 20 youth concerts. The remainder of its annual activities includes as many as ten year-end performances of Beethoven's Ninth and many trips to perform some 40 concerts throughout Japan.

It has a formal policy to be an orchestra composed only of men, with the sole exception in recent years of the harpist, and accordingly claims for itself a high reputation for its full sound. Its members are almost entirely Japanese, and its principal conductors are foreigners.

Most YNSO musicians teach, and some play in chamber ensembles organized by the musicians themselves. Roughly half of the orchestra's 100 players are graduates of the Tokyo National University of Fine Arts, and most others are from the Musashino Music Academy. Great status is accorded to the orchestra's concertmasters and solo players, talented Japanese musicians who have brought back to their country experience in similar positions in orchestras of Europe.

The YNSO relies on a trio of conductors to fulfill the main conducting duties, as do both other orchestras among Tokyo's "big three" (the NHK Symphony Orchestra* and the Tokyo Metropolitan Symphony Orchestra*). For the 1985 season, subscription concerts were under the direction of Principal Conductor Heinz Rögner and Honorary Conductors Kurt Sanderling and Kurt Masur. Raphael Frühbeck de Burgos serves as principal guest conductor, and Seiichi Mitsuishi and another ten or so guest conductors divide the remaining performances.

In order to attract the conservative audience, the YNSO leans heavily on the German romantics for the backbone of its repertoire. The management thus accounts for an increase in recent years in the numbers and proportion of young ticket-holders in the 20s and 30s to roughly 50% of a total audience of some 300,000.

The administration is also conservative in its no-deficit operation of YNSO finances. Total expenses for the 1985 season amounted to ¥1.2 billion. Approximately ¥400 million is realized in ticket sales, ¥180 million in business contributions, and ¥30 million from the Japanese Cultural Affairs Agency. Nearly 50% of the budget and the third largest such subsidy in Japan, ¥550 million, is the operating subsidy from the Yomiuri Group.

Headed by a Board of Directors, the YNSO's administration is in the hands of a managing director (Toshiharu Kubo) who oversees policy, a general manager (Jiro Kametaka) who supervises operations, and ten staff members. Yomiuri News Vice-President Tsuneatsu Isato serves as general director. In view of the critical shortage of concert halls in the Tokyo region, the administration has set as its major goal the acquisition of its own concert hall.

At present, major concerts of the YNSO are physically limited to once a month at best in two of the city's busiest concert halls, and artistic development, audience development, and earned income are seriously curtailed. Only the financial sustenance of the Yomiuri Group has made possible the orchestra's existence and remarkable development. The cost is high, however—the full price of every ticket is more than matched by the Yomiuri funds. Yomiuri Concert Hall, too, will be costly, but it is nonetheless perhaps the most practical goal the YNSO could devise to insure its future.

The *Yomiuri Shimbun* is the largest newspaper in Japan, with a total daily circulation of approximately nine million. The Yomiuri Group also owns television stations, printing companies, golf links, a professional baseball team, and a major entertainment center, Yomiuriland. In 1961 *Yomiuri Shimbun* owner Matsutaro Shoriki decided that the Yomiuri Group should include a symphony orchestra, to complement its popular baseball club, then 30 years old, and in order to continue its policy of "developing with our readers." Within six months, on September 26, 1962, American conductor Willis Page led the new orchestra, the city's fifth, in a program of Beethoven, Brahms, and Richard Strauss. Page remained as music director for the first season.

In order to carry out Shoriki's wish to create the best orchestra in Japan, the YNSO offers one of the country's highest orchestral salaries (with NHK). Tutti players earned an average of about ¥5 million during 1984. The orchestra's list of guest conductors has included Sergiu Celibidache, Antál Doráti, Aram Khachaturian, Zubin Mehta, Leopold Stokowski, and others of similar renown.

The YNSO made the first of its international tours in 1967, performing over 40 concerts under Arthur Fiedler in the United States and Canada. Month-long tours were also made in Europe: in 1971 under Hiroshi Wakasugi, and again in 1981 under Rafael Frühbeck de Burgos to represent Japan at the first International Orchestra Festival in Leipzig. The orchestra's many recognitions include a Grand Prix awarded by the Cultural Affairs Agency of Japan, making this the first time the distinction has been conferred on a Japanese orchestra.

RECORDING HISTORY AND SELECTIVE DISCOGRAPHY: The orchestra made an estimated 100 discs during its first decade under the Victor, Columbia, London, and other labels in Japan. Japanese composers and ''home concert'' programs made up the programming; about half of the recordings were conducted by Hiroshi Wakasugi. With the impression that the market for classical recordings in Japan was both small and saturated, recording was discontinued thereafter.

Beethoven, Symphonies (Wakasugi): Toshiba AA47/75/78/82. Bizet, *Carmen Suite* (Serge Baudo): Victor VX55. Dvořák, Symphony No. 8 (Theodore Guschlbauer): Errato STU70942. Mozart, Flute Concertos Nos. 1 and 2 (Rampal/Otto Steiner): Columbia MS1131M. Masau Ohki, *Night Meditation*; works of Fukai, Kiyose, Yamada (Shigenobu Yamaoka): Varèse/Sarabande 81061.

CHRONOLOGY OF MUSIC DIRECTORS: Willis Page, 1962–1963. Otto Matzerath, 1963. Hiroshi Wakasugi, 1965–1975. (Guest conductors, 1975–1980.) Rafael Frühbeck de Burgos, 1980–1985. Heinz Rögner, 1985-present.

BIBLIOGRAPHY: Jun Asaka, ed., *Ongaku Nenkan* (Music Yearbook) (Tokyo: Ongaku-no-Tomo Sha, 1984). Keiji Masui, ed., *Data Ongaku Nippon* (Music Data Japan) (Tokyo: Minon Music Library, Minsu Ongaku Kyokai, 1980). Matsue Nakasone, ed., *Sekai no Okesutora Jiten* (Dictionary of Orchestras of the World) (Tokyo: Geijitsu Gendai Sha, 1984). Takashi Ogawa, ed., *Nippon no Kokyo Gakudan* (Symphony Orchestras of Japan) (Tokyo: Minon Music Library, Minshu Ongaku Kyokai, 1983). Masahisa Sakisaka, ''Orchestras in Japan,'' in *New Japan* (Tokyo: Mainichi Shimbun Sha, 1968). Kazuko Yasukawa, gen. ed., *Ensokai Nenkan 1984* (Concert Yearbook) (Tokyo: Shadanhojin Nippon Enso Remmei, 1985). *Yomiuri Nippon Symphony Orchestra, 1967–1972* (Tokyo: Yomiuri Shimbun Sha, 1972). *The Yomiuri Shimbun: The World's Biggest Daily Newspaper* (Tokyo: Yomiuri Shimbun Sha, 1983).

ACCESS: Yomiuri Nippon Symphony Orchestra, Yomiuri Shimbun Building 8F1, Ohtemachi 1–7–1, Chiyoda-ku, Tokyo 100. (81) 03–270–6191. Toshiharu Kubo, Managing Director.

ROBERT RŸKER

Korea ─────────────────────────────────

SEOUL (8,364,000)

Seoul Philharmonic Orchestra

The history of Western classical music in Korea is quite short, in practical terms spanning just over 50 years. Throughout most of this period the Seoul Philharmonic Orchestra (SPO) has stimulated the burgeoning interest there in symphonic and instrumental music. One of the most widely reputed orchestras in Asia, its evolution closely parallels the economic development and westernization of South Korea.

The SPO is a full-time, 95- to 110-piece orchestra playing two subscription concerts per month, each with six rehearsals of two hours and 40 minutes. In addition to regular concerts, the orchestra performs many extra concerts, educational broadcasts for MBC Television, and a fall festival. The SPO rarely performs outside of Seoul. Many members teach at universities. With salaries ($300 to $1,100 monthly), extra-concert fees, and lucrative remuneration for private teaching, SPO musicians are able to live comfortable, middle-class lives.

The management structure of the orchestra is unusual. Since 1957 complete funding has been provided by the city of Seoul, itself an administrative unit of the federal government. The managing director of Sejong Center, Park Wi-Min, is a government appointee and functions as a cultural czar over all the organizations housed at the Center. The SPO budget, which in 1984 was $875,000 in domestic currency and $50,000 in hard currency for foreign guest performers, is administered through Park.

Beyond budgetary matters, music director Chung Chai-Dong (b. 1928) has complete control. He is advised by a committee of principals from the orchestra including the personnel manager (called "inspector"). Unfortunately, the SPO does little or no long-range planning. Some observe that effective planning is not indigenous to Korean culture; however, it is largely government control over Sejong Center and the budget that prevents the orchestra from planning any farther ahead than it does.

Under Japanese colonial rule (1910–1945), the provincial government held tight control over all cultural activities. Most Korean musicians studied in Japan. From the late 1920s, newly formed music societies in Seoul had begun to sponsor concerts by fledgling orchestras, but no permanent ensembles were created until after the effective end of Japanese occupation.

In 1945, 45 musicians from the Seoul Chamber Music Society formed an orchestra that was destined to attain prominence as the SPO. In 1948 the group was adopted by the Seoul Symphony Association and gave its first concert under their auspices in February of that year. It was conducted by the concertmaster and newly appointed music director, John Kim (b. Kim Saengryo, 1912). Because of his parturient role in its formation, Kim is credited as the founder of the SPO.

The outbreak of war in June 1950 disrupted the nascent musical life of Seoul. During the course of the conflict control of the capital exchanged hands several times. When it was last held by communist forces, the local intelligentsia were rounded up en masse and taken north. According to Kim, "the communists' sudden invasion made [it] impossible to continue . . . All the instruments and music were taken by them and even the musicians were kidnapped." The ensemble—decimated—regrouped and became part of the Navy Symphony and Chorus with Kim as its head.

In the postwar period the orchestra, like the nation, began to rebuild itself. In 1957, traveling in battleships, it made a two-month good-will tour of Hong Kong, Taipei, and Saigon. That year the Seoul City Council approved the adoption of the 82-member orchestra and named it Shi-Hyang, the Seoul-City Orchestra, by which name the SPO is still known in Korea. For international purposes the orchestra uses the name Seoul Philharmonic Orchestra.

John Kim resigned in 1961 and was replaced by Kim Man-Bok (b. 1925), who in 1965 took the orchestra to Japan. Won Kyung-Soo (b. 1928), who assumed the post of director in 1970, was the first conductor of the SPO who had considerable international training and professional experience.

When Won resigned in 1972, his assistant, Chung Chai-Dong, assumed control. Chung, a studious musician, has grown to become the most distinguished conductor living and working in Korea. Under Chung the orchestra made an Asian tour in 1975 that helped to establish its international reputation. In 1981 he took the orchestra to Hawaii and California.

With the building of Sejong Cultural Center in 1978, the SPO was provided with a permanent home. The Center supports a 550-seat recital hall and a 3,895-seat main concert hall, which despite its acoustical problems has become the nucleus of all musical life in Korea. The audience at Sejong Center is affluent; a significant portion is composed of high-school and college students.

The SPO performs much of the standard romantic repertoire as well as a good sampling of contemporary Korean works. It tunes to an A of 442 cps. While it consistently presents very respectable performances, it cannot yet compare to the better orchestras of the West. Korea produces many capable string players, but the level of woodwind, brass, and percussion playing is not well developed. Korea also suffers a paucity of good-quality instruments. Musical training there, especially in ensemble, is not yet of the highest international standard.

Despite these problems, the SPO is making great strides forward. Its director and members are committed to artistic development. One aid in that development is its unique affiliation with the United States Fulbright Program, through which the SPO offers Performing Artist Awards to Fellows who perform as principals with the orchestra and coach their respective sections. The orchestra toured the United States in 1986, performing in New York, Washington, Chicago, Los Angeles, and San Francisco.

CHRONOLOGY OF MUSIC DIRECTORS: Kim (John) Saengryo, 1945–1961. Kim Man-Bok, 1961–1970. Won Kyung-Soo, 1970–1972. Chung Chai-Dong, 1972–present.

BIBLIOGRAPHY: *A Handbook of Korea*, 4th ed. (Seoul: Ministry of Culture and Information, 1982). *Korea Annual* (Seoul: Yonhap News Agency). Kim (John) Saengryo, correspondence with author, 1984. Anthony Scelba, Fulbright Report (filed with USIA, Washington, D.C., 1984). Anthony Scelba, "The Road to Better Orchestras in Korea" (in Korean) *Auditorium Magazine* (Seoul) (October 1984). *Seoul Philharmonic Orchestra* pamphlet (Seoul: Sejong Cultural Center, 1981).

ACCESS: Seoul Philharmonic Orchestra, Sejong Cultural Center, Seoul, Korea (011–82–2) 722–720. Park Wi-Min, Managing Director.

ANTHONY SCELBA

Mexico ─────────────────────────

MEXICO CITY (14,750,000*)

Mexico City Philharmonic Orchestra

The Mexico City Philharmonic (MCPO; Orquesta Filarmónica de la Ciudad de México) is the latest addition to the growing list of fine orchestras in Mexico. Its main concert venue is the newly renovated Ollin Yoliztli Hall, but the orchestra also plays in other locations in Mexico City and its environs, including the Nezahualcoyotl Hall, the Fine Arts Palace, the City Theatre, and the Chapultepec Palace. Additionally, the orchestra is required to make regular appearances in the municipal auditoriums, churches, and movie theatres of the 16 administrative divisions comprising the Federal District of Mexico City. The MCPO rarely stages outdoor performances as Music Director Enrique Bátiz finds the vagaries of temperature, wind, humidity, and the unsatisfactory sound system unsuitable to the attainment of desirable artistic results. Otherwise, the MCPO makes an annual tour taking it to some 20 major population centers in Mexico.

The MCPO was originally composed of 111 musicians, but the economic downturns in Mexico's oil revenues have forced the budget-conscious orchestra to reduce its size to 95. Initially, the orchestra counted in its ensemble a number of students; today, however, the MCPO is composed entirely of professionals. The MCPO is fully subsidized by the Federal District, with its budget depending, though not strictly, upon ticket sales. Private donations, while not uncommon, play but a minor part in the orchestra's budgetary projections. As artistic director, Bátiz absorbs most of the administrative responsibility for programming and promotion. He is assisted by an associate music director, an assistant administrative director, and a general coordinator of activities. A corps of accountants maintains an economic liaison with the appropriate agency in the Federal District bureaucracy.

The MCPO works on a weekly schedule, running from Tuesday to Sunday, for approximately ten months of the year. Each weekly program involves four or five rehearsals, the same program being performed from two to four times within the week. The MCPO describes its yearly activities as comprising three sessions of eight pairs of concerts, plus an "opera season" whose repertoire includes such works as *The Barber of Seville*, *Carmen*, and *La Bohème*, performed in concert version.

The orchestra's concert repertoire is otherwise not unusual, with the bulk of its selections coming from the mainstream of the classic and romantic eras. During its remarkably short existence, the MCPO has held a stable and vociferously enthusiastic audience, a diverse group with representation from all social strata. By a 1979 decree of Mexico's President José Lopéz Portillo, the orchestra has a definite symphonic character and mission and therefore does not sponsor the typical adjunct chamber ensembles. While individual players are encouraged by the management to participate in such activities, they do so without official sanction.

In 1977, Enrique Bátiz, a ubiquitous figure in the development of symphonic music in Mexico, urged Mexican officials to create a symphony orchestra to fill the musical needs of the nation's burgeoning capital. The city's regent, Carlos Hank Gonzalez, who had been instrumental in the development of the Symphony Orchestra of the State of Mexico,* submitted the proposal to President Portillo, who found the necessary support to form the orchestra in January 1978.

The orchestra gave its first series of concerts in September 1978. Eight months later President Portillo again entered the scene, decreeing that, as of May 15, 1979, the Philharmonic was the official orchestra of the city. The founding music director was Fernando Lozano, who held this position for slightly over four years. In addition to the MCPO music directorship, Lozano held other posts, including the directorship of the National School of Music in Mexico City and an influential appointment in the Department of Civic Affairs, Culture, and Tourism. Following a change in political leadership late in 1982, however, Lozano rather hurriedly resigned and his entire staff was subsequently replaced.

Lozano was replaced in January 1983 by Enrique Bátiz. Bátiz brought the same vision and energy to his new role as he had shown previously as the founding music director of the Symphony Orchestra of the State of Mexico. He has conducted over 80 orchestras around the world and has an impressive discography of 66 recordings.

Bátiz was influential in spearheading a number of architectural modifications to the orchestra's principal performance site, the Ollin Yoliztli Hall. Originally a movie house, it will now accommodate 1,214, having been adapted in 1979 as a concert hall. It also provides room for administrative offices, individual or group score reading, a recording studio, and a music library. Plans are underway for further modifications to rid the hall of acoustical deficiencies, part of a pledge by both Bátiz and the orchestra management to make it the finest in Mexico. Other plans for the future include further recordings as well as tours beyond

Mexico's borders. The ensemble looks confidently ahead to international recognition by the end of the decade.

RECORDING HISTORY AND SELECTIVE DISCOGRAPHY: Four discs were produced for EMI in 1984, one each of Mexican concert music, Spanish music, music of Aaron Copland, and guitar concertos by Castelnuovo-Tedesco and Villa-Lobos. As of 1985 the MCPO planned to record ten more discs for EMI, six devoted to Mexican composers, four to the standard repertoire.

Silvestre Revueltas, *La Noche de los Mayas*, *Musica para charlar* (Bátiz): EMI (1985). Music of Blas Galindo, Rodolfo Halffter, Silvestre Revueltas, and Miguel Bernal Jiminez (Bátiz): EMI (1984).

CHRONOLOGY OF MUSIC DIRECTORS: Fernando Lozano, 1978–1983. Enrique Bátiz, 1983–present.

BIBLIOGRAPHY: Correspondence with MCPO Music Director Enrique Bátiz, 1985. MCPO fact sheets, 1984–1985. "Mexico City Philharmonic: Loud and Lusty," *The News* [Mexico City], 8 Nov. 1984.

ACCESS: Orquesta Filarmónica de la Ciudad de México, Periferio Sur #5141 esquina Zapote, México D. F. (655) 25–82 or 25–65. Enrique Bátiz, Artistic Director. José Luis Calderon Vasquez, General Coordinator.

STEPHEN H. BARNES

National Symphony of Mexico

The National Symphony Orchestra (NSO), as it is known today, was created by presidential decree in 1947. Initially called the Symphony Orchestra of the National Conservatory, it operated under the auspices of the National Institute of Fine Arts and Literature. In 1949 the name was changed to the current one to better reflect its public mission. The newly reformed National Institute of Fine Arts was given bureaucratic control of the ensemble. Despite its history of being buffeted by national political changes, the NSO is regarded as the primary symphonic institution in the country. It is the ensemble called upon to represent Mexico at Pan American music festivals and at international music festivals. It appears extensively throughout the country and has established the Spring Music Festival at Oaxaca and the Summer Music Festival in Aguascalientes.

The foundation for audience and governmental acceptance of this ensemble and for symphonic activity in general had been laid by earlier groups having the same title. None of these, apparently, had the stability or continuity to endure, nor did these antecedent groups have their mission well enough defined to survive the economic and political machination characteristic of developing countries. The connecting tissue between these groups and the present orchestra was the musicians themselves—upon the demise of these fledgling ensembles, the players would simply move on to the next group. Such was precisely the case after the Symphony Orchestra of Mexico, a private (i.e., nongovernmental) organization, which had been directed for 21 seasons by Carlos Chávez, offered its last concert series between February and April of 1948. The musicians of the defunct Symphony Orchestra of Mexico were assimilated almost totally into the new group.

Eduardo Hernandez Moncada conducted the NSO (as the Symphony Orchestra of the National Conservatory) in its first concert on October 30, 1947, but its first official season was in 1948–1949. That season the orchestra divided its services about equally between concerts for the general public and a series of youth concerts. The mission set forth for the ensemble was threefold: to program works from the standard repertoire; to present new works never before heard in Mexico; and to program the works of Mexican composers. With the name change in 1949 to National Symphony Orchestra, came the NSO's first permanent director, José Pablo Moncayo, who served until 1954.

Luis Herrera de la Fuente took the reins of the orchestra in 1955 following a season of guest conductors, a move that had been nearly a foregone conclusion following his highly acclaimed work with the Fine Arts Chamber Orchestra. Herrera de la Fuente's 17-year tenure as music director allowed the ensemble to grow and mature. By 1958 the NSO was ready to embark on an international tour; the ensemble performed in the United States, London, Paris, and in Brussels at the World's Fair. The programming was distinctly Mexican: works of Carlos Chávez, Silvestre Revueltas, José Pablo Moncayo, Manuel Ponce and other native composers were significantly represented.

A foundation established in 1961 under the direction of Eva Samarro de Lopez Mateos pledged financial, organizational, and artistic assistance to the NSO. Its impact was felt immediately; a chamber orchestra was formed out of the symphony, and a second series of concerts was offered featuring contemporary music. Audiences were exposed for the first time to music of Otto Luening, Vladimir Ussachevsky, Krzysztof Penderecki, and György Ligeti. The foundation also assisted the NSO in establishing festivals of Mexican art music. The foundation ceased to exist in 1964, but by that time many of its programs and festivals were able to stand alone, especially the Contemporary Music Festival.

The political climate changed, however, in 1973 with the presidency of Luis Echeverria Alvarez. He fired Herrera de la Fuente and named Carlos Chávez to the dual posts of director of the Fine Arts Institute and music director of the NSO. Ambitious plans were laid for the group but were abandoned when Chávez unexpectedly resigned. Chávez, it appears, was unable to come to terms with the orchestra's personnel, who desired a shared administration. The NSO was essentially without a music director until 1979. From 1973 to 1976 a committee consisting of the orchestra personnel and administrators of the National Institute of Fine Arts set the programming and selected guest conductors. This shared administration continued until the presidency changed, whereupon all programmatic and conducting decisions reverted to the bureaucrats in the institute.

Finally, in 1979, Sergio Cardenas was named music director of the NSO, a position he held until 1984. Cardenas followed the NSO's historic mission by offering balanced programs: the standard symphonic fare was matched by performances of music by Mexican composers and contemporary composers of all nationalities. Cardenas was also influential in reviving Mexican art music of the colonial period. José Guadalupe Flores succeeded Cardenas and now leads the orchestra under the title of director in residence. Flores, like Herrera de la Fuente before him, came to the attention of the Mexican musical public via his work with the Fine Arts Chamber Orchestra.

RECORDING HISTORY AND DISCOGRAPHY: Under Cardenas the orchestra has recorded the music of José Pablo Moncayo and Candelario Huizar.

Chávez, *Daughter of Colchis* (Chávez): Varèse/Sarabande 81055.

CHRONOLOGY OF MUSIC DIRECTORS: Eduardo Hernandez Moncada, 1947–1949. José Pablo Moncayo, 1949–1954. Luis Herrera de la Fuente, 1955–1972. (Guest conductors, 1973–1979.) Sergio Cardenas, 1979–1984. José Guadalupe Flores, 1984–present (Director in Residence).

BIBLIOGRAPHY: Correspondence with NSO Director in Residence José Guadalupe Flores, 1985. NSO fact sheets, 1984–1985.

ACCESS: Orquesta Sinfónica Nacional, Institute Nacional De Bellas Artes, Regina No. 52020. Piso México 1, D.F. (510) 91–80. Rogelio Rueda Alcocer, Manager.

STEPHEN H. BARNES

TOLUCA (421,000)

Symphony Orchestra of the State of Mexico

Despite its relatively short history, the Symphony Orchestra of the State of Mexico (SOSM; Orquesta Sinfónia del Estado de México) is today a busy ensemble, offering a ten-month season with about 120 concerts per year. A typical week includes four rehearsals per program and three concerts per week. Tours are confined to the various municipalities in the state of Mexico, lasting up to a week at a time, with a repertoire of standard symphonic fare.

The SOSM has more than 90 members, 82 of whom are identified as full-time musicians. The orchestra has, in addition to its music director, both an associate and an assistant conductor. With a staff consisting of a general manager, an administrator, three secretaries, two accountants, a music librarian, and a personnel director, the organization is completely subsidized by government funding. The SOSM maintains, in addition to the full symphony orchestra, a chamber orchestra, a string quartet, and a woodwind quintet.

The SOSM was created in June of 1971 by executive order of Professor Carlos Hank Gonzales, the constitutional governor of the State of Mexico. He had been approached by Enrique Bátiz, who later became the first music director, to create a symphony orchestra to meet the needs of the people of the State of Mexico, that territory surrounding the Federal District of Mexico (the latter having been set aside in the nineteenth century as the seat of government of the United States of Mexico. The State of Mexico has an area of approximately 8,200 square miles, and the 1980 census determined its population to be over 7.5 million.

Following the June 1971 executive order, the ensemble began rehearsing with 63 musicians selected by Enrique Bátiz and Manuel Suárez, one of the most prominent Mexican violinists of all time. The players were selected from the rosters of other orchestras in Mexico. Staffing the orchestra proved not too difficult, since it could promise stability and financial security for its players, owing in no small part to state funding. The SOSM moved rapidly from rehearsal hall to concert stage: its first performances were given on August 27 and 28, 1971, in the Morelos Theatre in Toluca (the state capital), and in the Fine Arts Palace in Mexico City.

Enrique Bátiz held the music directorship from 1971 to 1983. The first audiences were composed of curious government employees and civil servants. Inexorably, Bátiz and the orchestra gathered new followers among the students and the general populace, and the orchestra fulfilled its mandated mission by appearing in not only the great concert halls of the region but in very modest venues as well, all with a high degree of professionalism and quality. The SOSM was the first symphony orchestra in Mexico to publish an annual repertoire program in advance, thereby providing its listeners with consistent, competent performances in a program that had the group appearing in nearly all of the cities and towns in the State.

Bátiz's influence was incalculable. He brought an intense spirit of discipline and focus to his work as music director. His organizational skills bordered on the remarkable. Bátiz had vision. Not only was he involved with finding new frontiers of artistic and social significance, but he maintained a dogged perseverance in his efforts to foster respect and support for the orchestra among government authorities. His primary objectives were twofold: to take concert music to all socio-economic levels of the citizenry without discrimination and to foster the orchestra's musical growth by securing the services of the largest possible number of guest soloists and guest conductors, both Mexican and foreign.

Bátiz left the Symphony in 1983 to take the helm of the Mexico City Philharmonic Orchestra.* His successor is Manuel Suárez. Suárez, educated in the United States (Bishop Neumann High School in Philadelphia, the Curtis Institute, and the Juilliard School), began concertizing at age nine. He has toured extensively as a conductor, violin soloist, and chamber musician, the latter with the Trio México. Suárez has been responsible for updating the music curriculum for the Mexican national school system and has assisted in raising the performance standards of the National Conservatory of Music. His standing as an artist of international repute was evidenced by his presence as a jury member at the Seventh Tchaikovsky Competition in Moscow. Suárez has continued his predecessor's outreach programs, with orchestral performances in various university settings, in Mexico City at the City Theatre and the Fine Arts Palace, in numerous churches and cathedrals in the State of Mexico, and in its home concert hall, the 2,150-seat Morelos Theatre in Toluca.

RECORDING HISTORY AND SELECTIVE DISCOGRAPHY: Under Bátiz the orchestra has made several recordings of Mexican, Spanish, and other music for the Varèse/Sarabande, Sine Qua Non, EMI, ASV, and Mexican RCA recording companies.

Chávez, selected works (Bátiz): Varèse/Sarabande VCDM–1000150. Falla, *Three Cor-*

nerd Hat and *Nights in the Gardens of Spain* (Maria Luisa Salinas, Eva Maria Zuk/Bátiz): Varèse/Sarabande VCD–47210 (CD).

CHRONOLOGY OF MUSIC DIRECTORS: Enrique Bátiz, 1971–1983. Manuel Suárez, 1983–present.

BIBLIOGRAPHY: Telephone interviews and correspondence with SOSM Music Director Manuel Suárez, 1985. Correspondence with former SOSM Music Director Enrique Bátiz, 1985.

ACCESS: Orquesta Sinfónica del Estado de México, Plaza Fray Andres de Castor, Edif. C. Primer Piso, Toluca. (721) 562–16 or 452–19. Manuel Suárez, Music Director.

STEPHEN H. BARNES

Netherlands _____

AMSTERDAM (950,000*)

Concertgebouw Orchestra

An important institution among the 15 orchestras of the Netherlands, the Concertgebouw Orchestra (Concertgebouworkest) is also highly regarded throughout the world.

As of 1985 the orchestra comprised 111 musicians, several fewer than its state-allowed maximum of 115. As in the other major Dutch orchestras, Concertgebouw musicians hail from many different countries. Management is effected by a three-man executive team and a staff of 11. The orchestra's budget of Dfl 14,000,000 derives from earned revenues, subsidies from the national and city governments, and a limited number of donors. Its state-employed musicians have an association that elects its own Board of Directors. Artistic decisions are made collectively by the principal conductor, artistic director, management, and the Artistic Committee of the musicians' association. An association representative also sits on the orchestra's highest governing body, the Concertgebouw Foundation Board, along with representatives from the Concertgebouw building's Board, the city of Amsterdam, and the Ministry of Culture of the central government.

The 1985–1986 season included some 115 concerts, among them a few opera performances: about 80 concerts in Amsterdam (mostly at the Concertgebouw), arranged into several series and combinations thereof; 15 in other Dutch cities (particularly The Hague and Utrecht); and 21 abroad (North and South America and Europe). Principal Conductor Bernard Haitink led somewhat fewer than half of the total, with major guest conducting duties shared by Riccardo Chailly and Hans Vonk. The orchestra's repertoire has broadened somewhat in recent years, and the 1985–1986 season included at least eight evenings devoted to recent composers, including a newly commissioned work of Luciano Berio. Several chamber groups are formed from within the larger ensemble, among them the Concertgebouw Chamber Orchestra.

The orchestra's recordings and tours are mainstays of its international reputation; the number of each has grown greatly in recent years, and the list of countries visited by the orchestra is very impressive, with numerous trips to the United States and throughout Europe, somewhat fewer to South America, the U.S.S.R., and the Far East.

The orchestra owes its beginnings to the Concertgebouw ("Concert Hall") from which it takes its name. One of the world's most venerable and acoustically responsive halls, the Concertgebouw comprises two auditoriums, one large (Grote Zaal, 2,000 seats) and one small (Kleine Zaal, 500 seats), within a striking exterior whose eclectic architectural details combine in a splendid harmony of brick and stone. The overall plan and impression of the Concertgebouw are similar to those of the since-destroyed Leipzig Gewandhaus and Boston's less ornate Symphony Hall (which it influenced). Since its inauguration in 1888, the building has undergone several interior renovations for structural reinforcement, acoustical tuning, and the comfort of the audience and performers. Today the Concertgebouw plays host to the Netherlands Philharmonic Orchestra, regularly performing chamber ensembles, and numerous visiting orchestras, in addition to its major occupant, the Concertgebouw Orchestra. It is also used on occasion, with seats removed, for nonmusical events such as large receptions.

Orchestral music was not a major influence in the cultural life of Amsterdam or Holland generally in the mid-nineteenth century. It was not until the 1880s, in the midst of a general cultural renaissance, that the decision was made to move deliberately in the direction of symphonic culture. The immediate impetus for change came from a group of private citizens—businessmen and wealthy civic leaders—whose goal was to enliven the city's culture, thereby raising civic pride and lifting Amsterdam's profile a bit among its rival European centers. Their vehicle was the Concertgebouw, for which ground was broken in a fenny area on the outskirts of the city in 1883.

As the building neared completion in 1888, the management set about hiring an orchestra to occupy it. Willem Kes was engaged as conductor, and his intention, which met with some resistance by the early audiences, was to instruct as much as to entertain. In effect, this meant that he would not only emphasize symphonic music (beyond the eclectic programs common at the time) but also enforce behavior to which Amsterdam audiences had heretofore been unaccustomed—no eating, no talking, no latecomers. Such intentions are implicit in the orchestra's first program of November 3, 1888: "Consecration of the House" Overture (Beethoven), *Variations on a Theme of Haydn* (Brahms), *Phaeton*, Op. 39 (Saint-Saëns), *Meistersinger* Overture (Wagner), and Symphony No. 3 (Charles Villiers Stanford). When Kes left in 1895 to conduct the Scottish Orchestra, he left behind a disciplined and competent ensemble.

The Concertgebouw Orchestra's reputation as one of the world's most polished and sensitive ensembles was made under its next music director, Willem Mengelberg, who would lead the group for nearly 50 years. A student at the conservatory in Cologne under Franz Wüllner, the 24-year-old Mengelberg was more accomplished as a pianist than as a conductor. Sympathetic to the postromantic masters, his career was to be closely identified with the music of Richard Strauss and (especially) Gustav Mahler, whose work he never ceased to champion.

Within a few years of his appointment, both he and the orchestra were winning a growing reputation in Europe. Strauss's *Ein Heldenleben* was dedicated to Mengelberg, who introduced it to the Concertgebouw audience in 1899. It became a mainstay of Mengelberg's repertoire, especially on the Concertgebouw's more and more frequent tours. As he grew with his orchestra, Mengelberg began to widen his circle of musical associations, later taking on a conducting post with the New York Philharmonic** as well as a variety of guest-conducting stints. Among the conductors who were regularly appointed substitutes during Mengelberg's jaunts abroad were Karl Muck, Pierre Monteux, and Bruno Walter. Mengelberg was an early proponent of recorded music, and the Concertgebouw benefited from this interest. Mengelberg more than fulfilled the vision of the Concertgebouw's founders, for he and his orchestra had made Amsterdam's concert hall a musical as well as architectural landmark.

Musically, Mengelberg was known for his adherence to the composer's intentions, as he interpreted them according to oral traditions and the composer's own notations, sometimes from manuscript originals. Nevertheless, his overall approach would today be considered highly interpretational, and even in his own day his critics pointed to the "intentional fallacy" in his approach. It is well known that Mengelberg (as did many of his contemporaries, including Arturo Toscanini) occasionally altered the scoring to conform to his own interpretation of what the composer intended. But his performances—which followed exceedingly disciplined and highly structured rehearsals—were widely acclaimed, and Mengelberg's demonstrative podium technique invariably signalled energetic and intense renderings, especially of his beloved Beethoven, Strauss, and Mahler.

With the coming of the Second World War, Mengelberg's political sympathies and national ties (at odds with his remaining loyalty to the music of Mahler) led him away from the Concertgebouw and into a working relationship with the Berlin power center. Upon liberation, in what must have been a terribly painful decision for all concerned, the Netherlands Honors Council barred Mengelberg from working in Holland for six years. Before the expiration of this term, Mengelberg died in 1951.

Following the war the Concertgebouw Orchestra was reorganized under state auspices and placed under the direction of Eduard van Beinum, whose affiliation with the orchestra went well back into the Mengelberg era. Van Beinum was of an entirely different temperament and philosophy from his predecessor. The Concertgebouw Orchestra's changed, postwar sound (characterized by fluidity and sensitive communication among instrument groups) has been attributed to van Beinum's more interactive rehearsal technique, in which he deliberately drew out the interpretive strengths of individual players and sections. Van Beinum also widened the orchestra's repertoire, adding works from the French composers, Anton Bruckner, and current Dutch contemporaries, the latter often in premiere performances.

Following van Beinum's sudden death at a rehearsal in 1959, conducting duties were shared largely by Eugen Jochum and Bernard Haitink. When Haitink became the sole chief conductor in 1946, the Concertgebouw Orchestra entered another long period of stability. Haitink has brought the orchestra to many countries throughout the world, and he has pursued a policy of prolific recording. Haitink's years also saw the establishment of the Concertgebouw Orchestra Chorus (1980), which is directed by Arthur Oldham. The repertoire has since reflected this addition in more frequent performances of orchestral/choral works. Several noted musicians have held posts as regularly returning guest conductors at the Concertgebouw during Haitink's tenure, among them Colin Davis, Antál Doráti, Hans Vonk, and Kiril Kondrashin (who shared with Haitink the post of permanent conductor from 1979 until Kondrashin's death in 1981). Collaboration with the conductor Niklaus Harnoncourt, who specializes in the baroque and classical periods, led to refinements in the Concertgebouw's performance of Bach's *St. Matthew Passion*, a Palm Sunday tradition since 1899. Since 1975 the *St. John Passion* and *St. Matthew Passion* have been heard in alternate years on Easter Sundays, both under Harnoncourt.

Current plans for a 100th anniversary celebration in 1988 include six performances of Mahler's Symphony No. 8 and the release of several special recordings. It was recently announced that Bernard Haitink will step down as of the 1988–1989 season, to be succeeded as principal conductor by Riccardo Chailly, who frequently appeared with the orchestra in the capacity of guest conductor.

RECORDING HISTORY AND SELECTIVE DISCOGRAPHY: The Concertgebouw Orchestra has been producing records since the 1920s. It currently makes about ten per year. Its many recordings appear on Decca, EMI, London, Odyssey, Pro Arte, Teldec, Telefunken, Turnabout, and other labels, but the great majority of its recent recordings appear on the Philips (Phonogram) label. It has been quite active in producing compact disc recordings. The orchestra's current recorded repertoire comprises largely masterworks, including complete symphonies of Beethoven, Brahms, Bruckner, Haydn (London Symphonies), Mahler, and Schumann. Other concentrations are found in the works of Mozart, Rachmaninoff, Shostakovich, and Tchaikovsky.

The occasion of the Concertgebouw Orchestra's centenary in 1988 will be marked by the release of a compact disc collection entitled *Historical Classics* on the Philips label (CDs 416 200–2 through 416 206–2; 416 210–2 through 416 214–2). The series of 14 CDs (digitally remastered by Nippon Phonogram, Ltd.) presents Mengelberg and the orchestra in programs recorded in 1939 and 1940. Included are works of Bach, Beethoven, Brahms, Franck, Mahler, Schubert, and Strauss.

Bach, *St. Matthew Passion* (Jochum): Philips Fest. 6770018 (4 records). Bach, *St. Matthew Passion* (Harnoncourt): Teldec 6.35668 (3 records); 8.35668 (3 CDs). Brahms, Symphony No. 1 (Van Beinum): Philips 411.179–4. Bruckner, Symphony No. 7; Wagner,

Siegfried Idyll (Haitink): Philips 6769028 (2 records). Bruckner, Symphony No. 8 (Haitink): Philips 6769080 (2 records). Chopin, Piano Concerto No. 2; Schumann, Piano Concerto (Schiff/Doráti): London 411942–1 LH; 411942–2 (CD). Mozart, Symphonies Nos. 25, K. 183, and 40, K. 550 (Harnoncourt): Telefunken 642935.

CHRONOLOGY OF MUSIC DIRECTORS (Principal Conductors): Willem Kes, 1888–1895. Willem Mengelberg, 1895–1945. Eduard van Beinum, 1945–1959. (Guest conductors, 1959–1961.) Bernard Haitink and Eugen Jochum, 1961–1964. Bernard Haitink, 1964–1979. Bernard Haitink and Kiril Kondrashin, 1979–1981. Bernard Haitink, 1984–1988. Riccardo Chailly to assume duties in 1988.

BIBLIOGRAPHY: Correspondence with Concertgebouw Orchestra Adjunct Director Sjoerd G.A.M. van den Berg, 1986. Concertgebouw Orchestra, miscellaneous press materials, 1980–1986. *Concertgebouw Orchestra Amsterdam: Profile of an Orchestra* (Amsterdam: Concergebouw Orchestra, n.d. [ca. 1980])—pamphlet. R. Hardie, *The Recordings of Willem Mengelberg* (Nashville, Tenn., 1972). Eduard Reeser, *Music in Holland* (Amsterdam: J. M. Meulenhoff/Foundation Donemus, 1959). *New Grove Dictionary of Music and Musicians* (New York: Macmillan, 1980). Harold C. Schonberg, *The Great Conductors* (New York: Simon & Schuster, 1967). Jan Taat, *Het Concertgebouw Amsterdam* (Amsterdam: Concertgebouw N. V., 1982)—pamphlet. Howard Taubman, *The Symphony Orchestra Abroad: A Report of a Study* (Vienna, Va.: American Symphony Orchestra League, 1970).

ACCESS: Concertgebouworkest, Jacob Obrechtstraat 51, 1071 KJ Amsterdam. 020–792211. H. J. van Royen, Director.

                                                                                          ROBERT R. CRAVEN

THE HAGUE   (677,757*)

Residentie-Orkest

The Residentie-Orkest (also known in English-speaking countries as The Hague Philharmonic) ranges, along with Amsterdam's Concertgebouw Orchestra* and the Rotterdam Philharmonic Orchestra,* among the best of small Holland's 15 professional symphony orchestras. Within the Netherlands it is generally admired for its innovative programming and for its unorthodox ways of presenting classical music in unusual contexts.

The Residentie-Orkest is the municipal orchestra of Holland's royal residence (hence its name) and government town of The Hague, adjacent to Scheveningen, one of the North Sea's main balnear resorts. Besides about 60 subscription concerts and many other incidental appearances in its own city, the Residentie-Orkest gives ten more subscription concerts in the old university town of Leiden, ten miles north of The Hague. It also appears regularly—about ten times per season in total—in Amsterdam, Rotterdam, and Utrecht.

Being the orchestra of the royal residence, the Hague musicians sometimes give gala concerts for royal or presidential guests of the Dutch Queen or the government. Also on the Queen's birthday and on the traditional ''Princes' Day'' (the official opening of Parliament) the orchestra gives special concerts for an innumerable crowd in a vast trade-fair hall. In recent years the Hague orchestra has occasionally accompanied Queen Beatrix on her official state visits abroad.

An important activity of the Residentie-Orkest is its many foreign tours. Before the orchestra was ten years old, it had already concertized in Brussels, Paris, and London. It was after World War II that The Hague orchestra devoted many weeks of every season to touring abroad. Most of the tours bring the orchestra to relatively nearby countries, but Hague musicians have visited virtually all of Western and Eastern Europe. Since 1963 six extensive tours have brought the orchestra to the United States. Many such trips have been financially supported by the Dutch government as well as by the city of The Hague, the Residentie-Orkest being considered a Dutch goodwill ambassador to the world. In recent less affluent times, however, the orchestra manages to travel without special subventions and often cooperates with The Hague Tourist Office in promoting The Hague and Scheveningen during its foreign tours.

The Residentie Orkest is a foundation, governed by a Board of about ten leading citizens and three musicians. The orchestra is administered by a staff of 12 office personnel and four technicians. Its general budget of some 10.5 million guilders is funded by the central government, which pays about 40% of the musicians' salaries and the city of The Hague, which pays the rest of the salaries and a further subvention. The orchestra is backed by the 2,500-member Association of Friends of the Residentie-Orkest, which supports the orchestra substantially where the authorities fail.

Residentie-Orkest musicians are united in the "Vereniging Het Residentie-Orkest," a union representing their material and social interests. Following retirement at age 65 they receive an inflation-related state pension, to which they have contributed while employed. The musicians have founded an instrument fund to pay for expensive instruments and a social fund, which supports those in financial trouble. About 20% of the members of the Residentie-Orkest are foreigners; in this The Hague orchestra is no exception in Holland. Dutch conservatories do not train a sufficient number of orchestra musicians, especially string and brass, to fill all of the vacancies in Holland's 15 symphony orchestras. In recent years the number of foreigners has begun to decrease.

The impact of the Residentie-Orkest extends beyond its concertizing. Its leading musicians are also teachers at the Royal Conservatory and the Municipal Music School; other orchestra members give private lessons, are involved in amateur music-making, or play chamber music. Another aspect of cooperation with amateurs is the regular accompaniment of several of Holland's many large choral societies. Many concerts of the Residentie-Orkest are broadcast by the national broadcasting companies.

The orchestra never had an adequate concert hall where it could freely develop its capabilities. Its first concert venue was the vast, multi-purpose, 2,300-seat "Gebouw voor Kunsten en Wetenschappen," which it used until the hall burned down in 1964. After a few years in the then-delapidated Kursaal in Scheveningen, the orchestra moved to the 1,800-seat hall of the new Nederlands Congresgebouw, which has very poor acoustics. After begging vainly to the authorities for over 15 years for a new hall, the Residentie-Orkest in 1983 made the desperate decision to build its own hall, at its own expense, right in the old city center. Finally, the authorities, the sponsoring Netherlands industry and trade, and individual Maecenases came to the rescue and raised 25 million guilders for the acoustically excellent "Dr. Anton Philipszaal," which will be opened in September 1987.

The Residentie-Orkest was founded in 1904 by a group of prominent citizens of The Hague who were no longer content with the fact that municipal musical life was ruled by the Amsterdam Concertgebouw Orchestra. With the help of Henri Viotta, director of The Hague's Royal Conservatory—who was eager to use and train his many talented pupils—a moderate-size orchestra was formed of professionals, amateurs, and students. After its first successes the ensemble was soon enlarged with the aid of several first-rate musicians from Amsterdam who had fled the Concertgebouw and its rather tyrannical conductor, Willem Mengelberg.

In this early period the Residentie-Orkest musicians had a part-time contract for the winter season; for the rest of the year they had to play in cafe and theatre orchestras to make ends meet. In 1914 the First World War came, in effect, to the rescue. In Scheveningen, then one of Europe's most elegant beaches, a large number of symphonic concerts was given each summer by foreign orchestras. When the war interrupted their visits, the Residentie-Orkest was invited to take over from May through September. Thus The Hague musicians could get a full year's contract, and the revenues for the orchestra were considerable. The orchestra continued its Scheveningen seasons until 1968, by which time the resort's international reputation had come to an end.

When after World War II, the Holland Festival was founded, the Residentie-Orkest played an important role in this yearly springtime event, playing unusual concert programs as well as accompanying opera performances with artists of Milan's La Scala and other such organizations. As the Holland Festival grew more and more into an Amsterdam affair, the Residentie-Orkest over the years retired from it, preferring to do its own special concerts.

Following its founder and first conductor Henri Viotta, six regular conductors have led the orchestra to its present international level. Viotta was succeeded by Peter van Anrooy (1917–1935), who consolidated the ensemble. In 1938 Frits Schuurman took over and tried to carry the orchestra through the war period. In 1949 young Willem Van Otterloo became regular conductor, a position he would hold for 24 years. His reign raised the group's artistic level to international standards and brought it worldwide recognition. His aims were greatly facilitated by growing governmental support, enabling the orchestra to engage more and better musicians and to invite the world's best guest conductors and soloists. After Van Otterloo resigned in 1973, Jean Martinon took over in 1974; after his untimely death in 1977 he was succeeded by Ferdinand Leitner, who passed on the baton in 1980 to the young Dutch conductor Hans Vonk, the Residentie-Orkest's present conductor. The orchestra's many guest conductors have included the world's most acclaimed maestros, among them Arturo Toscanini, who appeared twice with the orchestra, the only Dutch ensemble he ever led. Such composers as Gabriel Pierné, Max Reger, Maurice Ravel, Paul Hindemith, Igor Stravinsky, Mauricio Kagel, John Cage, Lucas Foss, Bruno Maderna, and Pierre Boulez have led the orchestra in their own works.

The Residentie-Orkest distinguishes itself from many others by its various special musical enterprises and innovative programming. Already in 1911 the orchestra had organized a Richard Strauss Festival at which the composer himself conducted. After decades of traditional Beethoven series in the springtime, the idea of special composer-related series was taken up in the 1960s, with concert series on Stravinsky and Bartók/Ravel, culminating in the world's first Schoenberg/Berg/Webern series in 1968, led by Boulez. On the occasion of this Second Viennese School Series the orchestra published a Schoenberg/Berg/Webern "newspaper," which attracted international attention. The 40-concert "Town Full of Music" project in 1972 was the first manifestation of the orchestra's policy of outreach toward those citizens who could not come to the concert hall—the musicians travel in various formations to audiences in senior citizens' homes, hospitals, and even in prisons.

In subsequent years the orchestra organized series of chamber concerts in The Hague's charming "Diligentia" recital hall, with programs repeated elsewhere in the city. The 1973 spring series "500 Years of Dutch Music" was the start of a courageous attempt to draw attention to Holland's own much-neglected music. These series have had a consistent follow-up in seasonal programming of numerous contemporary and classical Dutch compositions. The program was crowned with the release of the six-record album *400 Years of Dutch Music* in 1979, which, with 26,000 copies sold, was an unexpected bestseller in Holland. Two years later a second album appeared: *400 Years, Part 2.*

In its normal subscription series the Residentie-Orkest also shows a wide repertoire. Willem Van Otterloo, having a special talent for nineteenth-century French as well as Austro/German compositions, specialized somewhat in composers such as Berlioz, Ravel, Debussy, Bruckner, and Mahler. The present conductor, Hans Vonk, continues this French-German tradition; in 1979 the orchestra won the Mahler Medal of the Internationale Mahler-Gesellschaft. Since so many expert baroque ensembles are specializing in Bach and his contemporaries, the Residentie-Orkest has almost stopped performing music from this period. Since about 1965 contemporary (including avant-garde) music has played an important role in the orchestra's program policy.

RECORDING HISTORY AND SELECTIVE DISCOGRAPHY: In the 1950s the Residentie-Orkest recorded an impressive number of discs for the Dutch Philips label. Several of these are available in various countries, mostly as re-releases. Philips having turned to other orchestras, the orchestra's recording history was thereafter reduced to incidental recordings for various other labels, including Erato, Decca, DGG, and EMI. After the unexpected success of the Dutch-music albums, the orchestra in 1985 released a large number of its own recordings of standard repertoire, aiming to raise money for the new concert hall.

Berlioz, *Symphonie fantastique* (Van Otterloo): Philips 411153–4. Bruckner, Symphony No. 7 (Carl Schuricht): Nonesuch 71127. *400 Years of Dutch Music*, vol. 1 and *400 Years of Dutch Music*, vol. 2 (various conductors): Residentie-Orkest (6 records per volume). Saint-Saëns, Symphony No. 3 (Feike Asma/Roberto Benzi): Philips 412295–4. Schubert, Symphony No. 9 (Vonk): Residentie-Orkest. Stravinsky, Symphony in C, Symphony in Three Movements, *Firebird* (Vonk): Residentie-Orkest (2 records).

CHRONOLOGY OF MUSIC DIRECTORS: Henri Viotta, 1904–1917. Peter van Anrooy, 1917–1935. (Guest conductors, 1935–1938.) Frits Schuurman, 1938–1949. Willem Van Otterloo, 1949–1973. Jean Martinon, 1974–1977. Ferdinand Leitner, 1977–1980. Hans Vonk, 1980–present.

BIBLIOGRAPHY: A.B.M. Brans and Evert Cornelis, *Het Residentie-Orkest 50 jaar* (The Hague: Residentie-Orkest, 1954). Eduard Reeser, ed., *Music in Holland* (Amsterdam: Meulenhoff/Foundation Donemus [1959]). P. W. Schilham, *Toj, Toj, Achter de schermen van het orkestbedrijf* (The Hague: Nijgh & van Ditmar, 1984). Joop Weyand, *De roman van een orkest* (The Hague, 1947).

ACCESS: Het Residentie-Orkest, Statenlaan 28, 2582 GM, The Hague. 070–548054. Dr. P. W. Schilham, General Secretary.

PIET W. SCHILHAM

ROTTERDAM (1,024,000*)

Rotterdam Philharmonic Orchestra

The Rotterdam Philharmonic Orchestra (RPhO) annually performs more concerts (75) in its hometown than any other Dutch orchestra. Its international character is revealed in its personnel, one-third of whom were born outside Holland, comprising musicians originating in 17 countries.

A typical recent concert season (1985–1986) includes 70 subscription concerts in Rotterdam, seven special concerts in Rotterdam (including a Beethoven cycle), 20 concerts elsewhere in the Netherlands, 18 concerts abroad, and seven opera accompaniments for the Netherlands Opera Foundation. Chamber ensembles from within the orchestra (Concerto Rotterdam and the Rotterdam Sinfonietta) offer chamber concerts, and smaller ensembles perform various youth concerts at schools. The season runs from late August to late June. Since 1949 the RPhO has performed abroad regularly. The orchestra has given concerts in more than 16 European countries, toured the United States four times (1970, 1975, 1977, and 1985), and in 1979 appeared in Hong Kong and Japan. In October 1987 the RPhO will become the first Dutch orchestra to have toured the People's Republic of China.

The Rotterdam Philharmonic Orchestra is a foundation (Stichting) with a Board of five members appointed by the city of Rotterdam and/or elected by the musicians and the Society of Friends of the Rotterdam Philharmonic. It comprises 107 musicians and a staff of 17. The orchestra's annual budget is Dfl. 13.5

million of which Dfl. 3.5 million is funded by the central state government, Dfl. 8 million by the city of Rotterdam, and Dfl. 2 million (about 15% of the budget) by its own receipts. It maintains excellent contacts with the other Dutch orchestras, all of whom are united in the "Contactorgaan van Nederlandse Orkesten." The orchestra cooperates with Rotterdam's other artistic institutions (theatres, museums, conservatory, art academy, and Arts Foundation) through regular meetings among the respective directors.

The Rotterdam Philharmonic had its beginnings in a meeting on Monday, June 10, 1918, above the Tivoli Theatre on the Coolsingel, held at the initiative of Rotterdam musician Jules Zagwijn, son of a famous musical family. The attending musicians—who longed to abandon their daily occupations as entertainment players in theatres, bars, or restaurants—formed themselves into the Society of Professional Musicians for the Mutual Performing of the Arts and chose as their conductor Willem Feltzer. After some initial all-string performances, auditions were held for winds and percussion and a small symphony orchestra was born, the basis of the present RPhO. In the next few years the orchestra assumed a permanent position in the city's musical life. In 1921 the City Council granted an annual subsidy of Dfl. 3,500 (now Dfl. 8 million), which enabled the orchestra to give popular Sunday afternoon concerts, followed soon afterward by the start of the so-called Workers' Concerts, where, at a very reduced price, one could listen to "easy listening" music.

In this period the orchestra performed alternately in the Groote Doele Hall and in the Circus-Schouwburg, but led another life as a wind band in the squares of the city. String players were thus obliged to play at least one wind instrument as well. Because Feltzer wanted to concentrate on symphonic performances, it was essential to find another conductor for outdoor activities. In 1926 the 30-year-old Eduard Flipse was appointed to this post. By the next year he had been promoted to associate conductor, and he immediately distinguished himself with original and adventurous programs. In 1928, when Feltzer resigned, the orchestra Board did not yet dare appoint Flipse in his place, but chose instead the violin virtuoso Alexander Schumuller as principal conductor. The success of this appointment was rather short-lived and on May 31, 1930, Eduard Flipse became Schumuller's successor.

The next ten years were among the most interesting in RPhO history. Realizing that his young orchestra, with its inherent lack of tradition, could hardly dare compare itself to the established ensembles in Amsterdam, The Hague, and Utrecht, Flipse decided to go his own way by paying a great deal of attention to contemporary music. Thereafter, hardly a single program lacked a premiere performance. Flipse invited composers to perform their own compositions (Béla Bartók, for example, introduced his Second Piano Concerto to Rotterdam), and he offered opportunities especially to young Dutch composers. Special rehearsals allowed them to listen to and edit their new works. With the composer Willem Pijper as director of the Conservatory of Music and Eduard Flipse as conductor of the Philharmonic, Rotterdam became a stronghold of new music. Moreover,

Flipse cultivated an understanding of music for a new generation of Rotterdam-mers with his famous youth concerts.

Contrary to the situation in the First World War, it was impossible for the Netherlands to remain neutral after the German invasion in May 1940. The center of Rotterdam disappeared in flames, and times were consequently most difficult for the RPhO. Of course, other orchestras donated instruments and scores, but the Koninginnekerk, a church, would have to serve temporarily as a concert hall, and not all the musicians were to survive the Nazi terrors. Flipse kept his orchestra going as long as possible, but this was not greatly appreciated by everyone later. However, he and his musicians provided consolation for thou-sands of people in trying circumstances.

In the first years after liberation the orchestra performed under other conduc-tors, but in 1947 Eduard Flipse took up the baton once more and continued with enthusiasm his daring program policy. One of the highlights in this period was the performance of Gustav Mahler's Symphony No. 8 ("Symphony of a Thou-sand") in the old Ahoy' Hall. In 1962 the Board appointed the German Franz-Paul Decker to serve along with Flipse. Three years later Eduard Flipse, at age 69, left the orchestra, but he was present on May 18, 1966, to open the gala concert at the inauguration of the new Doelen Hall ("de Doelen").

The realization of this new home for the nomadic orchestra is quite a story. In the beginning only a few realized exactly what the three Rotterdam architects Herman and Evert Kraaijvanger and Rein Fledderus meant with their plans to build a hall with over 2,000 seats. With the efforts of City Councillor Nancy Zeelenberg and the indefatigable Flipse, the once-reluctant city fathers finally approved of the plan, and indeed the optimists proved right. Build a good concert hall and the people will flock to it. Overnight, subscriptions quadrupled from fewer than 4,000 to 15,000. Extra subscription series were added, and the newly-confident RPhO flourished.

In 1967 the orchestra engaged then-26-year-old Edo de Waart. When in 1968 Franz-Paul Decker terminated his contract to leave for Canada, a situation arose similar to that of 40 years before: the Board deemed a chief conductorship for the young de Waart to be, though tempting, too risky, and appointed instead a Frenchman, Jean Fournet. Five years under Fournet's distinguished leadership contributed greatly toward determining the RPhO's own specific style. In 1973 the no-longer reluctant orchestra appointed Edo de Waart as its chief conductor. He devoted himself energetically to bringing the RPhO up to international stan-dards. Under his leadership a regular flow of recordings was produced, and his symphonic successes were matched with operatic successes as well—impressive productions of Verdi, Wagner, and Richard Strauss.

From 1975 onward de Waart became more and more involved with engage-ments in the United States, and Rotterdam had to start looking for a successor. In 1979 an American, David Zinman, who had been permanent guest conductor in the previous two years, took over as principal conductor from de Waart (who has since been associated with the San Francisco Symphony** and Minnesota

Orchestra**). Zinman was responsible for a number of important RPhO recordings. When Zinman returned to the United States in 1982, the orchestra played
under guest conductors for a year until a very talented young conductor, the 33-
year-old James Conlon, was appointed principal conductor. His arrival promised
the orchestra a new élan and marked the beginning of a new series of recordings.

Conlon's repertoire features many landmarks of the classical, romantic, and
early-twentieth-century repertoire. The RPhO still has many contacts in the world
of contemporary music, however. Luciano Berio has conducted the orchestra
regularly since 1972. The RPhO has commissioned works from Tadeusz Baird,
Luciano Berio, Frank Martin, Per Nørgård, Alexandre Tansman, and others,
including many Dutch composers.

RECORDING HISTORY AND SELECTIVE DISCOGRAPHY: The RPhO's recording
history began hesitatingly in the early 1950s, resulting, however, in the memorable 1954
world premiere recording of Mahler's Symphony No. 8 (a live recording of Flipse's
performance in the Ahoy' Hall). A subsequent lull in recording activity came to an end
in 1973 when, due above all to the efforts of Edo de Waart, an exclusive contract was
signed with Phonogram International. The result was a series of interesting recordings
on the Philips label. Special mention should be made of the 1976 recording of *Der
Rosenkavalier* under de Waart (the first integral recording of an opera in Holland) and
the 1980 album of *Pelléas et Mélisande* (works of Fauré, Schoenberg, and Sibelius) under
David Zinman. The latter was awarded two Grands Prix du Disque. The first tangible
fruits of the recording efforts of James Conlon (who brought a contract for the French
label Erato) appeared in 1984 in the form of Liszt's *Faust-Symphony* (Grammy nomi-
nation, 1986). More Liszt, Janáček, Poulenc (Grand Prix du Disque, 1986), Debussy,
and Stravinsky are in production. The complete works of Willem Pijper, performed by
the RPhO under various conductors, will appear in a three-record set on the Donemus
label in 1987.

Liszt, *A Faust Symphony* (John Aler, tenor/Conlon/Bratislava Male Chorus): Erato
751582; ECD 88068 (CD). Liszt, *Dante Symphony* (Conlon): Erato 75245; ECD 88162
(CD). Poulenc, Works for Piano and Orchestra (Françoise-Rene Duchable, Jean-Philippe
Collard/Conlon): Erato 75203; ECD 88140 (CD). Poulenc, Organ Concerto and *Concert
champêtre* for cembalo (Marie-Claire Alain, Ton Koopman/Conlon): Erato 75310; ECD
88141 (CD). Rimsky-Korsakov, *Tsar Saltan Suite; Le Coq d'or suite* (Zinman): Philips
6514163, Philips 411435–2 (CD).

CHRONOLOGY OF PRINCIPAL CONDUCTORS: Willem Feltzer, 1918–1928. Alexander Schumuller, 1928–1930. Eduard Flipse, 1930–1965. Franz-Paul Decker, 1962–
1968. Jean Fournet, 1968–1973. Edo de Waart, 1973–1979. David Zinman, 1979–1982.
James Conlon, 1983–present.

BIBLIOGRAPHY: Eduard Reeser, ed., *Music in Holland* (Amsterdam: Foundation
Donemus/J. M. Meulenhoff [1959]). Willem Vos, ed., *Eeen Spiegel van Diamant* (Amsterdam: RPhO, 1978)—60 interesting RPhO programs reproduced in facsimile with
commentary. W. A. Wagner, *Muziek aan de Maas* (Amsterdam, 1968).

ACCESS: Rotterdam Philharmonic Orchestra, de Doelen, Kruisstraat 2, 3012 CT Rotterdam. 010–4142911. Hans van Beers, Managing Director. Willem Vos, Artistic
Adviser.

WILLEM VOS

New Zealand _____

New Zealand Symphony Orchestra

As the country's first and only fully-professional symphony orchestra, the NZSO holds a pre-eminent place in New Zealand's cultural life. From its rehearsal studio in Symphony House in Wellington, it travels over 15,000 miles annually to meet its obligation to a population that, scattered over two islands, barely exceeds 3 million. Concert performances average 100 a year in up to 20 towns and cities, with ten subscription series in seven centers, as well as radio and television studio performances.

The NZSO enjoys unusual financial security yet receives no government grants, no local-body funding, and has never had to raise funds. Since its inception it has been the responsibility of New Zealand's public broadcasting system, with funds made available by the television license fee and radio/television advertising profits. The private sector now shares some of this financial burden, and business sponsorship makes a significant contribution to ever-rising concert costs.

The NZSO's 89 players are employed on a permanent (not a seasonal or contractual) basis. A general manager and staff of 15 maintain all aspects of the orchestra's operation, including the orchestral training source, Schola Musica (first of its kind in the world), and the annual New Zealand Youth Orchestra. A former resident conductor, John Hopkins, established them both, in 1961 and 1959, respectively, to assist recruitment in a country without a music conservatory. The success of the Schola—under Ashley Heenan, music director for its first 23 years—is confirmed by the presence of 22 former trainees in the present

NZSO. Resident or returning New Zealanders now fill most rank-and-file positions, although front-desk and some principal positions are advertised overseas.

Another uniquely NZSO scheme has for 20 years helped overcome a sense of isolation by providing overseas bursaries. Currently, one player per year receives return air fare and full salary for six months to undertake advanced study of his or her instrument and to observe contemporary orchestral trends.

New Zealand's first century of European settlement was celebrated in 1940. Plans were to retain permanently the acclaimed orchestra of its Music Festival, but World War II forced the disbandment of all but its 12-piece string ensemble. The dream became reality on October 24, 1946, when 59 players of the new National Orchestra assembled for rehearsal. Despite some criticism of both the cost and conductor Andersen Tyrer, the first concert—in Wellington's Town Hall on March 7 1947—was a resounding public success and was later repeated in each of the other three metropolitan centers of its triumphant inaugural tour.

Tyrer, with typical energy and enthusiasm, had personally auditioned hundreds of hopeful musicians up and down the country. Many, like their virtuoso leader, Vincent Aspey, had played for silent movies; others came from military or brass bands, but few had earned their living by music; most had never seen or heard a professional orchestra. An enormous amount of work was necessary to build up a symphonic repertoire, and the seemingly endless rehearsals frustrated more experienced musicians. Touring was long and arduous. Outside of the main centers, halls and theatres lacked proper facilities, and meals were unobtainable after a concert. Yet all this and more the orchestral pioneers bore with enthusiasm.

A succession of resident conductors followed Tyrer, notable among them James Robertson and John Hopkins. But by 1969, with high calibre conductors reluctant to commit themselves to one musically isolated orchestra, the guest conductor system began. There had always been important guests, including Igor Stravinsky (at his own request), but the new system annually brought eight or more guests of international reputation. The appointment for several seasons of a chief or principal guest conductor, currently Franz-Paul Decker, provided continuity.

The orchestra, as a result, is as noted for its adaptability as for its musical versatility. In one year offerings may include the symphonic repertoire of the subscription season, major choral works, ballet or opera accompaniment, and the complexity of a Festival of Modern Asian and Pacific Music. Major concerts are broadcast live or recorded for future broadcast on radio and/or television. Concerts range from the precise formality of a Royal Concert for visiting royalty to the relaxed informality of "Cushion," "Family," or "Shoppers" concerts. Consequently, the NZSO's appeal is widely spread, as evident in its light-hearted summer series. These began in the 1950s and were inspired by the BBC Proms, but the equally popular New Zealand version has developed along different lines. Light classics and showpieces such as the *1812 Overture* were presented outdoors or, if inside, with seating removed for predominantly young audiences to relax informally on cushions, blankets, or even mattresses. Gradually, Proms gave way to "Summer Pops" offering familiar music (by George Gershwin or John Williams, for example), often under the baton of New Zealand's favorite summertime host, the English conductor/composer/arranger Ron Goodwin.

New Zealand artists are actively encouraged. International opera stars Kiri te Kanawa and Donald McIntyre performed first with the orchestra, and today's emerging talent has the same opportunities. The work of New Zealand composers is frequently heard in concert or studio performance, and a major work is commissioned each year for either the NZSO, NZYO, or Schola Musica. Young listeners are encouraged as well, with programming geared to their level of experience.

Distance has restricted the orchestra to only two overseas tours—nine Australian concerts in 1974 under Brian Priestman and ten concerts as the featured orchestra at the 1980 Hong Kong Arts Festival under the direction of Michiyoshi Inoue and Orwain Arwel Hughes.

RECORDING HISTORY AND SELECTIVE DISCOGRAPHY: The first commercial recording was *Festive Overtures* (HMV, 1959) under John Hopkins. *The Great Classics* for Deutsche Grammophon under Hopkins (1976) was the first classical recording ever to reach number one on New Zealand's Top 40 national sales chart.

Invitation to the Dance (Hopkins): Kiwi Pacific Records TRL–020. Music by Lary Pruden (Susskind, Hopkins, Matheson, Waters, Heenan): Kiwi Pacific Records SLD–66.

CHRONOLOGY OF MUSIC DIRECTORS: Andersen Tyrer, 1946–1949. Michael Bowles, 1950–1953. Warwick Braithwaite, 1953–1954. James Robertson, 1954–1957. John Hopkins, 1958–1963. Juan Matteucci, 1964–1969. Brian Priestman (Chief Conductor), 1973–1975. Michiyoshi Inoue (Principal Guest Conductor), 1977–1980. Franz-Paul Decker (Principal Guest Conductor), 1984–1985, 1987–1988.

BIBLIOGRAPHY: *Concert Pitch* Magazine of the NZSO, 1980–1987. Keith Hambleton, ed., *Concord of Sweet Sounds: The New Zealand Symphony Orchestra at 30* (Wellington: BCNZ, 1977). Owen Jensen, *NZBC Symphony Orchestra* (Wellington: Reed, 1966). Joy Tonks, *New Zealand Symphony Orchestra: The First Forty Years.* (Aukland: Reed Methuen, 1986).

ACCESS: New Zealand Symphony Orchestra, Symphony House, 132 Willis Street, Wellington, New Zealand. (64–4) 851–735. Peter Nisbet, General Manager.

JOY TONKS

Norway ————————————————————

BERGEN (220,000)

Bergen Philharmonic Orchestra

The Bergen Philharmonic Orchestra (Musikselskabet "Harmoniens" Orkester) maintains a season of one to three performances every week from the end of August to the end of June, for a total of some 110 performances per year.

Nearly all performances take place in the Grieghallen concert hall, named after composer Edvard Grieg, the orchestra's most illustrious conductor and benefactor. The Grieghallen was opened only in 1978 but represents many years of hopes and planning. Plans for a proper concert hall were launched in 1894 by Grieg himself, but were delayed, fought over, and finally altered into the scheme of today's multipurpose hall. Its enormous stage of 800 square meters can be enlarged by the addition of 100 square meters otherwise occupied by an orchestra pit. There is seating capacity for an audience of 1,500.

The orchestra performs numerous concerts in schools and outlying places in Bergen. Extensive tours were made in the United States in 1965, Great Britain in 1972, Belgium and West Germany in 1975, Sweden and Denmark in 1977, the Soviet Union in 1979, and France in 1984. Tours are planned for Italy in 1987 and the United States in 1989. All of the regular home concerts are broadcast by the Norwegian Broadcasting Company.

The orchestra's budget for 1986–1987 is 26 million Norwegian kroner, of which 16.6 million go for wages, 1.6 million for guest artists, and 4.6 million for the rental of the concert hall. Income from broadcasts finances 34% of the total budget. After monies from ticket sales, donations from foundations, and broadcasting receipts are applied to the budget, the remainder is supplied by the Norwegian government (60%) and the municipal government of Bergen (40%). The orchestra has a permanent endowment of 15.5 million Norwegian kroner.

Ninety musicians are employed full-time, and the administrative staff under Managing Director Laila Kismul numbers nine. Tor Ivar Andreassen is chairman of the Orchestra Committee. Programs are selected by the Artistic Director (currently Aldo Ceccato), the Concertmaster (currently David Stewart) and two members from the orchestra. The governing body, the Philharmonic Society, is presided over by a President, currently Per Grieg.

At the time of the orchestra's founding, October 8, 1765, Bergen was the largest and most important city in Norway, carrying on a lively mercantile trade with England and other communities in Europe and farther away. The Bergen Philharmonic proudly traces its history back to a meeting held by gentlemen of different social backgrounds to found the Philharmonic Society (Musikselskabet Harmonien). Their leader, Jens Boalt, was the headmaster of the Cathedral School, and an amateur of the arts. He was reported to have been "an extraordinarily bad poet and an equally bad composer" but apparently was a successful organizer, establishing an academy which was given Royal support and founding an institution, "The Useful Society" which is still going today, as useful as ever.

A protocol still treasured in Bergen contains the discussions of the Society as far back as 1769. A record of the Society's musical scores from 1792 shows that their library contained—and the orchestra performed—numerous compositions of Haydn as well as works of Mozart during the composers' lifetimes.

The orchestra's first concertmaster was Niels Haslund, maternal great-grandfather of Edvard Grieg. He was appointed the first Honorary Member of the Harmonien, a distinction which was also granted his great-grandson. At the age of eight the child prodigy, Ole Bull, made his debut in the Harmonien, which had by then become the owner of a concert hall second to none in Scandinavia. In 1850 Bull founded Den Nationale Scene, the first permanent Norwegian theatre, inviting Henrik Ibsen to Bergen. Gessine Gaferup, an accomplished concert pianist, the Norwegian mother of Edvard Grieg (his father was Scottish) often appeared as a piano soloist with the Musikselskabet Harmonien. Edvard himself appeared on a program with the Society in 1863, at the age of 19. In subsequent years he was a frequent guest soloist, playing his own works as well as those of other composers. In 1880 Grieg became artistic director of the Harmonien and conductor of the orchestra. His tenure brought the orchestra and its chorus to a standard never reached earlier. When he died childless, he made the Harmonien the heir to his entire estate and to all future income from his compositions. Income from the Grieg inheritance continues to fund the orchestra to this day.

Later important conductors included Johan Halvorsen (1893–1899), Harald Heide (the conductor with the longest tenure in Bergen, 1907–1948), and Karsten Andersen (1965–1985). The current music director and permanent conductor, Aldo Ceccato, was appointed in 1985.

The Bergen International Festival, founded in 1953, takes place annually at the end of May. It is an intensive 12-day series of performances in music, dance and drama. Four to six presentations each day feature visiting orchestras, opera companies, dance groups, and solo and ensemble performers from Europe and America. The Philharmonic Society organizes and supports these events and the Bergen Orchestra acts as host group, appearing in orchestra concerts, and accompanying choral and dance groups.

Several chamber concerts are performed by musicians selected from the larger orchestra. In addition a number of smaller ensembles are constituted from the large group: the Bergen Wind Quintet, the Bergen Brass Ensemble, the Bergen New String Quartet, and the Harmonien Chamber Orchestra. Until 1979 the orchestra also had the duty of playing at the theatre in Bergen.

RECORDING HISTORY AND SELECTIVE DISCOGRAPHY: The Bergen Philharmonic Orchestra has recorded only music by Norwegian composers, mostly under the labels of the Norwegian Composers Society and The Norwegian Contemporary Music.

Grieg, Concerto in A Minor for Piano, Op. 16 (Audun Kayser/Andersen): TROLD 03. Grieg, Symphony in C Minor (Andersen): Decca SXDL 7537. Halvorsen, *Suite Ancienne*; *Two Rapsodies* (Andersen): Impetus/NKF 30030. Bull, Selected Works (Andersen): Impetus/NKF 30041. Tubin, Symphony No. 4 (Jarvi): BIS 227.

CHRONOLOGY OF MUSIC DIRECTORS: Samuel Lind, 176?–1769. Benjamin Ohle, 1769–1770. Niels Haslund, 1770–1785. Ole Pedersen Rødder, 1785–1805. J. Hindrich Paulsen, 1805–1806 and 1809–1820. C. M. Lundholm, 1820–1827. Ferdinand Giovanni Schediwy, 1827–1844. Ferdinand August Rojahn, 1856–1859. August Christian Johannes Fries, 1859–1862 and 1864–1873. Amadeus Wolfgang Maczewsky, 1862–1864. Richard C. Henneberg, 1873–1875. Adolf Blomberg, 1875–1878. Hermann Levi, 1879–1880. Edvard Grieg, 1880–1882. Iver Holter, 1882–1884 and 1885–1886. Per Winge, 1886–1888. Georg Washington Magnus, 1892–1893. Johan Halvorsen, 1893–1899. Christian Danning, 1899–1901 and 1902–1905. Harald Heide, 1907–1948. Olav Kielland, 1948–1950. Sverre Jordan, 1950–1952. Carl von Garaguly, 1952–1958. Arvid Fladmoe, 1958–1961. Sverre Bergh, 1961–1964. Rudolf Schwarz, 1964–1965. Karsten Andersen, 1965–1985. Aldo Ceccato, 1985–present.

BIBLIOGRAPHY: Correspondence with Laila Kismul, Bergen Philharmonic Orchestra Managing Director. Bergen Philharmonic Orchestra, miscellaneous documents. Olav Mosby, *Musikselskabet "Harmonien"* (Bergen, n.d.), 2 vols. Kåre Fasting, *Musikselskabet "Harmonien" During Two Hundred Years* (Bergen, n.d.).

ACCESS: Bergen Philharmonic Orchestra, Musikselskabet "Harmonien," Grieghallen, Lars Hillesgt. 3a, 5000 Bergen. (46–5) 32 04 00. Laila Kismul, Managing Director.

JOHN WILLIAM WOLDT

Panama ————————————————————

PANAMA CITY (386,000)

National Symphony Orchestra of Panama

Panama's National Symphony (OSN: Orquesta Sinfónica Nacional de Panama), founded in 1941 by Panamanian-born conductor and composer Herbert de Castro, is the sole professional symphony orchestra in the Republic of Panama. The OSN is administered and supported by the Ministry of Education through the Department of Fine Arts and is part of a large-scale cultural movement whose goal is to bring all of the fine arts to all parts of the country.

The regular season of the OSN involves approximately 40 concerts from April to December. These are divided into four types of performance runs: the traditional concert season held in the Italianate Teatro Nacional in Panama City; popular concerts presented on tour throughout the country; educational concerts for secondary-school and National Conservatory of Music students; and various individual festivals. In addition, the OSN plays a so-called Winter Season during January/February, consisting of five open-air concerts in parks and churches of the capital. Since one of the OSN's primary functions is that of a national orchestra, involving much touring throughout Panama, it has a large following in the provinces, where its concerts are presented free of charge.

For the most part, the general administration of the OSN is left to the Department of Fine Arts. Artistic decisions, however, are in the hands of the music director. In 1972 the OSN, along with orchestras in Cost Rica, Nicaragua, and Guatemala, formed the Gira Centroamerica, which coordinates efforts in the fine arts in those countries. OSN musicians are a mixture of native Panamanians and imported artists, with new members being trained at the National Conservatory. The annual budget is B 250,000, the majority provided by the Panamanian government.

The orchestra was formed on government order in 1941 as an auxilliary to the National Conservatory founded the previous year. Prior to that time Panama had a sporadic musical life; the main musical establishment consisted of numerous bands, and there was no cohesive cultural policy coordinating efforts to create a truly national symphony orchestra. Herbert de Castro's appointment as the newly formed group's first conductor brought to the orchestra a man with skill, knowledge, and dedication to the position, and due to his efforts a firm foundation was laid. Between 1952 and 1965, however, the orchestra went into eclipse. Few concerts were given, and there was no permanent director.

Following the transfer of the administration to the Ministry of Education and the establishment of a national fine arts policy in 1965, the OSN was reestablished on a more permanent basis, and the following year the present concert schedule was instituted. The repertoire of the OSN is similar to that of other symphony orchestras throughout the world. In addition, compositions by Panamanian composers are featured on the regular programs. The OSN has not recorded.

CHRONOLOGY OF MUSIC DIRECTORS: Herbert de Castro, 1941–1943. Walter Meyers, 1944–1952. (Guest conductors, 1952–1965.) Roque Cordero, 1965. Eduardo Charpentier, 1966–present.

BIBLIOGRAPHY: Interview with Eduardo Charpentier, 1985. *Cultural Policy in the Republic of Panama* (Paris: UNESCO, 1978). Richard F. Nyrop, ed., *Panama: A Country Study* (Washington, D.C.: GPO, 1981). Nicholas Slonimsky, *Music of Latin America* (New York: Da Capo, 1972).

ACCESS: Orquesta Sinfónica Nacional, Apartado 9190, Panama 6. Eduardo Charpentier, Music Director.

BERTIL H. VAN BOER, JR.
MARGARET L. FAST

Poland

KATOWICE (364,000)

Polish Radio National Symphony Orchestra

Together with the National Philharmonic in Warsaw,* the Polish Radio National Symphony (WOSPRiT) is a premiere symphonic ensemble in Poland. It was founded in March 1945, two months before the end of World War II, and it quickly achieved a high musical level.

The ensemble presents 20 to 40 concerts, 10 to 20 television programs, and 1,000 to 1,500 minutes of archival recordings per year. Especially popular are its cyclic television programs such as *Quodlibet* or *Music Mornings WOSPRiT*. For several years the orchestra has organized monographic festivals in Poznan, devoted, for example, to Beethoven, Brahms, Tchaikovsky, and Schumann.

WOSPRiT has spent much time touring the world—including Europe, Australia, and the United States. It has become traditional to hear the ensemble during the Warsaw Autumn Festival (Warszawska Jesián), where excellent playing has very often brought awards for the best contemporary music performances. WOSPRiT's season is from September through June, with the exception of concert tours. Its music hall, the 1,000-seat Grzegorz Fitelberg Auditorium in the Cultural Center in Katowice (1980), offers good acoustics. Like all the orchestras in Poland, WOSPRiT is a state ensemble and has a centrally planned budget.

From the very beginning the orchestra played a lot of Polish music, and it has done many archival recordings. Post-romantics and twentieth-century figures such as Karol Szymanowski, Krzysztof Penderecki, Witold Lutosławski and others are the most-often heard in WOSPRiT performances, but works of Stanislaw Moniuszko, Frédéric Chopin, and even some eighteenth-century Poles are included in the repertoire. The orchestra has presented many choral works in conjunction with the choruses of the Silesian Philharmonic Orchestra* or the Krakow Radio. Such concerts assemble massive audiences from throughout the Silesian industrial region. Tickets are sold out many days in advance because each concert is considered a major musical event. The whole of Poland has often heard them on television.

In 1956 WOSPRiT organized the first composers' competition for young Polish people. Twenty such competitions have taken place since, a further example of the orchestra's policy of supporting Polish music. Among past winners have been such well-known Polish composers as Kazimierz Serocki, Tadeusz Baird, and Krzysztof Penderecki.

For many years there have been active subgroups composed of WOSPRiT musicians, currently including the WOSPRiT Wind Quintet, Silesian Baroque Trio, WOSPRiT String Quartet, and others. They take part in concerts, broadcasts, and recordings.

On March 19, 1945, a group of 16 musicians with conductor Witold Rowicki arrived in Katowice to establish a radio orchestra. The first public concert took place on March 25, and by 1946 the ensemble had sufficient musicians to play classical works. In 1947 conductor Grzegorz Fitelberg conducted his first concert with the ensemble, and as music director he would build the orchestra to a high musical level. Then known as the Polish Radio National Symphony Orchestra (WOSPR), it earned an international reputation. The orchestra's first foreign tour took place in 1948, to Czechoslovakia. Archival recordings soon followed, and according to the Polish composer Wawrzyniec Zuławski, the orchestra became the best in Poland.

Following Fitelberg's death in 1953 Jan Krenz became music director, and in 1955 the orchestra began to perform in the new Radio Music Hall. During his directorship there were important changes in the life of the ensemble, one being the advent in 1956 of the group's first general manager, Piotr Perkowski. After a long break in touring, the orchestra once again went abroad, this time to Yugoslavia, Bulgaria, Romania, and Hungary. It presented its first performance for the Warsaw Autumn Festival and for the first time visited the West in a tour to Belgium. In the 1960s the 102-piece ensemble toured Europe, China, Japan, Australia, and the U.S.S.R., presenting Polish music to a truly international public.

In 1967 Jan Krenz left for the Grand Theatre in Warsaw, and after a brief interregnum Bohdan Wodiczko became music director. He organized the first cyclic television programs, and under his direction WOSPR became the radio/television orchestra WOSPRiT, seen in concert with famous Polish and foreign soloists. When Wodiczko left due to illness in 1968, his place was assumed by Kazimierz Kord, who brought to the repertoire choral music rarely played until then. Tadeusz Strugała became music director in 1974 and continued Kord's policy of frequent recording. In 1976 WOSPRiT made a two-month concert tour of the United States and Canada and shortly thereafter instituted the monographic festivals in Poznan under music director Stanislaw Wislocki.

In 1984 current music director Antoni Wit organized an interesting festival of Polish contemporary music, comprising portraits of Witold Lutosławski, Tadeusz Baird, Wojciech Kilar, and Krzysztof Penderecki. With its 30-year anniversary in 1985, the orchestra thanked Grzegorz Fitelberg for bringing it to excellence so quickly and giving it the foundation for its successful history.

RECORDING HISTORY AND SELECTIVE DISCOGRAPHY: WOSPR made its first radio archival recording in 1949 and its first record in 1951. The ensemble made recordings for the BBC in the early 1960s. Under Kord the orchestra intensified its recording work, with seven works by Penderecki for EMI in quadraphonic sound (1972). In the following years Penderecki made recordings of five more works for EMI, and Jose Serebrier made a film recording of Charles Ives's Fourth Symphony. In 1976, in conjunction with Polish Radio, EMI produced the first recording of the original version of Mussorgsky's *Boris Godounov* under the direction of Jerzy Semkow; this won the German Record Award. An International Record Critics Award was received in 1977 for a recording of Lutosławski's symphonic music.

Chopin, Piano Concerto No. 1; *Krakowiak* (Ohlsson, Maksymiuk): Angel RL–32092. Mussorgsky, *Boris Godounov* (Semkow): Angel SX–3844 (4 records). Penderecki, *Magnificat* (Penderecki) Angel S–37417. Piston, Concerto for Orchestra; Ruggles, *Men and Mountains* (Strickland); Hively, *Icarus* (Wodiczko): CRI S–254. Stravinsky, *Sacre du printemps* (Wodiczko): Stolat 0106.

CHRONOLOGY OF MUSIC DIRECTORS: Witold Rowicki, 1945–1947. Grzegorz Fitelberg, 1947–1953. Jan Krenz, 1953–1956, 1958–1967. Bohdan Wodiczko, 1968–1969. Kazimierz Kord, 1969–1973. Tadeusz Strugała, 1974–1976. Jerzy Maksymiuk, 1976–1977. Stanisław Wisłocki, 1977–1981. Antoni Wit, 1983–present.

BIBLIOGRAPHY: Irena Siodmok and Leon Markiewicz, *WOSPRiT, 1945–1975* (Katowice: WOSPRiT, 1975). WOSPRiT season retrospectives, 1973–1984.

ACCESS: Wielka Orkiestra Symfoniczna Polskiego Radia i Telewizji Poland Katowice, Plac Dzierżyńskiego, Katowice. 51–52–21. Marian Wallek-Walewski, General Manager. Irena Siodmok, Director of Promotion.

ADAM JASINSKI

Silesian State Philharmonic Orchestra

The Silesian State Philharmonic (Panstwowa Filharmonia Śląska) supports the Silesian Philharmonic Orchestra (Orkiestra Filharmonii Śląskiej), and although the institution dates back to May 26, 1945, the traditions of its orchestra revert to the era between the two world wars.

A conservatory of music flourished in the industrial city of Katowice for many years and provided highly qualified musicians who constituted the foundation of former orchestras. The musical traditions of Katowice and Silesia included numerous musical groups, especially wind ensembles associated with mining and industrial enterprises. The diversity of such musical performances established the basis for the creation of a symphony orchestra, which also filled the need for a social/cultural entity.

The activities of the Silesian Philharmonic institution during the initial postwar years fulfilled the important role of propagating musical culture. Along with weekly concerts in its own city, the Philharmonic Orchestra conducted concerts in various localities of Silesia, performing in factory halls, in houses of culture, or in the open air. With the passage of time, the function of the Silesian Philharmonic stabilized itself, spreading out in three directions: weekly symphonic concerts, popular concerts, and school performances.

The first type of concert is intended for a critical, labor-class audience accustomed to regular association with music. These performances are repeated in the larger cities of Silesia and encompass a repertoire drawn from every musical epoch from the Renaissance through the present, together with copyrighted works of prominent Polish composers. Many of the concerts are recorded on tape and are broadcast on Polish radio. The orchestra has been directed by nearly all the well-known Polish conductors and also by many others, including Leopold Stokowski and Roberto Benzi. Soloists appearing with the orchestra have been Polish and other virtuosos, including Witold Małcużyński, Svyatoslav Richter, Igor Oistrakh, Henryk Szeryng, and others.

The second type of concert currently instituted by the Silesian Philharmonic is the popular concert, geared to the novice listener and usually supplemented with explanatory comments. Such concerts are presented not only in Katowice but also in houses of culture and the club houses of various labor organizations. The current campaign of school concerts completes the Philharmonic's performance schedule. These cyclic concerts acquaint school children with both Polish and worldwide literature.

The artistic leadership of the Silesian Philharmonic Orchestra during the years 1945–1946 rested in the hands of Anatol Zarubin, followed by Witold Krzemieński (1946–1949) and Stanisław Skrowaczewski (1949–1953). Since 1953 the orchestra has been directed by Karol Stryja, a graduate of the Silesian Conservatory of Music and the State Lyceum of Music in Katowice. During this period the artistic level of the orchestra was raised considerably, its technical efficiency was advanced, and the scope of its repertoire was broadened, especially in the field of contemporary music.

The Silesian Philharmonic institution is the organizer of a series of musical enterprises such as the International Festival of Russian and Soviet Music, the All-Poland Competition of Young Directors, and the Festival of Organ Music. The Silesian Philharmonic Orchestra belongs to the groups that perform frequently in the "Warsaw Autumn" International Festival of Contemporary Music ("Warszawska Jesień"), recognition of its stature among Polish orchestras. The Silesian Philharmonic Orchestra also earned high approbation for its artistic standards during its foreign appearances in Czechoslovakia, Bulgaria, Romania, Italy, East Germany, West Germany, and the U.S.S.R.

The orchestra owns the full range of orchestral instruments; it tunes to A at 440 cps. In performing oratorios and other choral/orchestral works, the orchestra has enjoyed the cooperation of several amateur choirs, among them "Ogniwo," "Kolejarz," "Siemianowice," the male choir "Echo," and the choir of the

Musical Lyceum in Katowice. At the present time the Silesian Philharmonic institution possesses a permanent, professional choral group, which allows it to perform major vocal/instrumental works.

SELECTIVE DISCOGRAPHY: Bizet, *L'Arlesienne Suites* (Stryja): Muza sxl 0233; Stolat 0102. Bolesław Szabelski, Symphony No. 4 (Stryja): Muza sx 1828. Mieczysław Karlowicz, Symphonic Poems (Jerzy Salwarowski) Wifon LP 064.

CHRONOLOGY OF MUSIC DIRECTORS: Anatol Zarubin, 1945–1946. Witold Krzemienski, 1946–1949. Stanisław Skrowaczewski, 1949–1953. Karol Stryja, 1953–present.

BIBLIOGRAPHY: *Katowice, ich dzieje i kultura na tle regionu* (Warszawa: Arkady, 1976).

ACCESS: Panstwowa Filharmonia Śląska, ul. A Zawadzkiego 2, 40–956 Katowice. 58–62–61.

ZDZISŁAW LIS
TRANS. FELICIA CRAIG

KRAKOW   (726,000)

Krakow Philharmonic

Krakow, the captial of Poland and the town of the Polish kings until 1596, was also the seat of the Jagiellonian University (founded 1364). These facts designated the town to be the cultural and scientific center of the country, and even after the transfer of political power to Warsaw, Krakow did not give up its ambitions, fighting effectively against political and economic adversity. Thus the creation of the Krakow Philharmonic (Pánstwowa Filharmonia "Karola Szymanowskiego") in 1945 found deep historical justification in a national tradition many years old.

Of the groups at the Philharmonic Institution, the orchestra is the most vital. It is headed by a chief managing director (Wieslaw Kolankowski) and is under the artistic direction of its principal conductor, Tadeusz Strugała, who is also head of the Institution's artistic groups. The orchestra has recently acquired a second permanent conductor as well, Joseph Radwan. An artistic council, the group inspectors, and the concertmasters of the groups are mediatory links between management and musicians. The Philharmonic is financed from state subsidies. The amount varies from season to season, depending on needs and resources.

The orchestra gives symphonic concerts every Friday and Saturday in its own building and often tours abroad. The Philharmonic choirs (mixed and boys') also take part in its concerts. Many oratorios are performed by these groups in Krakow's ancient churches. The Philharmonic orchestra's artistic season, like that of other Polish orchestras, lasts from September to June, with summers given over to recitals, evening serenades, and the like. In addition to its symphonic and oratorio/cantata concerts, the Philharmonic presents symphonic concerts for students, ancient music concerts in the old Senators' Hall at Wawel (Wawel Evenings), recitals of eminent virtuosi (Masters' Recitals), organ recitals, chamber concerts, children's concerts, and popular concerts teaching the love of music. Furthermore, the Philharmonic organizes festivals such as the Organ Music Days (Dni Muzyki Organowej; since 1966), Krakow Music Spring (Krakowska Wiosna Muzyki; a festival of musical competition laureates, since 1962), and festivals of the music of Karol Szymanowski and Krzysztof Penderecki.

The orchestra's home, Krakow Philharmonic Hall, was not constructed specifically for concerts but nevertheless satisfies the needs of the Philharmonic's activities. The hall's 816 seats are generally filled to between 80% and 90% of capacity, and young people form a considerable part of the audience.

The Krakow Philharmonic Orchestra repertoire is the result of many circumstances, among them didactic considerations, the likes and dislikes of the audience, performers' suggestions, and musical occasions such as composers' anniversaries. The concern of the artistic management is to present all styles and epochs in adequate proportions in the programs of each season. The basis of the repertoire, however, is in the internationally recognized masterworks. Philharmonic groups specialize to some extent in the music of Szymanowski and Penderecki, particularly when the ensembles are on tour. Another special interest in repertoire is the music of other leading Polish composers. Generally speaking, twentieth-century music accounts for about 20% of the repertoire of Krakow Philharmonic ensembles.

The Wawel Evenings concerts, whose programs present only old music—exclusively composed at the king's castle or performed there—represent the verbatim historical trend in the Philharmonic's repertoire. This element gains a special importance, too, in didactically conceived programs destined for school audiences. They show, for example, the development of individual stylistic trends or musical forms, instruments, and the like.

The first concert of the Krakow Philharmonic took place on February 3, 1945, two weeks after the town's liberation. Since that time the Krakow Philharmonic groups have continued their concert activity without interruption. The birth of the orchestra was an imperative of the great interest in cultural values forbidden by the occupation of the Third Reich, especially the desire for performances of the great works of the Polish national repertoire. The legal act fundamental for the present orchestra's status was its nationalization and its being granted the rank of "Philharmonic" in April of 1945. Legal normalization of the mixed choir took place at the beginning of 1950, and the boys' choir has been active since 1952. During its 40 years of existence each of the orchestra's conductors has added an individual dimension to the repertoire and its performance.

Historically, many chamber groups have been active within the Philharmonic, among them Andrzej Markowski's Orchestra, Leszek Izmaiłow's String Quartet, and the Capella Cracoviensis (which has had independent status since 1983). At present two wind trios are active. The relatively small share of musicians in the chamber groups is dictated by living conditions on the one hand and a relatively low interest among local music lovers in chamber music on the other.

Because tours allow an orchestra to compare its own standards to those of other groups, and thus stimulate its strides toward perfecting its own skills of execution, the Krakow Philharmonic has made concert trips a priority. As of July 31, 1985, the Philharmonic has visited 24 countries throughout Eastern and Western Europe, Iran, the U.S.S.R., and the United States, making a total of 51 trips for the orchestra, 44 for the mixed choir, and 38 for the boys' choir. The orchestra has also appeared at a great many of the principal music festivals of Europe.

Krakow Philharmonic activity exerts a decisive influence on the musical life and musicality of the community, for the institution is Krakow's leading musical organization. Its contacts with Krakow's other musical institutions are manifold. The Polish Radio and Television Orchestra and Choir in Krakow have their main residence in the Philharmonic building, and some Philharmonic musicians participate in their activities as well as in opera and operetta performances. There are numerous common initiatives among the institutions, including exchange concerts, cooperation among choirs, and coordination of programming.

The institution is also active in educational work. Many of its members are active teachers, and the Philharmonic undertakes numerous programs for children and youth of different ages and degrees of preparation. Preschool and primary-grade concerts are given, as are school programs of the institution's symphonic concerts in the south of Poland (called "Music—ars amanda"). The latter are accompanied by folders, talks, and meetings with the performers and, above all, attractive programs especially prepared for the occasion. The cooperation of the Philharmonic with school authorities is very close.

It is difficult to define unequivocally the sound of an orchestra set to execute different repertoires and working with different conductors, but the Philharmonic Orchestra seems to find itself most at home with those romantic and late romantic works calling for wide melodic lines and a mellow sound. The Philharmonic is probably the only orchestra in Poland with nine double basses at its disposal (built by the Mayer firm). Its musicians have many precious string instruments, having a marked influence on the sound of the quintet; they are under the care of a violinmaker whose work has won many international prizes.

Following the resignation of Music Director Tadeusz Strugała in 1986, Krzysztof Penderecki will assume the role of principal guest conductor.

RECORDING HISTORY AND SELECTED DISCOGRAPHY: The Krakow Philharmonic has not made a great many discs, for the city is without a recording studio, and the Philharmonic building is located disadvantageously for such undertakings, being at the corner of two very busy streets that make recording—even at night—impossible. The orchestra's recordings of Penderecki and Szymanowski, however, have won it acclaim, particularly the 1966 recording of Penderecki's *Passion According to St. Luke*, (conducted by Henryk Czyż), which won the 1967 Grand Prix de Disque). The Krakow Philharmonic choir participated in a series of recordings by the Polish Radio and Television Symphony Orchestra* (WOSPRiT) in Katowice.

Liszt, *Polonica* (Strugała): Polskie Nagrania. Penderecki, *Canticum Canticorum*, Cantatas, and Stanzas (Jerzy Katlewicz): Polskie Nagrania. Szymanowski, *Kurpie Songs* (Józef Bok): Polskie Nagrania.

CHRONOLOGY OF MUSIC DIRECTORS: Zygmunt Latoszewski, 1945. Jan Maklakiewicz, 1945–1947. Walerian Bierdiajew, 1947–1949 (Principal Conductor, 1945–1949). Piotr Perkowski, 1949–1951 (Principal Conductor, Witold Krzemieński). Bohdan Wodiezko, 1951–1955. Bronisław Rutkowski, 1955–1956 (Principal Conductor, Stanisław Skrowaczewski). Jerzy Gert, 1957–1962 (Principal Conductor, Witold Rowicki). Andrzej Markowski, 1962–1965 (Principal Conductor, 1959–1965). Henryk Czyż, 1965–1968. Jerzy Katlewicz, 1968–1980. Tadeusz Strugała, 1981–1986.

BIBLIOGRAPHY: Jacek Berwaldt, *Filharmonia Krakowska, 1945–1980* (Krakow: Krakow Philharmonic, c. 1980). Krakow Philharmonic programs. Lucjan Kydryński, *Filharmonia Krakowska* (Krakow: 1965). Stefan Starzyk, *40-lecia choru Filharmonii Krakowskiej*. (Krakow: Krakow Philharmonic, c. 1985).

ACCESS: Państwowa Filharmonia im. Karola Szymanowskiego, ul. Zwierzyniecka 1, 31–103 Krakow. 22–94–77. Wiesław Kolankowski, Chief Director.

JACEK BERWALDT

LODZ (844,000)

Symphony Orchestra of the Artur Rubinstein Philharmonic of Lodz

This orchestra gives two concerts per week, on Friday and Saturday evenings, from September through June. Its other annual events are a festival of organ music, oratorios and cantatas (late September), popular carnival concerts (December and January), Easter oratorio performances, and outdoor popular programs in June. Its repertoire is dominated by works of the classical and romantic periods, a selection in compliance with the preferences of the local audience and the musical character of the ensemble—its sound and romantic style of performing. Contemporary music, that of Polish composers in particular, is also of importance.

At present the orchestra consists of 90 players, mostly young graduates of the Lodz Academy of Music, who have been playing with the group no longer than ten years. The orchestra maintains some string and wind chamber ensembles that perform occasionally in neighboring towns and at school concerts. The Philharmonic Choir of 70 voices performs with the orchestra and sometimes on its own.

The Philharmonic of Lodz is a state institution headed by a managing director and a music director whose position is simultaneously that of chief conductor. The managers set repertoire, secure conductors and soloists (in the case of foreigners, through the mediation of the Polish Agency of Art), hire musicians, organize concerts and tours, and perform other duties. The playing members, choir singers, and management staff are permanent employees receiving a regular salary. The 1984 budget was 55 million zlotych. It is funded through endowments of the state institution (85%) and income from the Philharmonic itself (15%), comprising ticket sales, recording and broadcast fees, and so forth.

The Philharmonic's permanent abode is its concert hall of 720 seats. Dating from the nineteenth century, the hall is currently in very poor condition, and there are plans to build a new one. The ensemble performs elsewhere as well. The September festival takes place in the Evangelical Church, which possesses a very good organ. Summer pops concerts are held in bandshells and amphitheaters. The orchestra has performed many times elsewhere in Poland, taking part in music festivals. It has toured internationally every year since the early 1970s, visiting the U.S.S.R., Italy, France, West Germany, Austria, Spain, and other countries. Recent plans for a tour of North and South America changed when negotiations were broken off in 1982.

The Philharmonic's management is very active in educating school children to become listeners of classical music. Many orchestra members take part in concerts at nursery, primary, and secondary schools. Some Philharmonic musicians teach in the schools of music in Lodz and neighboring towns, and there are close relationships between the orchestra and the local academy of music. Student choirs perform with the Philharmonic, and the best graduates of the academy play annual concerts with the group. The Philharmonic has also fostered the work of local composer/teachers at the academy.

The Philharmonic of Lodz is the successor to an orchestra established spontaneously in 1915 by musicians unemployed because of war. Their first concert took place on February 11 of that year. Between the wars they formed a union of musicians headed by the management. Main decisions were made by a general meeting of the membership. They had no concert hall; from 1922 on they had no permanent music director. Their budget was unsteady, consisting of ticket sales, private donations, and a small subsidy from the local government. Artistic standards thus suffered, and during periods of recession concerts were reduced or even suspended for months at a time. During World War II the ensemble was dissolved; Jewish members were deported to a ghetto and most were killed.

Immediately after the city's liberation, the surviving musicians gave their first concerts, performing voluntarily in unheated theatres, clubs, and factory halls during mass meetings. In February 1945 the government granted them a State Orchestra status and appointed Zdzisław Górzyński director. In 1948 the orchestra found a home of its own and was named the State Philharmonic of Lodz. Many musicians from destroyed Polish cities filled vacant seats in the Philharmonic, as they did in the other reviving ensembles around the country.

In the postwar period music by Polish composers was uppermost in the repertoire, and there were a great many premiere performances of contemporary pieces. Since the mid–1950s the programming has been extended and balanced for its period and stylistic content. After 15 years of changes (both of the management and musicians) the orchestra began perfecting its timbre and ensemble playing. In the 1970s, under the direction of Henryk Czyż, the orchestra achieved its current high musical standards.

In June of 1984 the Philharmonic was given the name of the Lodz-born pianist Artur Rubinstein. Thanks to Mrs. Rubinstein's donation of the great artist's memorabilia, the Artur Rubinstein Museum was founded, with contributions from the Philharmonic.

RECORDING HISTORY AND SELECTIVE DISCOGRAPHY: In the 1970s the orchestra recorded a cycle of concerts entitled "The Devil Is Not So Black" for the all-Polish television network, accompanied by commentaries by conductor Henryk Czyż, with the intention of popularizing classical music. The Philharmonic has also recorded sound tracks for about 70 motion pictures. It has not made many commercial recordings, however.

Szymanowski, Symphony in B-flat Major (Czyż): Polskie Nagrania SX 0981. Teresa Wojtaszek-Kubiak, recital (Czyż): Polskie Nagrania SX 1144.

CHRONOLOGY OF MUSIC DIRECTORS: Tadeusz Mazurkiewicz, 1915–1916. Bronisław Szulc, 1916–1922. Zdzisław Górzyński, 1945–1948. Włodzimierz Ormicki, 1948–1950. Władysław Raczkowski, 1950–1953. Witold Krzemieński, 1953–1956. Henryk Czyż, 1957–1960. Stefan Marczyk, 1960–1972. Zdzisław Szostak, 1971–1972. Henry Czyż, 1972–1980. Jacek Kasprzyk, 1980–1981. Zdzisław Szostak, 1982–1983. Andrzej Markowski, 1983–1986. Tomasz Bugaj, 1987–present.

BIBLIOGRAPHY: "Państwowa Filharmonia w Łodzi, 1915–1975" (collected monographs, Lodz, 1975).

ACCESS: Państwowa Filharmonia w Łodzi im. Artura Rubinsteina, ul. Narutowicza 20, 90–135 Lodz. 36–82–32. Andrzej Markowski, Artistic Director.

JACEK SZERSZENOWICZ

WARSAW (1,621,000)

National Philharmonic Orchestra in Warsaw

The National Philharmonic Orchestra is one of the most prominent Polish symphonic ensembles. Its annual activities include about 300 live performances before nearly a million people. The orchestra's main activity consists of routine concerts organized twice a week (Fridays and Saturdays) during the fall, winter, and spring, plus Tuesday concerts of chamber music and Sunday matinees. It also organizes and participates in such events as the Warszawska Jesień International Festival of Contemporary Music and the International Piano Competition of Chopin's Music.

The orchestra also concertizes for audiences in various Polish towns—mainly in regional symphonic festivals—plus conducting numerous tours abroad. To date the National Philharmonic has visited about 30 countries in all regions of the world, including several visits to the United States. In total it has given about 300 performances abroad. The orchestra makes many recordings and broadcasts each year.

Direct supervision of the orchestra is the responsibility of the artistic manager, who, on the whole, is the chief conductor as well. His tasks include, among others, selection of musicians, programming, and opening contracts with guest conductors and soloists (both Polish and foreign). Other administrative areas are managed by a superior corporate body that, in the orchestra's long history, has undergone substantial modifications and reshaping. Until World War II it had been a joint stock company named "Filharmonia Warszawska." After the war all its functions were taken over by the Polish State, under direction of the Ministry of Culture and Fine Arts, which became responsible for financial matters and the administration of the National Philharmonic. Today the artistic manager reports directly to the Ministry.

The National Philharmonic Orchestra employs 115 musicians plus a mixed choir of 120 voices. Most of its musicians are graduates of the musical college in Warsaw; however, this is not a rule, and graduates of other Polish musical schools are also employed, provided they have excellent abilities. The orchestra's repertoire generally comprises great classic works and contemporary compositions. Polish symphonic music is regarded separately, and the orchestra has premiered and repeated works of such Polish contemporaries as Karol Szymanowski, Tadeusz Baird, Kazimierz Serocki, Witold Lutosławski, and Krzysztof Penderecki.

The orchestra enters into contracts with various conductors in addition to the chief conductor. In its personnel structure it has principal players and soloists who are especially visible in the separately organized National Philharmonic Chamber Music Ensemble. In order to obtain its characteristic sound the orchestra tunes at an A of 440 cps.

The National Philharmonic plays an eminent role in the musical life of Poland. Its existence contributed—especially in the difficult periods of Poland's history—to the maintenance and preservation of Polish tradition and culture.

In the nineteenth century Poland did not exist, either as a separate country or as an independent political unit, Warsaw being then the capital of a province included in the Russian Empire. The political situation at that time inspired no interest in the residing authorities to create cultural centers that could make Warsaw a source of artistic and cultural influence affecting significantly the area of Poland remaining in the Russian sector of partitioned Poland. Nevertheless, due to the energy and efforts of Polish activists, the Grand Theater was founded in Warsaw; here opera dominated the many dramatic performances. The foundation of the Grand Theater significantly backed the already-existing Warsaw Musical Society and the Warsaw Conservatory. Thus Warsaw, despite the entirely different intentions of the authorities, became a cultural center whose influence spread into the German and Austrian sectors of what is today known as Poland.

The Grand Theater employed outstanding instrumentalists, singers, and conductors, both Polish and from abroad; its orchestra demonstrated a very high performance level. Still, the musical circles of Warsaw felt the lack of a symphony orchestra in the city. The Warsaw Musical Society tried to fill the gap and organized live performances of the orchestra borrowed from the Grand Theater several times a year. The Warsaw Conservatory also gave symphonic concerts, mainly between 1850 and 1890, using its own orchestra.

In 1890 such presentations underwent a rapid decline as the Grand Theater management increased the frequency of opera performances to at least once a day, thus making its orchestra unavailable for symphonic performances. The Conservatory also stopped its concerts. Only the visit in 1898 of Arthur Nikisch made the Grand Theater lend its orchestra for two symphonic concerts under Nikisch himself. Their enormous popularity and the very energetic activity of the Grand Theater's new artistic manager, Emil Młynarski, resulted in a revival of routine symphonic concerts. Simultaneously, Młynarski began to lay the foundation of a regular symphony orchestra in Warsaw, his idea being supported by Polish musical activists and by the Polish aristocracy.

The arrival of Ignacy Paderewski in 1899 and his concert on January 14 of that year offered the impetus to found an organizational committee aimed at creating a regular symphony orchestra in Warsaw, with its own philharmonic hall. The committee included, among others, Count Władysław Tyszkiewicz, Princess Natalia and Prince Stefan Lubomirski, and musicians Emil Młynarski and Ludwik Grossman. The funds for the concert hall were obtained from aristocrats and also from collections organized by the musicians themselves. Since the construction of both the building and the orchestra progressed quickly, the organizational committee was reshaped into a joint stock company. The orchestra's existence was inaugurated in a concert of all-Polish music held in the new hall on November 5, 1901. It was conducted by the group's first artistic manager—Emil Młynarski—with Ignacy Paderewski as soloist.

In its beginnings the Warsaw Philharmonic flourished. Concerts were sold out, Młynarski's skill and the executive body's efficiency brought high profits and high incomes. Edvard Grieg, Richard Strauss, and Ruggiero Leoncavallo premiered their masterpieces in Warsaw. However, prosperity did not last long. In 1903 Młynarski went abroad, the political situation curtailed concert activities, profits diminished, and stockholders withheld endowments. An attempt to save the orchestra by merging with the opera orchestra led once again to a scarcity of symphonic concerts in Warsaw. When the concert hall faced the auctioneer's block only the intervention of Prince Lubomirski prevented the worst. By paying musicians' salaries he sustained the ensemble as "Prince Lubomirski's Symphony Orchestra." Under the eminent Polish conductor Grzegorz Fitelberg, the repertoire was dominated by works of classical composers—Mozart and Beethoven—with few Polish works.

After one season Lubomirski withdrew his support and the musicians themselves reorganized as the Association of the Warsaw Philharmonic Orchestra and paid expenses in part by leasing the hall out for showing the then-fashionable, and new, moving pictures. After Fitelberg the new artistic manager was Zdzisław Birnbaum, under whom Karol Szymanowski's music was heard for the first time in Warsaw.

Following the outbreak of World War I, some musicians from partitioned sectors were interned. Thus the greatly diminished group began to perform in a motion picture theatre housed in the former Warsaw Philharmonic Hall, accompanying musically such features as the film *Life of Christ*. Only in 1916 was it possible to revive normal activity, and the ensemble, now known as the "Warsaw Philharmonic Orchestra," started a new season with a concert of Polish music. Polish composers would prevail in the repertoire until 1918, when under Polish independence the joint stock venture again took over finances and the orchestra returned to normal activities. Roman Chojnacki became the first artistic manager after the war, holding the position until 1938. Conductors in that period were Emil Młynarski, Zdzisław Birnbaum, and, from 1923, Grzegorz Fitelberg.

In 1924 the orchestra again fell into conflict with its corporation and once again began independent activity, this time as "An Association of the Warsaw Philharmonic Artists." Despite enormous financial troubles, the orchestra's artistic level remained very high, and Polish music was again heard at its concerts. Works of contemporary composers—Stravinsky, Prokofiev, Ravel, Honegger, and others—received first Polish performances. In 1927 the orchestra organized the First International Piano Competition of Chopin's Music. Grzegorz Fitelberg greatly increased the number of playing musicians, bringing the artistic level of the orchestra to prevailing European standards.

The outbreak of World War II completely stopped all activity of the Warsaw Philharmonic. In the first days of the war, fire destroyed the concert hall and, following the march of German troops into Warsaw, the orchestra ceased to exist, its members being scattered. At first the German occupation authorities forbade any musical presentations by Poles; later, however, they allowed performances in cafes and restaurants. This was a chance at survival for the remaining Philharmonic musicians as chamber music ensembles were organized in some small cafes. They played music of some Polish composers, though Chopin was strictly forbidden. In all, though, only seven Philharmonic musicians survived the war.

In 1944, after the liberation of the Right Bank of Warsaw, a musical ensemble called "The Representative Symphony Orchestra of Warsaw Capital City" was created, with Jerzy Wasiak as its first director and Olgierd Straszyński as its first artistic manager. Its finances were handled by the municipal authorities and, from 1946 on, by the state government. On September 10, 1948, the Ministry of Culture and Fine Arts dissolved the joint stock venture "Warsaw Philharmonic," taking over both the orchestra's patronage and its actual management. Witold Rudziński was appointed artistic manager, and the orchestra received the "Roma," the only undamaged hall in the city. The repertoire at this time included classical and romantic works, as well as works of Polish romantics and some turn-of-the-century moderns. When, for lack of a better location, the Warsaw

Opera Theater also sought shelter at "Roma," the authorities in 1949 fused its orchestra with that of the Warsaw Philharmonic and formed a new entity, the "State Enterprise of Opera and Philharmonic in Warsaw."

In 1950 Witold Rowicki was appointed director and artistic manager of the Warsaw Philharmonic Orchestra (still fused with the opera). This famous conductor and outstanding organizer first of all separated the two ensembles and then set about rebuilding the Philharmonic's old hall, which had been completely ruined in the war. Under his care and attention to musical quality, the Philharmonic became the best in Poland, its repertoire enriched by contemporary masterpieces, both Polish and foreign. The opening ceremony of the new, 1,100-seat concert hall took place in 1955, and the orchestra took a new name, the "National Philharmonic." The inaugural concert of all-Polish music conducted by Rowicki was repeated to open the Fifth International Piano Competition of Chopin's Music. In the same year the position of director and artistic manager was taken by Bohdan Wodiczko, who helped organize the 1956 First International Festival of Contemporary Music (Warszawska Jesień). The orchestra's repertoire was thus automatically enriched.

In 1958 Rowicki returned to his post with the Philharmonic, and the orchestra soon began to gain international fame. Rowicki introduced Tuesday chamber music concerts and organized performances for young audiences. International tours brought very positive reviews, and Rowicki was careful to include in programs for foreign audiences works by Polish composers. The orchestra began its numerous studio recordings, and the National Philharmonic Concert Hall hosted performances by the best world orchestras. The position of director and artistic manager was assumed in 1977 by Kazimierz Kord, whose leadership brought the orchestra to the highest national prominence. The orchestra continues in that role and today makes frequent broadcasts in addition to its many live performances.

RECORDING HISTORY AND SELECTIVE DISCOGRAPHY: The orchestra's first postwar recording, Chopin's First Piano Concerto with Fou Ts'ong as soloist, was conducted by Zdsisław Górzyński (1949) and edited by the Polskie Nagrania recording company (XL 0010). Since then the National Philharmonic has made many recordings for Polskie Nagrania, as well as for broadcast purposes.

Brahms, Piano Concerto No. 2 (Rubinstein/Rowicki): Polskie Nagrania SX 1862–62. Handel, *Messiah* (Kord): Polskie Nagrania SX 1691–1694. Handel, *Judas Maccabaeus* (Kord): Polskie Nagrania SX 1901–1904.

CHRONOLOGY OF MUSIC DIRECTORS: (Most were also chief conductors): Emil Młynarski, 1901–1905. Zygmunt Noskowski, 1906–1908. Henryk Malcer, 1908–1909. Grzegorz Fitelberg, 1909–1911. Zdzisław Birnbaum, 1911–1914, 1916–1918. Roman Chojnacki, 1918–1938. Jozef Ozimski, 1938–1939. Olgierd Straszyński, 1945–1946. Andrzej Panufnik, 1946–1947. Jan Maklakiewicz, 1947–1948. Witold Rudziński, 1948–1949. Władysław Raczkowski, 1949–1950. Witold Rowicki, 1950–1955. Bohdan Wodiczko, 1955–1958. Witold Rowicki, 1958–1977. Kazimierz Kord, 1977–present.

BIBLIOGRAPHY: Marian Gołębiewski, *Filharmonia w Warszawie* (Krakow: PWM, 1976). Zygmunt Mycielski, *Otwarcie roku jubileuszowego Filharmonii Narodowej* (Ruch

Muzyczny, 1976, nr 4). Andrzej Piber, *Narodziny Filharmonii Narodowej* (Ruch Muzyczny, 1976 nr 24). Teodor Zalewski, *Z powojennych dziejów Filharmonii* (Ruch Muzyczny, 1976 nr 23).

ACCESS: Filharmonia Narodowa, ul. Jasna 5, Warszawa. 26–72–81. Kazimierz Kord, Director and Artistic Manager.

JERZY ZAMUSZKO

Polish Chamber Orchestra and Sinfonia Varsovia

The Polish Chamber Orchestra (PCO; Polska Orkiestra Kameralna) was formed in 1972 originally as the accompaniment ensemble for performances of the Warsaw Chamber Opera. However, the musicians' ambitions to play concerts on their own led them to become artistically and organizationally independent. Since the formation of the ensemble under Jerzy Maksymiuk, its young, well-qualified musicians (most of whom are participants in international competitions) have worked very hard to attain their present high artistic level.

The ensemble is widely regarded as one of the most skilled and interesting of its type. Its fame began with its first tours abroad, to Italy in 1976 and to Great Britain in 1977. Subsequently, the orchestra visited most of the European countries as well as the United States, Canada, Japan, and Australia, playing in major halls and participating in major music festivals. The PCO regularly performs with eminent artists, among them Nikolas Kraemer, Neville Marriner, Yehudi Menuhin, Henryk Szeryng, Ruggiero Ricci, and Fou Ts'ong. PCO members perform as soloists as well. Having no permanent concert hall of its own, the PCO is typically a "guest orchestra," giving about 30 concerts per year in Poland and some 80 abroad. The ensemble also broadcasts concerts on radio and television and records for both Polish and foreign companies.

The group's wide-ranging repertoire includes masterpieces of the baroque, classical, and twentieth-century periods. The romantic composers produced little for chamber orchestra, and the period is represented in the PCO repertoire only by the Mendelssohn String Symphonies, Tchaikovsky's Serenade for Strings, the Grieg *Holberg Suite*, and the Dvořák Serenade. Many compositions have been written in recent years especially for the PCO.

The identifying characteristic of PCO interpretations is the great intensity of musicality gained through the unity that has arisen among the musicians and their leader during years of permanent work. Faultless proportioning of sound qualities combined with the ensemble's high pitch (A at 442 cps) make the orchestra's timbre rich and clear. Owing to their virtuosity, they play fast tempos showily, manifesting rhythm, dynamics, and effects of tone color. Far from "cool perfection," however, their music is full of tension and concentration, youthful mettle and controlled expression. Their interpretation of baroque and classical music is based on an aesthetic combining a love for period styles with the modern conceptions of musical beauty.

The PCO is a state orchestra subsidized by the government. However, during its tours abroad it is financially self-sufficient. It consists of 19 string players grouped 6–5–3–3–2, and its permanent rank is sometimes enlarged with paired winds to accommodate the repertoire (Mozart piano concertos, for example). The orchestra is headed by a music director and managing director. From the start it was led by Jerzy Maksymiuk, who, until leaving in 1986, functioned as both music director and conductor. Since 1982 Wojciech Michniewski has been principal guest conductor. Concertmaster Jan Stanienda is responsible for preparing the group technically in works to be led by guest conductors.

In August of 1983 the PCO performed together with Yehudi Menuhin and Mira Zakai for Pope John Paul II at Castel Gandolfo. Some months later Menuhin was invited by the PCO management to Warsaw to appear with the orchestra as both conductor and violinist. For this event the ensemble was obliged to expand its ranks by adding some young string and wind players. The concerts were met with such an enthusiastic response by critics and audience that the decision was made to give a permanent series of concerts by the enlarged group, which was subsequently named "Sinfonia Varsovia" (SV; "Varsovia" being the Latinate version of Warsaw). Menuhin was signed as principal guest conductor in the contracts of formation.

The SV has received many offers from throughout Europe, and Columbia Artists has engaged them for a tour of the United States and Canada. It has been invited to numerous festivals as well. Like the PCO, the SV is a state-subsidized ensemble acting under the aegis of the Art Center Studio in Warsaw.

Although Polish Chamber Orchestra personnel form the core of the Sinfonia Varsovia, the two are distinct organizational entities. The SV groups its 24 strings in the pattern 8–6–4–4–2 and comprises as well eight woodwinds, two trumpets, two horns, and tympani. The orchestra is administered by a managing director. It has no music director or permanent conductor, but rather a principal guest conductor (today as in the past, Yehudi Menuhin). The orchestra has been conducted by Volker Schmidt-Gertenbach, Claudio Abbado, and Jerzy Maksymiuk (among others), in addition to Yehudi Menuhin. Its repertoire, determined by guest conductors and managers, is almost unlimited, but music from the classical to contemporary periods is a bit more preferred. The orchestra recently performed, for example, *Prometeo* by Luigi Nono.

RECORDING HISTORY AND SELECTIVE DISCOGRAPHY: In the 1970s the Polish Chamber Orchestra entered into a five-year exclusive recording contract with EMI and about a dozen discs have been recorded since (Bach's *Brandenburg Concertos*, Vivaldi's *Four Seasons*, Haydn symphonies, Mozart serenades, and other works). Since the expiration of the exclusive clause for EMI, the PCO has recorded for other studios such as Penta Promotion (Holland), Addes (France), and MDG and Apperto (West Germany). The orchestra was twice awarded the Wiener Flöten Uhr for best recording of Mozart: in 1978 for the *Salzburg* Symphonies and in 1983 for piano concertos (with Christian Zacharias as soloist), both on EMI labels.

During its short history the Sinfonia Varsovia has recorded three discs in addition to its recordings for Polish radio and television. It has signed a five-record contract with the MDG recording company.

Bartók, *Divertimento*; Britten, *Frank Bridge Variations* (PCO, Maksymiuk): MDG G 1180. Grieg, *Holberg Suite*; Tchaikovsky, *Serenade for Strings* (PCO, Maksymiuk): Seraphim S–60355. Leclair, Violin Concerto; Tartini, Violin Concertos (PCO, Menuhin/Maksymiuk): Angel DS 38039. Mozart, Piano Concerto No. 12, K. 414 and Piano Concerto No. 14, K. 449. (PCO, Zacharias/Maksymiuk): EMI 1C 067–46437. Mozart, Symphony No. 35, K. 385, and Symphony No. 31, K. 297 (SV/Volker Schmidt-Gertenbach): Apperto 86004.

CHRONOLOGY OF MUSIC DIRECTORS: Jerzy Maksymiuk, 1972–1986.

BIBLIOGRAPHY: Interview with PCO Managing Director Franciszek Wybrańczyk. Miscellaneous PCO/SV documents.

ACCESS: Polska Orkiestra Kameralna and Sifonia Varsovia, Centrum Sztuki Studio, Palac Kultury i Nauki, 00–901 Warszawa. 20–43–69. Franciszek Wybrańczyk, Managing Director.

JACEK SZERSZENOWICZ

WROCLAW   (BRESLAU; 624,000)

Wroclaw State Philharmonic

The Wroclaw State Philharmonic originated in 1954, the result of efforts of a group of musicians active at that time. Wroclaw municipal authorities were the first to sponsor it, hence its original name, the Wroclaw Philharmonic Orchestra. Its concert activity was inaugurated on October 21, 1954. Having no permanent home, it usually gave concerts in the chambers of Wroclaw University or Technical University. In 1958 it was nationalized and given the name of Wroclaw State Philharmonic. Ten years later it acquired its own 501-seat hall (known by the name of the orchestra) on Swierczewskiego Street, where it has performed ever since.

Today's orchestra employs 95 musicians and two permanent conductors. The season comprises some 80 symphonic concerts, 16 chamber concerts, 18 concerts for students, numerous recitals, chamber concerts in clubs, and a great many school concerts: 72 performances for children of kindergartens in and around Wroclaw and nearly 300 chamber concerts in some 30 schools in the same region. Other recent events include special performances for the orchestra's 30th anniversary in 1984, participation in international festivals, and various tours.

Like the other philharmonic organizations in Poland, the Wroclaw Philharmonic is administered through the posts of manager, artistic director, and chief conductor(s), which generally, though not always, are manned by one individual. The Wroclaw State Philharmonic owes its artistic standard mainly to the late Adam Kopyciński and his students. Kopyciński, professor of conducting at Wroclaw Music Academy, led the orchestra since 1961, and one of his students, Tadeusz Strugała, was its director for over 11 years (to 1980). Since then the orchestra has been under the leadership of two of Strugała's students: Marek Pijarowski (its director, artistic manager, and primary chief conductor) and Mieczysław Gawroński (its secondary conductor). Kopyciński's school thus influenced the orchestra for more than 22 years, bringing it continuous and harmonious artistic development.

During the seven years between the management of Kopyciński and Strugała, the orchestra was led first by Radomir Reszka (1961–1963), then his professor, the late Włodzimierz Ormicki (1963–1965), and finally by Andrzej Markowski, a man of exceptional merit who made the Philharmonic one of the top Polish orchestras.

The Wroclaw State Philharmonic may be regarded as a unique institution in some respects. Its activity is distinguished by unusual incentive. It has founded three festivals, one of them international, which, even on the national scale, has had no precedence. The oldest is the Festival of Polish Modern Music, reaching back to 1962 and already organized 14 times. The next is the annual Days of Organ Music (1964–1969), changed by Markowski into ''Days of Organ and Clavecin Music'' (1969–1978). This tradition was broken by a fire at St. Elizabeth Church, which destroyed Wroclaw's best organ.

In 1966 Markowski initiated the annual International Oratorio/Cantata Festival ''Wratislavia Cantans,'' which, in 1980, was listed in the register of the European Association of Music Festivals (only two Polish festivals were ranked so high). Every September the festival draws thousands of artists, about 20 orchestras from all over the world, many specialized groups, and numerous soloists and conductors. Concert programs of oratorios, cantatas, masses, Stabat Maters, Magnificats, psalms, hymns, songs, madrigals, motets, and other forms are given in the ancient interiors of museums and churches. They are distinguished by high performance standards and are enhanced with lectures and symposia.

The Wroclaw Philharmonic introduced to Poland the practice of arranging a season's programs according to a common theme. Initiated by Markowski and developed on a large scale by Strugała, the practice has generated over 30 thematic cycles. Examples are the complete piano works of Bach, Ravel, or Szymanowski; the symphonic poems of Richard Strauss; Haydn's ''Paris'' and ''London'' symphonies; and basic cycles such as Beethoven's symphonies. One very original series, the Concert of Concerts, featured a single soloist appearing in three concerts. Another, Conductor Recitals, offered symphonic concerts without a soloist. The orchestra has also performed series directed toward high school students.

All concerts under the State Philharmonic's purview are included in a season's ticket, and audiences thus have a guaranteed entrance not only to Philharmonic concerts (many of which feature international soloists) but to performances by visiting symphonic and chamber orchestras as well. Many top ensembles have visited Wroclaw. The Philharmonic also has made numerous tours throughout Europe and has itself participated in many festivals.

The foundation of the chamber choir Cantores Minores Wratislavienses, another of Markowski's initiatives, is a further contribution of the Philharmonic to Wroclaw's cultural life. Under the leadership of the eminent choirmaster

Edmund Kajdasz, the singers enjoy an excellent reputation. Presently the choir functions as a separate institution.

The Philharmonic has also made a reputation for its publications, among which are the ''Wratislavia Cantans'' programs, which are considered collectors' items. The orchestra appears often on Polish radio and television, and its concerts are regularly taped. Although the Philharmonic has its own recording studio, few of its tapes have been made into records. The orchestra has won awards from both regional and national Polish institutions, including the Commander's Cross of the Order of Poland's Resurrection in 1984.

CHRONOLOGY OF MUSIC DIRECTORS: (Chief Conductors): Adam Kopyciński, 1954–1961. Radomir Reszka, 1961–1963. Włodzimierz Ormicki, 1963–1965. Andrzej Markowski, 1965–1968. Tadeusz Strugała, 1969–1980. Marek Pijarowski, 1980–present.

BIBLIOGRAPHY: Wroclaw State Philharmonic, miscellaneous publications, 1954–1985.

ACCESS: Wroclaw State Philharmonic, U1. Swierczewskiego 19, 55–044 Wroclaw. 442001.

EWA KOFIN

Portugal ─────────────────────────────

Gulbenkian Orchestra

The Gulbenkian Orchestra (GO) is one of the most important ensembles of Portugal. It was founded by—and continues under financing and direction of—the Gulbenkian Foundation. The Foundation was created in 1956 as willed by Calouste Sarkis Gulbenkian (b. Istanbul, 1869; d.1955), who was a philanthropist with interests in the arts. Centered in Lisbon, the Foundation supports artistic endeavors in numerous countries. In addition to the Gulbenkian Orchestra, other orchestras performing regularly in Portugal include the Symphony Orchestras of the Portuguese Radio in both Lisbon and Porto, and the São Carlos Theatre Orchestra.

The GO's concert season from October through May consists of biweekly concerts performed at the 1,200-seat Grand Auditorium in the Foundation's main edifice in Lisbon. In addition to its concert season in Lisbon, the GO has yearly concert tours throughout Portugal and other parts of the world. Its foreign tours have included countries in Europe, Africa, South America, and the Near and Far East, including China and India. It has also done recording, with 24 discs to its name, several of which include Portuguese composers and/or soloists.

The nucleus of the GO was established by the Gulbenkian Foundation in 1962 with the aim of presenting regular concerts to Portuguese audiences. At first comprising 11 strings plus harpsichord, the initial ensemble was gradually increased until 1971 to its present size of 41. In the same year it was officially designated the GO. Due to the shortage of qualified Portuguese instrumentalists, the GO initially hired a majority of its members from outside Portugal. However, foreign members were gradually replaced, and at present 85% of the musicians are Portuguese. Throughout its history the GO has invited an international array of notable guest conductors and soloists, among them some of the very first rank.

The music department of the Gulbenkian Foundation, the GO's only sponsor, oversees all of the orchestra's activities and carries out the necessary administrative tasks. In addition, the "maestro titular" or "titled conductor" is primarily responsible for artistic matters and collaborates with the Foundation's music department on many decisions.

The repertoire performed by the GO is influenced by its size, location, and traditional instrumental makeup. Ranging from the baroque to the twentieth century, it generally excludes those nineteenth-century compositions requiring a large orchestra. A special effort is made to incorporate within the regular concert season Portuguese compositions from various epochs as well as contemporary music by Portuguese and other composers. Contemporary music is also offered daily in May for a fortnight in a series named "Encounters of Contemporary Music." Some modern compositions were commissioned by the Foundation and/or premiered by the GO. Examples include Luciano Berio's *Recital (for Cathy)*, Darius Milhaud's *Musique pour Lisbonne*, Krzysztof Penderecki's *Canticum Canticorum Salomonis*, Iannis Xenakis's *Cendrées*, and works by Frederico de Freitas, Armando José Fernanes, Joly Braga Santos, Constança Capdeville, Emmanuel Nunes, Jorge Peixinho, Filipe Pires, Álvaro Cassuto, Cándido Lima, Maria de Lourdes Martis, and Paulo Brandão.

The GO collaborates in several performances with the Gulbenkian Chorus, a 20-year-old ensemble also sponsored by the Foundation. Portuguese musical life is also enriched by the orchestra's various chamber music ensembles, which perform independently. These include a 13-member chamber orchestra, two string quartets, a wind quintet, and a wind octet. The cultural impact of the GO has been considerable, especially in Lisbon. Its concert season attracts a diversity of listeners and has become a staple of Lisbon's cultural life. Several orchestra members teach at the Lisbon Conservatory and other musical institutions in and around the city.

RECORDING HISTORY AND SELECTIVE DISCOGRAPHY: The GO began recording in 1966. Of its 24 recordings, six are dedicated to Portuguese music, comprising part of the "Portugalia Musica" series of the Gulbenkian Foundation, produced in collaboration with Philips and DGG Archiv Producktion. Records of non-Portuguese music, a few featuring Portuguese soloists, were produced by the Foundation in collaboration with Erato. Several GO discs have won international awards, including three Grand Prix International du Disque (Académie Charles Cros): 1972, 1974, 1980. GO recordings for Philips and Archiv are no longer available, but most Erato recordings are in some European countries. A complete list of GO recordings is available from the Foundation.

Charpentier, *Beatus vir* (Corboz; Gulbenkian Chorus): Erato STU 70943. Mendelssohn, Psalms Nos. 42 and 95 (Corboz; Gulbenkian Chorus): Erato STU 71101. Mozart, *Requiem*: (Corboz; Gulbenkian Chorus): Erato STU 70943.

CHRONOLOGY OF MUSIC DIRECTORS: ("Maestros Titulares"): Lamberto Baldi, 1962–1963. Urs Voegelin, 1963–1964. Renato Ruotolo, 1964–1965. Trajan Popesco,

1965. Adrian Sunshine, 1966–1967. Gianfranco Rivoli, 1968–1971. Werner Andreas Albert, 1971–1973. Michael Tabachnik, 1973–1975. Juan Pablo Izquierdo, 1976–1977. Claudio Scimone, 1979–present.

BIBLIOGRAPHY: Interview with Gulbenkian Foundation Assistant Director of the Department of Music Dr. Carlos Pontes Leca, 1985. *Catalogo de Edicões* (Lisbon: Fundação Calouste Gulbenkian, 1984). GO Program Notes. "Gulbenkian Foundation," *New Grove Dictionary of Music and Musicians* (London: Macmillan, 1980).

ACCESS: Gulbenkian Orchestra, Fundação Calouste Gulbenkian, Servico de Música, Avenida de Berna, 1000 Lisboa, Portugal. (351–1) 735131/730160. Dr. Luis Pereira Leal, Director.

SALWA EL-SHAWAN CASTELO-BRANCO

Romania

George Enescu Philharmonic Orchestra in Bucharest

Founded in 1868 and today comprising 110 musicians, the George Enescu Philharmonic Orchestra (GEPO) is part of the organization known as the George Enescu Philharmonic, a music complex established by the Romanian government in 1950. The Philharmonic organization also includes a 60-member choir, virtuoso vocal and instrumental soloists, and chamber ensembles formed by the GEPO's musicians: two chamber orchestras; two string quartets; a baroque woodwind trio; the Armonia brass quintet; an early music ensemble, the Consortium Violae; and Musica Nova, a contemporary music group. These may perform alone or in collective recitals with the GEPO.

Annually the organization is responsible for over 400 concerts of diverse types. The GEPO subscription season includes two weekly concerts with a repeated program and several special concerts from mid-September until early July. Chamber concerts and sound/light shows on music-history themes take place during the summer months. Performances are held in the Romanian Athenaeum built in 1888, a beautiful, neoclassical structure with superb acoustics in a circular hall seating 810. Chamber concerts are held in the Athenaeum's two smaller halls. Audience figures reflect a steady growth, and they reached an annual total of 150,000 during the 1984–1985 season. GEPO concert subscribers are well educated, and many of their families have been subscription holders for generations. The orchestra has been described as one of Europe's best, and its playing has been characterized as brilliant, sonorous, and precise.

The administration of the GEPO is overseen by an artistic council of ten people led by Philharmonic Director Mihai Brediceanu and an administrative managerial board of the Philharmonic comprising seven people. Their program planning and philosophical direction adheres to a balanced selection of the fundamental works of classical, romantic, and contemporary composers. Additionally, about 40 to 45 outstanding symphonic works of contemporary Romanian composers are presented each season, 25% to 30% of which are premiere performances. The GEPO has traditionally aimed at preserving and cultivating the nation's musical heritage.

The varied and challenging Philharmonic programs attest to a flourishing musical institution. A representative program of May 1985 contained Alfred Alessandrescu's *Autumn Dusk*, Arnold Schoenberg's *Transfigured Night*, the Luigi Boccherini Cello Concerto in D Major, and Richard Strauss's *Til Eulenspiegel*. Unique programming possibilities are made available, since the state subsidizes 70% of the budget, with the remaining 30% deriving largely from ticket sales. The Romanian public can continually be exposed to new and/or unusual works. Audience reaction is taken into consideration and ascertained by questionnaires distributed at the end of the concert season.

Young people's concerts, a significant part of the Philharmonic's activity, are structured by age group and include theme-cycles related to the school curriculum: "Genres and Forms of Instrumental and Symphonic Music," for example. These are held every Sunday morning, mid-September to late June, for general and high school students. There are also ten monthly concerts, at accessible prices, for university students.

Bucharest is an important cultural, scientific, and economic center (as well as the capital city) of Romania, a country of music and music lovers, supporting 15 symphony orchestras. The nation was a monarchy from 1866 until December of 1947, when it was declared a People's Republic. In the summer of 1948 its industry and agriculture were nationalized, and in 1965 it was declared a Socialist Republic.

The George Enescu Philharmonic Orchestra, originally known as the "Filarmonica Romana" (The Romanian Philharmonic Society) was created for the purpose of exposing the Romanian people to symphonic music, including that of young Romanian composers. Court orchestras had existed in eighteenth-century Romania, and in the nineteenth century "Symphonic Concerts" were established. In 1865 the Bucharest Conservatory Orchestra was formed by a remarkable musician, Conservatory Professor Eduard Wachmann, who conducted its first concert on April 1, 1866. The group's first publicly acknowledged concert, however, was three weeks later, at the National Theatre, and included works of Haydn, Mozart, and Beethoven performed by 30 musicians.

By 1868, when the Romanian Philharmonic Society was formed, the orchestra had grown to 56 musicians, mostly professionals, with first chairs occupied by heads of their instruments at the Conservatory. With public donations, a permanent cultural palace, the Romanian Athenaeum, was built; it was inaugurated on March 5, 1889, with a performance of Beethoven, Schumann, Schubert, and Wagner, to a capacity audience. Eduard Wachmann, who headed the new Philharmonic and was to remain until 1906, gave the group its early direction. Under

Wachmann concert life blossomed; he developed orchestral programs that included classical, romantic, and contemporary composers, in addition to festivals devoted to Beethoven, Berlioz, and Wagner. An especially important event occurred on March 15, 1898—the debut of 17-year-old Romanian composer/ conductor George Enescu, violinist and child prodigy, who conducted on that occasion his Romanian Poem No. 1. The orchestra was now well on its way to achieving its educational goals, including its prime concern, attaining recognition for Romania and its people as rightful members of cultured Europe.

From 1906 to 1920 the young, talented Romanian conductor Dimitrie Dinicu further diversified the orchestra's repertoire with more frequent performances of Brahms, Tchaikovsky, Dvořák, Franck, Debussy, Ravel, Richard Strauss, Prokofiev, Schoenberg, and Shostakovich, as well as contemporary Romanian composers. Enescu's Second and Third Symphonies premiered in 1915 and 1919.

The orchestra's concert schedule was interrupted during World War I, but Dinicu and Enescu resumed conducting once again in 1919. Due to Dinicu's illness, a new conductor was appointed, Georges Georgescu, a student of Arthur Nikisch, who was already famous in European circles.

Georgescu's period with the orchestra, from 1920 to 1949 and again from 1954 to 1964, is considered the third stage of its development, for by the end of his tenure he had effectively elevated the orchestra to meet the highest standards. Initially he expanded its size to 80 musicians, and from 1923 to 1943 the orchestra was obliged to contribute to all performances of the Bucharest Opera House. Programming was further developed, and more premieres of Romanian composers' works took place, including Mihail Jora's Symphony (1937) and Dinu Lipatti's *Concertino* (1939).

Successful tours were undertaken to much of Eastern and Western Europe, the U.S.S.R., and England. An international dimension was further advanced by the frequent guest appearances of conductors and soloists of the highest renown, including Pierre Monteux, Ernest Ansermet, Herbert von Karajan, Béla Bartók, Yehudi Menuhin, and a great many more. During this period too a good number of Romanian virtuoso performers appeared with the orchestra, some of whom—such as the conductor Sergiu Celibidache—would go on to make important international contributions themselves. The increase in audience interest during this period is evident from increased attendance—from 15,000 in 1938–1939 to 62,000 in 1952–1953.

The social and cultural objectives of the Philharmonic were greatly advanced after 1945 when a 60-member choir, permanent soloists, two chamber orchestras, and a musicology department were added to the institution. In 1954 the Romanian government recognized the institution's growth, bestowing the title of "Merited Artistic Group" upon the Philharmonic Orchestra, and on May 4, 1955, after the death of George Enescu, the government renamed the orchestra the "George Enescu Philharmonic."

The musical institution housed in the Athenaeum had been carefully planned to meet its educational objectives, while steadily diversifying its activities, concerts, recitals, and "lesson concerts" for students. An example is the triennial Geroge Enescu International Festival established in 1958 by the Romanian government; the GEPO participates actively in its programs.

From 1964 to 1968 the GEPO's head was conductor Mircea Basarab. On the occasion of its centennial in 1968 the GEPO was awarded the order of "Cultural Merit" first class by the Romanian government. From 1968 to 1972 the GEPO's conductor was the composer Dumitru Capoianu, who was followed until 1982 by violinist Ion Voicu. Well-known guest soloists and conductors continued to appear.

Presently the GEPO has three permanent conductors, while four to six additional guest conductors and 30 guest soloists, foreign and Romanian, perform each season. Mihai Brediceanu, with the GEPO since 1958, has been director of the George Enescu Philharmonic Institution since 1982. A scholar, composer, and international guest conductor, Brediceanu favors conducting large-scale, monumental symphonic works. Among the Romanian works he has premiered with the GEPO is Wilhelm Berger's Concerto for Violin, Cello, and Orchestra (1983). Mircea Cristescu, GEPO conductor since 1962, actively conducts throughout Romania. A professor at the Bucharest Conservatory, guest lecturer, and author, Cristescu is known for his varied, rich concert programs. He premiered Theodor Grigoriu's *Symphony Cantabile* in 1954. Mircea Basarab, a composer and GEPO conductor since 1962, also teaches, writes, lectures, and guest-conducts. His repertoire ranges from the preclassical period through the twentieth century, and he too has premiered Romanian works, for example Pascal Bentoiu's First Symphony (1966). All three conductors have led the GEPO on its foreign tours. Especially successful among recent tours throughout Europe was the orchestra's visit to the 1981 Festival of Lucerne.

The cultural and educational impact and the wide scope of the Philharmonic's highly creative activities continue to enrich the cultural life of the Romanian people and also make the George Enescu Philharmonic Institution and all its musical organizations a deserving component of the best in international culture.

RECORDING HISTORY AND SELECTIVE DISCOGRAPHY: The GEPO has made numerous recordings since 1926 with Romanian conductors George Georgescu, Brediceanu, Cristescu, Basarab, and Constantin Silvestri, and guest conductors Sir John Barbirolli, John Pritchard, and Benzi, among others, under the Romanian Electrecord (ECE) label as well as for Deese, Company-Paris, EMI-Pathé-Marconi, and HMV. These recordings span from the preclassical to the twentieth-century musical periods. The complete symphonies of Beethoven were recorded under Georgescu's direction.

Berlioz, *Symphonie fantastique* (Brediceanu): ECE 02447. Cuclin, Symphony No. 13 (Basarab): ECE 02326. Dumitrescu, *Tudor Vladimirescu*, Part 1 (Georgescu): ECE 035. Enescu, Rhapsodies Nos. 1 and 2, Op. 11 (Georgescu): ECE 23. Enescu, Suite for Orchestra No. 1, Op. 9 (Georgescu): ECE 91. Enescu, Symphony No. 1 (Georgescu): ECE 58; (Brediceanu): ECE 01037.

CHRONOLOGY OF MUSIC DIRECTORS: Eduard Wachmann, 1868–1906. Dimitrie Dinicu, 1906–1920. Georges Georgescu, 1920–1949. George Cocea, 1944–1945. Emanoil Ciomac, 1945–1947. Constantin Silvestri, 1947–1953. Georges Georgescu, 1954–1964. Mircea Basarab, 1964–1968. Dumitru Capoianu, 1968–1972. Ion Voicu, 1971–1982. Mihai Brediceanu, 1982–present.

BIBLIOGRAPHY: Interviews with GEPO Arts Council Consultant Dinu Petrescu, Bucharest, 1985. Viorel Cosma, *Filarmonica "George Enescu" din Bucureşti, 1868–1968* (*George Enescu Philharmonic in Bucharest*) (Bucharest, 1968). Viorel Cosma, *Romania Muzicala* (*Musical Romania*) (Bucharest: Musical Edition, 1980). *The George Enescu Philharmonic in Bucharest* (Bucharest: Scientific and Encyclopedic Publishing House, 1985). GEPO program collection.

ACCESS: George Enescu Philharmonic Orchestra, Romanian Athenaeum, 1 Franklin Street, Bucharest. 70149. (011–400) 14–41–83. Radu Gheciu, GEPO Adjunct Artistic Director. Petree Codreanu, Persida Espirescu, and Dinu Petrescu, GEPO Artistic Counselors.

VIOLET VAGRAMIAN-NISHANIAN

Singapore —————————————

SINGAPORE (2,517,000)

Singapore Symphony Orchestra

One of the most important orchestras of Southeast Asia, the Singapore Symphony Orchestra (SSO) is the first and only professional symphony orchestra in Singapore, succeeding several semiprofessional orchestras of the past.

The SSO is headed by a music director and a general manager. Choo Hoey has been music director since the orchestra's founding in 1979. Management staff hires and negotiates with musicians and soloists; it sees to general administrative functions and public relations. Supported by both the Singapore government and the private sector, the SSO employs both domestic and foreign players. The SSO performs regularly at the National Trade Union Center and the Victoria Concert Hall.

The SSO performs a broad repertoire with concert programs usually aiming at a balance between the conventional classics and modern works. It is one of the few symphony orchestras outside China to perform a good many Chinese works, although it has been said by some critics that its performances of them are not authentic. *The Butterfly Lovers* violin concerto by He and Chen and *The Dance of Yao* by Liu and Mao are among its more popular Chinese works. The general public considers the SSO to be the representative musical institution of this island nation. Many foreign players and soloists also look to the SSO as a major opportunity to embark on a career in Asia as well as in the rest of the world. To date the SSO has engaged a wealth of internationally acclaimed soloists from Asia, Europe, and the United States, including Liu Shi-kun, Fou Ts'ong, Ruggiero Ricci, and others. It has toured Southeast Asia and Europe.

Numerous semiprofessional orchestras have existed in Singapore since the 1960s. The establishment of the SSO in 1979 was considered a giant step forward taken by the government and supporting groups in recognizing the importance of cultural development to societal growth. Choo Hoey, the SSO's first music director, was instrumental in establishing the orchestra. A Singapore Sinfonia Company was formally established to manage the SSO, and the music director has personally been actively involved in recruiting players from all over the world, particularly from the United States and the People's Republic of China. In 1980 the Singapore Symphony Choir was established. With a current roster of 80, it plans to expand its membership to about 100.

CHRONOLOGY OF MUSIC DIRECTORS: Choo Hoey, 1979–present.

BIBLIOGRAPHY: Personal communications with Singapore music critics. Numerous articles in Singapore newspapers.

ACCESS: Singapore Sinfonia Company, Victoria Concert Hall, Empress Place, Singapore 0617. 338–1230. Henry Lau, General Manager.

SIN-YAN SHEN

Spain _____

MADRID (3,188,000)

National Orchestra of Spain

The National Orchestra of Spain (ONE: Orquesta Nacional de España) is the nation's most prestigious orchestra. The geographical compass of the ONE is all of Spain, even though its regular concert season takes place in Madrid, where it has performed since 1966 in the 2,400-seat Royal Theatre, the former opera house, which was remodeled and converted into a concert hall. (A plan is afoot to reconvert the Royal into an opera house, with the ONE to move to the much larger Auditorium on Prince de Vergara Street, now under construction.

The ONE offers some 90 concerts in Madrid during the annual season. Adding to those performances in festivals and tours, the total comes to about 120 per year to live audiences numbering about 250,000. The regular concert season runs from October through April, and weekly programs take place on Friday and Saturday afternoons and Sunday mornings in the Royal Theatre. The ONE performs the standard international repertoire and contemporary works but also recognizes the importance of Spanish music by playing classical and modern Spanish composers' works rendered by Spanish performers. In its foreign tours the ONE usually performs Spanish music with folk roots, as is expected by foreign audiences, but lately it has also performed the works of modern national composers who are less identifiably "Spanish."

Administratively, the ONE is under the authority of the National Institute of Visual Arts and Music (INAEM: Instituto Nacional de las Artes Escenicas y de la Musica) within the ministry of Culture. As the National Orchestra and Chorus of Spain (the complete name of the organization, which also has a large professional chorus, conducted at present by two chorus masters), the ONE has a manager, an artistic coordinator, and 15 office personnel (among them an archivist and other specialists who report to the secretary). The ONE maintains a roster of 98 musicians and operates under the combined orchestra/chorus budget of 481,000,000 pesetas. The relationship between management and the musicians is coordinated by an inspector elected by the orchestra every two years. There is a committee of five orchestra members and a governing board from the orchestra to deal with matters of great importance.

The arrival of Jesus Lopéz Cobos as music director (following some years without a regular conductor) has brought about noticeable improvement in the internal discipline and organization of the orchestra, even though the latter improved when the composer Tomás Marco served as general manager. Better judgment in the makeup of programs can also be noted. Nevertheless, the repertoire is still rather conservative, featuring classical and romantic works to a great extent, with very little modern music by foreign composers and little baroque music. Contemporary Spanish composers are played, however, and there exists a "Center for the Diffusion of Contemporary Music" within the INAEM charged with programming new works.

The ONE is a center of Spanish musical life, and in turn the aspirations of many young instrumentalists revolve around it, particularly with regard to the National Youth Orchestra of Spain (JONDE: Joven Orquesta Nacional de España). The ONE maintains relationships with many cultural organizations and broadcasts courses for adults and students in collaboration with the Cultural Council of the Community of Madrid, under whose auspices rehearsals, musical explications, and similar events are presented.

All through the ONE's history diverse chamber groups have emerged, though unofficially. At present there are, for example, the Spanish Chamber Orchestra (conducted by ONE Concertmaster Victor Martín and dedicated principally to baroque and contemporary music), and the Town of Madrid Orchestra directed by Mercedes Padilla.

To explain the ONE's origins, it is necessary to go back to the middle of the nineteenth century, when a restlessness for pure symphonic music (apart from the operatic) began to stir in Madrid. In 1859 Francisco Asenjo Barbieri conducted an orchestra of 96 and a chorus of 93 in the Zarzuela Theatre; the following year the Mutual Aid Artistic Musical Society (Sociedad Artístico Musical de Socorros Mutuos) was established. This Concert Society, whose executive committee consisted of Hilarión Eslava, José Inzegna, and Joaquín Gaztambide, organized concerts of some importance (for example, in 1862 Jesús Monasterio conducted the March from *Tannhäuser*, which Barbieri had brought from Germany). The success of these concerts led Barbieri to found the Concert Society, inaugurated on April 16, 1866, with a varied program in the fashion of the period, featuring Beethoven's Symphony No. 7. The Concert Society Orchestra aroused the taste for music in the capital. It was conducted by the finest Spanish musicians of the time and also by foreigners such as Luigi Mancinelli, Charles Lamoureux, Camille Saint-Saëns, and Richard Strauss.

The failure of the Lyric Theatre at the turn of the century led to the collapse of the Concert Society; upon its disbandment its best musicians joined the new Symphony Orchestra of Madrid (Orquesta Sinfóncia de Madrid), which first appeared in Madrid's Royal Theatre in February of 1904. Its leadership quickly fell to Enrique Fernandez Arbós (1868–1939), a distinguished figure who introduced contemporary music to the people of Madrid.

Alongside the Symphony Orchestra of Madrid (performing in the National Zarzuela Theatre) was the Philharmonic Orchestra of Madrid founded and conducted by Bartolomé Perez Casas (1873–1956), a man who premiered 200 symphonic works by Spanish composers during his tenure. The National Orchestra of Spain emerged from the fusion of these two orchestras in 1940, shortly after the Civil War (1936–1939); Perez Casas became its conductor. The ONE made its debut performance on March 13, 1942, in Madrid's Maria Guerrero Theatre.

Perez Casas stepped down as director in 1947, and on January 2 of that year the tenure of Ataulfo Argenta (1913–1958) began, under whose leadership the ONE attained international status and began regular international tours. During that era the ONE was strengthened as a symphonic ensemble and maintained close relations with conductors Carl Schuricht and Ernest Ansermet.

After the death of Argenta and a period without a regular conductor, Rafael Frühbeck de Burgos took charge of the orchestra's musical direction. During this period the ONE performed many concerts both in and out of Spain, with notable successes in Italy, Switzerland, Germany, Belgium, France, Portugal, Hong Kong, Mexico, and other countries. On February 27, 1976, Queen Sofia accepted the honorary presidency of the orchestra. The most famous conductors have performed with the orchestra, as have the most prestigious soloists.

Antoni Ros-Marbá succeeded Frühbeck de Burgos for three seasons, 1978–1981, and following Marbá the orchestra had no regular conductor, although both Jesus Lopéz Cobos and Peter Maag held the title of principal visiting conductor. Since January 1, 1984, Jesus Lopéz Cobos (like Frühbeck de Burgos, born in the Castille-Léon region) has been the regular conductor, with Luis Aguirre Colón as assistant conductor and the Chilean maestro Maximiano Valdés as principal visiting conductor.

RECORDING HISTORY AND SELECTIVE DISCOGRAPHY: There are many recordings of the ONE from the time of Ataulfo Argenta and of Rafael Frühbeck de Burgos, sometimes with hypothetical names, to avoid problems with the Franco government (for example, the many recordings of zarzuelas done by Argenta on the Columbia label, reedited several times). Some of the exceptional historical recordings are Tomás Breton's *La verbena de la Paloma* (Columbia, SCE 966); José Maria Usandizaga's *Las golondrinas* (Columbia C30016/17); or Francisco Asénjo Barbieri's *Jugar con fuego* (Columbia C30029).

Falla, *Noches en los jardines de España* (Argenta): Columbia SCLL 14000. Palau, Guitar Concerto (Alonso/Yepes): London 6201; Columbia CS 8565. Parish-Alvars, Concerto for Harp and Orchestra (Frühbeck de Burgos/Nicanor Zabaleta): EMI 065–002.514; Angel S–37042. Maurice Ohana, Guitar Concerto; Rodrigo, *Fantasia para un gentilhombre* (Frühbeck de Burgos/Yepes): London 6356. Works of Arambarri, Gerhard, José, Turina (Ros-Marbá): Inter-American OEA–008.

CHRONOLOGY OF MUSIC DIRECTORS: Bartolomé Perez Casas, 1942–1946.
Ataulfo Argenta, 1947–1958. (Guest conductors, 1958–1962.) Rafael Frühbeck de Burgos, 1962–1978. Antoni Ros-Marbá, 1978–1981. (Guest conductors, 1981–1984.) Jesus Lopéz Cobos, 1984–present.

BIBLIOGRAPHY: Luis Alonso, *40 años Orquesta Nacional* (Madrid, 1982). Enrique Fernandez Arbós, *Arbós: memorias, 1863–1903* (Madrid, 1963). *Ataulfo Argenta, el músico, el hombre, el mito:* Exhibition Catalog (Santander, 1981). Antonio Fernandez-Cid, *Ataulfo Argenta* (Madrid, 1958). Antonio Fernandez-Cid, *Músicos qu fueron nuestros amigos* (Madrid, 1967). Enrique Franco, "Concierto homenaje a Bartolomé Perez Casas . . . en el trigésimo aniversario de su fallecimiento," program notes (Madrid, 18 January 1986). Gaspar Gomez de la Serna, *Gracias y desgracias del Teatro Real* (Madrid, 1976).

ACCESS: Orquesta y Coro Nacionales de España, Calle Carlos III s/n, 28013 Madrid. 2473242. Javier Muñiz, Manager. Ricardo Parada, Artistic Coordinator.

ANDRÉS RUIZ TARAZONA
TRANS. DAVID BRADT

Radio-Television Symphony Orchestra of Spain

The Radio-Television Symphony Orchestra of Spain (ORTVE: La Orquesta Sinfónica de Radiotelevisión Española; also known abroad as the Spanish National Radio and Television Orchestra) was created in 1964 by an order of the Ministry of Information and Tourism to increase cultural activities appropriate to the department with regard to symphonic music.

The official introduction of the ORTVE took place on May 27, 1965, in the Zarzuela Theatre in Madrid, under the direction of Igor Markevitch, who later was made its honorary musical director. Under the guidance of this distinguished conductor, the young group soon acquired prestige through its numerous performances in cities throughout Spain, thanks also to the National Radio of Spain and Spanish Television broadcasts of its concerts, both live and recorded.

During its normal season (October through April), the ORTVE offers a total of 46 concerts (23 programs taking place on Thursday afternoons and Friday evenings in the Royal Theatre of Madrid). To these must be added the dress rehearsals on Wednesdays, open to the public at 75 pesetas per ticket, and the numerous special concerts, Spanish and foreign tours, festivals, and recordings made expressly for radio and television. However, the ORTVE does not have its own venue for rehearsals (it uses the hall of Arts Promotion) nor for concerts (the Royal Theatre is the seat of the National Orchestra of Spain*), a situation creating at times an obstacle to superior performance.

The ORTVE also includes a professional chorus, presently directed by Pascual Ortega. Under the authority of Spanish Public Radio/Television (Ente Público Radio Televisión Española), the ORTVE has a management committee made up of representatives of the orchestra and chorus to deal with relations with the administration. There are 15 administrators. The general representative of the ORTVE is Miguel Alonso, a composer. Each orchestral musician receives a monthly recompense of 160,000 pesetas. Several informal chamber groups have emerged from within the ORTVE; among them a brass ensemble and the Spanish Quintet (piano and strings) have distinguished themselves in Spanish music circles.

The orchestra tours frequently, having performed in France, Britain, Belgium, and North and Central America. In 1971 the ORTVE made a long tour through the United States and Mexico with both critical and popular success. In the spring of 1975 an invitation came for a second tour of the United States, which was immediately followed by performances in London and Brussels. In 1978 the ORTVE was invited to participate in the International Cervantes Festival in Guanajuato, Mexico and later performed in Mexico City and Puebla. A tour of Switzerland in 1986 brought critical acclaim for the ensemble's interpretation of Mozart, Joaquín Rodrigo, and Manuel de Falla, as well as the purity of its performances. At present the ORTVE is preparing to depart for invited tours of Japan and the Federal Republic of Germany.

The ORTVE has also been a leader in its service to contemporary Spanish music, with premiere performances of the works of several national composers. Among these are works by young composers and the winners of the annual Queen Sofia Prize for composition (Joan Guinjoan, 1984; Claudio Prieto, 1985; Witold Lutosławski, 1986). The orchestra frequently collaborates with universities, city councils, and autonomous entities.

The first regular conductors were Antoni Ros-Marbá and Enrique Garcia Asensio, who obtained the position through competition. Ros-Marbá left the orchestra in 1967 and was replaced by Odón Alonso, who was also selected through merit competition. Asensio and Alonso left the ORTVE on October 1, 1984. The next regular conductor was Miguel Angel Gomez Martinez, a Spanish maestro who for six years had been the regular conductor of the Vienna Opera, and who is a professor in his native city of Granada. In this Andalusian conductor's two years with the orchestra, its prestige has grown considerably, and there have been improvements in the string section and in the performances of more technically difficult passages. Foreign guest conductors have included Lorin Maazel, Sergiu Comissiona, Mstislav Rostropovich, and others.

RECORDING HISTORY AND SELECTIVE DISCOGRAPHY: In addition to its routine recordings for rebroadcast, the ORTVE has recorded for several commercial labels, including Deutsche Grammophon, Philips, RCA, and Hispavox. In 1975 and 1976 *Record World* awarded the ORTVE the Orchestra of the Year prize. Its most important recorded legacy is the collection *Music of Spain*, which includes in a six-record album works of Manuel de Falla, Emmanuel Chabrier, Maurice Ravel, Isaac Albeniz, Ernesto Halffter, Enrique Granados, Federico Mompou, Tomas Luis de Victoria, Jerónimo Giminez, Amadeo Vives, Tomas Bretón, Federica Chueca, Francisco Asenjo Barbieri, and others, conducted by Markevitch (Philips 671105/06).

Joaquín Rodrigo, *Aranjuez Concerto* and *Fantasia para un gentilhombre* (Alonso/ Yepes): DG 139440.

CHRONOLOGY OF MUSIC DIRECTORS: Antoni Ros-Marbá, 1965–1967. Enrique Garcia Asensio, 1965–1984. Odón Alonso, 1968–1984. Miguel Angel Gomez Martinez, 1984-present.

BIBLIOGRAPHY: Miguel Angel Gomez Martinez, "Veinte brillantes años de la Orquesta Sinfónica de Radiotelevisión Española," *Diario "ABC" de Madrid*, 26 May 1985. *Orquesta Sinfónica y Coro de la Radio y Television Espanola*, Twentieth Anniversary Publication (Madrid: Ministerio de Información y Turismo, 1970). Program of the Royal Theatre, 27 May 1985. ORTVE documents.

ACCESS: Orquesta Sinfónica y Coro de Radiotelevisión Española, Calle Sor Angela de la Cruz 2, Edificio Cuzco 3, 7th floor, 28020 Madrid. 2707003. Miguel Alonso, General Representative.

ANDRÉS RUIZ TARAZONA
TRANS. DAVID BRADT

Sweden _____

GÖTEBORG (693,000*)

Göteborgs Symfoniker

The Göteborgs Symfoniker (GSO: Gothenburg Symphony) is one of Scandinavia's oldest. It performs about 90 concerts per year and reaches some 110,000 concertgoers. Six subscription series are offered, as well as additional radio performances, tours in western Sweden, and guest performances at home and abroad. The orchestra makes several records per year. At events in the Scandinavium Sports Arena, it plays before as many as 14,000 spectators.

Since 1969 the orchestra has been permanently lodged in Göteborg's Teater-och Konsert AB, which houses both the Stora Teatern (Great Theatre) and Konserthuset (Concert Hall). The Concert Hall, on Götaplatsen, is considered one of the world's foremost concert halls, ranking with Amsterdam's Concertgebouw, Boston's Symphony Hall, and the great hall of the Vienna Musikverein. It was inaugurated on October 4, 1935, to replace the earlier one (1905), which had burned down on Friday, January 13, 1928. Architect Nils Einar Eriksson's entirely wood-panelled hall, built in a fan shape with pleated walls on either side, accommodates 1,290 listeners.

The orchestra is financed primarily through the state and the municipality. The Volvo Automobile Company, which has its headquarters in Göteborg, paid for (among other things) the orchestra's transportation expenses for its recent United States tour. It has also undertaken for the years 1983–1988 to defray the expenses of the orchestra's build-up from 78 to 100 players, provided that the municipality thereafter bears the expenses for the new employees. The Concert Hall employs 115 persons, and the budget totals Kr 20 million.

For many years the orchestra has participated in concert planning and program scheduling. Administrative work is handled by the Concert Hall manager and a sales department. An orchestra manager deals with employee and personnel problems. The present head conductor, Neeme Järvi, directs somewhat more than every fourth concert, with guest conductors taking care of the rest.

Through grants the orchestra has been able to found a library of musical scores of nearly 10,000 orchestral works and thus two-thirds of the repertoire is played without renting music. In order to maintain continuity and steady activity after the remarkable rejuvenation of the orchestra that has occurred in recent years, there has been an effort during the 1980s to establish a basic repertoire of standard works, with an emphasis on composers such as Jean Sibelius, Carl Nielsen, Wilhelm Stenhammar, and Anton Bruckner. The orchestra tunes to A at 442 cps.

Since the end of the 1960s there has been cooperation with school administrations to see that every pupil in the municipality attends at least two special school concerts during his or her first six school years. Older students (up to and including the gymnasium level) can obtain free tickets to ordinary evening concerts, thus accounting for 2,000 to 3,000 concert visits annually. In 1983 a preschool educational program was established in order to permit the youngest child to come into contact with classical music.

A series of chamber music ensembles has formed within the orchestra, including the Göteborg Ensemble (five winds, five strings), the Stenhammar (String) Quartet, a woodwind quintet, a brass quintet, a wind ensemble, two piano trios (the Garcia Trio and the Wybraniec Trio), the Gothia (Percussion) Ensemble, and various duos, for a total of ten groups. Nonetheless, none of their musicians is paid by the corporation.

Göteborg, Sweden's second largest city, was founded in 1621 and is a commercial port with vital foreign connections that have influenced its musical life. After a musical revitalization following Czech conductor Joseph Czapek's settling in Göteborg in 1847 (with his compatriot Bedřich Smetana at his side from 1856 to 1862), several efforts were made to begin regular concert activity, especially in the 1890s. A donation from the Fürstenberg family led to the construction of a concert hall. For this hall (inaugurated in 1905), a 50-man orchestra was formed from the remainder of the ensemble Czapek had formed earlier, along with newly recruited musicians, mostly of foreign origin.

After the first director, German conductor Heinrich Hammer, left his post in 1907, the composer Wilhelm Stenhammar was persuaded to become the orchestra's director. During his directorship from 1907 to 1922 he built the orchestra to such a point that Göteborg was considered the foremost musical city of Northern Europe. From the earliest years music of contemporary composers such as Hugo Alfvén and Jean Sibelius was played. Young Swedish composers such as Ture Rangström, Josef Jonsson, Hilding Rosenberg, Edvin Kallstenius, and Algot Haquinius were performed by Stenhammar in Göteborg. His composer friends became frequent guest conductors; Sibelius directed his second, third, fifth, and sixth symphonies with the orchestra. Carl Nielsen conducted many of his own works and also introduced Claude Debussy and Maurice Ravel. In the meantime, Stenhammar himself chose his composer friend Ture Rangström as his successor. Rangström's directorship (1922–1925) favored Swedish music while at the same time introducing Albert Roussel, Hans Pfitzner, Ferruccio Busoni, Paul Hindemith, and Darius Milhaud.

A new period of greatness arrived under the leadership of Tor Mann (1925– 1939). Mann's interpretations of Gustav Mahler were renowned, as were his performances of Schreker's Chamber Symphony and Arnold Schoenberg's *Verklärte Nacht*. His "Nordic Concerts" (1936–1939) sparked heated debates; every new performance of Gösta Nystroem's music was a major event. The orchestra now had a reputation as the foremost and most radical in Northern Europe.

From 1937 to 1959 the orchestra also appeared as "Göteborg's Radio Orchestra." Under Sixten Eckerberg's leadership it performed about 1,000 radio concerts and dominated the radio's musical offerings before the Radio Orchestra in Stockholm was formed in the early 1950s.

During the period in the 1940s under Issay Dobrowen, however, the orchestra was sarcastically called "Göteborg's Tchaikovsky Association," and its fame as an outpost of the avant-garde came to an end. Toward the close of the 1950s attendance decreased. This situation lasted throughout the 1960s. The trend changed in 1970 after an intensive public relations project, and since 1973 attendance has been about 90% of capacity, nearly always standing room only.

Chief conductors responsible for the orchestra's revitalization have been Sergiu Comissiona, with a magnificent contribution to Swedish music (during his ten years in Sweden he directed about 90 Swedish works), and Charles Dutoit, who initiated the orchestra's corresponding growth in quality, which has blossomed since 1982 under the enthusiastic, powerful, and artistic musicality of its current music director, Neeme Järvi.

The orchestra's new vitality is mirrored in its extensive, new recording contracts and its recent tours. Warmly received in England and Ireland (1980) and the United States (1983), the orchestra received invitations for new tours, including one to the Soviet Union (1985).

RECORDING HISTORY AND SELECTIVE DISCOGRAPHY: Before 1982 a small selection of records was published through Philips and Caprice. The orchestra's current output (through previous Concert Hall Manager Bjørn Simensen) calls for 40 to 50 LPs and CDs on the BIS label in the ten to 15 years following 1983, including about 25 with all of Sibelius's orchestral music, eight with all of Nielsen's orchestral music, and several with music by Stenhammar. In 1985 a recording debut took place on Deutsche Grammophon with Franz Berwald's four symphonies on two compact discs, which received great critical acclaim in Europe.

Nielsen, Symphony No. 2 (Myung-Whun Chung): BIS LP–247; BIS CD–247 (CD). Sibelius, Symphony No. 2 (Järvi): BIS LP–252; BIS CD–252 (CD). Stenhammar, Symphony No. 2 (Järvi): BIS LP–251; BIS CD–251 (CD).

CHRONOLOGY OF PRINCIPAL CONDUCTORS: Heinrich Hammer, 1905–1907. Wilhelm Stenhammar, 1907–1922. Ture Rangström and Tor Mann, 1922–1925. Tor Mann, 1925–1939. Issay Dobrowen, 1939–1953. Dean Dixon, 1953–1960. Sten Frykberg, 1960–1967. Sergiu Comissiona, 1967–1972. Sixten Ehrling, 1973–1975. Charles Dutoit, 1976–1979. Neeme Järvi, 1982-present.

BIBLIOGRAPHY: Gustaf Hilleström, *Göteborgs Symfoniker 75 år* (Göteborg: Göteborgs Teater-och Konsert AB, 1980). *Upptakt* (program magazine for Goteborg Symphony with four issues per concert year, 1968–1982 and 1985-present).

ACCESS: Göteborgs Symfoniker, Stenhammarsgatan 1, S–412 56 Göteborg. (031) 20–01–30 (concert information) or 16–70–00 (tickets). Bengt Hörnberg, Managing Director. Lennart Dehn, Director of Promotion.

ROLF HAGLUND
TRANS. LAWRENCE GILLOOLY

STOCKHOLM   (1,386,000)

Stockholm Philharmonic Orchestra

Like the other Scandinavian capitals, Stockholm has several large orchestras. The Royal Opera Orchestra (with 115 members) is Sweden's largest and also its oldest, having been established more than 450 years ago, but it seldom gives symphonic concerts. The majority of public concerts in Stockholm are performed by the Stockholm Philharmonic Orchestra (with some 100 members), but the orchestra of Radio Sweden (also with 100 members) is also quite active.

Normally, the Stockholm Philharmonic gives two to three concerts per week between the middle of September and the end of May (usually one production a week). Normal concert times are Wednesdays and Thursdays at 7:30 P.M. and Saturdays at 3 P.M. Ticket sales are based on a subscription plan originated in the 1920s. At present there are two Wednesday series (9 and 12 concerts, respectively), three Thursday series (6, 8, and 12 concerts), and two Saturday series (5 and 8 concerts). Nine Saturdays per season the orchestra also performs a family concert (sometimes repeated) at 2 P.M. Summer concerts during June and August emphasize popular classics and some contemporary music. The Stockholm Philharmonic also makes numerous recordings.

Concerts for children have been given since the 1910s, first on Wednesdays and later on Saturdays. A new school-concert scheme was initiated in 1967 and involves setting aside one entire week per season for pupils in Stockholm schools to come to the concert hall during the day with their teachers. These 45-minute concerts have programs with clear instructional value, and they are announced well in advance. Recently a similar one-week program for preschoolers has been expanded to two weeks. A total of between 30,000 and 40,000 children hear Stockholm Philharmonic concerts each year.

The orchestra performs annually in other Swedish locations outside Stockholm, either in single concerts or extensive tours. This activity is of particular cultural importance since many Swedes live far away from a community with a professional symphony orchestra. The Philharmonic has also undertaken a considerable number of foreign tours of varying duration. Since 1966 it has visited the United

States four times, the U.S.S.R. once (1979), and various countries in both Eastern and Western Europe on many occasions.

The orchestra both rehearses and performs in the large auditorium of the Concert Hall. This has a 1,600 seating capacity, plus 200 seats made available on the choir gallery behind the orchestra. Attendance is considered quite good, about 80% of capacity, since extensive efforts were initiated a few years ago both to widen and renew the orchestra's audience. For example, concerts have been arranged in collaboration with large daily newspapers and cities elsewhere in the country. Also, special informational material has been distributed and meetings set up with composers and musicians before the start of a concert. One of the highlights of the concert season is an open-air concert in August, which attracts audiences of up to 30,000. Unfortunately, Stockholm's climate is too unpredictable, and perhaps too cool, for a regular series of outdoors concerts.

The Stockholm Philharmonic collaborates with the 140-member, community-based Stockholm Philharmonic Chorus (Stockholms Filharmoniska Kör), which has had only four conductors since its inception in 1907. Since 1980 the chorus has been contractually subordinated to the Concert Hall Society. It takes part in four or five productions each season, primarily in traditional oratorio works, but increasingly in modern works as well.

The orchestra's activities and operations are administered by the Stockholm Concert Hall Foundation (Stockholms Konserthusstiftelse), which also owns and administers the Stockholm Concert Hall. The managing director of the Foundation is also the general manager of the orchestra and the chairman of the orchestra's Program Committee. He bears artistic responsibility for all orchestral and chamber-music concerts arranged by the Foundation. The Program Committee also includes the planning manager, three orchestra members, a composer, and the leader of the Stockholm Philharmonic Chorus. The general manager maintains constant contact with the principal conductor, who participates in the work of the program council when he is able.

The orchestra's activities are financed largely by grants from the national government and the Stockholm County Council (prior to 1983, by the city of Stockholm). These grants cover about three-quarters of the foundation's total expenses. The remainder must be covered through the sale of tickets and by leasing the premises for other activities. In addition, a limited income is acquired from rent paid by a number of commercial establishments located on the street level of the building.

It is because of the large national and county grants that ticket prices can be kept as low as they are; the top single-ticket price for the 1984–1985 season is Kr 60. Guest performances by foreign orchestras are not subsidized, and ticket prices soar to a rather high international level, as high as about Kr 400. Up to and including the orchestra's tour of Spain in 1984, tour financing came from national and municipal grants in addition to what the host nation paid. The tour to North America in 1984 was the first for which a large part of the financial support came from Swedish industry. It now appears as if this type of sponsorship will be absolutely necessary for any future foreign tours. Industrial sponsorship of cultural activities is an entirely new phenomenon in Sweden but is growing rapidly in many sectors. For orchestras such sponsorship can make possible (in particular) short-term, expensive projects that are outside the regular seasonal activities.

Characteristic of the musical scene in Sweden today is the serious shortage of Swedish conductors of international standing. Two well-known Swedish conductors, however, Sixten Ehrling and Herbert Blomstedt, made their debuts with the Stockholm Philharmonic, and especially during the 1950s, conducted very often in the Stockholm Concert Hall. During the 1970s and 1980s most of the orchestra's concerts have been conducted by foreign conductors, including many luminaries. Antál Doráti, since 1981 the orchestra's Conductor Laureate, makes guest appearances every season.

The Stockholm Philharmonic is not solely dependent on foreign soloists; its ranks include some first-rate home talent in several instrumental groups. Moreover, there are two string quartets, a string ensemble, a woodwind quartet, a percussion ensemble, and an internationally renowned brass ensemble made up only or mainly of orchestra members. Many Philharmonic musicians participate in one or more of the excellent new chamber orchestras established in Stockholm in recent years. The orchestra's management takes a rather liberal stance in granting members time off to perform in small groups or as soloists. It is felt that such activity can stimulate and help develop orchestra members. The majority of the musicians are Swedes, but a good number of them are foreign, particularly from the other Nordic countries and from Eastern Europe. The orchestra is expected to reach 105 members within a few years.

The Stockholm Philharmonic has a warm, taut sound, darker in color than their colleagues' at the Radio Sweden orchestra. The strings have refined their sound during recent years, but the orchestra's profile owes much to its outstanding woodwind and brass sections. Thus, the orchestra is well suited for alte-romantic works, its traditional favorites. The orchestra's pitch is an A of 442 cps.

While the orchestra no longer has a special series devoted to modern music, contemporary works are frequently incorporated into the regular programs. Since the late 1970s the orchestra has commissioned two or three compositions each season from Swedish composers. The aim is that works given their premieres with the orchestra shall, as far as possible, be reperformed within a few seasons and, preferably, under another conductor. Naturally, the Program Committee also recognizes the importance of featuring older Swedish composers. During the 1984 tour to Spain, the orchestra performed Wilhelm Stenhammar's 50-minute-long Second Symphony before very enthusiastic audiences.

At the turn of the century Stockholm was a city with long-standing musical traditions. King Gustaf III, whose assassination provided the plot for Verdi's *Un ballo in maschera,* was a music lover and patron of the arts who founded the Royal Academy of Music during the late 1700s. He built a new opera house in Stockholm, established the world-renowned Drottningholm Court Theater, and promoted opera in a number of other ways. In addition, he founded a music conservatory attached to the academy. Stockholm also had rich traditions in choir singing.

However, the growing interest in orchestral concerts was not satisfied. Stockholm's only symphony orchestra was the Royal Opera Orchestra, which at that time also gave concerts. But it was a golden age for international orchestra music, and greater resources had to be created in order to provide a broad public with the opportunity to hear the new symphonic music of the late nineteenth and early twentieth centuries.

Tor Aulin (1866–1914) was a violinist, composer, and conductor who saw the need for a special symphony orchestra in Stockholm. Together with his friend the composer and pianist Wilhelm Stenhammar (1871–1927) and a number of interested amateurs, Aulin founded in 1902 a society for giving orchestral concerts, the Concert Society (Konsertföreningen). A group of professional musicians were gathered to perform six to eight concerts a year. Most of these were conducted by Aulin, and Stenhammar was often piano soloist.

Under these rather primitive circumstances, with no income other than that from the sale of tickets and private grants, a satisfactory activity was carried on until the spring of 1910. By then the orchestra had been disbanded and the season's concerts were being given by the Göteborgs Symfoniker* under the baton of Stenhammar. The ambitious undertakings of these early years resulted in the first Stockholm performances of significant symphonic works of Bruckner, Liszt, Max Reger, Sibelius, and Berlioz. On January 10, 1905, Aulin conducted the world premiere performance of Franz Berwald's *Sinfonie Singulière*—60 years after it had been composed.

Concerts were held in the Great Hall of the Music Academy, which despite its name was too small for the concerts to be profitable. A new concert hall was sought and soon found in an almost round auditorium in the city's very center. The acoustics were nothing to speak of and there was no room for the musicians behind the stage, but conditions were nevertheless sufficiently satisfactory to begin seriously considering the establishment of a permanent symphony orchestra.

On Thursday, January 15, 1914, the first concert was held with a new 70-member orchestra. This day is considered the birthday of the Stockholm Philharmonic Orchestra. The first conductor was the powerful and prominent Finn, Georg Schnéevoigt. During his leadership the orchestra developed rapidly into an ensemble of good quality with an interesting repertoire. Schnéevoigt's strength lay primarily in the heavier, mainly Austro-German repertoire, but he also made noteworthy efforts to introduce Swedish music and conducted many premiere performances. Naturally, Sibelius figured prominently in the early repertoire; the Stockholm Philharmonic's Sibelius tradition stems from this period. On March 24, 1924, Sibelius himself conducted the world premiere of his Seventh Symphony with the orchestra in Stockholm.

During Schnéevoigt's tenure many famous conductors made guest appearances with the orchestra. Arthur Nikisch led a cycle of Beethoven symphonies in 1919, and three years later Felix Weingartner did the same thing. In February of 1917 Richard Strauss conducted a concert of his own works. Front-rank soloists of the day also appeared with the orchestra—among them Henri Marteau, who had resided in Stockholm since 1910.

The Concert Society's orchestra finally acquired its own home on April 7, 1926, when Stockholm's Concert Hall was inaugurated. Still the home of the Philharmonic, Concert Hall is the versatile focal point for the music life of Sweden's capital city and also the site of the annual Nobel Prize ceremonies. In 1982 a new, large, modern organ was added.

In the fall of 1926 the orchestra got a new principal conductor, Vaclav Talich, who, with his fine feeling for artistry and psychology, improved orchestral quality. The previous, somewhat heavy repertoire became lighter and considerably broadened. The early 1930s also saw a steadier stream of internationally renowned guest artists, among them Bartók and Stravinsky. Guest appearances peaked in the 1936–1937 season (when Talich resigned), with appearances by Ernest Ansermet (13), Fritz Reiner (5), Thomas Beecham (2), Fritz Busch (2), Erich Kleiber (2), Hans Knappertsbusch (2), Bruno Walter (2), Eugene Ormandy (1), and Arturo Toscanini (1).

Fritz Busch succeeded Talich as principal conductor starting with the 1937–1938 season. Because of World War II his tenure was limited to only three seasons. One of the orchestra's violinists, Carl von Garaguly, became his successor in 1941 and remained in that post until the mid–1950s. He, in turn, was succeeded by Hans Schmidt-Isserstedt in 1955. The orchestra adopted the name Stockholm Philharmonic Orchestra in 1956. The immediate postwar period saw a stream of international guest conductors and solosits, including Willem Mengelberg, Wilhelm Furtwängler, Herbert von Karajan, Otto Klemperer, Bruno Walter, and others. Such figures helped raise the orchestra's already high quality. Of inestimable value was Igor Markevitch, who was a frequent guest for many seasons.

Of particular importance was the period from 1966 to 1974, when the orchestra was led by Antál Doráti as principal conductor. During those years the orchestra grew to more than 90 members and started to make serious foreign tours and recordings featuring Swedish as well as classical works. The repertoire grew and the the orchestra stabilized its high quality standards. From 1975 to 1977 the orchestra was under the musical direction of Gennady Rozhdestvensky. Since 1982 the principal conductor has been Yuri Athronovich.

RECORDING HISTORY AND SELECTIVE DISCOGRAPHY: The orchestra made its first recordings in the 1950's, notable a number of Sibelius symphonics conducted by Sixten Ehrling. From the 1960s on a more regular cycle was launched, with an annual output of some three or four recordings, mainly of Swedish music. A few interesting Mahler and Sibelius works were included. The bulk of the records were released on the government-owned Caprice label and on Phono Succia.

Karl-Birger Blomdahl, Symphony No. 3; Broman, Overture for Orchestra; Hilding

Rosenberg, Dance Suite from *Marionetter* (Ehrling): Caprice 1251. Ingvar Lidholm, *Kontakion* (Segerstam): Caprice 1167, Mahler, Symphony No. 6 (Horenstein): Unicorn RHS 320-1. Allan Pettersson, Symphony No. 7 (Doráti): Swedish Society Discofil SLT 33194. Sibelius, Symphony No. 2 (Doráti): Victrola 1318. Stenhammar, Serenade in F Major; Erland von Koch, Oxberg Variations (Kubelik and Westerberg): Swedish Society Discofil SLT 33 227. Stenhammar, Symphony (No. 2 (Stig Westerberg): Caprice 1151.

CHRONOLOGY OF PRINCIPAL CONDUCTORS: Georg Schnéevoigt, 1914–1924. (Guest conductors, 1924–1926.) Vaclav Talich, 1926–1937. Fritz Busch, 1937–1941. Carl von Garaguly, 1941–1953. (Guest conductors, 1953–1955.) Hans Schmidt-Isserstedt, 1955–1965. Antál Doráti, 1966–1974. Gennady Rozhdestvensky, 1975–1977. (Guest conductors, 1977–1982.) Yuri Ahronovitch, 1982–present.

BIBLIOGRAPHY: Bengt Olof Engström, *75 Years with the Orchestra Society of Stockholm* (Stockholm Concert Hall Foundation, 1977; in Swedish). *The Stockholm Concert Hall* (Stockholm 1977). Stockholm Concert Hall Foundation, seasonal programs, concert programs, records, and annual reports.

ACCESS: Stockholm Philharmonic Orchestra, Box 7083, S–103 87 Stockholm. 22–18–00. Åke Holmquist, General Manager.

BENGT OLOF ENGSTRÖM

Switzerland ———————————

BASEL (210,000)

Basel Chamber Orchestra

Located in close proximity to the French and German borders, Basel is a cosmopolitan town rich in cultural heritage, with a musical vitality it owes in some measure to one of its leading citizens, Paul Sacher (b. 1906), founder and leader of the Basel Chamber Orchestra (BKO: Basler Kammerorchester).

A native of the city, Sacher founded the Basel Chamber Orchestra in 1926. His other contributions include the foundation of the Schola Cantorum Basiliensis (1933), an institution for the study and performance of ancient music, which he saw merge with the Basel Musikschule and Conservatory in 1954 to form the Academy of Music of the City of Basel (Musik-Akademie der Stadt Basel). Although Sacher relinquished the directorship of the Academy in 1969, he and the Basel Chamber Orchestra still maintain an office there.

In addition to pursuing his interest in "old" music, Sacher has been a leader in the propagation of modern works, befriending many Swiss and foreign composers, commissioning their music, and helping to administer the Internationale Gesellschaft für Neue Musik (IGNM). The Paul Sacher Foundation, which occupies a building on Cathedral Square in Basel, has become an important resource for scholars, particularly since its acquisition in 1983 of the Stravinsky Archive, purchased at a cost of $5.25 million from the Stravinsky estate. Sacher has also been associated since 1941 with the Collegium Musicum Zurich and is a frequent guest conductor elsewhere in Europe.

The Basel Chamber Orchestra's season comprises six regular chamber orchestra concerts at Basel's Musiksaal Stadtcasino, plus two or three performances under its auspices by other ensembles (including the Basel Symphony Orchestra). Although Sacher continues to conduct several concerts per year, about half of the performances in recent years have been under the direction of such guest conductors as Luciano Berio, Pierre Boulez, Cristóbal Halffter, Heinz Hollliger, Witold Lutosławski, Krzysztof Penderecki, Hans Werner Henze, all of whom have led the orchestra in presenting their own compositions. The orchestra is overseen by a 13-member Board of Directors that includes Sacher and (traditionally since the ensemble's early years) several faculty of the university and/ or Basel Music Academy.

Since its founding the orchestra has followed a unique practice of presenting concerts that juxtapose preromantic and modern works—a tradition reflecting the musical interests of its founder. The BKO's first performance, on January 21, 1927, set the pattern for future programs, presenting works of Handel, Bach, and Mozart, in addition to the premiere performance of the Swiss composer Rudolf Moser's Suite for Cello and Chamber Orchestra (1926). In following years the orchestra would continue to feature new composers—at first mainly those of Switzerland but in succeeding years others as well—and seldom-heard works of earlier epochs. The Basel Radio began carrying BKO performances in 1927, making them a regular feature by 1931.

The orchestra soon gained recognition for its unique approach to both the old and new. As its stature rose it began touring to neighboring cities and countries, frequently introducing new works or older works never before heard in the cities it visited. The Basel Chamber Chorus was added in the 1927–1928 season, effectively extending the performance of old music back to the preorchestral periods.

By the early 1930s the ensemble had become somewhat more professionalized, and its concert season had expanded to a maximum of eight concerts by subscription, plus several special performances, frequently in collaboration with other musical institutions. Much of the organizational success of the group in this period has been attributed to its secretary, Dr. August Vortisch. Concerts were held in various halls, including the Hans-Huber-Saal, the Neuer Casino-Saal, and Martinskirche. Important premiere performances included works of Bohuslav Martinů, Wolfgang Fortner, Willy Burkhard, Béla Bartók, and Arthur Honegger. In the 1940s the orchestra's schedule contracted somewhat but its basic program format continued, as did its practice of presenting first performances. Prominent composers whose works were dedicated to and/or commissioned by Sacher and the BKO in this period include Béla Bartók, Arthur Honegger, Jacques Ibert, Ernst Křenek, Bohuslav Martinů, and Igor Stravinsky.

BKO programming is often very inventive and purposeful. One example may be found in the programs juxtaposing numerous short pieces by various composers, creating a suite of works from a single period or from one period through the transition to another. A hallmark of BKO programming is its attention to a large number of individual composers. In the ensemble's 327 performances in its first 25 years, it presented works of more than 180 composers. In all programming, however, Sacher and the orchestra are said to have as their foremost criterion the inherent quality of the music presented. The performance policy for older periods emphasizes interpretation according to historical principles, a goal much facilitated by the organization's close association (and at times somewhat overlapping personnel) with the Schola Cantorum Basiliensis.

At the time of the BKO's pioneering efforts, the concept of a chamber ensemble dedicated to the old and new was an influential one. The BKO was a leader in the movement toward scaled-down baroque and classical performances in a time when romantic interpretation was the more popular approach.

As of 1986, 60 of Paul Sacher's 80 years had been spent with the BKO, and his work with the orchestra was scheduled to continue for 1986–1987, once again presenting both old and new. The "old" (i.e. works of Haydn, Mozart, and Purcell), however, is of a more recent vintage than in the early years and the "new," in acknowledgement of the orchestra's fortieth anniversary, comprises a greater percentage of program time. World premieres of works by Pierre Boulez, Henri Dutilleux, Cristóbal Halffter, Rudolf Kelterborn, Wolfgang Rihm, and Sándor Veress are scheduled.

RECORDING HISTORY: Although the *Schwann* and *Gramophone Classical* record catalogs list no currently in-print commercial discs, the BKO has recorded occasionally, making its first recordings in 1931 for His Master's Voice. It has recorded as recently as 1972.

CHRONOLOGY OF MUSIC DIRECTORS: Paul Sacher, 1926 - present.

BIBLIOGRAPHY: *Alte und Neue Musik: Das Basler Kammerorchester unter der Leitung von Paul Sacher, 1926–1951* (Zurich: Atlantis, [1952]). *Alte und Neue Musik: Das Basel Kammerorchester unter der Leitung von Paul Sacher, 1926–1976* [vol. II] (Zurich: Atlantis, [1976]). Basel Chamber Orchestra, miscellaneous documents, 1985–1986. H. J. Jans, *Komponisten des 20. Jahrhunderts in der Paul Sacher Stiftung* (Basel: Paul Sacher Stiftung, 1986). Herbert Mitgang, "Paul Sacher Foundation Bought Archive for $5.25 Million," *New York Times*, 24 June 1983. Reidemeister, *Alte Musik: Praxis und Reflexion zum 50. Jubiläum der Schola Cantorum Basilienses* (Winterthur: Amadeus Verlag, 1983). M. F. Rich, "The Stravinsky Legacy," *Opera Quarterly* 3, no. 1, 1985. Paul Sacher, correspondence with author, 1986. Tilman Seebass, "Basle," in *The New Grove Dictionary of Music and Musicians* (New York: Macmillan, 1981). Jurg Stenzl, "Paul Sacher," in *The New Grove Dictionary of Music and Musicians* (New York: Macmillan, 1981).

ACCESS: Basler Kammerorchester, Leonhardsstrasse 4, Postfach, 4001 Basel. (061) 25–82–28. Prof. Dr. Marc Sieber, President of the Board of Directors.

ROBERT R. CRAVEN

GENEVA (335,000*)

Orchestre de la Suisse Romande

The Orchestre de la Suisse Romande (OSR), established in 1918 by Ernest Ansermet, has allowed the French Swiss (*Suisse romande*) to be endowed with a large symphonic group, providing the region with access to major symphonic and operatic works.

Ernest Ansermet understood how to define regional service to the French Swiss. The plan, still known by his name, has given the OSR a mission combining activity in three distinct areas: symphonic concerts (primarily in Geneva and Lausanne, but also in Neuchâtel, La Chaux-de-Fonds, Montreux, Vevey, Fribourg, Biel, and Sion); radio programs for the Radio Suisse Romande; and ballet or opera performances at the Grand Théâtre de Genève. Such variety requires flexibility in the use of musicians and much imaginative planning; the resultant concept of "variable geometry" enables the OSR to ensure availability as a large symphonic orchestra or in various smaller configurations for work in radio, television, or the theatre, as required by the institutions involved.

Each season the OSR's 117 musicians, sometimes with reinforcements, provide Geneva with two subscription series of ten concerts each, ten of which are repeated in Lausanne. One additional postseason concert is presented in each city. The orchestra also accompanies some 70 operas or ballets at the Grand Théâtre de Genève and offers joint concerts with choral societies at both Geneva and Lausanne. Five winter symphonic performances are organized by the Geneva municipality, along with eight summer serenade concerts. The OSR functions as well at the trials for the International Competition of the Exécution Musicale de Genève and at the annual concert offered by the city of Geneva for United Nations Day. It also provides six additional symphonic concerts in variable group sizes. To all this are added recording sessions for Radio-Télévision Suisse Romande, commercial recording sessions, and international tours comprising ten to 15 concerts every two years. The OSR's early international reputation as a champion of new music has been widened by its tours, since 1968 to the United States four times, twice to Japan and South Korea, three times to Germany and Austria, and on several occasions to France, Greece, Italy, Great Britain, and Hungary.

The OSR Foundation (FOSR) is a private institution headed by a Board of Directors of 22 voting members representing the state and municipality of Geneva, the French cantons, the city of Lausanne, the Grand Théâtre Foundation, Friends of the OSR in both Geneva and Vaud, representatives from the musicians in the orchestra and the Swiss Musicians Union. The Foundation recruits another eight Board members at large. The Board delegates to its Executive Committee all power necessary for management of both the Foundation and the orchestra; the Foundation's president, vice-presidents, and treasurer are de facto members of the Executive Committee.

OSR administration is headed by a secretary general who is aided by administrative and staff personnel totaling 12 persons. Artistic administration falls under the artistic director through various commissions, including, among others, COPRO—the commission charged with programming at those subscription concerts coproduced by FOSR and the Radio-Télévision Suisse Romande (RTSR)—and the city of Geneva's symphonic commission for city-sponsored concerts. At the Foundation level artistic direction is the responsibility of the secretary general.

Budgeted at $7 million U.S. in 1984, the financing reflects the variety of the orchestra's functions and its regional mission. The city and canton of Geneva supplied 39% and 31% of the total, respectively, with the RTSR giving 20%. Other cities and the Friends of the OSR supply most of the rest, and industrial and commercial support, once an important financial resource, is once again beginning to become significant. Administrative plans include an effort to broaden the base of support and reinforce the perception of the orchestra as an indispensible cultural arm of the French Swiss.

Indeed, OSR impact in that regard is considerable, especially in Geneva, where the various music conservatories train a significant number of musicians. General rehearsals are often open to the conservatories, especially the rehearsals for the Grand Théâtre de Genève, which produces a dozen operas each year featuring international opera stars. The Radio Suisse Romande records and broadcasts all OSR concerts as well as operas at the Grand Théâtre.

The orchestra itself is made up of musicians from many different countries. About 60% are Swiss, the remainder principally from Germany, France, the United States, and the Orient. Tryouts are open to all. Various orchestra members have formed chamber groups, including the Geneva Quartet, Ensemble Serenata, Romand Wind Quintet, Swiss Chamber Players, and Soloists of the OSR. Concertmaster Robert Zimansky has formed a piano trio with Michael Ponti and Jan Polasec. The various groups have recorded several albums, most recently the complete Arthur Honegger quartets by the Geneva Quartet.

From the provincialism of the latter 1800s, Geneva—and all French Switzerland—emerged, thanks to Ernest Ansermet and the OSR, as an early twentieth-century bastion for contemporary works—the original center where new works were immediately presented to the public. Ansermet, whose earlier training as a mathematician had given way to musical studies, had in a very few years of conducting attained a position of artistic stature. Befriended by Stravinsky, Ansermet from 1916 on conducted the orchestra of Serge Diaghilev's Ballets Russes. In 1918 he established the OSR in Geneva. Attracted by his growing reputation, the greatest virtuosos and conductors appeared with the orchestra in Geneva's venerable, 1,850-seat Victoria Hall (which dates from the 1890s and possesses one of Europe's best acoustical environments).

From its inception the OSR gave remarkable stimulus to Swiss composers, who could witness their works performed by the ensemble. These included Arthur Honegger, Ernest Bloch, Jean Binet, Aloys Fornerod, Henri Gagnebin, André-François Marescotti, and especially Frank Martin, who had more than 20 works performed by the OSR under the Ansermet baton. The tradition carries through today, but with reduced emphasis, with such musicians as Jean Derbès, Eric Gaudibert, Norbert Moret, and Michel Wiblé, to name a few.

Although in his later years Ansermet allowed some broadening of the repertoire, from 1918 to 1968 the OSR was best known as an outstanding French orchestra. Its style and orchestral color were firmly bound to works by Debussy, Ravel, and Stravinsky. Indeed, several composers have written especially for the OSR. Stravinsky revised his *Firebird* ballet into an orchestral suite for the ensemble. Honegger dedicated *Pacific 231* to Ansermet and *Chant de Joie* to the OSR. Other works dedicated to the OSR include Jean Binet's *Musique de mai,* Michel Wiblé's *Ouverture pour grand orchestra,* Frank Martin's *Les 4 Eléments,* Heinrich Sutermeister's *Consolae Philosophae,* Norbert Moret's *Tragiques,* and Eric Gaudibert's *L'Echarpe d'Iris.*

After the founder's death in 1969 the OSR passed through a difficult and unstable period, testimony to Ansermet's influence. Following an interim under Paul Klecki, the OSR witnessed its repertoire change under such conductors as Wolfgang Sawallisch and Horst Stein. Performances came almost exclusively from the major German repertoire to the detriment of what had originally been the orchestra's specialty. Currently, the OSR seems to have found the perfect accommodation in Armin Jordan, a Swiss conductor who seeks to reintroduce works from the group's original repertoire, at the same time retaining the "newer" (i.e. Germanic) works. Jordan thoroughly possesses both French and German cultures, allowing for better-than-optimistic predictions for the group's continued success.

Today the OSR has an extensive repertoire, from Bach to the most contemporary. The orchestra seeks to satisfy all tastes; nevertheless, new music is quite a minor part of current programming, limited to about a dozen works per season. The public seems satisfied, as the subscription concerts usually play to sold-out houses.

RECORDING HISTORY AND SELECTIVE DISCOGRAPHY: The OSR is known worldwide for its numerous recordings, more than 300, on the London "ffrr" label, all recorded in the Victoria Hall of Geneva. The first record for London, devoted to Debussy (*La Mer*), was made in 1947. Of the many that followed, 17 were awarded the Grand Prix du Disque. The orchestra was the first to record the major symphonic works of Stravinsky as well as the complete "Paris" symphonies of Haydn. The nine Beethoven symphonies were a sensation when they appeared at the beginning of the 1960s. Ansermet's recordings have a unique historical value as points of reference because the conductor was friends with so many composers—Debussy, Ravel, Manuel de Falla, Albert Roussel, Frank Martin, Honegger, Bartók, Prokofiev, Stravinsky—with whom he discussed in depth the style and tempo of each work recorded. In 1985 London began to make some of Ansermet's historic renderings available in re-releases on compact discs, a project that is expected to continue into the future.

Beethoven, Nine Symphonies (Ansermet): London STS–15464–9 (six records). Berlioz, *Nuits d'été*; Ravel *Shéhérazade* (Régine Crespin/Ansermet): London 25821. Debussy, *La Mer, Prélude á l'après-midi d'un faune* (Ansermet): London STS–15109. Dukas, *La Péri* and Symphony in C (Jordan): Erato ECD 88089 (CD). Falla, *Three Cornered Hat* and *La Vida Breve* Interlude and Dance (Ansermet): London 414 039–2 (CD). Ravel, *Bolero, La Valse* (Ansermet): London STS–15109. Stravinsky, *The Firebird* (Ansermet): London STS–15139. Stravinsky, *Pulcinella* (Ansermet): London STS–15218. Stravinsky, *Rite of Spring* (Ansermet): Turnabout 34384-E. Stravinsky, Symphony in C and Symphony in 3 Movements (Dutoit): London STS–15490.

CHRONOLOGY OF ARTISTIC DIRECTORS: Ernest Ansermet, 1918–1967. Paul Klecki, 1967–1970. Wolfgang Sawallisch, 1970–1980. Horst Stein, 1980–1985. Armin Jordan, 1985-present.

BIBLIOGRAPHY: Jacques Horneffer, *Orchestre de la Suisse Romande 1918–1968* (Geneva, 1968). François Hudry, *Ernest Ansermet, Pionnier de la musique* (Lausanne/Paris: L'Aire musicale/PUF, 1983). Allan Kozinn, "Exploring the Legacy of Ansermet," *New York Times*, 2 June 1985. Claude Tappolet, *La vie musicale à Genève au XXème siècle* (Geneva: Georg, 1978).

ACCESS: Orchestre de la Suisse Romande, Promenade du Pin, 3, CH 1204 Genève. (22) 292–511. Ron Golan, General Manager, Jean-Bernard Houriet, Director of Promotion.

FRANÇOIS HUDRY
TRANS. THERESA SNOW TOY

ZURICH   (706,000)*

Tonhalle Orchestra

The Tonhalle Orchestra Zurich presents about 100 concerts per year to a live audience of some 100,000. In addition to its seven subcription series, which are regularly sold out, the orchestra presents a special series in May and June as part of the Zürcher Juni-Festspiele. Since 1977 the orchestra's schedule has included regular foreign touring, with visits to the United States, South America, the Far East, and European countries.

Founded in 1868, the Tonhalle Orchestra is headed today by a Board of Directors (partly named by the City Council, partly by the musicians, and partly elected at the annual meeting), an Audit Committee, and the Music Commission, including the music director and managing director. Due to its collaboration with the opera house, the Tonhalle Orchestra was until recently one of Europe's largest. Since 1985–1986, its 167 musicians have been divided into two independent ensembles, one for the Tonhalle (with 87 positions shared by 89 musicians), the other for the Opera House. Before 1985 a special orchestra management was necessary to hire and dismiss members of the orchestra, arrange for temporary changes in assignments, and negotiate general terms of employment, salaries, vacations, and the rights of employees to participate in the decision-making processes of management. The Tonhalle Orchestra is funded through public endowments, ticket sales, the Friends of the Tonhalle (the Gönnerverein), private donations, and an increasing number of broadcasts and recordings.

The Tonhalle enjoys a tradition of diversity in its personnel. Women joined the orchestra for the first time in 1946, and today there are about 20, most playing string instruments. The orchestra is international. During the nineteenth century and until World War I, many musicians came from Germany and Austria because it still was difficult to educate enough musicians at Swiss conservatories. During the difficult periods of the world wars and the Great Depression, the number of foreigners was reduced, but today's orchestra comprises musicians of many different countries. The Tonhalle Orchestra has always gained from the steady confrontation between musicians from different countries and different musical styles. There is a clear influence of the French style in the woodwind section, whereas the sonorous quality of the string sections is in the tradition of German and Austrian orchestras. As in many orchestras today, the A is higher than 440 cps.

Over the years Tonhalle Orchestra members have formed a number of chamber music groups, examples being the Tonhalle Quartett, the Zürcher Streichquartett, the Mendelssohn-Trio Zürich, the Zürich Violincellist, the Kammermusik-Ensemble Zürich, the Stalder Quintett and the Pro Arte Quintett (both classical wind quintets). Many Tonhalle musicians also appear as soloists in Switzerland and abroad, and some play in smaller local orchestras such as the Collegium Musicum conducted by Paul Sacher. One of the few big orchestras in Switzerland, the Tonhalle Orchestra has an important cultural influence. Its musicians teach privately and at the conservatories and music schools of Zurich and other cities.

The first Musikkollegium of Switzerland was founded in 1613 at Zurich, and Zurich's first society to hire partly professional musicians for public concerts was founded in 1812 under the name Allgemeine Musikgesellschaft (AMG). Its concerts, which included works by Haydn, Mozart, and Beethoven, were held in the Casinosaal (now Obergericht). The foundation of the Actien-Theater (the city's first permanent stage), the appearance of the political refugee Richard Wagner who came from Dresden in 1849, and a number of important music festivals during the following years finally convinced the city fathers of the necessity to found a permanent orchestra. During the seasons of 1849–1853 Wagner had conducted several concert and opera performances featuring his own works and performances of several Beethoven symphonies, but he finally declined any further activity after the climax of three subscription concerts with 70 mostly foreign professional musicians. In spite of his great successes, Wagner's proposal for a permanent orchestra was turned down as too costly. Zurich's devoted amateurs remained the heart of the orchestra for another seven years. The preparation of the summer festival of 1861 led to the foundation of the Orchesterverein, with 31 professional members for eight concerts and four to five opera performances per year. The first of these concerts took place on September 25, 1862, to celebrate the 50th anniversary of the AMG. A first but modest public fund was donated by the city.

During the next 41 years another great German musician was to play an important role in the city's musical life: Friedrich Hegar (1841–1927), concertmaster since 1863, Kapellmeister of the Orchestergesellshaft and director of the mixed chorus since 1865. In preparation for the music festival of 1867, the Kornhaus (a makeshift hall) was changed into a concert hall, the old Tonhalle. A new corporation was founded that was artistically and financially responsible for the activities in the new hall, and Hegar was elected music director and permanent conductor. After a first season of six subscription and some extra concerts, the dedication concert for the new hall took place on August 23, 1868. Hegar was responsible for many achievements in Zurich's musical life. A devoted friend of Johannes Brahms, Hegar included much of his music in concert programs, conducting the German Requiem in Zurich three months after its first performance in Leipzig and inviting Brahms himself to conduct in Zurich. Other famous composers—including Franz Liszt—were drawn to the city.

In 1887 the Viennese architects Fellner & Helmer were at work on the new opera house behind the Sechseläutenplatz. The old Tonhalle-Gesellschaft was closed and the Neue Tonhalle-Gesellschaft was founded. At the same time the decision was made that the Viennese architects should build a new concert hall on the other side of the river to do proper justice to the increased cultural standards of the city. Opening celebrations were held on October 19–22, 1895, and the guest conductor was once more Johannes Brahms. Everybody was happy about the excellent acoustics of the new 1,546-seat hall.

On his retirement at the age of 65 in 1906, Hegar was succeeded by an equally strong personality, the 27-year-old Swiss composer and conductor Volkmar Andreae (1880–1962). Turning down an offer in 1911 to be Gustav Mahler's successor conducting the New York Philharmonic,** Andreae preferred to dedicate his musical life to the Tonhalle Orchestra. Over a period of more than 40 years, from 1906 to 1949, he developed a quality of orchestral sound that could do justice to the finest music of his time. A great Anton Bruckner admirer, Andreae started a Bruckner tradition that would bring international fame to the orchestra. In addition to featuring the late romantic and modern German schools of music, Andreae also supported a diversity of modern composers such as Richard Strauss, Mahler, Ferruccio Busoni, Ravel, Debussy, and contemporary Swiss composers. In 1944 Zurich's Radio Orchestra rejected a plan for reorganization and was dissolved. This led to a welcome expansion of the Tonhalle Orchestra and to the creation of a separate opera section.

In 1949 musical direction of the Tonhalle Orchestra passed into the hands of a former student of Arnold Schoenberg, the 42-year-old Swiss conductor Erich Schmid (b. 1907), while Hans Rosbaud (1895–1962) was named permanent guest conductor with equal responsibility for program planning. Schmid's merits were best realized in contemporary music. He inaugurated a new series called "Musica Viva." The climax of his work with the orchestra was the Festival of the International Society for New Music, held in Zurich in 1957. Two months before the Festival, Schmid was invited to become permanent conductor of the re-established radio orchestra, Radio Orchester Beromünster.

Now in sole charge of the Tonhalle Orchestra, Hans Rosbaud made Zurich a forum for twentieth-century music. The city gained international recognition when Rosbaud conducted the first staged performance of Schoenberg's *Moses and Aaron* at the Zurich Opera House. In 1960–1961 his complete cycle of Mahler symphonies, given together with Erich Schmid, aroused considerable interest. Rosbaud's sudden death in 1962 left a painful void.

Rudolf Kempe, chief conductor of the Royal Philharmonic Orchestra* of London, was immediately named the Tonhalle's permanent conductor. Kempe's interests lay largely in the great romantic symphonic repertoire. His interpretations of Tchaikovsky, Brahms, and Dvořák were of exceptionally high standards. He took the orchestra on its first foreign tours in 1967 and 1972 and made records that reached a worldwide audience. In 1967 Kempe was joined by Charles Dutoit as assistant conductor. Dutoit's efforts were to be devoted especially to French and to contemporary music, thus continuing a tradition reaching back to Andreae and even earlier. Dutoit left the Tonhalle Orchestra at the end of 1970–1971, and with Kempe resigning at the end of the 1972–1973 season, it was not until 1975–1976 that a new music director came to Zurich.

This was Gerd Albrecht (b. 1935), who since 1972 had been permanent director of the Deutsche Oper Berlin. He was elected by the Board of Directors of the Tonhalle Gesellschaft in 1973. Albrecht's five-year tenure brought many innovations. Having created about 30 television films mainly for children, he led the Tonhalle Orchestra to film work and to concerts for young people. His special interests were devoted to new music in the series "The Composer and His Public" and to massive works such as the Berlioz Requiem, Mahler's Third, Schoenberg's *Gurrelieder*, as well as concert performances of operas such as Berlioz's *Les Troyens*, Jules Massenet's *Thérèse*, and Arrigo Boito's *Mefistofele*. It was also under Albrecht that the Tonhalle Orchestra started worldwide foreign touring.

In 1981 Christoph Eschenbach, world-famous piano soloist and guest conductor, took the position of principal guest conductor. He was appointed chief conductor and music director in 1982 and has rapidly developed the orchestra's touring and recording activities. The orchestra's 1985 schedule included an extensive tour to Taiwan, Hong Kong, and Japan. Eschenbach will leave Zurich at the end of 1985–1986. His successor is Hiroshi Wakasugi.

RECORDING HISTORY AND SELECTIVE DISCOGRAPHY: Numerous recordings were made in the late 1950s and early 1960s for a Swiss record club but were never widely distributed. In 1971 recordings conducted by Kempe for the same club gave convincing proof of the artistic quality of the orchestra. Recordings of Beethoven's Fifth, Dvořák's Ninth, and Bruckner's Eighth symphonies were later distributed in some European countries and in Japan (Tudor TUD 74 0 03/04 Q) and are still available. Many members of the Tonhalle Orchestra record individually.

Musikinstrumente und wie man sie spielt (Albrecht): Atlantis/Schwann 95 001/002 (two discs). Mendelssohn, Violin Concerto; Tchaikovsky, Violin Concerto (Teiko Maeashi/ Eschenbach): CBS/Sony (in preparation).

CHRONOLOGY OF MUSIC DIRECTORS: Friedrich Hegar, 1865–1906. Volkmar Andreae, 1906–1949. Erich Schmid, 1949–1957. Hans Rosbaud, 1950–1962. Rudolf Kempe, 1965–1972. Charles Dutoit, 1967–1971. Gerd Albrecht, 1975–1980. Christoph Eschenbach, 1981–1986.

BIBLIOGRAPHY: H. Conradin, "Zürich," *New Grove Dictionary of Music and Musicians* (London: Macmillan, 1980). H. Erismann, *Johannes Brahms und Zürich: ein Beitrag zur Kulturgeschichte von Zürich* (Zurich, 1971). M. Fehr, *Friedrich Hegar als Zürcher Theaterkapellmeister* (Zurich, 1934). M. Fehr, *Richard Wagners Schweizer Zeit*, 2 Vols. (Aarau, 1934 and 1953). G. Fierz, *The Zurich Tonhalle: A History of the Zurich Tonhalle-Gesellschaft and the Tonhalle Orchestra* (Zurich, 1978—also in German). A. Haefeli, *Internationale Musikfeste in Zürich* (Zurich, 1977). E. Isler, *Das Zürcher Kon-*

zertleben seit der Eröffnung der neuen Tonhalle 1985 (Zurich, 1935–1936). F. A. Pfenninger, *Zürich und sein Theater im Biedermeier* (Zurich, 1980). F. A. Pfenninger, *Zürich und sein Theater auf dem Weg zur Belle Epoque* (Zurich, 1981). R. Schoch, *Hundert Jahre Tonhalle Zürich: Festschrift zum 100 jahrigen Bestehen der Tonhalle-Gesellschaft Zürich* (Zurich, 1968). P. Sieber, "Zürich," *Die Musik in Geschichte und Gegenwart* (Kassel: Bärenreiter, 1968). *Schweizer Musik-Handbuch 1983: Information uber Struktur und Organisation des Schweizewr Musiklebens*, (Zurich: Schweizerisches Musikarchiv, 1983). A. Steiner, *Aus dem zürcherischen Konsertleben der II Halfte des vergangenen Jahrunderts* (Zurich, 1904/1905). A Steiner, *Aus der Vorgeschichte der Allgemeinen Musik Gesellschaft* (Zurich, 1912/1913). H. Weber, *Zürichs Musikleben von 1812–1850* (Zurich, 1874/1875). W. G. Zimmermann, *Brahms und die Schweiz* (Zurich, 1983).

ACCESS: Tonhalle-Gesellschaft Zürich, Gotthardrstr. 5, CH–8001 Zurich. (01) 201–15–81. Hans J. Bär, President. Richard Bachi, Managing Director.

DOROTHEA BAUMANN

Taiwan ────────────────────────

TAIPEI (1,769,000)

Taipei City Symphony Orchestra

Founded on May 10, 1969, the Taipei City Symphony Orchestra is organized under the supervision of the Education Bureau of the Taipei City government. The orchestra is headed by a director, under whom are an assistant director, conductor, secretary, performance section, research and promotion section, and management staff. The orchestra employs over 100 playing members and presents about 100 concerts annually. Its activities include formal concerts, festival concerts, educational concerts, tours, outdoor summer concerts, lectures and master classes, and the presentation of the Taipei Arts Festival. The orchestra's concerts are largely devoted to traditional European symphonic repertoire.

Headed by Teng Chang-kuo, the orchestra was composed of only 30 members when it was organized in 1969. Its temporary home was then in the Municipal Fu-hsin Public School. In 1971 ten more members were added, and musical instruments and scores were purchased. The orchestra also acquired a home on Kai-feng Street. Concerts became more frequent and tours around Taiwan were arranged.

In September 1973 Teng left the orchestra, and the city government appointed Chen Tun-chu as director. The change instilled new vitality into the ensemble, enabling it to improve its artistic quality and management. The orchestra assisted in setting up the Taipei Teachers Choir and a program for musically talented children in Taipei. A further development plan for the orchestra was approved in 1978 to expand its membership to 100. Plans included a permanent home on Pah-teh Road, and construction soon followed.

In 1979 the orchestra was given the mission of organizing the Taipei Music Festival, in which 28 events of opera, ballet, and concerts were staged with unprecedented attendance. The 1980 Festival was equally successful. In 1981 this annual event was named the "Taipei Arts Festival," to include modern dance and drama performances. To date the Festival has presented some 300 performances, including large-scale romantic operas, Chinese regional operas, ballets, and Chinese classical music. All events were enthusiastically received and contributed a great deal to the cultural life of Taipei.

In October 1983 the orchestra's new home, the 2,000 seat auditorium of the Social Education Center, was finally completed. It has more than 2,000 square meters of usable area, comprising, in addition to its performance area, a large rehearsal hall, nine small practice rooms, a storage room for instruments, a recording room, and a meeting room. In the spring of 1984 the orchestra established a youth symphony.

Today the Taipei City Symphony Orchestra has not only developed into a complete symphony orchestra but also assumes the social responsibility of educating the public in the arts. It functions as impresario to foreign performing groups and has also begun research in the Chinese orchestral tradition. To date, however, it has not played much music outside of the Western idiom.

CHRONOLOGY OF RESIDENT CONDUCTORS: Teng Chang-kuo, 1969–1973. Chen Tun-chu, 1973–1978. Chen Chiu-sen and Hsu Sung-jen, 1984–present.

BIBLIOGRAPHY: Personal communications with Chang Tse-min and Chen Chiu-sen, 1984.

ACCESS: Taipei City Symphony Orchestra, 25 Pa-teh Road, Section III, Taipei. 752–7731. Chen Tun-chu, Director.

SIN-YAN SHEN

Union of Soviet Socialist Republics _____

KIEV (2,144,000)

Academic Symphony Orchestra of the Ukrainian S.S.R.

The Academic Symphony Orchestra of the Ukrainian S.S.R. (formerly known as the Ukrainian State Orchestra) was established in 1937 from an already existing radio orchestra in Kiev. Its first artistic director was Nathan Rakhlin, who, with the exception of the war years 1941–1945, when the orchestra was evacuated to Dushanbe and Ordzhonikidze, was principal conductor from its inception until 1962. From 1962 to 1977 the conductor was Vladimir Kozhukhar.

The repertoire of the orchestra is a wide one, embracing standard works by Western and Slavonic composers, though, as is to be expected, special attention is paid to the performance of Ukrainian compositions. The premieres of works by Ukrainian composers include Boris Lyatoshinksky's Third, Fifth, and Sixth Symphonies, Georgi Maiboroda's Second Symphony, and the Fifth and Seventh Symphonies of the prolific composer Gleb Taranov.

Notable conductors of the orchestra have been Leopold Stokowski, Nikolai Malko, Karel Ančerl, and Igor Markevitch, as well as Soviet musicians such as Alexander Gauk, Evgeny Mravinsky, Nikolai Anosov, Konstantin Ivanov, and Kiril Kondrashin. Ukrainian conductors have included Stefan Turchak, Oleksandr Klimov, Mikhailo Krechko, Venyamin Tolba, Pavlo Muravsky, and others. Soloists to appear with the orchestra have included Isaac Stern, Claudio Arrau, Jośe Iturbi, Van Cliburn, Annie Fischer, and Gaspar Cassado, as well as notable Soviet artists such as Emil Gilels, Lev Oborin, Svyatoslav Richter, Mstislav Rostropovich, and David Oistrakh.

In 1979 the orchestra consisted of approximately 100 players, most of whom were graduates of the Kiev Conservatory, while a number were recipients of state honors. In 1964 the orchestra was given the citation of Zasluzhenny Orkestr

Uk.S.S.R. (literally "esteemed orchestra of the Ukrainian S.S.R.") and in 1976 the honor of Academic Symphony Orchestra.

The orchestra has undertaken several tours of Eastern Europe, including Bulgaria (1968 and 1979) and Poland (1980), and has participated in various cultural festivals held in Moscow, among which may be mentioned the Decade of Ukrainian Literature and Art (1960), Ukrainian Days Concerts (1968), and the Russian Winter Festival (1975).

RECORDING HISTORY AND SELECTIVE DISCOGRAPHY: The Academic Symphony Orchestra is little represented on records outside the U.S.S.R., and though there are numerous Ukrainian recordings of indigenous composers such as Vadim Homolyaka, Victor Kosenko, Boris Lyatoshinsky, Platon Maiboroda, Vladimir Nakhabin, Dmitri Revutsky, Miroslav Skorik and others, only a small portion of this music is known outside the Ukrainian-speaking world and centers of Ukrainian culture.

Lyatoshinsky, Symphony No. 3 (Kozhukhar): 06079/80. Maiboroda, Symphony No. 2 (Kozhukhar): 027543/4.

CHRONOLOGY OF MUSIC DIRECTORS: Nathan Rakhlin, 1937–1962. V. Kozhukhar, 1962–1977. F. Glushenko, 1977–present.

BIBLIOGRAPHY: J. R. Bennett, *Melodiya. A Soviet Russian L. P. Discography* (Westport, Conn.: Greenwood Press, 1981). O. N. Kaydalova, ed., *Muzykal'naya zhizn' SSSR Spravochnik* (Musical Life of the USSR: A Book of Reference) (Moscow, 1970). Yu. V. Keldysh, ed., *Muzykal'naya entsiklopediya* (Musical Encyclopedia), Vol. 5 (Moscow, 1981). A. L. Ostrovsky, ed., *Sputnik muzykanta* (*The Musician's Companion*), 2d ed. (Leningrad, 1969).

ACCESS: Ukrainian S.S.R. State Symphony Orchestra, Vladimirsky spusk 2, Kiev.

GERALD R. SEAMAN

LENINGRAD   (4,779,000)

Leningrad Philharmonic Orchestra

The Leningrad Philharmonic Orchestra is the oldest orchestral collective in the Soviet Union. Its centenary was celebrated in 1982. In its long history the orchestra has followed a complex route from an ensemble gathered at the imperial court for the merely utilitarian needs of court life to an orchestra that has long been considered one of the best in the world.

Concerts of the Philharmonic take place in the main building of the Great Hall on the Square of the Arts, in the Little Hall (or, since 1949 Glinka Hall, formerly Engelhardt Hall), and in the October Concert Hall, as well as in regional Palaces of Culture. Concerts are given in the factories and towns of Leningrad Province and guest performances are also given in major cities of the Soviet Union. The Philharmonic maintains a library of musical scores, a members' room, and two reading rooms. Exhibitions are organized and educational programs are offered.

The orchestra has frequently gone abroad. Its first guest performances took place in Finland in 1946, and from that time to 1972 the orchestra visited 23 countries, reaching about 120 cities, including some in the United States. The orchestra visited New York City in 1962 and 1973 as part of its tours of the United States. Tours continue at the present time, but much more infrequently, as is the case with other major Soviet collectives, apparently due to the frequency with which artists request political asylum. An example is the defection of two musicians—Valentin Malkov and Natalya Koloskova—during the Leningrad Philharmonic's 1979 tour to Japan.

Administratively, the orchestra is a unit of the larger Philharmonic institution, which is governed by a director and artistic supervisor. Among the latter were, in their time, such outstanding musical impresarios as Boris Asafyev (pseud. Igor Glebov), Alexander Ossoovsky, and Ivan Sollertinsky. At the head of the orchestra stands a principal musical director. The Great and Little Halls have their own administrative directors as well. The Philharmonic is supported from the state budget and, with regard to wages, the Philharmonic Orchestra is on an equal footing with artists of the Bolshoi Theatre, that is, at top scale.

The Leningrad Philharmonic Orchestra has emerged from what might be considered a distinguished school of the highest artistry, in which world-class conductors and artists—such figures as Arthur Nikisch, Richard Strauss, Felix Weingartner, Otto Klemperer, Hans Knappertsbusch, Vaclav Talich, Serge Koussevitzky, and many others—served as teachers. From their leadership was developed the high professional art of the ensemble.

In the years of work with master directors, the Philharmonic Orchestra performed an immense quantity of work both of the classical and the contemporary repertoires. Mastery of the styles of diverse composers enriched the orchestra's palette, and, in the opinion of directors who have performed with it, the ensemble is a most sensitive and responsive instrument. This long tradition of close ensemble playing was carried down from generation to generation. No matter how much the orchestra was subsequently strengthened with new personnel, the new players were subjected to its educational influence and creative atmosphere. At its height the ensemble stood in the forefront with four or five other symphony orchestras in the world. Its sound, most lush, full, and soft, never became strident in the most intense fortissimo nor blank in the most barely audible pianissimo. In the years following World War II, however, the orchestra underwent a period of artistic decline from which, in the opinion of some, it has never fully recovered.

In 1882 Alexander III organized the Court Musicians' Orchestra, intended specifically for performance at the imperial court. From elements of the then-existing musicians' bands of the regiments of the Horse Guards and the Mounted Life Guard were drawn 53 musicians. Preference was given to whoever played two instruments since it was necessary to have two ensembles, a wind group and a symphony orchestra. The first concerts took place soon after the establishment of the Musicians' Orchestra (Khor) was ratified on June 17, 1882: that of the wind ensemble on August 31 and that of the symphony orchestra on December 25.

The ensembles' makeup was purely military. Musicians were ranked as sub-officers and privates; army recruits previously trained in music could do their military service in the ensemble. Thus many talented musicians with special training were inducted into the group, which was headed by a Baron K. Stackelberg. The first orchestra leader was M. Frank, transferred from the Preobrazhensky Life Guard Regiment, who conducted until he was replaced by G. Varlikh. In September 1882 the Khor's leader, G. Flige, was invited to head the symphony orchestra, and after his death in 1907, Varlikh remained as senior orchestra leader, while E. Belling was named to the post of junior leader in 1910.

It became part of the responsibility of the Musicians' Orchestra to play at the court luncheons, dinners, and suppers of the imperial family. Programs were not very rich in content and consisted for the most part of hymns and also Guard marches and fanfares. In addition, the Khor performed music for functions in the theatres at Gatchina, Tsarskoye Selo, Peterhof, and at St. Petersburg's Hermitage Theater. In the summer it played in the Peterhof Lowergarden on an open stage.

Throughout those early years the Khor gradually widened its audience, and after its first 20 years it had begun to appear in the halls of the Singers' Chapel (Pevcheskaya Kapella) and the Court Assembly. In 1896 the orchestra was freed of its military organization and was reorganized as the Court Orchestra. Its artists received the privileges pertaining to artists of the imperial theatres.

Although in 1898 the orchestra was granted the right to give open, public, advertised programs, it was not until 1902 that its concert work intensified, when it offered a series of major concerts in celebration of Schumann, Mendelssohn, Haydn, Mozart, Wagner, and Borodin. Also, then regularly scheduled "orchestral gatherings of musical innovations" began in which for the first time works of contemporary Western composers were performed. Attempted with only a single rehearsal, such programs were lost ventures. By 1912, however, the concerts of the Court Orchestra had attained a high degree of artistic quality, and major foreign artists began to appear on the podium—Richard Strauss, Arthur Nikisch, and others.

Immediately following the February Revolution of 1917—on March 3—there was a general meeting of the orchestra personnel. From that date the Court Orchestra renamed itself the State Orchestra. As early as March 18 the State Orchestra appeared in the hall of the Singers' Chapel and presented Tchaikovsky's Fifth Symphony. In the spring of 1917 the State Orchestra appeared three more times, and on May 15 it chose as its conductor Serge Koussevitzky, on whose initiative the wind ensemble was disbanded on October 1, 1917. That day is considered the day of the founding of the State Orchestra. For the summer season of 1918 the orchestra played in Pavlovsky Vokzal concert hall.

On October 19, 1920, the title "State Philharmonic Orchestra" was conferred on the group. In place of Koussevitzky, who had emigrated, A. Khessin was named music director, and after him Emil Cooper. On May 13, 1921, the "Statute concerning the State Philharmonic" was ratified. At that time the orchestra took possession of the incomparable concert hall of the former Court Assembly.

This white-columned hall, with its splendid acoustics, was built by the architect P. Jacot according to the plans of C. Rossi. It leads into the complex of the Mikhailovsky Palace, nowadays the Russian Museum on the Square of the Arts. The hall has 1,300 seats with a total capacity of nearly 2,000. Its acoustical merits permitted from the very start its use as a concert hall. Here Liszt and Anton Rubinstein had performed in solo concerts, the concerts of Russian musical society had taken place, and many great musicians had conducted—von Bülow, Wagner, Berlioz, Nikisch, Tchaikovsky, and many others.

On June 12, 1921, the triumphant opening of the Great Hall of the Philharmonic took place. Emil Cooper directed the symphonic concert. In the course of the three summer months, 54 symphonic concerts were held before full houses. For some of them (Beethoven's Ninth Symphony, for example), the number of participants reached 500. In addition to Cooper's concerts, performances were led by Alexander Glazunov, Mikhail Klimov, Nikolai Malko, and others. The winter season opened on December 4, 1921, and 46 concerts were held in the period between then and May 14, 1922. On June 7 of that year the Philharmonic was awarded the designation "Academic." The Glazunov Quartet became part of its structure at that time, as well as the Academic Choir—both were subsequently detached as independent organizations.

In July 1923 Cooper left for abroad, and in the 1923–1924 season distinguished conductors both Russian and Western were invited, among which was Oskar Fried. In the 1924–1925 season Valery Berdyaev was invited as conductor. The following season Mikhail Klimov was named director, later to head only the Chapel Chorus. That season saw many guest conductors, among them the likes of Milhaud, Klemperer, Monteux, Weingartner, and Suk. A new regulation, signed on November 9, 1925, recognized the Philharmonic as a "State Cultural and Instructional Institution"; it was granted the right to organize concerts outside Leningrad and also to play guest performances abroad.

In December 1926 Klimov departed since he was engaged with the Chapel and the Conservatory, but Nikolai Malko was named in his place; that and the following seasons' concerts again saw a procession of famous conductors, new names among them being Arthur Honegger, Hans Knappertsbusch, Alexander Gauk, Bruno Walter, and Ernest Ansermet. By the end of the 1920s the Leningrad Philharmonic Orchestra had become one of the world's best, characterized by harmony of ensemble, virtuosic technique, beautifully emotional sonorities, and an amazing stylistic sensitivity.

When Malko emigrated in 1929 Alexander Gauk was named principal director. Though not possessing an outstanding creative talent, Gauk was an experienced musician, an excellent teacher, and an expert in musical literature. Gauk showed serious interest in the contemporary music of Russian composers, and by the early 1930s he began to introduce new compositions of Shostakovich, Prokofiev, Nicolai Miaskovsky, Yuri Shaporin, and a number of other Soviet composers. Under his direction many undeservedly forgotten or rarely performed works of Russian classical music were heard, as well as a number of oratorio productions of both Russian and contemporary Western composers. Starting in 1930 the orchestra began to travel in the summers to Kislovodsk, Baku, and, later, to Sochi. This considerably increased its audience. Even in Leningrad, extramural concerts at cultural centers and factories became ordinary occurrences. By the mid–1930s the Leningrad Philharmonic Orchestra had attained a high renown throughout the whole country.

In 1934 Fritz Stiedry, for some years a guest conductor with the orchestra, was invited to become its director. He worked hard with the orchestra, notably heightening its clarity of line and its rhythmic precision. On April 29, 1934, the orchestra was awarded the title of Deserving Collective of the Republic. It is the only symphonic collective in the U.S.S.R. possessing such a title.

A notable event of 1937 was the November celebration of Soviet music, the principal event of which was the premiere of the Fifth Symphony of Shostakovich under the direction of Evgeny Mravinsky. Stiedry ended his work with the Philharmonic in 1937—he went on leave to Switzerland but was not allowed back. At that time the Iron Curtain was being lowered and the years of cruelest repression began in the U.S.S.R. In September 1938 Mravinsky was named principal director; he was shortly thereafter to become the prizewinner in the first Conductors' Competition in Moscow.

During the war years (autumn 1941 to autumn 1944), the Leningrad Philharmonic Orchestra worked in Novosibirsk, where it had been evacuated and where it played a major role in musical education. In those years the orchestra put on guest performances in Tashkent, Tomsk, and the cities of the Kuzbass. Returning to Leningrad in September 1944, the orchestra opened the concert season in January 1945. Anyone who had not heard the orchestra in the years it was away was struck upon its return by how much it had deteriorated. The reason lay not only in the death of many of its older musicians, but of younger ones who never returned from the front. The alteration in the performing style of the entire collective was striking. The single bright spot was the director Kurt Sanderling, who had begun to work with the orchestra during this period.

In earlier years work with many directors had accustomed the orchestra to two or three rehearsals to master scores and allowed it great versatility in orchestral performance. Only an insignificant portion of the library had been saved, and the group now lacked a chorus. The resulting skimpiness of repertoire, combined with years under few conductors (mainly Kurt Sanderling and Evgeny

Mravinsky), led to the loss of freedom and adaptability in performance. Public appearances dwindled, and even after unlimited rehearsal time the orchestra's utmost limit was ten concerts per month. When Western musicians began to arrive as the Iron Curtain slid open a bit, the orchestra's deterioration became obvious. A period of emigration weakened the orchestra's ranks even more. Out of 60 string players the best 18 left, including the orchestra's concertmaster.

The change had been compounded by the conducting style and procedures of its music director since 1938, Evgeny Mravinsky (who still today, in his 80s, is at least the titular music director). To one who knew the Leningrad Philharmonic Orchestra in the prewar years, Mravinsky's new, subdued approach was a great and unwelcomed contrast to the effusive styles of those who had preceded him. In addition, Mravinsky's repertoire has been limited, principally to such standards as Shostakovich's Fifth Symphony; Tchaikovsky's Fourth, Fifth, and Sixth Symphonies; *Francesca da Rimini* and *Romeo and Juliet*; and the suites from the *Sleeping Beauty* and *Nutcracker* ballets. Mravinsky is not the orchestra's only regular conductor, and his second in command is assisted by as many as three others.

It should be noted that in its tours to the West the Leningrad Philharmonic Orchestra has generally provoked high praise from Western critics, more so in the 1970s than in the 1960s. Despite their isolated complaints about the Russian approach to tone color in the brass, writers from various Western countries have commended the lushness of the orchestra's strings, its ability to maintain full tone over a wide dynamic range, and the group's fine ensemble playing. On tour, the orchestra has frequently featured works of Shostakovich and Tchaikovsky, and although the critics are nearly unanimous in their praise of such performances, their responses to Leningrad Philharmonic renderings of Germanic literature have been mixed.

Within the structure of the Leningrad Philharmonic, there has existed since 1953 a second orchestra, the former Leningrad Radio Orchestra. For years this group (sometimes confused abroad with the first orchestra, and occasionally referred to as the Leningrad Symphony) had fully equalled the first, and in the period in which Yuri Tmirkanov was its principal director, it even surpassed the first organization to some degree. Chamber ensembles once allied to the main orchestra have since been detached, including the Sergei Taneyev Quartet (since 1946), the Chamber Orchestra (since 1962), and the Leningrad Chamber Orchestra under the direction of Lazar Gozman (since 1961). This last ensemble to all intents vanished following the emigration of its leader and several of its members; in recent times Gozman revived his chamber ensemble in the United States under the name of the Soviet Emigré Orchestra.

It is difficult to exaggerate the importance of the Philharmonic in the life of Leningrad. Subscriptions for Philharmonic concerts are bought up in the course of a few days; for concerts of favorite musicians they are reserved for many months (even years) and round-the-clock queues are set up. Its popularity extends to all ages. From its first days, regardless of any changes or even decline in its artistic quality, the Philharmonic has been a temple of art, fulfilling an otherwise unmet spiritual need.

RECORDING HISTORY AND SELECTIVE DISCOGRAPHY: Unfortunately, no inventory of recordings is maintained by the orchestra, and although its recording history is quite long and full, information is not available. In his discography *Melodiya* (1983), J. R. Bennett lists more than 100 works committed to discs by the Leningrad Philharmonic. The following are from the 1985 *New Schwann Artist Issue* catalog.

Beethoven, Piano Concerto No. 5 (Gilels/Sanderling): Monitor 2033E. Schumann, Cello Concerto (Rostropovich/Rozhdestvensky): DG 2532357. Shostakovich, Violin Concerto (Oistrakh/Mravinsky): Monitor S–2014E. Tchaikovsky, Symphony No. 4 (Mravinsky): DG 2535235. Tchaikovsky, Symphony No. 6 (Mravinsky): DG 2535237.

CHRONOLOGY OF MUSIC DIRECTORS: G. Flige, 1882–1907. G. Varlikh, 1907–1917. Serge Koussevitzky, 1917–1920. A. Khessin, 1920. Emil Cooper, 1920–1923. Valery Berdyaev, 1924–1925. Nikolai Malko, 1926–1927. Alexander Gauk, 1930–1933. Fritz Stiedry, 1934–1937. Evgeny Mravinsky, 1938–present.

BIBLIOGRAPHY: J. R. Bennett, *Melodiya. A Soviet Russian L. P. Discography* (Westport, Conn.: Greenwood Press, 1981). *Desayat' lyet simfonicheskoi muzyki 1917–1927* (Ten Years of Symphonic Music 1917–1927) collection of articles (Leningrad: Academic Philharmonic, 1928). *Leningradskaya Filharmoniya 1934–1935* (The Leningrad Philharmonic 1934–1935) collection of articles (Leningrad: Leningrad Philharmonic, 1935). *Leningradskaya gosudarstvennaya ordena Trudnovogo krasnogo znameni Filharmoniya— Stat'i, Vospominaniya, Materialy* (Leningrad State Philharmonic of the Order of the Red Flag of Labor—Articles, Memoirs, Materials) (Leningrad: "Muzyka" Izdatyel'stvo, 1972). *New Schwann 1985 Artist Issue* (Boston: Schwann, 1985). Boris Schwarz, *Music and Musical Life in Soviet Russia* (Bloomington: Indiana University Press, 1983). Numerous reviews in *Current Musicology, The Musical Times, The Nation, Neue Zeitschrift fur Musik, New York Times, New Yorker,* and other periodicals.

ACCESS: Orchestra of the Leningrad Philharmonic, Ul. Brodskogo 2, Leningrad 191011.

ALEXANDRA ORLOVA
TRANS. LAWRENCE GILLOOLY

MOSCOW (8,396,000)

Grand Orchestra of the All-Union Radio and Television

The Grand Orchestra of the All-Union Radio and Television (better known in the Western world as the Moscow Radio Symphony Orchestra) differs from most other Soviet orchestras in its large number of recordings and the fact that it is also used (like the orchestra of the Moscow Bol'shoy Theatre) for opera performances. Consisting of approximately 110 players, it has an extremely busy schedule, while its repertoire is probably the most extensive of any orchestra in the Soviet Union.

Broadcasting was first introduced in Russia in 1922, this being from a transmitter in Moscow, followed by other stations in Leningrad, Kiev, and Nizhny-Novgorod two years later. The Radio Symphony Orchestra was established over the period 1930–1931, coinciding with the advent of music broadcasting. Though Alexander Orlov and Georges Sebastian were the first conductors of the orchestra (1931–1937), a more important part was played by its next conductor, Nikolai Golovanov, who did much to establish the orchestra on a firm professional footing over the years 1937–1953. From 1953 to 1961 the regular conductor was Alexander Gauk, who was succeeded by Gennady Rozhdestvensky in the period 1961 to 1974. Since that time the orchestra has been conducted regularly by Vladimir Fedoseev. From the very beginning the orchestra fulfilled a double role as a broadcasting ensemble and a concert organization, and this policy has persisted to the present day.

During the course of its existence the orchestra has attracted outstanding Western conductors, including Erich Kleiber, Fritz Stiedry, Leopold Stokowski, André Cluytens, Lorin Maazel, as well as notable Russian musicians such as Samuil Samosud, Evgeny Mravinsky, Alexander Melik-Pashaev, Nathan Rakhlin, Boris Khaikin, Maxim Shostakovich, Yuri Ahronovitch, Konstantin Ivanov, and others.

Apart from its role as a vehicle for the publicizing of the work of Russian composers and performers, the orchestra, which acquired its present name in 1958, performs frequently in radio concerts, on television, and in open public concerts, playing both classical and contemporary Soviet music and, to a lesser extent, music by Western composers. Among the Russian composers who have conducted their own works with the orchestra may be mentioned Reinhold Glière, Aram Khachaturian, Dmitri Kabalevsky, and others, while notable premieres have included Nicolai Myaskovsky's Twenty-Seventh Symphony, Glière's Concerto for Voice and Orchestra, Serge Prokofiev's Seventh Symphony and his secular oratorio *On Guard for Peace,* Khachaturian's *Festive Poem,* Kabalevsky's Second Symphony, Otar Taktakishvili's First and Second Symphonies, Rodion Shchedrin's Second Symphony and *Poetoriya,* and works by composers such as Boris Chaykovsky and Al'fred Shnitke, to cite only a few. The orchestra was also responsible for the first performance of Dmitri Shostakovich's Fifteenth Symphony, under Maxim Shostakovich in 1972.

With the orchestra appeared at various times many distinguished Russian singers such as the coloratura soprano Antonia Nezhdanova, the mezzo-soprano Nadezhda Obukhova, the basses Alexander Pirogov and Maxim Mikhaylov, and the tenor Ivan Kozlovsky, the pianists Emil Gilels and Svyatoslav Richter, the violinist Leonid Kogan, the cellists Mstislav Rostropovich and Svyatoslav Knyushevitsky, and many other eminent musicians. Encouragement of young artists and of budding composers has always been regarded as a high priority. Among the orchestra's players are a number of international prize winners and recipients of state decorations.

The Radio Symphony Orchestra is also renowned for its concert performances of operas, among them being Mozart's *Don Giovanni, Le Nozze di Figaro,* and

Il Seraglio; Beethoven's *Fidelio*; Wagner's *Die Walküre*; Ambroise Thomas's *Mignon*; and works by Britten, Bernstein, Hindemith, Bartók, and other Western composers. Concert performances of works by Russian and Soviet composers have included Alexander Dargomyzhsky's *The Stone Guest*, Rimsky-Korsakov's *Mlada*, Tchaikovsky's *The Oprichnik*, Prokofiev's *Love for Three Oranges*, and others. It was also the first Russian orchestra to give a complete performance of Prokofiev's opera *The Gambler* and to present and record in Russia Ravel's *L'Heure espagnole, L'Enfant et les sortilèges*, and Carl Orff's *Die Klüge*.

In addition to its regular concert and broadcasting commitments, the Radio Orchestra has also undertaken a number of international tours, including visits to Austria, Belgium, Holland, and Britain, as well as Czechoslovakia, Hungary, Romania, Bulgaria, and Poland. Speaking of the orchestra's performance of Prokofiev's Second Symphony during its tour of Britain, the music critic of the London-based *Musical Times* (October 1966) spoke of the strings' "energy and unanimity," while another critic in the same periodical described how the orchestra was "rapturously received" at the final concert of the Edinburgh Festival. The sometimes strident sound of the orchestra, though no doubt pleasing to Russian audiences, has not always found favor, however, with Western critics.

RECORDING HISTORY AND SELECTIVE DISCOGRAPHY: The Radio Symphony Orchestra is quite well represented on American and Western European discs. In 1968 the orchestra won the Grand Prix du Disque for the complete recording of Prokofiev's ballet *Cinderella* and also for the first complete world recording of all the Prokofiev symphonies. However, although most of its records are devoted to works by Russian and Soviet composers, some recordings of works by Western composers are periodically made available for sale in the highly competitive world market. A recording of the Brahms Second Piano Concerto was issued in 1971 with John Lill (joint-winner of the 1970 Tchaikovsky Competition) as soloist, conducted by Rozhdestvensky, and a number of records of works by Berlioz, Grieg, Bizet, Sibelius, and Richard Strauss have also appeared.

A notable event in 1981 was the visit to Moscow of a group of Japanese technicians who produced Digital tapes for Melodiya (the Soviet State Record Company), some of which were issued in the West on chromium dioxide cassettes. These included Stravinsky's *Le Sacre du Printemps* (VX-D-VCS–9054) and Tchaikovsky's Sixth Symphony, both conducted by Vladimir Fedoseev.

Glazunov, The Eight Symphonies (Fedoseev): Ariola-Eurodisc 999.000. Glière, Symphony No. 3 ("Ilya Murometz") (Rakhlin): CBS/Melodiya MG–33832. Khachaturian, Violin Concerto (Oistrakh/Khachaturian): Odyssey/Melodiya Y–34608. Prokofiev, Symphonies Nos. 1 and 7 (Rozhdestvensky): Quintessence 7138. Rimsky-Korsakov, Overture on Russian Themes; Sadko, Sinfonia on Russian Themes (Maxim Shostakovich): Eurodisc 200441. Stravinsky, *Le Sacre du Printemps* (Fedoseev): Vox D-VCL–9054; Moss Music MCD–10029 (CD). Tchaikovsky, Symphony No. 6 (Fedoseev): Vox VCL–9053; Moss Music MCD–10028 (CD).

CHRONOLOGY OF MUSIC DIRECTORS: Alexander Orlov, 1931–1937. Nikolai Golovanov, 1937–1953. Alexander Gauk, 1953–1961. Gennady Rozhdestvensky, 1961–1974. Vladimir Fedoseev, 1974–present.

BIBLIOGRAPHY: J. R. Bennett, *Melodiya. A Soviet Russian L.P. Discography* (Westport, Conn.: Greenwood Press, 1981). O. N. Kaydalova, ed., *Muzykal'naya zhizn' S.S.S.R. Spravochnik* (Musical Life of the U.S.S.R.: A Book of Reference) (Moscow, 1970). Yu. V. Keldysh, ed., *Muzykal'naya entsiklopediya* (Musical Encyclopedia), vol. 1 (Moscow, 1973). A. L. Narochnitsky, ed., *Moskva: Entsiklopediya* (Moscow: An Encyclopedia) (Moscow, 1980). A. L. Ostrovsky, ed., *Sputnik muzykanta* (The Musician's Companion), 2d ed. (Leningrad, 1969). G. Shneerson, *Bol'shoy simfonichesky orkestr Vsesoyuznogo Radio* (The Grand Symphony Orchestra of the All-Union Radio) (Moscow, 1955). L. Sidel'nikov, *Bol'shoy simfonichesky orkestr Tsentral'nogo televideniya i Vsesoyuznogo Radio* (The Grand Symphony Orchestra of Central Television and All-Union Radio) (Moscow, 1981).

ACCESS: Grand Orchestra of the All-Union Radio and Television, Broadcasting House, 24 Kachalova Street, Moscow.

GERALD R. SEAMAN

Moscow Chamber Orchestra

The Moscow Chamber Orchestra came into being in 1955 and gave its first public performance the following year. Founded by violist Rudolf Barshai, it was modelled on West European chamber groups of the baroque and classical periods and was formed initially of 14 instrumentalists, subsequently increased to 23.

Consisting of a core of string players, to which other instruments may be added as required, its repertoire is drawn largely from compositions of the seventeenth and eighteenth centuries, especially works by Bach, Handel, Telemann, and Mozart, though from the very beginning the orchestra has always paid attention to pieces by twentieth-century composers as well. Among works by Soviet composers to receive their premieres with the Chamber Orchestra may be mentioned compositions by Dmitri Shostakovich, Yury Levitan, Moisey Vainberg, Vladimir Bunin, Georgy Sviridov, the Estonian composer Jaan Rääts, and others.

In the course of its 30 years' existence, the Moscow Chamber Orchestra has attracted prominent Soviet performers, including the violinists David Oistrakh and Leonid Kogan, the cellists Mstislav Rostropovich and Daniel Shafran, the pianists Emil Gilels and Svyatoslav Richter, the mezzo-soprano Zara Dolukhanova, and some notable Western artists. Within the U.S.S.R. the orchestra has received many state decorations. It has also won a number of national and international prizes.

Apart from its local commitments the ensemble is also noteworthy from the point of view of its extensive international tours, including visits to the United States and Japan, as well as much of Western and Eastern Europe. Referring to a concert given in New York by the Chamber Orchestra on November 8, 1963, the *Musical America* reviewer described a performance of the Bach Double Concerto with David and Igor Oistrakh as soloists, as ''a miracle of ensemble,'' while the performance of Vivaldi's *The Four Seasons* evoked the comment that "this was no orchestra but a band of virtuosos who think and react as one."

Administratively the orchestra falls under the management of the Moscow Philharmonic, the body which supervises and coordinates the activity of the State Academic Symphony Orchestra of the U.S.S.R.,* the Symphony Orchestra of the Moscow Philharmonic,* the Borodin and Beethoven String Quartets, and several other musical organizations. Following Rudolf Barshai's emigration from the Soviet Union in 1976, the Chamber Orchestra has been under the direction of Igor Bezrodny.

RECORDING HISTORY AND SELECTIVE DISCOGRAPHY: The Moscow Chamber Orchestra is quite well represented on American and West European record labels, issues including works by Bach, Handel, Pergolesi, Mozart, Schubert, and Debussy. Among its recorded works by Russian and Soviet composers, special mention should be made of Sviridov's Music for Chamber Orchestra and the accompaniment to Shostakovich's opera *The Nose*. Rudolf Barshai is himself the soloist in the Concerto in C Major for Viola and Orchestra by the gifted eighteenth-century Russian composer Ivan Khandoshkin.

Haydn, Trumpet Concerto; Hummel, Trumpet Concerto (Dokschitser/Barshai): Quintessence 7135. Khandoshkin, Concerto in C Major for Viola and Orchestra; works of Rameau and Vivaldi (Barshai/Barshai): Monitor 2018E. Mozart, Concerto for Flute and Harp, K. 299 (Aleksandr Korneev/Olga Erdeli/Barshai): Westminster WGS–8334. Mozart, Symphonies Nos. 35, K. 385, and 38, K. 504 (Barshai): Allegro 88102.

CHRONOLOGY OF MUSIC DIRECTORS: Rudolf Barshai, 1955–1976. Igor Bezrodny, 1976–present.

BIBLIOGRAPHY: J. R. Bennett, *Melodiya. A Soviet Russian L. P. Discography* (Westport, Conn.: Greenwood Press, 1981). O. N. Kaydalova, ed., *Muzykal'naya zhizn' SSSR Spravochnik* (Musical Life of the USSR: A Book of Reference) (Moscow, 1970). A. L. Ostrovsky, ed., *Sputnik muzykanta* (The Musician's Companion), 2d ed. (Leningrad, 1969).

ACCESS: Moscow Chamber Orchestra, Ul. Gertzena 13, Moscow K9.

GERALD R. SEAMAN

State Academic Symphony Orchestra of the U.S.S.R.

The State Academic Symphony Orchestra of the U.S.S.R. (SSO; also known as the State Orchestra of the U.S.S.R., the State Symphony Orchestra of the U.S.S.R., or the U.S.S.R. Symphony Orchestra) is one of the chief orchestras of the Soviet Union and also one of the most active. Apart from an intensive program of regular concerts in its home base in Moscow, the orchestra spends much of its time on tour, such events often taking place during the summer months, when concert life in the capital is at its lowest ebb. The orchestra totals approximately 110 players, and its guest conductors have included many distinguished foreign musicians, among them Otto Klemperer, André Cluytens, Sir Malcolm Sargent, Charles Munch, Lorin Maazel, and many others.

The SSO was founded in 1936 on the basis of an already existing radio ensemble, its first conductor being Alexander Gauk. The first concert took place on October 5, 1936, in the Great Hall (Bol'shoy Zal) of the Conservatory, the program consisting of the "International" and Beethoven's First and Third Symphonies. In 1941 Nathan Rakhlin was appointed music director, being succeeded by Konstantin Ivanov in 1946 and by Evgeny Svetlanov in 1965. The orchestra acquired the distinction of "Academic Orchestra" in 1970.

The repertoire of the orchestra is extensive, comprising works by Western European, Russian, and Soviet composers, though works by indigenous composers tend to prevail. The orchestra is notable for the fact that it has premiered many important Soviet pieces, including Prokofiev's Fifth Symphony, Shostakovich's Eighth, Ninth, and Eleventh Symphonies, and his Second Piano Concerto, as well as numerous works by Nicolai Miaskovsky, Yuri Shaporin, Aram Khachaturian, Tikhon Khrennikov, Vissarion Shebalin, Otar Taktakishvili, Kara Karayev, Sergei Slonimsky, Sulkhan Tsintsadze, and pieces by younger composers. As one of the principal Russian orchestras it has been conducted by most of the leading Soviet conductors, such as Nikolai Golovanov, Samuil Samosud, Evgeny Mravinsky, Alexander Melik-Pashaev, Boris Khaikin, Nikolai Anosov, Kiril Kondrashin, Gennady Rozhdestvensky, Vladimir Fedoseev, Veronika Dudarova, and others, while some of the artists to appear with the orchestra have included the pianists Annie Fischer, Marguerite Long, Lev Oborin, Emil Gilels, Svyatoslav Richter, the violinists Yehudi Menuhin, Isaac Stern, Leonid Kogan, David Oistrakh, and many others. For a number of years Maxim Shostakovich served as assistant conductor.

The quality of the orchestral musicians is high, many of the players holding state decorations such as "Zasluzhenny artist" (literally "esteemed artist") or being prize-winners in national and international contests. Such honors are highly rated in the Soviet Union and are accordingly included in one's official title, for example "Zasluzhenny Artist RSFSR Concertmaster G. M. Fridgeym (Violin)" or "Laureat of All-Union Concourse N. M. Tolstaya (Harp)."

Perhaps no other orchestra in the Soviet Union has toured as extensively as the SSO, its visits including the United States, Canada, England, Mexico, Austria, Belgium, West Germany, Holland, Norway, Switzerland, Japan, the People's Republic of China, to say nothing of frequent visits to Eastern European countries. It gave concerts in Australia and New Zealand in 1986. Musically it is noted for its depth and breadth of tone, its emotional intensity, and its high degree of technical achievement; indeed, when the orchestra toured the United States in 1960, the reviewer for *Musical America* (January 1960) spoke of the "electrifying effect" it created among the capacity audience, producing a sound unlike that of American orchestras. This different sound, he decided, lay in the "uncommonly fat tone" of its woodwinds; the brightness and brassiness of the horns, trumpets, and trombones; and the strong, solid sound of the strings.

Financially the orchestra is under the control of the state, which is also responsible for ensuring adequate pensions for orchestral players upon their retirement. The orchestra itself is under the aegis of the Moscow Philharmonic, the name given to the organization that supervises the activities of the S.S.O., the Symphony Orchestra of the Moscow Philharmonic,* the Moscow Chamber Orchestra,* the Borodin Quartet, the Beethoven Quartet, and other ensembles.

RECORDING HISTORY AND SELECTIVE DISCOGRAPHY: The S.S.O. is represented on American and Western European records to a modest extent, recordings including various symphonies by Mily Balakirev, Tchaikovsky, Vasily Kalinnikov, Alexander Glazunov, Alexander Scriabin, and Dimitri Shostakovich, orchestral works by Modest Mussorgsky, Alexander Borodin, and Sergei Rachmaninov. One of the orchestra's latest ventures has been a recording under Rozhdestvensky of some of Shostakovich's early works, including *Two Fables by Krylov*, Op. 4, and arrangements of songs by Rimsky-Korsakov, scored by him while still a student at the Petrograd Conservatory.

Borodin, Symphony No. 2 (Svetlanov): Quintessence, 7165. Shchedrin, Concertos Nos. 1 and 3 for Piano and Orchestra (Shchedrin/Svetlanov): Westminster Gold WG–8359. Shostakovich, Festive Overture (Svetlanov): Ar. 200 539–366. Tchaikovsky, Symphony No. 4 (Svetlanov): Allegro 88099.

CHRONOLOGY OF MUSIC DIRECTORS: Alexander Gauk, 1936–1941. Nathan Rakhlin, 1941–1946. Konstantin Ivanov, 1946–1965. Evgeny Svetlanov, 1965.

BIBLIOGRAPHY: J. R. Bennett, *Melodiya. A Soviet Russian L. P. Discography* (Westport, Conn.: Greenwood Press, 1981). O. N. Kaydalova, ed., *Muzykal'naya zhizn' SSSR Spravochnik* (Musical Life of the USSR: A Book of Reference) (Moscow, 1970). Yu. V. Keldysh, ed. *Muzykal'naya entsiklopediya* (Musical Encyclopedia), vol. 2 (Moscow, 1974). A. L. Narochnitsky, ed., *Moskva: Entsiklopediya* (Moscow: An Encyclopedia) (Moscow, 1980). A. L. Ostrovsky, ed., *Sputnik muzykanta* (The Musician's Companion), 2d ed. (Leningrad, 1969). I. E. Popov, "Gosudarstvenny simfonichesky orkestr SSR" (The State Symphony of the USSR) in L. Grigor'ev and Ya. Platek, eds., *Moskovskaya gosudarstvennaya filarmoniya* (The Moscow State Philharmonic) (Moscow, 1973), pp. 185–191.

ACCESS: State Academic Symphony Orchestra of the USSR, Ul Gertzena 13, Moscow K9.

GERALD R. SEAMAN

Symphony Orchestra of the Moscow Philharmonic

The Symphony Orchestra of the Moscow Philharmonic (also known as the Moscow Symphony Orchestra or the Academic Symphony Orchestra of the Moscow Philharmonic) first came into being in 1953 when the orchestra of the All-Union Radio was placed under the management of the Moscow State Philharmonic.

A "Philharmonic," in Soviet terminology, is not solely an orchestra but the name given to a regional organization that sponsors specific musical events as well as serving as a publishing house and library. There are roughly 138 Philharmonics in the Soviet Union. The Moscow State Philharmonic was established in 1925.

The first conductor of the orchestra was Samuil Samosud, who directed from 1953 to 1957 and was succeeded by Nathan Rakhlin (1957–1960). The conductor from 1960 to 1976 was Kiril Kondrashin and since 1976 Dmitry Kitaenko. The Symphony Orchestra of the Moscow Philharmonic received the distinction of "Academic Orchestra" in 1973. It should not be confused with the less important Moscow State Symphony Orchestra, founded in 1943, nor with an earlier existing "Moscow Philharmonic" orchestra, founded in 1928.

The orchestra is highly regarded both in the Soviet Union and abroad and has been conducted by notable virtuosi such as Igor Markevitch, André Cluytens, and others, as well as by leading Soviet musicians. Like all Soviet orchestras, it is funded by the state, which is also responsible for the provision of pensions to players on completion of their musical service.

The Symphony Orchestra of the Moscow Philharmonic gives frequent concerts in venues such as the Bol'shoy Zal (Grand Hall or Great Hall) of the Conservatory, the Kremlin Palace of Congresses, or in the various Palaces of Culture. Its repertoire is diverse, and in recent times has included twentieth-century works by Arnold Schoenberg, Anton Webern, Alban Berg, and other Western composers. Prices of admission are moderate, rarely exceeding $5.00 (the average monthly wage in the U.S.S.R. is about $250).

As is to be expected, works by Russian and Soviet composers figure largely in the orchestra's programs, notable past events having been the premieres of Serge Prokofiev's secular oratorio *Ivan the Terrible,* Aram Khachaturian's Rhapsody for Violin and Orchestra, Dmitri Shostakovich's Fourth Symphony, Second Violin Concerto and secular cantata *The Execution of Stepan Razin,* Georgy Sviridov's *Poem in Memory of Sergey Esenin,* and others.

The orchestra itself comprises about 110 players, many of whom hold state decorations or prize awards, and during its years of existence it has been associated with many outstanding Western and Soviet performers, including the pianists Artur Rubinstein, Van Cliburn, Svyatoslav Richter, and Emil Gilels; the violinists David Oistrakh and Leonid Kogan; the cellists Mstislav Rostropovich and Svyatoslav Knushevitsky; and the singers Alexsander Pirogov, Mark Reizen, and Vitaly Gromadsky, to mention only a few.

Apart from its role in providing accompaniment for the Moscow Tchaikovsky Competition, the orchestra also participates regularly in festivals of contemporary music held in Zagreb, Warsaw, Kursk, Gor'ky, and elsewhere. Tours abroad have included the United States, Cuba, England, Finland, France, West Germany, Norway, Sweden, Turkey, and throughout Eastern Europe.

RECORDING HISTORY AND SELECTIVE DISCOGRAPHY: A number of recordings by the Moscow Philharmonic Orchestra have been issued in the Western world, among which may be mentioned Hindemith's *Symphonic Metamorphoses on Themes by Weber* and Khachaturian's Third Symphony (both under Kondrashin), miscellaneous works by Tchaikovsky, and many symphonies by Shostakovich. The performance of Shostakovich's Fifteenth Symphony under Kondrashin was highly acclaimed.

Rachmaninoff, *The Bells* (Kondrashin): Quintessence 7173. Shostakovich, Symphony No. 15 in A, Op. 141 (Kondrashin): ABC AB–67024. Tchaikovsky, *Romeo and Juliet* and other works (Kondrashin): Quintessence 7175. Tchaikovsky, *The Storm,* Op. 76 (Dudarova): Angel SR–40271.

CHRONOLOGY OF MUSIC DIRECTORS: Samuil Samosud, 1953–1957. Nathan Rakhlin, 1957–1960. Kiril Kondrashin, 1960–1976. Dmitry Kitaenko, Veronika Dudarova, 1976–present.

BIBLIOGRAPHY: J. R. Bennett, *Melodiya. A Soviet Russian L. P. Discography* (Westport, Conn.: Greenwood Press, 1981). O. N. Kaydalova, ed., *Muzykal'naya zhizn' SSSR Spravochnik,* (Musical Life of the USSR: A Book of Reference), vol. 5 (Moscow, 1981). A. L. Narochnitsky, ed., *Moskva: Entsiklopediya* (Moscow: An Encyclopedia) (Moscow, 1980). A. L. Ostrovsky, ed., *Sputnik muzykanta* (The Musician's Companion), 2d ed. (Leningrad, 1969). M. Sokol'sky, "Simfonichesky orkestr Moskovskoy filarmonii" (The Symphony Orchestra of the Moscow Philharmonic) in L. Grigor'ev and Ya. Platek, *Moskovskaya gosudarstvennaya filarmoniya* (The Moscow State Philharmonic) (Moscow, 1973).

ACCESS: Symphony Orchestra of the Moscow Philharmonic, Ul. Gorkogo 31, Moscow.

GERALD R. SEAMAN

United Kingdom ─────────

BELFAST, NORTHERN IRELAND (444,000*)

Ulster Orchestra

Under Music Director Vernon Handley, the Ulster Orchestra numbers 63 players and plays throughout the year, except for a break in July. Its main venue is the Ulster Hall in Belfast, designed by W. J. Barre and built in 1862, a hall with a capacity of 1,215 (plus choirstalls) and fine acoustics. Concerts are also given in Armagh, Ballymena, Coleraine, Craigavon, Enniskillen, Londonderry, Newry, and Omagh. The average attendance was 91% in the 1983–1984 season. The orchestra regularly performs in the Republic of Ireland and toured England and Wales in 1983. A European tour is planned for 1986. School concerts and opera form part of the orchestra's activities, and the strong working relationship that has been established with the BBC means that 25% of the working year is spent doing studio work.

The orchestra is administered by a company limited by guarantee, with a Board of Directors, General Purposes and Finance Committee, and administrative staff of 17. The major funding bodies are the Arts Council of Northern Ireland (ACNI), the British Broadcasting Corporation, Belfast City Council, Gallaher Ltd., and other commercial sponsors. The working budget for 1984–1985 was £1.15 million. As with other British regional orchestras, the players are on the Symphony Orchestras Standard Contract.

The orchestra's repertoire is mainly the standard romantic one, for Ulster audiences, perhaps even more than most, are wary of the new and unfamiliar; but there is a cautious policy of introducing new works, and as a spin-off from its recording activities the orchestra has featured music by Hamilton Harty and Arnold Bax.

The key factor leading to the formation of the Ulster Orchestra in 1966, and which has governed its development since, is the geographical isolation of Northern Ireland from the rest of the United Kingdom. Whereas other regions of the United Kingdom are served by touring orchestras, the stretch of water between Britain and Ireland has always meant that visits to Northern Ireland by British orchestras are very expensive and therefore rare. At the same time, it has never been possible for professional orchestras based in the South (Republic) of Ireland to serve the musical needs of the North. Hence the need for the province to have its own professional orchestra, despite the small size of the population (about 1.5 million) and the paucity of large population centers outside Belfast.

Prior to 1966 the main orchestra in Northern Ireland was the City of Belfast Orchestra, which was made up of the small BBC Northern Ireland Light Orchestra augmented by freelance musicians. There was a desire to replace the slightly ad hoc CB Orchestra with a regular full-time complement of players. From the outset the Ulster Orchestra was a fully professional body of 37 salaried players, augmented for special occasions. It gave its inaugural concert on September 28, 1966, and continued to give regular concerts during the 1960s and 1970s in Belfast and other towns. It also gave school concerts, played in the productions of the Northern Ireland Opera Trust and Studio Opera Group, and accompanied choral concerts, notably those of the Belfast Philharmonic Society. Successive principal conductors were Maurice Miles (who had previously conducted the City of Belfast Orchestra), Sergiu Comissiona, Edgar Cosma, Alun Francis, and Bryden Thomson.

The creation of the Ulster Orchestra coincided with a long period of civil unrest in Northern Ireland, which affected all aspects of life there. Despite formidable difficulties the orchestra continued to perform throughout the unrest, and there are few players of those days who do not have memories of the hazards encountered in traveling to and from venues. However, other problems also cast a cloud over the ensemble's artistic achievements. Its small audience was attributed to the unrest and also to the classical-sized orchestra's lack of romantic repertoire. It was funded and administered directly through the Arts Council of Northern Ireland, and although it gained from the Council's protection, it was also inhibited from seeking business and commercial sponsorship to boost its funds. Furthermore, it had few opportunities to broadcast, since the BBC had its own studio orchestra in Belfast, the BBC Northern Ireland Orchestra.

During the 1970s there were various attempts to merge the two orchestras. The intention was to seek a relationship between the Arts Council and the BBC in Northern Ireland similar to that in Wales, with an orchestra managed by the BBC but operating under a joint BBC/Arts Council nominated Board, carrying out broadcasting and public concert engagements and funded jointly by the two bodies. This accorded with BBC policy as defined in *Broadcasting in the Seventies*.

In 1979–1980 several developments occurred that led to the transformation of the Ulster Orchestra. First, when negotiations with the BBC over a merger had finally been abandoned in 1979, the Arts Council decided that the time had come to set the orchestra up as an independent company. The result was the formation, on April 1, 1980, of the Ulster Orchestra Society Ltd. Second, in the summer of 1980 the BBC—as part of a move to reduce the number of its house orchestras—announced that it proposed disbanding the Northern Ireland Orchestra. This left the way free for the newly independent orchestra to negotiate taking on BBC players and financing in return for broadcasting. Third, a major financial involvement on the part of the tobacco firm of Gallaher Ltd. and the Belfast City Council enabled the orchestra to enlarge to 55 players and to plan more substantial and prestigious concerts. The result was an immediate boost to the orchestra's image, a change reflected in dramatically improved box-office figures.

Another development enhancing the orchestra's reputation was its entry into the record catalogs. Bryden Thomson, permanent conductor (1977–1985), played an important part in the artistic success of the orchestra during the period of change. But a major share of the credit is due to the Arts Council of Northern Ireland, which maintained the orchestra throughout the 1970s despite formidable problems and which was untiring in seeking its betterment.

RECORDING HISTORY AND SELECTIVE DISCOGRAPHY: The Ulster Orchestra began recording in 1979 with a centenary album of music of Hamilton Harty. This was followed soon by recordings of Harty, Bax, and Edward Elgar. The orchestra's entry into the recording field owed much to the enterprise of the Friends of the Ulster Orchestra and Chandos Records Ltd. and to the artistic direction of Bryden Thomson.

Harty, Violin Concerto, Irish Symphony, *Children of Lir,* Piano Concerto, and other works (Ralph Holmes, violin/Malcolm Binns, piano/Thomson): Chandos DBRD 4002 (4 records, also available separately). Bax, *November Woods, The Happy Forest, The Garden of Fand, Summer Music* (Thomson): Chandos ABRD 1066. Bax Symphony No. 4, *Tintagel* (Thomson): Chandos ABRD 1091.

CHRONOLOGY OF MUSIC DIRECTORS: Maurice Miles, 1966–1967. Sergiu Comissiona, 1967–1969. Edgar Cosma, 1969–1974. Alun Francis, 1974–1977. Bryden Thomson, 1977–1985. Vernon Handley, 1985–present.

BIBLIOGRAPHY: Arts Council of Northern Ireland: minutes of the Board and the Ulster Orchestra Management Committee, 1966–. Ulster Orchestra Society Ltd.: minutes of the Board and the General Purposes and Finance Committee, 1980–. Miscellaneous documents on file with ACNI and the orchestra.

ACCESS: Ulster Orchestra Society Ltd., 181a Stranmillis Road, Belfast BT9 5DU. (0232) 663591. Roger L. Lloyd, General Manager.

DAVID GREER

BIRMINGHAM, ENGLAND   (920,000)

City of Birmingham Symphony Orchestra

The City of Birmingham Symphony Orchestra (CBSO) presently employs 90 players on full-time contracts and gives approximately 140 concerts a year. About half of that total is given in Birmingham, while a further quarter is given within a radius of 50 miles. Concert series are held in Bedworth, Cheltenham, Kidderminster, and Worcester, for example. The remaining concerts are given in other parts of the United Kingdom or on the orchestra's regular overseas tours. Birmingham is centrally located at the hub of the British transport system and, given Britain's population distribution, the orchestra is within easy reach of 80% of the population and therefore travels frequently to various centers.

CBSO concerts given in Birmingham are wide-ranging and include much twentieth-century music. They are concentrated into a Tuesday and a Thursday series, a Saturday family series, with inducements for youth of the area, and summer seasons of "CBSO Proms," which began in 1945. Attendances are among the best in the country, and an efficient, effective marketing system aims to continue that trend.

An independent body, the CBSO Society Limited, elects a management council and appoints a principal conductor and secretary/general manager. The organization is funded by the Arts Council, the West Midlands County Council, the city of Birmingham, a growing number of sponsors (mainly local businesses), and, of course, box-office revenue. The orchestra's current turnover is about £1,750,000.

Home to the orchestra is the Birmingham Town Hall, which was built to house the Triennial Festivals. It accommodates about 1,750 people, and, though somewhat cramped and acoustically less than perfect, it is very much a product of Victorian civic pride. A new concert hall is planned, scheduled for completion toward the end of the decade, and a new rehearsal complex is soon to be completed.

Calling itself "The Orchestra of the West Midlands," the organization sees itself very much as the region's cultural ambassador, and its numerous broadcasting engagements and recordings help make its name widely known. Its wide-ranging and catholic programs attract many people, and its impact on the community is immeasurable. A youthful CBSO Chorus as well as the longer-established City of Birmingham Choir joins the orchestra in several major concerts each year. There are some smaller instrumental groups formed from within the CBSO's ranks, though these are privately administered and give small, local recitals.

Birmingham, England's second city, is a true product of the Industrial Revolution. Little more than a market town in the mid-eighteenth century, it grew at a phenomenal rate so that now the whole West Midlands conurbation is home to some 3,000,000 people. The existence of an orchestra in Birmingham is, however, a fairly recent innovation. The main musical event for which the city was renowned was its Triennial Festival, principally a choral festival to which composers such as Mendelssohn, Dvořák, Charles Gounod, and Edward Elgar contributed works. Mendelssohn's *Elijah* and Elgar's *Gerontius* were first performed in Birmingham, for example. The great musicality and enthusiasm of the British, coupled with the strong choral tradition so common in industrial cities, served to put Birmingham firmly on the musical map.

Choral music held sway through the nineteenth century. It was not until 1920 that a permanent orchestra was founded. Various attempts to establish some sort of orchestra had been made prior to that date, and not without some successes, but it was largely the post-World War I euphoria that led to the orchestra's establishment. Instrumental in its launching were the composer Granville Bantock and Neville Chamberlain, later prime minister but then a considerable force in Birmingham politics. The first concert was conducted by Elgar in Birmingham Town Hall on November 10, 1920.

The actual nucleus of the orchestra was formed in 1918 when Appleby Matthews, a local musician, added a string section to the Police Band of which he was conductor and started his own series of Sunday concerts. After the inception of the CBSO, Matthews became its principal conductor and remained so for four years, after which Adrian Boult took over. Boult, who steered the orchestra through the difficult depression years, departed to the BBC in 1930, and his place was taken by the truly gifted Leslie Heward, who stayed until his premature death in 1943.

The year 1944 marked a new departure, as the City Council, whose grant had steadily been increasing, placed the orchestra on full-time contract, playing 25 hours a week. Concerts were given on Thursday evenings and Sunday afternoons, and the orchestra initiated educational activities and also played beyond the boundaries of the city. The City of Birmingham Symphony Orchestra, as it was renamed in 1948, grew in size and reputation under George Weldon and subsequently under Rudolf Schwarz. The Polish composer Andrzej Panufnik took the reins between 1957 and 1959, after which Sir Adrian Boult returned for a year.

It was at this stage that the John Feeney Charitable Trust (founded after a wealthy Birmingham businessman) began to commission new works for the CBSO, particularly works by British composers. This trend continues and now averages about one new work each year. Hugo Rignold conducted during the 1960s, to be succeeded in 1969 by the French-born Louis Frémaux, who introduced a wider repertoire than had hitherto been heard. He left in 1978 and was succeeded by the young British conductor Simon Rattle.

RECORDING HISTORY AND SELECTIVE DISCOGRAPHY: The orchestra has a long and distinguished recording history, making its first 78-rpm disc in 1925 (Granville Bantock's *Hebridean Symphony*), and subsequently making a large number of similar discs of a wide-ranging repertoire right through the war years. Today recordings are made principally for EMI, and several recent issues have been particularly well received, especially those made by Frémaux and Rattle.

Britten, *War Requiem* (Rattle): EMI-SLS 1077573, Angel DS3949. Saint-Saëns, Symphony No. 3 (Frémaux): Decca ESD 7038; Klavier 526.

CHRONOLOGY OF MUSIC DIRECTORS: Appleby Matthews, 1920–1924. Sir Adrian Boult, 1924–1930. Leslie Heward, 1930–1943. George Weldon, 1944–1951. Rudolf

Schwarz, 1951–1957. Andrzej Panufnik, 1957–1959. Sir Adrian Boult, 1959–1960. Hugo Rignold, 1960–1968. Louis Frémaux, 1969–1978. Simon Rattle, 1979–present.

BIBLIOGRAPHY: CBSO Diamond Jubilee Yearbook (CBSO, 1980). CBSO Society, Ltd., miscellaneous notes. Michael Hurd, *The Orchestra* (London: Phaidon, 1975). Lyndon Jenkins and Beresford King-Smith, *The Birmingham 78s* (CBSO,1983). Beresford King-Smith, *1920–1970: The First 50 Years: A History of the CBSO* (CBSO, 1970). *The New Grove Dictionary of Music and Musicians* (London: Macmillan, 1980).

ACCESS: City of Birmingham Symphony Orchestra, 9, Margaret Street, Birmingham, B3 3RP. (021) 236–1555. Edward Smith, General Manager.

GLYN MÔN HUGHES

BOURNEMOUTH, ENGLAND   (144,000)

The Bournemouth Symphony Orchestra and Bournemouth Sinfonietta

The genteel South Coast resort town of Bournemouth is today, as it was early in the century, an important musical center. Under the management of the Western Orchestral Society Limited, the Bournemouth Symphony Orchestra (BSO) and the Bournemouth Sinfonietta employ 120 musicians, making this company the largest British employer of musicians outside the BBC.

The orchestras serve the Southwestern triangle of England, a mainly rural area lacking large population centers. The Bournemouth Symphony Orchestra gives over 300 concerts a year in ten main subscription series in Bournemouth, Poole, Bristol, Paignton, Exeter, Plymouth, Portsmouth, Southampton, Swindon, and Weymouth. In addition, many "one-off" concerts are given at smaller venues, as well as on the London concert platforms. In recent years the BSO has travelled abroad and has appeared in concert halls as far afield as Hong Kong. The orchestras record and broadcast regularly, and often appear at the Henry Wood Promenade Concerts in London each summer. Each season sees a wide representation of the repertoire, from Elgar's *Gerontius* through *Porgy and Bess* to a pops series tapping the summer visitor. Programs are carefully selected to suit the venue. A regular concert pattern can afford to be more adventurous than an isolated performance in a small town. It is significant that, as in the past, the orchestra still champions British music but rather shies away from new music.

The orchestra is funded from a consortium of local councils (comprising the South-Western Concerts Board), as well as by the Arts Council of Great Britain, local arts associations, the Bournemouth Council (supplying a cash grant and services in kind), other elements of sponsorship, and, of course, box-office revenue. An administrative staff of 22 looks after a budget in excess of £2,000,000 as of 1984. The orchestra's home base is the Winter Gardens in Bournemouth, though given the current working pattern, it has several homes. The present Winter Gardens is a multi-purpose conversion, serving several kinds of entertainment. It replaced a much-maligned but endearing pavilion.

The BSO's sound is probably best described as traditional. It has no special effects, but one characteristic worthy of note is its splendid string sound, a feature since the early days, but developed particularly during Constantin Silvestri's period of office. The organization has a great impact on its region, bringing top-class performances, a rapidly developing educational program, and the opportunity for local choirs—the Bournemouth Symphony Chorus, cathedral choirs, and others—to perform with the orchestra several times a year.

The Bournemouth Sinfonietta, formed in 1968, is one of Britain's foremost chamber orchestras. Run totally separately from its sister orchestra, it is managed by the same organization and gives concerts both locally and further afield. It appears regularly in British and overseas festivals and its name is well known in the United Kingdom by virtue of its many broadcasting engagements. Its catalog of recording is extensive, as is its pattern of music-making. Its great virtue is its accessibility, taking top-class music to areas where little live music is heard. In addition, the Sinfonietta is heavily involved in the rapid expansion of music education, occasionally devoting a whole week to one town, giving a selection of concerts, with its members undertaking workshops, lectures, and other activities.

The first concert by the Bournemouth Municipal Orchestra was given on May 22, 1893. Under the baton of Dan Godfrey, this group of 30 musicians was engaged to play on the pier and in the old Winter Gardens Pavilion, in order to add to the amenities of a rapidly developing seaside resort. In 1895 Godfrey began a weekly series of symphony concerts and was soon renowned for his championing of British music, particularly concerts in which composers conducted their own works. There was even one occasion in 1927 when a concert took place in which an all-British team of women composers conducted their works. Godfrey's tireless commitment to the orchestra for over 40 years earned him a knighthood and sowed the seeds of the orchestra we know today.

Godfrey's place was taken in 1934 by Richard Austin, who remained until just after the outbreak of World War II. During the war the orchestra nearly disappeared, but in 1947 the Bournemouth Corporation breathed new life into the organization and appointed Rudolf Schwarz principal conductor. Schwarz revitalized the orchestra and established a new audience pattern. He was succeeded in 1951 by Charles Groves, during whose conductorship a radical change took place.

Finances had, from the very beginnings, been a point of controversy in the Council Chamber, but in 1954 the orchestra faced its worst-ever financial crisis. It was at this point that control of the orchestra passed from Bournemouth Corporation to the newly formed Western Orchestral Society Ltd., changing its name to the Bournemouth Symphony Orchestra, widening the geographical area in which it would play, and, perhaps most important, spreading the cost over a wider area.

Groves was succeeded in 1951 by Constantin Silvestri, who helped establish the international reputation of the orchestra and initiated the BSO's first foreign tours as well as making a number of acclaimed recordings. He died in 1969, and in 1972 Paavo Berglund took over. Under Berglund the orchestra toured widely and made many recordings, notably of Sibelius and Shostakovich. In 1980 Uri Segal was appointed principal conductor, succeeded in 1982 by Rudolf Barshai.

RECORDING HISTORY AND SELECTIVE DISCOGRAPHY: The orchestras make many recordings, several of which are regarded as definitive, particularly the Sibelius recordings under Berglund. Over the years one of the main characteristics of the recorded repertoire has been the prominent place given to British music, as well as to Sibelius and Shostakovich. An exclusive contract was signed with EMI in 1974.

Boyce, Symphonies No. 1 through 8 (Ronald Thomas/Sinfonietta): CRD–1056/ CRDC4056. Sibelius, Symphonies No. 3 and 5 (Berglund): HMV Green Label ESD/TC-ESD 7094. Walton, Violin Concerto; Britten, Violin Concerto (Ida Haendel/Berglund): HMV ASD/TC-ASD 3483.

CHRONOLOGY OF MUSIC DIRECTORS: (Bournemouth Symphony Orchestra): Dan Godfrey, 1893–1934. Richard Austin, 1934–1940. Montague Birch, 1940–1946. Rudolf Schwarz, 1947–1951. Sir Charles Groves, 1951–1961. Constantin Silvestri, 1961–1969. George Hurst, 1969–1972. Paavo Berglund, 1972–1980. Uri Segal, 1980–1982. Rudolf Barshai, 1982–present.

BIBLIOGRAPHY: Michael Hurd, *The Orchestra* (London: Phaidon, 1975). Geoffrey Miller, *The Bournemouth Symphony Orchestra* (Dorset: Dorset Publishing Co., 1970). *New Grove Dictionary of Music and Musicians* (London: Macmillan, 1980). Western Orchestral Society, miscellaneous fact sheets.

ACCESS: Western Orchestral Society Ltd., 2, Seldown Lane, POOLE, Dorset, BH15 1UF. (0202) 670611. David Richardson, Chief Executive.

GLYN MÔN HUGHES

GLASGOW, SCOTLAND   (760,000)

Scottish National Orchestra

In the 1984–1985 season the Scottish National Orchestra (SNO) gave 73 concerts, including 25 in Edinburgh and 32 in Glasgow. The orchestra performs in several concert halls in Scottish cities, including the City Hall, Glasgow (1,216 seats); Usher Hall, Edinburgh (2,438 seats); Caird Hall, Dundee (2,680 seats); His Majesty's Theatre, Aberdeen (1,445 seats); and Music Hall, Aberdeen (1,267 seats). In 1986 the Proms in Glasgow will be held for the first time in Hall Three of the new Scottish Exhibition and Conference Centre, with a seating capacity in excess of two thousand. The orchestra is supported and financed by grants from the Arts Council of Great Britain and from local authorities in the four main cities in which it regularly performs.

The Scottish National Orchestra was formed and founded in July 1950 in direct succession to the Scottish Orchestra, which had been in existence since 1890. In the last years of the nineteenth century and the early years of the present century, that orchestra's main conductors included George Henschel, Sir Arthur Sullivan, Hans von Bülow, and Sir August Manns. It was also led by many celebrated guest conductors. It may seem strange that the orchestra maintained its existence for over 40 years without engaging a permanent conductor, but such was the case until 1933, when John Barbirolli assumed that post. His charm and engaging, dynamic personality endeared him to concertgoers in the mid–1930s, and both the prestige of the orchestra and its financial stability were much enhanced. Although the programs remained rather conservative and limited in range, it was during this period that Arnold Schoenberg's *Verklärte Nacht* and William Walton's Viola Concerto and First Symphony were first played in Scotland.

When Barbirolli left in 1936, his successor, George Szell, arrived from Prague. One of the highlights of his years with the orchestra was the first performance in Scotland of Mahler's *Das Lied von der Erde*. Szell's flair and brilliance as a conductor were much admired in Scotland by the time he left in 1939 to take up the music directorship of the Cleveland Orchestra** in the United States.

During the war years the fortunes of the Scottish Orchestra were largely guided by Warwick Braithwaite, a New Zealander who had already spent some years as the music director of the BBC's Western Region. He was a tireless worker and popular for his exuberance and verve. The orchestra's activities seemed to have increased rather than diminished during the war, for between 1941 and 1943 it and the BBC Scottish Orchestra worked in association with the Carl Rosa Opera Company, and in 1943 the Scottish Orchestra was able to extend its season to six months with a total of 53 concerts on Saturday and Sunday evenings in Glasgow. Thomas Beecham was a welcome guest conductor in 1944–1945, when he directed seven concerts for children in Glasgow.

In the immediate postwar years the orchestra's popularity and fame increased, and eventually, on July 8, 1950, the Scottish National Orchestra Society, Ltd., was founded in response to the need and desire throughout Scotland to establish a permanent symphony orchestra that would perform throughout the year. The new foundation was supported by grants from the corporations of the four main cities in Scotland—Glasgow, Edinburgh, Aberdeen, and Dundee. Concerts began to be held regularly in these cities, especially in the first two, and the association that the orchestra had made with the Edinburgh Festival since its establishment in 1947 was greatly enhanced from that time.

During Walter Susskind's period with the orchestra (1946–1951), several recent compositions were first heard in Scotland, including Vaughan Williams's Sixth Symphony and Bartók's Concerto for Orchestra and Third Piano Concerto. Karl Rankl directed the orchestra between 1952 and 1957, but his programs tended to be surprisingly unenterprising for a musician of his experience, and he showed little interest in contemporary music. The important feature of Rankl's time in Glasgow was the introduction of Promenade Concerts to the city; they have remained a popular element of the summer season ever since. Rankl was followed by Hans Swarowsky, the Hungarian musician who had studied with both Schoenberg and Anton Webern, and who held the appointment with the SNO in combination with that of chief conductor of the Vienna State Opera. He stayed only two years in Glasgow, and on his departure in 1959 he was succeeded by Alexander Gibson.

Gibson had made his first appearance with the orchestra in 1954 when he had conducted a performance of Jean Sibelius's Seventh Symphony. He was the first Scot to be appointed conductor of the SNO, and he was the first to be appointed with the designation "Musical Director and Principal Conductor." The Musica Viva concerts that he introduced to Scotland with the SNO on the Viennese pattern in 1959 enabled audiences to sample many contemporary works, and these included Schoenberg's Violin Concerto (in 1959) and Karlheinz Stockhausen's *Gruppen* (in 1961, together with the BBC Scottish Orchestra).

Scottish Opera was founded in 1962, and with the SNO it gave performances of *Pelléas and Mélisande* and *Madam Butterfly* in its first season. The close association of opera and orchestra has been maintained ever since, and operas that they have presented at the Edinburgh Festival have included *The Rake's Progress* (1967) and *Peter Grimes* (1968). Later productions that have made a particular impact include the operas of the *Ring* cycle as well as *Otello* and *Wozzeck*.

In the course of the 1960s the size of the SNO was gradually increased, from 74 players in 1959 to 96 in 1966. These increases were made possible by the foundation of the SNO Endowment Trust and increased grants from other authorities in Scotland.

In October 1967 the orchestra made its first extended tour abroad, visiting Holland, Germany, and Austria with Janet Baker and Jacqueline du Pré as soloists. Fourteen concerts were given in 12 cities in 16 days, and the venture was an outstanding success. The solo items were two song cycles by Mahler and cello concertos by Dvořák, Edward Elgar, and Robert Schumann. Later tours took the orchestra to Norway (the Bergen Festival of 1969); to Belgium and Holland, where concerts were given in Brussels and Rotterdam in 1973 as part of *Europalia* (a series of events designed to celebrate Britain's entry into the European Economic Community); and to the United States in 1975, which was the orchestra's longest and most ambitious tour to date.

The concerts in Glasgow had for many years been presented in St. Andrew's Hall, where the acoustics were judged to be among the finest in the world for orchestral performance. Disaster, however, struck on August 25, 1962, when the hall was destroyed by fire. Interim venues were arranged until the relatively small, old City Hall in the center of Glasgow was refurbished and reopened in 1968. Since the war the orchestra had suffered many difficulties in finding a suitable rehearsal center in Glasgow, and it was not until 1979 that a permanent home was established. On January 19, 1979, the new SNO Centre was officially opened by Princess Margaret, and the main hall there was named in memory of Sir Henry Wood. The building that was redesigned for this purpose was the Trinity Church, Claremont Street.

Another important venture in more recent years has been the series of concerts of new music given under the title "Musica Nova." These are presented by the SNO Society and Glasgow University with the support of the Calouste Gulbenkian Foundation. The programs in 1971, for instance, included music by Luciano Berio, Iain Hamilton, Thea Musgrave, and Thomas Wilson, and the works presented were rehearsed, discussed, and performed in public.

In 1984, after 25 years' service, Alexander Gibson retired, and he was succeeded by Neeme Järvi as musical director and principal conductor. Järvi is an Estonian who had studied in Leningrad and who had won an important conductor's prize in Rome in 1971. He has been much admired for his performances of the symphonies of Mahler and the Russian composers of the last 100 years.

The SNO today is an orchestra of first-class international status and reputation, and the fact that this is so is due very largely to the prestige that the orchestra gained during Gibson's tenure. The range of music undertaken in the seasons' programs has become remarkably full and wide and has embraced all areas of the orchestral repertoire.

SELECTIVE DISCOGRAPHY: Elgar, *The Dream of Gerontius* (Gibson): CRD 1026–7 (2 records). Elgar, Cello Concerto; Walton, Cello Concerto (Ralph Kirschbaum/Gibson): Chandos ABRD 1007. Rimsky-Korsakov, Miscellaneous Orchestral Pieces (Järvi): Chandos 8327–9 (3 records). Sibelius, Seven Symphonies (Gibson): Chandos DBRD 4003 (4 records). Sibelius, Complete Tone Poems (Gibson): Chandos CBR 1027–8 (2 records). Stravinsky, The Three Symphonies and *Ode* (1943) (Gibson): Chandos 8345–6 (2 records). Walton, Symphony No. 1 (Gibson): Chandos ABRD 1095. Prokofiev, Symphony Nos. 2 and 6 and other pieces (Järvi): Chandos ABRD 1122 and 1134.

CHRONOLOGY OF MUSIC DIRECTORS: (Scottish Orchestra.) Sir John Barbirolli, 1933–1936. George Szell, 1936–1939. Warwick Braithwaite, 1940–1945. Walter Susskind, 1946–1951. (Scottish National Orchestra established, 1950.) Karl Rankl, 1952–1956. Hans Swarowsky, 1957–1959. Alexander Gibson, 1959–1984. Neeme Järvi, 1984–present.

BIBLIOGRAPHY: Correspondence with SNO Press and Publicity Officer Lynne Walker, 1985. George Bruce, *Festival in the North: The Story of the Edinburgh Festival* (London: Robert Hale, 1975). Robert W. Grieg, "The Story of the Scottish Orchestra." An Address given in Glasgow on 12 March 1945 (Glasgow: Choral and Orchestral Union of Glasgow, [1945]). Roger Witts, Robert Ponsonby, and Paul Kingsley, eds., *SNO 1971: An Anniversary Study of the SNO* (Glasgow: SNO Society, Ltd. [1971]).

ACCESS: Scottish National Orchestra, 3 La Belle Place, Glasgow, G3 7LH. (041) 332–7244. Fiona Grant, General Administrator. Lynne Walker, Publicity Officer. SNO Society, Ltd., 12 Hope Street, Charlotte Square, Edinburgh, EH2 4DD. (031) 226–2561. G. K. V. Clarke, Secretary.

GWILYM BEECHEY

LIVERPOOL, ENGLAND   (510,000)

Royal Liverpool Philharmonic Orchestra

Always known locally as "The Phil," the Royal Liverpool Philharmonic Orchestra (RLPO) is one of three major symphony orchestras operating in the northwest of England, the others being the Hallé* and the BBC Philharmonic (principally a broadcasting unit), both based in Manchester. Despite the close proximity of their home cities, the two civic orchestras serve largely separate communities, the Hallé providing for the densely populated areas of central Lancashire, and the RLPO drawing its regular audiences mainly from Merseyside, North Wales, and the coastal regions of North Lancashire.

The RLPO (currently with some 82 players) is fortunate in having a first-rate concert hall, the Philharmonic Hall in Liverpool, permanently at its disposal for rehearsals and concerts. The building has excellent acoustical properties and a seating capacity in excess of 1,800. Each season upward of 80 concerts are held there. These are organized mainly on a subscription basis (including special Industrial Concerts for those engaged in industry or commerce in the locality). In addition, there are concerts for schools and events undertaken in conjunction with the principal choral societies in the city—the Philharmonic Choir and the Liverpool Welsh Choral Union, each comprising about 180 voices. Including its extensive work outside Liverpool, the orchestra gives a total of about 140 concerts each year. It performs regularly at the BBC Henry Wood Promenade Concerts and at the Festival Hall in London. It broadcasts, records, and has undertaken distinguished foreign tours in many parts of Europe.

Decision-making and planning, together with the day-to-day business affairs of the orchestra, are the concern primarily of the director and his administrative staff; on all artistic matters they work closely in association with the principal conductor. However, the chief controlling body to whom, ultimately, all these persons are responsible is the Management Committee. Although soon to be affected by changes in local government organization, the Committee consists at present of eight members of the Philharmonic Society, together with five full-time employees of the Society (drawn from the orchestra and administrative staff), five members of the local authorities of Merseyside, and one person nominated by the Arts Council of Great Britain. In addition to box-office receipts and subventions from local councils, the RLPO is funded by a substantial annual grant from the Arts Council. Furthermore, a number of business concerns in the area regularly give toward the cost of particular concerts and unusually enterprising (and expensive) events. A Special Activities Fund is maintained to underwrite these ventures. Local support for the orchestra is excellent, with ticket sales averaging 80% to 90% of capacity.

The RLPO makes a strong impact on the Merseyside region. It supports a flourishing youth orchestra, whose members receive regular coaching from their senior colleagues, attaining in the process performances of high artistic calibre. Individual RLPO musicians also undertake tuition with students at the university and at local colleges.

Founded in January of 1840, "The Phil" is among the oldest surviving concert societies. At first it gave only occasional concerts, with a mixed orchestra of amateurs and professionals and assorted madrigal and glee singers, using, as a rather unsatisfactory venue, the Collegiate Hall on Shaw Street. However, in

August 1849 a decisive advance was made when the first Philharmonic Hall (rapidly to gain a reputation for its near-perfect acoustics) was opened and became the orchestra's permanent home. The inaugural celebration involved a four-day festival of music, for which Felix Mendelssohn was to have composed and conducted a choral setting of part of John Milton's *Comus*; however, the work remained unfinished at his death in 1847. During the remainder of the nineteenth century, despite periods of financial crisis, the Society prospered artistically, numbering among its distinguished musical directors Julius Benedict, Max Bruch, and Sir Charles Hallé. Records of the period reveal a somewhat conservative choice of music, but increasing enterprise was to be shown under the guidance of Frederick Cowen, who, as conductor from 1895, gradually introduced works by Brahms, Franck, Richard Strauss and, eventually, Debussy, Elgar, and Rachmaninov.

After the start of World War I, visits by conductors and soloists from abroad virtually ceased, and for a considerable period the orchestra relied on a number of outstanding guest conductors of native origin, such as Sir Henry Wood, Eugene Goossens, and Sir Thomas Beecham. With the return of peace, however, the situation changed, and during the 1920s world-famous soloists such as Pablo Casals and Alfred Cortot were drawn to Liverpool, together with numerous foreign conductors of the highest renown—Ernest Ansermet, Serge Koussevitzky, and others.

In July of 1933 tragedy struck. The famous Philharmonic Hall in Hope Street was completely destroyed by fire. However, by June of 1939 dedicated efforts by the Management Committee came to fruition, and a new Philharmonic Hall was inaugurated under Beecham in a concert designed to test its acoustics thoroughly; these were pronounced excellent. With the help of Sir Hamilton Harty, Sir Adrian Boult, and others, the orchestra's high artistic level was sustained through World War II, and full-time status was eventually achieved in 1943, with Sir Malcolm Sargent as principal conductor.

In more recent times, under the direction of such notable musicians as Sir John Pritchard, Hugo Rignold, Sir Charles Groves, Walter Weller, and David Atherton, the orchestra has built a reputation second to none in the British provinces. The accolade "Royal" was bestowed on the orchestra in 1957. Under Groves the RLPO specialized to a marked degree in the performance of modern British music and gave several notable premieres, including William Mathias's Concerto for Orchestra (1966), Gordon Crosse's *For the Unfallen* (1967), Roger Smalley's *Gloria tibi Trinitas I* (1969), Edmund Rubbra's Symphony No. 8 (1971), Hugh Wood's Violin Concerto (1972), and Benjamin Frankel's Symphony No. 8 (1972).

Another special feature in recent years has been the presentation of complete cycles of works: all the symphonies of Mahler, Sibelius, and Vaughan Williams, for example, and the entire orchestral output of Ravel. These have provided some notably adventurous examples of program planning. In an effort to advance the cause of contemporary music, annual seminars (involving concerts, lectures, and discussion periods) have been arranged in conjunction with the University of Liverpool. Each is devoted to the work of a particular composer (successively, since 1981, Alexander Goehr, Peter Maxwell Davies, William Mathias, Edward Cowie, and Michael Tippett), and at each the composer himself has participated fully in the activities.

RECORDING HISTORY AND SELECTIVE DISCOGRAPHY: The great majority of the RLPO's recordings are of British music, an early and famous example being Sir Michael Tippett's *A Child of Our Time* (1958), conducted by John Pritchard (Argo, DPA 571).

Elgar, *Caractacus* (Groves): EMI SLS–998. Elgar, Violin Concerto (Groves): EMI CFP–40322. Holst, *At the Boar's Head* (Atherton): EMI ASD 4387. Wood, Cello Concerto and Violin Concerto (Atherton): Unicorn, RHS 363.

CHRONOLOGY OF PRINCIPAL CONDUCTORS: William Sudlow and John Russell, 1840–1844. Zeugheer Herrman, 1844–1865. Alfred Mellon, 1865–1867. Julius Benedict, 1867–1880. Max Bruch, 1880–1883. Sir Charles Hallé, 1883–1895. Sir Frederick Cowen, 1895–1913. Sir Henry Wood and Sir Thomas Beecham, 1913–1942. Sir Malcolm Sargent, 1942–1948. Hugo Rignold, 1948–1955. Efrem Kurtz and Sir John Pritchard, 1955–1957. Sir John Pritchard, 1957–1963. Sir Charles Groves, 1963–1977. Walter Weller, 1977–1980. David Atherton, 1980–1984. Marek Janowski, 1983–1987. Libor Pešek, to assume duties in 1987.

BIBLIOGRAPHY: Stainton de B. Taylor, *Two Centuries of Music in Liverpool,* Ch. 2, "The Royal Liverpool Philharmonic Society" (Liverpool: Rockliff, 1976). "Liverpool," *New Grove Dictionary of Music and Musicians* (London: Macmillan, 1980).

ACCESS: Royal Liverpool Philharmonic Society, Philharmonic Hall, Hope Street, Liverpool L1 9BP. (051) 709–2859.

                                                                                BASIL SMALLMAN

LONDON, ENGLAND   (6,696,000)

The Academy of St. Martin in the Fields

The Academy of St. Martin in the Fields (ASMF) is one of the most distinguished orchestras to have emerged in Britain since World War II. With the English Chamber Orchestra* it has dominated the recording catalogs since the early 1960s and continues to be in worldwide demand. The orchestra has no permanent concert location but appears annually for short seasons at the Royal Festival Hall and at the church in Trafalgar Square from which it gets its name.

Since its incorporation in 1970 the orchestra has existed in three forms. The largest is a group of about 45 players conducted only by Neville Marriner. The "little band" of 16 players undertakes the majority of the tours and has been directed from the violin by Marriner, Iona Brown, or Kenneth Sillito. The Chamber Ensemble dates from 1967 and was formed to present large-scale string chamber music. All three groups are presently administered by a general manager. Players are not affiliated with the orchestra on a full-time basis but are engaged for specific projects as appropriate. Funding is achieved through the Arts Council of Great Britain, the British Council (for foreign tours), residual royalties on recordings, and business sponsorship.

The orchestra's original repertoire derived largely from string music of the baroque era but now encompasses four centuries. The group's attitude toward "authenticity" is that this is an area best left to more specialized ensembles. Their interest in contemporary music is only limited by the realities of their schedules and the managements that employ them. In recent years they have commissioned and recorded a number of important pieces including works by Alexander Goehr, Nicholas Maw, William Walton, and Michael Tippett.

The desire to work outside the main symphonic repertoire and an interest in baroque music prompted the violinist Neville Marriner in 1958 to invite a small group of players to rehearse together. A year later, ignoring superstition, the ensemble of 12 players gave its first recital on Friday the 13th of November at the Church of St. Martin in the Fields. The players were all virtuosi (capable of playing concertos, when invited) and shared a desire to achieve the highest standards of ensemble playing without a conductor. From the outset Marriner aimed to achieve a corporate, almost family, approach with a strong emphasis on bright, energetic playing. Noting the decline of the London Chamber Orchestra and others and the success of such ensembles as the Stuttgart Chamber Orchestra,* Marriner saw an opportunity to meet what he termed "a heavy demand for a top-quality British chamber orchestra. . . . Promoters soon found that they could fill large halls just as easily with the Academy as with a big symphony orchestra" (*Classical Magazine*).

Finding little support for such a specialist group amongst music clubs in the United Kingdom, the orchestra attempted to seek recognition through other channels, notably recordings. As one writer has neatly, if overenthusiastically, described it, "The history of the Academy of St. Martin-in-the-Fields has been the history of the L.P. record" (*Hi-Fi News and Record Review,* quoted by Harries). Certainly part of the unorthodox story of the orchestra was its development first as a recording group and only second as a concert-giving ensemble. The millionairess Mrs. Louise Hanson Dyer, founder of L'Oiseau Lyre Company, offered the orchestra its first contract in 1961 as part of her policy to encourage an unusual repertoire and new talent. Three years later Argo, another specialist label, recorded Handel's Concerti Grossi, Op. 3, which attracted sufficient interest for the company to offer a five-year contract in October of 1965. This was also the year in which two television films were made (of Vivaldi's *Seasons* with Alan Loveday and of Wagner's *Siegfried Idyll*), and the orchestra made its first two appearances at the BBC Proms. By 1966 there were financial uncertainties at Argo arising from the policy of recording this rather specialist repertoire, but happily a year later confidence was restored by an Audio Award for Rossini's String Sonatas (the first of several such distinctions confirming the orchestra's importance in the eyes of the record-buying public).

In 1970 the Academy was formed into a limited company with Marriner and four other founding members as directors. This development reflected the increasing activities of the group, which now required the services of a full-time manager and additional office staff. Touring, first in Europe and then worldwide (after 1972), was now possible, as were expansions of the orchestra's work program. Among the most important of these was the association with Philips, which began in 1971 with the release of a four-record box entitled *The Rise of the Symphony*. Produced by Erik Smith, the set featured Marriner in the new role of conductor and established the orchestra as a force in symphonic repertoire. A cycle of Mozart concertos with Alfred Brendel was also significant in developing this area of the Academy's work.

The year 1975 was in many ways a milestone in the orchestra's development. Philips issued separate contracts for the orchestra and for Marriner as conductor, and as a result Iona Brown assumed direction of the group for its baroque recordings and for chamber music. Her performances of Vivaldi (especially the *Four Seasons*) attracted worldwide interest, as did her direction of the Chamber Ensemble. In the same year Marriner was appointed to coordinate London's prestigious South Bank Summer Music while the orchestra's German agent requested the formation of a "Chorus of the Academy of St. Martin in the Fields" under Laszlo Heltay to perform Bach's B-Minor Mass on tour.

Since the 21st Anniversary Season of concerts at St. Martin's Church in July 1980, the orchestra has maintained its activities in all the major areas of classical music. As well as an increased number of U.K. recitals, European and world tours are now a regular feature of the calendar. In the studio projects such as the Schubert and Beethoven symphony cycles progress alongside further recordings of baroque music and film work (for example, *Amadeus,* 1984). An initial operatic venture for Philips in 1983 (*Barber of Seville*) is to be followed by Mozart's *Marriage of Figaro* in 1985–1986.

RECORDING HISTORY AND SELECTIVE DISCOGRAPHY: The Academy of St. Martin in the Fields has produced more than 300 discs to date, including many award-winning recordings. Major companies associated with the group are Argo, ASV, EMI, Decca, and Philips. A recent estimate suggested each serious music station in the United States broadcasts, on the average, 30 minutes of the Academy's work every day. The orchestra holds numerous recording awards.

A Baroque Festival (various conductors): Argo D69 D3. *English Music for Strings* (Marriner): Angel S–36883. Handel, Concerti Grossi (Marriner): Argo 5400. Haydn, *The Seasons* (Marriner): Philips 6769068 (3 records), Philips 411428–2 (CD) (2 discs). Mozart, Piano Concertos Nos. 20, K. 466, and 24, K. 491 (Brendel/Marriner): Philips 6500–533. Poulenc, Concertos (Malcolm, Brown): Decca Jub. 410 172–1. Schoenberg, *Verklärte Nacht* (Marriner): Argo ZRG 763. Tippett, Concerto for Double String Orchestra (Marriner): Argo ZRG 680. Trumpet Concertos of Stolzel, Telemann, and Vivaldi (André/Marriner): Angel DS 37984; Angel CDC 47012 (CD). Vivaldi, *The Four Seasons* (Brown): Philips 9500–717. Wagner, *Siegfried Idyll*; works of Boccherini, Fauré, Grieg, and Tchaikovsky (under title, "Digital Concert") (Marriner): Angel DS 37758.

CHRONOLOGY OF MUSIC DIRECTORS: Neville Marriner, 1959-present.

BIBLIOGRAPHY: E. Greenfield, R. Layton, and I. March, *Penguin Stereo Record and Cassette Guide* (London: Penguin, 1984). Meiron and Susie Harries, *The Academy of St. Martin in the Fields* (London: Michael Joseph, 1981). R. Morrison, "The Academy of St. Martin in the Fields," *Classical Music* (277), 1985.

ACCESS: Academy of St. Martin in the Fields, 109 Boundary Road, London, NW8 ORG. (01) 625–8698. Hilary Keenlyside, General Manager.

DENIS MCCALDIN

BBC Symphony Orchestra

With a roster of 111 musicians, the BBC Symphony can now claim to be the largest in the United Kingdom, and its worldwide reputation places it among the most important as well, particularly in its commitment to contemporary and little-known works.

Its yearly activities include a great many performances for direct and rebroadcast principally on BBC Radio 3; upward of 70 public concerts in various halls in London; and tours that have taken it to many foreign countries. Its main concert venues for the regular season (which it terms its "winter" season) are the Barbican Concert Hall and the Royal Festival Hall, and it has participated substantially in the summer Henry Wood Promenade Concerts, which take place at the Royal Albert Hall. In 1984–1985 (as a sample year) the BBC's tours took it to many cities in England, Ireland, Scotland, and Wales, often in conjunction with music festivals. It also toured Spain, France, Italy, Switzerland, and Scandinavia. A visit to the United States is planned for January 1987.

Because the orchestra is funded and administered through the BBC, under government sponsorship, the BBC Symphony is far less affected by the financial insecurities endured by the four self-governing, self-sustaining major London orchestras. The orchestra's administration is in two sections, both responsible to the BBC Controller of Music (currently John Drummond). Operational administration, conducted from offices at the BBC Maida Vale Studios, is overseen by the BBC Symphony Manager. Artistic policy and liaison to the overall BBC structure are carried out through an office at London's Yalding House, under supervision of a producer responsible for artistic planning. Although the orchestra is not represented by the Association of British Orchestras, the majority of its musicians are members of the Musicians' Union. Many engage themselves with chamber music and other work outside of the BBC. Primary performance conducting responsibilities are currently shared by a staff of four: Chief Conductor Sir John Pritchard, Chief Guest Conductor Gunter Wand, and Principal Guest Conductors David Atherton and Peter Eötvös.

The BBC Symphony's historical affinity for contemporary music continues to characterize its repertoire, which nevertheless includes works of the romantic and post-romantic composers, with classical composers less often represented. Concert programs regularly feature premiere performances, some of which are BBC commissions. In addition to its performances in regular winter concerts, for example, the BBC participated in the series "Music of Eight Decades." A typical program in this series occurred on March 14, 1986, conducted by Peter Eötvös. Following a pre-concert lecture by composer Harrison Birtwistle, Eötvös presented Stravinsky's *Threni*; Bernd Alois Zimmermann's *Dialoge* in a first United Kingdom performance; and Birtwistle's *Earth Dances,* a BBC commission receiving its world premiere. BBC Symphony Prom concerts are equally challenging.

The British Broadcasting Company was formed in 1922, and its first official broadcast took place on November 14 of that year. A policy for the broadcasting of music evolved gradually at first but soon gathered momentum when Percy Pitt took up a part-time appointment as music adviser in May 1923, when the Company moved to new headquarters in Savoy Hill. His appointment became full-time in 1924. In 1926 he was joined by Edward Clark, who came to London from Newcastle and who became a major force in forming the Company's musical policy. By 1924 an orchestra of the BBC (the 2L0 Wireless Orchestra) had been formed, with Dan Godfrey as its conductor and with 22 players on contract.

On January 1, 1927, the Company became a corporation, with John Reith as director-general. Concerts were organized in London by a "National Orchestra" of about 130–150 players, and there were some first-rate programs, which included performances of Arthur Honegger's *King David* and Richard Strauss's *Alpine Symphony.* In 1928 Arnold Schoenberg came to London to conduct the British premiere of his *Gurrelieder.* Plans to form a permanent BBC Orchestra began in 1927, when Walford Davies and Landon Ronald were in touch with Thomas Beecham. Discussions were elaborate, prolonged, and contentious, and no real progress was made until Adrian Boult was appointed director of music in January 1930, succeeding Percy Pitt. Auditions began in 1930, and a few months later the orchestra gave its first concert at Queen's Hall, on October 22, with Arthur Catterall as leader. The program, which included Wagner, Brahms, and Ravel, received enthusiastic reviews. Boult's successes in the early concerts led to his being appointed chief conductor on May 15, 1931. He held this position until he retired in 1950 but relinquished the post of director of music in 1942.

The BBC Orchestra's early years saw much new music. The International Society for Contemporary Music Festival was held in Oxford and London in 1931 and ended with two BBC concerts at Queen's Hall. Parts of these concerts were broadcast, and one included Anton Webern's Symphony, Op. 21. In 1931–1932 there were 22 concerts, and in that season Strauss conducted his tone-poems *Macbeth, Don Juan,* and *Tod und Verklärung*; Schoenberg conducted his *Verklärte Nacht* and his *Variations,* Op. 31; and Béla Bartók visited London to play his *Rhapsody,* Op. 1, under Henry Wood, who also conducted his *First Suite,* Op. 3, and *The Miraculous Mandarin.* Other important programs of contemporary music in the 1930s included studio performances of Igor Stravinsky's *Mavra* and *Les Noces,* parts of Alban Berg's *Lyric Suite* (arranged for string orchestra), and the first performance in England of his Violin Concerto, with the composer conducting. Boult conducted the Szymanowski Memorial Concert on October 8, 1937, which included the Second Violin Concerto and the ballet *Karnase*, Op. 55. Music by British composers has always been given an important and significant place in the BBC concert seasons, and early years saw first performances, first broadcasts, and all-British programs involving music of Constant Lambert, Edward Elgar, Ralph Vaughan Williams, Arnold Bax, and Arthur Bliss.

Boult believed that the appearances of guest conductors would greatly enhance the orchestra's status and standards, and in the early years there were visits from Felix Weingartner, Bruno Walter, Serge Koussevitzky, and in 1935, for his first appearance with any British orchestra, Arturo Toscanini, whose appearances with the BBC were called "the most important events that have occurred for years in the orchestral life of this country" (*Manchester Guardian*, June 7, 1935).

For the start of the 1934–1935 season, the orchestra moved to new headquarters at the more spacious Maida Vale Studios in North London. In 1935 a critical investigation and review of broadcasting and of musical broadcasts was made by the Ullswater Committee when the BBC's charter was due for renewal. There was some adverse comment regarding repertoire, but the orchestra's programs in the studio and concert hall continued to be adventurous, with works by composers such as Constant Lambert and William Walton. In the following year the orchestra made its first continental tour, visiting Paris, Vienna, Zurich, and Budapest. Its programs featured music of English and other contemporaries, but the programming for the Budapest concert (Elgar, Bax, and Bartók) so infuriated Edward Clark that he resigned in 1936. It was not until the 1960s, and the arrival of William Glock as BBC controller of music, that the orchestra sought to present as wide a range of repertoire, particularly in terms of contemporary music.

Toscanini came to London again in 1937 and in 1938, and in the last of the London Music Festivals (1939), on the eve of war, he conducted all the Beethoven symphonies and gave two performances of the *Missa Solemnis*. All made lasting, unforgettable impacts.

The first years of World War II found the orchestra working in and around Bristol and from 1941 to 1943 in Bedford. Broadcast concerts took place on Wednesdays and Sundays, and monthly concerts were given before invited audiences. When in 1943–1944 it became propitious to return to London, concerts were planned there as well as in Bedford. The permanent return to London, however, was fraught with difficulties, and it was not until April 1947 that the new "Studio 1" at Maida Vale was ready for use. The immediate postwar years were hard, and the orchestra had to compete with the new Royal Philharmonic Orchestra* and the Philharmonia Orchestra,* both of which began life in 1946–1947. Forty of the BBC's 90 players had left between 1939 and 1946.

The new BBC Third Program (a new channel of broadcasting, supplementing the two main existing BBC channels) began in September 1946, and on September 29 Boult conducted a concert at Maida Vale consisting entirely of English music. In April 1947 the orchestra was reconstituted with 96 members and a continental tour was undertaken. The following year the orchestra made its first visit to the Edinburgh International Festival.

Boult's long period of highly distinguished service came to an end in 1950. He was sad to have to retire, and there were protracted problems in finding a successor. Sir Malcolm Sargent was eventually appointed. He was a masterly and brilliant choral conductor, but his very limited interests in twentieth-century music were to prove an unfortunate drawback in planning orchestral programs. While the BBC, and especially their Third Program, played a full part in exploring the music of neglected composers and bringing new music to public attention, the BBC Orchestra took only a very limited part in such enterprises.

The Royal Festival Hall was opened during the Festival of Britain in 1951, and the new hall proved a remarkable success in giving a feeling of intimacy to an audience of some 2,900. The BBC Orchestra took part in the opening concert with Sargent, who conducted Vaughan Williams's Sixth Symphony and Debussy's *La Mer*. The orchestra had been associated with the Henry Wood Promenade Concerts since the 1930s, first at Queen's Hall and then at the Royal Albert Hall. The Proms were among Sargent's favorite concerts, and toward the end of his tenure he was appointed, in 1956, conductor-in-chief of the Promenade Concerts and chief guest conductor of the BBC Orchestra. One of the highlights of Sargent's career was the BBC Orchestra tour in 1956 to Scandinavia, where it took part in the Sibelius Festival in Helsinki and also performed a Royal Concert in Stockholm.

In 1957 Sargent was succeeded by Rudolf Schwarz, who had done admirable work with The Bournemouth Symphony Orchestra* and The City of Birmingham Symphony Orchestra* before going to London, and his appointment was warmly welcomed. The repertoire was broadened and now contained more various and contemporary music. One new work for which Schwarz had a special enthusiasm was the Benjamin Britten *Nocturne,* Op. 60, which was first given at the Leeds Festival on October 16, 1958.

William Glock held the position of BBC controller of music from 1959 until his retirement in 1972. Orchestral and chamber concert programs at once became more adventurous and wide-ranging. For example, Stravinsky came to the Festival Hall and to the Maida Vale studio in 1959 to conduct his *Oedipus Rex*. In 1963 Glock gave a lecture in the BBC Concert Hall entitled "The BBC's Music Policy," in which he reviewed past achievements, took a look at the current scene, and laid forth his ideals, ideas, and plans for the following years. It had become clear that orchestral programs were now to give much greater prominence to the music of the Second Viennese School and to distinguished contemporary composers such as Roberto Gerhard. Gerhard's *The Plague* (1964), for example, was a BBC commission. In spite of these timely developments, however, the measures to improve the status and image of the orchestra were frustrated in the 1960s by financial restrictions.

The arrival of Pierre Boulez gave an unmistakable spur and jolt to the BBC Orchestra's performance of contemporary music. In one of his first appearances with the orchestra (1964), he presented the first British performance of his *Soleil des Eaux* at the Festival Hall in a program including Anton Webern's *Six Pieces, Op. 6*. In the ensuing years the whole concept of the concert program was to change radically and fundamentally, coming to particular fruition during Boulez's tenure as chief conductor from 1971 to 1975.

It was Antál Doráti, however, who was Schwarz's immediate successor at the BBC, and it was he who took the orchestra on its first American tour (1965). An outstanding success, its demanding repertoire consisted almost entirely of twentieth-century music, including Gerhard, Bartók, Stravinsky, and members of the Second Viennese School. Doráti shared the podium with Boulez, for whom the tour occasioned his debut performance in New York City, whose Philharmonic Orchestra** he would one day lead as music director. The tour of Eastern Europe in 1967 was similarly successful but hard-going, with many frustrations and confusions in the U.S.S.R.

Boulez's appointment as permanent conductor of the BBC was announced in 1969, though it did not take effect until 1971. It was about this time that Karlheinz Stockhausen's association with the BBC began to be more frequent. His *Gruppen* had been heard at the Proms in 1967, and on January 14, 1970, he was at Maida Vale for a concert of his own works that included *Setz die Segel zur Sonne,* a work that requires total improvisation from all the players.

Concerts at the Round House in North London began in 1972. New works were a constant feature here, with verbal introductions and spontaneous post-performance discussions. These concerts were in many ways informal and, on the whole, warmly received. In 1974 they adopted a new and more clearly defined form, comprising one new work, one revival of a recent work, and one acknowledged twentieth-century masterpiece in each program. These imaginative concerts came to an end in 1976, although they eventually changed form and sequence under the title "College Concerts," which were broadcast from the various London colleges of music.

Boulez took the orchestra on a tour of Japan in May 1975. His period with the orchestra was one of intense energy, activity, and vitality, and one in which the orchestra's repertoire and experience widened to an exceptional degree. The tenure of Boulez's successor, Rudolf Kempe, was very short, brought to an end by his sudden and untimely death in May 1976. He was followed in 1978 by Gennady Rozhdestvensky, one of whose particular triumphs was the performance of Tchaikovsky's complete *Sleeping Beauty* at the Festival Hall in 1979. Rozhdestvensky proved to have very real sympathy with the music of British composers as well. He was succeeded in 1982 by John Pritchard.

SELECTIVE DISCOGRAPHY: The BBC Symphony Orchestra has a published discography comprising hundreds of works and representing commercial recordings made in many formats, beginning with 78 rpm shellac discs. Among the latter are historic recordings by Beecham (Sibelius's *Karelia Suite,* for example), Boult, Fritz Busch, Edward Elgar, Serge Koussevitzky, Bruno Walter, and Arturo Toscanini (whose BBC discography includes about a dozen unissued discs recorded by EMI). Its recorded repertoire, like its concert offerings, stresses large romantic works, twentieth-century classics, and works of living composers. A four-record set was issued to mark the 50th anniversary of the founding of the BBC Symphony Orchestra (BBC Artium 4001), including Boult's recordings of Bliss and Vaughan Williams, Elgar's recording of his *Cockaigne* Overture, and Toscanini's performance of Beethoven's Sixth Symphony. Other currently available discs appear on such labels as Angel, Arabesque, Argo, CBS, Deutsche Grammophon, Mercury, Pearl, Philips, Seraphim, and Turnabout.

Bartók, *The Miraculous Mandarin* (Doráti): Mercury 77012 (3 records). Beethoven, Symphonies Nos. 1, 4, and 6; Overtures (Toscanini): Seraphim 601 (3 records). Berg, *Chamber Concerto* (Boulez): CBS MS 7179. Boulez, *Pli selon pli* (Boulez): NUM 75050. Boulez, *Le soleil des Eaux* (Boulez): Argo ZRG 756. Haydn, *The Seasons* (Colin Davis): Philips Fest. 6770035 (3 records). Tippett, *A Child of Our Time* (Davis): Philips 6500985.

CHRONOLOGY OF MUSIC DIRECTORS: (Chief Conductors): Sir Adrian Boult, 1930–1950. Sir Malcolm Sargent, 1950–1957. Rudolf Schwarz, 1957–1962. Antál Doráti, 1963–1966. Colin Davis, 1967–1971. Pierre Boulez, 1971–1975. Rudolf Kempe, 1975–1976. Gennady Rozhdestvensky, 1978–1981. Sir John Pritchard, 1982–present.

BIBLIOGRAPHY: Correspondence with Ms. Caroline Gant, BBCSO Orchestral Promotions and Publicity Officer, 1986. Asa Briggs, *The History of Broadcasting in the United Kingdom,* 4 vols. (London: BBC, 1961–1979). Adrian Boult, *My Own Trumpet* (London: Hamish Hamilton, 1973). David Cox, *The Henry Wood Proms* (London: BBC, 1980). William Glock, *The BBC's Music Policy* (London: BBC, 1963). Nicholas Kenyon, *The BBC Symphony Orchestra: The First Fifty Years, 1930–1980* (London: BBC, 1981). Ates Orga, *The Proms* (Newton Abbot: David & Charles, 1974).

ACCESS: BBC Symphony Orchestra, BBC Maida Vale Studios, Delaware Road, London W9 2 LG. (01) 580–4468. Lawrie Lea, Manager.

GWILYM BEECHEY

English Chamber Orchestra

The English Chamber Orchestra (ECO) is generally considered one of the finest and most versatile ensembles in the world. It began in 1948 as the Goldsbrough Orchestra with the aim of specializing in music of the baroque era. Since then its work has widened considerably to include the whole chamber orchestra repertoire. Like the Academy of St. Martin in the Fields,* the ensemble believes that the area of "authentic performance" is better covered by more specialized bodies. The group soon became established on radio and television and appeared at many important festivals, including Aldeburgh, Bath, and Cheltenham. The ECO exists without state subsidy and is flexible both in repertoire and in size (24 to 38 players).

From the beginning the orchestra has exported its music not only to European countries but across the world. It has appeared in nearly 300 venues outside the United Kingdom, including Australia, Hong Kong, India, Israel, Japan, South America, Mexico, New Zealand, the United States, and the West Indies. The ECO records copiously.

In the late 1950s it became clear that the original name was no longer appropriate and that a new one was needed to reflect the orchestra's growing reputation. On October 11, 1960, the English Chamber Orchestra gave its inaugural concert in London's Queen Elizabeth Hall with a program of excerpts from Monteverdi operas, realized and directed by Raymond Leppard. At the same time the English Chamber Orchestra and Music Society was formed as a promoting body for the orchestra, with a special emphasis on the presentation of a London concert series.

In common with many other chamber orchestras, the ECO has avoided employing players on a contract basis. There are good reasons for this. To begin with, the orchestra's development has always been directed by market forces. It has never sought state subsidies, except for its London series, and only in recent years has business sponsorship become an important element. Furthermore, in London it appears that the finest players give of their best when free to accept a variety of work: as soloists in chamber ensembles, as well as in recording, film, and television work. Today the ECO averages 430 sessions a year, including 140 concerts; it is management's aim to provide a worthwhile pattern of work using a system of stable coprincipal groupings. In normal circumstances two principal players share each chair and agree to be available for a certain number of engagements in each contract period.

Another distinguishing feature of the ECO is its policy (until 1985) of working without a principal conductor. Instead, the orchestra has consistently invited great interpreters (both established and new talents) to perform it. Its record of giving young conductors important opportunities has been admirable. Among the earliest to benefit from this philosophy was the young Sir Colin Davis. In 1961, as well as conducting the ECO's first United Kingdom tour, he also directed the orchestra's first recording of two Mozart divertimenti. Since that time the ECO has cultivated special relationships with many artists, including Britten, Raymond Leppard, Daniel Barenboim, Murray Perahia, Pinchas Zuckerman, and Vladimir Ashkenazy.

The year 1967 was notable for several important occasions, including the inaugural concert at the Queen Elizabeth Hall in the presence of the Queen, the first color television recording of music for the BBC, and the first networked concert across Europe via the European Broadcasting Union. In the 1980s the ECO continues to be recognized by its appearances at many prestigious events, such as the Royal Wedding for the Prince and Princess of Wales in 1981 and the opening of Barbican Centre (London) a year later. It celebrated its own 25th anniversary in 1985. This was the occasion on which the orchestra also announced the appointment of Jeffrey Tate as its first principal conductor.

RECORDING HISTORY AND SELECTIVE DISCOGRAPHY: The orchestra has always attracted a heavy schedule of recording sessions from the major companies. Over the years it has recorded music from nearly 800 works, and its discography lists a wealth of discs of historic interest. The ECO has appeared on the EMI, Phonogram, Philips, CBS, Decca, Claves, Chandos, ASV, RCA, Vox, Hyperion, and other labels. To date it has released more than 350 discs. Among its recording awards are several for collections of works, including the Deutsche Schallplatten Award (Handel Arias, Baker/Leppard),

Edison Award (Handel Orchestral Works, Leppard), Prix de l'Académie Charles Gros (Cycle of Mozart Piano Concertos, Perahia), and others, some of which are listed below.

Bach, *Brandenburg* Concertos (Leppard): Philips 6746166. Britten, Symphony for Cello and Orchestra; Haydn, Concerto in C for Cello and Orchestra (Rostropovich/Britten): Decca SXL 6641; London 6419. Cantaloube, *Songs of the Auvergne (Kiri Te Kanawa/ Tate*: London LDR–71104 and London 410004–2 (CD) (Best British Classical Recording 1983). Handel, Concerti Grossi, Op. 6 (Leppard): Philips 7699157 (2 records). Mendelssohn, Symphony No. 4 (Leppard): Erato EPR 15533. Mozart, Piano Concertos Nos. 15, K. 450, and 16, K. 451 (Perahia): CBS IM–37824 (Edison Award 1984). Vivaldi, *Complete Sacred Music* (Negri): Philips 6700116 (2 records), 6769032 (2 records), Philips 6769046 (2 records) (Stereo Review Award, Cecilia Prize). Vivaldi, *Four Seasons* (Zuckerman): CBS 60010.

CHRONOLOGY OF PRINCIPAL CONDUCTORS: Jeffrey Tate, 1985–present.

BIBLIOGRAPHY: *ECO into the Eighties* (London: Spencedata, 1983). Nicholas Kenyon, *ECO Pictorial Review* (London: Bruton Hay, 1978). Many articles in the national press.

ACCESS: English Chamber Orchestra, 1 Bloemfontein Way, London W12 7BU. (01) 749–3866. Quintin Ballardie, Director.

DENIS MCCALDIN

London Philharmonic Orchestra

The London Philharmonic Orchestra (LPO) is one of London's and the world's best-known and admired ensembles. Though currently favoring quite strongly the most popular works of the romantic and post-romantic composers, its repertoire includes works from the baroque through the contemporary periods as well as some lesser-known items from the romantic masters.

In the 1985–1986 season the orchestra presented its London concerts in two major series. The International Series at the Royal Festival Hall, funded largely by the Arts Council and the Greater London Council, ran from September through May for a total of 29 concerts, each with its own program. A shorter, lower-priced Royal Festival Hall Series, "Classics for Pleasure," presented ten concerts (five programs in pairs) derived nearly wholly from the romantic repertoire. Other concerts took place at the Barbican Hall and various other halls in, around, and outside of London. The LPO participates each year in the Henry Wood Promenade Concerts (four concerts in 1986) and at festivals in the United Kingdom. It tours abroad regularly (to Italy and West Germany in 1985–1986) and records prolifically. Of the LPO's 93 live concerts in the 1985–1986 season, 16 were under the direction of its principal conductor, Klaus Tennstedt. Other conductors included LPO Conductor Emeritus Sir Georg Solti, Principal Guest Conductor Jesus López-Cobos, and Associate Conductor Vernon Handley, who has since left the position and has been replaced by Carl Davis in 1987.

An important part of the orchestra's season and an important source of revenue is its participation as the accompanying orchestra for the prestigious Glyndebourne Festival Opera each summer in Sussex. For the 1986 Glyndebourne season the orchestra performed nearly nightly from May through mid-August in five productions representing a wide diversity of periods and styles.

The orchestra undertakes a modest though growing program of musical education for school children, at present comprising school visits by individual orchestra members who give lecture/demonstrations and invite students to concerts at reduced rates.

One of London's four major self-governing orchestras, the LPO is administered by a Board of Directors comprising seven orchestra members and the managing director. The orchestra's 90 musicians fall into two categories of membership: full members (of which there are 73) and associate members (of which there are 17). Paid on a per-service basis rather than a yearly salary, they are considered self-employed through the orchestra and are therefore able to occasionally pursue other work as players and/or teachers. Several teach at the Royal College of Music, the Royal Academy of Music, or the Guildhall School of Music and Drama.

According to the orchestra's administrative office, the LPO's annual budget of over £2 million is largely self-generated: 30% from engagements such as the orchestra's annual work for the Glyndebourne Festival; 20% from self-promoted concerts at the Royal Festival Hall; 20% from recording fees and royalties; 5% from overseas tours. Support from the Arts Council accounts for 15% and corporate sponsorship (often in the form of direct support for series and individual concerts) makes up the remaining 10%.

In the past few years the LPO has suffered from the financial insecurity felt by London orchestras generally. This has necessitated concessions by players of, in the words of LPO Board Chairman David Marcou, "small but hard-won benefits." Following recent Arts Council funding cuts and the dissolution of the Greater London Council in April 1986, the LPO, like the other London orchestras, is turning a greater effort toward generating corporate support and self-reliance.

The orchestra's history goes back more than 50 years, and it is heir to a tradition extending back to the early nineteenth century. In 1931, a year after the founding of the BBC Symphony Orchestra,* Thomas Beecham began to discuss with Robert Mayer and art collector Samuel Courtauld (both avid music patrons) the possibility of founding a new orchestra. Upon the founding of the BBC Symphony Orchestra, Beecham had been disappointed not to be as closely involved with it as he might have expected to be, and he soon decided to launch a new orchestra of his own. Thus the London Philharmonic Orchestra came into being in September 1932, with a force of 106 players. They were guaranteed 70 to 80 concerts a year as well as the opportunity to take part in the International Opera season at Covent Garden. The new orchestra began life under the auspices of the Royal Philharmonic Society, whose 121st season it was in 1932–1933. Beecham had attracted some of the best instrumentalists of the period after his proposals had been announced. The orchestra made its debut on October 7, 1932, at the Queen's Hall with a program consisting of music by Berlioz, Mozart, and

Frederick Delius, together with Richard Strauss's *Ein Heldenleben*. The success of this concert was brilliant, and the reviews were full of encouragement and praise.

Beecham ensured that the new orchestra and the long-established Society should remain closely connected as time went on. The Royal Philharmonic Society was established in London in 1813 as the "Philharmonic Society," an association of 30 members together with an unlimited number of associate members and with directors to manage its concerts. Until 1897 society members gave a season of eight concerts between February and June of each year. The title "Royal" was added in 1911. The difficulties that the Society had faced in 1914 had been largely relieved by Beecham's generosity, but there was no permanent orchestra associated with the Society until 1932 when the (independent) LPO was founded. The Society and the London Philharmonic Orchestra were closely linked until 1946, when new seasonal plans were laid. The LPO then played three of the season's eight concerts, while other orchestras (the BBC Symphony Orchestra, London Symphony Orchestra,* Royal Liverpool Philharmonic Orchestra,* and the Hallé Orchestra*) also contributed. Later the Society continued to engage other orchestras for its concerts, even after the Royal Philharmonic Orchestra* had been founded in 1946.

One of the first soloists to appear with the LPO was the 16-year-old Yehudi Menuhin, who played three concertos in a program at the Royal Albert Hall on November 20, 1932. Beecham conducted concertos by Bach and Mozart (K. 271a, discovered in 1907 and receiving its first London performance), and Edward Elgar, then 75, conducted a historic performance of his own B-Minor Concerto.

In 1935 Thomas Russell joined the orchestra as a viola player, and from 1939 to 1952, when the orchestra became self-governing, he was at first secretary and then, from 1945, managing director of the orchestra. By 1935 the orchestral players were guaranteed a regular income, and their activities before the outbreak of the war included some visits abroad, including one to Berlin in 1936, in which they performed in the presence of Hitler. As the Nazi grip tightened over Europe, refugees began to arrive from Germany. Among them was Dr. Berta Geissmar, Furtwängler's secretary in Berlin; she came to London to act as Beecham's secretary.

There were serious financial problems for the orchestra in 1938–1939, but it survived the opera season, and Beecham conducted nearly half of the performances himself. A liquidation meeting was held in 1939 but the determination to remain in force brought about the foundation of a company called "Musical Culture Ltd.," with Thomas Russell as secretary. Another venture of this period to which Russell devoted his energies was the new bimonthly magazine, *The London Philharmonic Post*, which he edited and for which he also wrote. This helped to keep the public aware of the orchestra's activities.

In January 1940 Beecham launched an appeal for the orchestra that resulted in the receipt of £2,000. Beecham, however, who planned to live in the United

States and Australia during the war, severed his active connection with the orchestra in April 1940. He finally broke away altogether in 1945 to found the Royal Philharmonic Orchestra.* J. B. Priestly launched "A Musical Manifesto" on behalf of the LPO on July 18, 1940, and the conductors who took part on that occasion (Adrian Boult, Basil Cameron, and Malcolm Sargent) were to take the greater share in the orchestra's direction in the next few years.

During the remaining war years there was a successful association with the band leader Jack Hylton, who presented the orchestra in many of the theatres he controlled in England. Their concerts then were especially appreciated in Manchester and other places in the north and in Wales. In 1942 the LPO made its first appearance at the Henry Wood Promenade Concerts, which had been transferred to the Royal Albert Hall after the bombing of Queen's Hall in 1941, when many LPO players lost their instruments. By 1943 the LPO had become the first full-time permanent symphony orchestra to balance its accounts without subsidies. It had found a home of its own at the Orpheum Theatre in Golders Green in North London.

The newly formed London Philharmonic Choir came into existence in 1947. Its founder, chorus master, and conductor for the next 22 years was Frederic Jackson. Also in 1947 the London County Council (LCC) made its first grant to the orchestra at about the same time as plans were first put in hand to build a concert hall to replace the Queen's Hall. The LCC looked upon the LPO as its "home" or "resident" orchestra, and Russell and others on the LPO Committee thus took an active share in the plans that were eventually to result in the building of the Royal Festival Hall. The LCC sponsored the orchestra in the late 1940s in the promotion of children's concerts, for which the guest conductor was Leslie Russell.

In 1948 the first permanent postwar principal conductor was appointed— Eduard van Beinum, whose association with the Concertgebouw Orchestra* in Amsterdam since 1931 had ensured him a wide reputation. He had first appeared as a guest conductor with the LPO in 1946. Beecham had returned at the end of the war and had conducted the orchestra for a further 18 months, but he found the position uncongenial, as he was no longer in overall control of its activities.

The credit goes to van Beinum for raising the standards of the orchestra in the late 1940s with his breadth of repertoire and superb rehearsal efficiency. A Dutch citizen, van Beinum was allowed to work in England only six months of the year, and this created problems with the organization of a full season's concerts. After he relinquished his position the LPO was fortunate to engage Sir Adrian Boult as its new permanent conductor in 1951, the year after he retired from the BBC. The orchestra made its first appearance on television, with Boult, on June 6, 1952, in a program called *The Conductor Speaks*.

In 1949 Russell had visited the U.S.S.R. (albeit as a private individual); this and his ensuing visit to the People's Republic of China in 1952 were not thought auspicious by orchestra leaders, and in the ensuing breach a few members of the orchestra resigned in sympathy with him. Thereafter the orchestral management was reconstituted and a general administrator, Thomas O'Dea, was placed at the helm.

About this time the orchestra began to make a more widespread impact around the country and was no longer content to confine its performances to London. Recordings too began to be more frequent. In 1956 the LPO became the first British orchestra to visit the U.S.S.R. Boult at first did not intend to go, but was persuaded finally to do so by the Foreign Office. There were ten concerts in all, six in Moscow and four in Leningrad. After this tour Boult retired as principal conductor, but appeared as a guest on numerous occasions. The mid–1950s were bad financial years for the orchestra, and matters had become serious by the 1957–1958 season. Contracts and pension arrangements had to be abandoned in favor of a fee-earning scheme. The new chairman of the orchestra's Board was Eric Bravington, the principal trumpet, and he produced a scheme for the foundation of the London Philharmonic Society. The orchestra survived through funds from the LCC for concerts given in London and from funds from the Arts Council for concerts given outside London.

In 1958 William Steinberg was appointed permanent conductor following Boult, but his interests in the United States caused him difficulties in organization, and he left in 1960. The orchestra went on a 26,000-mile tour of the Far East and Australia in 1962, when the conducting was shared by Malcolm Sargent and John Pritchard. At the time this was the longest tour ever undertaken by a British orchestra, and its overall success was an important factor in the appointment of Pritchard as the orchestra's permanent conductor in that year. In the early 1960s the orchestra underwent some new shaping with the appointment of several new young players of considerable talent. Tastes were changing too, and the programs had a wider range and were making a fresh impact with Pritchard in control. The highlight of 1963 was the visit of Pablo Casals, who conducted the first performance in Great Britain of his oratorio *El Pessebre* (1960) in the Royal Festival Hall on September 27. This was a very moving occasion, and it proved to be Casals's last appearance in London.

In 1964 the orchestra was engaged as the resident orchestra of the Glyndebourne Opera (with whom Pritchard had been associated since 1947). The ten-week summer season involved some 60 performances, and the orchestra has maintained this congenial and fruitful association over many years. When in 1965 the LPO Council was formed with Lord Shaftesbury as chairman, the orchestra's work and reputation were afforded a surer and more solid footing. The financial situation improved considerably, and there was a noticeable advance in performing standards once again with the appointment of Bernard Haitink as principal conductor in 1967. He remained for 12 years, longer than any previous LPO conductor. Haitink's wide sympathies and his energetic ebullience endeared him to British players and British audiences. Tours continued and widened, the 1973 tour to China being a special highlight.

When Haitink's busy schedule at Glyndebourne and his commitments in Holland caused him to relinquish his appointment with the LPO in 1979, he was succeeded by Georg Solti, who has achieved a wide reputation for his many vivid and exciting performances. Boult's long association with the orchestra came to an end finally in 1978, and in April of the following year the LPO gave two concerts to celebrate his 90th birthday. Two months later the LPO and its choir gave a concert at Royal Festival Hall to celebrate the 100th birthday of Sir Robert Mayer, one of the guarantors at the founding of the orchestra nearly 50 years before. Sir Robert had chosen the music for the occasion, which included Hector Berlioz's *Nuit d'Été*, sung by Dame Janet Baker; at intermission the Queen conferred on Sir Robert the distinction of Knight Commander of the Royal Victorian Order.

In 1982 Klaus Tennstedt, who had made his London debut in 1976, took over from Georg Solti as principal conductor. Tennstedt has been especially admired for his performances of the music of Gustav Mahler. The year 1985 saw the appointment of the LPO's first managing director chosen from outside the orchestra's own organization. This was John Willan, whose stated goals for the orchestra include "more congenial working conditions and absolution from financial stress."

RECORDING HISTORY AND SELECTIVE DISCOGRAPHY: The LPO's first records had been made in 1933, but they had been few and far between until the 1950s, when the Nixa Company signed a contract with the orchestra. In 1953 Boult recorded William Walton's *Belshazzar's Feast* with the LPO chorus and orchestra. By the end of 1953 Boult had recorded all of Ralph Vaughan Williams's symphonies for Decca with the assistance of the composer, who had warm praise for their performances. An anniversary album entitled *Fifty Years' Recordings* contains various pieces conducted by Beecham, van Beinum, Haitink, Pritchard, and Solti (LPJ 50). In recent years the orchestra has recorded for Deutsche Grammophon, EMI, Erato, London, Philips, Quintessence, RCA, and others. Major recording projects include a nearly complete cycle of Mahler symphonies under Tennstedt, Haydn symphonies under Solti, and a series of English music planned for recording under Bryden Thomson.

Bartók, Piano Concertos Nos. 2 and 3 (Vladimir Ashkenazy/Solti): London 7167. Berlioz, *Requiem* (André Previn): EMI SLS 5029, Angel DS–3902 (2 records). Cavalli, *La Calisto* (Raymond Leppard): Decca/Argo ZNF 11. Elgar, *The Apostles* (Boult): EMI SLS 976. Elgar, *The Kingdom* (Boult): EMI SLS 939. Mahler, Symphony No. 4 (Popp/Tennstedt): Angel DS–37954, CDC 47024 (CD). Parry, *Symphonic Variations* and Symphony No. 5 (Boult): EMI/HMV ASD 3725. Shostakovich, Symphony No. 4 (Haitink): London 7160.

CHRONOLOGY OF MUSIC DIRECTORS: (Principal Conductors): Sir Thomas Beecham, 1932–1940. (Guest conductors, 1940–1948.) Eduard van Beinum, 1948–1950. Sir Adrian Boult, 1950–1957. William Steinberg, 1958–1960. Sir John Pritchard, 1962–1966. Bernard Haitink, 1966–1979. Sir Georg Solti, 1979–1983 (now Conductor Emeritus). Klaus Tennstedt, 1983–present.

BIBLIOGRAPHY: Interview between Robert R. Craven and LPO Publications Editor Frances Cook, 1986. Adrian Boult, *My Own Trumpet* (London: Hamish Hamilton, 1973). Robert Elkin, *Royal Philharmonic* (London: Rider, 1946). William Kellaway, *London Philharmonic* (London: Kenneth Mason, 1972). *LPO Yearbook '85/86*. Jerrold N. Moore,

Philharmonic Jubilee, 1932–1982 (London, 1982). Thomas Russell, *Philharmonic* (London, 1942). Thomas Russell, *Philharmonic Decade* (London, 1945). Thomas Russell, *Philharmonic Project* (London, 1952). Ursula Vaughan Williams, *RVW: A Biography of Ralph Vaughan Williams* (London: Oxford University Press, 1964).

ACCESS: The London Philharmonic Orchestra, 35 Doughty Street, London, WC1N 2AA. (01) 833–2744. John Willan, Managing Director.

GWILYM BEECHEY

London Symphony Orchestra

Of all the orchestras in Great Britain, the London Symphony Orchestra (LSO) can rightly claim to be a pioneer. It was the first self-governing orchestra in England, the first British orchestra to tour the United States and Canada, and the first to be sponsored by a commercial firm. These are just a few of the remarkable achievements by a body of musicians born out of conflict.

The LSO's symphonic season runs from the end of September to the beginning of December, then from mid-January to the end of April, with more popular concerts over the Christmas period and during the summer, for a total of 160 working days in its home hall, the Barbican Centre. Audiences generally fall into the pattern of those who attend on Saturday evenings and Sunday afternoons in a relaxed weekend mood, wanting to hear familiar, well-loved music, and those who prefer a mid-week concert where they look for mental stimulation.

The LSO's repertoire ranges over the whole spectrum of orchestral history, although there have recently been highly acclaimed performances of contemporary music, including a Webern Centenary Festival (conducted by current music director Claudio Abbado and heard in London, Paris, and Vienna), Karlheinz Stockhausen's *Gruppen,* and Michael Tippett conducting his own works. Future plans include music by Hans Werner Henze and Pierre Boulez, conducted by the composers.

Since its first trans-Atlantic tour (1912) the LSO has been a frequent visitor overseas and now plays regularly throughout North America and Europe, having made 13 trips in 16 years, more than any other British or European orchestra. For a world tour in 1983 a British Airways plane was chartered to take the orchestra to seven countries in 34 days to play 21 concerts. The 1984–1985 season saw tours of Germany, Austria, France, Italy, Switzerland, North America, and India.

Because the musicians are not paid unless they play, the orchestra has to be commercially competitive and has developed the flexibility to play as backing for television commercials, films, and pop records, in addition to its distinguished recording career in the symphonic repertoire. Because it is known that London orchestras can read music better and get it recorded faster than any other orchestras in the world, the LSO is in demand for commercial work required within a tight schedule. This ability to sight-read and respond quickly is not a new phenomenon. Arthur Nikisch said of the LSO, "They are not only such fine players and first-sight readers, but they are so extraordinarily quick to catch my meaning.'' The LSO's recordings are closely linked to its touring policy, as its worldwide public appearances encourage the sale of records. One of the world's most prolific recording ensembles, the LSO has hundreds of titles currently in print. The orchestra also appears regularly on television.

Chamber ensembles have been formed from within the orchestra, players join groups unconnected with the LSO, and principals and coprincipals regularly play with other orchestras as soloists. Players are not required to take on extra work, but many find it necessary to supplement their average weekly earning of £250. Outside work is encouraged because it helps players enlarge their repertoire and demonstrates to the public that this orchestra contains players of high professional standing and reputation. The allied London Symphony Chorus does not work solely with the LSO but sings with all the major London orchestras, and in 1984 joined with the U.S.S.R. State Symphony Orchestra* in Moscow for the first performance in that country of William Walton's *Belshazzar's Feast* conducted by the choir's director of music, Richard Hickcox, and Edward Elgar's *Dream of Gerontius* conducted by Evgeny Svetlanov.

In 1948 the orchestra entered into an agreement, now discontinued, with Harrow Education Authority to provide concerts for schoolchildren, and educational work still forms part of the annual program. The most important scheme is the Shell-LSO Music Scholarship for young musicians. Begun in 1977, the orchestra undertakes an annual national tour during which it is joined by young musicians between the ages of 14 and 21 who have reached regional finals for the scholarship. At a final judging in London a single winner emerges. Each year a different family of orchestral instruments is judged: percussion/tympani in 1984, for example, and woodwinds in 1985. In tandem with this scholarship is the newly developed idea of noncompetitive workshops that take place in public, during which principals work with young players on orchestral repertoire. The LSO has also arranged for a 1985 British-American scholarship to provide study for an American student at the Royal Academy of Music in London, with a reciprocal arrangement for a British student at the Juilliard School in New York City in 1986.

To supplement its income from ticket sales, recording, and broadcasting, the orchestra must rely heavily on financial support from many sources. This comes in a variety of forms, including grants toward staging particular concerts, sponsorship of tours, and endowments of some principals' chairs. The Arts Council of Great Britain and the City of London combine to contribute some £500,000 toward 80 concerts per year that the LSO plays at its Barbican Centre home. The orchestra is also supported by the LSO Club, with its membership advantages of priority booking and reduction on concert tickets as well as its fund-raising and publicity work.

Having been chosen as the resident orchestra in London's Barbican Centre has helped the LSO to consolidate its position as a leading orchestra of the world. Barbican Hall, where the orchestra performs, is part of a complex that includes blocks of flats as well as the Barbican Centre itself, with its two cinemas, Art Gallery, Sculpture Court, conference facilities, public library, exhibition halls, and restaurants. The hall's 2,226-seat, fan-shaped auditorium provides a feeling of intimacy, and no listener is far from the orchestra. The Barbican Theatre is the home of the Royal Shakespeare Company, with which the orchestra has formed strong performance links. On the same site is the Guildhall School of Music and Drama, where some 20 members of the orchestra are employed as teachers. The Guildhall also benefits from a scheme whereby conductors who are engaged by the LSO work with student orchestras. Tickets are given to music students for specific concerts, and they attend LSO rehearsals.

The self-governing structure pioneered by the LSO remains virtually unchanged today. Each of the present 86 players has to hold 40 shares in the orchestra, which carry the entitlement to full voting rights and participation in the running of the company. Shares are returned when a player leaves or dies. The nine Board members are elected annually by the shareholders, three members resigning by rotation each year but still being eligible for re-election. It is hoped that all sections of the orchestra will be represented on the Board, but this is not always achieved. The Board annually elects its chairman, vice-chairman, and officers and is responsible for appointing a managing director and an administrator from outside the orchestra. It is possible for a percentage of members to call a special meeting, but apart from the necessary formal annual general meeting and Board meetings, other issues are generally discussed on a friendly, less formal basis within the orcherstra, where rank-and-file members enjoy equality with the Board of Directors. In this way many issues can be settled quickly, but it is also possible for members to be unaware of decisions that have been taken. Occasional periods of discontent have rocked this management structure, as in a 1967 dispute over the degree of authority that might be exercised by the administrator relative to that of the elected Board.

In 1937 a category of associate membership was introduced, available to first-call extras who have to hold themselves free from permanent engagements in order to deputize for full members. The LSO works to a schedule of approximately 580 three-hour sessions per year, excluding traveling, with no corporate holiday period, and because there is no pay unless a musician attends a working session, substitutes are required for the player who falls sick or has worked many days, even weeks, without a break. The use of regular deputies who understand the nuances of the orchestra helps to achieve a balanced sound. Entry to LSO membership is by audition before a panel of ten, made up of LSO players and the conductor, if he is available. A prospective member can be invited to play with the orchestra, allowing an assessment of his or her musical skill and personality. As well as employing coprincipals for most instruments, the LSO has the title of principal for English horn, piccolo, bass clarinet, and contrabassoon. Of the LSO's 15 support staff, librarians and transport staff are vitally important, as this orchestra regards travel as an essential part of its ongoing life.

At the beginning of the 1900s orchestral players, especially in London, found work wherever it was available for the highest fee. Permanent members of an orchestra would send deputies to concerts and rehearsals, and it was possible for a performance to contain a large percentage of musicians who had not attended any rehearsals. By 1904 Henry Wood was no longer prepared to work on these terms with his Queen's Hall Orchestra. In return for a guaranteed wage he offered his players 100 engagements over nine months, provided that the deputy system was abandoned except in the case of sickness. Many of the musicians had long-standing, better-paid engagements outside the orchestra and, faced with a loss of earnings through this restriction, 46 of them resigned to adopt a self-management scheme. On June 9, 1904, the London Symphony Orchestra thus began its long career, in the same hall where players had so often performed as members of the Queen's Hall Orchestra.

An outline of the self-management scheme was sent to Hans Richter, who agreed to become the first principal conductor, with the proviso that the orchestra should contain at least 100 players. He offered his services free for the first concert, which opened with Richard Wagner's *Die Meistersinger* Overture, included Edward Elgar's *Variations on an Original Theme (Enigma),* and concluded with Beethoven's Symphony No. 5. From October 1904 to March 1905 monthly concerts attracted great contemporary conductors—Arthur Nikisch, Fritz Steinbach, Sir Charles Villiers Stanford, Édouard Colonne, and Elgar—and established in England the new idea of the guest conductor.

As early as 1906, just two years after its foundation, the LSO gave two concerts in Paris, conducted by Stanford, Colonne, and André Messager. In 1912 Nikisch agreed to conduct in the United States and Canada if he could take the LSO, which thus became the first British orchestra to tour North America, giving 28 concerts in 21 days, beginning and ending in New York's Carnegie Hall, visiting Witchita (Kansas), Toronto, Montreal, and Boston, and being received in the White House by President Taft. For the players it was a tour never to be forgotten, as last-minute travel arrangements prevented the orchestra from sailing aboard the *Titanic*.

In 1922 Walter Wanger, head of Hollywood's United Artists, engaged the LSO to accompany silent films in Covent Garden Opera House. The orchestra has had a working relationship with the film industry ever since. Representative highlights are its performance of film scores to *Things to Come* (1934) and *Star Wars,* for which the LSO was awarded a Platinum Disc.

The orchestra's involvement with the British Broadcasting Corporation stretches back to February 1924, when Ralph Vaughan Williams conducted his recently written *Pastoral* Symphony in the first of many broadcasts which gave regular employment to the orchestra until the formation of the BBC Symphony Orchestra* in 1930.

The LSO has had a long line of international conductors, some of whom held regular positions with the orchestra, while others worked for intermittent periods without the title. Many of the LSO's guest and permanent conductors have left their mark on the orchestra, but in recent years the traditional style of French playing developed by Pierre Monteux, the training given by Sergiu Celibidache, the energy of André Previn, and the depth of interpretation provided by Claudio Abbado have brought the orchestra to its high performance standard.

The orchestra has been associated with leading composers, and many first performances now in the standard repertoire form part of the orchestra's heritage. Particular conductors have each in their own way widened the repertoire. In 1969 Pierre Boulez presented a series of concerts under the title of "The Second Viennese School," with five concerts in London and two in Vienna as part of the Vienna Festival. Colin Davis and Sergiu Celibidache introduced more French music and André Previn included additional Russian repertoire. Claudio Abbado has a particular feeling for the music of Gustav Mahler, and the orchestra is responding to this with performances of his symphonies.

The LSO is assured of its home at the Barbican and of Abbado's direction until at least 1990. It is the first of the world's orchestras to be marketed by the firm of International Management Consultants, marketers of events such as the Olympic Games, and so looks forward to a busy future.

There is, however, the continuing worry about financial support. One scheme that had to be abandoned as too expensive was the Composer-in-Residence, begun in 1982 when the orchestra moved to the Barbican. Nevertheless, the orchestra still encourages direct work with composers and is looking forward to a creative period with Boulez. The LSO employs a support staff of 15, including librarians and a transport team, and hopes to be able to retain these employees. Through its advertising policy and international recognition the orchestra is able to attract sponsorship, but more will be needed in the future. Special recognition was given to the orchestra in 1984 when the BBC presented a four-hour television documentary on the work and life-style of the LSO and its members. This was the longest documentary program to feature a single arts establishment and is a measure of the status that the LSO retains on the national and international musical scenes.

RECORDING HISTORY AND SELECTIVE DISCOGRAPHY: Recording has been a feature of the LSO's work since 1912, when records were made with the Edison Bell Co. In 1920 a contract was signed with Columbia, and famous conductors such as Felix Weingartner, Bruno Walter, and Richard Strauss conducted a variety of works. In the 1930s the orchestra began recording for Decca, with whom it issued many memorable performances, including in 1935 William Walton's First Symphony conducted by Hamilton Harty. Sir Edward Elgar remained closely associated with the LSO and conducted his symphonic poem *Falstaff* at the opening of EMI's Abbey Road Studios in 1931. The bulk of his later recordings for HMV was made with the LSO. Today the orchestra puts out more new records for top labels (such as Deutsche Grammophon, CBS, and EMI) than any other London orchestra. These amount to some 30 to 40 per year.

Bartók, *The Miraculous Mandarin* (Abbado): DG 410598. Berg, *Lulu—Symphonic Suite* and *Three Pieces* (Abaddo): Polygram 2534–804. Brahms, Piano Concerto No. 2 (Ashkenazy/Mehta): Polygram SXL6309. Britten, Choral Works (LSO Chorus & Soloists/ Marriner): Polygram ZRG 947. Mahler, *Song of the Earth* (Colin Davis): Philips 6514– 112. Mozart, Piano Concertos Nos. 9 and 17, K. 271 and K. 453 (Rudolf Serkin/Abbado):

DG 2532–060. Shostakovich, Symphony No. 10 (Previn) EMI ASD–4405, Angel DS–37955. Strauss, Tone Poems (Abbado): DG 410518 (CD). Stravinsky, *The Rite of Spring* (Abbado): DG 2530–635. Webern, Complete Works of Webern (Boulez): CBS M4–35193 (4 records).

CHRONOLOGY OF PRINCIPAL CONDUCTORS: Hans Richter, 1904–1911. Sir Edward Elgar, 1911–1912. (Guest conductors, 1913–1915.) Sir Thomas Beecham, 1915–1916. (Guest conductors, 1916–1919.) Albert Coates, 1919–1922. (Guest conductors, 1922–1932.) Sir Hamilton Harty, 1932–1935. (Guest conductors, 1935–1950.) Josef Krips, 1950–1954. (Guest conductors, 1954–1961.) Pierre Monteux, 1961–1964. (Guest conductors, 1964–1965.) Istvan Kertesz, 1965–1968. André Previn, 1968–1979. Claudio Abbado, 1979–1983, 1983–present (as Music Director).

BIBLIOGRAPHY: Linda Blandford, *The LSO: Scenes from Orchestral Life* (London: Michael Joseph, 1984). Hubert Foss and Noel Goodwin, *London Symphony: Portrait of an Orchestra* (London: Naldrett Press, 1954). Maurice Pearton, *The LSO at 70* (London: Gollancz, 1974). Alan Smyth, ed., *To Speak for Ourselves* (London: Kimber, 1970).

ACCESS: London Symphony Orchestra, Barbican Centre, London EC2Y 8DS. (01) 588–1116. Anthony Camden, Chairman.

ANNE DUNN

Philharmonia Orchestra

Generally regarded as one of the finest in the United Kingdom, the Philharmonia Orchestra presents a season of nearly 50 concerts in London's 2,900-seat Royal Festival Hall as well as numerous programs to full and enthusiastic audiences throughout the country. The orchestra appears frequently at the major international festivals, including the BBC Promenade Concerts, and makes regular visits to Europe. It is justly renowned for its fine commercial recordings.

Originally under the care of one man, Walter Legge, the Philharmonia is now organized on a basis similar to most of London's other orchestras. A Board of Management drawn from players in the orchestra works in conjunction with the principal conductor and managing director. Policy decisions and program planning are arrived at through fairly democratic means, although recent financial constrictions have inevitably quashed more adventurous projects. Concerts and recording sessions are managed on a strictly contractual basis with no fixed annual salary for orchestral players. In common with most of the other orchestras in the United Kingdom, the Philharmonia is largely dependent on industrial sponsorship for its financial security, although it receives an annual grant from the Arts Council of Great Britain and the London Orchestral Concert Board.

Since the members of the orchestra are in effect paid per concert or recording session, they are given some opportunity to take a greater part in London's extensive freelance musical scene. Some players have secured professorships at the leading music colleges in London. Others appear regularly with specialist ensembles such as the London Sinfonietta. Many of the principals appear as soloists with other orchestras throughout the country.

The Philharmonia is a relatively young orchestra, yet its immediate association with some of the greatest conductors of this century has resulted in a reputation founded on the finest traditions of orchestral discipline. While the orchestra undoubtedly lacks the tonal brilliance most commonly associated with the London Symphony Orchestra,* its string section possesses a warmth unrivaled in the country. Despite the tremendous pressures affecting musical life in London, the orchestra has never compromised its uniformly high standard of performance.

During World War II Walter Legge, who had spent much time arranging concerts and entertainments for the troops (under the national organization ENSA) harbored one driving ambition: to form in Britain one of the finest recording orchestras in the world. With the cessation of hostilities in 1945, orchestral life in the country was naturally in disarray. However, as controller of EMI's Columbia record label, Legge could offer substantial contracts to soloists and conductors, at the same time guaranteeing regular work for an orchestra. Using his background in ENSA, he combed Europe for the most promising talent, and then he set about making records. His first efforts with the "Philharmonia Quartet" established from the start both the ensemble's title and principal string positions.

The Philharmonia Orchestra made its first public appearance in a concert of Mozart works conducted by Sir Thomas Beecham in October 1945 at the Kingsway Hall, London (still used for the orchestra's numerous recording sessions). According to contemporary anecdotes Sir Thomas was so impressed by the first rehearsal that he offered to renounce his fee. The orchestra rewarded him with a box of cigars. Beecham's generosity was, however, tempered with a certain amount of self-interest, as he was keen to become the orchestra's principal conductor. Legge had different ideas, and, determined to attract the best European conductors, he quite deliberately initiated a tradition that is still maintained: the orchestra has never had a principal conductor born in England.

Despite the inevitable financial crises of the postwar period, the Philharmonia's rise to prominence was astonishingly rapid. Lucrative recording sessions attracted the finest players. Legge himself established a string section emulating the warmth promoted by the best orchestras of Berlin and Vienna. For the winds he secured the services of a number of outstanding soloists including flautist Gareth Morris and the legendary horn virtuoso Dennis Brain. In addition, Legge, who was recording for EMI in Vienna, played a vital role in breaking down hostility to artists who had worked under the Nazi regime. Before long both Wilhelm Furtwängler and his arch rival, Herbert von Karajan, were lured to London to work with the orchestra—this naturally reinforced a relationship with great European traditions. Karajan in particular secured his postwar reputation with the orchestra both in public concerts and an extensive series of recordings. Karajan was acknowledged as the orchestra's first unofficially appointed principal conductor, even though he gave only one or two public concerts with the Philharmonia each season.

Although Karajan dominated the orchestra's fortunes at this time, Legge was keen to explore other avenues. When at his own request Arturo Toscanini led the Philharmonia in a series of concerts at London's newly opened Royal Festival Hall (1952), critical response was rapturous. Toscanini introduced his young protégé Guido Cantelli to Legge and the orchestra, reinforcing a connection with the Italian tradition that is maintained to the present day. Cantelli's stormy yet electrifying relationship with the orchestra brought immense rewards in the recording studio until his career was tragically cut short in an air crash in 1956.

In addition to its work with renowned conductors, the Philharmonia enjoyed a fairly close liaison with a number of leading composers. Richard Strauss, William Walton, and Paul Hindemith all conducted the orchestra in their own compositions. At the same time, Nicolas Medtner (the Russian composer now resident in Britain) and Constant Lambert enjoyed the patronage of the orchestra in a series of recordings.

In the 1954–1955 season Karajan succeeded Furtwängler as principal conductor of the Berlin Philharmonic Orchestra,* thereby relinquishing his close ties with the Philharmonia. Once again, Legge demonstrated extraordinary vision in his choice of successor: he persuaded the 70-year-old Otto Klemperer to become the orchestra's first principal conductor (a post he retained until his retirement in 1971). Although Klemperer, as a disciple of Gustav Mahler, had enjoyed a reputation as one of the greatest conductors in Berlin during the 1920s, his career after the war was really in the doldrums. However, the chance to work with Legge and the Philharmonia produced a veritable transformation in fortunes that had a profound impact on both conductor and orchestra.

Earlier in the century Klemperer had built his career around the espousal of modern composers such as Arnold Schoenberg, Igor Stravinsky, Kurt Weill, and Hindemith, but with the Philharmonia he concentrated his attention on the great symphonic literature from Haydn to Mahler and Strauss. However, his approach was far from reactionary. Offering radical insights into the established repertoire, he brought to the orchestra an increased weightiness of sound balanced by an astonishing clarity of texture and ensemble. Unlike Karajan, Klemperer established a regular series of concerts with the Philharmonia, regarded by both critics and audiences without reservation as the high spots of London's musical life during the late 1950s and early 1960s. Many of his recordings are available to this day.

A further development for the orchestra occurred in 1955 when Legge invited Wilhelm Pitz, choir master at Bayreuth, to direct the newly formed Philharmonia Chorus. Collaboration with Klemperer on such works as Bach's *St. Matthew Passion*, Beethoven's Ninth Symphony, and Mahler's *Resurrection* Symphony further enhanced the choir and orchestra's growing reputations.

Legge wielded autocratic power over the orchestra, which was dependent on him for financial and artistic security. However, by 1964 Legge had reduced his recording commitments with EMI, and realizing that he could no longer maintain the orchestra as he wished, he threatened to disband the Philharmonia. Fearing this, the players responded immediately by forming themselves into a self-governing cooperative and adopting the name ''New Philharmonia Orchestra.''

Klemperer encouraged the orchestra in this move, the BBC responded by offering regular studio work, and while EMI committed themselves to future recording contracts with Klemperer, other recording companies (who had for so long envied EMI's virtual monopoly with the Philharmonia) relished the prospect of using the orchestra. In practical terms, a trust was set up to provide financial help and secure a new library of orchestral parts, while the London Orchestral Concert Board agreed to fund public concerts. A major link with the Edinburgh International Festival was set up, and in 1955 the Festival's director, the Earl of Harewood, was appointed the orchestra's first artistic director.

By the following year the New Philharmonia had amassed sufficient funds to undertake a major tour of South America, and during the late 1960s it performed with increasing frequency at major European festivals, including Salzburg and Lucerne. A particularly moving occasion was an invitation from the West German government to Klemperer and the orchestra to perform in the Beethoven bicentenary year at the composer's birthplace in Bonn.

In 1971 Klemperer was forced to retire from the concert platform due to ill health, and his absence caused an inevitable vacuum. It was at Klemperer's suggestion that the young American conductor Lorin Maazel was offered an associate position in 1971. For two years the fiery and brilliant personality of Maazel battled with the orchestra, but morale was low and standards of orchestral discipline suffered. In the end it was the imaginative appointment in 1973 of a young and relatively unknown Italian, Riccardo Muti, that restored the New Philharmonia to its former eminence. With Klemperer the emphasis was directed almost exclusively toward German repertoire, but Muti's tastes were more obviously catholic, based upon his wide experience in the opera house. Muti drew a more brilliant sound from the orchestra but never sacrificed traditional warmth of tone. His predilection for fast tempi and emotionally charged interpretations produced a mixed reception from the critics, who sometimes accused him of superficiality, though audiences were large, enthusiastic, and often adulatory. An exclusive contract with EMI cemented the partnership between Muti and the orchestra.

In 1977 the orchestra reverted to its original name, "Philharmonia" and reestablished close association with Carlo Maria Giulini, who had made a number of highly acclaimed recordings with it in the early 1960s. At the same time Muti continued to tour with the orchestra in Europe and the United States. He was appointed principal music director in 1979 and eventually conductor laureate in 1982. In 1980 the Prince of Wales became the orchestra's first patron.

The past five years have brought a sense of consolidation to the orchestra after its turbulent reputation in the early 1970s. Although the future seems uncertain because of vicissitudes of government funding, the Philharmonia continues to draw fuller audiences to London concerts than any of its rivals. Its tours continue at a brisk pace—in the 1983–1984 season, for example, the orchestra visited Canada, the United States, Australia, and almost every country in Europe. Despite the fact that its repertoire has long remained relatively conservative, contemporary music has begun to play a greater part in program planning. A notable event was the world premier of Peter Maxwell Davies's First Symphony in 1978. More recently, collaboration between the industrial sponsor Du Maurier and the Society for Promotion of New Music has resulted in the orchestra participating in the "Music of Today" concerts featuring works by Witold Lutosławski, György Ligeti, Morton Feldman, Michael Finnissy, Jacob Druckman, and the Philharmonia's own composer-in-residence, Oliver Knussen.

The appointment in 1984 of Giuseppe Sinopoli as principal conductor to succeed Riccardo Muti can also be seen as part of this trend, for the young Italian is also a composer whose music demonstrates radical sympathies. Moreover, Sinopoli's obsession with a limited repertoire (specializing in Mahler, Brahms, Schumann, Mendelssohn, Schubert, and selected moderns) and his penchant for idiosyncratic interpretations have already aroused a healthy if controversial response from audiences, critics, and players.

RECORDING HISTORY AND SELECTIVE DISCOGRAPHY: The Philharmonia's first commercial recording for EMI was made late in 1945 when French violinist Ginette Neveu recorded the Sibelius Violin Concerto, with the orchestra conducted by Walter Susskind. Karajan's extensive series of recordings (1948–1960), including his first complete cycle of Beethoven's symphonies (1953), did much to secure his postwar reputation with the orchestra. Guido Cantelli's recording in the early 1950s of Tchaikovsky's *Pathetique* Symphony is one of the finest ever committed to disc. William Walton's recordings of his own First Symphony and oratorio *Belshazzar's Feast* (HMV SLS 5246) and Hindemith's recordings of his own works are especially noteworthy. Klemperer's reputation as a recording artist is built around the cycle of Beethoven symphonies as well as those by Brahms, Bruckner, and his mentor, Mahler. The fact that most of these recordings are still available after 20 years says a great deal for their lasting quality.

Close ties with EMI were maintained up to 1964, but after Legge's departure recordings were made with Decca, Deutsche Grammophon, Philips, CBS, Lyrita, RCA, Erato, and Unicorn. In the 1970s Riccardo Muti's recordings of a series of Verdi's operas as well as symphonies by Tchaikovsky, Mendelssohn, and Schumann won many international accolades.

Beethoven, Symphonies Nos. 1–9 (Klemperer): HMV SLS 788. Cherubini, Requiem in C Minor (Muti): HMV ASD 4071; Angel DS 37789. Copland, Symphony No. 3 (Copland): CBS 61869, CBS M 35113(.) Debussy, *La Mer, Nocturnes* (Guilini): HMV SXLP 30146, Angel RL 32033. Hindemith, *Symphonia Serena, Horn Concerto* (Brain/ Hindemith): Angel S 35491. Mahler, Symphony No. 2 (Klemperer): HMV SLS 806 (2 records). Mendelssohn, Symphony No. 4; Schubert, Symphony No. 8 (Sinopoli): DG 4108621 GH. Mendelssohn, *Elijah* (Rafael Frühbeck de Burgos): HMV SLS 935, Angel S–3738 (3 records). Horn Concertos Nos. 1–4 (Brain/Karajan): Angel 35092. Rachmaninov, Piano Concerto No. 4; Ravel, Piano Concerto in G (Arturo Beneditti Michelangeli/ Ettore Gracis): HMV SXLP 30169, Angel S–35567. Sibelius, Symphonies Nos. 5 and 7 (Karajan): HMV SXLP 30430. Tchaikovsky, Symphony No. 5 (Ashkenazy): Decca SXL 6884, London 7107. Wagner, *Tristan und Isolde* (Furtwängler): HMV RLS 684 (4 records).

CHRONOLOGY OF MUSIC DIRECTORS: (Various titles): Herbert von Karajan, 1948–1954. Otto Klemperer, 1955–1971. Lorin Maazel, 1971–1973. Riccardo Muti, 1973–1983. Giuseppe Sinopoli, 1984–present.

BIBLIOGRAPHY: Stephen J. Pettit, *The Philharmonia Official History* (London: Gollancz, 1985). *Philharmonia Orchestra Year Books*. Elisabeth Schwarzkopf, *On and Off the Record: A Memoir of Walter Legge* (London: Faber, 1982).

ACCESS: Philharmonia Orchestra Limited, 12 de Walden Court, 85, New Cavendish Street, London W1M 7RA. (01) 580–9961. Christopher Bishop, Managing Director.

ERIK LEVI

Royal Philharmonic Orchestra

Recognized as one of the four leading independent orchestras based in London, the Royal Philharmonic Orchestra (RPO) presents a season of some 30 concerts in the capital's Royal Festival Hall (seating capacity 2,909), ten at the Barbican Hall (seating capacity approx. 2,200), and 15 at Croydon's Fairfield Hall (seating capacity 1,850). With the permanent membership of 85 players, the orchestra gives numerous concerts throughout the United Kingdom and tours widely abroad. In the 1984–1985 season, for example, it visited more than a dozen countries including the United States, Canada, Japan, France, East Germany, Austria, and Greece. Under its recent music director, André Previn, the RPO has launched a music festival on London's South Bank with the orchestra in permanent residence for over two weeks. Throughout its history the RPO has held a long and fruitful association with recording and film companies.

In organization the RPO falls into line with most of London's other major orchestras in the sense that it is financed by a limited company governed by an elected Board of Directors, most of whom are playing members of the orchestra. The Board works in conjunction with the music director and managing director in hammering out policies and programs for the forthcoming season. A fairly sophisticated office organization is employed to back up the Board's decisions— a concerts department organizes all the RPO's day-to-day work; a financial department pays the orchestra's salaries (on the basis of fees per rehearsal and concert rather than an annual salary); and a public relations office looks after concert promotions and sponsorship. In addition, the orchestra receives an annual grant from the London Orchestral Concert Board and (until 1986) the Greater London Council.

Since the orchestra was for so long indelibly associated with its founder and principal conductor, Sir Thomas Beecham, its identity and special characteristics may well have been lost in recent years. Despite claims made in the official yearbook that the orchestra is now London's busiest, there is no doubt that the RPO cannot rival either the Philharmonia Orchestra* for warmth of tone or the London Symphony Orchestra* for virtuosity and brilliance. The orchestra has suffered some criticism for its seemingly conservative and unadventuresome artistic policy.

After the end of World War II, Sir Thomas Beecham was anxious to found a new orchestra that would be run under his sole direction. At first he approached Walter Legge, controller of EMI's Columbia gramophone label, with the proposal that he might take over the newly formed Philharmonia Orchestra, but when this plan was rebuffed, Beecham assembled his own group of players. His first move was to reach an agreement with the Royal Philharmonic Society that this new orchestra would be engaged exclusively by them for their next season of concerts. The proposed title of Royal Philharmonic Orchestra was then approved directly by King George VI. After their first concert at the now destroyed Davis Theatre in Croydon (September 15, 1946), Beecham promised his players a secure future with guaranteed recording contracts and a regular series of fortnightly concerts. In the following year the Thomas Beecham Concerts Society was formed to present the RPO in both London and the regions and to coordinate the Royal Philharmonic Society season.

It took less than two years for the RPO to establish itself as one of the finest in London. Beecham had persuaded a number of outstanding instrumentalists (including, in the wind section, Reginald Kell, Archie Camden, and Dennis Brain) to join his orchestra, and his concerts attracted a great deal of interest and enthusiasm. As the orchestra's reputation grew, it began to form close ties with the Edinburgh Festival and a regular association (until 1963) with the Glyndebourne Opera Company.

In 1950 the RPO became the first English orchestra to visit the United States since the London Symphony Orchestra's tour of 1912. Under Beecham the orchestra gave no fewer than 51 concerts in 45 different cities. However, the programs, based almost exclusively on the conductor's favorite composers (Handel, Mozart, Bizet, Sibelius, and Delius), were criticized in the American press for their failure to introduce any contemporary English music. Nevertheless, the tour was a resounding success, and the orchestra continued to make great strides despite the fact that Beecham appeared less frequently with it. His interest in the RPO had by no means waned, but he claimed that harsh British tax laws forced him to live almost exclusively outside his native country. By 1960 Beecham's health had in fact deteriorated and he made his final appearance with the orchestra in May of that year. Following Beecham's death in 1961, the German conductor Rudolf Kempe was appointed his successor, but it was clear that a glorious chapter in the orchestra's history had closed.

The RPO's work continued much as before with a full list of engagements, but within two years there were ominous signs of uncertainty regarding its future. In February 1963 the Thomas Beecham Concerts Society proposed a possible amalgamation of the RPO with the orchestra of the Royal Opera at Covent Garden, but nothing came of this scheme. Meanwhile, Rudolf Kempe announced that he would resign as principal conductor following the Royal Philharmonic Society's decision not to engage the RPO for its forthcoming season of concerts. By this time the orchestra had already been excluded by the Royal Festival Hall from a scheme in which the three other independent orchestras (the London Philharmonic Orchestra,* London Symphony Orchestra, and the then ''New Philharmonia'') were to cooperate.

The summer of 1963 was a crisis point in the orchestra's history. Facing the

threat of extinction, the RPO decided to form itself into a new, independent
organization run by the players themselves. A Board of Directors drawn from
the orchestra was elected and its chairman invited Rudolf Kempe to return as
artistic director. Despite the rigors of reorganization the RPO presented from
September through December 1963 a strenuous series of 52 concerts through
the Americas with Sir Malcolm Sargent and Georges Prêtre as the principal
conductors.

When the RPO returned to England in 1964, the new company had been
established but its future was by no means secure. For one thing, the orchestra
was to be excluded from appearing at the Royal Festival Hall for a further two
years, and a series of concerts presented at a London cinema (the Odeon, Swiss
Cottage) could not really offer a satisfactory alternative. Moreover, the Royal
Philharmonic Society threatened repeatedly to withdraw the orchestra's title,
maintaining that without Beecham or the Society's services it was invalid. Eventually, however, these problems were resolved when the Queen herself conferred
definitively upon the orchestra the title "Royal . . . in its own right."

During the mid–1960s the whole question of London's orchestras was discussed by a government-sponsored report chaired by Lord Goodman. In rec-
ommending that the RPO should remain active and receive adequate subsidies,
Goodman gave the orchestra a new lease on life, quashing finally any rumors
of its impending demise. The RPO's development since that time has been steady
if unremarkable. Kempe remained principal conductor for the next ten years;
yet he curiously failed to mold the orchestra into a really individual ensemble,
having achieved much more success with the Munich Philharmonic Orchestra*
and Dresden Staatskapelle.*

In 1975 Kempe was succeeded by Antál Doráti, who now holds the post of
the orchestra's first conductor laureate. Doráti's extremely versatile repertoire
was to some extent modified by the orchestra's conservative disposition toward
programming (many Beethoven, Brahms, and Tchaikovsky cycles, for instance).
Since Doráti left in 1979, to be succeeded by the Austrian conductor Walter
Weller, the orchestra seems to have adopted a rather anonymous role in London's
concert life. Nevertheless, a continual stream of tours around the world and
regular appearances at major international festivals have served to maintain the
RPO's high profile. Indeed, a number of distinguished conductors have worked
with the orchestra on a regular basis (Lawrence Foster, Hans Vonk, Yuri Tem-
irkanov, and Sir Yehudi Menuhin, for example). However, there can be no doubt
that the arrival of André Previn as the RPO's principal conductor in 1985 had
an immediate impact. So too did his dramatic resignation late in 1986, in protest
of the overburdened schedules under which RPO and other London orchestra
players must work. It has been announced that Vladimir Ashkenazy will become
the new music director.

With its prior history of fighting for survival, the RPO has taken a lead in
exploiting industrial sponsorship, a policy very much supported by the present
Conservative government. Commercial considerations have come to play an ever-

increasing role in determining the sort of programs that are presented to the public—it may be a factor in the relative absence of contemporary works or those of such composers of Arnold Schoenberg, Edgard Varèse, Charles Ives, or Anton Webern in current RPO programs. Undoubtedly the aggressive marketing policy adopted by the RPO's managing director will continue to hold sway. The orchestra seems to be more heavily committed to providing backing for the popular music industry than any of its London rivals. The RPO's *Hooked on Classics* series, for example, has sold over 9 million albums throughout the world. The orchestra's recent appearance at the spectacular half-time show of the Orange Bowl football game in Miami, Florida, was beamed to an estimated 80 million people.

RECORDING HISTORY AND SELECTIVE DISCOGRAPHY: The RPO's most enduringly famous recordings were made with Sir Thomas Beecham and were released on a variety of labels including HMV, Columbia, Philips, and RCA. Their first ensemble recording (Frederick Delius's Dance Rhapsody No. 2, October 3, 1946) was not commercially issued at first, but it was followed by a long series of records that in the orchestra's early years included a diversity of works. From 1946 to 1959 Beecham made over 250 different recordings with the RPO. On the whole, his repertoire was catholic, despite the absence of Brahms, a Beethoven cycle, or works of twentieth-century composers (with the exception of Delius). Beecham revived many neglected nineteenth-century works, including Karl Goldmark's *Rustic Wedding* Symphony and Mily Balakirev's *Tamar* and First Symphony. The recording highlights of his final years were undoubtedly the complete series of Haydn's "Salomon" Symphonies (1957–1959), Sibelius's *Tapiola* (1955), Liszt's *Faust* Symphony (1958), and Rimsky-Korsakov's *Scheherezade* (1957), all issued by HMV and re-released on many occasions.

Following Beecham's death, the RPO made records with many conductors, although those under its principal conductors have generally lacked the distinction of earlier efforts. Kempe preferred to record with German orchestras and his output with the RPO is small; Doráti recorded a complete cycle of Beethoven symphonies and (on the Decca label) a well-received series of Haydn oratorios. Weller recorded little. An imaginative recording project sponsored by RCA and *Readers Digest* featured the RPO under such eminent musicians as Fritz Reiner and Jascha Horenstein. Single issues conducted by Rafael Kubelik, Leopold Stokowski, and Paavo Berglund all received considerable critical acclaim.

In May 1986 the RPO took the unique step of producing and marketing its own performances on its exclusive RPO label. The first releases in Great Britain on the RPO label include William Walton's *Belshazzar's Feast* (Previn) and Handel's *Water Music* (Menuhin).

Brahms, Symphony No. 4 (Reiner) Quintessence 7182. Delius, *Brigg Fair* and other works (Beecham): HMV ASD 357. Haydn, *The Creation* (Doráti): Decca D50 D2; London 12108 (2 discs). Haydn, Symphonies No. 103 and 104 (Beecham): HMV SXLP 30257. Rimsky-Korsakov, *Scheherezade* (Beecham): Angel RL–32027. Sibelius, Symphony No. 2 (Barbirolli): Quintessence 7008. Stravinsky, *The Rake's Progress* (Stravinsky): CBS 77304. Tchaikovsky, Symphony No. 5 (Previn): TELA DG 10107.

CHRONOLOGY OF MUSIC DIRECTORS: Sir Thomas Beecham, 1946–1961. Rudolf Kempe, 1961–1975. Antál Doráti, 1975–1979. Walter Weller, 1979–1985. André Previn, 1985–1986.

BIBLIOGRAPHY: Neville Cardus, *Sir Thomas Beecham: A Memoir* (London: Collins, 1961). Michael H. Gray, *Beecham: A Centenary Discography* (London: Duckworth, 1979). H. Proctor-Gregg, *Beecham Remembered* (London: Duckworth, 1977). Royal Philharmonic Orchestra Yearbooks. Howard Taubman, *The Orchestra Abroad: A Report of a Study* (Vienna, Va.: American Symphony Orchestra League, 1971).

ACCESS: Royal Philharmonic Orchestra Limited, 34 Red Lion Square, London WC1R 4SG. (01) 404–0017. Ian Maclay, Managing Director.

ERIK LEVI

MANCHESTER, ENGLAND   (449,000)

Hallé Orchestra

A major symphonic ensemble, the Hallé Orchestra gives up to 190 concerts each season, including two subscription series at Manchester's Free Trade Hall, which is let by the Greater Manchester Council at a favorable rate. The October-to-May season consists of a Thursday series of 16 fortnightly concerts, a Sunday series of 15 concerts, and the Opus One series (three series of seven concerts presented monthly). Each summmer, usually in June and July for four weeks, a series of popular concerts at popular prices is presented in the Free Trade Hall.

The Hallé broadcasts regularly for the BBC and aims to produce at least two commercial recordings per year. The Hallé Choir, a fine amateur group, has an integral role in the orchestra's activities, appearing in several concerts each season.

The orchestra travels widely in the United Kingdom and in particular makes frequent visits to Bradford and Sheffield in the north of England. Its overseas tours began in the Christmas/New Year period of 1944–1945 for the benefit of British troops in Belgium, France, and Holland. Thereafter it embarked on a major tour every few years. The most ambitious so far was a tour to South America in 1968, featuring 28 concerts in eight countries.

The Hallé Concerts Society, whose principal aim is "the maintenance of the Hallé Orchestra and the presentation of Hallé concerts," is a company limited by guarantee and is also a registered charity. The Society is controlled by the General Committee of the Hallé Concerts Society, comprising 15 elected members and eight coopted members who for the time being include four representatives of the Greater Manchester Council, two representatives of the Manchester City Council, the chairman of the Hallé Choir, and the chairman of the Hallé Club. This committee determines the policy of the Society, including the appointment of permanent conductors and leaders of the orchestra and the general manager, each of whom is responsible to the committee for the execution of policy.

The annual budget is over £1.5 million, approximately 61% of which is allotted for the orchestra's costs, 32% for promotion costs, including conductors and soloists, and 7% for administration. Part of the cost of the orchestra is met by the Arts Council of Great Britain, the Greater Manchester Council, Manchester Corporation, and the Counties of Lancashire and Cheshire. The remainder (55% of the Society's income) is derived from the box office and from fees received for hiring the orchestra.

The Hallé Trust Fund was established in 1964 to mark the late Sir John Barbirolli's 21st season with the orchestra. Its purpose is to enable the Society to undertake those activities not financed by national or local authorities; these include foreign tours, opportunities for young artists and composers, and special concerts for young people.

Charles Hallé, the orchestra's founder, was born on April 11, 1819, and first attracted attention when he gave a piano recital at the age of nine under the patronage of Louis Spohr. In his teens he moved to Paris to study with Friedrich Kalkbrenner, where he also soon came to know Berlioz, Chopin, Liszt, and Wagner. He moved to London with his family following the Revolution of 1848 and visited Manchester for the first time in June, returning to play Beethoven's *Emperor* Concerto at the prestigious Gentlemen's Concert on September 13th. In November 1849 the Committee appointed him conductor of their orchestra, giving him wide powers to make changes in personnel, rehearsal schedules, and concert programs. Following the Manchester Exhibition of 1857, for which Hallé was engaged to provide daily concerts with an expanded orchestra in Edward Walton's new Free Trade Hall, the conductor determined, as he wrote later in his memoirs, "to give weekly concerts during the autumn and winter at my own risk and peril." Thus the Hallé Concerts began on January 30, 1858, and by 1866 profits had risen from a few pence to over £2,000. As the Hallé concerts grew in importance, though, the Gentlemen's Concerts declined. They finally disbanded in 1920.

From the outset of his remarkable period of 37 years as director, Hallé aimed to educate the public by providing a large number of cheap seats and by performing new music along with established works. He was also Foundation Principal of the Royal Manchester College of Music. Hallé appeared at almost every concert, playing the piano as well as conducting. Because of his wide contacts he was instrumental in bringing many famous executants to Manchester, including Jenny Lind, Joseph Joachim, Hans von Bülow, George Henschel, and Vladimir de Pachmann. Berlioz's *Symphonie Fantastique* had its British premiere on January 9, 1878, and ten years later Grieg conducted his Piano Concerto with Hallé as soloist.

After Hallé's death in 1895, Hans Richter, principal conductor of the Vienna Opera and Vienna Philharmonic,* was approached. He accepted the position, and until his appointment was confirmed in 1899 Frederick Cowen acted as conductor, with the understanding that the position was only temporary. When the newly formed Hallé Concerts Society endorsed Richter's appointment, there was considerable feeling expressed at the lack of sensitivity towards Cowen's position.

Richter's 12 seasons began controversially and this trend continued. Although his appointment carried great prestige, there were soon complaints about the predominance of German music in the program. Beethoven, Brahms, and Wagner were joined by new works of Richard Strauss, Anton Bruckner, and others—while Claude Debussy, Frederick Delius, and César Franck were largely neglected. Richter's championship of Edward Elgar was immensely gratifying to the composer, who dedicated his First Symphony (1908) to the conductor. When Richter resigned for health reasons in 1911, there was considerable pressure to appoint a leading British conductor such as Henry Wood, Thomas Beecham, or Landon Ronald as his successor. The members looked again to Germany, and after Richard Strauss declined, the offer was finally accepted by Michael Balling. His two seasons saw a number of new works including Mahler's First Symphony. He was also the first conductor of the Hallé Orchestra to seek municipal aid to obtain a weekly salary for the players and to propose the building of an opera house.

The outbreak of war in 1914 found Balling conducting in Bayreuth, from whence he did not return. Guest conductors, especially Beecham, provided some continuity to the orchestra's programs, but the inevitable lack of overall direction was only one of several factors contributing to a difficult postwar period for the Hallé.

Hamilton Harty's appointment as permanent conductor in 1920 revitalized the orchestra and its repertoire: Arnold Bax, Debussy, Gustav Holst, Maurice Ravel, Jean Sibelius, Igor Stravinsky, and William Walton were only some of the composers now represented. Two notable symphonies receiving their English premieres under his baton were Mahler's Ninth and Shostakovich's First. It was also the beginning of the orchestra's broadcasting and recording activities. Harty resigned in 1933 after a quarrel with the Committee over guest engagements.

A year later the society came to an arrangement with the BBC whereby the best players were guaranteed year-round employment rather than the 40 concerts that the Hallé itself could offer during the depression. Without this collaboration the orchestra would almost certainly have collapsed. However, no artistic director was appointed after Harty until Malcolm Sargent became conductor-in-chief in 1939. His association with other orchestras and the outbreak of World War II prevented him from exerting much influence on the Society's plans. The government, recognizing the morale-boosting value of the orchestra, subsidized tours of schools, military camps, and munitions factories, thus exposing the rigidity of the Hallé/BBC agreement. Moreover, in 1942 Sargent accepted the Royal Liverpool Philharmonic Orchestra's* offer to form a permanent autonomous orchestra rather than continue to share players with the Hallé, a practice that had been established for almost a century. The bombing of the Free Trade Hall forced the orchestra into a gypsylike existence in school halls and suburban cinemas. Once again the Hallé Orchestra was in decline, but Philip Godlee, the new chairman, decided to make some bold decisions. He agreed to sever the BBC connection, offer the players a new 200-concert-per-year contract, and engage a major conductor. John Barbirolli was approached and he accepted, but on arrival in 1943 from New York (where he had briefly taken over the New York Philharmonic** following Toscanini's years there), he discovered that only four players had agreed to remain with him on the new terms.

Nevertheless, Barbirolli's 27-year association with the orchestra has become legendary. In spite of wartime difficulties, he worked tirelessly to rebuild the orchestra into one of the finest in the world, one with a reputation for versatility and fiery enthusiasm. It toured regularly both at home and abroad with a wide range of programs, including Barbirolli's specialties such as the symphonies of Bruckner, Elgar, Mahler, Carl Nielsen, Sibelius, and Vaughan Williams. In 1958, the Hallé's centenary, Barbirolli reduced his commitments, becoming conductor-in-chief and delegating some of the work to George Weldon, Laurence Leonard, and Maurice Handford. In 1968 he was appointed Conductor Laureate, a title he held until his death in 1970. A report by *New York Times* critic Howard Taubman in that year suggested that standards had descended to an indifferent level.

Barbirolli's successor was James Loughran, a versatile musician who, as well as maintaining the traditional Hallé repertoire, also brought many new composers before the Manchester public, including Gordon Crosse, Alexander Goehr, Charles Ives, György Ligeti, John McCabe, Schoenberg, and Shostakovich. Conductor Laureate since 1983, Loughran also built up an interest in the Hallé choir and issued more than 24 discs with the orchestra during his 12-year association. The Polish conductor Stanisław Skrowaczewski began his contract with the orchestra on September 1, 1984.

RECORDING HISTORY AND SELECTIVE DISCOGRAPY: The orchestra's recording career is among the longest of any in the world. The historic 1930 recording of Constant Lambert's *Rio Grande* with the Hallé Choir, conducted by the composer and with Harty as solo pianist, has been reissued on World Records SH 227. Berlioz's overture *Le Corsaire* and the *Royal Hunt and Storm* from *The Trojans*, both recorded at 78 rpm in 1931 and 1932, respectively, are also available on World Records No. 248 SH. The Hallé's main discography dates from Barbirolli's era; their first recording together was of Arnold Bax's Third Symphony (8H-C 3380–5) on December 31, 1943, for HMV. Later they moved to Pye Records from 1955 to 1960, returning to HMV in 1964 with Elgar's Symphony No. 2. Barbirolli's last recording was of Delius's *Brigg Fair* on H-ASD–2637 (Appalachia), on July 18, 1970. In 1974 Loughran directed Serge Rachman-inov's Second Symphony for EMI's Classics for Pleasure, heralding a new chapter in the orchestra's history of regular visits to the studio. Full details of the Hallé's recording history are found in Michael Kennedy's *Hallé, 1858–1980*.

Berlioz, *Symphonie Fantastique* (Barbirolli): PRT GSCG/2CGC 2025. Brahms, Symphony No. 2 (Loughran): Classics for Pleasure 4388. Delius, *Summer Night* and other works (Barbirolli): Angel S–36588, ASD 2477. Elgar, Symphony No. 2 (Barbirolli): HMV SXLP 30287. Elgar, Symphony No. 2 (Loughran): Nonesuch 71406, ALH 907. Sibelius, Symphonies Nos. 5 and 7 (Barbirolli): EMI EMX 41 2050–4.

CHRONOLOGY OF PRINCIPAL CONDUCTORS: Sir Charles Hallé, 1858–1895. Sir Frederick Cowen, 1896–1899. Hans Richter, 1899–1911. Michael Balling, 1912–1914. Sir Thomas Beecham, 1915–1920. Sir Hamilton Harty, 1920–1933. Sir Malcolm Sargent,

1939–1942. Sir John Barbirolli, 1943–1970. James Loughran, 1971–1983. Stanisław Skrowaczewski, 1984–present.

BIBLIOGRAPHY: Thomas Batley, ed., *Sir Charles Hallé's Concerts in Manchester: A List* . . . (Manchester, 1896). Sir Neville Cardus, *The Delights of Music: A Critic's Choice* (London, 1966). David Freer, ed., *Hamilton Harty, Early Memoirs* (Belfast, 1979). David Freer, *Hamilton Harty, His Life and Music* (Belfast, 1979). *Hallé Magazine* (Manchester Hallé Club and Hallé Concerts Society), 1946–1981. Alan Jefferson, *Sir Thomas Beecham* (London, 1979). Michael Kennedy, *The Hallé Tradition* (Manchester, 1960). Michael Kennedy, *Barbirolli: Conductor Laureate* (London, 1971). Michael Kennedy, ed., *The Autobiography of Charles Hallé* (London, 1972). Michael Kennedy, *The Hallé, 1958–1983* (Manchester: Manchester University Press, 1982). Michael Kennedy, *Hallé Orchestra* (Manchester, 1983). Nicholas Kenyon, *The BBC Symphony Orchestra: The First Fifty Years, 1930–1980* (London, 1981). Charles Reid, *John Barbirolli* (London, 1971). John F. Russell, *A History of the Hallé Concerts, 1858–1939* (serialized in the *Hallé Magazine*, Manchester, 1948–1956). Howard Taubman, *The Symphony Orchestra Abroad* (Vienna, Va.: American Symphony Orchestra League, 1970).

ACCESS: Hallé Concerts Society, 30 Cross Street, Manchester M2 7BA. (061) 834–8363. Clive F. Smart, General Manager.

DENIS MCCALDIN

Uruguay ———————————————

SODRE Symphonic Orchestra

The SODRE Symphonic Orchestra (OSSODRE) and the Municipal Symphonic Orchestra (OSM) are the two government-supported institutions that normally perform in Montevideo, capital of the República Oriental del Uruguay. Founded in 1959 by Carlos Estrada, the OSM has as its goals allowing conductors and soloists of Uruguay to get in touch with large audiences and giving Uruguayan composers the opportunity to have their pieces played by a skilled and fully competent orchestra. Tickets for the OSM's performances are inexpensive so as to attract a large audience. Additionally, a Student Orchestra of the Ministry of Education and Culture fosters young instrumentalists who are later expected to become part of the major ensembles.

The activity of the OSSODRE since its foundation in 1930 has not been restricted to symphonic concerts. Its members participate also in the yearly opera seasons and in 20 to 30 ballet exhibitions annually. Its performances take place during the winter season at the 1,200-seat Solis Theatre (since 1971, when the Estudio Auditorio was destroyed), but the orchestra also goes on tours to the rest of the country. During the summer there are outdoor concerts in the east, especially at important seaside resorts such as Punta del Este and Piriapolis. In these and other concerts (given in the capital), lighter music is included so as to attract a larger audience.

Some 20 to 30 symphonic performances are held mostly on Saturdays from April or May to August in cycles of 12 or 14 concerts usually booked as subscriptions. These concerts are usually broadcast by the SODRE radio and are shown live on SODRE television. The audience that attends OSSODRE's performances is considerable, especially during the opera seasons (12 to 15 performances) and when programs feature international figures. The orchestra also performs five or six orchestral/choral programs. The role of the SODRE broadcasting station is important, and the recordings of all the performances that have been given are now part of a large collection of tapes. Additionally, the institute has a most important archive of scores that nurture OSSODRE's programs.

The SODRE is a government institution with government support channeled through the Ministry of Education and Culture. Programs are selected by the artistic director with the approval of the Board of Directors. Many important musicians have held the position of artistic director, among them Carlos Estrada, Hugo Balzo, and Pedro Ipuche Riva.

The orchestra had its beginnings in the evenings of old Montevideo, when the colonial parlor and the theatre were the center of all social, cultural, and artistic activities in the recently founded Spanish colony. The first theatre, the Casa de Comedias, founded in 1793, was of paramount importance to music, for it housed an orchestra conducted by Tiburcio Ortega, who was also in charge of religious music (at St. Francis Church, Charity Chapel, etc.). During this formative period there were also philharmonic societies and incipient orchestras that reached peaks in their activities. Among their many leaders was Francisco José Debali (from 1838 to 1848), author of the music for the Republic's national anthem.

Another local leader was Count Luis Preti Bonatti, a superb violinist of European education who conducted the orchestra on August 25, 1856, for the inauguration of the Solis Theatre in the performance of Verdi's opera *Ernani*. Thereafter the Solis was to become the axis around which all the city's cultural activities would revolve. Preti also conducted the first performance in Uruguay of Beethoven's Third Symphony and founded one of the most important philharmonic societies. In 1868 and 1869 Uruguay received the American composer/ pianist Luis Moreau Gottschalk, who took part in a concert for 16 pianos and later composed a symphony entitled "Montevideo."

Other institutions developed, including several conservatories and The Beethoven Society, which performed from 1897, first under the direction of Pérez Badía and later under Luis Sambucetti, Jr., who would have great influence in the continued development of this and later orchestras. Through these years an interest in composition had developed, and Sambucetti's National Orchestra included Uruguayan composers in its concerts. In the early 1920s the Uruguayan Orchestral Society held a series of successful performances. On August 5, 1923, Montevideo enjoyed an unforgettable experience with the visit of the Vienna Philharmonic Orchestra conducted by Richard Strauss, who performed some of his own pieces as well as others from the international repertoire. Strauss made an important impression on all, magnified by his asking for the symphonic poem called *Campo* (a description of Uruguayan country landscapes) by the Uruguayan composer Eduardo Fabini, to become part of the program the orchestra would present at the Colòn Theatre in Buenos Aires.

With the death of Sambucetti in 1926, the time seemed ripe for the creation of a national orchestra. On December 18, 1929, the legislature created the Official Broadcasting Service (Servicio Oficial de Difusión Radioeléctrica—SODRE). Its first broadcast was on April 1, 1930, from a room at the Palacio Legislativo, but in June of that year it moved to a much more adequate building, the Urquiza Theatre, thereafter called the Estudio Auditorio, which would become the site of uninterrupted symphonic seasons until 1971, when a fire destroyed the stage and concert hall. Thirteen years would pass before the old structure was demolished to leave room for the new Estudio Auditorio.

The OSSODRE's inaugural concert, June 20, 1931, involved 105 musicians in a program of Bach, Ferruccio Busoni, Eduardo Fabini, Liszt, and Beethoven. The conductor was Vincente Pablo, assisted by Virgilio Scarabelli and Lamberto Baldi, who would occupy until 1941 the position of permanent conductor. That first program meant the achievement of a permanent goal of the institution: including at least one composition by a Uruguayan composer. In following years many Uruguayan composers have had their work premiered by OSSODRE, among them Alfonso Broqua, César Cortinas, and Jaurés Lamarque Pons. Another feature of that first year was the presence of Ernest Ansermet as guest conductor—one of a multitude of international conductors who would lead and praise the group in the following years. The orchestra also continues today to feature international soloists as well as those of Uruguay.

The most memorable of the early seasons was 1938–1939, which saw a cycle of Beethoven's nine symphonies conducted by Erich Kleiber. In the words of Cyro Scoseria, a master among Uruguayan critics (*El Día*, July 19, 1939), "It was a most interesting and exciting experience to watch Kleiber rehearsing! How conscientiously he 'taught' the way of executing each inflection and each accent. . . . Kleiber was a fanatic of fidelity to the original composition. And that was why the extraordinary personality that was revealed in his versions was all the more marvelous."

Over the years the OSSODRE has continued with its performances in spite of economic problems, which have precipitated the loss of many of its members, who have been hired by orchestras in neighboring countries. Concert seasons have continued to feature many first auditions of pieces from the national and international repertoires, striving to fulfill one of the aims the orchestra's founders had in mind—to convey and spread culture and information.

CHRONOLOGY OF PRINCIPAL CONDUCTORS: Complete information unavailable.

BIBLIOGRAPHY: Lauro Ayestarán, *La Música en el Uruguay* (Montevideo: SODRE, 1953). Rolando Scoseria, *Literatura de los programas del SODRE, Anos 1954–1979* (Montevideo, [1980]). SODRE archives.

ACCESS: OSSODRE, Sarandí 444 esq. Misiones, Montevideo. 907662. Homero Toriani, Director de Espectáculos.

YOLANDA PÉREZ ECCHER DE SCOSERIA
TRANS. ELEONORA SCOSERIA

Yugoslavia ——————————

BELGRADE   (774,000*)

Belgrade Philharmonic

The Belgrade Philharmonic is one of the leading Yugoslav symphonic orchestras, certainly the best orchestra in the Republic of Serbia. It performs for an annual live audience of about 30,000, with 56 concerts per season, and offers subscription series in Belgrade, as well as giving concerts in other Yugoslav towns. It makes occasional broadcasts.

The orchestra is controlled by its council, one of whose members acts as the orchestra's administrative director (a post distinct from that of artistic director, though sometimes filled by the same person). An art council controls program selection. With an annual budget of 65 million dinars, the Philharmonic employs 65 musicians and a staff of nine; musicians' salaries vary from 1,800 to 3,500 dinars per year. Current administrative problems center on complementing the orchestra with the necessary players, ensuring musicians' salaries, and providing them with living quarters if necessary.

The orchestra's main concert hall is the Kolarac Memorial Center (sometimes known as the "University of Kolarac"), named after its founder, Ilija Kolarac. This 1,200-seat hall has very good acoustics and is set in an old building comprising as well a small art gallery and small halls for lectures and foreign language courses. Philharmonic musicians participate as soloists and chamber players, and the orchestra has been the founder and protector of various chamber ensembles, such as the Belgrade Wind Quintet and the Belgrade Chamber Ensemble. Two books and many articles have been written about the Philharmonic.

In the beginning of the nineteenth century, after the newly constituted state had delivered the Serbs from Turkish domination, Belgrade became the capital of the Kingdom of Serbia. The Serbs reorganized their cultural life; soloists, choirs, and various orchestras (of the army, theatres, and amateurs) became active in the period after 1840. Orchestras of Baron Hallenbach and Johann Strauss the Younger played in Belgrade in 1844 and 1847, respectively. Thus an orchestral tradition had been well established in the city when the Belgrade Philharmonic arose in 1923 as the answer to the city's felt need for a regularly performing symphony orchestra.

The orchestra's growth toward homogeneous playing and sophisticated interpretation may be traced from 1923 to 1941. The first director, Stevan Hristić, succeeded in maintaining the orchestra in very difficult circumstances. His follower, Lovro von Matačić, managed to bring the ensemble to a remarkable artistic level. Austro/German classical and romantic repertoires were performed; also included were works by Slavic composers, among them, Igor Stravinsky, Josip Slavenski, Leoš Janáček, and others. Famous conductors such as Dimitri Mitropoulos, Josef Krips, and others, as well as renowned soloists appeared with the orchestra. Rising Yugoslav musicians also were given the opportunity to perform with the group. Orchestral activities were suspended from 1941 to 1945, during the Second World War.

After 1945 the Belgrade Philharmonic shared its cultural impact with two other orchestras—the Belgrade Radio Orchestra and the Artistic Ensemble of the Yugoslav Army Orchestra. Immediately after the war the Philharmonic appeared occasionally to celebrate some political events; the intention was often pedagogical, with accompanying lectures. Gradually, the repertoire expanded and the Belgrade Philharmonic continued with real concerts based on classical and romantic compositions, especially those of Russian, Czech, Soviet, and Yugoslav works. Oskar Danon and Mihailo Vukdragović were among the leading conductors.

The conductor and composer Krešimir Baranović was nominated director and chief conductor in 1952. From then on the Philharmonic began the modern phase of its history, which is still unfolding. Živojin Zdravković was elected director and chief conductor in 1961. At that time there were six subscription concerts, which included both standard repertoire and works of Yugoslav composers. Famous musicians were once again employed. A separate series was dedicated to single composers, either on a whole-series or single-concert basis. Another series presented famous instrumental and vocal soloists, often with young performers as well. Some of these were organized by the organization Jeunesses Musicales. Under the title "vozom na koncert" ("by train to the concert"), youths from the provinces were brought to Belgrade to attend Philharmonic concerts.

Many well-known and capable conductors have left their mark on the orchestra, and their suggestions helped orchestra members overcome the quotidian pace of routine concerts by bringing interpretations of remarkable artistic value. Among them: Sir John Barbirolli, Kiril Kondrashin, and Leopold Stokowski. There is hardly a competent Yugoslav conductor, instrumentalist, or singer who has not performed with the Belgrade Philharmonic Orchestra. Some of the finest of these have been violinists Marije Mihailović and Branko Pajević, and clarinetist Milenko Stefanović. The orchestra continues to invite world-renowned artists such as Pierre Rampal, Yehudi Menuhin, and Mstislav Rostropovich to participate in its concerts.

The orchestra's repertoire is wide-ranging, from baroque to contemporary, and often features large works encompassing soloists and choir. These range from J. S. Bach's B-Minor Mass to Arthur Honegger's *Jeanne d'Arc au bûchet*, Janáček's *Glagolska mse* and Benjamin Britten's *War Requiem*. Special attention is paid to compositions by such Yugoslav composers as Petar Konjović, Stevan Hristíc, Krešimir Baranović, Milan Ristić, Ljubica Marić, Vasilije Mokranjac, and many younger composers.

Since its reorganization in 1952 the Belgrade Philharmonic has made tours in Europe, Asia, northern Africa, and Latin America. It often participates in festivals, especially in Germany and Austria.

RECORDING HISTORY: The Philharmonic has recorded for RTB (Radio-Television Belgrade), Jugoton (Yugoslav discographic house), and commercially for Philips, Decca, and Electrola. Its recordings, however, are not currently listed in the Schwann or Gramophon Classical catalogs.

CHRONOLOGY OF MUSIC DIRECTORS: Stevan Hristić, 1923–1938. Lovro von Matačić, 1938–1941. Krešimir Baranović, 1952–1961. Živojin Zdravković, 1961–1972. Miroljub Milovanović, 1972–1976 (Administrative Director). Angel Šurev, 1977–1978. Jovan Šajnović, 1984–present.

BIBLIOGRAPHY: *Belgrade Philharmony, 1957–1971 (Belgrade, 1971)* Roksanda Pejović, *Fifty Years of the Belgrade Philharmony . . . 1923–1973* (Belgrade, 1977).

ACCESS: Belgrade Philharmonic, Studentski trg 11, 11000 Belgrade. (38–11)635–518. Davor Kuljarić, Manager (c/o Living Art, Inc., 9 Boulevard Montmartre, Paris 75015, France).

ROKSANDA R. PEJOVIĆ

LJUBLJANA   (213,000*)

Slovene Philharmonic Orchestra

The Slovene Philharmonic Orchestra is the central orchestra of the Slovene nation, which (not including the Slovene minorities in Italy, Austria, and part of Hungary) is an independent republic incorporated in the federation of Yugoslavia. As such, the orchestra is one of Yugoslavia's busiest, giving about two concerts per week. In the main fall/winter/spring season it offers in addition three consistently sold-out subscription series. It also tours regularly in Slovenia, elsewhere in Yugoslavia, and abroad. It has visited most European countries as well as the United States (1977 and 1980). It often participates in music festivals in Yugoslavia, Austria, Italy, Poland, and elsewhere.

Until 1982–1983 the Philharmonic gave its concerts in its 550-seat Philharmonic Hall, which today it still uses for chamber concerts, recording, and rehearsals. The new, 1,440-seat hall in the Ivan Cankar Cultural and Congress Centre boasts an organ by Schuke of West Berlin and has ameliorated the ensemble's working conditions and enhanced its ability to engage in concert exchanges.

The Slovene Philharmonic is administered by a general manager who, together with the "external" president of the General Board, is in charge of general as well as artistic decisions prepared by the consultative Artistic Board under the artistic director (a post distinct from that of conductor). Since World War II the list of artistic directors reads: Marjan Kozina (1948–1950), Lucijan Marija Škerjanc (1950–1956), Marijan Lipovšek (1956–1964), Ciril Cvetko (1965–1969), Darijan Božič (1970–1974), Marijan Gabrijelčič (1975–1979), and Ivo Petrič (1980-present). The permanent chief conductor is Uros Lajovič, whereas the permanent visiting conductor is Milan Horvat. Numerous visiting Yugoslav and foreign conductors and soloists appear with the orchestra. The orchestra is supported by the Slovene Cultural Community (Kulturna skupnost Slovenije), the Ljubljana Cultural Community (Ljubljanska kulturna skupnost), its own income, archival recordings, and broadcasts on radio and television.

The orchestra performed with a Slovene Philharmonic Chorus up to 1976 and the Youth Chorus of the Slovene Philharmonia (1949–1952). Today the Philharmonic maintains various chamber groups, such as the Slavko Osterc Ensemble, the Ljubljana Wind Trio, the Slovene Brass Quintet, the Slovene Philharmonic String Quartet, and others. Since 1951 a concert magazine has been regularly published. The orchestra keeps strictly to an A of 440 cps., and in recent decades, as proven by many a positive review of its foreign tours, it has developed into a temperamental and technically refined instrumental body.

Under its current name, Slovenska filharmonija, the orchestra was not founded until 1908, although culturally and de jure it is carrying on the rich musical tradition of Ljubljana, which experienced one of its peaks of development in the baroque era, with the founding in 1701 of the Academia Philharmonicorum Labacensis, the first such institution outside the Latin and Anglo-Saxon areas. It was a testimony to the vigor of the humanistically oriented spiritual atmosphere of Ljubljana at that time. The Academia Philharmonicorum Labacensis numbered at the utmost 31 amateur or partly trained musicians of aristocratic and bourgeois descent, under a director and vice-director who, in accordance with statute, had to be experienced in leading the orchestra and/or the choir. For public engagements professional musicians enlarged the group to 50 performers. Each year, when celebrating its patroness Saint Cecilia (symbolized with an organ and the motto *"Recreat mentique perennia monstrat"*—"Forever rejuvenate and enlighten the mind"—in its coat of arms) the Academia Philharmonicorum organized a musical regatta on the Ljubljanica River. However, in the mid–1760s, because of social and political changes, the organization's once-rich musical activities had to cease.

In 1794 that organization's bright tradition found its continuation in the Philharmonic Society (Philharmonische Gesellschaft), which grew out of a string quartet of local dilettantes. The group's organizing Statute of 1794 fixed weekly private concerts as well as public performances for special occasions and also distinguished between performers and listeners (women were admitted as performers in 1801, and listeners became ''members'' in 1849). The programs were executed by the Society's orchestra, by soloists, chamber ensembles, and at times the choir. Regular chamber music evenings, instead of the traditional pell-mell programs, came into being only after 1882. The Philharmonic Society was at first an explicitly bourgeois institution, though successively both aristocracy and clergy joined its ranks, contributing to its prestige. Thus, among its honorary members are to be found such personalities as J. Haydn (1800), Beethoven (1819), W. A. Mozart (posthumously, 1821), and Nicolō Paganini (1824). In spite of periodical crises, such as the French occupation of 1809–1813 (during which the Society closed its doors) and reorganizations, which hurt the level and stylistic orientation of its programs, the Society reached its final consolidation after 1856 under Anton Nedvěd.

This culmination was also the beginning of the Society's end. Until the up-welling of nationalism in the mid-nineteenth century, the institution was more or less cosmopolitan. However, at that time an independent Slovene culture in the narrower sense of the word began to force a split in the city's musical and nonmusical life. On one hand, there remained the high musical level of the Philharmonic Society (in 1881–1882 Gustav Mahler, then conductor of the Lju-bljana Provincial Theatre, performed with the group); on the other hand an independent musical culture of a forming nation was to be detected. Whereas strong economic support from the German-oriented middle classes, bureaucracy, and aristocracy ensured the status quo as regards the Society's artistic standards down to the end of the Hapsburg Empire, the emerging Slovene culture was yet developing its musical institutions. That development bore fruit with the successive founding of the versatile Glasbena Matica (1872), the Slovene Opera (1892), and, last but not least, the Slovenska Filharmonija.

This orchestra was founded on October 23, 1908, and continued with the efforts of the Ljubljana Band Society (Ljubljanska društvena godba), established in 1900 as one of the latest amateur instrumental ensembles that since the mid–1800s had tried to lay the foundations of a permanent Slovene orchestra. The musical level was secured by a number of visiting Czech musicians, beside whom local instrumentalists learned their profession. Especially important were the orchestra's conductor Václav Talich and visiting artist Fritz Reiner (1910–1911). The repertoire was rather traditional, though with a special emphasis on Slav and native composers. The orchestra's activity was diverse from the very beginning: regular symphonic concerts with local and foreign soloists, popular concerts in restaurants, vocal concerts with the Glasbena Matica Chorus, and opera productions. Unfortunately, financial and political discord—which destroyed the Slovene Opera—led also to the disbandment of the Philharmonic on September 27, 1913.

The period of the Kingdom of Serbs, Croats, and Slovenes (after 1918) saw some not-very-successful endeavors toward restoration. The Philharmonic Society was nationalized (1919) and integrated into Glasbena Matica, which did not succeed in forming its own professional instrumental ensemble, so that symphonic concerts in Ljubljana took place in a rather unorganized manner. They were given from time to time by the Glasbena Matica Orchestral Society (Orkestralno društvo Glasbene matice, 1919–1941), the Drava Division Orchestra (Muzika dravske divizije, 1919–1941), and finally, by the Ljubljana Philharmonia (Ljubljanska filharmonija, 1935–1941), none of which flourished.

It was only after the liberation that the Slovenska Filharmonija, refounded on December 28, 1947, was given a position befitting such an institution within the culture of its nation. It now saw conditions for an adequate development, which led the orchestra into the waters of internationally tested professionalism, especially under such chief conductors as Bogo Leskovic, Samo Hubad, Lovro von Matačić, Oskar Danon and, lately, Uroš Lajovic. The orchestra has since performed with many leading international artists.

RECORDING HISTORY AND SELECTIVE DISCOGRAPHY: Since 1955 the Slovene Philharmonic has maintained its own recording studio and recording service. It has thus compiled a rich record of its development. Numerous Philharmonic records have been published by Helidon (Ljubljana), Produkcija kaset in plošč RTV-Ljubljana "PK" (Ljubljana), Jugoton (Zagreb), and RTB (Belgrade).

Bruckner, Symphony No. 7 (Matačić): PK (1985). Dvořák, Symphony No. 8 (Anton Nanut): PK (1981). Haydn, Symphonies Nos. 100 and 102 (Uroš Lajovic): PK (1982). Uros Krek, *Rhapsodic Dance*; Strauss, *Till Eulenspiegel*, Prokofiev, *Romeo and Juliet* (Horvat): PK (1984).

CHRONOLOGY OF MUSIC DIRECTORS: Complete data unavailable.

BIBLIOGRAPHY: Dragotin Cvetko, *Academia Philharmonicorum Labacensis* (Ljubljana: Cankarjeva založba, 1962). Freidrich Keesbacher, *Die philharmonische Gesellschaft in Laibach* (Ljubljana, 1862). Primož Kuret, "Slovenska filharmonija 1908–1913," in *Koncertni list SF* (Ljubljana, 1968–1969), vol. 3–6. *Leksikon jugoslavenske muzike I-II* (Zagreb: Jugoslavenski leksikografski zavod, 1984).

ACCESS: Slovenska Filharmonija, Trg osvoboditve 9, 61000 Ljubljana. 61–213 554. Ivo Petrić, Artistic Director.

ANDREJ RIJÁVEC

ZAGREB   (566,000)

Zagreb Philharmonic Orchestra

The Zagreb Philharmonic Orchestra, whose roots go back into the nineteenth century, is one of the busiest in Yugoslavia, presenting regular weekly concerts with the participation of top domestic and foreign artists, often of the youngest generation, at its permanent home, the 1,851-seat Vatroslav Lisinski Concert Hall (1973). It yearly offers subscription series in its regular September-June season and makes frequent tours at home and abroad during the season and in summers as well, taking part, in particular, in the summer festivals along Yugoslavia's Adriatic Coast (in Dubrovnik, Split, Zadar, and Osor). Its summer concerts in Zagreb are given at the Atrium of the Jesuit Monastery, built in the seventeenth century. Performances of oratorios and similar works are arranged in cooperation with choral societies. All told, the Philharmonic presents about 60 concerts per year to a live audience of some 90,000.

Comprising more than 100 instrumentalists (80 of whom are full-time), the orchestra employs about 172 persons on an annual budget of 40,000,000 dinars. It is funded through Zagreb city grants and ticket sales. The Philharmonic is headed by a self-management board (called the Workers' Council), under whom is the director. The orchestra also maintains an Artistic Council that deals primarily with artistic policy.

In the period from 1970 to 1976 the Zagreb Philharmonic maintained a chamber orchestra named the "Chamber Studio of the Zagreb Philharmonic." In May of 1984 the orchestra began publishing an informative bulletin.

Noted in particular for its specific orchestral timbre, an innate feeling for melody and rhythm, as well as cultivated, disciplined performance, the Zagreb Philharmonic has since its beginning played a leading role in the cultural life of the Southern Slavs. It has carefully preserved classical and romantic repertoires, but also gives much attention to contemporary music and to music of Yugoslav composers, providing a valuable stimulus for their continued work. The orchestra thus educates the tastes of its audience, whose horizons are spreading and whose evaluation of music is becoming more critical. Its musicians teach at the Zagreb Music Academy as well as at other music schools, and some of them perform as soloists. Orchestra performances are often broadcast on the radio and occasionally on television.

The history of the Zagreb Philharmonic is closely connected with the Opera of the Croatian National Theatre in Zagreb. In the first half of the nineteenth century (the period of national revival), orchestral concerts in Zagreb were performed by amateur instrumental groups. Ivan Zajc's arrival in Zagreb in 1870, when the first permanent Zagreb Opera was founded, had a favorable effect on music performance in the city. He started his work as the Zagreb Opera director but he was also the first Croatian professional musician to introduce special concerts (*quodlibets*). These were given in the theatre building, usually with vocal and orchestral operatic passages and later with symphonic passages or, though seldom, entire symphonies. As far as is known, the first concert of this kind was organized on February 2, 1871, and it is possible to consider it as the beginning of professional orchestra activity in Zagreb. The title "A Philharmonic Concert" for such a quodlibet was used for the first time on April 8, 1884. A survey of the repertoire shows Zajc's strong preference for Italian music.

When in 1894 Stjepan Miletić became the general manager of the Croatian Theatre, more attention was paid to the activity of the Zagreb Opera Orchestra. January 1, 1896, began a new period in the development of orchestral playing, for that orchestra became the first in Croatia to give regular symphonic concerts.

The Opera Orchestra is thus considered a direct forerunner of the Zagreb Philharmonic. Its recorded concert activity culminated February 5, 1916, when a so-called historic concert took place. Indeed, this concert stimulated many new Croatian composers, mostly trying to bring their musical idiom close to folk music while displaying their interest in orchestral forms. The conductor was Fridrik Rukavina and the program included compositions by Krešimir Baranović, Antun Dobronić, Franjo Dugan, Dora Pejačević, Svetislav Stančić, and Božidar Širola.

Finally, after World War I (in 1919) at the initiative of viola player Dragutin Arany, the members of the Zagreb Opera Orchestra founded the Zagreb Philharmonic of the Theatre Orchestra, renamed the Zagreb Philharmonic on October 3, 1920. The foundation of the orchestra is generally considered one of the most significant events in the musical life of the region and period. For over 20 years the Zagreb Philharmonic gave regular symphonic concerts. The artistic director during this period was cellist Umberto Fabbri, and the busiest conductors were Krešimir Baranović, Milan Sachs, and Lovro von Matačić. In 1928 the Croatian Philharmonic Society was founded in order to support the orchestra's work financially. Its president was for a long time the prominent jurist, Marko Kostrenčić.

After World War II Zagreb continued its long tradition of being the main center of Croatian orchestral music. The former Zagreb Radio Orchestra was renamed the State Symphony Orchestra in 1948, to become again the Zagreb Philharmonic Orchestra in 1955. Under new conditions, that is, as an independent musical institution, the Zagreb Philharmonic developed into a fine orchestra. Its artistic directors (as distinct from chief conductors) since 1955 have been Ivan Brkanović, Milan Horvat, Josip Depolo, and Toma Prošev. It has toured to seventeen countries, including Great Britain, the United States, and the U.S.S.R., and its roster of guest conductors includes some of the world's finest. As of 1985–1986 the post of chief conductor has been discontinued, and the former chief conductor, Pavle Dešpalj, has become "permanent conductor."

RECORDING HISTORY AND SELECTIVE DISCOGRAPHY: The Zagreb Philharmonic's first recording (Tchaikovsky's *Nutcracker*) was made in 1956. It has produced over 20 recordings since then.

Beethoven, Concerto for Violin (Horvat): CMS Summit 1017. Lhotka, *Davo Uselu* (The Devil in the Village) (Dešpalj): Jugotron LSY 61819–20. Rimsky-Korsakov, *Scheherezade* (Dešpalj): Jugotron, LSY 68089.

CHRONOLOGY OF MUSIC DIRECTORS (Chief Conductors): Fritz Zaun, 1945–1956. Milan Horvat, 1956–1970. Lovro von Matačić, 1970–1980. Pavle Dešpalj, 1980–present.

BIBLIOGRAPHY: Josip Andreis, *Music in Croatia* (Zagreb: Institute of Musicology, Academy of Music, 1982). Krešimir Kovačević, *Zagrebačka filharmonija* in *Muzička enciklopedija* (Zagreb: Jugoslavenski leksikografski zavod, 1974–1977).

ACCESS: Zagrebačka filharmonija, Trnjanska bb, 41000 Zagreb. (041) 539–399 or (041) 539–699. Ivan Kunej, Director.

SANJA MAJER-BOBETKO

Chronology of Foundings for Orchestras Profiled _____

The foundings of many of the profiled orchestras involved mergers, false starts, periods of suspended operations, antecedent organizations, and other complexities that defy a tabular format. Specifying the "founding dates" of the orchestras frequently involves historical interpretation, as may be inferred from the profiles themselves. This is particularly true of those orchestras with closely linked antecedent organizations; in a few unclear cases the founding date is supplemented with the antecedent organization's founding (in parentheses following orchestra name).

Bavarian State Orchestra	1530
Berlin State Orchestra	1572
Dresden Staatskapelle	1584
Stuttgart State Orchestra	1617
Weimar State Orchestra (1482)	1683
Bergen Philharmonic Orchestra	1765
Leipzig Gewandhaus Orchestra (1743)	1775
Linz Bruckner Orchestra	1803
City Opera and Museum Orchestra of Frankfurt am Main (1792)	1808
Orchestre de Paris	1828
Gürzenich Orchestra of the City of Cologne	1840
Royal Liverpool Philharmonic Orchestra	1840
Mozarteum Orchestra (Salzburg)	1841
Vienna Philharmonic	1842
Budapest Philharmonic Orchestra	1853
Strasbourg Philharmonic Orchestra	1855
Hallé Orchestra (Manchester)	1858

Berlin Philharmonic Orchestra	1862
George Enescu Philharmonic Orchestra in Bucharest	1868
Tonhalle Orchestra (Zurich)	1868
Dresden Philharmonic	1870
Lamoureux Orchestra (Paris)	1881
Helsinski Philharmonic Orchestra	1882
Leningrad Philharmonic Orchestra	1882
Concertgebouw Orchestra (Amsterdam)	1888
The Bournemouth Symphony Orchestra	1893
Munich Philharmonic Orchestra	1893
Czech Philharmonic Orchestra (Prague)	1901
London Symphony Orchestra	1904
Residentie-Orkest (The Hague)	1904
Göteborgs Symfoniker	1905
Toronto Symphony Orchestra	1906
Beethovenhalle Orchestra (Bonn)	1907
Orchestra of the National Academy of St. Cecilia (Rome)	1907
Slovene Philharmonic Orchestra (Ljubljana)	1908
Stockholm Philharmonic Orchestra	1914
Orchestre de la Suisse Romande (Geneva)	1918
Rotterdam Philharmonic Orchestra	1918
City of Birmingham Symphony Orchestra	1920
El Salvador Symphony Orchestra (San Salvador)	1922
Vienna Symphony Orchestra	1922
Belgrade Philharmonic	1923
Hungarian State Symphony Orchestra (Budapest)	1923
Danish Radio Symphony Orchestra	1925
Radio Telefís Éireann Symphony Orchestra (Dublin)	1925
Basel Chamber Orchestra	1926
NHK Symphony Orchestra (Tokyo)	1926
Wuppertal Symphony Orchestra	1926
BBC Symphony Orchestra (London)	1930
SODRE Symphonic Orchestra (Montevideo)	1930
Grand Orchestra of the All-Union Radio and Television (Moscow)	1931
Vancouver Symphony Orchestra	1931
London Philharmonic Orchestra	1932
National Orchestra of France (Paris)	1934
Prague Symphony Orchestra	1934

Montreal Symphony Orchestra	1935
Belgian National Orchestra (Brussels)	1936
Israel Philharmonic Orchestra	1936
Jerusalem Symphony Orchestra	1936
State Academic Symphony Orchestra of the U.S.S.R.	1936
Symphony Orchestra of the RAI of Rome (1924)	1936
Academic Symphony Orchestra of the Ukrainian S.S.R. (Kiev)	1937
Symphony Orchestra of Brazil (Rio de Janeiro)	1940
National Symphony Orchestra of Costa Rica (San Jose)	1941
National Symphony Orchestra of the Dominican Republic (Santo Domingo)	1941
National Symphony Orchestra of Panama (Panama City)	1941
Symphony Orchestra of Chile (Santiago)	1941
National Orchestra of Spain (Madrid)	1942
Philharmonic Orchestra of Guatemala (Guatemala City)	1944
Symphony Orchestra of the Artur Rubinstein Philharmonic of Lodz (1915)	1945
Krakow Philharmonic	1945
Orchestra of the Hungarian Radio and Television (Budapest)	1945
Philharmonica Orchestra (London)	1945
Polish Radio National Symphony Orchestra (Katowice)	1945
Seoul Philharmonic Orchestra	1945
Silesian State Philharmonic Orchestra (Katowice)	1945
Bamberg Symphony	1946
Buenos Aires Philharmonic Orchestra	1946
New Zealand Symphony Orchestra (Wellington)	1946
Royal Philharmonic Orchestra (London)	1946
Sydney Symphony Orchestra (1932)	1946
National Symphony of Mexico (Mexico City)	1947
Osaka Philharmonic Symphony Orchestra	1947
Winnipeg Symphony Orchestra	1947
Southwest Radio Symphony Orchestra (Baden-Baden)	1948
Zagreb Philharmonic Orchestra	1948
National Philharmonic Orchestra in Warsaw (1901)	1949
Bavarian Radio Symphony Orchestra (Munich)	1948
Hamilton Philharmonic Orchestra	1949
National Symphony Orchestra of Argentina (Buenos Aires)	1949
Iceland Symphony Orchestra (Reykjavik)	1950

Melbourne Symphony Orchestra	1950
Scottish National Orchestra (Glasgow)	1950
I Musici (Rome)	1951
Prague Chamber Orchestra	1951
Symphony Orchestra of the Moscow Philharmonic	1953
Wroclaw State Philharmonic	1954
Moscow Chamber Orchestra	1955
Cairo Symphony Orchestra	1956
Gulbenkian Orchestra (Lisbon)	1956
The Academy of St. Martin in the Fields (London)	1959
Philharmonia Hungarica (Marl)	1959
English Chamber Orchestra (London)	1960
The Philharmonic Orchestra of Liège and of the French-Speaking Community of Belgium	1960
Württemberg Chamber Orchestra (Heilbronn)	1961
Radio-Television Symphony Orchestra of Spain (Madrid)	1962
Yomiuri Nippon Symphony Orchestra (Tokyo)	1962
Tokyo Metropolitan Symphony Orchestra	1965
Ulster Orchestra (Belfast)	1966
Lyon Symphony Orchestra	1967
National Arts Centre Orchestra (Ottawa)	1967
Austrian Radio Symphony (Vienna) (1945)	1969
Taipei City Symphony Orchestra	1969
Symphony Orchestra of the State of Mexico (Toluca)	1971
New Japan Philharmonic Symphony Orchestra (Tokyo)	1972
Polish Chamber Orchestra and Sinfonia Varsovia (Warsaw)	1972
Hong Kong Philharmonic Orchestra	1974
Central Philharmonic Orchestra (Beijing) (1956)	1977
Mexico City Philharmonic Orchestra	1978
Singapore Symphony Orchestra	1979

Selected Bibliography ─────

80 Jahre Wiener Symphoniker. Vienna: Doblinger, 1980.

Alonso, Luis. *40 anos Orquesta Nacional*. Madrid, 1982.

Alte und neue musik: das Basler Kammerorchester. Zurich: Atlantis, [1952]. Festschrift.

Alte und neue musik: das Basler Kammerorchester. Vol. II. Zurich: Atlantis, [1977].

Bech, Lutz. *Bamberger Symphoniker, 1946–1976*. Bamberg, 1976.

Bekker, Paul. *The Story of the Orchestra*. New York: Norton, 1936.

Biba, Otto. *100 Jahre Wiener Philharmoniker in Salzburg*. Salzburg, 1977.

Bitter, Christoph. *Sinfonieorchester des Südwestfunks Baden-Baden*. Baden-Baden, 1980.

Blandford, Linda. *The LSO: Scenes from Orchestra Life*. London: Michael Joseph, 1984.

Boult, Adrian. *My Own Trumpet*. London: Hamish Hamilton, 1973.

Brans, A.B.M., and Evert Cornelis. *Het Residentie-Orkest 50 jaar*. The Hague: Residentie Orchestra, 1954.

Breuer, Janos. *The Budapest Philharmonic Orchestra*. Budapest: BPO, 1981. Pamphlet.

British Music Yearbook. London: Rhinegold, 1985. Annual.

Brook, Donald. *Conductors Gallery*. London: Rockliff, 1946.

Buttrose, Charles. *Playing for Australia: A Story about ABC Orchestras and Music in Australia*. Melbourne, 1982.

Caamano, Roberto. *La Historia del Teatro Colón, 1908–1968*. Buenos Aires: Cinetea, 1969.

Carse, Adam von Ahn. *The Orchestra from Beethoven to Berlioz*. Cambridge: Heffer, 1948.

──────. *The Orchestra in the Eighteenth Century*. Cambridge: Heffer, 1950.

Cosma, Viorel. *Filarmonica "George Enescu" in Bucharest*. Bucharest, 1968.

Cox, David. *The Henry Wood Proms*. London: BBC, 1980.

20 Let Pražského Kohorního Orchestru (1951–1971). Prague: Prague Chamber Orchestra, 1971.

350 Jahre Württembergisches Staatsorchester. Stuttgart, 1967.

Edinborough, Arnold. *A Personal History of the Toronto Symphony*. Toronto, 1972.

[Egypt]: Ministry of Culture and National Guidance, *Urqistra Al-Qāhirah Al-Simfūni*. Cairo, 1960.

Elkin, Robert. *Royal Philharmonic: The Annals of the Royal Philharmonic Society*. London: Rider, 1946.

Endler, Franz. *Musik auf Reisen*. Vienna: Österreichischer Bundesverlag, 1982.

Engström, Bengt Olof. *75 Years with the Orchestral Society of Stockholm*. Stockholm: Stockholm Concert Hall Foundation, 1977. In Swedish.

Ewen, David J. *Dictators of the Baton*. Chicago: Alliance, 1943.

————. *The Man with the Baton: The Story of Conductors and Their Orchestras*. New York: Thomas Crowell, 1936. Rpt., Freeport: Books for Libraries Press, 1968.

Fauchaux, Pierre. *Orchestre national de France*. Paris: ONF, 1981. Pamphlet.

Fierz, G. *The Zurich Tonhalle: A History of the Zurich Tonhalle-Geselschaft and the Tonhalle Orchestra*. Zurich, 1978.

Freer, David. *Hamilton Harty: His Life and Music*. Belfast, 1979.

Gatti, G. M., et al. *Orchestra Sinfonica e il Coro di Torino RAI 1933–1983*. Turin: ERI e Cassa di Risparmio di Torino, 1983.

The George Enescu Philharmonic in Bucharest. Bucharest: Scientific and Encyclopedic Publishing House, 1985.

Gołębiewski, Marian. *Filharmonia w Warszawie*. Krakow: PWM, 1976.

Grigor'ev, L., and Ya. Platek. *Moskovskaya gosudarstvennaya filamoniya*. Moscow, 1973.

Hamilton Philharmonic Orchestra: 100 Years of Music. Hamilton [Canada]: Wentworth, 1984.

Harries, Meiron, and Susie Harries. *The Academy of St. Martin in the Fields*. London: Michael Joseph, 1981.

Hart, Philip. *Conductors: A New Generation*. New York: Scribner's, 1979.

Härtwig, Dieter. *Die Dresdner Philharmonie: Ein Chronik des Orchesters 1870–1970*. Leipzig: Deutscher Verlag für Musik, 1970.

————. *Die Dresdner Philharmonie*. Leipzig: Bibliographischer Institut, 1985.

Helsinki Philharmonic Orchestra 1882–1982. Helsinki: Helsinki Philharmonic, 1982. Pamphlet.

Hilleström, Gustaf. *Göteborgs Symfoniker 75 år*. Göteborg: Göteborgs Teater-och Konsert AB, 1980.

Holzknecht, V. *Česká filharmonie, příběh orchestru*. Prague, 1963.

Horneffer, Jacques. *Orchestre de la Suisse Romande 1918–1968*. Geneva, 1968.

Hudry, François. *Ernest Ansermet, Pionnier de la musique*. Lausanne/Paris: L'Aire musicale/PUF, 1983.

Hurd, Michael. *The Orchestra*. New York: Facts on File, 1980.

Hydes, Cynthia, et al. *Celebration*. Hong Kong: Hong Kong Philharmonic, 1984.

Ibbeken, I., and Tzvi Avni. *An Orchestra [Israel Philharmonic] Is Born*. Tel-Aviv, 1969.

International Music Guide. London: Tantivy, 1985. Annual.

Jefferson, Alan. *Sir Thomas Beecham*. London, 1979.

Kallman, Helmut, et al., eds. *Encyclopedia of Music in Canada*. Toronto: University of Toronto Press, 1981.

Kaydalova, O. N., ed. *Muzykal'naya zhizn' S.S.S.R. Spravochnik* (Musical Life of the USSR: A Book of Reference). Moscow, 1970.

Kellaway, William. *London Philharmonic*. London: Kenneth Mason, 1972.

Kennedy, Michael. *Barbirolli: Conductor Laureate*. London, 1971.

————. *The Halle: A History of the Orchestra from 1858 to 1983*. Manchester: Manchester University Press, 1983.

Kenyon, Nicholas. *The BBC Symphony Orchestra: The First Fifty Years*. London: BBC, 1981.

King-Smith, Beresford. *1920–1970: The First 50 Years: A History of the CBSO*. Birmingham: City of Birmingham Symphony Orchestra, 1970.

Kydryǹski, Lucjan. *Filharmonie Krakowska*. Krakow, 1965.

Leningradskaya gosudarstvennaya ordena Trudnovogo krasnogo znameni Filharmoniya— Stat'i, Vospominaniya, Materialy. Leningrad: "Muzyka" Izdatyel'stvo, 1972.

Lieberwirth, Steffen. *Dokumente sur Gewandhausgeschichte*. Leipzig: Gewandhaus, 1986. 3 vols.

Matheopoulos, Helena. *Maestro: Encounters with Conductors of Today*. New York: Harper & Row, 1982.

Mayerhofer, Alfred. *Städisches Orchester Wuppertal 1862–1962*. Wuppertal: Girardet, 1962.

Memoria 10 años Orquesta Sinfónica Nacional, 1966–1976 [Dominican Republic]. Santo Domingo, 1976.

Memoria 25 años Orquesta Sinfónica Nacional, 1941–1966 [Dominican Republic]. Santo Domingo: Editorial Arte y Cene, 1966.

Miller, Geoffrey. *The Bournemouth Symphony Orchestra*. Dorset: Dorset Publishing, 1970.

Mittag, Erwin. *The Vienna Philharmonic*. Vienna: Gerlach & Wiedling, 1950.

Monteux, Doris. *It's All in the Music: The Life and Work of Pierre Monteux*. New York: Farrar, Straus and Giroux, 1965.

Moore, Jerrold. *Philharmonic Jubilee, 1932–1982*. London: Hutchinson, 1982.

Muck, Peter. *100 Jahre Berliner Philharmonisches Orchester I-III*. Berlin and Tutzing, 1982.

Munch, Charles. *I Am a Conductor*. London: Oxford University Press, 1955.

Museum: 175 Jahre Frankfurter Museums-Gesellschaft. Frankfurt: Lembeck, 1984.

Nakasone, Matsue, ed. *Sekai no Okesutora Jiten* (Dictionary of Orchestras of the World). Tokyo: Geijitsu Gendai Sha, 1984.

Nettel, Reginald. *The Orchestra in England: A Social History*. 1948; rpt., St. Clair Shores, Michigan: Scholarly Press, 1972.

Novotná, O., and Peter Zapletal, comps. *The Prague Symphony Orchestra*. Prague: Prague Symphony, 1984.

Oehlmann, Werner. *Das Berliner Philharmonisch Orchester*. Berlin and Kassel, 1974.

Ogawa, Takashi, ed. *Nippon no Kokyo Gakudan* (Symphony Orchestras of Japan). Tokyo: Minshu Ongaku Kyokai, 1983.

Das Orchester: Zeitschrift für Orchesterkultur und Rundfunk-Chorwesen. Mainz: Schott. Monthly.

Orga, Ates. *The Proms*. Newton Abbot: David & Charles, 1974.

Osaka Philharmonic Orchestra. Osaka: Osaka Philharmonic, 1983.

Pâris, Alain. *Concerts Lamoureux*. Paris: Guerin, 1981.

Pearton, Maurice. *The LSO at 70*. London: Gollancz, 1974.

Pejović, Roksanda. *Fifty Years of the Belgrade Philharmony . . . 1923–1973*. Belgrade, 1977.

Pettit, Stephen J. *The Philharmonia Official History*. London, 1985.

Peyser, Joan, ed. *The Orchestra: Origins and Transformations*. New York: Scribners, 1986.

Pospíšil, V. *S Ceskou filharmonií třemi světadíly*. Prague, 1961.

Potvin, Giles. *Les 50 premières années* [Montreal Symphony]. Montreal: Editions A. Stanke, 1984.

Proctor-Gregg, H. *Beecham Remembered*. London: Duckworth, 1977.

Raynor, Henry. *Music and Society: Since 1815*. New York: Schocken, 1976.

———. *The Orchestra*. New York: Schocken, 1972; Scribners, 1978.

———. *A Social History of Music: From the Middle Ages to Beethoven*. New York: Schocken, 1972.

Reid, Charles. *John Barbirolli*. New York: Taplinger, 1971.

Reeser, Eduard, ed. *Music in Holland*. Amsterdam: Meulenhoff/Foundation Doremus, 1959.

Rodzinzki, Helena. *Our Two Lives*. New York: Scribner's, 1976.

Russell, Thomas. *Philharmonic*. London, 1942.

Sadie, Stanley, ed. *The New Grove Dictionary of Music and Musicians*. London and New York: Macmillan, 1980–1981.

Schilham, Piet W. *Toj, Toj, Achter de schermen van het orkestbedrijf*. The Hague: Nijgh & van Ditmar, 1984.

Schonberg, Harold C. *The Great Conductors*. New York: Simon & Schuster, 1967.

Schonfeld, Christl. *The Vienna Philharmonic*. Vienna: Bergland, 1957.

Schröcksnadel, Joseph. *Salzburgs Musikalische Botschafter: Das Mozarteum Orchester*. Salzburg: Verlag Alfred Winter, 1984.

Schwartz, Erwin. *Humanität durch Musik: Vierzig jahre Stuttgart Kammerorchester*. Stuttgart, [1985].

Scoseria, Rolando. *Literatura de los programas del SODRE, Años 1954–1979*. Montevideo, [1980].

Seoul Philharmonic Orchestra. Seoul: Sejong Cultural Center, 1981. Pamphlet.

Sidel'nikov, L. *Bol'shoy simfonichesky orkestr Tsentral-nogo televideniya i Vsesoyuznogo Radio*. Moscow, 1981.

Siodmok, Irena, and Leon Markiewicz. *WOSPRiT, 1954–1975* [Polish Radio National Symphony Orchestra]. Katowice: WOSPRiT, 1975.

Smith, Moses. *Koussevitzky*. New York: Allen, Towne & Heath, 1947.

Smyth, Alan, ed. *To Speak for Ourselves: The London Symphony Orchestra*. London: Kimber, 1970.

Strasser, Otto. *Und dafur wird man noch bezahlt. Mein Leben mit den Wiener Philharmonikern*. Vienna, 1974.

Stresemann, Wolfgang. *The Berlin Philharmonic Orchestra from Bülow to Karajan*. Berlin: Heinman, 1981.

Taubman, Howard. *The Orchestra Abroad: A Report of a Study*. Vienna, Va.: American Symphony Orchestra League, [1970].

Terry, Charles Sanford. *Bach's Orchestra*. London: Oxford University Press, 1932.

Tobischek, Herbert. *25 Jahre Philharmonia Hungarica*. Marl: Breitfeld & Biermann, 1982.

Tonks, Joy. *New Zealand Symphony Orchestra, 1946–1986*. Aukland: Reed Methuen, 1986.

Veselý, R. *Dějiny České filhamonie v letech 1901–1924*. Prague, 1935.

Vos, Willem, ed. *Een Spiegel van Diamant* [Rotterdam Philharmonic programs]. Amsterdam: Rotterdam Philharmonic, 1978.

Weigel, Hans. *Das Buch der Wiener Philharmoniker*. Vienna, 1967.

Witts, Roger, et al. *SNO 1971: An Anniversary Study of the SNO*. Glasgow: Scottish National Orchestra Society, [1971].

Wolschke, Martin. *Von der Städtpfeiferei zu Lehrlingskapelle und Sinfonieorchester: Wandlungen im 19. Jahrhundert*. Regensburg: Bosse, 1981.

Wooldrige, David. *Conductors' World*. New York: Praeger, 1970.

Zapletal, Petar. *FOK: Fifty Years of the Prague Symphony Orchestra*. Prague: Editio Supraphon, 1984.

Index ———————————————————

About the Contributors _____

BERNARD W. ANDREWS, Ed.D., is Visiting Professor of Education at the University of Toronto, where he teaches Program Organization. He has extensive experience as an educator and is active as a writer, composer, and bandleader.

STEPHEN H. BARNES, Ph.D., is Dean of the College of Fine Arts at Eastern New Mexico University. His area of scholarly interest is the sociological and social-psychological foundations of aesthetic education in the United States.

DOROTHEA BAUMANN, Dr.phil., stand.wiss.Mitarbeiter at the University of Zurich, teaches Acoustics, History of Performing Practice, and Bibliography there. The author and editor of books and articles on many musical subjects, she has written program notes for the Tonhalle-Gesellschaft Zurich since 1972. She is also a pianist and harpsichord player.

WARREN A. BEBBINGTON, M.A., M.Mus., Ph.D., is Dean of Music at the University of Queensland, Australia. The author of two musical editions and various articles, he is also a conductor who has appeared with various orchestral and choral groups around Australia.

GWILYM BEECHEY, M.A., Mus.B., Ph.D., is a music historian and editor with special interests in music of the seventeenth and eighteenth centuries. He is also an organ recitalist with wide interests in the history of organ and other keyboard music.

JACEK BERWALDT, a graduate of Jagiellonian University (Musicology), has been an editor with Polish Music Publishers and has served since 1974 as Program Section Manager of the Krakow Philharmonic. He is a member of the Association of Polish Composers.

LUCIO BUCCARELLA, double-bass player in (and President of) I Musici, teaches double-bass at the Santa Cecilia Conservatory of Music in Rome.

KRISTIN CARMICHAEL, B.A., is an editor, writer, and translator who has written on a wide variety of subjects, including legislative procedures, music, drama, literature, science, demographic studies, and business.

SALWA EL-SHAWAN CASTELO-BRANCO, Ph.D., is Associate Professor of Music at the Universidade Nova de Lisboa, where she teaches ethnomusicology. Her publications include articles, reviews, and books (in preparation) on the musical life of Egypt and Portugal. Dr. Castelo-Branco is also record review editor for the *Yearbook of Traditional Music*.

MARJORIE ANN CIARLILLO, M.A., Musicology, Director of the China Music Project (Cleveland, Ohio), studied Chinese music at The Shanghai Conservatory of Music during 1982–1983. She also travelled through seven provinces and conducted research on Western influences on Chinese music.

CESARE CORSI, Dipl. in Organ and Organ Composition, is completing advanced musicological studies at the University of Rome under the guidance of Professor Pierluigi Petrobelli.

ROBERT R. CRAVEN, Ph.D., Professor of English, teaches multidisciplinary humanities at New Hampshire College. A horn player and community orchestra Board member, he is the author of books and articles on a variety of subjects and Editor-in-Chief of the present volume's companion, *Symphony Orchestras of the United States: Selected Profiles*.

DALE P. DICKIE, Mus.B. (Hons.), is a college lecturer, a communicator, educator, and therapist working mainly through music.

JOACHIM DORFMÜLLER, Dr.phil.habil., Professor of Musicology at the University of Münster, is an organist and pianist with many international tours and more than 25 records to his credit. A prolific writer as well, Dr. Dorfmüller has produced five books and more than 300 other works, including articles, editions, and transcriptions.

MILENA DOSOUDILOVA is a scientific worker of the Cabinet for Czech Theatre Studies of the Czechoslovak Academy of Sciences. She specializes in opera production. As a critic she especially follows contemporary music and performing arts.

CATHERINE DOWER, Ph.D., Professor of Music at Westfield State College, author of a book and numerous articles, is a Corporator of the Springfield Symphony Orchestra Association and Life Member of the Women's Symphony League.

ANNE DUNN, M.Phil., Head of Streatham (London) Adult Education Institute, organizes nonvocational studies for adults and teaches music. She has written articles on many subjects and is a leading authority on the teaching of music appreciation.

BENGT OLOF ENGSTRÖM has been General Manager and Artistic Director of the Stockholm Philharmonic Orchestra since 1976. A teacher and consultant,

Mr. Engström is the author of several books and is a member of the Royal Swedish Academy of Music.

MARGARET L. FAST is a Humanities Reference Librarian at the University of Utah in Salt Lake City.

BRIAN G'FROERER, B.Mus., Ed.Cert., is Third/Associate Principal Horn in the Vancouver Symphony Orchestra and Principal Horn in the CBC Vancouver Orchestra. A horn instructor at the University of British Columbia and Vancouver Academy of Music, he is pursuing postgraduate studies in Urban Geography.

DAVID GREER is Professor of Music at the University of Durham, England. His publications include *English Madrigal Verse*, *Hamilton Harty: His Life and Music*, and editions of sixteenth- and seventeenth-century music.

ROLF HAGLUND is a music journalist whose credits include radio programs, program notes for the Göteborgs Symfoniker, and articles in such publications as Sohlman's *Dictionary* and the *New Grove Encyclopedia*.

FREDERICK A. HALL is Associate Professor and former chairman of the Department of Music, McMaster University. He has contributed articles on Canadian music history to the *Encyclopedia of Music in Canada*, *Canadian Encyclopedia*, and several research journals.

JEHOASH HIRSHBERG, Ph.D., is Professor of Musicology at Hebrew University in Jerusalem. He is the author of *Ben-Haim: His Life and Works* (Tel-Aviv, 1983) as well as articles in historical musicology, sociology of music, and ethnomusicology.

JAROSLAV HOLECEK studied piano at the Prague Conservatory and musicology at the Charles University in Prague. Librarian of the Czech Philharmonic, he has written a book and several articles in addition to many program annotations and record sleeve notes.

D. KERN HOLOMAN, Ph.D., is Professor and Chairman of Music at the University of California, Davis, where he conducts the University Symphony. He is Chief Program Annotator for the Sacramento Symphony and an authority on the music of Berlioz.

FRANÇOIS HUDRY, musicologist, is the author of a book on Ernest Ansermet and of numerous articles. Producer/administrator of the Radio Suisse Romande in Geneva, he is also the archivist and editor responsible for the program annotations for the Orchestra of the Suisse Romande.

GLYN MÔN HUGHES, B.Mus., ARCM, ARCO, an organist and harpsichordist, is a journalist and freelance writer on music and the arts. He lives in South Wales.

ADAM JASINSKI, M.A., is a violist and conductor who has performed in many Polish cities. He now works for the Opera House in Lodz and is Assistant at the Academy of Music in Lodz.

BERNARDA JORGE is a scholar in socio-musicology, pianist, music teacher, and *docente* at the Autonomous University of Santo Domingo. She is also Director of the Music Department of the Santiago Center for Culture, Dominican Republic.

CAROL KOCH carries degrees from Mercy College (Communication Arts), the Juilliard School (piano), and the Vienna Academy (organ). She teaches piano and performs, in addition to her broadcasting work with the Austrian Radio.

EWA KOFIN, Ph.D., is Professor of Musicology at the Institute of Cultural Sciences of the University of Wroclaw. A music critic as well, she is the author of the book *Television Music* and many articles.

ALFONSO LETELIER, composer and educator, studied at the National Conservatory of Music in Santiago, Chile. Professor of Composition and Music History, he later became Dean of the Faculty of Arts at the University of Chile. Winner of the National Prize in the Arts, 1968, he is now Professor Emeritus.

ERIK LEVI, Lecturer in Music (London University), also pursues an active career as a professional accompanist.

ROBERT M. LINDELL, Ph.D., teaches music history for foreign study programs in Vienna and pursues a research interest with emphasis on late sixteenth-century music. In addition to a dissertation and articles on the secular music of Filippo di Monte, he is currently preparing a biography of this composer.

ZDZISŁAW LIS, M.A., is a teacher of Music Theory at the Academy of Music in Lodz.

RUT MAGNÚSSON, GGSM, LRAM, was born in England and pursued a singing career there until moving with her husband to Iceland in 1966. Since then she has been employed as a singer, teacher, conductor, and organizer; she now runs Tonverk, a music information and concert agency.

SANJA MAJER-BOBETKO, M.A., musicologist and Professor of Russian Language, is Research Assistant in the Zagreb Music Academy Library, teaches music at the Zagreb University, collaborates in research projects of the Institute of Musicology of the Yugoslav Academy of Sciences and Arts, and is the author of *Aesthetics of Nineteenth-Century Music in Croatia*.

DENNIS MCCALDIN, Ph.D., is Director of Music at the University of Lancaster, England. A conductor and Director of the Haydn Society of Great Britain, he is at present researching a book on the chamber orchestra.

YOSHIHIRO, OBATA, Ph.D., is Associate Professor of Music at Florida International University and the author of books and articles on musical subjects ranging from orchestral music to the concert band. He formerly played clarinet as an extra and substitute member of the NHK Symphony Orchestra.

ALEXANDRA ORLOVA, musicologist, is the author of a number of books, articles, and other works about Russian composers (Glinka, Tchaikovsky, Mussorgsky, Rimsky-Korsakov, and others). Since immigrating to the United States from the Soviet Union in 1979, she has continued to publish, both in the Russian language and in English translation.

ROKSANDA R. PEJOVIĆ, Mus.D., musicologist and art historian, teaches History of Music at the Faculty of Music, Belgrade, and is the author of books on medieval musical instruments, Yugoslav music history, and world music history—in addition to numerous articles.

FRANK REINISCH (Dr.), musicologist, has been actively associated with the publishing firm of Breitkopf and Härtel since 1983. His publications mainly deal with questions of the history and reception of opera (particularly with regard to the nineteenth century).

ANDREJ RIJAVEC, Ph.D., Professor of Musicology, teaches Music History (concentration in the twentieth century) at the University of Ljubljana. He is the author of books and numerous articles covering a broad range of subjects and published in various periodicals and encyclopedias.

ROBERT RŸKER is active in Japan as a conductor and commentator of educational concerts. Formerly tubist of the Montreal Symphony, Conductor of the Calcutta Symphony, and Community Musician for the Canada Council, he has written major proposals for a music festival (1984) and for educational concerts (1985) in Japan.

GUILLERMO E. SCARABINO is Professor of Music at the National University of Cuyo (Mendoza, Argentina), where he also is Music Director of the University Symphony Orchestra. He has conducted nearly all the symphony orchestras of Argentina, including, on numerous occasions, the Colón Theater Orchestra and the National Symphony Orchestra.

ANTHONY SCELBA, D.M.A., is a concert double bassist. A graduate of Juilliard School of Music, he is a Fulbright Performing Artist Award winner. He has taught at the Hartt, Manhattan, and Baylor University Schools of Music.

PIET W. SCHILHAM, Doctor Juris, is General Secretary of the Residentie-Orkest, The Hague. He is the author of books and articles as well as a lecturer on music-related subjects.

YOLANDA PÉREZ ECCHER DE SCOSERIA, Licenciada en Musicologia, pianist and teacher, is a well-known lecturer, writer, and scholar in the history of music in Uruguay. She directed the Musicology Department of the University Conservatory of Music until her retirement in 1984.

GERALD R. SEAMAN, M.A., D.Phil., is Professor of Musicology at the University of Aukland, New Zealand. Well known as a writer and lecturer, he has published a *History of Russian Music*.

SIN-YAN SHEN, Ph.D., is President of the Chinese Music Society of North America and Editor-in-Chief of the international quarterly journal *Chinese Music*. The author of over a hundred papers and articles on music, acoustics, and physics,

Dr. Shen is also Music Director of the Orchestra of the Chinese Music Society of North America.

LADISLAV ŠÍP, Producer and Director of the Gramophone Records Department of the Supraphon Company (1949–1973), Chief of the Prague National Theater Opera (1973–1976), is now Director of the Prague Symphony Orchestra and author of publicity books on music.

BASIL SMALLMAN, Emeritus Professor of Music (University of Liverpool), is the author of books and articles on a variety of musicological topics. Active as a pianist and harpsichordist and as a conductor of opera and oratorio, he is a long-standing member of the RLPO Management Committee.

JACEK SZERSZENOWICZ, Ph.D., Lecturer, Chair of Aesthetics at the University of Lodz, is a music critic as well.

ANDRÉS RUIZ TARAZONA, writer and music critic for the Madrid newspaper *El Pais*, is the author of numerous books and articles on musical subjects. He also collaborates with the Spanish National Radio and Television in Madrid.

JOY TONKS, B.A. (Eng. Lit.), is the New Zealand Symphony Orchestra's personnel manager, editor of its tri-annual magazine *Concert Pitch*, and author of the orchestra's fortieth anniversary history. She also writes fiction.

JANET TURKOVIĆ is a freelance writer and violinist living in Salzburg, Austria. Before moving to Europe, she was Dean of Students at the Curtis Institute of Music in Philadelphia.

LUCA TUTINO studies philosophy at the University of Rome "La Sapienza." The author of articles on baroque music, he is a graduate in composition of the Conservatory A. Casella of L'Aquila.

VIOLET VAGRAMIAN-NISHANIAN, Ph.D., is Professor of Counterpoint, Form and Analysis, and Music History at Florida International University. The author of journal articles and compositions, she is also a pianist.

BERTIL H. VAN BOER, Jr., Ph.D., is Assistant Professor of Musicology at Brigham Young University. He is the author of numerous editions and articles on eighteenth-century music.

HENRI VANHULST, Ph.D., is Professor of Musicology at the Free University of Brussels. The Secretary of the Belgian Musicological Society, he has contributed to the *New Grove* and is the author of articles published in the *Revue belge de musicologie*.

WILLEM VOS studied musicology in Amsterdam and Utrecht. Formerly the musicological collaborator and program annotator for Het Gelders Orkest (Arnhem), he has since 1968 been Artistic Adviser of the Rotterdam Philharmonic

Orchestra. He has published numerous program notes and articles on contemporary music.

JOHN WILLIAM WOLDT, Ph.D., Professor of Music at Texas Christian University in Fort Worth, was formerly Principal Horn in the Fort Worth Symphony and the Fort Worth Opera Orchestras.

JERZY ZAMUSZKO, M.A., is a teacher of Music Theory at the Musical Academy in Lodz.

About the Translators _____

DAVID BRADT, Ph.D., teaches English and Psychology at New Hampshire College and has published several English translations of Spanish poetry.

KRISTIN E. CARMICHAEL, B.A., is an editor, writer, and translator who has written on a wide variety of subjects, including legislative procedures, music, drama, literature, science, demographic studies, and business.

FELICIA CRAIG, B.A. (Fine Arts) was raised in a Polish- and English-speaking environment. She is a native of Manchester, New Hampshire.

JULIA DISTEFANO, Ph.D., Associate Professor of English at New Hampshire College, has published in *The Bulletin of Research in the Humanities* and *African Literature Today* and has presented papers in Europe and North America on a variety of subjects including William Blake, the Wordsworths, women's studies, and communication.

LAWRENCE J. GILLOOLY is Professor of Romance Languages and Literatures at Merrimack College, North Andover, Massachusetts.

SUSAN ELIZABETH HOAGLUND, B.M. (mus.), Dipl. (German), held a full professorship at the Stadt. Musikschule, Düsseldorf, and also taught at the American International School, Düsseldorf. The former Director of Scheduling at Boston University Tanglewood Institute, she is presently on the faculty of St. Paul's School, Concord, New Hampshire.

PETER JÄHNE, born in Bidefeld, Germany, and a resident of Caracas, Venezuela, is fluent in four languages. He is preparing for a career in the hospitality industry by studying at New Hampshire College and Belvoirpark Hotel School, Zurich.

ELEONORA SCOSERIA is a teacher of English as well as a student and teacher of Chemistry at the Universidad de la Republica in Montevideo. Most of her experience as a translator has been in scientific, technical, and musical topics.

DON W. SIEKER, Ph.D., is Associate Professor of English at New Hampshire College. His interest in the eighteenth century includes keyboard music, and he is the author of the article on Boston's Haydn and Handel Society in *Symphony Orchestras of the United States*.

THERESA SNOW TOY, M.S. in Library Science, spent three years in the Peace Corps (Tunisia). Her music training was put to use in her years as the Music Librarian at the Manchester, N.H., City Library.

ANNELIESE YIENGST was born and educated in Munich, Germany. Living in the United States since 1952, she has taught conversational German at St. Anselm College (Manchester, New Hampshire) since 1976. Her writings appear in several German newspapers and magazines.